THE THEORY, PRACTICE, AND INTERPRETATION OF CUSTOMARY INTERNATIONAL LAW

Although customary international law (CIL) has been central to international law from its inception, it is often misunderstood. This edited volume remedies that problem by tracing the history of CIL, and providing an in-depth study of its theory, practice, and interpretation. Its chapters tackle the big questions which surround this source of international law such as: what are the rules that regulate the functioning of CIL as a source of international law? Can CIL be interpreted? Where do lines between identification, interpretation, application, and modification of a rule of CIL lie? Using recent developments, this volume revisits old debates and resolves them by proffering new and innovative solutions. With detailed examples from international and national courts, it places CIL in a range of settings to explain, explore and reflect upon this developing and highly significant field. This title is also available as Open Access on Cambridge Core.

PANOS MERKOURIS is Professor at the University of Groningen. He holds a Chair on Interpretation and Dispute Settlement in International Law. He is the Principal Investigator of the TRICI-Law project. Professor Merkouris has written extensively on interpretation, most recently co-authoring *Treaties in Motion* (Cambridge, 2020) with Professor Malgosia Fitzmaurice.

JÖRG KAMMERHOFER is Senior Research Fellow at the University of Freiburg, Germany, and *Privatdozent* for international law and legal theory at the Vienna University of Economics. He is a generalist international law scholar, specialising in legal theory, and has published widely, including, recently, *International Investment Law and Legal Theory: Expropriation and the Fragmentation of Sources* (Cambridge, 2021).

NOORA ARAJÄRVI is Postdoctoral Fellow with the ERC funded project ‘Cultural Expertise in Europe: What is it useful for?’, and Associate at the Hertie School. She is the author of *The Changing Nature of Customary International Law* (2014) and several journal articles and book chapters on customary international law and other key questions of international law.

THE RULES OF INTERPRETATION OF CUSTOMARY INTERNATIONAL LAW

Established in 2021, the *TRICI-Law Book Series* is a limited series that aims to publish monographs and edited volumes on topics that shed light on legal interpretation in international law, with a particular emphasis on the interpretation of customary international law. Titles appearing in the series examine the interpretation of customary international law from a theoretical and practical perspective, and compare the characteristics of legal interpretation in international law across courts, regimes and sources as they have evolved and continue to do so through time. The *TRICI-Law Book Series* is a joint initiative between Cambridge University Press, the European Research Council and the University of Groningen. The titles in this series are available as Open Access.

THE THEORY, PRACTICE, AND INTERPRETATION OF CUSTOMARY INTERNATIONAL LAW

Edited by

PANOS MERKOURIS

University of Groningen

JÖRG KAMMERHOFER

University of Freiburg

NOORA ARAJÄRVI

The Hertie School and Panthéon Sorbonne University

Assistant Editor

NINA MILEVA

University of Groningen

CAMBRIDGE UNIVERSITY PRESS

CAMBRIDGE
UNIVERSITY PRESS

Shaftesbury Road, Cambridge CB2 8EA, United Kingdom

One Liberty Plaza, 20th Floor, New York, NY 10006, USA

477 Williamstown Road, Port Melbourne, VIC 3207, Australia

314–321, 3rd Floor, Plot 3, Splendor Forum, Jasola District Centre, New Delhi – 110025, India

103 Penang Road, #05–06/07, Visioncrest Commercial, Singapore 238467

Cambridge University Press is part of Cambridge University Press & Assessment, a department of the University of Cambridge.

We share the University's mission to contribute to society through the pursuit of education, learning and research at the highest international levels of excellence.

www.cambridge.org
Information on this title: www.cambridge.org/9781009505505

DOI: 10.1017/9781009025416

First published 2022
First paperback edition 2024

A catalogue record for this publication is available from the British Library

ISBN 978-1-316-51689-8 Hardback
ISBN 978-1-009-50550-5 Paperback

CONTENTS

CONTRIBUTORS

NOORA ARAJÄRVI works at the Hertie School in Berlin, and in the ERC-funded project 'Cultural Expertise in Europe: What Is It Useful For? (Panthéon Sorbonne University). She has conducted research as a postdoctoral fellow with the Berlin Potsdam Research Group 'The International Rule of Law – Rise or Decline?', held teaching positions at UCLan Cyprus and the University of the West Indies, visiting fellowships at MPIL and Fordham University, and worked at the UN Rule of Law Unit in New York. She received her PhD from the European University Institute and is the author of *The Changing Nature of Customary International Law* (Routledge 2014) and several journal articles and book chapters on customary international law and other key questions of international law.

ROMEL REGALADO BAGARES teaches international law at the Lyceum of the Philippines University College of Law and the San Sebastian College Recoletos Manila Graduate School of Law. At the Manila-based Center for International Law, where he was Executive Director for nearly a decade, he litigated many public interest and human rights cases before Philippine courts and UN human rights mechanisms. Mr Bagares has an LLB from the University of the Philippines and an MA (*cum laude*) from the Vrije Universiteit Amsterdam, where he hopes to finish a PhD applying H Dooyeweerd's *Encyclopedia of the Science of Law* to international law.

ANNA IRENE BAKA is a Greek jurist, senior legal associate at the Greek National Commission for Human Rights and postdoctoral fellow at the Philosophy Department of the University of Crete, where she focuses on the implications for Law of the Phenomenology of Edmund Husserl. She is adjunct lecturer of Jurisprudence, EU Law and Human Rights at the University of London International LLB Programme in Greece. She holds a PhD in international law and legal philosophy from the University of

Hong Kong, for which she was awarded a scholarship by the University of Hong Kong and the Hellenic National Scholarship.

MARKUS P BEHAM is Assistant Professor at the Chair of Constitutional and Administrative Law, Public International Law, European and International Economic Law of the University of Passau, Germany, and an adjunct lecturer in international law at the University of Vienna, Austria. He holds a joint doctoral degree from the Université Paris Nanterre and the University of Vienna and a doctoral degree in history from the latter as well as an LLM degree from Columbia Law School in New York. Prior to returning to academia, Markus was part of the International Arbitration Group of Freshfields Bruckhaus Deringer LLP, resident in the firm's Vienna office.

FREDERICK COWELL is a Senior Lecturer in law at Birkbeck College, University of London. His research interests are in the enforcement of international law and he is currently writing a book on the philosophy of treaty withdrawal. He has previously worked in an advisory capacity at an NGO helping civil society groups with the Universal Periodic Review process.

LUIGI CREMA is Associate Professor of International Law at the Law School of the Università degli Studi of Milan. He holds a PhD in public international law from the Universities of Geneva and Milan and he did postdoctoral work as a fellow at the Jean Monnet Center of the New York University School of Law. He has numerous publications in the field of international law, and he has dedicated himself in recent years to a broad project of institution building, helping to establish and implement an LLM programme on sustainable development and a PhD on law, ethics and economics.

JEAN D'ASPREMONT is Professor of International Law at Sciences Po Law School and at the University of Manchester. He is General Editor of the Cambridge Studies in International and Comparative Law and Director of Oxford International Organizations (OXIO). He writes on questions of international law and international legal theory.

MARIANA CLARA DE ANDRADE is Postdoctoral Fellow at the University of Milano-Bicocca (Italy). She holds a PhD in public international law from the same university, and a bachelor's and LLM from the Federal University of Santa Catarina (Brazil). Mariana has been a guest researcher at the Max Planck Institute Luxembourg for International, European and Regulatory Procedural Law, the University of Geneva and the PhD Support Programme at the WTO.

RICCARDO DI MARCO is a PhD researcher at the University of Rome Tor Vergata and the University of Paris Nanterre (joint PhD). Under the supervision of Professor Alessandra Gianelli and Professor Jean-Marc Thouvenin, he focuses his research on the interpretability of customary international law and the methods of its interpretation. A member of the Rome Bar Association, after obtaining an LLB from Sapienza University of Rome, he has studied law at the University of Cambridge, at the European University Institute as well as at The Hague Academy of International Law with an emphasis on sources of international law and international legal theory.

ANDREAS FOLLESDAL is Professor of Political Philosophy at the Faculty of Law, University of Oslo. He is the co-director of PluriCourts, a Centre of Excellence for the Study of the Legitimate Roles of the Judiciary in the Global Order, and the Principal Investigator of European Research Council Advanced Grant MultiRights 2011–16, on the Legitimacy of Multi-Level Human Rights Judiciary. He holds a PhD in philosophy from Harvard University. Føllesdal publishes in the field of political philosophy, mainly on issues of international political and legal theory, globalisation/Europeanisation, human rights, and socially responsible investing.

EMILY FORBES graduated LLB Hons and bachelor of international studies from Deakin University, Victoria, Australia. Her honours thesis on the ICJ *Chagos* Advisory Opinion has been published in the *Monash University Law Review*. She is currently an LLM student at Melbourne Law School, University of Melbourne.

MARINA FORTUNA is a PhD researcher at the University of Groningen. Her PhD research focuses on the interpretation of customary international law in the practice of international courts and tribunals. Marina's research is conducted under the supervision of Professor Panos Merkouris within the TRICI-Law project funded by the European Research Council under the European Union's Horizon 2020 Research and Innovation Programme (Grant Agreement No. 759728). Her area of interest and research includes judicial reasoning and interpretation, international courts and tribunals, customary international law, judicial impartiality, international criminal law, human rights and the intersection between international law and social sciences.

KOSTIANTYN GOROBETS is Assistant Professor of International Law at the University of Groningen. He specialises in analytical jurisprudence and philosophy of international law, as well as in their interplay. He is currently finalising his PhD dissertation on 'Beyond Validity: Authority of International Law'.

ANDREAS HADJIGEORGIU is a Cypriot practicing lawyer and an aspiring academic. He has received education from various European universities including the Universities of Vienna (Austria), Glasgow (UK), Utrecht (Netherlands), and the Aristotelion University of Thessaloniki (Greece). He has completed his doctoral training, in (international) law and (legal) philosophy, at the Universities of Antwerp (Belgium) and Groningen (Netherlands). Internationally, his research revolves primarily around the ontology and evolution of (international) law, while on the national level he writes on human rights and their various infringements within the Cypriot legal system. He has been a member of the Human Rights Committee of the Cyprus Bar Association since 2020.

GERARD HOOGERS is a senior lecturer at the department of Constitutional Law, Administrative Law and Public Administration of the University of Groningen, the Netherlands. He holds an honorary professorate in comparative constitutional law at the Carl von Ossietzky University of Oldenburg, Germany. His research focuses on comparative constitutional law, the history of political theory and the constitutional law of the transatlantic Kingdom of the Netherlands.

JÖRG KAMMERHOFER is Senior Research Fellow at the University of Freiburg, Germany, and *Privatdozent* for international law and legal theory at the Vienna University of Economics. He is a generalist international law scholar and specialises in theory, sources, use of force, dispute settlement and investment law as well as the theory of law, in particular the Pure Theory of Law. He has published widely, including *International Investment Law and Legal Theory: Expropriation and the Fragmentation of Sources* (Cambridge University Press 2021). He is erstwhile member and chair of the ESIL's Interest Group on International Legal Theory and Philosophy Co-ordinating Committee.

VLADYSLAV LANOVOY is Assistant Professor of Public International Law, Law Faculty, Université Laval, Quebec, Canada. Prior to this, he was an associate legal officer at the International Court of Justice in the Hague. He has held visiting academic positions at Lille Catholic University and Queen Mary University, London. He holds a PhD in international law from the Graduate Institute of International and Development Studies in Geneva and has published widely. He is the author of *Complicity and its Limits in the Law of International Responsibility* (Hart 2016), which was awarded the 2017 Paul Guggenheim Prize in International Law.

ZHUO LIANG is a doctoral candidate in international law at the Graduate Institute of International and Development Studies, Geneva. He obtained an LLB and an LLM from China University of Political Science and Law, and an Advanced LLM from Leiden University. His research interests centre on international humanitarian law, international criminal law and use of force. He has been an intern at the International Committee of the Red Cross, the Special Tribunal for Lebanon and the International Criminal Court, and a research assistant at the UN International Law Commission.

LETIZIA LO GIACCO is Assistant Professor of Public International Law at the Grotius Centre for International Legal Studies of Leiden University. Her research explores structural questions of international law, with a focus on courts and judicial practices in global governance. Letizia is the co-founder of the Leiden Hub on the Theory and History of International Law, an interdisciplinary platform for theoretical and/or historical questions on international law and is a founding member and co-chairperson of the European Society of International Law interest group on international criminal justice.

DIEGO MEJIA LEMOS, LLM, PhD, serves as a scholar and practitioner of international law and dispute resolution. He holds graduate degrees from New York University and the National University of Singapore (NUS) among others. He has participated in the representation of states in proceedings before international courts, including while working as a *juriste international* at Freshfields Bruckhaus Deringer's Paris office.

Furthermore, he has provided support to arbitral tribunals conducting proceedings under the Permanent Court of Arbitration's auspices. Latterly, he has held a postdoctoral fellowship at NUS and been appointed as Distinguished Research Associate Professor within Xi'an Jiaotong University's 'Young Talent' programme.

PANOS MERKOURIS is a Professor at the University of Groningen. He holds a Chair on Interpretation & Dispute Settlement in International Law. He is the Principal Investigator of the TRICI-Law project (ERC Grant Agreement No. 759728). Professor Merkouris has written extensively on law of treaties and on interpretation, has been cited in international reports and cases, and has advised as expert on these issues.

NINA MILEVA is a PhD researcher of the TRICI-Law project (ERC Grant Agreement No. 759728) under the supervision of Professor Panos Merkouris, at the Department of Transboundary Legal Studies of the University of Groningen. Her research focuses on the interpretation of customary international law, and in particular the development of a theory of interpretation of customary international law. Her research interests relate to the role of international law in the practice of domestic courts, the relationship between international and domestic law, international legal theory and critical approaches to international law. She is also a lecturer in public international law at the University of Groningen.

JOHN MORSS grew up in London, studying in Sheffield and Edinburgh and teaching in the north of Ireland and then the south of New Zealand. He is currently Senior Lecturer in International Law at Deakin Law School. He is author, co-author or co-editor of seven books.

CEDRIC RYNGAERT (PhD Leuven 2007) is Chair of Public International Law at Utrecht University (Netherlands) and Head of the Department of International and European Law of the university's law school. His research interests relate to the law of jurisdiction, immunities, the role of international law before domestic courts, sanctions, international responsibility and international organisations. Among other publications, he authored *Jurisdiction in International Law* (Oxford University Press 2015, 2nd ed) and *Selfless Intervention: The Exercise of Jurisdiction in the Common Interest* (Oxford University Press 2020). He is a member of the Dutch Advisory Council on International Law and editor-in-chief of the *Utrecht Law Review*.

PREFACE

This edited volume finds its origin in a conference on the theory and practice of customary international law (CIL) and its interpretation, held in May 2019 at the University of Groningen. The conference was co-organised by the TRICI-Law project and the Interest Group on International Legal Theory and Philosophy (IGILTP).

The TRICI-Law project, headed by Professor Panos Merkouris, is a five-year research project funded by the European Research Council (ERC) Horizon 2020 program (Grant Agreement No. 759728). The project is dedicated to the in-depth study of CIL interpretation, and the identification of the rules that guide this process. It is the first of its kind, introducing the lens of interpretation as a separate process to be studied in the life cycle of a CIL rule.

The IGILTP is one of the interest groups of the European Society of International Law (ESIL). It seeks to facilitate research into all areas, approaches and questions of a theoretical and philosophical nature with a bearing on international law. In the IGILTP the TRICI-Law project found a willing ally for the organisation of the conference and the collection of this edited volume. It was during our time as co-members of IGILTP's Coordinating Committee that we exchanged many of the ideas that inspired the theoretical questions tackled in this volume.

The conference presented an ambitious programme. We invited scholars and practitioners to engage with questions that hit at the core of our selected subject: what are the rules that regulate the functioning of CIL as a source of international law? Is the classical paradigm of state practice and *opinio juris* still valid today? Can CIL be interpreted? Is there a difference between the interpretation of state practice and the interpretation of a customary rule? Where do lines (if any) between identification, interpretation, application and modification of a rule of CIL lie? And what potential lessons may we learn from domestic approaches to these questions?

We were delighted to receive over 100 abstracts in response to our call for papers; a testament to the continued interest that the theory of CIL inspires among scholars and practitioners of international law. We were particularly encouraged to see that many of the abstracts were willing to engage with the novel lens of interpretation alongside the more traditional subjects of CIL genesis and identification. Thus, in our selection of abstracts we were careful to strike a balance between contributions which examined more traditional issues related to the theory of CIL, and contributions which went outside these familiar frameworks. Moreover, attention was paid to bring together a complementary diverse set of contributions which deal with the theory, practice, and interpretation of CIL respectively. The conference, and ultimately the chapters of this edited volume, reflect this balance.

The edited volume boasts twenty-three chapters, organized into five parts. Part I, dedicated to the theory of CIL, deals with the fault lines in CIL theory and the need for new approaches. This part contains chapters which examine some of the issues emerging from the theory of CIL, commentaries on the validity of the traditional 'state practice and *opinio juris*' model, and suggestions for alternative theoretical approaches. Part II is dedicated to an examination of CIL as a source of international law, with a focus on the doctrine and history of custom. This part contains chapters that critically engage with questions of doctrine, the historical development of CIL, and the contribution of some seminal historical scholars to the way we understand CIL today. Part III turns to the practice of CIL. The chapters in this part present studies of the ways various institutions and actors engage with the application of CIL, and offer commentaries on how these practices shape the way CIL operates in international law. Part IV then introduces the notion of interpretation as a separate stage in the life cycle of a customary rule. This part contains chapters which persuasively illustrate the need to account for interpretation in the operation of a CIL rule, and offer suggestions as to how this may be done. Finally, Part V provides insight into the way domestic courts deal with custom. The chapters in this final part trace the jurisprudence of various domestic courts and illustrate that interpretation of custom (both international and domestic) is regularly engaged in by domestic judges, and that there are valuable lessons to be learned from these approaches for the purposes of international law.

We are deeply grateful to the contributors of this edited volume for their impressive scholarly efforts reflected in each chapter. We also thank the other speakers and chairs of the conference, whose presentations and comments during the 2019 conference no doubt inspired many of the discussions developed in this volume. We are particularly grateful to His Excellency Judge Raul Pangalangan for his engaging keynote speech on the constraints on codified rules and the enduring power of custom.

This edited volume is the first in a line of publications that will deal with the various issues emerging for the study of CIL interpretation. We are very grateful to Cambridge University Press for hosting this pioneering research collection under the heading of the "TRICI-Law Book Series". In particular, a special thanks is owed to Ms Finola O' Sullivan, with whom we fleshed out the idea for this book series on a sunny day in Athens during one of the breaks of the ELSA Conference, and who went above and beyond the call of duty in ensuring that this volume and the book series would get off the ground. We are also indebted to Ms Marianne Nield for her invaluable support and unending patience throughout this process and for those that are still to come, and to Mr Tom Randall and the Cambridge University Press editing team for their continued support through the publication process. A special place of mention is also owed to the ERC and the University of Groningen, without whose generous financial help this edited volume, as well as the TRICI-Law Book Series, would not have been possible.

Finally, we thank Ms Nina Mileva for her assistance in the organisation of the conference and the editing of this volume, as well as Mr Konrad Turnbull for his immense help in all practical matters related to the production of this volume.

This publication has been made open access thanks to the generous funding from the European Research Council (ERC) under the European Union's Horizon 2020 Research and Innovation Programme (Grant Agreement No. 759728) and the University of Groningen.

ABBREVIATIONS

AB	Appellate Body
ACHEA	The Association for Christian Higher Education in Australia
AG	Advocate General
AJIL	*American Journal of International Law*
Amer Sociol Rev	*American Sociological Review*
Am J Juris	*The American Journal of Jurisprudence*
Am U Int'l L Rev	*American University International Law Review*
AppPEN	Approximately Plausible Empowerment Norm
APSR	*American Political Science Review*
ARIEL	*Austrian Review of International and European Law*
ARSIWA	Articles on Responsibility of States for Internationally Wrongful Acts
ASCM	Agreement on Subsidies and Countervailing Measures
Asian JIL	*Asian Journal of International Law*
ASIL	*American Society of International Law*
Aust YBIL	*Australian Yearbook of International Law*
BC Int'l & Comp L Rev	*Boston College International and Comparative Law Review*
BIOT	British Indian Ocean Territory
BJ Pol S	*British Journal of Political Science*
Brook J Int'l L	*Brooklyn Journal of International Law*
BVerfGE	*Die Entscheidungen des Bundesverfassungsgerichts*
B-VG	*Bundes-Verfassungsgesetz*
BVG	*Bundesverfassungsgesetze*
BYBIL	*The British Yearbook of International Law*
Cal W Int'l LJ	*California Western International Law Journal*
Can YBIL	*Canadian Yearbook of International Law*
Cardozo L Rev	*Cardozo Law Review*
CEDAW	Convention on the Elimination of all forms of Discrimination Against Women
Chin J Int Law	*Chinese Journal of International Law*
ChJIL	*Chicago Journal of International Law*

CIL	Customary International Law
CJIL	*Cambridge Journal of International Law*
CJLJ	*Canadian Journal of Law & Jurisprudence*
CLJ	*Cambridge Law Journal*
CLP	*Current Legal Problems*
CLR	*California Law Review*
CMLJ	*Capital Markets Law Journal*
Colum J Transnat'l L	*Columbia Journal of Transnational Law*
Const Comment	*Constitutional Commentary*
Cornell Int'l LJ	*Cornell International Law Journal*
CRC	Convention on the Rights of the Child
Crim LF	*Criminal Law Forum*
DSM	Dispute Settlement Mechanism
DSU	Dispute Settlement Understanding
Duke J Comp& Int'l L	*Duke Journal of Comparative and International Law*
Duke LJ	*Duke Law Journal*
EC	European Communities
ECCC	Extraordinary Chambers in the Courts of Cambodia
Ecology LQ	*Ecology Law Quarterly*
EJIL	*European Journal of International Law*
Emory Int'l L	Rev *Emory International Law Review*
FCAFC	The Full Court of the Federal Court of Australia
FRG	Federal Republic of Germany
FYBIL	*Finnish Yearbook of International Law*
Ga J Int'l & Comp L	*Georgia Journal of International and Comparative Law*
GDR	German Democratic Republic
Geo LJ	*Georgetown Law Review*
Georget J Int Law	*Georgetown Journal of International Law*
Geo Wash Intl L Rev	*George Washington International Law Review*
GLR	*Griffith Law Review*
GYIL	*German Yearbook of International Law*
Harv Hum Rts J	*Harvard Human Rights Journal*
Harv Int'l LJ	*Harvard International Law Journal*
Harv L Rev	*Harvard Law Review*
HE His/Her	Excellency
HHR	Journal *Health and Human Rights Journal*
HPCR	*Humanitarian Policy & Conflict Research*
HRC UN	Human Rights Council
HR&ILD	Human Rights & International Legal Discourse
HRLR	*Human Rights Law Reports UK Cases*
HYIL	*Hague Yearbook of International Law*
ICC	International Criminal Court

ICJ	International Court of Justice
ICLQ	International & Comparative Law Quarterly
ICLR	*International & Comparative Law Review*
ICTR	International Criminal Tribunal for Rwanda
ICTY	International Criminal Tribunal for Yugoslavia
ICs	International Courts
IDI	Institut de Droit International
IJIL	*Indian Journal of International Law*
IL	International Law
ILA	International Law Association
ILC	International Law Commission
ILDC	International Law in Domestic Courts
ILR	*International Law Reports*
ILS	International Law Studies
Ind J Global Legal	Studies *Indiana Journal of Global Legal Studies*
Int CLR	*International Criminal Law Review*
Int CL Rev	*International Community Law Review*
IO	International Organisation
IOLR	*International Organizations Law Review*
IP	International Peacekeeping
IRRC	International Review of the Red Cross
Isr YB Hum Rts	*Israel Yearbook on Human Rights*
ITLOS	International Tribunal for the Law of the Sea
IYIL	*Italian Yearbook of International Law*
J Conflict Resol	*Journal of Conflict Resolution*
JC&SL	*Journal of Conflict and Security Law*
JICJ	*Journal of International Criminal Justice*
JIDS	*Journal of International Dispute Settlement*
JIHLS	*Journal of International Humanitarian Legal Studies*
J Intl Econ L	*Journal of International Economic Law*
JLS	*Journal of Legal Studies*
J Med Ethics	*Journal of Medical Ethics*
JMWP	*Jean Monnet Working Paper*
JWT	*Journal of World Trade*
LEG	Legal Theory
LGDJ	The Librairie générale de droit et de jurisprudence
Liverpool LR	*Liverpool Law Review*
LJIL	*Leiden Journal of International Law*
Lond rev int law	*London Review of International Law*
Loy LA Int'l & Comp L Rev	*Loyola of Los Angeles International and Comparative Law Review*
L& Phil	*Law and Philosophy*

LPICT	*The Law & Practice of International Courts and Tribunals*
Mich J Intl L	*Michigan Journal of International Law*
Mich L Rev	*Michigan Law Review*
Minn L Rev	*Minnesota Law Review*
MJIL	*Melbourne Journal of International Law*
MPEPIL	*Max Planck Encyclopedia of Public International Law*
NILR	*Netherlands International Law Review*
Nord J Intl L	*Nordic Journal of International Law*
NWULR	*Northwestern University Law Review*
NYIL	*Netherlands Yearbook of International Law*
NY L Sch J Hum Rts	*New York Law School Journal of Human Rights*
NZ L Rev	*New Zealand Law Review*
OHCHR	Office of the United Nations High Commissioner for Human Rights
OJLS	*Oxford Journal of Legal Studies*
OU	University of Oklahoma
Pace Int'l L Rev	*Pace International Law Review*
PCIJ	Permanent Court of International Justice
Phil & Pub Aff	*Philosophy & Public Affairs*
Phil Rev	*Philosophical Review*
PROC	*Proceedings of the Annual Meeting*
RBDI	*Revue Belge de Droit International*
RD	*Revista de Derecho e Jurisprudencia y Ciencias Sociales*
RDC	Recueil des Cours (Abbreviation for collected courses of the Hague Academy, in references and bibliography)
RGDIP	*Revue générale de droit international public*
RIAA	*Reports of International Arbitration Award*
RIO	*Review of International Organizations*
Riv Dir Int	*Rivista di diritto internazionale*
RQDI	*Revue Québécoise de Droit International*
RStGH	*Staatsgerichtshof für das deutsche Reich*
RV	*Reichsverfassung*
Santa Clara L Rev	*Santa Clara Law Review*
S Cal L Rev	*Southern California Law Review*
Stan J Intl L	*Stanford Journal of International Law*
Stan L Rev	*Stanford Law Review*
STL	Special Tribunal for Lebanon
SYBIL	*Singapore Year Book of International Law*
TRICI-Law	The Rules of Interpretation of Customary International Law
TWQ	*Third World Quarterly*

U Chi L Rev	*University of Chicago Law Review*
UCDavis JInt'l L& Pol'y	*UC Davis Journal of International Law & Policy*
U Ill L Rev	*University of Illinois Law Review*
UN	United Nations
UNC	University of North Carolina
UNCRC UN	Committee on the Rights of the Child
UNDP	United Nations Development Programme
UNHRC	United Nations Human Rights Council
UNYB	*Max Planck Yearbook of United Nations Law*
UPR	*Universal Periodic Review*
UTLJ	*University of Toronto Law Journal*
Va J Int'l L	*Virginia Journal of International Law*
Vand J Transnat'l L	*Vanderbilt Journal of Transnational Law*
VCDR	Vienna Convention on Diplomatic Relations
VCLT	Vienna Convention on the Law of Treaties
VfGH	*Verfassungsgerichtshof*
VUWLR	*Victoria University of Wellington Law Review*
WdW	*De Wijsbegeerte der Wetsidee*
WTO	World Trade Organization
Yale J Int'l L	*Yale Journal of International Law*
Yale LJ	*Yale Law Journal*
YBILC	*Yearbook of the International Law Commission*
ZaöRV	*Heidelberg Journal of International Law*

TABLE OF CASES

International Court of Justice (ICJ)

Permanent Court of International Justice (PCIJ)

International Tribunal for the Law of the Sea (ITLOS)

Arbitration

International Criminal Tribunal for the Former Yugoslavia (ICTY)

International Criminal Tribunal for Rwanda (ICTR)

International Criminal Court (ICC)

Extraordinary Chambers in the Courts of Cambodia (ECCC)

Special Tribunal for Lebanon (STL)

Special Court for Sierra Leone (SCSL)

European Court of Human Rights and European Commission of Human Rights

Court of Justice of the European Union

Inter-American Court of Human Rights

Advisory Opinion on Juridical Condition and Human Rights of the Child, Advisory Opinion OC-17/2002, IACtHR (28 August 2002); 337
Domingues *v.* United States (Merits) (2002) IACmHR Report No 62/02; 335

Human Rights Committee

Toonen *v.* Australia (1994) UN Doc CCPR/C/50/D/488/1992; 325

WTO

WTO, Brazil – Desiccated Coconut, Panel Report (17 October 1996) WT/DS22/R 75; 281
WTO, Chile – Price Band System, Appellate Body Report (23 September 2002) WT/DS207/AB/R; 280
WTO, China – Publications and Audiovisual Products, Appellate Body Report (21 December 2009) WT/DS363/AB/R 166; 282
WTO, EC – Approval and Marketing of Biotech Products, Panel Report (29 September 2006) WT/DS291/R; 458
WTO, EC – Hormones, Appellate Body Report (16 January 1998) WT/DS26/AB/R; 249, 279–80, 282, 286, 293
WTO, EC and Certain Member States – Large Civil Aircraft, Appellate Body Report (18 May 2011) WT/DS316/AB/R; 282, 285
WTO, EC—Measures Affecting the Approval and Marketing of Biotech Products (EC – Biotech), Panel Report (21 November 2006) WT/DS291/R, WT/DS292/R, WT/DS293/R; 249, 358
WTO, Japan – Alcoholic Beverages, Appellate Body Report (4 October 1996) WT/DS8/AB/R; 280
WTO, Japan – Alcoholic Beverages II, Appellate Body Report (4 October 1996) WT/DS8/AB/R; 282
WTO, US – 1916 Act (EC), Appellate Body Report (28 August 2000) WT/DS136/AB/R WT/DS162/AB/R; 279
WTO, US – AD and CVD (China), Appellate Body Report (11 March 2011) WT/DS379/AB/R; 284–86
WTO, US – Carbon Steel, Appellate Body Report (28 November 2002) WT/DS213/AB/R; 281
WTO, US – Cotton Yarn, Appellate Body Report (8 October 2001) WT/DS192/AB/R; 283, 287–88, 294
WTO, US – Cotton Yarn, Panel Report (31 May 2001) WT/DS192/R; 294
WTO, US – Gasoline, Appellate Body Report (29 April 1996) WT/DS2/AB/R; 280, 282
WTO, US – Gasoline, Panel Report (29 January 1996) WT/DS2/R; 280
WTO, US – Line Pipe, Appellate Body Report (15 February 2002) WT/DS202/AB/R; 283, 294–95

Domestic Cases

TABLE OF INTERNATIONAL TREATIES, DOCUMENTS AND NATIONAL LEGISLATION

Treaties

1997 Convention on the Prohibition of the Use, Stockpiling, Production and Transfer of Anti-Personnel Mines and on Their Destruction (adopted 18 September 1997, entered into force 1 March 1999) 2056 UNTS 211; 317

1998 Rome Statute of the International Criminal Court (adopted 17 July 1998, entered into force 1 July 2002) 2187 UNTS 3; 55–56, 163, 168, 354, 503

International Documents

General Assembly and Security Council

UNGA Res 1514(XV) 'Declaration on the Granting of Independence to Colonial Countries and Peoples' (14 December 1960) UN Doc A/RES/1514(XV); 244, 269–70, 321, 326, 428, 445

UNGA Res 2066 'Question of Mauritius' (16 December 1965) UN Doc A/RES/2066 (XX); 436

UNGA Res 2749(XXV) 'Declaration of Principles Governing the Sea-Bed and the Ocean Floor, and the Subsoil Thereof, Beyond the Limits of National Jurisdiction' (12 December 1970) UN Doc A/RES/2749(XXV); 331

UNGA Res 60/251 'Resolution Adopted by the General Assembly: 60/251 Human Rights Council' (3 April 2006) UN Doc A/Res/60/251; 326

UNGA Res 62/61 'Responsibility of States for Internationally Wrongful Acts' (6 December 2007) UN Doc A/62/446; 164

UNGA Res 63/123 'Report of the International Law Commission on the Work of its 60th session' (11 December 2008) UN Doc A/RES/63/123; 168

UNGA Res 69/118 'Report of the International Law Commission on the Work of its 66th Session' (10 December 2014) UN Doc A/RES/69/118; 167

UNGA Res 71/292 'Request for an Advisory Opinion of the International Court of Justice on the Legal Consequences of the Separation of the Chagos Archipelago from Mauritius in 1965' (22 June 2017) UN Doc A/71/PV.88; 436

UNGA Res 73/203 'Identification of Customary International Law' (11 January 2019) UN Doc A/RES/73/203; 233, 236

UNGA Res 74/180 'Responsibility of States for Internationally Wrongful Acts' (18 December 2019) UN Doc A/RES/74/180; 164

UNGA 'Report of the International Court of Justice 39th Plenary Meeting' (27 October 2005) UN Doc A/60/PV.39; 146

UNGA 'Report of the International Court of Justice – 42nd Plenary Meeting' (1 November 2007) UN Doc A/62/PV.42; 146

UNGA 'Resolution Adopted by the General Assembly: 60/251 Human Rights Council' (3 April 2006) UN Doc A/Res/60/251; 326

UNGA 'Review of the Role of the International Court of Justice: Report of the Secretary-General' (15 September 1971) UN Doc A/8382; 145

UNGA 'Review of the Role of the International Court of Justice (*concluded*)' (5 November 1974) UN Doc A/C.6/SR.1492; 145

International Law Commission

ILC, 'Final Report: Working Group on the Obligation to Extradite or Prosecute (aut dedere aut judicare)' (5 May–6 June and 7 July–8 August 2014) UN Doc A/CN.4/L.844; 167

ILC, 'Final Report: Study Group on the Most-Favoured-Nation Clause' (4 May–5 June and 6 July–7 August 2015) UN Doc A/CN.4/L.852; 168

ILC, 'First Report on Formation and Evidence of Customary International Law by Michael Wood, Special Rapporteur' (17 May 2013) UN Doc A/CN.4/663; 4, 46, 142

ILC, 'First Report on State Responsibility by Mr James Crawford, Special Rapporteur' (24 April 1998) UN Doc A/CN.4/490 and Add 1–7; 171

ILC, 'First Report on the Law of Treaties by Sir Humphrey Waldock, Special Rapporteur' (26 March 1962) UN Doc A/CN.4/144 and Add.1 reproduced in [1962/II] YBILC; 351

ILC, 'Formation and Evidence of Customary International Law, Elements in the Previous Work of the International Law Commission that Could Be Particularly Relevant to the Topic, Memorandum by the Secretariat' (5 May–7 June and 8 July–9 August 2013) UN Doc A/CN.4/659; 169

ILC, 'Fourth Report on Identification of Customary International Law by Michael Wood, Special Rapporteur' (8 March 2016) UN Doc A/CN.4/695; 47

ILC, 'Fourth Report on the Law of Treaties by Gerald Fitzmaurice, Special Rapporteur' (17 March 1959) UN Doc A/CN.4/120, reproduced in [1959/II] YBILC 37; 112

ILC, 'Fourth Report on Peremptory Norms of General International Law (*Jus Cogens*) by Dire Tladi, Special Rapporteur' (31 January 2019) UN Doc A/CN.4/727; 312

ILC, 'Fragmentation of International Law: Difficulties Arising from the Diversification and Expansion of International Law. Report of the Study Group of the International Law Commission' (1 May-9 June and 3 July-11 August 2006) UN Doc A/CN.4/L.682; 167, 289, 356

ILC, 'Guide to Practice on Reservations to Treaties, with Commentaries' (26 April–3 June and 4 July–12 August 2011) UN Doc A/66/10/Add.1; 164, 167, 181

ILC, 'Guiding Principles Applicable to Unilateral Declarations of States Capable of Creating Legal Obligations with Commentaries Thereto' (1 May-9 June and 3 July-11 August 2006) UN Doc A/61/10 reproduced in [2006/II – Part Two] YBILC 160; 164, 166, 353, 456–57

ILC, 'Identification of Customary International Law: Comments and Observations received from Governments, Comments and Observations by the Kingdom of the Netherlands submitted on 23 January 2018' (14 February 2018) UN Doc A/CN.4/716; 46, 398

ILC, 'Identification of Customary International Law: Comments and Observations received from Governments' (14 February 2018) UN Doc A/CN.4/716; 398

ILC, 'Identification of Customary International Law: Text of the Draft Conclusions Provisionally Adopted by the Drafting Committee' (30 May 2016) UN Doc A/CN.4/L.872; 150, 323

ILC, 'Long-term Programme of Work: Review of the List of Topics Established in 1996 in the Light of Subsequent Developments, Working Paper Prepared by the

Secretariat' (2 May-10 June and 4 July-12 August 2016) UN Doc A/CN.4/679/ Add.1; 170

ILC, 'Peremptory Norms of General International Law (*jus cogens*): Draft Conclusions' (29 May 2019) UN Doc A/CN.4/L.936; 362

ILC, 'Programme, Procedures and Working Methods of the Commission, and its Documentation' (6 May-26 July 1996) Un Doc A/51/10 (Part 2), reproduced in [1996/II – Part Two] YBILC 84; 168

ILC, 'Provisional Summary Record of the 3225th Meeting' (18 September 2014) UN Doc A/CN.4/SR.3225; 398

ILC, 'Provisional Summary Record of the 3338th Meeting' (2 May 2017) UN Doc A/ CN.4/SR.3338; 398

ILC, 'Report of the International Law Commission on the Work of its 58th Session' (1 May-9 June and 3 July-11 August 2006) UN Doc A/61/10; 166–67

ILC, 'Report of the International Law Commission on the Work of Its 59th session' (7 May–5 June and 9 July–10 August 2007) UN Doc A/62/10; 112

ILC, 'Report of the International Law Commission on the Work of its 65th Session' (6 May-7 June and 8 July-9 August 2013) UN Doc A/68/10; 35

ILC, 'Report of the International Law Commission on the Work of its 69th Session' (1 May-2 June and 3 July-4 August 2017) UN Doc A/72/10; 168

ILC, 'Report of the International Law Commission on the Work of its 70th Session' (30 April – 1 June and 2 July – 10 August 2018) UN Doc A/73/10; 4, 416

ILC, 'Report of the International Law Commission on the work of its 71st session' (29 April–7 June and 8 July–9 August 2019) UN Doc A/74/10; 164, 166

ILC, 'Report of the Study Group, Fragmentation of International Law: Difficulties Arising from the Diversification and Expansion of International Law: Conclusions' (18 July 2006) UN Doc A/CN.4/L; 403

ILC, 'Report on Fragmentation of International Law: Difficulties Arising from the Diversification and Expansion of International Law, Finalized by Martti Koskenniemi' (13 April 2006) UN Doc A/CN.4/L.682; 167, 289, 356

ILC, 'Report on the Law of Treaties by Mr GG Fitzmaurice' (14 March 1956) UN Doc A/CN.4/101 reproduced in [1956/II] YBILC 104; 352

ILC, 'Second Report on General Principle of Law, by Marcelo Vázquez-Bermúdez, Special Rapporteur' (9 April 2020) UN Doc A/CN.4/741; 368

ILC, 'Second Report on Identification of Customary International Law by Michael Wood, Special Rapporteur' (22 May 2014) UN Doc A/CN.4/672; 4, 46

ILC, 'Second Report on the Question of Treaties Concluded between States and International Organizations or between Two or More International Organizations by Mr Paul Reuter, Special Rapporteur' (15 May 1972) UN Doc A/CN.4/271 reproduced in [1972/II] YBILC 75ILC; 352

ILC, 'Summary Record of the 668th Meeting' (26 June 1962) UN Doc A/CN.4/ SR.668; 352

ILC, 'Summary Record of the 729th meeting' (22 May 1964) UN Doc A/CN.4/SR.729 reproduced in [I/1964] YBILC 34; 290

ILC, 'Summary Record of the 3150th Meeting' (26 July 2012) UN Doc A/CN.4/SR.3150; 398

ILC, 'Summary Record of the 3151st meeting' (27 July 2012) UN Doc A/CN.4/SR.3151; 417

ILC, 'Summary Record of the 3183rd meeting' (19 July 2013) UN Doc A/CN.4/SR.3183; 398, 417

ILC, 'Summary Record of the 3184th Meeting' (23 July 2013) UN Doc A/CN.4/SR.3184; 398

ILC, 'Summary Record of the 3185th meeting' (24 July 2013) A/CN.4/SR.3185; 417

ILC, 'Survey on Liability Regimes Relevant to the Topic International Liability for Injurious Consequences Arising Out of Acts Not Prohibited by International Law: Study Prepared by the Secretariat' (23 June 1995) UN Doc A/CN.4/471; 146

ILC, 'Third Report on Identification of Customary International Law by Michael Wood, Special Rapporteur' (27 March 2015) UN Doc A/CN.4/682; 4, 34, 47, 440

ILC, 'Third Report on the Law of Treaties by Sir Humphrey Waldock, Special Rapporteur' (3 March, 9 June, 12 June and 7 July 1964) UN Doc A/CN.4/167 reproduced in [1964/II] YBILC 5; 290

ILC, 'Title and Texts of the Preamble and the Draft Principles on the Allocation of Loss Arising Out of Hazardous Activities Adopted by the Drafting Committee on Second Reading' (1 May-9 June and 3 July-11 August 2006) UN Doc A/CN.4/L.686 and Corr.1; 164

International Law Association

Committee on Formation of Customary (General) International Law, 'Final Report of the Committee: Statement of Principles Applicable to the Formation of General Customary International Law' (London Conference 2000); 60, 233

ILA Committee on Non-State Actors, 'Third Report of the Committee: Non-State Actors' (Washington Conference 2014); 304

Study Group on Content and Evolution of the Rules of Interpretation, 'Preliminary Report' (Johannesburg 2016); 461

Institut de Droit International

IDI, 'Resolution: Problems Arising from a Succession of Codification Conventions on a Particular Subject' (1995) 66 AIDI 435; 233

IDI, 'Resolution: The Elaboration of General Multilateral Conventions and of Non-Contractual Instruments Having a Normative Function or Objective' (1987) 62 AIDI 274; 233

IDI, 'Resolution: The Intertemporal Problem in Public International Law' (1975) 56 AIDI 536; 361

Other Reports

Advisory Committee of Jurists, *Procès Verbaux of the Meetings of the Advisory Committee of Jurists: 16 June 24 July 1920 with Annexes* (van Langenhuysen 1920); 231, 355, 400

Advisory Committee on Issues of Public International Law, 'Advisory Report on The Identification of Customary International Law' (Advisory Report No 29, 2017) https://bit.ly/3Dx6tcX;398

CEDAW Committee, 'Concluding Observations on the Combined Fourth and Fifth periodic Reports of Maldives' (11 March 2015) UN Doc CEDAW/C/MDV/CO/4–5; 327

Gujadhur S & Limon M, 'Towards the Third Cycle of the UPR: Stick or Twist' (2016) Policy Report: Universal Rights Group 31; 329

Human Rights Council, 'Report of the Working Group on the Universal Periodic Review: Maldives' (4 January 2011) UN Doc A/HRC/16/7; 327

Human Rights Council, 'Review of the Work and Functioning of the Human Rights Council' (12 April 2011) UN Doc A/HRC/RES/16/21; 334

Human Rights Council, 'Report of the Working Group on the Universal Periodic Review: Algeria' (5 July 2012) UN Doc A/HRC/21/13; 338

Human Rights Council, 'Report of the Working Group on the Universal Periodic Review: Brazil' (9 July 2012) UN Doc A/HRC/21/11; 328

Human Rights Council, 'Report of the Working Group on the Universal Periodic Review: Benin' (11 December 2012) UN Doc A/HRC/22/9; 342

Human Rights Council, 'Report of the Working Group on the Universal Periodic Review: Indonesia' (5 July 2012) UN Doc A/HRC/21/7; 342

Human Rights Council, 'Report of the Working Group on the Universal Periodic Review: France' (21 March 2013) UN Doc A/HRC/23/3; 338

Human Rights Council, 'Report of the Working Group on the Universal Periodic Review: Dominican Republic' (4 April 2014) UN Doc A/HRC/26/15; 320

Human Rights Council, 'National Report Submitted in Accordance with Paragraph 5 of the Annex to Human Rights Council Resolution 16/21: Indonesia' (20 February 2017) UN Doc A/HRC/WG.6/27/IDN/1; 342

Human Rights Council, 'Report of the Working Group on the Universal Periodic Review: Indonesia' (14 July 2017) UN Doc A/HRC/36/7; 342

Human Rights Council, 'Report of the Working Group on the Universal Periodic Review: India' (17 July 2017) UN Doc A/HRC/36/10; 328

Human Rights Council, 'National Report Submitted in Accordance with Paragraph 5 of the Annex to Human Rights Council Resolution 16/21: Benin' (7 August 2017) UN Doc A/HRC/WG.6/28/BEN/1; 342

Human Rights Council, 'Report of the Working Group on the Universal Periodic Review: Switzerland' (29 December 2017) UN Doc A/HRC/37/12; 338

Human Rights Council, 'Report of the Working Group on the Universal Periodic Review: Benin' (3 January 2018) UN Doc A/HRC/37/10; 342

Other International Documents

ICRC, 'Practice Relating to Rule 104 Respect for Convictions and Religious Practices' (*ICRC IHL Database*, 2021) https://bit.ly/3DAOIt8;220

ICRC, 'Rule 1 The Principle of Distinction between Civilians and Combatants' (*ICRC IHL Database*, 2021) https://bit.ly/3v70hVT; 12

Negotiating Group on Institutions, 'Meeting of 26 September 1991 – Note by the Secretariat' (18 October 1991) GATT Doc MTN.GNG/IN/1; 280

Yoo J, 'The Soleimani Strike: The President Has the Constitution and Precedent on His Side' (6 January 2020) National Review; 57

National Legislation

1945 US Presidential Proclamation No 2667, 'Policy of the United States with Respect to the Natural Resources of the Subsoil and Sea Bed of the Continental Shelf' 10 Fed Reg 12303 (1945) 13 DSB 485; 374

Bundesverfassungsgericht (Entscheidung vom 23 Oktober 1951) BVerfGE 1; 516, 518, 520, 522

Bundesverfassungsgericht (Entscheidung vom 30 Januar 1973) BVerfGE 34; 520–21

Bundes-Verfassungsgesetznovelle vom 30 Juli 1974, BGBl nr 444/19749; 525

Greek Code of Civil Procedure, ΦΕΚ Α 182 19851024; 356

Grundgesetz für die Bundesrepublik Deutschland vom 23. Mai 1949, BGBl 1949, S 1; 516

Judicature Act, The Official Law Reports of the Republic of Kenya https://bit.ly/2YLRay8; 472–74

Law of Obligations, Official Gazette of R Macedonia No 18 of 5.03.2001 https://bit.ly/3mOqrZU;470

Reichsgesetz vom 9 Juli 1921 (Federal Act of July 9 1921) RGBl 1921, S 905; 510

Staatsvertrag zwischen den Freistaaten Bayern und Coburg vom 20. Februar 1920, GVBl 1920, S 335; 520

Verfassung des Deutschen Reichs vom 11 August 1919, RGBl 1919, S. 1383; 509

Verfassung des Landes Baden vom 22 Mai 1947, GVBl 1947, S 129; 517

Verfassung des Landes Württemberg-Baden vom 28 November 1946, RegBl 1946, S 277; 517

Verfassung des Landes Württemberg-Hohenzollern vom 18 Mai 1947, RegBl 1947, S 1; 517

Verfassungsgerichtshof (Entscheidung vom 15 Oktober 1998) VfSlg 15.309/1998; 527

Verordnung vom 27 Dezember 1971 zur Neugliederung Bayerns in Landkreise und kreisfreie Städte GVBl 1971, S 495; 520

PART I

The Theory of Customary International Law

Fault Lines and the Need for New Approaches

1

Between Pragmatism and Disenchantment

The Theory of Customary International Law after the ILC Project

JÖRG KAMMERHOFER

1 Introduction

There is a fundamental, eternal and unresolvable conundrum at the heart of customary international law (CIL) – the 'source', if the pun may be excused, of the enigma that is customary law. It is that we do not know on what we can – or are allowed to – base our arguments for or against one or another concept. Authors frequently note the lack of discipline in our debates on the foundations of this source of international law, even as they fail to show any themselves. Plenty of old wine is poured into new bottles as we seem to periodically rediscover arguments which generations upon generations before us have made – sometimes all the way back to Roman law.

Debates on the theory of CIL continue unabated, inter alia because there is a continuing, strong, urgent and foundational belief that we *need* CIL in order to keep international law working. Instead of being able to see customary law as a primitive method of norm-creation which is severely limited in its utility and dismissing it – as their domestic colleagues are wont to do – as entirely unsuitable for modern legal orders which tend to be complex and technocratic, an important sub-group of international lawyers wish to see and/or create international law as such a complex legal order. To this group belong practitioners and international legal scholars with a stake in the actual functioning of the law. They imagine customary law to be capable of performing the complex functions analogous to legislation in domestic law.[1] They do so not out of a sense of pride or ego, but because

[1] M Wood, 'The Present Position within the ILC on the Topic "Identification of Customary International Law": In Partial Response to Sienho Yee, Report on the ILC Project on "Identification of Customary International Law"' (2016) 15 Chin J Int Law 3, 5:

they genuinely believe that we cannot rely on treaties alone, that we *must* have CIL[2] (and therefore do) in order to achieve the political goals international society or politics needs to progress (or those which they imagine do). But the question is whether that is reason enough to consciously or subconsciously change the mechanics of customary law to suit these perceived needs and whether CIL has the flexibility to react to these perceived needs.

Two events have prompted my writing of this chapter. The first is that the International Law Commission (ILC) concluded its project on the Identification of Customary International Law in 2018.[3] Ably directed by Michael Wood, it has from the very beginning been suffused with the spirit of pragmatism. The project primarily wanted to provide guidance to decision makers, particularly those not professionally trained in international law. Engaging in depth with the theory of CIL was consciously avoided as far as possible. Yet, for all its self-avowed pragmatism, the ILC could not avoid taking a stance on the theoretical aspects of this source, even if only in a roundabout, subconscious manner. On the other side of the equation we find foundational critiques of CIL, with Jean d'Aspremont's 2018 *International Law as a Belief System* as well as recent articles on CIL[4] as excellent recent contributions to this *genre*. In these writings, CIL is downgraded to a set of doctrines within the canon of folk tales international lawyers tell themselves – our 'bed-time stories', so to speak.

Both methods have virtues, but both have very dangerous vices and both, in a sense, contain the seeds of their own destruction. One aim of this contribution will therefore be an effort to show the relative merits and

'Customary international law continues to play a significant role . . . In uncodified fields, it has proven itself able to adapt to the ways of modern international life.'

2 DH Joyner, 'Why I Stopped Believing in Customary International Law' (2019) 9 Asian JIL 31, 38–41, gives a range of examples from humanitarian law. I have also previously written on this phenomenon: J Kammerhofer, 'Orthodox Generalists and Political Activists in International Legal Scholarship' in M Happold (ed), *International Law in a Multipolar World* (Routledge 2011) 138.

3 Documents cited in this chapter: ILC, 'Report of the International Law Commission on the Work of its 70th Session' (30 April–1 June and 2 July–10 August 2018) UN Doc A/73/10; ILC, 'First Report on Formation and Evidence of Customary International Law by Michael Wood, Special Rapporteur' (17 May 2013) UN Doc A/CN.4/663; ILC, 'Second Report on Identification of Customary International Law by Michael Wood, Special Rapporteur' (22 May 2014) UN Doc A/CN.4/672; ILC, 'Third Report on Identification of Customary International Law by Michael Wood, Special Rapporteur' (27 March 2015) UN Doc A/CN.4/682.

4 J d'Aspremont, *International Law as a Belief System* (Cambridge University Press 2018); J d'Aspremont, 'The Four Lives of Customary International Law' (2019) 21 Int CL Rev 229.

demerits of these two approaches, exemplified in the ILC Report and d'Aspremont's work. I will focus on what they can tell us about the theoretical foundations of customary law as a source of international law. I am sympathetic to both: CIL is on shakier ground than mainstream writers and practitioners assume, but the point cannot be to employ a brutal reductivism. In this chapter, I will show where the quicksand lies and why our reliance on this source is problematic. To paraphrase Carl Schmitt: whoever invokes customary international law wants to deceive.[5]

The second event to spark this chapter is that at the time of writing fifteen years had passed since I first published an article in the *European Journal of International Law* on the fundamental 'uncertainties', as I called them, of customary international law-making.[6] This anniversary and the conclusion of the ILC project have prompted me to rethink the argument made then and to reconceptualise the foundation of this source whose importance for international lawyers is eclipsed only by their frustration in the face of the manifold *aporia* with which they are confronted when wishing to research and/or apply it. My work usually stops at the recognition that we cannot find the law which tells us what the rules on customary international law-making are. In this chapter, I will attempt to go a step further.

Accordingly, Section 2 will summarise what I consider to be the salient features of the two approaches, exemplified by the writings of its two champions, Wood for the pragmatists and d'Aspremont for the iconoclasts. This section is brief because these traits are better discussed using specific examples. Indeed, the example in Section 3 is the pivot point for this chapter, because it is both an illustration of the two approaches as well as an expression of the high-level problem: the 'meta-meta law' and the problem of finding what its content is. Section 4 will focus on this problem and will discuss my proposal for a new method for conceptualising this elusive level.

2 Two Approaches to Customary International Law

There are, of course, more than two possible approaches to customary (international) law and the choice of these two is arbitrary. Yet, they are

[5] Schmitt's aphorism is: *Wer Menschheit sagt, will betrügen*. 'Whoever invokes humanity wants to deceive.' C Schmitt, *Der Begriff des Politischen* (first published 1932, 7th ed, Duncker & Humblot 1991) 55.

[6] J Kammerhofer, 'Uncertainty in the Formal Sources of International Law: Customary International Law and Some of Its Problems' (2004) 15 EJIL 523; later incorporated, rewritten and expanded in J Kammerhofer, *Uncertainty in International Law: A Kelsenian Perspective* (Routledge 2010) 59–86, 195–240.

well-known and well-respected archetypes for two essential directions the debates on this topic have taken in the past decade or so – both in terms of the sharp divergences that characterise them as well as the fact that they are surprisingly close on some points. Wood is typical of those scholars and practitioners who wish to construe CIL in a practicable manner from a 'generalist' perspective; d'Aspremont is the most adept communicator among the younger generation of scholars who seek to deconstruct the theoretical-philosophical foundations of the stories we tell about custom. Both approaches have merits, but both suffer from significant defects: Wood is right to focus on the positive law, but wrong to dismiss CIL's problems so easily. His generalist-pragmatic understanding leads to an indistinct view of what CIL is and how it comes about; an impish soul might call him 'the astigmatic pragmatist'. D'Aspremont is right to criticise that aspect, but the way forward in legal scholarship cannot lie in a reduction of law to collective psychology; he, in turn, could be called a 'frustrated iconoclast'. My argument is, and has been for more than fifteen years, that both methods have a point, but that we require a combination of factors in order to make headway in international legal scholarship on customary law: it should be a theory-conscious analysis of the positive law in force.

2.1 *Astigmatic Pragmatists*

From the beginning of the ILC's project on CIL, Michael Wood as the special rapporteur was committed to pragmatic goals, rather than to exploring theoretical (or even many doctrinal) questions. Wood's First Report is clear about the project's goal, namely 'to offer some guidance to those called upon to apply rules of CIL on how to identify such rules in concrete cases',[7] that is 'especially those who are not necessarily specialists in the general field of public international law', because it is 'important that there be a degree of clarity in the practical application of this central aspect of international law, while recognizing of course that the customary process is inherently flexible'.[8] On that *pragmatic* level, concerned with the 'usefulness of its practical consequences',[9] the project has to some extent succeeded. In this sense, the ILC's work has a stabilising function and Wood is to be commended for his contribution. If he had remained

[7] Wood, 'First Report' (n 3) [14].
[8] Wood, 'Second Report' (n 3) [12].
[9] *Oxford English Dictionary* (3rd ed, Oxford University Press 2004): pragmatism, n 4a, available at: <https://oed.com>.

on this pragmatic level, it would not have made for a good example for this chapter; however, there are indications that there is more to this mindset. For example, in a 2016 article, Wood (writing in his private capacity), argues: 'Work on the topic has also shown that *several longstanding theoretical controversies related to customary international law have by now been put to rest*. It is no longer contested, for example, that verbal acts, and not just physical conduct, may count as "practice."'[10] One can take issue with statements such as this on several levels. For one, it is less than certain that 'theoretical controversies', including the verbal practice problem, have been 'put to rest' (which itself can mean a number of things). On another level, however, I submit that this type of statement is indirectly expressive of a particular view popular with practitioners and practice-leaning scholars, mistakenly believing that practice solves theoretical problems. While neither Wood nor the ILC texts openly declare it, one could argue that there is a subconscious belief that the eternal problems of customary law can be solved by the Commission declaring one side the winner – or that it should try. It is trivial to say that the ILC is not a lawmaker which could modify the law on customary international lawmaking. It is perhaps not so trivial to say that the role of the ILC as epistemic 'authority' – as an institution whose pronouncements can be presumed to accurately represent the state of international law – is equally problematic, particularly given the narrow range of sources and arguments on which it, like most orthodox international lawyers, relies.

Partially, this can be explained by the peculiar, if widespread use of the word 'theory' in English legal language. Whereas for example in German, *Theorie* or *Rechtstheorie* refers to legal theory, in English it tends also to be used for doctrinal statements about the material content of the positive law. The 'theory of customary international law' of which Wood writes tends to be concerned with questions like the relative value of domestic court judgments as state practice or the requisite number of instances of *opinio juris*.[11] Those are not the core research areas of legal theorists, but of international legal scholars – *Rechtsdogmatik* in German. If those topics are 'theory', then it is not surprising that legal theory properly so called finds no place in the ILC project and that a pragmatic project assumes that it has made changes to the 'theory' of customary law.

[10] Wood (n 1) 8 (emphasis added).

[11] O Sender & M Wood, 'The Emergence of Customary International Law: Between Theory and Practice' in C Brölmann & Y Radi (eds), *Handbook on the Theory and Practice of International Lawmaking* (Edward Elgar 2016) 133, 137–45.

Largely, however, it is the *culture of orthodoxy*[12] which moulds this mindset. Orthodoxy is understood here as respect for conventional authority (acceptance by peers). International lawyers with their largely (but not consistently) 'positivist' outlook tend to exhibit three elements as part of the culture of orthodoxy: (1) submission: international lawyers submit to an apology of international tribunals (foremost the ICJ) as almost unquestioned authorities; (2) realist pragmatism: the pragmatic impetus unites with a belief in being 'realistic' and accommodating the 'realities' of international life, particularly practice – we know that practice is relevant because practice tells us that practice is relevant; (3) problem-solving: their pragmatic bent leads naturally to a tendency to try to solve problems, rather than analyse the law, even when they are not authorised to 'solve' the problems themselves.

On this basis, Wood's reports combine a certain (small-c) conservatism on substantial issues, for example on international legal subjectivity,[13] with a pragmatic *modus operandi*. As mentioned above, the problem arises when there is even the tacit assumption that this is the right way to cognise or change the law – the result is an unclear cognition, an astigmatism.

2.2 *Frustrated Iconoclasts*

Like myself, Jean d'Aspremont has critiqued the *naïveté* inherent in the ILC project, which cannot escape the theoretical problems of what he calls the 'monolithic understanding of customary law'.[14] This is obvious in manifold ways, including the central problem of verbal practice which we have both criticised in similar terms. His is a theoretical approach to (customary) international law; it is heterodox in the sense that theoretical coherence is more important to him than his arguments being in line with what is generally accepted. However, even the briefest look at his current theory, summarised in the 2018 book *International Law as a Belief System*, shows that its radical reductivism borders on non-cognitivism and threatens to destroy more than false assumptions. In this book, d'Aspremont argues with some justification that much of the (orthodox) discourse about what CIL is and how it functions – 'the articulation of international legal

[12] I have tried to outline this in a recent publication as part of international legal scholarship's 'default positivism': J Kammerhofer, 'International Legal Positivist Research Methods' in R Deplano & N Tsagourias (eds), *Research Methods in International Law: A Handbook* (Edward Elgar 2021), 95, 97–103.

[13] Wood, 'Third Report' (n 3) [70].

[14] D'Aspremont, 'The Four Lives of Customary International Law' (n 4) 231.

discourses around fundamental doctrines', as he puts it – has the hallmarks 'of a belief system'.[15] That, in turn, is characterised in the following manner:

> [A] belief system is a set of mutually reinforcing beliefs prevalent in a community or society that is not necessarily formalised. A belief system thus refers to dominant interrelated attitudes of the members of a community or society as to what they regard as true or acceptable or as to make sense of the world. In a belief system, truth or meaning is acquired neither by reason (rationalism) nor by experience (empiricism) but by the deployment of certain transcendental validators that are unjudged and unproved rationally or empirically.[16]

The 'fundamental doctrines', such as (our talking about) CIL are 'organised clusters of modes of legal reasoning that are constantly deployed by international lawyers when they formulate international legal claims about the existence and extent of the rights and duties of actors',[17] which sounds reasonable as a *sociological description* of the *language use* by international law professionals. And indeed, on first blush, d'Aspremont seems to carefully guide us through the problems of this deconstructive enterprise. This new view of customary law doctrine as part of a belief system and as a cluster of reasoning is supposedly a 'heuristic undertaking' 'with a view to raising awareness about under-explored dimensions of international legal discourse'. By this method, he posits the possibility of 'a temporary suspension of the belief system' and 'a falsification of the transcendental character of the fundamental doctrines to which international lawyers turn to generate truth, meaning or sense in international legal discourse'.[18] In more conventional terms, by realising that the (dominant) way in which we *talk* about international law and the widespread acceptance of certain doctrines does not equal 'truth', the authority of orthodox assumptions can be questioned. So far so good: questioning the unspoken assumptions of legal scholars is the main task of all legal theory and I would happily count myself among those who participate in this form of 'radical' critique in the word's original sense: pertaining to the *radix*, the root or foundation, of our knowledge.

Yet at this point the critique turns to iconoclasm, despite d'Aspremont's avowed aim of avoiding 'apostasy', which 'is neither possible nor desirable'.[19] Let us look at what d'Aspremont does *not* (wish to) talk about: international law itself and the relationship of the doctrines/belief system to the body of

[15] D'Aspremont, *International Law as a Belief System* (n 4) 1.
[16] ibid 4–5.
[17] ibid 8.
[18] ibid 17–18.
[19] ibid 20.

rules/norms that is the law. The open question is as to the reason for this reluctance, which he shares with many other postmodernist international legal theorists. My interpretation of this peculiar state of affairs – peculiar from my theoretical vantage point – is that for d'Aspremont, two foundational beliefs strongly discourage talking about the law itself in any meaningful way: (1) a general noncognitivism; (2) a specific aversion to the 'ruleness of sources'.

(1) For d'Aspremont, the title of his book is enough to show the radical reductivism of this strain of thought: it is *international law* that is a belief system. Despite considerable vacillation between the possibility of rules/norms and their denial, in the end, international law is identified with and reduced to 'law-talk' – the way we talk about the law is the law. The 'existence' in any sense of the word of international law as body of rules (as legal order) is half-negated. It seems – although it is difficult to pinpoint in the text – that, on the one hand, substantive rules are rules properly speaking, but on the other hand, sometimes certain parts of the law and the law in general is doctrine. Law is doctrine, law is a socio-psycho-linguistic phenomenon, law is reducible to (a special kind of) facts and apprehensible only by social-scientific methods. Even when d'Aspremont's approach was still closer to Hartian legal positivism, it tended to favour reductivist, legal realist and anti-metaphysical readings of Hart.[20] With this book, this trend is strengthened and he is now closer to the postmodernist orthodoxy in international legal theory.

(2) Denying the idea that the law regulates its own creation (i.e. sources *sensu stricto*), and that sources are not themselves law unites certain post-Hartian and postmodernist theoretical approaches with a long tradition of state-centred thought in international legal doctrine. Whereas the former would rather, as d'Aspremont does, reduce sources to a doctrine – to teachings and to methods of law ascertainment[21] – the latter see the source of law immediately founded in facts.[22]

[20] J Kammerhofer, 'International Legal Positivism' in F Hoffmann & A Orford (eds), *The Oxford Handbook of the Theory of International Law* (Oxford University Press 2016) 407, 414–25.

[21] D'Aspremont, *International Law as a Belief System* (n 4) 55–63; see already J d'Aspremont, *Formalism and the Sources of International Law: A Theory of the Ascertainment of Legal Rules* (Oxford University Press 2011).

[22] I have analysed this aspect in J Kammerhofer, 'Sources in Legal Positivist Theories: The Pure Theory's Structural Analysis of the Law' in S Besson & J d'Aspremont (eds), *The*

The problems which this approach engenders are, at least potentially, destructive not just of false orthodox narratives, but of the very idea of law. It does not really matter that d'Aspremont asks us only for 'a temporary suspension'[23] of the belief system. The very possibility that we can simply suspend belief destroys the underlying concept and is probably self-contradictory – as if we could temporarily suspend belief that half, but not all, of the audience members are in an auditorium. Reductivism of this sort must face up to the enormous problem that it cannot distinguish between the belief system of doctrines about the law and the possibility that the law itself is no more than a belief system. This idea is indeed more than a heuristic tool to critique baseless orthodox taboos and fetishes, it is more than 'apostasy'; it negates the very possibility of law as something separate from what actually happens in the physical world, its counterfactual nature. 'The argument that in the end . . . the "existence" of law "is a matter of fact" is a negation of the very possibility of Ought. Ideals cannot be deduced from reality alone.'[24] It does not really matter that perhaps the reductivism which d'Aspremont wishes to promote is not anti-norm-ontic, merely epistemic. As long as the mediatisation of law by way of beliefs and discourse is watertight, law is still reduced to facts. If we adopt such reductivism, we are throwing the baby (the notion that 'you ought not to kill' makes sense as a claim to regulate behaviour) out with the bathwater (the true observation that many of our most cherished doctrines have little to do with the content of the positive law). But there is some 'hope' that orthodoxy's serene pragmatism will domesticate and ultimately frustrate this iconoclasm – as it tends to do with all theoretical arguments, whether they are right or wrong.

3 Verbal Practice as Example

How do the two approaches deal with an issue which is not always acknowledged as problem, but which (from a theoretical vantage point) is far from problem-free? From a range of potential topics I have chosen verbal practice, because it allows me to demonstrate the strengths and weaknesses of both approaches introduced in Section 2 – but also because it is an ideal candidate to show the fundamental problem of all CIL theory (Section 4).

Oxford Handbook of the Sources of International Law (Oxford University Press 2017) 343, 349–51.

[23] D'Aspremont, *International Law as a Belief System* (n 4) 17.

[24] Kammerhofer, *Uncertainty in International Law* (n 6) 226.

Verbal acts have become incredibly important for international law and we have increasingly turned to texts to support our claims to the emergence, change and destruction of customary law. That is because our world has become more complex whereas customary law as ancient law-creation mechanism originally based on raw actions has not. The classical controversy about the role of verbal utterances as practice has abated and it is virtually universally admitted that statements can be state practice.[25] In customary international humanitarian law, for example, reliance on verbal practice has far eclipsed 'battlefield practice' – take the ICRC study's almost exclusive use of verbal emanations such as manuals as example for this trend. For example, the 'Practice' section for the principle of distinction contains a vast amount of material. As far as I can tell, all of these are statements and not a single instance of battlefield practice is mentioned;[26] for example under 'Other National Practice', the study quotes the following '"[i]t is the *opinio juris* of the United States that ... a distinction must be made"' – *opinio juris* is thus made practice. The entire project seems to be aimed at reporting statements, rather than acts.

The pragmatic temperament of colleagues has meant that they are unwilling to exclude any factor that might possibly be useful. Accordingly, verbal acts are now universally recognised, including by Wood. He is dismissive of those who problematise the use of statements; those 'views ... are too restrictive. Accepting such views could also be seen as encouraging confrontation and, in some cases, even the use of force.'[27] That is a strongly emotive argument – you better accept verbal practice or we may end up at war – but in terms of a dispassionate legal argument it cannot convince. Yet orthodoxy's pragmatic impetus pushes Wood and the ILC to focus on the fact of widespread acceptance by peers:[28] "it is now *generally accepted* that verbal conduct ... may also count as practice."[29] The only substantive argument is negative; Wood quotes Mark Villiger's 1997 monograph, which contains the following argument: 'the term "practice" ... is general enough ... to cover any act or behaviour ... it is not made entirely

[25] N Petersen, 'Customary Law Without Custom? Rules, Principles, and the Role of State Practice in International Norm Creation' (2007) 32 AmUInt'l LRev 275, 278.

[26] ICRC, 'Practice Relating to Rule 1 The Principle of Distinction between Civilians and Combatants' (*ICRC Customary IHL Database*, 2005) sect A <https://ihl-databases.icrc.org/customary-ihl/eng/docs/v2_rul_rule1> accessed 1 March 2021.

[27] Wood, 'Second Report' (n 3) [37].

[28] Which, in turn, is the decisive element of the 'culture of orthodoxy' that characterises orthodox (positivist) international legal scholarship (and practice): Kammerhofer (n 12) 97–101.

[29] ILC Report (n 3) Conclusion 6, Commentary 2 [66].

clear in what respect verbal acts originating from a State would be lacking'.[30] Neither argument is particularly strong. Why, on the one hand, should general acceptance by peers be a decisive factor in the creation or cognition of law? Cognition is not a matter for plebiscites; scholarship is not a dictatorship of the majority. This argument has pragmatic value – it is difficult to argue against it, certainly – but is weak in terms of scholarship. On the other hand, a whole school of thought in the classical debate on verbal practice has made it its business to set out what, exactly, this form of practice is 'lacking'; we are, I think, not really confronted by a dearth of argument against verbal practice.

And, indeed, there are two (partially overlapping) avenues to problematising verbal practice: one is doctrinal and another theoretical. D'Aspremont's critique is, I submit, rather on the doctrinal than the theoretical side. When he argues that 'the International Law Commission's formal acceptance that practice and *opinio juris* can be extracted from the very same acts collapses the distinction between the two tests',[31] I would argue that he is more concerned with a question of language-use, whereby we do not keep apart the two elements and the evidence for them. As I argued in my 2004 article (and as is obvious by the ICRC counting a clear instance of *opinio juris* as practice), the word 'practice' seems to lead a double life.[32] Villiger, in another section of the monograph mentioned above, gives us an indication of this double meaning. When he argues that those denying the validity of verbal acts 'cannot support their views *on* State practice *with* State practice',[33] a critical reading would see him commit a circular argument; on a more charitable reading, however, it is obvious that the two meanings of 'state practice' differ markedly.

The most common use of the word 'state practice' is wide. Discussing the special problem of treaties as state practice, Villiger notes that 'the acceptance of a convention['s] . . . significance as State practice, namely as an expression of *opinio juris*, is lessened for three reasons'.[34] Quoting another classical author, Michael Akehurst puts it to us that 'State practice means any act or statement by a State from which *views about*

[30] ME Villiger, *Customary International Law and Treaties: A Manual on the Theory and Practice of the Interrelation of Sources* (2nd ed, Kluwer Law International 1997) 21, cited by Wood, 'Second Report' (n 3) [37].

[31] D'Aspremont, 'The Four Lives of Customary International Law' (n 4) 249.

[32] Kammerhofer, 'Uncertainty in the Formal Sources of International Law' (n 6) 525–30; Kammerhofer, *Uncertainty in International Law* (n 6) 62–70.

[33] Villiger (n 30) 19–20.

[34] ibid 27.

customary law can be inferred'.[35] We can see that state practice on this reading can express *opinio juris*; it can be the basis for inferences to what states believe to be the state of customary law. I believe that there is a conceptual (but still doctrinal) case to be made that we need to distinguish between evidences/proofs of custom-forming elements and the elements themselves. Critics are certainly right that this commingling almost inevitably leads to problems. I join d'Aspremont, however, in arguing that – on this level – the problem is more practical and more a question of internal incoherence of the orthodox position:

> [T]he Special Rapporteur, while showing some awareness for the problem of double counting, had no qualms defending the idea that practice and *opinio juris* could be extracted from the very same acts. . . . it must be emphasized how difficult it is to reconcile the claim made in Conclusion 3 that each of the two elements must be verified separately with the explicit possibility that practice and opinio juris may be extracted from the same acts.[36]

As pragmatic argument, however, this line of critique is liable to be rebuffed by equally pragmatic assurances that *in practice* this does not matter and will not be problematic: 'distinctions between "constitutive acts" and "evidence of constitutive acts" . . . are artificial and arbitrary because one may disguise the other'.[37] Wood's equivocating between his insistence on the separation of the two elements and his willingness, to admit 'state practice' as evidence of *opinio juris*[38] is borne of that pragmatic impulse. Nothing would be easier than to give in to the idea that we could just 'take some scholars' use of the term "state practice" with a pinch of salt'.[39] This 'state practice', as it were, is merely a slightly inaccurate use of the word, given that 'state practice' is also the technical term for the objective element of customary law creation. 'State practice and *opinio juris* may be categorically different things, but we may look for proof of either element in the same place'[40] – problem solved.

However, these pragmatic manoeuvres hide the real theoretical problem which only the second avenue of critique is able to clarify. Neither the

[35] M Akehurst, 'Custom as a Source of International Law' (1975) 47 BYBIL 1, 53(emphasis added).

[36] D'Aspremont, 'The Four Lives of Customary International Law' (n 4) 250, 252.

[37] K Zemanek, 'What Is State Practice and Who Makes It?' in U Beyerlin et al (eds), *Recht zwischen Umbruch und Bewahrung: Völkerrecht, Europarecht, Staatsrecht: Festschrift für Rudolf Bernhardt* (Springer 1995) 289, 292.

[38] Wood, 'Second Report' (n 3) [38].

[39] Kammerhofer, *Uncertainty in International Law* (n 6) 69.

[40] ibid 68.

orthodox international lawyer nor the 'international law as argumentative practice' theory espoused by d'Aspremont and others – the 'post-ontological ... mindset'[41] – are likely to be able to distil the fundamental legal theoretical problem of verbal practice. The classical canon of generalist international legal writings is once more on point. I still[42] believe that Karol Wolfke's argument expresses the true theoretical problem of verbal practice, whether or not a theoretical, rather than doctrinal argument was intended. For him, admitting verbal practice 'neglects the very essence of every kind of custom, which for centuries has been based upon material deeds and not words. ... customs arise from acts of conduct and not from promises of such acts'.[43] Wolfke is correct: the utterance 'I will do x' does not mean physically doing 'x': 'repeated verbal acts ... can give rise to international customs, but only to customs of making such declarations, etc., and not to customs of the conduct described in the content of the verbal acts'.[44]

The theoretical basis for Wolfke's argument is that at least in the civil tradition of customary law, despite just about everything being contentious about this source, one thing is reasonably clear: customary law must be based on customs. Customs, *usus*, *actus frequens*,[45] in turn must be an observance of the budding prescription or exercise of the budding right. Without the manifestation in a behavioural regularity of what will become binding, there can be no usage; without usage, the law-making of unwritten laws is not customary law. Customary law must be about *customs*. It is predicated on customs being or becoming obligatory. Only the behaviour that is (or is to become) the content of the norm – the 'practical exercise of the legal rule'[46] – can serve as the objective element. Only doing or abstaining from 'x' can count as *usus* for a customary norm which prescribes 'x'. Talking about doing/abstaining from 'x', in contrast, can be content forming only for a norm which prescribes talking. For norms which specify actual

[41] D'Aspremont, 'The Idea of "Rules" in the Sources of International Law' (2014) 84 BYBIL 103, 109.

[42] Kammerhofer, 'Uncertainty in the Formal Sources of International Law' (n 6) 527–28; Kammerhofer, *Uncertainty in International Law* (n 6) 65–66.

[43] K Wolfke, *Custom in Present International Law* (2nd ed, Martinus Nijhoff 1993) 42.

[44] ibid 42.

[45] '*dicitur enim consuetudo, quia in communi est usu ... quomodo autem esse potest in usu communi sine actuum frequentia.*' 'for "custom" is so called because ... it is usage in common. But how can it be common usage except through a repetition of actions?' F Suárez, 'De legibus ac Deo legislatore' (first published 1612) in GL Williams, A Brown, J Waldron & H Davis (trs), *Selections from Three Works of Francisco Suarez – Vol 2* (Clarendon Press 1944) 529–30, lib 7 cap 10, sect 1.

[46] 'Das Erfordernis der praktischen Uebung des Rechtssatzes' S Brie, *Die Lehre vom Gewohnheitsrecht: Eine historisch-dogmatische Untersuchung* (Marcus 1899) 12.

behaviour, none but actual behaviour will do as *usus*. With respect to state practice, the prohibition of torture is not constituted by states *saying* that they will not torture, only by the actual omission of torture. Customary law is a primitive form of law-making and cannot do all we ask of it in modern international legal debate.

The force of this argument is not undermined by the theory of speech acts.[47] Sometimes, speech can be more than descriptive: 'I name this ship "Queen Victoria"' or 'I now pronounce you man and wife.' One could therefore argue that verbal state practice is largely composed of such acts – the content, rather than the fact of uttering, is determinative. In certain cases, this may be true: it is conceivable that there are customary norms whose *usus* is a series of speech acts. However, not all speech is speech acts and this supplanting cannot happen for all, or indeed, for most legal rules. For example, 'I am putting a chicken in the oven to be roasted' is not a speech act; what is more, the chicken will firmly remain on the kitchen counter once I have uttered the sentence. The putting of the chicken into the oven can only happen in the real world; only when I have physically moved the chicken from the kitchen counter to the oven will the sentence be true. The same applies a fortiori to the *usus* with respect to customary norm-creation: uttering the words: 'we are not torturing' is not a speech act, but a (possibly accurate) description of the behaviour by state organs. It is not the actual omission of torture and – even if we accept the theory of performative utterances – cannot replace it as *usus/actus frequens* in the process of custom-formation *for a norm regulating actual behaviour*, as the prohibition of torture is.

However, this argument is predicated on customary (international) law being a type of norm that has two essential criteria: (1) the creation of customary norms requires a repetition of behaviour; (2) this behavioural regularity – the sum-total of behaviours attributed to the law-creation process – is the content of the prescription (*Tatbestand*) of the norm. Yet how do we know that this is the legally correct predicate? The concept of customary (international) law is not unitary, as d'Aspremont points out for international legal doctrine.[48] There are strong currents, from Roman law all the way to the drafting of the Permanent Court of International Justice (PCIJ) Statute in 1920, of a different basis for customary law: 'acts . . . of a specific kind were . . . considered as custom-creative . . . only, because

[47] For example JR Searle, *Speech Acts: An Essay in the Philosophy of Language* (Cambridge University Press 1969).

[48] D'Aspremont, 'The Four Lives of Customary International Law' (n 4).

these acts evidenced the *consensus tacitus* in an adequate form',[49] writes Siegfried Brie; the PCIJ/International Court of Justice (ICJ) Statute speaks of 'a general practice accepted as law'. There are, however, also strong indications that over the course of the development of western (particularly civil) law, *usus* understood as behaviour which forms the content has been regarded as essential for the very idea of customary norms. Yet, even if we ignore countervailing arguments made over the course of the more than 1,500 years of our debating customary law, the legal-structural question remains: why is this the correct (or incorrect) reading of what customary (international) law is? On this level, we cannot effectively counter the orthodox insistence that verbal practice is part of state practice because it is accepted by all those who matter with the essentialist argument that customary law is necessarily shaped in a specific manner which conflicts with the majority opinion. That would mean succumbing to a metaphysical realism. If we do not wish to absolutise and reify concepts such as this, we must at least admit that this source of law *could* be different. Bin Cheng's proposal to rename customary international law to 'general international law' once he eliminates practice from the conditions for law-creation, is consistent.[50] Whether CIL *is* different, however, is a question for the meta-meta law (Section 4).

4 Source-Creating International Law?

4.1 Law-Identification versus Law-Making

Therefore, as mentioned above, I strongly believe that on a truly legal-scholarly (rather than pragmatic) perspective, the real problem is the exact content of those rules which regulate the creation of CIL. Yet, instead of tackling it head-on, recent writings on CIL, the ILC project among them, engage in what looks to me like an exercise in avoidance: they speak of customary law 'identification' or 'ascertainment'. Law-*creation*, not to mention the *law* of law-creation, is not discussed. This is understandable, given the widespread feeling among international lawyers that attempts at solving the problems of customary law have been unsuccessful, also given their resignation that they can ever be

[49] *Handlungen … von einer gewissen Beschaffenheit galten … als erforderlich für Bildung eines Gewohnheitsrechts … nur deshalb, weil in ihnen der für Entstehung eines Gewohnheitsrechts erforderliche consensus tacitus in geeigneter Weise sich bekunde.* Brie, *Die Lehre vom Gewohnheitsrecht* (n 46) 142.

[50] B Cheng, 'Custom: The Future of General State Practice in a Divided World' in RStJ Macdonald & DM Johnston (eds), *The Structure and Process of International Law: Essays in Legal Philosophy Doctrine and Theory* (Martinus Nijhoff 1983) 513, 548.

solved. Focusing on law-identification may seem like a legitimate alternative, particularly on the basis of the success of anti-metaphysical, radically reductivist and non-cognitivist Anglo-Saxon (legal) philosophy; d'Aspremont's 'post-ontological . . . mindset'.[51]

Take the ILC project. The 2018 ILC Conclusions open with the bold statement that they 'concern the way in which the *existence and content* of rules of CIL *are to be determined*';[52] the commentary explains that the conclusions 'concern the *methodology* for identifying rules of CIL, seeking to 'offer *practical guidance*' regarding this determination, which, in turn, means that 'a structured and careful process of legal analysis and evaluation is *required* to ensure that a rule of customary international law is properly identified'.[53] For the ILC, the objective and subjective elements, state practice and *opinio iuris*, respectively, are identification elements: 'to identify the existence and content of a rule of customary international law each of the two constituent elements must be found to be present': 'practice and acceptance as law (*opinio juris*) *together supply the information necessary for the identification of customary international law*'.[54] The ILC conclusions explicitly do not wish to address law-creation, which is seen as different from law-identification: 'Dealing as they do with the identification of rules of customary international law, the draft conclusions do not address, directly, the processes by which customary international law develops over time.' Yet the ILC seems to distance itself from law-creation properly (ie legally) speaking even in its disavowal. The 'consideration of the processes by which [customary international law] has developed', the 'formation of rules'[55] which the ILC does not want to look at, seems to be one of the social or socio-psychological forces at play in physical reality, matters usually studied by legal sociologists, rather than legal scholars *sensu stricto*.

This raises a number of issues concerning both internal coherence and external justification. I have italicised a number of phrases in the previous paragraph to indicate some of the issues, for example the incoherence of arguing that it is a methodology, yet that we should follow them not merely to ensure proper 'identification' or 'determination' (a sort of 'correct cognition'), but also *qua* rules to be followed: 'as in any legal system, there must in public international law be *rules* for identifying the sources of the law'.[56]

51 D'Aspremont, 'The Idea of "Rules" in the Sources of International Law' (n 41) 109.
52 ILC Report (n 3) Conclusion 1 [65] (emphasis added).
53 ILC Report (n 3) General commentary 2 [66] (emphasis added).
54 ibid Conclusion 3, Commentary 6 [66] (emphasis added).
55 ibid Conclusion 1, Commentary 5 [66].
56 Wood, 'First Report' (n 3) [38] (emphasis added).

This seems to be belied by the project's aim of (merely) providing 'practical guidance' to law-appliers. While the ILC's pragmatic impetus may excuse some of this theoretical imprecision, d'Aspremont's taking-on-board of this preference is particularly problematic. Discussing the ILC project in a recent paper, he harks back to an understanding of sources he had held earlier – before his recent sceptical turn – of the 'sources' as 'law-ascertainment'.[57] In *International Law as a Belief System*, he mentions 'the establishment of two distinct facts, that is, practice and *opinio juris* (acceptance as law)' which are 'the dominant modes of legal reasoning to *determine the existence and content* of a rule of customary international law'[58] – determine the existence, not create. Law-creation is thus robbed of its legal character, harking back to old, yet still popular ideas of the sources of law as not themselves law.[59]

This sustained privileging of the law-cognising over the law-creative function has wide theoretical implications. If the 'state practice plus *opinio juris*' formula is merely, but necessarily, the only legitimate method for determining the existence and content of CIL, is it not peculiar that this process is so rigid, formal and so much like a form of law-creation? Is it not much more likely that a whole range of (epistemic) 'methods', which may not have much to do with the two elements, allow us to cognise whether CIL exists and how it is shaped? Is it not much more likely (and does it not accord better with the mainstream understanding of customary law) that state practice and *opinio juris* are the two elements of law-*creation* – the two conditions which international law prescribes for the creation of norms of the type 'customary international law' – rather than 'mere' law-ascertainment or law-identification?

How likely is it that state practice and *opinio juris* are purely of epistemic interest, rather than factors of law-creation? On that view, state practice and *opinio juris* would be the microscope with which we can observe cell division, not the cell division itself. If we assume that state practice and *opinio juris* are mere epistemic tools, how does CIL come about, then? Do we not need customs and a belief or consent to be bound? Even on the epistemic level, would it not be much more sensible to argue that the cognition of CIL involves, as I put it in earlier writings, 'a re-creation of its genesis',[60] that is, an analysis of the various instances of state practice and *opinio juris*, precisely because these two elements are legally required to create CIL? If this were a debate about domestic legislation, nobody would

[57] D'Aspremont, 'The Four Lives of Customary International Law' (n 4) 254.

[58] D'Aspremont, *International Law as a Belief System* (n 4) 88.

[59] Kammerhofer (n 22) 349–50.

[60] Kammerhofer, *Uncertainty in International Law* (n 6) 60.

be tempted to ascribe the label 'means of law-identification' to the approval of the bill by the Houses of Parliament or to the sanction by the head of state.

Neither the ILC nor d'Aspremont tell us what, exactly, this 'identification', 'determination' or 'ascertainment' is. Are they properly part of the cognitive faculties – epistemic processes of law-cognition? How can they then be rule-governed? Probably a similar shift in meaning has taken place as for what I have called 'interpretation$_B$' – a process preparatory to application, to be performed by organs, guided by rules somehow inherent to the legal order, but utterly muddled by confounding it with real cognitive processes (interpretation$_A$). In our case, we would get custom-identification$_A$ versus custom-identification$_B$. Probably also, the idea of 'rules' of custom-identification is as misguided as the idea of rules of interpretation which can somehow determine the hermeneutic process.[61]

4.2 *The Problem of Source-Law (Meta-meta Law)*

Law-identification is important, but it cannot be part of the law. I believe that the whole debate is either a conscious strategy to avoid tackling the problems of law-creation without a written constitution (as a form of avoidance behaviour) or a subconscious category mistake. Figure 1.1 illustrates the different levels which many confound, partly because it is more convenient to do so, partly because of a genuine belief in the post-ontological and anti-metaphysical mindset. As argued in Section 2.2: in order to be able to see law as counterfactual and in order to be able to speak of 'you ought to do/abstain from doing "x"' in any meaningful sense, law (norms) cannot be reducible to facts, whether linguistic, factual or psychological. We cannot supplant law and law-making for ascertainment, for linguistic practices and for an analysis of the way we talk about the law – as much as we need to talk about these issues as well. If we follow this reductivist path, the whole idea of rules becomes precarious. What is left of law as *standard setter* if all we can do is look at linguistic practices?

On a non-reductivist reading, then, there are at least three levels of legal-scholarly discussion: (1) legal scholarship analyses (cognises) which norms are valid, particularly (1a) empowerment norms, that is 'source law'.[62] (2) It may be possible to speak of a separate discussion about law-identification where the various proofs or evidences for the validity of various norms

[61] See J Kammerhofer, 'Taking the Rules of Interpretation Seriously, but not Literally? A Theoretical Reconstruction of Orthodox Dogma' (2017) 86 NordJIntlL 125.

[62] Kammerhofer (n 22) 346–49.

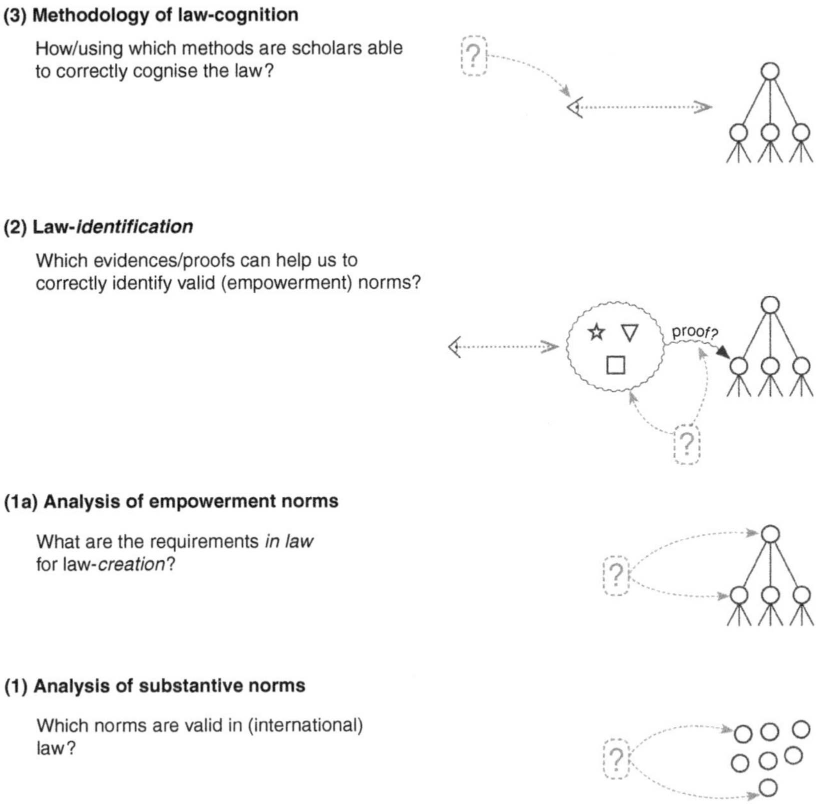

Figure 1.1 Levels of discussion.

(particularly empowerment norms) are discussed. This is unlikely, however, because this pragmatic issue will probably be subsumed under (1) or (3). (3) Legal methodology, then, discusses the (proper) methods which legal scholarship may use/uses in order to correctly cognise the law.[63]

In contrast, Figure 1.2 shows the different 'levels' of the law itself – the hierarchy of empowerment norms ('sources') and law created under it.[64] This is the object of cognition for legal scholarship as 'structural analysis'[65] of legal orders (level (1) above). 'The legal order is not a system of coordinate legal norms existing alongside each other, but a hierarchical ordering of various strata of legal norms,' writes Hans Kelsen. For him, 'a norm which

[63] Kammerhofer (n 12) 95–6.

[64] Kammerhofer (n 22) 346–49.

[65] H Kelsen, *General Theory of Law and State* (Harvard University Press 1945) xiv.

has been created according to the terms of another norm derives its validity from that latter norm',[66] 'validity' being the specific form of existence for norms/law. Also, however, such a derivation is necessary: 'a norm [is] valid, if and when it was created in a certain fashion determined by another norm',[67] because we need to keep apart the norms (Ought) as claims to determine human behaviour from 'mere' reality.

The structure of international law might approximate that given in Figure 1.2:

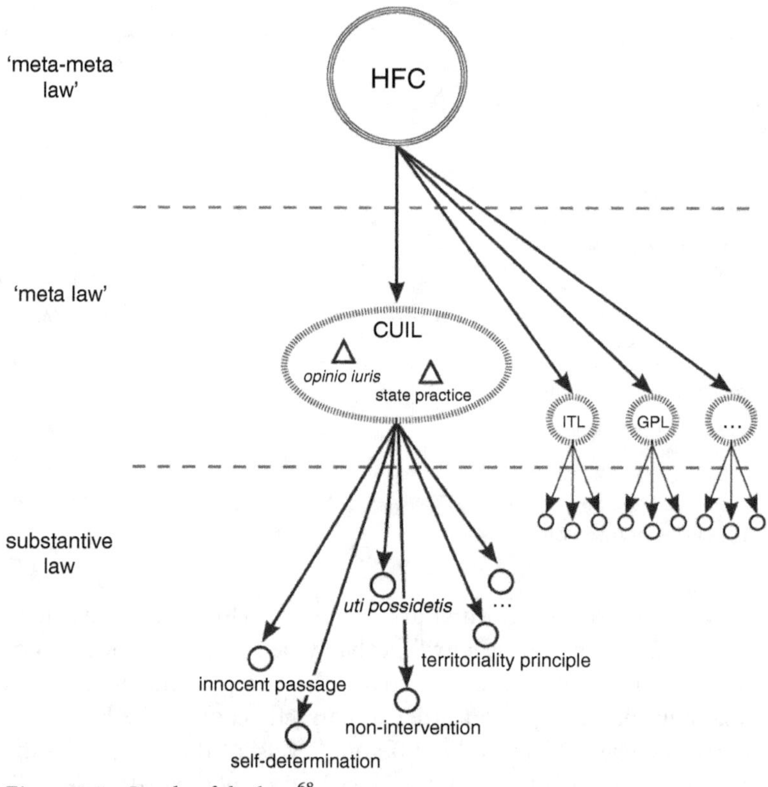

Figure 1.2 Levels of the law.[68]

[66] *'Die Rechtsordnung ist nicht ein System von gleichgeordneten, nebeneinanderstehenden Rechtsnormen, sondern ein Stufenbau verschiedener Schichten von Rechtsnormen ... die Geltung einer Norm, die gemäß einer anderen Norm erzeugt wurde, auf dieser anderen Norm beruht'* H Kelsen, *Reine Rechtslehre* (2nd edn, Deuticke 1960) 228.

[67] *'eine Norm [gilt] darum ..., weil und sofern sie auf eine bestimmte, das heißt durch eine andere Norm bestimmte Weise erzeugt wurde'* Kelsen, *Reine Rechtslehre* (n 66) 228.

[68] Legend: HFC = historically first constitution; CUIL = customary international law; ITL = international treaty law; GPL = general principles of law.

- The level of substantive norms contains a number of CIL norms, like *uti possidetis* or the right to innocent passage, but also a multitude of 'cousins' from other sources, such as the treaty norms like the prohibition on the threat or use of force in Article 2(4) UN Charter or the prohibition of expropriation in Article 13(1) Energy Charter Treaty 1994.
- The meta-law contains a number of 'sources': the empowerment norms to create substantive norms. One such (complex) norm for CIL must be part of international legal order for substantive customary law norms to be able to 'exist', that is: be valid. On the traditional reading, then, this empowerment norm prescribes two conditions – state practice and *opinio juris* – to be fulfilled in order for a customary norm to be created.
- If customary and treaty law as well as general principles are to be equals, yet if all of international law is to be *one* legal order, a further norm is required, since creation according to the same empowerment norm constitutes unity among a multitude of norms.[69] This could be what Kelsen calls 'historically first constitution' (*historisch erste Verfassung*):[70] the hierarchically highest positive norm of a positive normative order. It is what I have called 'meta-meta law',[71] the legal determinant for which sources the international legal order contains.

The distinction between these levels is crucial, as our arguments about the content of the empowerment norm for CIL can *only* be grounded on this level. In other words, if author A were to argue that state practice is not a required element for the creation of CIL and that this is the case because many morally valuable (proposed) norms would not exist otherwise,[72] A must fail. A could succeed only if they could prove that the meta-law for custom-creation is shaped that way. A's arguments regarding the meta-law, in turn, depend on the shape of meta-meta law: A's claim that customary international law-making does not require state practice is true if the meta-law is shaped that way; the meta-law is shaped that way if it has been created according to the meta-meta law.

On a truly legal-theoretical perspective, the solution must lie within the law, as law regulates its own creation. The coming-about of CIL is and has to be based on law. Hence, we *must* find that meta-law, the law on

[69] Kelsen, *Reine Rechtslehre* (n 66) 228.

[70] H Kelsen, *Principles of International Law* (Rinehart 1952) 411.

[71] For example Kammerhofer 'Uncertainty in the Formal Sources of International Law' (n 6) 549; Kammerhofer, *Uncertainty in International Law* (n 6) 231–37.

[72] See for example BD Lepard, *Customary International Law: A New Theory with Practical Applications* (Cambridge University Press 2010).

customary international law-making. Yet the tragedy which I have frequently decried is that while we must proceed in this manner in order to generate legal-scholarly knowledge, we cannot do so. Those 'empowered to will the highest echelons of international law . . . are unlikely to ever have'[73] created meta-meta law. There are also limits to what we can say about international law at this high level. Our epistemological horizon is too limited to answer this question with more than a presumption. As long as we are presupposing, we could presuppose any 'method' to create customary law, even an absurd one. Whatever the case, our knowledge of the content of meta law suffers, because there is little we can do to improve our knowledge of the historically first constitution.

What will never do is to say that this justifies basing our arguments (eg on whether state practice is required) on considerations of pragmatic expediency, political legitimacy or moral necessity: even if there were no meta-meta law (and CIL were to be its own legal order with the *Grundnorm: consuetudines sunt servanda*), arguments of this type would still be based on category mistake. What will also not do is the ILC's 'optimistic' approach: the attempt to trivialise and minimise the problems of CIL by maximising the leverage of the most widely accepted positions. This is combined with the acceptance of the factual influence of the orthodox position, foremost the ICJ's *jurisprudence constante*. When asked what the 'rules for identifying the sources of the law' are, Wood's answer is this: 'These can be found . . . by examining in particular *how States and courts set about* the task of identifying the law.'[74] While Wood uses the word 'identifying', rather than 'creating', identification supplants creation in the ILC project (Sections 2.1 and 4.1).

4.3 *Approximately Plausible Empowerment Norm*

As mentioned above, this is the point where my analysis usually ends: little more can be said, from a legal-theoretical point of view. We cannot know more; those who purport to do so base their arguments on ineligible grounds. In this, we must face a particular problem for the international legal order which permeates all normative orders: how to proceed when the law is 'sparse'? In other words, what is the 'default' position when there is little in the way of (proven or provable) law? This question may look a lot like

[73] Kammerhofer, 'Uncertainty in the Formal Sources of International Law' (n 6) 550; Kammerhofer, *Uncertainty in International Law* (n 6) 239.

[74] Wood, 'First Report' (n 3) [38] (emphasis added).

a burden of proof in the strict sense (ie which of the parties to a judicial procedure has the burden for specific arguments), but it is not. The default position question may or may not arise in judicial proceedings, but it is found on a different level than the standards of proof required by the procedural law for a particular tribunal. It is connected, in a contingent way, to the scholarly 'burden of proof', a burden of proof in a very wide sense: what does scholarship have to do in order for its arguments to satisfy the requirement of generating knowledge about the law? For example, scholarship usually does not have to prove a contention that a proposed norm is *not* valid (although there may be situations where it does); if a scholar claims, however, that 'x' is a norm of, say, CIL, this needs to be proven to be accepted as a 'true' legal-scholarly statement, rather than wishful thinking.

The default position question may also remind us of the 'residual negative principle' and the (in)famous *dictum* in *Lotus* that '[r]estrictions upon the independence of States cannot ... be presumed'.[75] The voluntarist strawman which has dominated much of international legal scholarly discussion of this passage is, I believe, mistakenly applied to it and another reading of the *dictum* is better-aligned with legal theory:[76] '"Restrictions" are only applicable if they are positive law of the normative system "international law". If there is no law, there is no law.'[77] Under that reading, the non-validity of norms is the default; it thus provides a partial answer to the question.

If we cannot prove the content of an empowerment norm for CIL, yet *arguendo* proceed from the presumption that 'customary international law' exists and that there is such an empowerment norm, what would be the 'default' position? In a 1970 book, Herbert Günther mentions that he would proceed on the basis of 'the assumption that custom ... has the power to create law':[78]

> If the norm empowering customary international law as source is thus called a 'hypothesis' or 'postulate', it is done only in the sense that this is conditional upon our being correct in that certain acts can create an Ought. The presumptive validity of particular norms of customary international law, derived as it is from the constituting norm [the source], is thus hypothetical as well: it is only possible to cognise a particular norm of

[75] *SS 'Lotus' (France v Turkey)* (Judgment) [1927] PCIJ Series A 10, 18.

[76] Kammerhofer (n 20) 412–13.

[77] J Kammerhofer, 'Gaps, the *Nuclear Weapons* Advisory Opinion and the Structure of International Legal Argument between Theory and Practice' (2010) 80 BYBIL 333, 343.

[78] *'die Annahme, daß die Gewohnheit ... rechtserzeugende Kraft besitzt'* H Günther, *Zur Entstehung von Völkergewohnheitsrecht* (Duncker & Humblot 1970) 87.

> customary international law as valid if the hierarchically higher norm on law-creation is seen as law and as norm.[79]

This solution sounds quite Kelsenian. There would be a *Grundnorm* with the content: *consuetudines sunt servanda*[80] for a small legal order, comprising CIL (and potential subordinate sources) only, but not international law as a whole. This is also very close to my proposal 'to incorporate all conditions for the creation of . . . customary law . . . into the postulated *Grundnorm* of . . . customary international law'. However, as I argued then, this cannot work, because the *Grundnorm* 'cannot create what is not already positive. It only gives validity as existence as Ought'.[81]

I propose a much weaker heuristic tool, which I will call the Approximately Plausible Empowerment Norm (AppPEN). If we assume (a) that international law contains a positive empowerment norm for 'customary international law' and if we assume (b) that the 'formal source' thereby constituted includes a creation mode of the customary type, then certain arguments/forms of regulation are made more plausible and certain others are less plausible. This is informed legal-theoretical *speculation* that the international legal order is shaped that way, not abstract deductive proof. However, there are degrees of plausibility, because the possible structure of normative orders and the idea of law as norms (Ought) is not completely arbitrary and because we can in some cases see constructs not based on logical fallacies as more plausible than those who celebrate inconsistency. Yet this idea is not orthodox majority following: constructs (such as the two-element theory) are not part of AppPEN because they are widely accepted by peers, but because they are more plausible than single-element theories. AppPEN is thus much weaker than 'ordinary' legal-scholarly proof of the validity (*vel non*) of a specific norm, but it may be the best we can hope for,

[79]

> *Wenn danach die das Völkergewohnheitsrecht einsetzende Norm als 'Hypothese' oder 'Postulat' bezeichnet wird, dann nur in eben diesem Sinne als bedingt durch die Richtigkeit der Entscheidung zugunsten der Soll-Geltung bestimmter Akte. In demselben Maße hypothetisch ist dann die Ableitung des angenommenen Sollens der Völkergewohnheitsrechtsnorm aus der sie konstituierenden Regel: Hat man sich dafür entschieden, eine Norm des Völkergewohnheitsrechts als verbindlich zu betrachten, dann ist dies nur möglich, wenn man zugleich die Rechtseigenschaft der ihr übergeordneten Kreationsnorm und überhaupt deren Normqualität anerkennt.*

Günther, *Zur Entstehung von Völkergewohnheitsrecht* (n 78) 100.

[80] See Kelsen (n 70) 418.

[81] Kammerhofer, *Uncertainty in International Law* (n 6) 238.

given our poor epistemic position vis-à-vis the highest echelons of the international legal order.

A few examples for this positive and negative plausibility might show how AppPEN would operate:

- *It is more likely that CIL is based on customs – repetition of behaviour – than not.* It is trivially true that an empowerment norm ('formal source') could prescribe norm-creation without requiring regular behaviour as basis, for example domestic legislation. However, whether or not we now propose renaming it,[82] it is more likely that a source called 'customary' law is based on customs than not, particularly since the more than 1,500 years of debate have been reasonably consistent on this point.
- *It is more likely that CIL is its own legal order than part of a complex hierarchically ordered international legal system.* If we cannot prove meta-meta norms incorporating CIL, international treaty law, general principles etc. as part of one legal order, it is more likely that no such norm is valid. Hence, 'international law' may refer to a family of legal orders, rather than to one.[83]
- *It is more likely that there is one source 'customary international law' than a whole range of sources.* It is possible that a number of empowerment norms is valid which allow for the creation of a whole range of non-treaty international law. Alfred Verdross proposes a variation on this scheme in a 1969 article: 'It is impossible to found all unwritten norms of international law on the same basis of validity'; 'yet, it is likely that there is some truth in all theories'[84] of how CIL is created. Hence, he argues to accept all those procedures which usually succeed in creating CIL. The theoretical basis for this argument is flawed – we cannot know that CIL has been created unless we know the law on creation, which is exactly what we set out to find. Yet it is also unlikely in terms of Occam's razor: the creation of one empowerment norm is incredibly difficult, see the endless debates about customary international law-making; it is less likely that a whole plethora of such

[82] Cheng (n 50) 548.

[83] Kammerhofer, 'Uncertainty in the Formal Sources of International Law' (n 6) 549–50; Kammerhofer, *Uncertainty in International Law* (n 6) 237–38.

[84] '*Es ist unmöglich, alle ungeschriebenen Normen des VR auf denselben Geltungsgrund zurückzuführen*' '*es aber wahrscheinlich ist, daß in jeder der verschiedenen Theorien ein richtiger Kern steckt*' A Verdross, 'Entstehungsweisen und Geltungsgrund des universellen völkerrechtlichen Gewohnheitsrechts' (1969) 29 Zeitschrift für ausländisches öffentliches Recht und Völkerrecht 635, 649, 636.

norms is valid, rather than one (or even none), particularly given that we have traditionally discussed only one.

5 Conclusion

I have only given a first impression of what AppPEN is and how it could be used. In particular, I foresee two types of use. The first is pragmatic, similar to the idea behind the ILC project: it allows those who have little time to study the various theories of and approaches to CIL and international legal theory – like judges of domestic and international courts and tribunals – to circumnavigate some of the problems by weeding out implausible and selecting plausible theories. The second, however, is legal-scholarly: doctrinal (international) legal scholarship cannot always question all its foundations and will have to make a number of assumptions. AppPEN helps to select those which are more plausible. Neither practitioners nor doctrinal scholars are, however, best served by the orthodox *modus operandi* visible in the ILC report. If, for example, a widely held argument is based on a *contradictio in adiecto*, the fact of the acceptance by peers cannot be better than an approach which consciously avoids solutions which are logically flawed or which are based on an incoherent legal theoretical stance. Legal theory's goal is not to provide a balanced theory, that is, a theory likely to be most widely accepted by international lawyers, because this implies that truth is to be found in compromise and majorities. Rather, it is meant to be consistent and consistently legal, a theory which takes the positive law seriously, yet shows where the law ends, where arguments are self-contradictory and where pragmatism becomes a fetish.

If we do not wish to operate on such a provisional basis, however, the most consistent course of action is to learn to live with much less CIL than we are used to imagining. At the very least we must acknowledge that customary law is a primitive mode of law-creation: we can do much less than we commonly assume. Customary law cannot be international law's 'saviour' or its 'future' – the *Zeitgeist* will never walk where it can run.

2

The Custom-Making Moment in Customary International Law

JEAN D'ASPREMONT

1 Introduction

Customary international law (CIL), as it is commonly construed in international legal thought and practice, is grounded in a particular social reality. In fact, the two constitutive elements of CIL, namely practice and *opinio juris*, correspond to two sides of the social reality which CIL is supposed to be grounded in. This is no new state of affairs. Even in the nineteenth century where CIL was thought to be the product of tacit consent, customary international law was construed as the product of social reality.[1] This social grounding of CIL is certainly neither spectacular nor unheard of. That CIL is grounded in a particular social reality

[1] For some illustrations of an understanding of custom built on tacit consent, as well as some remnants thereof, see H Triepel, *Völkerrecht und Landesrecht* (Scientia Verlag 1899); K Strupp, *Elements du droit international public* (Rousseau & Co 1927); T Lawrence, *The Principles of International Law* (7th ed, Heath & Co 1915); J Westlake, *International Law* (The University Press 1904) 14; D Anzilotti, *Scritti di diritto internazionale pubblico* (Cedan Padova 1956–57) 1, 38, 95 ff; GI Tunkin, *Theory of International Law* (Harvard University Press 1974) 124; C Chaumont, 'Cours général de droit international public' (1970) 129 RdC 333, 440; for an attempt to modernise the consensual conception of customary international law, see A Orakhelashvili, *The Interpretation of Acts and Rules in Public International Law* (Oxford University Press 2008) 70–107; A D'Amato, 'Treaties As a Source of General Rules of International Law' (1962) 3 HarvIntlLJ 1. For an overview of nineteenth-century understanding of customary law as tacit consent, see A Carty, *The Decay of International Law: A Reappraisal of the Limits of Legal Imagination in International Affairs* (Manchester University Press 2019) 61–65. For an illustration of the resilience of the association between custom and consent in international legal thought, see J Tasioulas, 'Custom, *Jus Cogens*, and Human Rights' in CA Bradley (ed), *Custom's Future: International Law in a Changing World* (Cambridge University Press 2016) 95; N Petersen, 'The Role of Consent and Uncertainty in the Formation of Customary International Law' in BD Lepard (ed), *Reexamining Customary International Law* (Cambridge University Press 2017) 111.

bespeaks a construction that has become rather mundane since the Enlightenment,[2] and according to which norms are no longer supposed to be received by their contemplating[3] addressees but are collectively produced[4] by them as members of a self-conscious social community.[5] Such an understanding of the making of CIL as originating in a process of *self-production*, where the authors and the addressees of the customary norm are conflated,[6] is a manifestation of modern thinking.

Although simple in principle, the grounding of a norm in a social reality is a construction that commonly calls for a number of discursive performances for this grounding to be upheld in the discourse.[7] The present chapter zeroes in on one of these discursive performances that is required for CIL to be grounded in social reality, namely the postulation of a moment in the past where the social reality actually engendered the norm. In fact, the grounding of CIL in a social reality captured through practice and *opinio juris* can only be upheld if there was a moment in the past where the practice and *opinio juris* of states – and possibly of other actors[8] – have coalesced in a way that

[2] The modernism of the way in which CIL is construed in international legal thought and practice does not contradict the fact that the generation of legal normativity through past behaviour has been known to many ancient societies. See DJ Bederman, *Custom as a Source of Law* (Cambridge University Press 2010). See also the remarks of E Kadens, 'Custom's Past', in CA Bradley (ed), *Custom's Future: International Law in a Changing World* (Cambridge University Press 2016) 11; H Thirlway, *The Sources of International Law* (2nd ed, Oxford University Press 2019) 60. The doctrine of sources itself was not totally absent from early thinking about international law. Indeed, theories of substantive validity of rules, as those found on scholastic theories, allowed for an autonomous concept of sources. Yet, the dualism – by virtue of which immanent considerations would trump any formal aspects of validity – at the heart of such theories of substantive validity inevitably demoted sources to a very secondary mechanism. See generally A Pagden & J Lawrence (eds), *Vitoria: Political Writings* (Cambridge University Press 1991); A Gentili, *On the Law of War* (JC Rolfe tr, Clarendon Press 1933). On Gentili, see generally B Kingsbury & B Straumann (eds), *The Roman Foundations of the Law of Nations* (Cambridge University Press 2011).

[3] This expression is from Hannah Arendt; H Arendt, *The Human Condition* (2nd ed, University of Chicago Press 1998) 14–21.

[4] On the idea that the question of production of human artefacts and human discourses is very modern, see M de Certeau, *L'écriture de l'histoire* (Gallimard 1975) 27–28.

[5] See the remarks of J Habermas, *The Philosophical Discourse of Modernity: Twelve Lectures* (F Lawrence tr, Polity Press 1987) 41.

[6] Thirlway (n 2) 61.

[7] I have studied these discursive performances elsewhere. See J d'Aspremont, *The Discourse on Customary International Law* (Oxford University Press 2021).

[8] On the question of the role of other actors in the formation of CIL, see S Droubi & J d'Aspremont (eds), *International Organizations, Non-State Actors, and the Formation of Customary International Law, Melland Schill Perspectives on International Law* (Manchester University Press 2020).

generates customary international law. In other words, for CIL to be grounded in social reality, there must have been a moment in the past where customary international law was actually made.

This chapter argues that, in international legal practice and literature, the actual moment where social reality has engendered a customary norm is never established or traced, but is always presupposed.[9] According to the argument developed here, the moment CIL is made is located neither in time nor in space. Customary international law is always presupposed to have been made through actors' behaviours at some given point in the past and in a given place. Yet, neither the moment nor the place of such behaviours can be found or traced. In other words, there is never any concrete moment where all practices and *opinio juris* coalesce into the formation of a rule and which could ever be 'discovered'. This means that the behaviours actually generating the customary rule at stake are *out of time* and *out of space*. Because the custom-making moment is out of time and out of space, it cannot be located, found, or traced, and it must, as a result, be presumed. This is why current debates on CIL in both practice and literature always unfold as if all actors' behaviours and beliefs had at some point coalesced into a fusional process leading to the creation of customary international law. However no trace of that fusional moment can ever be found, condemning this original fusion of all behaviours and beliefs to be presumed.[10] This presumption of a moment in the past where the social reality creates the norm is called here *the presumption of a custom-making moment*. Most

[9] On the idea of an illusory historicism in customary international law see A Carty, *The Decay of International Law? A Reappraisal of the Limits of Legal Imagination in International Affairs* (MUP 2019) 59–80; A Carty, 'The Need to be Rid of the Idea of General Customary Law' (2018) 112 AJIL Unbound 319, 321:

> CIL is merely the lens whereby lawyers choose to describe that society, which Chimni generously recognizes in citing me. By this I mean that within the field of international legal jurisprudence, international lawyers came to talk of States as having a collective *opinio juris*, but as Guggenheim and Ago have already shown, this is an illusion of historicism. Since the international system is still broadly based upon nation States that are aggressively distrustful of others, there is simply no possibility of any CIL of significance emerging.

[10] See however the understanding of CIL as a rule short of a law-making fact defended by Roberto Ago. See R Ago, 'Positive Law and International Law' (1957) 51 AJIL 691, 723 ('those so-called elements of custom ... are nothing but the external data by which the existence and efficacy of a customary norm can be recognized'). In the same vein as Ago, see B Stern, 'Custom at the Heart of International Law' (2001) 11 DukeJComp&IntlL 89, 93.

debates on CIL in practice and in the literature are built on such a presumption of a custom-making moment. As was said, this presumption of a custom-making moment is necessary for CIL to present itself as being grounded in a certain social reality.

This chapter is structured as follows. It first sketches out some of the main manifestations of this presumption of a custom-making moment (1). It then sheds light on some of the discursive consequences of presuming a custom-making moment, including those consequences for the interpretation of CIL (2). The chapter ends with a few observations on what the presumption of a custom-making moment entails for foundational debates about CIL as a whole (3).

Before elucidating the manifestations of the presumption of a custom-making moment and its consequences, a preliminary observation is warranted in light of the presumptive character of the custom-making moment. It could be claimed that the presumption of a custom-making moment is, like *opinio juris*,[11] yet another fiction around which CIL is articulated. In that sense, the custom-making moment would be a fiction about the origin of CIL. It is submitted here that claiming that the custom-making moment is a fiction says basically nothing about what such a presumption stands for and actually does. Indeed, it could be said that international law's representations of both the reality and the past are always fictitious constructions.[12] What is more, fictions have always been

[11] This is a charge made by most of those who approach *opinio juris* with suspicion. See for example A D'Amato, *The Concept of Custom in International Law* (Cornell University Press 1971) 7, 52, 471; see also Carty (n 9) 59–60; A Carty, *The Philosophy of International Law* (Edinburgh University Press 2007) 26–27; H Kelsen, 'Théorie du Droit International Coutumier' (1939) 1(4) Revue Internationale de Theorie du Droit 253, 263; P Guggenheim, 'Les deux elements de la coutume en droit international' in *La Technique et les Principes du Droit Public: Éudes en I'Honneur de Georges Scelle*, Vol 1 (LGDJ 1950) 275 ; M Virally, 'The Sources of International Law' in M Sorensen (ed), *Manual of Public International Law* (St Martin's Press 1968) 116, 134–5; M Meguro, 'Customary International Law and Non-State Actors: Between Anthropomorphism and Artificial Unity' in S Droubi & J d'Aspremont (eds), *International Organizations, Non-State Actors, and the Formation of Customary International Law, Melland Schill Perspectives on International Law* (Manchester University Press 2020); S Droubi, '*Opinio Juris*: Between Mental States and Institutional Objects' in S Droubi & J d'Aspremont (eds) *International Organizations, Non-State Actors, and the Formation of Customary International Law, Melland Schill Perspectives on International Law* (Manchester University Press 2020).

[12] On the reality-making performances of international law, see M Hakimi, 'The Work of International Law' (2017) 58 HarvIntlLJ 1; D Kennedy, *A World of Struggle: How Power, Law, and Expertise Shape Global Political Economy* (Princeton University Press 2016); M Koskenniemi, 'The Politics of International Law: 20 Years Later' (2009) 20 EJIL 7; I Venzke, *How Interpretation Makes International Law: On Semantic Change and*

a common mode of representing the real.[13] That CIL rests on a fictitious representation of the moment of its making can thus not be demoted to just another fiction of international legal reasoning. It is a powerful discursive performance without which CIL could not do all what it does.

2 The Custom-Making Moment in the International Legal Discourse

The following paragraphs mention a few of the manifestations of the presumption of a custom-making moment in international legal thought and practice. It is, for instance, noteworthy that practice and scholarship continuously set aside the question of the duration of practice, as the determination of a minimum threshold would bring back the question of the custom-making moment.[14] The recurrence of the metaphoric shorthand of 'crystallisation' to describe the formation of customary law in the literature similarly epitomizes the continuous avoidance of finding a custom-making moment and the presumption of the latter.[15] In the same vein, it is striking that courts always locate the practice and *opinio juris* they find *in the present*,[16] thereby constantly avoiding the tracing of a custom-making moment.

Normative Twists (Oxford University Press 2012); S Pahuja, 'Decolonization and the Eventness of International Law' in F Johns, R Joyce & S Pahuja (eds), *Events: The Force of International Law* (Routledge 2011) 91. See also the success of the so-called constructivist approaches to world-making, J Brunnée & S Toope, 'Constructivism and International Law' in JL Dunoff & MA Pollack (eds), *Interdisciplinary Perspectives on International Law and International Relations: The State of the Art* (Cambridge University Press 2012) 119–45; J Brunnée & S Toope, 'International Law and Constructivism: Elements of an International Theory of International Law' (2000) 39 ColumJTransnat'lL 19; N Onuf, *World of Our Making: Rule and Rules in Social Theory and International Relations* (University of South Carolina Press 1989); N Onuf, 'The Constitution of International Society' (1994) 5 EJIL 1, 6.

13 On the idea that scientific modes of inquiries have no distinct superiority over literary ones see H White, *Tropics of Discourses: Essays in Cultural Criticism* (Johns Hopkins University Press 1986) 121–22, 142–43; SL Winter, *A Clearing in the Forest: Law, Life and Mind* (University of Chicago Press 2001) 65–66; R Barthes, *L'aventure sémiologique* (Seuil 1985) 14.

14 See ILC, 'Draft Conclusions on identification of customary international law, with commentaries' (30 April–1 June and 2 July–10 August 2018) UN Doc A/73/10, reproduced in (2018/II - Part Two) YBILC, Conclusion 8.1 (hereinafter *ILC Draft Conclusions*); *North Sea Continental Shelf Cases (Federal Republic of Germany/Netherlands; Federal Republic of Germany/Denmark)* (Judgment) [1969] ICJ Rep 3 [74]; see also Thirlway (n 2) 74.

15 See for example Thirlway (n 2) 77.

16 *Military and Paramilitary Activities in and against Nicaragua (Nicaragua v USA)* (Merits) (1986) ICJ Rep 14 [184]: 'The Court must satisfy itself that the existence of the rule in the *opinio juris* of States is confirmed by practice'. This is also the case of the more rigorous ascertainment of practice and *opinio juris*. See *Jurisdictional Immunities of the State (Germany v Italy: Greece intervening)* (Judgment) ICJ Rep 99, 127–35 [64–78].

The presumption of a custom-making moment has occasionally been touched on in the literature. For instance, the famous discussion on the chronological paradox of CIL is a question that, although focused only on *opinio juris*, is all about the abovementioned presumption of a custom-making moment.[17] Yet, those debates on the chronological paradox of CIL never explicitly acknowledge the presumption of a custom-making moment. Reference could also be made to scholarly discussions about the relations between a customary international legal rule with a corresponding existing treaty provision.[18] In this situation, the treaty seems to provide some indication of the time and place of the making of CIL.[19] And yet, here too, despite the treaty providing some vague direction in this regard, there is

[17] GJH van Hoof, *Rethinking the Sources of International Law* (Kluwer 1983) 99 (who seeks to explain the chronological paradox on the basis of an idea 'mistake') or H Meijers, 'How is International Law Made? The Stages of Growth of International Law and the Use of Its Customary Rules' (1978) 9 NYIL 1. For some critical observations about how this discussion is being conducted in international legal scholarship, see H Charlesworth, 'Customary International Law and the Nicaragua Case' (1984–87) 11 AustYBIL 9. See also M Byers, *Custom, Power and the Power of Rules: International Relations and Customary International Law* (Cambridge University Press 1999) 130–33; CA Bradley, 'Customary International Law Adjudication as Common Law Adjudication' in CA Bradley (eds), *Custom's Future: International Law in a Changing World* (Cambridge University Press 2016) 34, 41–43; B Lepard, 'Customary International Law as a Dynamic Process' in CA Bradley (eds), *Custom's Future: International Law in a Changing World* (Cambridge University Press 2016) 62, 69; J Tasioulas, '*Opinio Juris* and the Genesis of Custom: A Solution to the "Paradox"' (2007) 26 AustYBIL 199; M Meguro, 'Distinguishing the Legal Bindingness and Normative Content of Customary International Law' (2017) 6(11) ESIL Reflections.

[18] See for example the debates on the so-called Baxter paradox. RR Baxter '*Treaties and Custom*' (1970) 129 RdC 36, 64, 73; J Crawford, *Chance, Order, Change: The Course of International Law, General Course of Public International Law* (The Pocket Books of The Hague Academy of International Law, Vol 21, Brill 2014) 128–74; H Thirlway, 'Professor Baxter's Legacy: Still Paradoxical?' (2017) 6(3) ESIL Reflections; M Forteau, 'A New "Baxter Paradox"? Does the Work of the ILC on Matters Already Governed by Multilateral Treaties Necessarily Constitute a Dead End? Some Observations on the ILC Draft Articles on the Expulsion of Aliens' (Forum on the ILC's 'Draft Articles on the Expulsion of Aliens', Harvard, March 2016); AM Weisburd, 'Customary International Law: The Problem of Treaties' (1988) 21 VandJTransnatlL 1; ILC, 'Third Report on Identification of Customary International Law by Michael Wood, Special Rapporteur' (27 March 2015) UN Doc A/CN.4/682 [41].

[19] *ILC Draft Conclusions* (n 14) Conclusion 11:

> 1. A rule set forth in a treaty may reflect a rule of customary international law if it is established that the treaty rule: (a) codified a rule of customary international law existing at the time when the treaty was concluded; (b) has led to the crystallization of a rule of customary international law that had started to emerge prior to the conclusion of the treaty; or (c) has given rise to a general practice that is accepted as law (*opinio juris*), thus generating a new rule of customary international law. 2. The fact that

no effort to identify a custom-making moment, the latter remaining presumed.

It is remarkable that the International Law Commission (ILC), in its work on the identification of CIL, consciously decided not to look into the custom-making moment either. Indeed, as it stated in the commentaries to its 2018 conclusions:

> Dealing as they do with the identification of rules of customary international law, the draft conclusions do not address, directly, the processes by which customary international law develops over time. Yet in practice identification cannot always be considered in isolation from formation; the identification of the existence and content of a rule of customary international law may well involve consideration of the processes by which it has developed. The draft conclusions thus inevitably refer in places to the formation of rules of customary international law. They do not, however, deal systematically with how such rules emerge, change, or terminate.[20]

Interestingly, it is this very choice to exclude the question of the formation of customary law from the scope of its work that entailed a change in the way in which the ILC described its own work.[21] It is submitted here that such a choice is not informed by the material impossibility to trace the formation of CIL or the irrelevance of the question for custom-identification, but by the very fact that this presumption is at the heart of the contemporary understanding of CIL. Being presumed, it does not even need to be traced. In the discourse on CIL, the question of establishing or tracing the custom-making moment simply never arises.

3 The Custom-Making Moment and its Doings

It is argued here that the presumption of a custom-making moment is not just a move of convenience to evade difficult methodological and evidentiary obstacles pertaining to the identification of CIL. Such a construction

> a rule is set forth in a number of treaties may, but does not necessarily, indicate that the treaty rule reflects a rule of customary international law.

20 *ILC Draft Conclusions* (n 14) 124.

21 At its 3186th meeting, on 25 July 2013, the commission decided to change the title of the topic from 'Formation and Identification of Customary International Law' to 'Identification of Customary International Law'. For a summary of the debate within the commission, see ILC, 'Report of the International Law Commission 65th Session' (6 May–7 June and 8 July–9 August 2013) UN Doc A/68/10, 64, 66.

is being perpetuated for its many discursive virtues. Indeed, as was indicated above, CIL could not be upheld as being grounded in social reality if it could not be presumed as being made at a certain moment in the past. If it were not presumed to be made at a given moment in the past where *opinio juris* and practice coalesce and generate CIL, it would not be possible to hold that CIL originates in some form of social reality.

In enabling the grounding of CIL in social reality, the presumption of a custom-making moment simultaneously allows some other discursive moves which are worthy of mention here. In particular, attention must be turned to the way in which the presumption of a custom-making moment enables a two-dimensional temporality in the discourse on CIL. In fact, it organizes the life of CIL around two distinct moments, namely: (i) the (presumed) moment of making of CIL in the past; and (ii) the application of CIL in the present.[22] If CIL has a past, albeit presumed, it can have a present distinct from that past. The postulation of a custom-making moment in the past thus allows the postulation of other 'moments'. In particular, this two-dimensional temporality enables the idea that CIL is a product made in the past and subjected to interpretation in the present. Because one presupposes a custom-making moment in the past, one can think of CIL as a tangible artefact in the present which

[22] On the idea that international lawyers, in the many activities in which they are engaged, are constantly historicising, even more so since the formalisation of a 'doctrine of sources' in the twentieth century, see R Parfitt, 'The Spectre of Sources' (2014) 25 EJIL 297, 298 ('The classical doctrine of sources, as it emerged in the 19th century, eventually to be codified in Article 38(1) of the ICJ Statute, leaves no doubt as to the historical character of international law's claim to authority and legitimacy – of its claim to be law'). See also A Orford, 'On International Legal Method' (2013) 1 LondRevIntLaw 166, 172 & 175 ('After all, as lawyers, particularly those of us with common law backgrounds, we are trained in the art of making meaning move across time'); A Orford, 'International Law and the Limits of History' in W Werner et al (eds), *The Law of International Lawyers: Reading Martti Koskenniemi* (Cambridge University Press 2015) 297; T Kleinlein, 'International Legal Thought: Creation of a Tradition and the Potential of Disciplinary Self-Reflection' (2016) 16(1) The Global Community: Yearbook of International Law and Jurisprudence 811–12; M Craven, 'The Invention of a Tradition: Westlake, The Berlin Conference and the Historicisation of International Law' in L Nuzzo & M Vec, *Constructing International Law: The Birth of a Discipline* (Klostermann 2012) 4; K Purcell, 'Faltering at the Critical Turn to History: "Juridical Thinking" in International Law and Genealogy as History, Critique, and Therapy' (2016) 02/15 JMWP Series, 13–15. It is interesting to note that such a claim has been made in relation to philosophy as well, for instance by Hegel. On this point, see T Rockmore, 'Hegel' in A Tucker (ed), *A Companion to the Philosophy of History and Historiography* (Wiley-Blackwell 2011) 468, 474. See the remarks of M Koskenniemi, 'Epilogue' in W Werner et al (eds), *The Law of International Lawyers: Reading Martti Koskenniemi* (Cambridge University Press 2017) 406–07.

can therefore be subject to an autonomous and neatly organised interpretive process.[23] This is why those scholars that argue that the interpretation of the content of CIL can be distinguished from the interpretation of its legal existence[24] extensively and systematically build on this two-dimensional temporality.[25] In that sense, the current scholarly attempts to distinguish the interpretation of the making of the CIL rule from the interpretation of its content can be seen as being predicated on this presumption of a custom-making moment.

There is another important consequence of the presumption of a custom-making moment that ought to be mentioned here. That is, the anonymity and impunity in argumentation about CIL that accompany the presumed custom-making moment and its abovementioned two-dimensional temporality. Indeed, since the custom-making moment is outside time and out of space, and simply presumed, those generating the custom-making behaviours cannot be known. The only possible

[23] For the idea that one should not distinguish law-ascertainment and content-determination regarding customary international law, see M Lippold, 'Reflections on Custom Critique and on Functional Equivalents in the Work of Jean d'Aspremont' (2019) 21 IntCLRev 257–82.

[24] On the distinction, see G Postema, 'Conformity, Custom, and Congruence: Rethinking the Efficacy of Law' in MH Kramer, C Grant, B Colburn et al (eds), *The Legacy of HLA Hart: Legal, Political and Moral Philosophy* (Oxford University Press 2008) 45; see also R Dworkin, *Law's Empire* (Harvard University Press 1986) who famously identified several interpretative stages. On the (non-)applicability of such a distinction to CIL, see O Corten, *Méthodologie du droit international public* (Editions de l'Université Libre de Bruxelles 2009) 213–15; J d'Aspremont, 'The Multidimensional Process of Interpretation: Content-Determination and Law-Ascertainment Distinguished' in A Bianchi, D Peat, & M Windsor (eds), *Interpretation in International Law* (Oxford University Press 2015) 111–29; M Meguro, Distinguishing the Legal Bindingness and Normative Content of Customary International Law (2017) 6(11) ESIL Reflections (2017); Lippold (n 23) 257–82.

[25] See P Merkouris, 'Interpreting the Customary Rules on Interpretation' (2017) 19 Int CL Rev 126; see also the TRICI Law project: www.TRICI-Law.com. It is interesting to note that the ILC has acknowledged to distinguish between identification and determination of content. See ILC Draft Conclusions (n 14) 124:

> The terms 'identify' and 'determine' are used interchangeably in the draft conclusions and commentaries. The reference to determining the 'existence and content' of rules of customary international law reflects the fact that while often the need is to identify both the existence and the content of a rule, in some cases it is accepted that the rule exists but its precise content is disputed. This may be the case, for example, where the question arises as to whether a particular formulation (usually set out in texts such as treaties or resolutions) does in fact correspond precisely to an existing rule of customary international law, or whether there are exceptions to a recognized rule of customary international law.

pedigree of customary international law comes to be reduced to 'all states at some point in the past'. Being presumed, the custom-making process is actually anonymised. This anonymity is explicitly confirmed by the ILC:

> The necessary number and distribution of States taking part in the relevant practice (like the number of instances of practice) cannot be identified in the abstract. It is clear, however, that universal participation is not required: it is not necessary to show that all States have participated in the practice in question. The participating States should include those that had an opportunity or possibility of applying the alleged rule.[26]

The above statement shows that it is not necessary for the sake of custom-ascertainment to even seek to identify who did (or said) what. The ILC is thus saying that the custom-making moment, because it is presumed, ought not to be traced, named and individualised. Being presumed, the making of CIL can stay anonymous.

The anonymity that accompanies the presumption of the custom-making moment is not benign. In fact, as a result of this anonymity, no one can ever be made responsible for the rule of CIL concerned and what is claimed under its name. In other words, as any customary rule enjoys a life of its own out of time and out of space, what is said under the discourse on CIL cannot be blamed for both the good and the suffering caused in the name of CIL. All those invoking CIL can accordingly present themselves as candid followers and observers who just walk behind CIL, be it for the good or the suffering made in the name of CIL.[27]

4 Concluding Remarks: The End of Foundationalism?

Customary international law epitomizes the idea of grounding. Indeed, by virtue of CIL, the rules to which a customary status is recognised are supposedly grounded in a past social reality. And yet, as has been argued in this chapter, such grounding can never be traced but can solely be presupposed.

It is submitted at this concluding stage that the question of whether this presumptive grounding of CIL is a satisfactory state of the discourse is irrelevant. It is particularly argued here that foundational debates about whether a customary international law rests on valid or invalid,

[26] *ILC Draft Conclusions* (n 14) 136.

[27] I have made a similar argument regarding the identification and interpretation of treaties. See J d'Aspremont, 'Current Theorizations about the Treaty in International Law' in D Hollis (ed), *The Oxford Guide to Treaties* (2nd ed, Oxford University Press 2020) 46.

consistent or inconsistent, legal or illegal, grounded or arbitrary, true or untrue, factual or imaginative foundations are bound to be sterile since the foundations of CIL are condemned to be presumptive.[28] As was shown by this chapter, venturing into foundational debates about the validity, truth, legality, consistency and factuality of the foundations of CIL is to condemn oneself to an inevitable defeat.

Yet, it must be emphasised that the limitations of foundational debates about CIL do not entail that one should verse into relativism, nihilism or even discourse vandalism. Although twenty-first-century post-truth delinquents feel they have made a groundbreaking discovery about the origin-less-ness of discourses, it has long been shown that modern discourses cannot meet their own standards in terms of origins and grounding.[29] The same holds for international law, and even more so for CIL.[30] That does not mean, however, that CIL, or all the discourses that cannot meet their own standards of origin and grounding, ought to be derided, disregarded or vandalised.[31] On the contrary, a discourse should be appreciated for how it does what it does, and especially for its origin-less and untraced performances. In that sense, it is once one is liberated from foundational debates about CIL that one can measure and appreciate both the discursive splendour and the efficacy of the latter.

[28] See J Derrida, 'Force de Loi: Le "Fondement Mystique de l'Autorité"' (1990) 11 CardozoLRev 920, 942; see also J Derrida, *L'écriture et la différence* (Editions du Seuil 1967) 410–11; J Derrida, *De la Grammatologie* (Editions de Minuit 1967) 53, 87.

[29] On the idea that modern discourses are always doomed from the start when it comes to their ultimate foundations and justification, see P Sloterdijk, *Critique of Cynical Reason* (University of Minnesota Press 1987); B Latour, *An Inquiry into Modes of Existence: An Anthropology of the Moderns* (C Porter tr, Harvard University Press 2013) 152; on the idea that the debate about modern discourses are always driven by foundational contradictions given that they claim some universality while seeking to ground themselves historically, see P Ricoeur, *La mémoire, l'histoire, l'oubli* (Seuil, 2000) 386–87, 399.

[30] On the correlative refuge in mechanisms like self-referentiality, see J d'Aspremont, *International Law as a Belief System* (Cambridge University Press 2017).

[31] R Unger, *The Critical Legal Studies Movement: Another Time. A Greater Task* (Verso 2015) 20 ('Deprived of light, [the ironical and strategic lawyer] easily becomes the victim of his own ironic distancing from the discourse that he deploys instrumentally. By this posture, he denies himself the benefit of a passage from faith to disillusionment to new faith. He finds himself imprisoned in half-belief'). On the idea that any alternative to the system will look like the system, see JF Lyotard, *La Condition Postmoderne* (Editions de Minuit 1979) 70.

3

Misinterpreting Customary International Law

Corrupt Pedigree or Self-Fulfilling Prophecy?

NOORA ARAJÄRVI

1 Introduction

This chapter explores the misinterpretation of customary international law (CIL) and its practical and normative consequences. I focus on three main questions: (1) what is misinterpretation? (2) how and why do different misinterpretations take place? and (3) what are the potential consequences of misinterpretation of CIL? These all converge in the underlying question of whether there are detectable objective standards for the determination of misinterpretation or whether such observation is a subjective one – anchored on a disagreement on the values which lie at the core of international law.

In exploring these questions, I combine doctrinal study with empirical examples. Additionally, the different potential consequences of misinterpretation call for a normative evaluation: whether misinterpretation renders a norm invalid or illustrates *lex ferenda*? Could misinterpretation create an authoritative verdict of the status of law, even against its flawed premise – 'a corrupt pedigree', a term coined by Fernando Teson?[1] And why does pedigree matter for CIL – is there something beyond institutional formality conferring authority and legitimacy?

By its nature, CIL is constantly evolving – the customary process is continuous. While in its purest form interpretation of CIL may consist of an analysis of an already ascertained rule (and its elements), interpretation of CIL in most cases inevitably includes an element of construction at that particular point in time – it is difficult to distinguish between the

[1] F Teson, 'Fake Custom' in BD Lepard (ed), *Reexamining Customary International Law* (Cambridge University Press 2017) 84.

formation, identification and interpretation of CIL.[2] As Anthony D'Amato has noted in relation to CIL: 'there is an interrelation between law-formation and law interpretation'.[3]

According to traditional methodology, CIL emerges spontaneously 'like a path in a forest'.[4] It has been suggested, somewhat convincingly, that the identification and interpretation of CIL have taken a strategic turn, potentially arising from the proliferation of international interactions and norm-interpreters and -entrepreneurs.[5] The theories of 'modern CIL'[6] have attempted to explain and justify the broadened methodology, which utilises CIL to advance political, ethical, economic and other aims. Some of such attempts may in fact encourage and expand potential misinterpretations of CIL, with reliance and application of elements far removed from the common understanding of state practice and *opinio juris*. The effect is not relevant only in the methodology but also in the outcomes: with the utilisation of different interpretative methodologies by different courts and other norm-interpreters,[7] the resulting identification of a rule of CIL and/or its subsequent interpretation could be highly inaccurate, due to either a genuine mistake in the interpretive methodology or an aspiration to apply a progressive norm disguised as customary rule for moral, ethical, policy, or other extra-legal reasons.

Following the 'CIL as a path' metaphor, the interpreter of a norm may misidentify, say, a dried-up stream as a path, designate a minor trail as a fully-fledged path, find a path where there is none, or call a man-made

[2] For example MH Mendelson, 'The Formation of Customary International Law' (1998) 272 RdC 155; Kammerhofer accurately notes that 'the cognition of customary international law' includes 'a re-creation of its genesis'. See Chapter 1 by Kamerhoffer in this volume.

[3] A d'Amato, 'The Neo-Positivist Concept of International Law' (1965) 59 AJIL 321, 323.

[4] K Wolfke, *Custom at Present in International Law* (2nd ed, Kluwer 1993) 54–55.

[5] M Byers, *Custom, Power, and the Power of Rules* (Cambridge University Press 1999); N Krisch, 'International Law in Times of Hegemony: Unequal Power and the Shaping of the International Legal Order' (2005) 16(3) EJIL 369; JL Goldsmith & EA Posner, *The Limits of International Law* (Oxford University Press 2005); LR Helfer & IB Wuerth, 'Customary International Law: An Instrument Choice Perspective' (2016) 37(4) MichJIntlL 563.

[6] For example A Roberts, 'Traditional and Modern Approaches to Customary International Law: A Reconciliation' (2001) 95 AJIL 757; A Seibert-Fohr, 'Modern Concepts of Customary International Law as a Manifestation of a Value-Based International Order' in A Zimmermann & R Hofmann (eds), *Unity and Diversity in International Law* (Duncker and Humblot 2006) 257; BD Lepard, *Customary International Law: A New Theory with Practical Applications* (Cambridge University Press 2010).

[7] For example A Bianchi, D Peat & M Windsor (eds), *Interpretation in International Law* (Oxford University Press 2015); I Venzke, *How Interpretation Makes International Law* (Oxford University Press 2012).

walkway a path. These present examples of misinterpretations without delving into their underlying motives. It is, however, useful to analyse reasons behind a misinterpretation as they may have a direct bearing on the consequences flowing from it, how it is received and responded to by the international community, and for the determination of whether it is representative of 'a corrupt pedigree' or a matter of sluggish methodology.

While Articles 31 to 33 of the Vienna Convention on the Law of Treaties (VCLT) serve as the starting point for addressing interpretation in international law – and these rules have crystallised as part of CIL in their own right[8] – they provide little guidance on how to interpret CIL rules. Just as well, courts have adopted and adapted their own approaches and methodologies on how to go on about interpreting CIL, and not always consistently even within the same institution. In this chapter I intentionally avoid delving into the discussion of what constitutes interpretation: this is accomplished by other authors in this volume.[9] One may criticise my approach for cutting corners or reversing the analysis while pursuing exactly the same result: exploring what interpretation is *not*. I accept that the critique may be warranted. The purpose here is, however, not to provide an ample understanding of the misinterpretation of CIL but to initiate conversation on how interpretation may go awry and what it may do to the validity and legitimacy of CIL.

Capturing the definition and examples of misinterpretation is like chasing a moving target – as with interpretation, the elements may be in flux, the circumstances and narratives changing, and the line between genuine and fake CIL – and correct interpretation and misinterpretation – often fluid. With CIL identification (and possibly subsequent interpretation), one can usually find evidence to support what one is looking for – but so can the opposite party. Transplanting a correct interpretation reached at a given point in time into a later case may in fact provide the very premise for misinterpretation even when the methodology of the initial interpretation has been accurate *per se*: the act of interpreting CIL requires the interpreter to analyse the practice and *opinio juris* at a specific point in time. By definition, CIL can develop continually and therefore the interpreter needs to look beyond the matter or dispute at hand to get a broader vision of the applicable evidence of the elements of CIL. This argument runs somewhat parallel to Article 30 of the VCLT on the application of successive

[8] See for instance Chapter 16 by Merkouris in this volume.
[9] See Chapters 16–22 in this volume.

treaties relating to the same subject matter and to its Article 31 (3) (a) and (b) on subsequent agreement and practice in the interpretation of a treaty: the commentaries call for consideration of what is appropriate in particular circumstances and for caution in resorting to effective interpretation, noting that 'even when a possible occasion for [principles and maxims'] application may appear to exist, their application is not automatic but depends on the conviction of the interpreter that it is appropriate in the particular circumstances of the case',[10] and that to resort to extensive or liberal interpretation 'might encourage attempts to extend the meaning of treaties illegitimately on the basis of the so-called principle of "effective interpretation"'.[11] The commentaries also touch upon consequences of such extensive interpretation, with a reference to the 1950 Interpretation of Peace Treaties Advisory Opinion of the International Court of Justice (ICJ), where the court emphasised that to adopt an interpretation which ran counter to the clear meaning of the terms would not be to interpret but to revise the treaty.[12] In a similar manner, to interpret CIL 'effectively' or in a way that runs counter to established practice and *opinio juris*, could either constitute a revision of the rule of CIL (if it is shown that new practice and *opinio* have emerged) or, as is the focus here, result in misinterpretation (if practice and *opinio* do not sufficiently support the new interpretation). As noted by the arbitrator in the *Island of Palmas* case: 'The same principle which subjects the act creative of a right to the law in force at the time the right arises, demands that the existence of the right, in other words its *continued manifestation*, shall follow the conditions required by the evolution of law.'[13]

Moreover, methodological questions on whether a solid definition of 'interpretation' ought to be stipulated in order to address misinterpretation cannot be dismissed. While the purpose of this chapter is not to extensively delve into these questions, they run in the background of this inquiry and occasionally surface; must we pre-determine the conditions of validity of CIL before we can analyse its misreadings? How, by whom and why should the interpretation of CIL rule be deemed invalid? What

[10] ILC, 'Draft Articles on the Law of Treaties with Commentaries' (4 May–19 July 1966) UN Doc A/CN.4/191, reproduced in [1966/II] YBILC 187, 218.

[11] ibid 219.

[12] ibid.

[13] The *Island of Palmas Case (or Miangas) (Netherlands v USA)* (1928) 2 UNRIAA 829, 845 (emphasis added).

can the examples of misinterpretation of CIL tell us about the rules of interpretation?

In discussing the substance of CIL, I use 'norms' when the legal validity is uncertain or they appear in a space of conceptual ambiguity – is it CIL or not, is it a legal rule or simply social practice or aspiration? 'Rules' refer to those norms which have, to the best of our knowledge and assessment, materialised or crystallised as a part of CIL.

2 From Methods of Interpretation to Misinterpretation

Interpretative exercises in customary international law have been described as 'methodological mayhem' resting on the flexibility of methodological uncertainty,[14] and creating an environment of ontological doubt.[15] The same goes for misinterpretation. The orthodox purpose of interpretation is to clarify the intentions of parties. While in treaty law this may be a feasible – if not an easy – task, in CIL identifying and clarifying the intentions of parties is practically impossible, not least for the absence of records of *travaux preparatoires*. This may depend, however, on the theory of formation of CIL: whether one accepts that CIL forms 'like a path in the forest' or whether CIL may arise through a focused, intended and continued practice of actors in international law. In the latter occasion, tracing cognisant practices may be possible, even if based on speculation.

As we know, in the *North Sea Continental Shelf* cases[16] the ICJ evaluated the basic parameters for CIL based on Article 38 (1) (b) of the ICJ Statute, which have become the reference point for the traditional account of CIL. The ICJ articulated the elements of CIL as follows: 'Not only must the acts concerned amount to a settled practice, but they must also be such, or be carried out in such a way, as to be evidence of a belief that this practice is rendered obligatory by the existence of a rule of law

[14] S Talmon, 'Determining Customary International Law: The ICJ's Methodology between Induction, Deduction and Assertion' (2005) 26(2) EJIL 417; S Talmon, 'Determining Customary International Law: The ICJ's Methodology and the Idyllic World of the ILC' (*EJIL: Talk!*, 3 December 2015). <https://bit.ly/3EQMgQ2> accessed 1 March 2021.

[15] N Banteka, 'A Theory of Constructive Interpretation for Customary International Law Identification' (2018) 39(3) MichJIntlL 301; see also L Blutman, 'Conceptual Confusion and Methodological Deficiencies: Some Ways that Theories on Customary International Law Fail' (2014) 25(2) EJIL 529.

[16] *North Sea Continental Shelf cases (Federal Republic of Germany v Denmark; Federal Republic of Germany v Netherlands)* (Judgment) [1969] ICJ Rep 3.

requiring it.'[17] This was adapted in the *Nicaragua* case,[18] which saw a more flexible approach, in particular regarding the relationship and the chronological order of emergence of practice and *opinio juris*. The ICJ reaffirmed the two-element approach in the *Jurisdictional Immunities of the State* case, stating, with a reference to its previous case law,[19] that 'the existence of a rule of customary international law requires that there be "a settled practice" together with *opinio juris*'.[20] Now, beyond the basic identification of CIL and its elements, the ICJ has not contributed a great deal to the science of interpretation of CIL, nor – luckily – does it offer obvious examples of misinterpretation either,[21] although some have claimed that 'the identification practice of the International Court of Justice for customary norms deviates from the traditional definition of customary law in Art. 38 (1) lit. b of the ICJ Statute'.[22] It has been suggested that 'progressive determinations of CIL [by courts] are generally unproblematic when States are in the dock [as opposed to international criminal law proceedings]'.[23] This statement is simplistic and misleading. First, determinations and interpretations of CIL, especially when delivered by a court with a high authority such as the ICJ, unavoidably influence not only the development of international law but also methods and techniques on how CIL is interpreted subsequently by other international and national courts. Second, while the principle of legality has a heightened relevance in (international) criminal proceedings,[24] it is not redundant in inter-state adjudication. In addition, the ICJ – and any other court deciding inter-state cases – has a duty to uphold core tenets of the rule of law, such as consistency, predictability and non-arbitrariness.

[17] ibid 44 [77].

[18] *Military and Paramilitary Activities in and against Nicaragua (Nicaragua v USA)* (Merits) [1986] ICJ Rep 14.

[19] *Continental Shelf (Libyan Arab Jamahiriya v Malta)* (Judgment) [1985] ICJ Rep 13.

[20] *Jurisdictional Immunities of the State (Germany v Italy: Greece intervening)* (Judgment) [2012] ICJ Rep 99, 122.

[21] See Talmon, 'Determining Customary International Law' (n 14) 417; P Merkouris, 'Interpreting the Customary Rules on Interpretation' (2017) 19(1) IntCLRev 126.

[22] N Petersen, 'The International Court of Justice and the Judicial Politics of Identifying Customary International Law' 28(2) EJIL 357; See also SJ Choi & M Gulati, 'Customary International Law: How Do Courts Do It?' in CA Bradley (ed), *Custom's Future: International Law in a Changing World* (Cambridge University Press 2016) 117.

[23] T Rauter, *Judicial Practice, Customary International Criminal Law and Nullum Crimen Sine Lege* (Springer 2017) 233.

[24] For example N Arajärvi, *The Changing Nature of Customary International Law: Methods of Interpreting the Concept of Custom in International Criminal Tribunals* (Routledge 2014) 120–42; K Gallant, *The Principle of Legality in International and Comparative Criminal Law* (Cambridge University Press 2008).

Adopting progressive determinations of CIL has the potentiality to obstruct these fundamental principles in international judicial decision-making, regardless of whether it is states or individuals in the dock.

Some have argued that the Draft Conclusions on Identification of Customary International Law by the International Law Commission (ILC) constitute a 'statement of the principles guiding the interpretation of CIL'.[25] This characterisation is inaccurate. The difference between 'formation' and 'identification' has been discussed at length in the ILC's Special Rapporteur's First and Second Reports on CIL,[26] but 'interpretation' has simply not received similar attention; while the work of Sir Michael Wood is invaluable in setting out the issues, controversies and principles for the *identification* of CIL, it does little to inform the interpretation of existing rules of CIL. This caveat was highlighted also, *inter alia*, in the Comments and Observations by the Government of the Netherlands to the Draft Conclusions in 2018, which notes that 'it does not become clear whether the process for identifying the existence of a rule is the same as the process for determining the content of that rule'.[27] As has been discussed in this chapter and extensively elsewhere over the course of the lifespan of international legal scholarship, the process of CIL interpretation, nevertheless, overlaps with the process of identification in a complex manner.

In my previous work,[28] I have addressed different categories of identification and interpretation of CIL: First, courts may find customary international law by employing the traditional method of assessing state practice supported by *opinio juris*. Second, they may place more weight on *opinio juris* over practice – often in this context understood to include a broad spectrum of different considerations. Third, they may

[25] For example O Ammann, 'On the Interpretability of Customary International Law: A Response to Nina Mileva and Marina Fortuna' (*Opinio Juris Blog*, 7 October 2019) <https://bit.ly/2YtuKSg> accessed 1 March 2021.

[26] ILC, 'First Report on Formation and Evidence of Customary International Law by Michael Wood, Special Rapporteur' (17 May 2013) UN Doc A/CN.4/663; ILC, 'Second Report on Identification of Customary International Law by Michael Wood, Special Rapporteur' (22 May 2014) UN Doc A/CN.4/672; see also N Arajärvi, 'The Requisite Rigour in the Identification of Customary International Law: A Look at the Reports of the Special Rapporteur of the International Law Commission' (2017) 19(1) IntCLRev 9.

[27] ILC, 'Identification of Customary International Law, Comments and Observations received from Governments, Comments and Observations by the Kingdom of the Netherlands submitted on 23 January 2018' (14 February 2018) UN Doc A/CN.4/716, 6.

[28] See Arajärvi (n 24) 75–119.

deduce customary rules from treaties, national legislation and other (binding or nonbinding) documents. And fourth, courts may refer to previous case law as a confirmation of the customary status of a norm, without in fact assessing the actual findings of practice and *opinio juris* at that point in time.[29] The main criticism regarding the CIL methodology concerns the lack of proper analysis of the elements of custom: courts rendering assertions without justifications, either intentionally, negligently, or, as often seems to be the case, rather casually. This serves as a background for the ensuing analysis of misinterpretation of CIL, which bridges the methodological considerations with the underlying rationales. Identifying examples of misinterpretation is to a large extent related to the way one perceives the functions and limits of international law. For those adopting traditional reading of CIL,[30] many more cases of misinterpretation may be detectable than to those with leanings towards the 'modern approach'[31] or 'the sliding scale approach'.[32]

There are two dimensions to misinterpretation. Misinterpretation can refer to, on the one hand, to the process and the outcome of the process, and on the other, to the law ascertainment and content determination:[33]

(1) The act of misinterpretation and its motives – affects institutional legitimacy.
(2) The substance of the misinterpretation and its consequences – affects the validity of the norm, depending on its reception by relevant actors, and hence, depends on the conditions of validity imposed by the normative framework.

While misinterpretation has an inherently negative sound to it, it can be a necessary stage in the development and normative change of CIL rules. For an existing CIL rule to change, the practice and/or *opinio juris* ought

29 ibid.

30 For example A D'Amato, *The Concept of Custom in International Law* (Cornell University Press 1971); Mendelson (n 2) 155; M Akehurst, 'Custom as a Source of International Law' (1974–75) 47 BYBIL 53; Wood (n 26); ILC, 'Third Report on Identification of Customary International Law by Michael Wood, Special Rapporteur' (27 March 2015) UN Doc A/CN.4/682; ILC, 'Fourth Report on Identification of Customary International Law by Michael Wood, Special Rapporteur' (8 March 2016) UN Doc A/CN.4/695; ILC, 'Fifth Report on Identification of Customary International Law by Michael Wood, Special Rapporteur' (14 March 2018) A/CN.4/717.

31 For example Roberts (n 6) 757; Seibert-Fohr (n 6) 257; Lepard (n 6).

32 F Kirgis, 'Custom on a Sliding Scale' (1987) 81 AJIL 146.

33 J d'Aspremont, 'The Multidimensional Process of Interpretation: Content-Determination and Law-Ascertainment Distinguished' in A Bianchi, D Peat & M Windsor (eds), *Interpretation in International Law* (Oxford University Press 2015) 111.

to differ from, contradict or go beyond *lex lata*, providing initially a consideration of *lex ferenda*. Now, even when practice and/or *opinio juris* may not have changed or the evidence thereof is mixed, the interpreters (usually courts) may pitch in to spearhead the change in a catalytic manner: such activity may constitute an example of misinterpretation of CIL, closely related to the misidentification and misevaluation[34] of the elements of CIL and leading to a potential misrepresentation of a norm. The interpreters may find evidence of practice and/or *opinio juris* where there is none, exaggerate their prevalence and impact, or declare a norm as CIL without further ado. The breadth, depth, scope and applicability of CIL may be incorrectly set out: for instance, a regional custom may be (mis)interpreted as universally applicable, a general principle of law may be mistakenly awarded customary status, or a *jus cogens* norm may be characterised as CIL even in the absence of widespread and consistent practice.[35] The same could occur in reverse: downplaying practice and/or *opinio juris*, to hinder the emergence of an undesired rule of CIL even when the elements would point to its crystallisation.

Does the finding of misinterpretation presuppose a cognisant misinterpreter? No: misinterpretation by definition is not concerned with motivations, but it simply refers to 'the act of forming a wrong understanding of something that is said or done, or an example of a wrong understanding'.[36] In any case, evidence of deliberate misinterpretation of CIL is rare and mostly misinterpreters have adopted a lazy methodology or ignored rules of interpretation in evaluating practice and/or *opinio juris*.

When analysing the notion of misinterpretation in CIL, we can also break it down to the elements: is it the CIL rule as a whole, or practice or

[34] For discussion on interpretation and evaluation see Merkouris (n 21) 138.

[35] While agreeing with Conclusion 5 of the Draft conclusions on peremptory norms of general international law (*jus cogens*) of the ILC ('Customary international law is the *most common* basis for peremptory norms of general international law'), I disagree with the claim that all peremptory norms are part of customary international law, as 'custom plus'. There may well be norms of such high importance to the community of states or as considerations of humanity as to be characterised as *jus cogens* but which lack sufficient requisite elements required to be identified as CIL, and where contradictory practice does not negate the validity and status of the norm. See for example A Cassese, 'For an Enhanced Role of *Jus Cogens*' in A Cassese (ed), *Realizing Utopia: The Future of International Law* (Oxford University Press 2012) 158, 165.

[36] Cambridge Dictionary, 'Misinterpretation' (2021) <https://bit.ly/3mZE0XP> accessed 1 March 2021.

opinio juris that is being misinterpreted? What is the relative relevance of misinterpreting practice or *opinio juris*? Misinterpreting the element of practice – being usually more quantifiable – may be more obvious than that of the more fluid, subjective, element of *opinio juris*. It may also be more consequential, as it is viewed – at least by many of us – as the very bedrock of custom.

Now, it is not terribly difficult to find cases of national courts taking liberties in their interpretation of the concept and rules of CIL,[37] although most often these courts 'simply assert, without citing persuasive practice authority, the existence of a customary norm'.[38] At the international level one may expect to see more cross-referencing and recognise potential consequences of misinterpretation for international law. The next section sets out categories, with selected examples, where international courts and tribunals have overstepped methodological limits to the effect that may constitute misinterpretation.

3 Categories of Misinterpretation

Based on my initial research findings, three types of misinterpretation are identifiable. First, the extension (or reduction) of CIL through *exitus acta probat* – the end-justifies-the-means approach – where analysis of the elements of CIL is modified to fit the desired outcome and the elements are substituted or complemented with resort to extra-legal tools and concepts. This approach often finds support among the more modern-liberal theories of CIL. Second, I have identified the negligent interpretation, which may amount to misinterpretation when the norm-interpreter labels a norm as CIL without further analysis of the elements and where in fact opposite practice and *opinio juris* might be observable. Finally – and luckily evidence of this remains scarce – there is the fallacious method of misinterpretation, where the interpreter finds false CIL or considers flawed or incomplete evidence of its elements. All the three categories contain overlapping dimensions – it may be hard to distinguish whether the norm-interpreter was merely negligent or

[37] See for instance PR Trimble, 'The Supreme Court and International Law: The Demise of Restatement Section 403' (1995) 89(1) AJIL 53, which refers to '[Supreme Court's] disregard or misinterpretation of international law, especially in the *Alvarez-Machain* and *Sale* cases'; see also SL David, 'A Foul Immigration Policy: US Misinterpretation of the Non-Refoulement Obligation under the Convention against Torture' (2003) 19 NYLSchJHumRts 769.

[38] For example CMJ Ryngaert & D Hora Siccama, 'Ascertaining Customary International Law: An Inquiry into the Methods Used by Domestic Courts' (2018) 65(1) NILR 1.

plain wrong, or where the end-justifies-the-means approach crosses over to the delivery of fallacious interpretation. In particular, regarding the latter example, ideological leanings may cloud the legal astuteness of determining whether the interpreter has acted in good faith or not, and wherein lies the line between an actual legal error and consequentialist bending of the rules of interpretation to achieve a morally desirable outcome. Also, a fallacious interpretation of CIL has a much higher chance of success to flourish through subsequent interpretations and practice when it leads to 'good' outcomes – for instance, an 'effective' interpretation expanding the scope of a human right can be expected to be met with more praise than an argument to the opposite effect.

A misinterpretation may be discoverable in subsequent proceedings by the same or another court. In May 2010, the Extraordinary Chambers in the Courts of Cambodia (ECCC) held that the mode of responsibility of Joint Criminal Enterprise (JCE III)[39] did not exist under CIL in 1975–79, and consequently was not applicable in the proceedings of that court.[40] The ECCC limited JCE III by declaring that there was not enough evidence of its customary nature, at least not in 1975–79, thus dismissing the ICTY's argumentation in *Tadić* by illustrating that the *Tadić* court had in fact invented that category of criminal responsibility.[41] In analysing the concept of JCE, the ECCC first noted that it must consider 'not only whether JCE existed under customary international law at the relevant time, thus being punishable under international criminal law, but also whether it was sufficiently foreseeable and accessible to the Charged Persons'.[42] It then examined the findings in *Tadić*, other ICTY cases, and case law dealing with the crimes committed in World War II, stating in relation to JCE III that '[h]aving reviewed the authorities relied

[39] '[A] common design to pursue one course of conduct where one of the perpetrators commits an act which, while outside the common design, was nevertheless a natural and foreseeable consequence of the effecting of that common purpose', *Prosecutor v Duško Tadić* (Appeal Judgment) IT-94-1-A (15 July 1999) [204].

[40] *Prosecutor v Ieng, Ieng and Khieu* (Pre-Trial Chamber Decision on the Appeals against the Co-Investigative Judges Order on Joint Criminal Enterprise) (D97/15/9) 002/19-09-2007-ECCC/OCIJ (PTC 35, 37, 38 & 39) (20 May 2010) [83].

[41] The appeals to the Pre-Trial Chamber argued that 'the *Tadić* Appeals Chamber wrongly determined that JCE liability existed under customary international law as it relied on too few cases. . . . JCE liability has never been a form of liability in general and consistent State use'. *Prosecutor v Ieng, Ieng and Khieu* [51]; and the defence further noted that 'the notion of JCE, as understood by the Trial Chamber, was "invented 20 years later by an (over-) activist ICTY Appeals Chamber" in the *Tadić* Case', NUON Chea's Appeal Brief referring to Trial Judgement [486].

[42] *Prosecutor v Ieng, Ieng and Khieu* [45].

upon by *Tadić* in relation to the extended form of JCE (JCE III), the Pre-Trial Chamber is of the view that they do not provide sufficient evidence of consistent State practice or *opinio juris* at the time relevant to Case 002'.[43] This approach was further confirmed in November 2016 by the Supreme Court Chamber of the ECCC.[44]

Earlier the same year, however, the Appeals Chamber of the ICTY reconfirmed its interpretation of JCE III as a mode of liability under CIL by noting that 'the third category of joint criminal enterprise has existed as a mode of liability in customary international law since at least 1992 and that it applies to all crimes consistently confirmed in the Tribunal's subsequent jurisprudence'.[45] In responding to the defendant's challenge of the customary nature of JCE III, the Appeals Chamber stated that 'this contention is essentially premised on his suggestion to depart from the existing jurisprudence on the basis of his *misconstruction* of the law'.[46] This could be viewed as the Appeals Chamber's reaction to the debate surrounding JCE III and presents a clear expression of its position vis-à-vis interpretation of CIL by the ECCC and many scholars.

Even when acknowledging that nearly twenty years passed between the commission of crimes in Cambodia and in the former Yugoslavia – and the applicable rule of CIL needs to be determined with reference to those points in time – these cases nonetheless show CIL's ambiguity and the challenges it poses to interpretation. The drastic departure of the ECCC from the ICTY jurisprudence brings uncertainty on the actual status of the rule and raises the question of the implications of such diverse interpretations for future cases dealing with modes of criminal liability.[47] This goes

[43] ibid [77]; for further analysis of the decision, see MG Karnavas, 'Joint Criminal Enterprise at the ECCC: A Critical Analysis of the Pre-Trial Chamber's Decision against the Application of JCE III and Two Divergent Commentaries on the Same' (2010) 21 Crim LF 445.

[44] *Prosecutor v Ieng, Ieng and Khieu* (Appeal Judgment) (DF/36) 002/19-09-2007-ECCC/SC (23 November 2016) [791].

[45] *Prosecutor v Mićo Stanišić and Stojan Župljanin* (Appeal Judgment) IT-08-91-A (30 June 2016) [599].

[46] ibid [966] (emphasis added).

[47] See for example V Haan, 'The Development of the Concept of Joint Criminal Enterprise at the International Criminal Tribunal for the Former Yugoslavia' (2005) 5 IntCLR 167; ME Badar, 'Just Convict Everyone! Joint Perpetration from *Tadić to Stakić* and Back Again' (2006) 6 IntCLR 293; JD Ohlin, 'Three Conceptual Problems with the Doctrine of Joint Criminal Enterprise' (2007) 5 JICJ 69; A Cassese, 'The Proper Limits of Individual Responsibility under the Doctrine of Joint Criminal Enterprise' (2007) 5 JICJ 109; S SáCouto, LN Sadat & P Viseur Sellers, 'Collective Criminality and Sexual Violence: Fixing a Failed Approach' (2020) 33(1) LJIL 207.

on to illustrate that there may not be objectively one right answer to how and what to interpret. The method and consequently the outcome may depend on the interpreter's approach to CIL: which element carries the most weight and which evidence is included in the assessment of practice and/or *opinio juris*. Both interpretations of the status of JCE III can be objectionable on these grounds. As noted by Verdier and Voeten, 'an attempt to justify a breach by reference to the rule's ambiguity is likely to be interpreted as a violation by the counterparty and (some) third parties'.[48] Regarding the treatment of the JCE III neither of the tribunals can be accused of sluggish methodology even if one could be persuaded to view ICTY's early judicial activism as falling into the *exitus acta probat* category. The interpretation of JCE III as CIL has, however, been repeated in the jurisprudence of the ICTY in numerous subsequent cases. Below, under 'Consequences of Misinterpretation', I will discuss the relevance of repetitive judicial practice in the context of potentially 'corrupt pedigree' of CIL.

Similar discourse involving possible misinterpretations of CIL took place internally between different chambers of the ICTY and the Special Court for Sierra Leone (SCSL), in relation to the requirement of specific direction as a part of the *actus reus* of aiding and abetting.[49] The ICTY and the SCSL, within a space of less than a year, interpreted this requirement under CIL reaching opposite outcomes: Whilst the ICTY Appeals Chamber held in *Perisić* that specific direction is a part of *actus reus* of aiding and abetting, it did not make any explicit reference to its status under CIL. The SCSL Appeals Chamber in *Taylor*, on the other hand, stated that:

> [i]n the absence of any discussion of customary international law, it is presumed that the ICTY Appeals Chamber in *Perisić* was only identifying and applying internally binding precedent. ... [T]he ICTY Appeals Chamber's jurisprudence does not contain a clear, detailed analysis of the authorities supporting the conclusion that specific direction is an element of the *actus reus* of aiding and abetting liability under customary international law.[50]

In effect, the SCSL called out the ICTY Appeals Chamber's misinterpretation of CIL. The ICTY Appeals Chamber, in a decision shortly after, adopted the

[48] PH Verdier & E Voeten, 'Precedent, Compliance, and Change in Customary International Law: An Explanatory Theory' (2014) 108(3) AJIL 389, 396, fn 43.

[49] *Prosecutor v Momćilo Perišić* (Appeal Judgment) IT-04-81-A (28 February 2013); *Prosecutor v Charles Taylor* (Appeal Judgment) SCSL-03-01-A (26 September 2013).

[50] *Prosecutor v Charles Taylor* [476–77].

SCSL interpretation, mending its own prior misinterpretation.[51] Hence, this is an example of the second category of misinterpretation where the ICTY had discussed a rule, presuming it part of CIL without a further analysis of its elements and when in fact a further analysis would have uncovered opposite practice and *opinio juris*.

Likewise, an example of misinterpretation, subsequently identified by another authority, can be found in the EU case law. The rules which constitute an expression of customary international law are binding upon the EU institutions and form part of the EU legal order and as such: '[CIL] is regularly interpreted and applied by the Court as an "integral part" of EU law'.[52] De Burca has observed that 'CIL was cited by the CJEU in twenty-one cases' (as of October 2015).[53] A recent search on EUR-LEX reveals that the number stands now at thirty.[54] Interestingly, the Court of Justice of the European Union and the Advocate General have made some remarks about misinterpretation of CIL. For example, without delving further into EU case law, in *Front Polisario*, the Advocate General considered and accepted[55] the argument put forth by the council and commission that 'the General Court misinterpreted customary international law, as it did not cite any legal basis requiring the EU institutions to verify that the other party to the agreement has complied with the principle of permanent sovereignty over natural resources and the primacy of the interests of the inhabitants of non-self-governing territories'.[56]

A striking example of a misinterpretation of CIL – or misidentification as the limits may be fluid – through flawed methodology undercutting

51 *Prosecutor v Šainović et al* (Appeal Judgment) IT-05-87-A (23 January 2014); for further analysis see Arajärvi (n 24) 115–17.

52 G de Burca, 'Internalization of International Law by the CJEU and the US Supreme Court' (2015) 13(4) IntJConstL 987, 990.

53 ibid 994.

54 Eur-Lex, 'Search Results: Customary International Law' (*Eur-Lex*, 16 April 2021) <https://bit.ly/3EXBQ11> accessed 16 April 2021.

55 Case C-104/16 P *Council of the European Union v Front Populaire pour la libération de la saguia-el-hamra et du rio de oro (Front Polisario)* ECLI:EU:C:2016:677 [2016] Opinion of Advocate General Wathelet.

56 ibid [283]. See also the judgment of the court in C-641/18 *LG and Others v Rina SpA, Ente Registro Italiano Navale* ECLI:EU:C:2020:349 [2020] [60]: 'The principle of customary international law concerning immunity from jurisdiction does not preclude the national court seised from exercising the jurisdiction provided for by that regulation in a dispute relating to such an action, where that court finds that such corporations have not had recourse to public powers within the meaning of international law.'

the element of practice took place in the ICTY Trial Chamber judgment *Prosecutor* v. *Kupreškić*, discussing the prohibition of reprisal attacks against civilians:

> Admittedly, there does not seem to have emerged recently a body of State practice consistently supporting the proposition that one of the elements of custom, namely *usus* or *diuturnitas* has taken shape. This is however an area where *opinio iuris sive necessitatis* may play a much greater role than *usus*, as a result of the aforementioned Martens Clause. In the light of the way States and courts have implemented it, this Clause shows that principles of international humanitarian law may emerge through a customary process under the pressure of the demands of humanity or the dictates of public conscience, even where State practice is scant or inconsistent.[57]

The court, going against the traditional understanding of CIL and its elements, allowed for inconsistent practice to suffice in its finding of CIL and suggested that *opinio juris* is of a higher value than state practice. It relied almost exclusively on *opinio juris* in its interpretation of the CIL rule on reprisals, while simultaneously broadening the internal nature of *opinio juris* and its limits to include extra-legal considerations, such as 'elementary considerations of humanity', which, the ICTY considered, should be fully used when interpreting and applying loose (customary) international rules.[58] It further noted a customary rule of international law had emerged 'due to the pressure exerted by the requirements of humanity and the dictates of public conscience'.[59]

Such misinterpretation originates, most likely, from two objectives: on the one hand, the court saw evidence of a horrific act which was, however, not explicitly covered by the rules of international law at the time and felt a moral duty to rectify this – to bring the perpetrators to account for their actions, to deliver justice for the victims, to contribute to deterring future atrocities and to enhance international criminal law as a social pedagogical imperative, and, possibly, to contribute to the development of the law. At the same time, the mandate of the ICTY limits its jurisdiction to the application of international humanitarian law that is 'beyond any doubt part of customary law so that the problem of adherence of some but not all States to specific conventions does not arise'.[60] Hence, the ICTY could only apply law that it considered to have already crystallised as CIL, which then led it down the

[57] *Prosecutor v Kupreškic et al* (Trial Judgment) IT-95-16 (14 January 2000) [527].

[58] ibid [524].

[59] ibid [531].

[60] UNSC 'Report of the Secretary-General Pursuant to Paragraph 2 of the Security Council Resolution 808' (3 May 1993) UN Doc S/25704 [34].

path of broadening the methodology of identifying and interpreting norms so as to fit them under the umbrella of CIL – at times like in *Kupreškić* amounting to misinterpretation of CIL at the intersection of an *exitus acta probat* (end-justifies-the-means) approach and the intentionally deceiving method of misinterpretation.

Another example of a potential misinterpretation of CIL stems from the 6 May 2019 judgment of the Appeals Chamber on the International Criminal Court (ICC) in the *Jordan Referral* in the *Al Bashir case.* The court discussed the customary status of Article 27 (2) of the Rome Statute and concluded that Head of State immunity under customary international law does not apply in international courts and tribunals.[61] It stated that: '[t]here is neither State practice nor *opinio juris* that would support the existence of Head of State immunity under customary international law vis-à-vis an international court. To the contrary, such immunity has never been recognised in international law as a bar to the jurisdiction of an international court.'[62] The decision was not unanimous and in their joint dissenting opinion Judges Luz Del Carmen Ibáñez Carranza and Solomy Balungi Bossa stated that '[i]t is thus clear that the international community as a whole has consistently rejected the invocation of Head of State immunity for the commission of international crimes', continuing somewhat contentiously, that '[u]nder customary international law, immunity can never result in impunity for grave violations of the core values consolidated in international human rights law'.[63]

Despite the ICC's approach that there is no CIL rule supporting the applicability of immunities for international crimes in an international court, there is no general understanding on the status of this rule, as illustrated by the several *amicus curiae* briefs submitted on the issue at the ICC, strong political resistance from the African Union,[64] and some

61 The precise question concerned the immunity of Heads of States from arrest by other states acting at the request of an international criminal tribunal. See D Akande, 'ICC Appeals Chamber Holds that Heads of State Have No Immunity Under Customary International Law Before International Tribunals' (*EJIL: Talk!*, 6 May 2019) <https://bit.ly/3H9rj4W> accessed 1 March 2021.

62 *The Prosecutor v Omar Hassan Ahmad Al Bashir* (Judgment in the Jordan Referral re Al-Bashir Appeal) ICC-02/05-01/09-397-Corr (6 May 2019) [1].

63 ibid, Joint Dissenting Opinion of Judge Luz Del Carmen Ibáñez Carranza and Judge Solomy Balungi Bossa ICC-02/05-01/09-397-Anx2 [12].

64 For example P Pillai, 'The African Union, the International Criminal Court, and the International Court of Justice: At the Fault Lines of International Accountability' (2018) 22(10) ASIL Insights; EY Omorogbe, 'The Crisis of International Criminal Law in Africa: A Regional Regime in Response?' (2019) 66(2) NILR 287; B Kahombo, 'Africa Within the Justice System of the International Criminal Court: The Need for a Reform'

previous jurisprudence of the court itself. For instance, in the *South Africa Decision* in the *Al Bashir* case, the ICC Pre-Trial Chamber II held that '[t]he Chamber is unable to identify a rule in customary international law that would exclude immunity for Heads of State when their arrest is sought for international crimes by another state, even when the arrest is sought on behalf of an international court'.[65] Further to this, the practice of states on the matter remains far from consistent, constant and uniform, and expressions of *opinio juris* are few and far between.[66]

The *Al-Bashir* case and its discussion on immunities touches on a core tenet of interpretation: it all hinges on the expectations. What tasks and results should international courts, other norm-interpreters and international law in general, deliver? For instance, while many scholars debate the ICC's recent decision on Heads of State immunity under CIL,[67] advocates for ending impunity, human rights organisations and several scholars have cheered at the decision, viewing it as very much the correct interpretation of CIL of immunities in international tribunals.[68] This is to show how different levels and categories of misinterpretation will be most definitely welcomed by one audience or another. Interpreters, of course, are aware of this and can strategically adjust the method of interpretation and, consequently, the ensuing norm, to address the target

(2016) KFG Working Paper Series No 2 <http://dx.doi.org/10.2139/ssrn.3129009> accessed 1 March 2021.

65 *The Prosecutor v Omar Hassan Ahmad Al Bashir* (Decision under Article 87(7) of the Rome Statute on the Non-compliance by South Africa with the Request by the Court for the Arrest and Surrender of Omar Al-Bashir) ICC-02/05-01/09-302 (6 July 2017) [68].

66 J Barkholdt & J Kulaga, 'Analytical Presentation of the Comments and Observations by States on Draft Article 7, paragraph 1, of the ILC Draft Articles on Immunity of State Officials from Foreign Criminal Jurisdiction, United Nations General Assembly, Sixth Committee, 2017' (April 2018) KFG Working Paper Series No 14 <https://bit.ly/3kn7QDP> accessed 1 March 2021; see also D Tladi, 'The International Law Commission's Recent Work on Exceptions to Immunity: Charting the Course for a Brave New World in International Law?' (2019) 32 LJIL 169.

67 See for example C Kress, 'Preliminary Observations on the ICC Appeals Chamber's Judgment of 6 May 2019 in the Jordan Referral re Al-Bashir Appeal' (2019) TOAEP's Occasional Paper Series; SMH Nouwen, 'Return to Sender: Let the International Court of Justice Justify or Qualify International-Criminal-Court Exceptionalism Regarding Personal Immunities' (2019) 78(3) CLJ 596.

68 For example Human Rights Watch, 'ICC: Jordan Was Required to Arrest Sudan's Bashir' (*HRW*, 6 May 2019) <https://bit.ly/300ozFL> accessed 1 March 2021; LN Sadat, 'Heads of State and Other Government Officials Before the International Criminal Court: The Uneasy Revolution Continues' in MM deGuzman, JE Beasley & V Oosterveld (eds), *The Elgar Companion to the International Criminal Court* (Edward Elgar 2020).

audience.[69] In this context, Andrea Bianchi has noted that 'interpretive strategies [are] adaptable and flexible enough to serve different purposes'.[70]

Finally, misinterpretations may be politically motivated with little legal foundation or objective. They may be just plain wrong, with flawed methodology and conclusion. As noted above, examples of such outrightly erroneous misinterpretation of CIL at the international level remain scarce. One example could be devised from the torture debate in the early 2000s in the USA.[71] Similarly, in vain, a few scholars tried to argue in 2003 that the Bush Doctrine – as some still recall meaning preventative war with pre-emptive strikes and so on – had developed into CIL, or even into instant CIL.[72] These misinterpretations did not come from internationally authoritative sources nor did they do much more than stir some debate and yield material for scholarly articles. They remain cautionary tales of getting CIL wrong but also attest to the resilience of traditional sources theory and the approach of international legal scholarship in preserving the core of what constitutes CIL, even when recognising that due to their morally distasteful nature they were bound to invoke strong opposition.

4 Consequences of Misinterpretation

The implications and consequences of misinterpretation vary depending on the original form of misinterpretation. Corrupt pedigree and self-fulfilling

[69] It has been noted that 'the "living instrument" or "evolutive interpretation" doctrines resonate better in human rights circles'. Bianchi (n 64) 50.

[70] ibid 52.

[71] US Department of Justice, 'Memorandum for Alberto R. Gonzales, Counsel to President "Re: Standards of Conduct of Interrogation under 18 USC §§ 2340-2340A"' (1 August 2002); compare E de Wet, 'The Prohibition of Torture as an International Norm of *Jus Cogens* and Its Implications for National and Customary Law' (2004) 15(1) EJIL 97; LPF Rouillard, 'Misinterpreting the Prohibition of Torture Under International Law: The Office of Legal Counsel Memorandum' (2005) 21(1) AmUIntlLRev 9.

[72] B Langille, 'It's "Instant Custom": How the Bush Doctrine Became Law After the Terrorist Attacks of September 11, 2001' (2003) 26 BCIntl&CompLRev 145; JA Cohan, 'The Bush Doctrine and the Emerging Norm of Anticipatory Self-Defense in Customary International Law' (2003) 15(2) PaceIntlLRev 283; compare L Piggott, 'The "Bush Doctrine" and the Use of Force in International Law' in MJ Morgan (ed), *The Impact of 9/11 and the New Legal Landscape: The Day that Changed Everything?* (Palgrave Macmillan 2009) 241; see also United States Mission to the United Nations, 'Letter to UN Security Council on Article 51' (8 January 2020) <www.passblue.com/wp-content/uploads/2020/01/Art-51-Letter.pdf> accessed 1 March 2021; John Yoo on the legality of targeted killings: J Yoo, 'The Soleimani Strike: The President Has the Constitution and Precedent on His Side' (*National Review*, 6 January 2020) < https://bit.ly/3wuBdZH> accessed 1 March 2020.

prophecy are by no means mutually exclusive but may complement one another in a fertile environment. They may be reflections of different stages of the customary process: originating from a corrupt pedigree, but resulting in a self-fulfilling prophecy when viewed with subsequent hindsight. What, then, are the consequences of misinterpretation?

Practice – as some examples set out in Section 3 and many in this volume illustrate – suggests that the interpretative rules of CIL may be fluid and open to interpretation themselves (just like Articles 31–33 VCLT have been given various interpretations). Hence, the methods do differ and even when employing the same set of methods or rules of interpretation, different interpreters may reach different outcomes. Interpretation is inevitably connected to cognitive frames and social needs,[73] and extra-legal considerations are omnipresent and impact the process and result. It depends, not least, on the interpreter's position towards CIL how explicitly these considerations inform his or her interpretative methodology.

Fernando Teson offers *Nicaragua*'s determination of the rule of non-intervention as an example of CIL based on corrupt pedigree, in which the court failed to cite practice, precedent or consensus.[74] The ensuing practice, precedents and consensus consolidate and perpetuate the legal error, and themselves become sort of precedents creating a corrupted chain of legal justification. As opposed to Teson, who claims that the only kind of fake custom that has the power to generate genuine custom is the false legal statements made by states if they are then clearly followed widely by the international community,[75] I argue that the same must go for decisions of international courts, but only if subsequent practice confirms the rule. This idea can be implicitly found also in the ILC Draft Conclusions, which note that while the practice of international courts and tribunals is not state practice, pleadings by states in those forums can be.[76] Hence, when a state

[73] See for example Venzke (n 7) 11.

[74] Teson (n 1) 96–100.

[75] ibid 106.

[76] Importantly, such pleadings can be viewed either as state practice or *opinio juris*. See Commentary on Conclusion 6 [5]: 'The expression "executive conduct" . . . refers comprehensively to any form of executive act, including . . . official statements on the international plane or before a legislature; and claims before national or international courts and tribunals' and Commentary on Conclusion 10 [4]: 'Among the forms of [opinio juris], an express public statement on behalf of a State . . . provides the clearest indication that the State has avoided or undertaken such practice . . . such statements could be made, for example . . . as assertions made in written and oral pleadings before courts and tribunals.'

would refer to the case law containing the 'corrupt pedigree' in front of a court, this could be viewed as constituting such a confirmatory subsequent practice. As Harlan Cohen notes, 'precedent must be understood within practice [– or community of practice –] of international law [and its] force derives solely from the desirability of the rule reflected in it'.[77] If the precedent is not cited, followed or endorsed in any way, it has very little authority on its own. At best, it can produce a strong presumption that the interpretation is in fact the rule, creating a compliance-pull. This depends on multiple factors: the quality of legal reasoning, the clarity of interpretation, adherence to prior interpretations, and how well the interpretation fits within the broader legal framework, the aspirations of the parties and the potential burden it imposes on those parties.[78] Thus, even with corrupt pedigree, a norm may under favourable conditions eventually spawn into real custom.

Antonio Cassese has suggested that acquiescence to a misinterpretation would have the same effect as affirmation through practice and consensus, as is the case with the formation of CIL[79] – where 'silence equals consent'. I am sceptical of this position for it sidesteps any requirement of actual practice, basing the existence of CIL merely on 'combination of a string of decisions … coupled with the implicit acceptance or acquiescence of all the international subjects concerned'.[80] Teson argues against such flex CIL methodology, stating that 'citing a multitude of non-binding documents does not turn a proposed norm into a binding customary norm because is neither anchored in state practice nor is the object of a universal and specific consensus'.[81] Repetition alone does not confer normativity or legitimacy! In order to sustain a level of legitimacy, the interpreter cannot exclusively refer to their own practice and create a cyclic self-asserting method of interpretation – an external confirmation or affirmation is required, even when the end result may be what I refer to as a self-fulfilling prophecy. While it may be likely that with multiple decisions discussing the same rule at least some would enter a detailed analysis of practice and *opinio juris*, we cannot base a coherent conceptual analysis of CIL merely on judicial practice, neglecting evidence of practice or its

[77] HG Cohen, 'Theorizing Precedent in International Law' in A Bianchi, D Peat & M Windsor (eds), *Interpretation in International Law* (Oxford University Press 2015) 268, 270–71.

[78] ibid 278.

[79] *In the Matter of El Sayed* (Decision on Appeal of Pre-Trial Judge's Order Regarding Jurisdiction and Standing) CH/AC/2010/02 (10 November 2010) [47].

[80] ibid.

[81] Teson (n 1) 93.

absence. This would place a completely new burden on states to react to decisions of courts (and potentially other norm-interpreters) in order to ensure they will not be bound by the so-called CIL arising from their decisions.

Subsequent state practice and consensus can legitimise the misinterpretation, which has then served as a catalyst for change. When this is the case, the discovery of past misinterpretation – classifying a norm under CIL when it has not yet so crystallised – does not denounce its subsequent normative validity, if it has been followed as if it were already part of CIL. So, in determining the consequences of misinterpretation, we must go back to the roots of CIL before and after the act of misinterpretation, to look at the practice and *opinio juris*, and to assess whether sufficient affirmation exists which renders the legal basis of the CIL rule. This affirmative consequence of misinterpretation was noted already at the International Military Tribunal for the Far East in 1953, with Judge Pal stating that 'law also can be created illegally otherwise than by the recognized procedures ... any law created in this manner and applied will perhaps be the law henceforth'.[82] Misinterpretation can, naturally, lead to positive as well as negative outcomes. It may be that a progressive approach and dynamic interpretation, even when considered incorrect either methodologically or substantively, directs the development of practices and beliefs towards more just processes and outcomes.[83] Even if the rule was not customary at the initial point, the subsequent practice may override the initially faulty interpretation as the norm gains wider usage, which is supported by illustrations of *opinio juris*.[84]

5 Concluding Remarks

Is it possible to avoid misinterpretation in international law and if not, how can the negative consequences be mitigated? For CIL to develop,

82 Quoted in T Rauter, *Judicial Practice, Customary International Criminal Law and Nullum Crimen Sine Lege* (Springer 2017) [237].

83 'Once a customary rule has become established, States will naturally have a belief in its existence: but this does not necessarily prove that the subjective element needs to be present during the formation of the rule,' ILA Committee on Formation of Customary International Law, 'Final Report of the Committee: Statement of Principles Applicable to the Formation of General Customary International Law' (London Conference 2000) 7.

84 As Patrick Norton quotes Junius in his paper, 'One precedent creates another. They soon accumulate and constitute law. What yesterday was fact, today is doctrine', in PM Norton, 'A Law of the Future or a Law of the Past? Modern Tribunals and the International Law of Expropriation' (1991) 85 AJIL 474.

some instances of misinterpretation may be inevitable, serving as test cases on what states and other actors perceive to be the acceptable limits of the law at a given time. Determining the relevance of misinterpretation is a retrospective exercise, and in that sense, if courts deliberately enter unknown, uncertain or even outright incorrect legal terrain, they risk facing accusations of judicial activism or 'effective interpretation', which may affect their institutional legitimacy; at the same time, if all plays out well, their (mis)interpretation may instigate the crystallisation of a new (and maybe better!) CIL rule.

Identifying misinterpretation is a challenging task, which depends on the underlying approach to CIL. If one concedes that CIL forms through various ways and that its elements rest on a broad range of evidence beyond settled understanding of what amounts to state practice and *opinio juris*, one is likely to also accept the wide-ranging methods of interpretation of CIL – and consequently, find less occurrences of misinterpretation. To remain faithful to the traditional notion of CIL – which is embodied in practice – and to preserve legal certainty and predictability, it is crucial to recognise that courts are not infallible, sometimes lacking the requisite methodological tools, and occasionally just getting CIL wrong. The indeterminacy of CIL renders futile the attempts to pin down precise conditions for its validity, and simultaneously, leaves open the definition of misinterpretation of CIL. Misinterpretation, in general, diminishes foreseeability and consistency of the law. It may also, however, push the actors to develop the law. With the inescapable constructive dimension of CIL, courts implicitly serve a key function in the development of CIL through their interpretations and their interpretative methodology.

The misinterpretation of a customary norm, which is subsequently followed by states and other entities as if it were part of CIL, creates a self-fulfilling prophecy – a self-generating crystallisation of a rule. Even if the rule was not customary law embedded in practice and *opinio juris* at its 'inception', the subsequent practice and acceptance eradicates the mishap of the initial faulty interpretation and legitimises the rule as part of CIL. On the other hand, as examples from international criminal tribunals illustrate, a later decision may denounce the misinterpretation and correct the course of the customary process and norm development, or the misinterpretation will remain an unfortunate but soon forgotten misstep, neither to be restored nor repeated.

4

The Logic of Absence in Customary International Law

An Open-System Approach

ANNA IRENE BAKA

1 Introduction

Customary international law (CIL) bears an *ab initio* element of absence and thus abstractness: the lack of written formality, which, as such, can spur multitudinous interpretative debates. The profound ambiguity surrounding all elements of CIL particularly as regards the subjective, psychological element of *opinio juris* is further accentuated by the prevailing element of absence, silence or non-action and their often-monolithic interpretation as non-objection or, even, acquiescence. There also appears to be a fundamental presumption against the existence of semantic voids in CIL – a presumption that attaches negativity to silence and positive value to affirmative propositions. Indeed, negative premises appear to be less valuable and less informative than affirmative ones, while affirmatives are given semantic priority and added value over negatives. But is that true, according to the rules of informal logic? If a positive statement corresponds to a positive affirmation, to what state of affairs does a non-statement refer or correspond? What is a negative fact? What is a non-fact? What is the value of non-doing? Non-acting or abstaining? Non-believing towards the formation of a certain *opinio juris*? Is every absence, or negation, necessarily a denial of a state of affairs?

International law does not provide any clear guidance as regards the legal effects that follow from state silence. This produces further difficulties with the polysemous nature of silence, which may have several meanings, from tacit agreement to absence of view or simple lack of interest. The legal positivist eagerness to evaluate and attach negativity to absence has its roots, on the one hand, in the Wittgenstenian, contextual and consensual origins of legal positivism, assumed in HLA Hart's theory and his subsequent rejection of metaphysics, that is the premise that there is no meaning outside communitarian semiotics.[1] On the other hand, Kelsen's *Grundnorm* theory assumes a complete normative order consisting only of positive norms, even if those positive norms are negatively deduced.[2] However, according to the rules of logic and the canons of reasoning, absence may correspond to multiple values, a variety of propositions and modalities, which in international jurisprudence have been either equated or largely ignored. The mainstream interpretation of CIL overlooks the quantifications and varieties of meaning in non-appearances, such as the conceivable neutrality of absence.

The modalities of absence are not mere academic exercises. They affect the rationality and soundness of international legal doctrine and even have a real impact on international relations when overlooked. This repositions the whole enquiry to the proper place of informal logic in international legal and judicial reasoning. The chapter suggests that the rational deficit in international legal reasoning has led to, or has been enhanced by, persuasive-teleological argumentation, in the sense that the person or agency elaborating on silence aims at a certain end and is thus characterised by a certain 'argumentative orientation' towards a preferred conclusion. In this spirit, the ICJ has developed several techniques of superficial, persuasive argumentation, teleologically governed by the *non liquet* principle, the containment of international crises and the effective resolution of international disputes. This is a form of judicial interventionism, further accentuated by the demonstrated judicial or scholarly difficulty to 'translate' silence and/or the absence of state practice by virtue of some justification that transcends a particular case, is intrinsic to the legal system and is construed logically, that is by virtue of specialised rules of deductive thought which rely on a highly logical systemisation. An open-system approach could shed light on these inconsistencies and/or political manoeuvres.

2 Setting Up the Standards: Is International Legal Reasoning a Scientific Method of Reasoning?

The answer to this question necessitates a twofold examination, namely (a) how science and the scientific method of reasoning are generally

[1] HLA Hart, *The Concept of Law* (2nd ed, Clarendon Press 1994) 123.

[2] H Kelsen, *Pure Theory of Law* (M Knight tr, 2nd ed, University of California Press 1967) 245–46.

defined and (b) whether law as a discipline, and international legal reasoning in particular, fit into these definitions.

To respond to the first question, science is traditionally considered to refer to any kind of methodical study that 'has a definite subject matter, is systemic and comprehensive and . . . its aim is to discover the truth as far as possible',[3] whereas scientific method 'is just taking things in order, simplifying as far as necessary and possible, endeavouring to leave out nothing that ought to go in, and distinguishing true from false'.[4] Science is characterised by systematisation, linguistic and conceptual accuracy, the application of rules of logic and a concrete methodology for the purpose of generating knowledge. The scientific method consists of techniques of 'argument, conceptual clarification, logic and discussion'[5] or, if the subject matter is the investigation of natural phenomena, the application of the empirical method, namely qualitative or quantitative techniques and the process of hypothesis testing and verification.[6] The process of concept formation is an essential part of scientific knowledge, which traditionally consists of a logically ordered, hierarchical pyramid of concepts.[7] In most disciplines this pyramid takes the form of axioms, principles and derived theories that subsequently produce valid deductive inferences, provided that the working concepts are clear and unambiguous.[8]

Regarding the second question, on the scientificity of international legal reasoning, it is necessary to first inquire into the object and method of law in general. One should first distinguish between such terms as 'the sociology of law' or 'sociological approaches to law' or 'socio-legal studies', and such prepositions as 'law as a social science'. Whereas the former form part of a distinct discipline that examines law as a social phenomenon[9] the latter investigates the scientificity of law as such. In universities, law is traditionally classified among the social sciences. It is, however, questionable whether such attribute is accurate. There have been arguments in favour, namely that law 'is not just a social science but one

[3] AD Ritchie, 'Scientific Method in Social Studies' (1945) 20 Philosophy 3, 4.

[4] ibid 4.

[5] C McCrudden, 'Legal Research and the Social Sciences' in M Del Mar & M Giudice (eds), *Legal Theory and the Social Sciences Vol II* (Routledge 2010) 633.

[6] ibid.

[7] E Oeser, *Evolution and Constitution: The Evolutionary Self-Construction of Law* (Kluwer Academic Publishers 2003) 40.

[8] ibid.

[9] R Cotterrell, 'Why Must Legal Ideas Be Interpreted Sociologically?' in M Del Mar & M Giudice (eds), *Legal Theory and the Social Sciences Vol II* (Routledge 2010) 101.

that is central to social thought in general,'[10] as well as arguments against, that law cannot be categorised as a social science because 'it is preoccupied with normative judgments and not with human interaction and behaviour'.[11] Another argument against law as a social science is that its theories cannot be falsified, according to Karl Popper's falsification test.[12]

It is useful, at this point, to apply an insider's approach and investigate how legal theory has dealt with this problem. Kelsen's formalism and his Pure Theory of Law have separated legal doctrine from social, moral and political theories. In his *Concept of Law*, HLA Hart has been somewhat less stringent in that he placed particular emphasis on the 'social functions' of law and considered his work to be both a legal theory as well as 'an essay in descriptive sociology'.[13] He applied a so-called internal and external attitude to law in different contexts and pointed out that there are elements of social psychology behind legal concepts.[14] Dworkin and Raz acknowledged the importance of the social scientific method for the study of legal institutions but both drew a clear line between jurisprudence and 'legal sociology' or 'sociological jurisprudence' as distinct disciplines.

The dominant view from both the legal and the sociological perspective is that law cannot be considered to be a social science (a) because of its very narrow subject matter which is distinct from the one of sociology and the sociology of law, and (b) because legal doctrine does not apply the traditional methods of the social sciences, that is, the qualitative and quantitative techniques. The narrow reading of law as a closed system of knowledge has attracted serious criticisms due to its isolation from the social and political settings, as well as its autopoietic nature and stringent self-referentiality.[15] Law as a closed, isolated system of knowledge inevitably leads to 'a body of knowledge [that] has nothing to contribute, epistemologically speaking, to

[10] G Samuel, 'Is Law Really a Social Science? A View from Comparative Law' in M Del Mar & M Giudice (eds), *Legal Theory and the Social Sciences Vol II* (Routledge 2010) 178.

[11] ibid 173.

[12] ibid 175.

[13] M Krygier, 'The Concept of Law and Social Theory' in M Del Mar & M Giudice (eds), *Legal Theory and the Social Sciences* (Routledge 2010) 7.

[14] ibid 16–17.

[15] 'From a legal internal perspective, modern law is formally a self-contained system that creates itself, amends itself, and justifies itself through itself.' N Kedar, 'The Political Origins of the Modern Legal Paradoxes' in O Perez & G Teubner (eds), *Paradoxes and Inconsistencies in the Law* (Hart 2006) 112; Helmut Willke argues that legal autoreferentiality leads to ontological perplexity and fragmentation. H Willke, 'The Autopoietic Theory of Law: Autonomy of Law and Contextual Transfer' in P Amselek & N MacCormick (eds), *Controversies About Law's Ontology* (Edinburgh University Press 1991) 108–19.

our knowledge of the world as an empirical phenomenon', whereas it is a narcissistic discipline that 'is of little interest intellectually speaking to those outside [it], save perhaps to those social scientists interested in studying the corps of lawyers as a social phenomenon itself'.[16]

No matter how one looks at it, law is not a social science. From this assertion alone it does not follow, however, that international legal reasoning should not conform to rules of informal logic. The scientific authority of law is a quasi-logical requirement for internal coherence and causality, which, together with other logical principles, have built a closed system of logic.[17] In this closed system of logic deductive inferences are produced from a matrix of consented legal axioms. This process forms the 'scientific' authority of the legal syllogism.[18] It is obvious that, from this perspective, legal reasoning is at best quasi-logical.

Apart from the quasi-logical nature of legal reasoning, the ambiguity of language, as well as the various legalist approaches that normally complement the legal syllogism, such as functional, hermeneutical and dialectical approaches, lead to an obscure model of reasoning that is not open to testability.[19] The legal syllogism is complemented by an erratic series of variables that include (a peculiar understanding of) logic, interpretation, functionalism and systematisation, as well as an abstract appeal to general principles such as democracy, legal certainty and the rule of law.[20] All these variables attract dialectical instrumentalism, inasmuch as they impose an additional burden to the legal theorist to be consistent 'with the multitudinous rules' of legal systems which 'should [also] make sense when taken together'.[21] It follows from the above that legal reasoning does not concur with logical reasoning. Then, our initial question needs to be reformulated thus: should this closed system of logic with its demand for coherence operate at the expense of logical rationality? And how is this logical rationality to be measured?

Kelsen himself claimed that law is a normative science and it is necessary for legal norms to be logically explained and connected.[22]

16 Samuel (n 10) 295.
17 ibid 197.
18 ibid.
19 ibid 198.
20 ibid.
21 N MacCormick, *Legal Reasoning and Legal Theory* (Clarendon Press 1978) 152; for the internal approach and demand for coherence, see also McCrudden (n 5) 150.
22 Oeser (n 7) 7; according to Kelsen it is 'common' logic and not some special, 'juridical' logic that is applied in legal science. For Kelsen, however, rules of syllogistic logic are inapplicable to prescriptive statements because

One can therefore observe a traditional association of law with the requirement of objective-external rationality. And rightly so: without objective standards of logic, legal theory and jurisprudence are contemned to drift into speculation. From the perspective of both legal theory and jurisprudence the requirement of rationality is always relevant. Such requirement, however, cannot be considered fulfilled at the narrow level of internal coherence.

To return to our reformulated question, namely whether law should be governed by something more than the superficial requirement of coherence, the chapter answers in the affirmative. Among the variables that determine the legal syllogism, namely interpretation, systematisation, functionalism and the appeal to abstract principles, the rules of informal logic appear to be the crucial constant, in the mathematical use of the term, which can direct the legal syllogism to rational, that is syllogistically sound, conclusions. It is only by transcending the closed logic of law and the limitations of legal formalism and coherence that the syllogistic credibility of law can be restored. Law cannot be rational if it operates autonomously and self-sufficiently. Law should not operate beyond logic; legal theorists need to resort to the classical understandings of logic in order to avoid superficial formal rationality (which may or may not coincide with logical rationality) as well as unscientific instrumentalist thinking. It has been argued that law has teleology and is both 'natural, in the sense that it has to be found out and is not made by any arbitrary act of will and rational because it is not solely a fact of observation'.[23]

The laws of thought and the so-called canons of reasoning[24] operate in accordance with a *natural* mind process, which is independent from social institutions. Whether such laws of thought can be applied in

> truth and falsity are properties of a statement, whereas validity is not the property of a norm, but is its existence, its specific ideal existence. That a norm is valid means that it is present. That a norm is not valid means that it is absent . . . the validity of a norm, which is the meaning of an act of will, is conditioned by the act which posits it.

H Kelsen, *Essays in Legal and Moral Philosophy* (D Reidel 1973) 230–31, 251. On the contrary, Kelsen argues, logical inference can be applied to descriptive statements, that is 'theoretical statements' about the validity of norms, see ibid 245; all this redirects to Hume's is-ought, fact-value distinction.

[23] Ritchie (n 3) 12.

[24] The three primary laws of thought are for Jevons the Law of Identity (whatever is, is), the Law of Contradiction (nothing can both be and not be) and the Law of the Excluded Middle (everything must either be, or not be). SW Jevons, *Elementary Lessons in Logic: Deductive and Inductive* (Macmillan 1948) 117.

social settings in the same way that they are applied in natural sciences has been the object of a heated debate, famously initiated by Hume with his fact-value/is-ought distinction. Although the purpose of the chapter is not to get into the details of the debate, it should be nonetheless noted that, even for traditional logicians like John Stuart Mill, the 'mathematical inexactness' of the humanities and the social sciences is not a conviction to unscientificity. For Mill 'whenever it is sufficient to know how the great majority of the human race or of some nation or class of persons will think, feel, and act, these propositions are equivalent to universal ones. For the purposes of political and social science this *is* sufficient'.[25] Likewise, in his *Novum Organum*, Francis Bacon insisted that his method is applicable to both normative and factual issues alike.[26]

3 Methods and Techniques for the Interpretation of Silence in ICL by the ICJ: Errors and Inconsistencies

International law does not provide any clear guidance as regards the legal effects that follow from state silence. This produces further difficulties with the interpretation of the polysemous nature of silence, which may have several meanings, from tacit agreement to absence of view or simple lack of interest.

Two scholarly debates are of particular relevance here. The first debate is a systemic one, relating to the nature of international law as a normative system and the question whether it is an open or a closed system of norms. Should we follow the hypothesis that international law is an open system, then one could then fathom the possibility of an absence of law, which could then open up the possibility for a *non liquet* declaration. For Jörg Kammerhofer the question is whether silence is simply a gap or a gap in law.[27] Kammerhofer argues that, since normative systems consist of positive norms, it is unthinkable to have a situation where there is an absence of norms within the legal system.[28] Accordingly, when we face a situation of non-regulation in international law, then the Lotus principle, that is, the presumption in

[25] JS Mill, *Philosophy of Scientific Method* (Hafner Publishing 1950) 313.

[26] J Cohen, *An Introduction to the Philosophy of Induction and Probability* (Clarendon Press 1989) 8.

[27] J Kammerhofer, 'Gaps, the Nuclear Weapons Advisory Opinion and the Structure of International Legal Argument between Theory and Practice' (2009) 80 BYBIL 333, 340.

[28] ibid 339, 358.

favour of state liberty to act, cannot be sustained because this liberty is essentially a factual state of affairs that falls completely outside the normative order.

The second debate relates to the epistemological tools that the international judge has at hand for the adjudication of a case: the inductive and the deductive methods of reasoning. For the purposes of law ascertainment, induction may be defined as empirical generalisation, 'as inference of a general rule from a pattern of empirically observable individual instances of State practice and *opinio juris*'.[29] The deductive method, on the other hand, is defined as inference of a specific rule from an existing and generally accepted rule or principle, that is, the process of deriving the specific from the general. With the exception of the common law tradition, legal academic reasoning is mostly based on deductive syllogisms, namely the application of general laws and principles to concrete cases. Indeed, both Kelsen's *Grundnorm* system and HLA Hart's model of the Rule of Recognition portray a stringently hierarchical arrangement of axiomatic concepts, which presumably produce a series of safe, deductive inferences. Interestingly, this is not the view of Georg Schwarzenberger who, in his *Inductive Approach to International Law*, famously praises the application of the inductive method and attacks the, as he says, eclectic and unreliable results of the deductive method of legal reasoning.[30] The rationale behind this paradoxical – from the logical point of view – thesis may be summarised as thus: the derivation of lesser axioms, the process of legal interpretation and the application of general principles to concrete cases can all end up being extremely subjectivist and logically misleading for they are unverifiable and often based on speculation and an arbitrary 'picking up and choosing' from both natural and positive law.[31] The speculative and eclectic nature of international legal deduction is, according to Schwarzenberger, underpinned by the obscure positivist borderline between *lex lata* and *lex ferenda*.[32] With respect to the naturalist approaches to law, Schwarzenberger is equally suspicious and notes that the 'law-finding' process of naturalist deduction is often a 'law-making' process in disguise.[33] He defends the

[29] S Talmon, 'Determining Customary International Law: The ICJ's Methodology between Induction, Deduction and Assertion' (2015) 26(2) EJIL 417, 420.
[30] G Schwarzenberger, *The Inductive Approach to International Law* (Oceana Publications 1965) 74.
[31] ibid 13.
[32] ibid 47, 65.
[33] ibid 12.

inductive method of international legal reasoning on grounds that it is an empirical device that secures international legal theory from 'the subjectivism of deductive speculation and eclectic caprice, and the vested interests prone to use – and abuse – both'.[34] He therefore treats all 'deduction, speculation, or intuition' as mere hypotheses until they are all inductively verified by reference to the 'law-creating processes' and the 'law-determining agencies' which are enumerated in Article 38 of the Statute of the ICJ.[35] Despite his extensive eulogy to inductive reasoning Schwarzenberger's formalism does not embrace an unrestricted use of induction in international legal theory. Instead, he submits all logical methods, the inductive method included, to the requirement of consistency and systemic coherence, as well as the standard verification process of 'the three law-creating processes of international law' which all come down to the principle of consent.[36]

Although, in practice, both the inductive and deductive methods are employed in judicial syllogistics, the ICJ rarely states explicitly the methodology that it uses for the determination of CIL, and, as we will see in Section 5, it is often the case that it applies the two methods of reasoning erroneously. In fact, it appears that there is a lot of confusion among jurists and legal theorists vis-à-vis the proper definition and application of the two logical methods of reasoning. It has been argued, for instance, that induction is employed in the application rather than the determination of the applicable law, which is a deviation from the typical definition of induction from the scope of informal logic.[37] A justification for this deviation is that logical reasoning should not be equated with legal reasoning, which is governed from an internal logic, a logic of its own. In the same vein, judicial deduction is regarded as not being the same as logical deduction.

There is widespread agreement that CIL is, as a rule of thumb, ascertained by means of induction, since according to the mainstream, or traditional, legal doctrine the two elements of CIL are gathered in an empirical and inductive way. Because this is not a mathematical exercise – and against Schwarzenberger's theory on the merits of the inductive method in international law – it has been suggested that the application of the inductive method for customary law ascertainment is prone to subjectivity, selectivity and law creation.[38] Since it is practically

[34] ibid 6.
[35] ibid 129.
[36] ibid 19, 50.
[37] Jevons (n 24) 202.
[38] Talmon (n 29) 432.

impossible to gather and assess the practice and *opinio juris* of states, the ascertainment of any customary rule entails a selection that is often 'supportive of a preconceived rule of customary law'.[39] Besides, it is for the ICJ to assess what counts as state practice, what counts as *opinio juris*, whether the state practice is consistent and uniform etc.

The two above-mentioned debates, that is, the question whether international law is an open or a closed system of norms, as well as the application of induction as the prominent tool for the ascertainment of CIL, intertwine in a new theoretical trend that involves deduction and assertion as alternative, or additional, methods for customary law ascertainment. In this new and ongoing debate there is a distinction between traditional and the so-called modern deductive CIL – a distinction between customary law that results from the traditional, inductive method of reasoning, and customary law that arises in instances where the inductive method is considered 'impossible to use' because state practice is non-existent, the legal question is too new and has not been dealt with etc.[40] In the latter case, it has been assumed that, because international law is a closed system of norms and *non liquet* is simply not a possibility for the ICJ, international legal theorists and judges are left either with deduction of customary law from other international legal norms and principles or, even, simple assertion of CIL, that is, statements regarding the existence of customary rules that are ungrounded or not properly explained. Both deduction and assertion emphasize *opinio juris* rather than state practice, and often reveal value judgements.[41]

Deduction and assertion are not only limited to 'positive' customary rules, but also the negation or absence of custom, where the ICJ simply denies the existence of customary law due to the, presumably, lack of (uniform) state practice and/or *opinio juris*. This is particularly true for cases of omission, abstention and absence of either state practice or *opinio juris*. One could recall, for instance, the *Gulf of Maine* case, where it was held that the lack of state practice precludes the formation of a customary rule.[42] In the *North Continental Shelf* cases, Judge Sørensen argued that '[i]n view of the manner in which international relations are conducted, there may be numerous cases in which it is practically impossible for one government to produce conclusive evidence of the motives which have prompted the action

[39] ibid 432.

[40] ibid 422.

[41] A Roberts, 'Traditional and Modern Approaches to Customary International Law: A Reconciliation' (2001) 95 AJIL 757, 758.

[42] *Delimitation of the Maritime Boundary in the Gulf of Maine Area (Canada/USA)* (Judgment) [1984] ICJ Rep 246, 290.

and policy of other governments'.[43] In other words, whereas the absence of state practice and/or *opinio juris* 'discourages' the effective application of the inductive method of reasoning as a tool for the ascertainment of CIL, the new category of the so-called deductive CIL allows for state silence to be interpreted on the basis of rules that are deduced from general principles such as the sovereign equality of states etc. Inevitably, the deductive or assertive character of this new CIL implies value judgements or even the personal preferences of the adjudicating judge, exposing the type of subjectivism and eclecticism that Schwarzenberger so viciously criticised.

From the above, it follows that there is no straightforward answer or at least an interpretative formula as regards the reading of absence of state practice or the silence of states in the process of CIL ascertainment. In relations among sovereign states, the lack of explicit protest often equals recognition, or at least formal non-objection to a certain legal state of affairs that is under law-creation. There is, for instance, the notion of acquiescence in custom formation and change, such as with territorial claims. Acquiescence is a negative concept related to state inaction or silence, whereby a state is faced with a situation constituting an infringement or threat to its rights. It could be the case that acquiescence be inferred from states' failure to react to certain claims or acts that call for a positive reaction from their part. Such failure to react thus signifies a non-objection to these claims or acts. In this context, passivity or state silence is tantamount to absence of opposition. The concept has particularly arisen in ICJ proceedings relating to border disputes, asylum, maritime claims and consular rights. For instance, in the process of annexing a new territory, the exercise of formal protest means that the objecting state does not acquiesce in the situation, and that it has no intention of abandoning its territorial rights over the region. Conversely, when a state does not raise an objection, such silence may often be considered as acquiescence.

A question that obviously arises is whether passivity or non-denouncement equals implicit approval. In the *Pedra Branca/Pulau Batu Puteh* case, the ICJ found, by means of induction, that the absence of reaction conveys acquiescence provided that the conduct of the other state calls for reaction.[44] This is part of the condition *si loqui debuisset ac potuisset*

[43] *North Sea Continental Shelf Cases (Federal Republic of Germany/Netherlands; Federal Republic of Germany/Denmark)* (Judgment) [1969] ICJ Rep 3, Dissenting Opinion of Judge Sørensen 246.

[44] *Sovereignty over Pedra Branca/Pulau Batu Puteh, Middle Rocks and South Ledge (Malaysia/Singapore)* (Judgment) [2008] ICJ Rep 12 [121].

(if one can and must act) that was previously articulated in the *Temple of Preah Vihear* case.[45] In the same vein, states whose rights are directly affected by a certain act are naturally expected to react. On the contrary, the ICJ ruled in the *Asylum* case that, as far as regional customary law is concerned, silence on the part of a state vis-à-vis an emerging regional practice equals objection or protest.[46] This goes against the general presumption implied in acquiescence and the persistent objector doctrine that states should be explicit if they wish not to be bound by an emerging international legal norm.

One could therefore conclude that, when interpreting state silence or inaction for the determination of rules of CIL, the case law of the ICJ is characterised by inconsistencies and an improper, that is non-technical, use of the inductive and deductive methods of reasoning. These disparities are hardly coincidental. Whereas there is, arguably, unfamiliarity among international jurists with the two methods of reasoning, both the interpreter of CIL and the CIL enforcer are often driven by a certain legal purposefulness: governments are naturally tempted to interpret state inaction and silence in a self-serving way, while the ICJ is driven by a combination of systemic considerations, such as the *non liquet* principle, and legal expediency, such as the preservation of the legal *status quo* or the management and dealing with international crises. This has been, for instance, the case with the Kosovo advisory opinion and the *Asylum* case, where the ICJ changed the normal calculus and opted for *ad hoc* solutions.

4 Lack of Formal Rationality and Recourse to Persuasive Argumentation

From the scope of informal logic, acquiescence is, in principle, quite problematic a concept since the absence of opposition to a state of affairs does not necessarily equal tacit approval. In fact it could be precisely that: absence of opposition. Although the ICJ aimed at addressing the deficiencies of the principle by construing a theory of intentional silence connected to the (natural law) idea that states are willing Leviathans, no robust methodology has been so far produced due to the inevitable subjectivism ensuing from the abstract psychologism pertaining to the will theory. Moreover, the mainstream opting for a closed system of norms precludes

45 *Case Concerning the Temple of Preah Vihear (Cambodia v Thailand)* (Preliminary Objections) [1962] ICJ Reports 17.

46 *Colombian-Peruvian Asylum Case (Colombia v Peru)* (Judgment) [1950] ICJ Reports 266 (*Asylum Case*).

the proper application to international legal reasoning of informal logic thus undermining the external rationality of international legal syllogisms.

The lack in international legal reasoning of external rationality and even internal consistency has paved the way to persuasive-teleological argumentation. Argumentation is teleological, in the sense that the person or agency producing the argument aims at a certain end and is thus characterised by a certain 'argumentative orientation' towards the preferred conclusion. In this spirit, the ICJ has developed several techniques of superficial, persuasive argumentation, teleologically governed by the *non liquet* principle, the containment of international crises and the effective resolution of international disputes. For instance, in the *Burkina Faso/Mali Frontier Dispute*, and without any substantive justification, the ICJ made a leap and asserted the general scope of the *uti possideti juris* although at that time the principle had only been applied in the context of Latin America and Africa: '[i]t is a *general principle*, which is logically connected with the phenomenon of the obtaining of independence, *wherever it occurs*'.[47] In the *Land, Island and Maritime Dispute* the *uti possideti juris* was extended to offshore islands and historic bays and in the *Territorial and Maritime Dispute in the Caribbean Sea*, to the territorial sea.[48] No substantive justification was sought in the *Construction of a Wall* case, where the ICJ asserted that the right of peoples to self-determination is a right *erga omnes*.[49] At no stage did the court examine the practice and *opinio juris* of states. Indeed, it is quite often the case that the court simply 'asserts' the rules of CIL.

The semantic abstractness of absence and silence constitutes the perfect ground for 'magic' argumentative tricks. A characteristic example of this is the *Asylum* case,[50] where the ICJ aimed at containing the global expanse of a regional custom in Latin America, namely a regional customary rule requiring a host state to grant safe passage from the embassy where a political refugee has sought diplomatic asylum to the asylum state. In order to suppress the international distillation of the regional custom, the ICJ reversed, without any substantive justification, its settled jurisprudence and ruled that, where a regional custom was concerned, state silence in the face of an emerging regional practice meant that states' *opinio juris*

[47] *Case Concerning the Frontier Dispute (Burkina Faso/Republic of Mali)* (Judgment) [1986] ICJ Rep 554.

[48] *Territorial and Maritime Dispute between Nicaragua and Honduras in the Caribbean Sea (Nicaragua v Honduras)* [2007] ICJ Rep 659.

[49] *Legal Consequences of the Construction of a Wall in the Occupied Palestinian Territory* (Advisory Opinion) [2004] ICJ Rep 136.

[50] *Asylum Case.*

was to object/protest to the emerging rule. This assertion, however, ran counter to the general, customary law presumption that states have to raise objections if they wish to avoid being bound by an emerging custom. A year later, in the *Fisheries* case,[51] Norway had attempted to claim ocean areas by mapping them through 'straight baselines', drawn from points along its coastline, and asserted that the enclosed areas were exclusively Norwegian. Norway's argument was also based on Britain's lack of protests, which according to Norway meant that Britain had waived its rights by not objecting. However, the ICJ asserted that Norway's straight baselines were not against international law, for the additional reason that '[t]he general toleration of foreign States with regard to the Norwegian practice is an unchallenged fact. For a period of more than sixty years the United Kingdom Government itself in no way contested it'.[52]

It seems that the ICJ rulings regarding the formation of CIL are particularly troublesome, and, with the exception of regional CIL, they favour aggression and proactiveness in staking claims, while other states' absence or silence is, as a rule, taken as acquiescence or implicit approval. However, the ICJ's argumentation techniques often lead to irrational or even absurd results. A typical example is the Kosovo advisory opinion, where the ICJ committed, among others, typical informal fallacies due to *argumenta e silentio*, as well as *argumenta ad ignorantiam*.

5 Logical Fallacies in the Kosovo Advisory Opinion: An 'Open-System' Approach

Absence and silence are not monosemic. They may signify a variety of things, from acceptance to opposition, or they may have no significance at all. I also need to clarify the following: by referring to absence, I distinguish – yet I mean both – (a) silence qua non-expressed *opinio juris* and (b) absence proper, qua the lack of (positive) state practice/action. The debate falls into the broader discourse relating to arguments from silence, or *argumenta e silentio*, as well as arguments from ignorance, or *argumenta ad ignorantiam*. These are normally classified as informal logical fallacies or weak arguments (weak types of induction) that are somewhat strengthened when evidence is produced at a later stage. Arguments from silence occur when someone interprets someone's silence as meaning anything other than silence, basically arguing

[51] *Fisheries Case (UK v Norway)* [1951] ICJ Rep 116.

[52] ibid 138.

that silence is either communicating implicit approval or disapproval. On the other hand, the fallacy *ad ignorantiam* occurs when someone argues in favour or against something, in our case state practice, because the opposite has not been proven to be the case.[53] In other words, something is said to be true because we do not know whether it is not true. The issue typically has to do with the so-called burden of proof or *onus probandi*: the ignorance fallacy is a dialectical manoeuvre aiming at unfairly shifting the burden of proof. Normally, in a legal debate between two parties, when one makes a claim that the other party disputes, then the party who makes the claim or assertion has the burden of proof, that is, needs to prove, justify or substantiate the claim.

The fallacy of ignorance occurs when the burden of proof is arbitrarily and unjustifiably reversed, that is, shifted towards the party who disputes the claim. The fallacy of ignorance assumes that something is the case because it has not yet proved to be false or vice versa. This is essentially a false dichotomy providing for forced options, inasmuch as it excludes the possibility that the truth is simply unknowable – not necessarily true or false – or that there has been insufficient investigation of the matter. A typical example in most legal traditions is the presumption of innocence: there is a benefit of assumption, that is, the accused is presumed to be innocent until, and if, evidence is produced to the contrary. Those who are accused of committing a crime are not burdened with proving themselves innocent. One can never shift the burden of proof, which generally rests on the one who sets forth a claim. In criminal proceedings, it is the prosecutor who must show, beyond reasonable doubt, that the accused person is guilty. Not providing adequate evidence of innocence is irrelevant to the verdict. Therefore, an *ad ignorantiam* fallacy of the type 'the defendant is guilty because he could not prove his innocence' would never stand in a criminal court. As we will see later on, in CIL the fallacy *ad ignorantiam* occurs when there is a judicial misinterpretation of the absence of evidence, that is, instances of state practice, and is normally tightly connected to the fallacy of silence.

From the above it follows that the lack of evidence, in our case, state practice, is not necessarily neutral. There are times when the absence of evidence may prove or disprove a claim. In that case, however, one needs to take into account the context of the case: suppose that John needs to rent an apartment in Groningen, Netherlands, but he needs to make sure that the house has no cockroaches. He hires a specialist who,

[53] B McCraw, 'Appeal to Ignorance' in R Arp, S Barbone & M Bruce (eds), *Bad Arguments: 100 of the Most Important Fallacies in Western Philosophy* (Wiley Blackwell 2019) 106.

after investigating the apartment, reaches the conclusion that it does not have any swarms or cockroaches or other insects. The lack of evidence in this case is not neutral. In the evaluation of evidence, the authority that makes a certain claim is taken into account. Moreover, although it appears as though we have a typical case of argument *ad ignorantiam*, the truth is that the negative inference (absence of cockroaches) is based on a positive evaluation of evidence. A fallacy *ad ignorantiam* occurs when there is no evidence and no proof whatsoever is offered for the claim, that is, when one argues that there are no cockroaches in the apartment simply because they have not seen any. The argument that there is no God simply because one cannot see Him, and vice versa, the argument that there is God because the atheists cannot disprove His existence, are both arguments from ignorance, and thus informal fallacies.

To bring this back to the Kosovo advisory opinion, the ICJ implicitly applied the Lotus principle and reformulated the legal question. Instead of examining whether unilateral declarations of independence are in accordance with international law, the court, without providing any substantive justification for this choice, decided to examine whether international declarations of independence are forbidden under international law, thus substantially changing the question, while at the same time committing the fallacy of false alternatives. Moreover, the judicial argument did not entail any substantial evaluation of evidence of state practice, *opinio juris*, or any substantial evaluation of absence or silence, but merely took note of the historical fact that:

> In no case . . . does the practice of States as a whole suggest that the act of promulgating the declaration was regarded as contrary to international law. On the contrary, State practice . . . points clearly to the conclusion that international law contained no prohibition of declarations of independence. During the second half of the twentieth century, the international law of self-determination developed in such a way as to create a right to independence for the peoples of non-self-governing territories and peoples subject to alien subjugation, domination and exploitation . . . A great many new States have come into existence as a result of the exercise of this right. There were, however, also instances of declarations of independence outside this context. **The practice of States in these latter cases does not point to the emergence in international law of a new rule prohibiting the making of a declaration of independence in such cases** . . . For the reasons already given, the Court considers that general international law contains no applicable prohibition of declarations of independence. Accordingly, it concludes that the declaration of

> independence of 17 February 2008 did not violate general international law.[54]

The ICJ examined the general law applicable to the case before it and asserted that there is no general rule of international law – either treaty law or customary law – that prohibits declarations of independence and that '[i]n no case . . . does the practice of States as a whole suggest that the act of promulgating the declaration was regarded as contrary to international law'.[55] Judges Yusuf and Simma criticised the court's conclusion on the ground that the Lotus principle is an outdated doctrine and the silence in international law should be understood and interpreted more broadly. Judge Simma asserted that according to the Lotus principle 'restrictions on the independence of States cannot be presumed because of the consensual nature of the international legal order'.[56] He criticised the court for being too formalistic in equating 'the absence of a prohibition with the existence of a permissive rule' and drew the attention to 'the possibility that international law can be neutral or deliberately silent on the international lawfulness of certain acts'.[57] The advisory opinion on Kosovo received robust criticisms and extensive commentaries from both the judiciary and the international legal scholarship.

We have seen that arguments from silence occur when someone automatically interprets someone's silence as meaning anything other than silence, basically arguing that silence is either communicating implicit approval or disapproval. Generally, when we are dealing with a silent authority (i.e. a state) we should ask ourselves: would the silent authority have known about the claim and consciously chose to remain silent? Is the silent authority definitely aware of the claim? Is the silent authority most likely to be honest about the claim? Do we have a complete record of everything written/done by the authority? Is this record true and reliable record, and not just a presumption based on lack of evidence? If the answer to any of the above questions is negative, it is quite possible that we are dealing with a fallacious argument from silence. However, even if we answer in the affirmative, even a good argument from silence is a weak argument that should be treated as inconclusive or uncertain when no other evidence is provided.

[54] *Accordance with International Law of the Unilateral Declaration of Independence in Respect of Kosovo* (Advisory Opinion) [2010] ICJ Rep 403 (*Kosovo Opinion*) [79].

[55] ibid.

[56] ibid, Declaration of Judge Simma [2].

[57] ibid [3].

From the perspective of informal logic, the argument from silence is also tightly connected to the relation between negation and belief. Let us assume that someone does hold a certain belief or *opinio juris*. Is it monosemic or could it express various modalities? Indeed, there are various modalities governing the belief-universe, a misunderstanding/misapplication of which could generate logical fallacies and lead to distortions. For instance, there are the so-called internal and external negations of belief, and thus, *opinio juris*. Let us diagnose the fallacy:

1. John believes that God does not exist. (Internal negation)
2. John does not believe that God exists. (External negation)
3. John believes that God exists.

These three examples depict the so-called withhold/deny fallacy.[58] The fallacy is to read 1 and 2 as meaning the same, whereas according to informal logic 1 entails 2, but not vice versa. Accordingly, the denial of 3 is sometimes wrongly taken to be 1 (case of false alternatives), whereas the contradictory/true denial of 3 is 2. In other words, one's denial to hold a belief does not affirm that one holds the opposite belief. Not believing does not amount to disbelieving. This is what distinguishes agnosticism from atheism: the choice between belief and disbelief is not a forced choice: there is a third way, the way of withhold or non-belief. In everyday argumentation, it is quite often the case that we commit the withhold/deny fallacy for the sole reason that the practical consequences are seemingly indistinguishable. However, that would only make sense if the object of belief was entirely factual/practical rather than conceptual. Generally, the occurrence of the withhold/deny fallacy also produces the fallacy of false alternatives: that is, a state either accepts a regional custom or not.[59] There is no in-between. The fallacy of false alternatives in CIL has been formally incorporated in legal doctrine via the Lotus principle, as it manifests itself in the Kosovo advisory opinion, among others. Let us assume that the assertion 'Anna believes in ghosts' is 'Ag'. The variations of negation can be further symbolised as those contained in Figure 4.1.

The richness of belief. There is also the problem of belief itself. Let us also take as a given that a state is an entity that can be conceptualised as a Leviathan who thinks and reasons, which is of course not the case, so the induction is already arbitrary so to speak. The state is an enormous political-bureaucratic machine, and so one may naturally wonder how

[58] J Adler, 'Belief and Negation' (2000) 20(3) Informal Logic 207, 222.
[59] ibid 212.

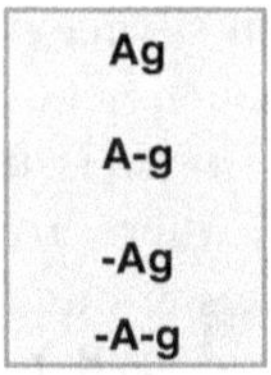

Figure 4.1

many beliefs by state-agents, legal advisors and high-ranking officials need to coordinate towards a certain belief or idea. Whose belief is of greater value, if so? How many views are considered enough to formulate the so-called *opinio juris* as a belief-reservoir? Or, even more profoundly, how will these individual beliefs be measured, attested and evaluated? Should we resort to official archives? Either official or unofficial communications? General Assembly Resolutions? How intense or strong should the negation or affirmation be in order to qualify as a positive or negative belief regarding the perceived bindingness of a norm? And what about plain indifference? What type of formality should be attached to this set of beliefs? Moreover, we cannot simply assume that a certain belief – *opinio juris* – is always in full awareness.

The richness of silence. Accordingly, we, as international lawyers, may indeed have to deal with either conscious silence or unconscious silence: intended or unintended silence. Should we assume that there are no variations in silence itself? What if silence qua the consciously or unconsciously omissive passage of time is not semantically homogenous throughout (the silent) time, that is, transforms into something semantically different at some point, given new circumstances? Judge Sørensen in the *North Sea Continental Shelf* noted '[i]n view of the manner in which international relations are conducted, there may be numerous cases in which it is practically impossible for one government to produce conclusive evidence of the motives which have prompted the action and policy of other governments'.[60]

Some of these questions have been addressed by the ICJ but most of them have not. For instance, in the 1951 *Fisheries* case, the ICJ seems to have taken into deeper consideration the context of British silence and ruled that '[t]he notoriety of the facts, . . . Great Britain's position in the North Sea, her own interest in the question, and her prolonged abstention would in any case warrant Norway's enforcement of her (straight

[60] See Judge Sørensen's dissenting opinion in *North Sea Continental Shelf Cases.*

baseline) system against the United Kingdom'.[61] Accordingly, in the *North Sea Continental Shelf Cases*, the court stated:

> [w]ith respect to the other elements usually regarded as necessary before a conventional rule can be considered to have become a general rule of international law, it might be that, even without the passage of any considerable period of time, a very widespread and representative participation in the convention might suffice of itself, *provided it included that of States whose interests were specially affected.*[62]

Normally, however, the evaluation of silence is much more superficial and narrow. In the *Military and Paramilitary Activities in and Against Nicaragua*, the court ruled that *opinio juris* may also be deduced from the attitude of states towards certain General Assembly resolutions.[63] This was confirmed in the *Nuclear Weapons* advisory opinion.[64] In the *Lotus* case, the Permanent Court of International Justice deduced from the freedom of the seas' principle that 'vessels on the high seas are subject to no authority except that of the State whose flag they fly'.[65]

We have seen that arguments from silence occur when someone interprets someone's silence as meaning anything other than silence, basically arguing that silence is either communicating implicit approval or disapproval. Again, when we are dealing with a silent authority, such as a state, we should ask ourselves: would the silent authority have known about the claim and consciously chose to remain silent? Is the silent authority fully aware of the claim? Do we have a complete record of everything written/done by the authority? Is this record true and reliable, and not just a presumption based on lack of evidence? If the answer is 'no' to any of the above, it is quite possible that we are dealing with a fallacious argument from silence. On the other hand, the fallacy *ad ignorantiam* occurs when someone argues in favour or against something, in our case state practice, simply because of lack of evidence, and not because of a positive evaluation of the absence of evidence.

In the Kosovo advisory opinion, the ICJ committed both fallacies. Without any substantial argumentation and with the ultimate goal to solve the Kosovo puzzle, the ICJ erroneously interpreted the absence of state practice as also implying a neutral *opinio juris* by the vast majority of

[61] *Fisheries Case (United Kingdom v Norway)* 139.
[62] *North Sea Continental Shelf Cases* (emphasis added).
[63] *Military and Paramilitary Activities in and Against Nicaragua (Nicaragua v United States of America)* [1986] ICJ Reports 14.
[64] *Legality of the Threat or Use of Nuclear Weapons* (Advisory Opinion) [1996] ICJ Rep 241.
[65] *SS 'Lotus' (France v Turkey)* (Judgment) [1927] PCIJ Series A No 10.

states vis-à-vis unilateral declarations of independence. The question that obviously arises here is this: how is it even possible for states to concur in a situation that would put their very existence in danger? One therefore notices a typical example of persuasive-teleological argumentation, oriented towards the effective resolution of an international dispute. The ICJ also construed the controversial perceived intent argument, that is, the argument that the authors of the declaration of independence did not seek to act within the constitutional framework of the interim administration for Kosovo (i.e., as the Assembly of Kosovo), but instead 'acted together in their capacity as representatives of the people of Kosovo'.[66] In particular, the ICJ held that 'the authors of that declaration did not act, or intend to act, in the capacity of an institution created by and empowered to act within that legal order but, rather, set out to adopt a measure the significance and effects of which would lie outside that order'.[67] Regarding the Serbian constitutional order, the ICJ concluded that the constitutional laws of Serbia were not applicable insofar as the object and purpose of the 1244 Security Council Resolution was to establish a temporary legal regime that would supersede the Serbian Constitution. In other words, the ICJ opted for the mainstream, closed-system approach, that is, departed from the premise that international law is a closed normative system, and treated the unilateral declaration of independence as a factuality lying outside that system. It also 'extended' the will theory to a non-state actor. By doing so, the ICJ also reached another paradoxical conclusion: one can act outside a normative order and thus avoid liability, simply by saying so.

Apart from the erroneous interpretation of silence and absence, the ICJ also committed an important syllogistic fallacy. Inference, or formal inference, is the logical process of understanding what is implied in a certain proposition; the process of deriving general or particular propositions, on the basis of something previously assented to, namely the 'derivation of one proposition, called the Conclusion, from one or more given, admitted, or assumed propositions, called the Premise or Premises'.[68] The objective of inference is the objective of reasoning: the examination of the validity of a statement by reason of certain facts or statements from which it is said to follow. Syllogism is the narrow concept of mediate inference, namely the inference for the completion of which we necessarily employ a medium or middle term.

[66] *Kosovo Opinion* [109].
[67] ibid [105] (emphasis added).
[68] W Minto, *Logic Inductive and Deductive* (John Murray 1915) 146.

The term 'syllogism' derives from the Greek words *σύν* (together) and *λόγος* (thought) and means the bringing together in thought of two Propositions in order to compose a third proposition, commonly referred to as Conclusion. For logician William Minto, '[t]he main use of the syllogism is in dealing with incompletely expressed or elliptical arguments from general principles'.[69] It is often the case where elliptical arguments are put forward, also known as enthymemes, whereby one premise is explicit and the other suppressed, namely held in the mind.[70] In this case, the purpose of the syllogism is practical: to expose the implications of the hidden premises in the most explicit, convincing and undeniable way possible, and challenge what is otherwise considered to be self-evident. There is such a fundamental, *hidden* syllogism in the Kosovo advisory opinion.[71] The syllogism goes as thus:

Premise 1 (P1):	All what is not forbidden (to states) is allowable.
Premise 2 (P2):	All declarations of independence (by non-state actors) are not forbidden.
Conclusion (C):	All declarations of independence are allowable (for non-state actors).

From the above scheme one immediately notices that the problem with the judicial syllogism does not only rest with the fallacious interpretation of absence and silence in international law according to the Lotus principle but also with a serious syllogistic fallacy. The conclusion of the deductive judicial syllogism is logically unsound because it does not follow from the premises. The syllogism suffers from the logical fallacy of equivocation. Equivocation is not a formal fallacy but a verbal or material fallacy, which implies that the same word or phrase is used in two different ways. The predicate term 'what is allowable' has a dual meaning: in P1 it means 'allowable for states' whereas in C it means 'allowable for non-state actors'. This is a typical sophist fallacy: 'an elephant has a trunk; a car has a trunk; therefore, an elephant must be a car'. This is equivocation. The rationality crisis is camouflaged because the judicial critique (i.e., the declarations, separate and dissenting opinions) focuses on the interpretation of silence.

69 ibid 209.

70 ibid.

71 This is generally acknowledged by international legal scholars. See for instance H Quane, 'Silence in International Law' (2014) 84(1) BYBIL 240.

Considering that the judicial syllogism does not have any external rationality, let us now turn to its internal consistency. As mentioned above, silence was attributed to the authors of the unilateral declaration of independence, it is therefore important to examine whether, from the scope of international law, silence could concern the conduct of non-State actors as well. In other words, the crucial question from an internal point of view is whether the Lotus principle applies to states and non-state actors alike. This particular question was neither posed nor addressed by the ICJ. At a first glance, it is debatable whether the principle applies to non-state actors at all due to their limited and derivative legal personality. In fact, in the same advisory opinion the ICJ concluded that the principle of territorial integrity is not applicable to, and thus does not bind, non-state actors. However, from an internal perspective and based on Kammerhofer's interpretation of Kelsen, that is, that a normative order can only be composed of positive norms, one can also go as far as to regard silence by states as well as non-state actors as merely factual, that is, as lying outside the normative order. From this perspective, what the ICJ then did was simply to acknowledge a factual state of affairs, namely a freedom that is normatively indifferent. However, it is difficult to argue in favour of such an interpretation, given that the ICJ did not simply acknowledge a freedom that is factual, but actually a freedom that is normative, insofar as it is accorded concrete legal consequences. Indeed, according to the ICJ, in the absence of a prohibitive rule, states (and non-state actors alike) are *legally* free to do as they wish. One can hardly argue that such an assertion is normatively indifferent, given that it clearly entails a positive legal permission as well as a corresponding legal entitlement.

6 Conclusion

It has been demonstrated that international law does not provide any clear guidance as regards the legal effects that follow from state silence. The prominent closed-system approach goes against the rules of logic and the canons of reasoning, according to which absence may correspond to multiple values, a variety of propositions and modalities. It has been argued that, in international jurisprudence, these modalities have been either equated or largely ignored. In the same spirit, the mainstream interpretation of CIL overlooks the quantifications and varieties of meaning in non-appearances. It has been suggested that an open-system perspective could shed light on inconsistencies and/or erroneous interpretations.

The modalities of absence affect the rationality and soundness of international legal doctrine and even have a real impact on international relations when overlooked. Due to the scarcity of proper inductive arguments in the process of CIL ascertainment, the striving for discursive truth and reason has been limited to an examination of superficial rationality, that is, a mere analytical and superficial testing of consistency. Even this internal consistency, though, is not a given. There is, for instance, a new distinction between the traditional and the so-called modern deductive CIL, that is, a distinction between customary law that results from the traditional, inductive method of reasoning, and customary law that arises in instances where the inductive method is considered impossible to use because state practice is non-existent, the legal question is too new and has not been dealt with etc. In those instances, deduction and assertion are often used. Both the absence of state practice and state silence are thus often interpreted on the basis of rules that are either deduced from general principles, or expressing simple assertions. Inevitably, the deductive or assertive character of this new CIL implies value judgements and/or the personal, political preferences of the adjudicating judge.

The lack in international legal reasoning of external rationality and even internal consistency has paved the way to persuasive-teleological argumentation. The ICJ has developed several techniques of superficial, persuasive argumentation, teleologically governed by the *non liquet* principle, the containment of international crises and the effective resolution of international disputes, thus producing and reproducing serious rationality deficits in the judicial treatment of silence in the framework of CIL. The existence of external and internal rationality deficits as well as the corresponding rhetorical manoeuvring increase the need for the legal system to appeal to a concrete legitimizing basis for the explanation of derogations, exemptions, ad hoc solutions or whatever argumentation games and gaps cannot be justified by virtue of the normative structure of the system itself or some generalised imperative of system maintenance, such as a state of emergency. This has been, for instance, the case with the Kosovo advisory opinion and the *Asylum* case, where the ICJ changed the normal calculus in the interpretation of silence and opted for ad hoc solutions. The anomaly in the Kosovo advisory opinion was pointed out by Judge Tomka, who in his Declaration argued that:

> [t]he legal régime governing the international territorial administration of Kosovo by the United Nations remained, on 17 February 2008, unchanged. What certainly evolved were the political situation and

> realities in Kosovo. The majority deemed preferable to take into account these political developments and realities, rather than the strict requirement of respect for such rules, thus trespassing the limits of judicial restraint.[72]

However, unless either an open-system approach is applied or robust coherence and consistency is systematically and methodologically pursued within a closed system, ad hoc and arbitrary judicial responses to non-appearances will persist.

[72] *Kosovo Opinion*, Declaration of Judge Tomka [35] (emphasis added).

5

Schrödinger's Custom

Implications of Identification on the Interpretation of Customary International Law

MARKUS P BEHAM

One can even set up quite ridiculous cases. A cat is penned up in a steel chamber, along with the following diabolical device (which must be secured against direct interference by the cat): in a Geiger counter there is a tiny bit of radioactive substance, so small, that perhaps in the course of one hour one of the atoms decays, but also, with equal probability, perhaps none; if it happens, the counter tube discharges and through a relay releases a hammer which shatters a small flask of hydrocyanic acid. If one has left this entire system to itself for an hour, one would say that the cat still lives if meanwhile no atom has decayed. The first atomic decay would have poisoned it. The ψ-function of the entire system would express this by having in it the living and the dead cat (pardon the expression) mixed or smeared out in equal parts.

Erwin Schrödinger, 'The Present Situation in Quantum Mechanics'[1]

[1] Translation taken from JD Trimmer, 'The Present Situation in Quantum Mechanics: A Translation of Schrödinger's "Cat Paradox" Paper' (1980) 124(5) Proceedings of the American Philosophical Society 323, 328. The original reads:

> *Man kann auch ganz burleske Fälle konstruieren. Eine Katze wird in eine Stahlkammer gesperrt, zusammen mit folgender Höllenmaschine (die man gegen den direkten Zugriff der Katze sichern muß): in einem Geigerschen Zählrohr befindet sich eine winzige Menge radioaktiver Substanz, so wenig, daß im Lauf einer Stunde vielleicht eines von den Atomen zerfällt, ebenso wahrscheinlich aber auch keines; geschieht es, so spricht das Zählrohr an und betätigt über ein Relais ein Hämmerchen, das ein Kölbchen mit Blausäure zertrümmert. Hat man dieses ganze System eine Stunde lang sich selbst überlassen, so wird man sich sagen, daß die Katze noch lebt, wenn inzwischen kein Atom zerfallen ist. Die ψ-Funktion des ganzen Systems würde das so zum Ausdruck bringen, daß in ihr die lebende und die tote Katze (s. v. v.) zu gleichen Teilen gemischt oder verschmiert sind.*

See E Schrödinger, 'Die gegenwärtige Situation in der Quantenmechanik' (1935) 23(49) Die Naturwissenschaften 807, 812.

1 Introduction

Normative efforts in international law – including interpretation – must be grounded on a sound ascertainment of the sources of legal obligation. What might appear as a comforting truism for followers of black letter law seems an almost unattainable quest when it comes to the identification of international custom. This chapter proposes a pragmatic positivist approach to the identification of non-consensual, unwritten law: Schrödinger's custom. If the classic textbook 'two-element' theory of customary international law (CIL) is valid – and the ILC still seems to think it is[2] – then at least half of the identification process consists of an empirical assessment. It requires to look at – to follow the title of Louis Henkin's seminal work[3] – how nations behave. Under the classical view of realism, states act according to a set of inherent interests. These may provide a compass for orientation through the haze of normative propositions. The chapter begins by characterising CIL among the sources from which international rights and obligations arise (Section 2). It then moves on to depict the process of identification referred to here as Schrödinger's custom including its implications for the issue of custom interpretation (Section 3). On that basis, it discusses how international relations theory may help predict the outcome of the identification process (Section 4). A conclusion rounds it all off. (Section 5).

2 Custom as a Source of Legal Obligation

If one accepts the catalogue of manifestations of international law in Article 38(1)(a)–(c) of the Statute of the International Court of Justice as an expression of universal state consensus,[4] one must look for 'international custom, as evidence of a general practice accepted as law'. Without overthinking the implications of the wording referring to custom *as* the evidence as opposed to being evidenced *by* 'a general practice

[2] See ILC, 'Draft Conclusions on Identification of Customary International Law, with Commentaries' (30 April–1 June and 2 July–10 August 2018) UN Doc A/73/10, reproduced in [2018/II – Part Two] YBILC 122, Conclusion 2.

[3] See L Henkin, *How Nations Behave. Law and Foreign Policy* (2nd ed, Columbia University Press 1979).

[4] See in this regard the slightly ambiguous wording of the ICTY in *Đorđević* considering Article 38(1) of the Statute of the International Court of Justice as customary international law, *Prosecutor v Vlastemir Đorđević* (Judgment) IT-05-87/1-A (27 January 2014) [33].

accepted as law',[5] one could simply take the provision at face value: references to custom as a source of legal obligation imply the existence of evidence as to 'a general practice accepted as law'. Invocation of custom proposes the possibility of identifying both state practice and *opinio juris*, making 'international custom' and 'evidence of a general practice accepted as law' synonymous sides of an equation.[6] In this view, 'international custom' comprises both the process of identification (*Rechtserkenntnis*) and the underlying acts of law creation (*Rechtserzeugung*).[7]

How may these underlying acts be characterised? The element of 'practice' reaches directly into international relations as they are conducted on a daily basis. In addition, for something to constitute custom, the respective behaviour must follow a sense of legal obligation. This has led certain strands in the literature to equate custom with tacit agreements.[8] Yet the general principles of law *ut res magis valeat quam pereat*[9] and *favor contractus*[10] carry the assumption that states adopting Article 38 of the Statute of the International Court of Justice intended to give meaning to its words. That custom is unwritten, unless it is codified, seems uncontested. But following 'international conventions, whether general or particular, establishing rules expressly recognized', 'a general practice accepted as law' must also mean something other than a consensual agreement. Unless one were to stretch the word 'convention' beyond its ordinary meaning under international law (for the lay use of the term might actually be synonymous with custom), Article 38(1)(a) refers to 'agreements'. As such, these may be written or unwritten, even implicit in the form of a tacit agreement.[11] When the Statute of the International Court of Justice requires that they establish 'rules expressly

5 See on this already M Beham, *State Interest and the Sources of International Law: Doctrine, Morality, and Non-Treaty Law* (Routledge 2018) 90.

6 The equation being 'international custom = evidence of a general practice accepted as law'.

7 On the distinction between creation and identification, see H Kelsen, *Reine Rechtslehre* (2nd ed, Franz Deuticke 1960).

8 See Beham (n 5) 81–83.

9 That a provision should rather be given effect than ignored.

10 That, in doubt, an agreement be upheld.

11 Confirming this understanding also American Law Institute, *Restatement of the Law. The Foreign Relations of the United States: Vol 1* (American Law Institute Publishers 1987) 149 [301] Comments a & b; ILC, 'Report on the Work of the Sixty-fifth Session' (6 May–7 June and 8 July–9 August 2013) UN Doc A/68/10, 32 [5] Commentary to Conclusion 4 'Definition of Subsequent Agreement and Subsequent Practice'.

recognized by the contesting states', this refers to the express recognition inherent in the process of reaching an 'agreement'.

If one were now to equate 'a general practice' with 'international conventions, whether general or particular' and 'accepted as law' with 'establishing rules expressly recognized', no sense would be given to the two separate provisions included in Article 38(1) of the Statute of the International Court of Justice. In short, *opinio juris* cannot simply be equated to an oral or tacit agreement. Still, it represents a quasi-consensual element, in that states could equally choose to answer the question 'did you just behave that way because you thought there is a legal obligation to do so' negatively.[12]

3 Identification

The state of CIL is in constant flux. The paradox that a customary norm must first be broken in order for a new one to arise, follows the Linnaean urge of scholars to sort and categorise their surroundings. But this approach does not do justice to the dynamic nature of a set of norms that is largely dependent upon the interaction of states.[13] While an awareness of certain trends within a particular area of law is both useful

[12] See however on the difficulties of determining *opinio juris* S Verosta, *Theorie und Realität von Bündnissen: Heinrich Lammasch, Karl Renner und Der Zweibund (1897–1914)* (Europa Verlag 1971) XXI:

> *Das Vorhandensein – oder Nichtvorliegen – der Rechtsüberzeugung kann aus den Regierungserklärungen und Parlamentsdebatten nicht immer eindeutig festgestellt werden. Sowohl die Rechtslage als auch die Tatsachen sind, wenn die Entscheidungen – meist unter Zeitdruck – gefällt werden, oft nur einer kleinen Zahl von Personen bekannt. Erst wenn die Akten, vor allem der Außenämter, freigegeben werden und Memoiren erschienen sind, läßt sich völkerrechtlich ein abschließendes Urteil bilden. Das erfordert ein eingehendes und mühseliges Studium, das oft überraschende Ergebnisse hat, wie sich auch aus dieser Untersuchung ergibt.* [The existence – or non-existence – of a legal conviction cannot always be clearly ascertained from governmental statements and parliamentary debates. When a decision is made – oftentimes under time pressure – the legal situation as well as the facts are mostly only known to a small circle of people. Only once the files, especially of foreign offices, are released and memoirs have been published, can there be a final determination as pertaining to international law. This requires detailed and arduous study that often brings forth surprising results as also evident from this analysis. Translation by the author.]

[13] Which does not imply that CIL is little more than a discursive recognition process. See for instance M Hakimi, 'Making Sense of Customary International Law' (2020) 118 MichLRev 1487.

and necessary to satisfy expectations towards the rule of law, a full assessment is only necessary once a specific argument is put forward. Like a snapshot photograph, CIL is identified at a certain point in time, be it within judicial proceedings or in a scholarly publication.[14] Since custom implies both identification and creation, their temporal dimensions collapse. The view that CIL is made in the past becomes a myth.[15]

Custom forms only in the present, once it is invoked and an observer is introduced. Explanatory aid may be sought from the famous thought experiment of Austrian physicist Erwin Schrödinger.[16] In his (for pet lovers luckily only theoretical) experimental set-up, a cat is placed in a steel chamber together with a vial of deadly acid that is released the moment an atom from a piece of radioactive material decays. However, it is equally probable that the radioactive material does not decay. Without an observer, there is no knowing whether the atom has decayed. Until that point in time, both the living and the dead cat must be assumed to exist. They are 'mixed or smeared' together.[17] What Schrödinger intended as an illustration of the paradox between reality and theoretical quantum-mechanics may easily be transposed to the problem of CIL formation. Until an observer is introduced, it is unclear how many states have already engaged in practice accompanied by *opinio juris*.

This should not be mistaken with the identification of an exact point in time at which a particular norm of CIL was created. The question is only as to the present existence of 'evidence of a general practice accepted as law'. As Maurice Mendelson pointedly illustrated,

> it makes no more sense to ask a member of a customary law society 'Exactly how many of you have to participate in such-and-such a practice for it to become law' than it would to approach a group of skinheads in the centre of The Hague and ask them, 'How many of you

[14] See in this sense also M Mendelson, 'The Subjective Element in Customary International Law' (1995) 66 BYBIL 177, 203:

> One way of dealing with this difficulty [the paradox of CIL formation] is to ignore it. Often, the 'consumer' of legal rules does not need to know when the fruit ripened, but simply whether it is ripe when he comes to eat it, or is still too hard or sour to eat. Indeed (to change the metaphor), to ask a follower of fashion at what point exactly something became the mode is in a sense to miss the point of informal rule-systems.

[15] See Chapter 2 by d'Aspremont in this volume.

[16] This analogy was first formulated by the author as a helpful illustration of the paradoxical formation of CIL in M Beham, M Fink & R Janik, *Völkerrecht verstehen* (Facultas 2015) 49; see also Beham (n 5) 91–93.

[17] Schrödinger (n 1).

> had to start wearing a particular type of trousers for it to become the fashion – and, indeed, *de rigeur* – for members of your group?' . . . The customary process is in fact a continuous one, which does not stop when the rule has emerged, even if one could identify that exact moment. To illustrate the point, I would like to introduce a simile. . . . My simile is the building of a house. It is often not easy or even possible to say exactly when a house has been created. Clearly, it is not when the first foundation stone is laid. But it is not when the last lick of paint has been added either. It is problematic at exactly what point we could say 'This is a house'. Do we have to wait for the roof to go on, for the windows to be put in, or for all of the utilities to be installed? So it is with customary international law.[18]

Rather than the point of formation, the observer will 'take a still photograph, so to speak, of the state of the (customary) law at a given moment',[19] the *lex lata.* The relevant question in practice – and in scholarship, for that matter – will mostly be the application of a certain rule to a particular set of circumstances, rather than a historic narrative of when and how a rule has formed.[20] In Charles De Visscher's words, '[i]n international relations more than elsewhere, the fact precedes its classification'.[21] The result is simply a manifestation of the dynamic character of international relations.

In our experiment, what do we imagine this observer to look like? Obviously, it cannot be a lobbyist or policymaker, nor an idealist international lawyer.[22] So, should it be a judicial robot, an algorithm fed with empirical data? While this idea of an objective assessment seems attractive at first, it is hard to see how this would deliver equitable results; more

18 M Mendelson, 'The Formation of Customary International Law' (1998) 272 RdC 155, 173–75, 284.

19 ibid 253.

20 G Scelle, 'Essai sur les Sources Formelles du Droit International' in C Appleton (ed), *Recueil d'Études sur les Sources du Droit en l'Honneur de François Gény: Tome III: Les Sources des Diverses Branches du Droit* (Sirey 1934) 400: '*Mais la source suppose une nappe souterraine, parfois inconnue ou mal connue, dont l'existence est pourtant indiscutable, puisque les sources sans elle n'existeraient pas*'. ['But the source assumes an underground water level, sometimes unknown or poorly known, though its existence is indisputable since the sources would not exist without it.' Translation by the author.] Of course, the establishment of CIL at a certain point in time will require engaging with the existing narrative.

21 C De Visscher, *Theory and Reality in Public International Law: Revised Edition* (Princeton University Press 1968) 153.

22 See, with regard to the efforts of the International Committee of the Red Cross in collecting and codifying customary international humanitarian law, JB Bellinger III & WJ Haynes II, 'A US Government Response to the International Committee of the Red Cross Study Customary International Humanitarian Law' (2007) 89 IRRC 443.

likely, such a sterile approach to law identification – which ultimately relies on the interaction of states as raw data – might result in a 'Bizarro World' image of international law. The fact that states torture with the conviction that they have a legitimate basis for doing so – one must only think of the 'ticking time bomb' scenario[23] – would result in a permissive rule allowing torture under such circumstances.

The analysis requires an underlying human corrective. It is in the same sense that Andreas Paulus and Bruno Simma speak of the need for an 'enlightened positivism'.[24] It would seem fitting to rely on the proverbial man on the Clapham omnibus. This reasonable – we might also imagine 'extra-terrestrial' – is neither an idealist, nor a cynic, neither a revisionist, nor an innovator. As little is he driven by a particular national interest, as by the ideal of the international community as a *civitas maxima*. Admittedly, this is a 'you know it, when you see it' approach, but in combination with the identification of CIL restricted to a certain point in time it will surely allow for a more grounded assessment of the body of CIL than any elaborate game theory model or natural law-based impulse. Occam's razor will easily help in the identification of state practice and *opinio juris*.[25]

What does this imply for the act of interpretation? If the temporal dimensions of creation and identification collapse, it can only result in 'instant interpretation'. As custom is frozen in the moment of its invocation, any statement about its future application becomes meaningless. Instead, custom must be repeatedly reassessed, unless there is a good faith assumption that the original invocation still constitutes 'evidence of a general practice accepted as law'. Any subsequent practice always paves the road towards new custom. Taking the example of a codification, if one were to 'interpret' its content for purposes of clarification, one would either be interpreting 'subsidiary means for the determination of rules of law'[26] to help identify such 'international custom, as evidence of a general practice accepted as law',[27] or again

[23] See in this respect for example *Gäfgen v Germany* [GC] ECtHR, App No 22978/05 (1 June 2010).

[24] AL Paulus & B Simma, 'The Responsibility of Individuals for Human Rights Abuses in Internal Conflicts: A Positivist View' (1999) 93(2) AJIL 302, 307.

[25] See JJ Paust, 'The Complex Nature, Sources and Evidences of Customary Human Rights' (1996) 25 GaJInt'l&CompL 147, 149–50.

[26] Article 38(1)(d) Statute of the International Court of Justice (adopted 26 June 1945, entered into force 24 October 1945) 33 UNTS 993.

[27] On the process of courts engaging in the interpretation of custom see Chapter 21 by Mileva in this volume.

engage in the identification of the underlying acts of law creation, thereby acting as an observer to 'Schrödinger's custom'.

4 State Interest

Are the implications of this mode of identification on the interpretation of CIL that it simply becomes unpredictable? As Malcolm Shaw writes, '[c]hange is rarely smooth but rather spasmodic'.[28] If state practice follows day-to-day world affairs, international relations theory might help. As Louis Henkin convincingly laid out in his seminal work *How Nations Behave*, states act according to carefully calculated interests and dependent upon the consequences of their conformity to or violation of international law.[29] This approach is, generally, quite similar to the economic theory of negligence that '[w]hen the cost of accidents is less than the cost of prevention, a rational profit-maximizing enterprise will pay tort judgments to the accident victims rather than incur the larger cost of avoiding liability'.[30]

The term 'interest' derives from the Latin *interesse*, which carries the meaning 'to differ' or 'to make a difference'. The interest is something that makes a difference to someone – or, if speaking of a juridical entity, to something. In discussing these issues, one is always confronted with the problem of anthropomorphising states.[31] Some writers have gone as far as to argue that states are not capable of holding such interests, 'as if artificial entities could have discernible motivations'.[32] However, this position overlooks the idea of statehood as represented through the collective of individual actors with a common agenda. Just as what makes a difference for an individual employee does not necessarily make a difference for a corporation, it does not necessarily make a difference for a state.[33]

[28] M Shaw, *International Law* (8th ed, Cambridge University Press 2017) 65.

[29] Henkin (n 3). For a rational choice version of this approach see JL Goldsmith & EA Posner, *The Limits of International Law* (Oxford University Press 2005). For a general overview of the various compliance theories see M Burgstaller, *Theories of Compliance with International Law* (Martinus Nijhoff 2005).

[30] R Posner, 'A Theory of Negligence' (1972) 1 JLS 32.

[31] See J Frankel, *National Interest* (Macmillan 1970) 115: 'More generally, the tendency to personalize the state and to compare its goals and needs with those the individuals, if pushed too far, inevitably leads to confusion.'

[32] A D'Amato, *The Concept of Custom in International Law* (Cornell University Press 1971) 271.

[33] Dino Kritsiotis sarcastically refers to this construction of states as 'corporate Hobbesian offspring'. D Kritsiotis, 'Reappraising Policy Objections to Humanitarian Intervention' (1998) 19(4) MichJIntlL 1005, 1008–13.

Each entity, the natural person as well as the juridical body, carries distinct goals and purposes. Some may correlate, some may differ. It is the nature of the respective actor that determines the interest.

The expression 'state interest' or 'national interest',[34] as it is sometimes found in the literature, confers the idea that there must be a common set of factors that are important to the existence of the abstract entity of the state. At the same time, it has been suggested that 'no agreement can be reached about its ultimate meaning'.[35] Still, it seems to be an important factor in decision-making of political stakeholders,[36] best reflected in the anecdotal quotes of Charles De Gaulle and Henry Kissinger that their respective states had 'no friends' but 'only interests'. That states ultimately strengthen and enrich themselves at the cost of others cannot shock an international lawyer since Emer de Vattel's 1758 publication of *Le Droit des Gens*.[37]

The idea that law formation follows the interplay of interests is also not particularly new. Carl Schmitt – the Dooyeweerd of German people[38] – already argued that public international law in the nineteenth century rested less on ideas of sovereignty than on a selection of specific state interests.[39] Jean d'Aspremont found that '[e]ven liberals and constitutionalists agree that States first strive to promote their own interests' and that 'they naturally act to maximize the interest of their constituency given their perception of the interests of other States and the distribution of State power'.[40] Martti Koskenniemi has called reference to this fact a 'truism, present since Vattel'.[41] Richard Steinberg convincingly showed how different schools of international legal thought and international relations theory resorted to realism whenever

[34] For a general caveat on the use and usefulness of the term 'state interest' see B Simma, *Das Reziprozitätselement im Zustandekommen völkerrechtlicher Verträge* (Duncker & Humblot 1972) 75–77.

[35] Frankel (n 31) 15.

[36] ibid 18.

[37] E de Vattel, *Le Droit des Gens: Ou Principes de la Loi naturelle, appliqués à la Conduite et aux Affaires des Nations et des Souverains. Tome 1* (London 1758) 268 [16] (misprinted as [17]).

[38] See Chapter 5 by Regalado Bagares in this volume.

[39] C Schmitt, *Der Begriff des Politischen: Text von 1932 mit einem Vorwort und drei Corollarien* (Duncker & Humblot 1963) 115.

[40] J d'Aspremont, 'The Foundations of the International Legal Order' (2007) 18 FYBIL 219, 228.

[41] M Koskenniemi, 'The Place of Law in Collective Security' in M Koskenniemi (ed), *The Politics of International Law* (Hart 2011) 79, 91.

they dealt with states.[42] Today, Martin Dixon begins his introductory textbook on international law by finding that '[i]t is true of all legal systems that vital interests of its subjects may prevail over the dictates of the law'.[43] According to Malcolm Shaw, the motivation behind an act of a state lies within the way in which 'it perceives its interests', which again depends upon 'the power and role of the State and its international standing'.[44]

What are these supposed interests that determine the probability of state action? For any realist, states are driven by two principal considerations: first, national security, comprising the protection of statehood, territorial integrity, as well as sovereignty, and, second, a functioning economy. Gerhard Hafner identified five traditional areas of state interest: 'the protection of statehood, territorial integrity, sovereignty, security and economic wealth'.[45] Nicholas Onuf speaks, in the Hobbesian tradition, of 'standing, security, and wealth'.[46] Recalling the definition of what constitutes a state, these 'traditional' interests are inextricably linked to its 'survival'.[47] Each student of international law knows that the 'primary subjects'[48] of international law consist of a permanent population, a defined territory and a government.[49] Recalling this definition, these

[42] See RH Steinberg, 'Wanted – Dead or Alive: Realism in International Law' in JL Dunoff & MA Pollack (eds), *Interdisciplinary Perspectives on International Law and International Relations* (Cambridge University Press 2013) 146.

[43] M Dixon, *Textbook on International Law* (7th ed, Oxford University Press 2013) 15.

[44] Shaw (n 28) 58.

[45] G Hafner, 'Some Thoughts on the State-Oriented and Individual-Oriented Approaches in International Law' (2009) 14 ARIEL 27, 29. He goes on: 'Under the traditional perspective, international law generated by states had to reflect a behaviour of states that was deemed to be reasonable. Such reasonable state conduct was expected to be motivated by the intention of maximising power, comparable with the REM hypothesis, *i.e.*, the conduct of a rational, egoistic and maximising man.' See ibid.

[46] N Onuf, *World of Our Making: Rules and Rule in Social Theory and International Relations* (USC Press 1989) 258–79.

[47] See Frankel (n 31) 131–32; Onuf (n 46) 278. See on this notion in jurisprudence also *Legality of the Threat and Use of Nuclear Weapons* (Advisory Opinion) [1996] ICJ Rep 241 [96–97]; furthermore, Article 25 of the Articles on Responsibility of States for Internationally Wrongful Acts 2001 (ARSIWA) allows necessity as a ground for precluding wrongfulness if the act 'is the only way for the State to safeguard an essential interest against a grave and imminent peril' and 'does not seriously impair an essential interest of the State or States towards which the obligation exists, or of the international community as a whole', ILC 'Draft Articles on Responsibility of States for Internationally Wrongful Acts with Commentaries' (23 April–1 June and 2 July–10 August 2001) UN Doc A/56/10, reproduced in [2001/II – Part Two] YBILC 31, art 25 (hereinafter ARSIWA).

[48] A Cassese, *International Law* (2nd ed, Oxford University Press 2005) 71.

[49] See G Jellinek, *Allgemeine Staatslehre* (3rd ed, O Häring 1914) 71.

'traditional' interests are inextricably linked to the 'survival' of a state. In a sense, to anthropomorphise states once more, this feature is not so different from the 'survival instinct' of individuals. The latter are equally interested in escaping the Hobbesian *bellum omnium contra omnes* before all else. The social contract that allows for this escape wants to be upheld. Thereby, state interest is equated with the survival of the state.[50] Without territory, without governmental control, it lacks its constitutive elements.

While states require individuals to take action on their behalf, these 'do not act on their own account but as State officials, as the tools of the structures to which they belong',[51] a view that is further reflected in the rules of attribution in the International Law Commission's Articles on State Responsibility.[52] The state organs are limited by the framework that is the respective state, even if this is little more than the collectivity of individual decisions. Its economy, social structure, and cultural heritage will largely determine what is opportune. Thus, states may weigh their interests differently and in accordance with additional factors such as ideology, be it liberal democracy, socialism, or some pan-territorial or ethnic component.[53] Still, the definition of the state is tainted by the fact that individuals act on its behalf. The way it is externally perceived is shaped by its successive governments. Therefore, it is important to differentiate between the state, its organs, and its population in making any determinations as to its character. Brierly defined the state exactly along these lines as 'a system of relations which men establish among themselves as a means of securing certain objects, of which the most fundamental is a system of order within which their activities can be carried on'. At the same time, he cautioned that the state 'should not be confused with the whole community of persons living on its territory', as 'it is only one among a multitude of other institutions, such as churches and corporations, which a community established for securing different objects'.[54] Yet

[50] See M Wight, 'Why Is There No International Theory?' (1960) 2 International Relations 35, 48: 'International theory is the theory of survival'; see also *Legality of the Threat or Use of Nuclear Weapons* [96–97].

[51] Cassese (n 48) 4.

[52] ILC, 'ARSIWA', arts 4–11.

[53] What Yadh Ben Achour calls 'civilisation', giving the states 'its cohesive spiritual power, its ideology' [translation by the present author]. YB Achour, *Le Rôle des Civilisations dans le Système International (Droit et Relations Internationales)* (Editions Bruylant/Editions de l'Université des Bruxelles 2003) 19.

[54] JL Brierly, *The Law of Nations: An Introduction to the International Law of Peace* (Humphrey Waldock ed, 6th ed, Clarendon Press 1963) 126.

this is little different from the way that multi- or transnational corporations such as Walmart, Royal Dutch Shell, or ExxonMobil are perceived against the background of a change in the board of directors. Only in extreme situations such as a revolution, is it likely that states entirely change their character on the initiative of a government or other persons or groups of persons exercising authority. States, as all other legal entities, are fictions to express the idea that individuals may come together to create an entity that pursues goals not necessarily representing their own and vice-versa. Even Immanuel Kant, one of those authors most championed for the cause of lofty values, pointed out that the wellbeing of the state – the '*Heil des Staates*' – does not necessarily correspond with the wellbeing or happiness of its respective citizens.[55]

A number of structural arguments have been brought against this view. For example, the need of states 'to include [NGOs] in their foreign policy analysis and respect their interests in the process of creating norms of international law' as a result of 'the power exercised by them through the use of media and similar means'.[56] However, these are means to an end:[57] the survival of states and, in this case, governments. These will likely set acts in the name of a state that aim at preventing civil unrest, cultivating a happy electorate,[58] attracting investment and highly skilled labour, securing development aid, gaining admission to an international organisation – the list goes on.[59] There is also still a certain impetus of morality determining action in the face of mass human rights violations or unrestrained warfare.[60] But this altruistic impulse seems often by itself too weak to spur any form of meaningful intervention.[61] Notwithstanding, the constitutionalist or Kantian argument still stands strong within international legal scholarship, spurred by Wolffian ideas

[55] I Kant, *Die Metaphysik der Sitten. Erster Theil: Metaphysische Anfangsgründe der Rechtslehre* (2nd ed, Friedrich Nicolovius 1798) 202.

[56] See Hafner (n 45) 35; Paulus & Simma (n 24) 306; Paust (n 25) 160–61.

[57] See PH Imbert, 'L'Utilisation des Droits de l'Homme Dans les Relations Internationales' in Société Française pour le Droit International (ed), *Colloque de Strasbourg: La Protection des Droits de l'Homme et l'Évolution du Droit International* (Éditions Pedone 1998) 282–83.

[58] See on these two considerations vis-à-vis foreign policy interests Frankel (n 31) 132.

[59] See Goldsmith & Posner (n 29) 109–19.

[60] See HJ Morgenthau & KW Thompson, *Politics Among Nations: The Struggle for Power and Peace* (6th ed, Alfred A Knopf 1985) 249–60; HJ Morgenthau, 'The Twilight of International Morality' (1948) 58(2) Ethics 79, 82.

[61] See in this regard also M Walzer, 'The Moral Standing of States: A Response to Four Critics' (1980) 9(3) Phil&PubAff 209, 226–27.

of a *civitas maxima*.[62] Its moral superiority is, after all, compelling.[63] Equally, state interest is not a one-way street. Interests of other states must be taken into account at some level, in particular in an international relations reality that has become dominated by a universal international organisation that is the United Nations.[64] Yet, this is a simple outcome of the discourse within which international relations take place,[65] already identified and incorporated by structural realism.[66] Yet 'subsidiary interests' will not necessarily predict what states will do, when competing core interests of survival arise. In such cases, states will usually resort to 'Realpolitik'.[67] They will, generally, not compromise on their interests out of altruistic motives – in this case vis-à-vis states – or out of concern for public opinion.[68] Even Gerhard Hafner, who takes a position that emphasises the role of the individual in international law, concedes that states take all the weight in this balance of interests when he writes that 'the reflection of the – nevertheless increasing – individual-oriented interests in norms of international law still depends on the will of states'.[69]

Equally, the constitutionalist argument does not stand empirical scrutiny. Just as states will bulldoze over public image considerations, whenever their survival interests are at stake, states will limit their activism with regard to *jus cogens* and *erga omnes* obligations to situations in which their own interests are concerned.[70] In the competition of 'first-order reasons', to borrow Joseph Raz's terminology,[71] interests related to the survival of the states will, naturally, prevail. In absence of an

[62] See for such a Wolffian *civitas maxima* view of the international community MC Bassiouni, 'Advancing the Responsibility to Protect Through International Criminal Justice' in RH Cooper & J Voïnov Kohler (eds), *Responsibility to Protect: The Global Moral Compact for the 21st Century* (Palgrave Macmillan 2009) 31, 36–37.

[63] See in this regard also A Somek, 'From the Rule of Law to the Constitutionalist Makeover: Changing European Conceptions of Public International Law' (2011) 18(4) Constellations 576, 578.

[64] See also the wording of Article 25 of ILC ARSIWA (n 47).

[65] MC Bassiouni, 'Revisiting the Architecture of Crimes Against Humanity: Almost a Century in the Making, with Gaps and Ambiguities Remaining – the Need for a Specialized Convention' in LN Sadat (ed), *Forging a Convention for Crimes Against Humanity* (Cambridge University Press 2011) 43.

[66] See fundamentally KN Waltz, *Theory of International Politics* (Addison Wesley 1979).

[67] See in this regard Imbert (n 57) 283; Frankel (n 31) 154–55.

[68] See Frankel (n 31) 152.

[69] Hafner (n 45) 28–29, 39.

[70] See Cassese (n 48) 210.

[71] See J Raz, *The Authority of Law: Essays on Law and Morality* (2nd ed, Oxford University Press 2009) 34.

exclusionary rule, a state will balance these interests in accordance with their respective 'strength' or 'weight'.[72] A ready example is the primacy that states accord to national security considerations over basic citizens' rights in the face of terrorism.[73] Altruistic obligations, in particular, do not seem likely candidates for custom.

How can these considerations on state interest help identify possible trends in CIL? Add to this effectivity and reciprocity, the catalysers of international law formation,[74] as the vertical and horizontal angles for the realist's theodolite and a credible prediction should be the likely result. After all, it is not just international law that guides the behaviour of states, but politics of interest. In turn, interest determines the formation of international law.[75] There might also exist areas of law in which compliance is not necessarily rewarded by reciprocal behaviour, but it seems that CIL will, at least, likely reflect an equilibrium of interests.[76]

72 See HS Richardson, 'Moral Reasoning', *The Stanford Encyclopedia of Philosophy* (Winter ed, 2014) <http://plato.stanford.edu/archives/win2014/entries/reasoning-moral> accessed 1 March 2021.

73 See also with regard to the balancing of interests of democratic states between ending human rights abuses abroad and the risk of its own citizens S McFarland & M Mathews, 'Who Cares About Human Rights?' (2005) 26(3) Political Psychology 365.

74 Reciprocity has been found to serve as a 'motivation' and a 'starting mechanism' that 'helps to initiate social interaction'. See AW Gouldner, 'The Norm of Reciprocity: A Preliminary Statement' (1960) 25(2) AmerSociolRev 161, 176; B Simma, *Das Reziprozitätselement in der Entstehung des Völkergewohnheitsrechts* (Wilhelm Fink 1970) 51; see also *Delimitation of the Maritime Boundary in the Gulf of Maine Area (Canada v USA)* (Judgment) [1984] ICJ Rep 246 [111].

75 See A Somek, 'Kelsen Lives' (2007) 18(3) EJIL 409, 446:

> The usual view is that international law is a check on state interests, causing a state to behave in a way that is contrary to its interests. In our view, the causal relationship between international law and state interests runs in the opposite direction. International law emerges from states' pursuit of self-interested policies on the international stage. International law is, in this sense, endogenous to state interests. It is not a check on state self-interest; it is a product of state self-interest.

This is not to say that interest alone is determinative of state behaviour, as some neo-realists have argued. See Goldsmith & Posner (n 29) 39. This view has been rightly criticised by Norman and Trachtman for ignoring that compliance with legal obligations may in itself be considered an 'exogenous influence' as Goldsmith and Posner say. G Norman & JP Trachtman, 'The Customary International Law Game' (2005) 99(3) AJIL 541, 571.

76 See A D'Amato, 'Trashing Customary International Law' (1987) 81 AJIL 101, 102; C Tomuschat, 'Obligations Arising for States Without or Against Their Will' (1993-IV) 241 RdC 195, 290–91.

5 Outlook

The 'cliché'[77] two-element theory of CIL can provide a simple solution against the legion of alternative theories. As a manifestation of international law that does not directly spring from the 'will' or 'consent' of states, it reflects their perpetual international relations. States do not voluntarily form a will at the international level but consciously or unconsciously influence its creation through their actions. Following the metaphor of 'Schrödinger's custom', until an observer is introduced to determine what the particular customary rule is in a certain moment, CIL remains 'mixed or smeared'.

Once an observer is introduced and the temporal dimensions of creation and identification collapse, 'interpretation' can only mean the assessment of 'evidence of a general practice accepted as law' at a certain point in time. Subsequent practice will always only ever pave the road towards new custom.

This should not suggest a nihilistic view of custom. While the literature may already now concede the instructive value of realism when dealing with states, stronger attention should be given to the interplay of this 'truism' with the formation of CIL. It is obvious that parties bring their interests to the table when negotiating a treaty. Strangely, it appears less obvious whenever scholars seek to harness custom for the normative project of international law. More even than other sources, CIL will most likely reflect an equilibrium of interests.

[77] L Condorelli, 'Customary International Law: The Yesterday, Today, and Tomorrow of General International Law' in A Cassese (ed), *Realizing Utopia: The Future of International Law* (Oxford University Press 2012) 148.

PART II

Customary International Law as a Source of International Law

Doctrine and History

6

The Significance of State Consent for the Legitimate Authority of Customary International Law*

ANDREAS FOLLESDAL

> experience has taught us, that human affairs would be conducted much more for mutual advantage, were there certain symbols or signs instituted, by which we might give each other security of our conduct in any particular incident.[1]
>
> the reasonable expectation produced by a promise ... [which is] a declaration of your desire that the person for whom you promise should depend on you for the performance of it.[2]

1 Introduction

Norms of customary international law (CIL) pose a dilemma for international courts. Rules (and principles) of CIL are unwritten sources of international law with two central constituent features: they form 'a general practice' which enjoys 'acceptance as law' (*opinio juris*).[3]

* Research for this chapter was partly supported by the Research Council of Norway through its Centres of Excellence Funding Scheme, project number 223274 – PluriCourts: The Legitimacy of the International Judiciary. A first version of the chapter was presented at the TRICI-Law conference on 'The Theory and Philosophy of Customary International Law and its Interpretation' Groningen 24–25 May 2019. I am grateful for comments received there from Matthias Brinkmann, Antoinette Scherz, Geir Ulfstein and Johan Wibye, from the editors and from anonymous reviewers.

1 'Of the Obligation of Promises' D Hume, *A Treatise of Human Nature* (first published 1739, Clarendon Press1960).

2 A Smith, 'Of Contract' in RL Meek, DD Raphael & PG Stein (eds), *Lectures on Jurisprudence* (Oxford University Press 1978) 263.

3 ILC, 'Draft Conclusions on the Identification of Customary International Law' (30 April–1 June and 2 July–10 August 2018) UN Doc A/73/10, reproduced in [2018/II – Part Two] YBILC 11, General Commentary 3 (CIL Conclusions); Statute of the International Court of Justice (adopted 26 June 1945, entered into force 24 October 1945) 1 UNTS 993, art 38(1); Vienna Convention on the Law of Treaties (adopted 23 May 1969, entered into force

Among CIL are various *jus cogens* norms, with a higher rank than treaty law and other CIL.[4] Judges and scholars may thus disagree about whether alleged CIL indeed is a rule of CIL – whether it satisfies both the two necessary conditions, its specific contents and whether it is *jus cogens*.

Customary international law appears to challenge the central role of state consent in accounting for the legitimacy of public international law (PIL) in general. Consider the immunity of foreign heads of state, the principle of non-refoulement, or *jus cogens* norms that outlaw slavery, torture, genocide, aggression, or crimes against humanity. Sovereign states are under a legal obligation to comply with these CIL norms, even though they have not explicitly consented to them. How should international courts accommodate non-consent-based CIL and state sovereignty? The following reflections outline one strategy that avoids or helps address challenges wrought against other attempts to create more consistency and coherence between CIL and the other sources of international law – whilst securing a central role for state consent.

Some argue to weaken the conception of state consent to include various 'tacit' forms in CIL. Challenges to these strategies are *legio*, including how to detect the sort of tacit consent that – unlike forced acquiescence or mindless habituation – can help account for the justificatory binding force of such consent.

Similar challenges arise when resorting to purely hypothetical consent. Thus, some argue that states sometimes have good reason to be bound to CIL norms precisely without their consent, in response to certain collective action problems.[5] Such functionalist rationales illuminate the reasons states may have to comply with specific CIL norms, but they stop short of explaining or justifying the authority of such norms over sovereign states: why are states bound by such norms, and

27 January 1980) 1155 UNTS 331, art 31(3)(c); *North Sea Continental Shelf Cases* (Federal Republic of Germany/Denmark; Federal Republic of Germany/Netherlands) (Judgment) [1969] ICJ Rep 3 [77].

[4] Some *jus cogens* norms may instead be 'general principles of law'; ILC, 'Draft Articles on Responsibility of States for Internationally Wrongful Acts with Commentaries' (23 April–1 June and 2 July–10 August 2001) UN Doc A/56/10, reproduced in [2001/II – Part Two] YBILC 31 (ARSIWA); ILC (n 3).

[5] AT Guzman & J Hsiang, 'Reinvigorating Customary International Law' in CA Bradley (ed), *Custom's Future: International Law in a Changing World* (Cambridge University Press 2016); L Helfer & I Wuerth, 'Customary International Law: An Instrumental Choice Perspective' (2016) 37(4) MichJIntlL 563.

bound by them rather than by other equally functional rules? Others seek consistency by arguing the reverse: consent-based treaty obligations themselves are but instances of CIL since they rest on custom. Such strategies beg the question of whether there are any relevant differences in kind between treaties and CIL – what role does state consent serve? And what to make of the various constraints on when consent binds states, such as in the Vienna Convention on the Law of Treaties (VCLT) Articles 48–53? Some instead bite the bullet and downplay CIL as a source of international law, because treaties have come to replace and strengthen such unwritten norms.[6] But such historical and causal claims are contested, and fail to account for all CIL – whether, for example, the authority of *pacta sunt servanda* only rests on states' consent 'all the way down'.

The following reflections pursue another answer to why and when non-consent-based CIL enjoys legitimate authority over states. A plausible account of why states have an obligation to honour treaties they consent to *also* contributes to justify states' obligation to honour CIL norms – which they have given normatively significant consent to. The shared normative basis for both sorts of obligations may be a 'Principle of Non-manipulation', a norm *to not violate intentionally created rightful expectations*. The account draws much on Scanlon, MacCormick and Hart.[7]

The aim of these reflections is limited to identifying one shared normative premise for the authority of treaties and of CIL: the principle of non-manipulation. This does not exhaust their normative premises – such as the justification of the *jus cogens* status of some CIL and their constraints on treaties. The account does not deny that state consent is often a valuable mechanism for states to commit to new obligations – to

[6] J Trachtman, 'The Growing Obsolescence of Customary International Law' in CA Bradley (ed), *Custom's Future: International Law in a Changing World* (Cambridge University Press 2016).

[7] HLA Hart, *Punishment and Responsibility: Essays in the Philosophy of Law* (Oxford University Press 1968) 28; TM Scanlon, 'The Significance of Choice' (1986) 7 The Tanner Lectures on Human Values 149, 211; N MacCormick, 'Voluntary Obligations and Normative Powers I' (1972) 46 Proceedings of the Aristotelian Society 59; J Raz, 'Promises and Obligations' in J Raz & PMS Hacker (eds), *Law, Morality and Society: Essays in Honour of HLA Hart* (Oxford University Press 1977); TM Scanlon, 'Promises and Practices' (1990) 19(3) Phil & Pub Aff 199; N Kolodny & RJ Wallace, 'Promises and Practices Revisited' (2005) 31(2) Phil & Pub Aff 119; a frequent alternative is to try to build on a duty of fair play, D Lefkowitz, 'The Legitimacy of International Law' in D Held & P Maffettone (eds), *Global Political Theory* (Polity 2016) discussed briefly below.

the contrary, there are reasons to endorse the consent mechanism for states to create legal obligation. But rather than regard it as the centre and normative bedrock of international law with some odd epicycles of exceptions and conditions, we should understand the consent mechanism as embedded in a broader normative structure for international law. Some such normative premises also allow us to justify some non-consent-based CIL.

Section 2 motivates the quest for the grounds for valuing state consent. Section 3 defends state consent as necessary to render certain PIL norms legitimate authorities for international judges and other compliance constituencies. The justification is partly based on a normative principle of non-manipulation, to not harm other actors who have formed reasonable expectations about our future conduct on the basis of our deliberate attempts to foster such expectations. States can use consent to send such complex signals to others, that it henceforth regards some norm as an exclusionary, somewhat content-independent reason for action.

Sections 4 and 5 considers why non-consent-based CIL may also enjoy legitimate authority over states. The same principle of non-manipulation may contribute to justify norms that bind states even though they have not performed any recognisable act of consent.[8] Section 6 brings this account to bear on some contested conclusions of the International Law Commission's (ILC) final report on the 'Identification of Customary International Law' (Conclusions or ILC Conclusions). This account may also guide the unavoidable broad discretion judges must exercise in discovering and creating CIL.[9] The concluding section responds to several of the apparent puzzles about the scope and conditions of state consent to valid treaties, and considers objections concerning the relationship between PIL and normative premises such as the principle of non-manipulation: that it is too vague or that the account is unhelpful adds nothing.

2 Some Challenges and Puzzles Concerning State Consent in PIL

Of particular concern here are several apparent puzzles concerning the relationship between CIL and state consent. A wide range of authors have sought to explain the binding nature of all traditional sources of PIL exclusively based on consent. Some claim that there are great benefits to

[8] I am grateful to Asif Hameed for prompting this clarification.
[9] ILC (n 3) Conclusion 9.

require state consent as the sole basis of the legitimate authority of international law. However, such a requirement also entails some costs: consent by all states serves to *prevent* agreement to 'global public goods', so that important human interests go unmet.[10] Leaving the cost-benefit issues aside, consider various claims about why consent enables states to create new legally binding obligations. Consent is often regarded as a central expression of state sovereignty, yet many challenge the central role of it in endowing international law with normatively legitimate authority in the following sense: how – if at all – and when, does state consent justify the claims of each of the sources of PIL to be legitimate authorities? That is: how does their consent give states new reasons to act otherwise, and judge new reasons when they interpret and adjudicate?

I shall suggest that CIL plays several roles with regard to when the mechanism of state consent creates valid PIL. The relevant conception of state consent should be consistent with and might help justify that source's claim to be a legitimate authority. That is, what are the scope conditions and background requirements for when state consent creates new rules that enjoy legitimate authority over particular subjects?

I submit that the roles for and constraints on state consent in current CIL may identify a broader normative framework for when CIL (and other sources of PIL) is a legitimate authority for states and international courts (ICs): when do these norms give the actors reason to act differently than they otherwise would, and what is the appropriate role of state consent? On closer scrutiny, it seems that states' consent is neither necessary nor sufficient for them to have or acquire legal obligations as a matter of PIL.

2.1 Challenges to State Consent as a Necessary Normative Basis for CIL

Several arguments based on the origins of such consent would appear to fail. Consider a frequent form of argument that draws from premises akin to 'the presumptive ability of State representatives to speak and act on behalf of nations and their citizenry'.[11] State consent on this account binds because it expresses the moral autonomy of its citizens. Such a democratic, person-based line of argument appears implausible for PIL, at least without further elaboration. It seems unable to account for

[10] N Krisch, 'The Decay of Consent: International Law in an Age of Global Public Goods' (2014) 108(1) AJIL 1.

[11] Y Shany, 'Assessing the Effectiveness of International Courts: A Goal-Based Approach' (2012) 106(2) AJIL 225, 241.

how authoritarian non-democracies can be bound – if at all. Their claims to act 'on behalf of' their citizenry seem blatantly false in the absence of any signalling or accountability mechanisms linking the executive to the citizenry's preferences.[12] Some may bite the bullet and conclude that non-democratic states cannot bind themselves by consent to treaties. Yet they – and other states – appear to hold otherwise, and there seems to be good reasons to hold non-democracies to be legally – and arguably morally – obligated to treaties when that is crucial to secure objectives such as combating climate change, piracy, or human rights violations. How can this be?

A second kind of challenge to claims that state consent is the sole reason that PIL binds states as a legitimate authority concerns the risk of infinite regress – a 'chronological paradox'.[13] In particular, why is it that their consent binds states? Appeals to the fact that states agreed to the legal norm '*pacta sunt servanda*' in the VCLT would appear relevant, but is insufficient. Several states have not consented to the VCLT. Moreover, how could states' act of consent to the VCLT *create* a state obligation, if state consent had no such magical consequences for the states prior to their consenting to the treaty? The binding force of the practice of state consent itself cannot only rest on the binding force of state consent 'all the way down'.[14]

In order to accommodate CIL as based on state consent, Suarez and many later scholars have appealed to versions of 'tacit' or 'presumed' consent.[15] Such strategies meet with a range of objections. Who has the authority to determine the specific content of norms that a state tacitly consents to?[16] Are these norms 'particular' among a limited group of

[12] T Christiano, 'Climate Change and State Consent' in J Moss (ed), *Climate Change and Justice* (Cambridge University Press 2015) 22.

[13] M Byers, *Custom, Power and the Power of Rules: International Relations and Customary International Law* (Cambridge University Press 1999) ch 9.

[14] H Lauterpacht, 'The Nature of International Law and General Jurisprudence' (1932) 37 Economica 301; JL Brierly, 'The Basis of Obligation in International Law' in H Lauterpacht & CHM Waldock (eds), *The Basis of Obligation in International Law and Other Papers by the Late James Leslie Brierly* (Clarendon Press 1958); A Pellet, 'The Normative Dilemma: Will and Consent in International Law-Making' (1989) 12 Aust YBIL 22; E Posner, 'Do States Have a Moral Obligation to Obey International Law?' (2003) 55(5) Stan L Rev 1901, 1910–11; R Collins, 'Consent, Obligation and the Legitimate Authority of International Law' in P Capps & HP Olsen (eds), *Legal Authority Beyond the State* (Cambridge University Press 2018) 206.

[15] F Suarez, *The Laws and God the Lawgiver* (Naples 1612); more recent contributions include K Wolfke, *Custom in Present International Law* (2nd ed, Martinus Nijhoff 1993).

[16] J Locke, *Two Treatise of Government* (first published 1690, The New English Library 1963) 2nd treatise, ch 8 [119].

states only, or general? How can we distinguish normatively binding tacit consent from 'tacit aquiescence',[17] or from submission as the only alternative to destruction?[18]

The ILC Conclusions explicitly dismiss state consent as a plausible ground for CIL. They note the *peculiar* nature of CIL as not based on formal consent. The Conclusions include the term '*opinio juris*' alongside 'accepted as law', because 'it may capture better the particular nature of the subjective element of customary international law as referring to legal conviction and not to formal consent'.[19]

Several authors argue that these foundational challenges and various peculiar features of the practice of state consent gives reason to question the significance of consent for issues of legitimate authority.[20] These concerns should not lead us to dismiss state consent too quickly. The topic at hand – of the legitimacy of CIL – can benefit from reflections on the reasons that may have led us to believe that consent in general, and state consent in particular, endows parts of PIL with legitimate authority – that is, so that states may have moral obligations to comply with PIL.[21]

2.2 *Puzzles of State Consent*

There are several striking features of the role of state consent. Standardly, a state's consent must be informed and voluntary to create an obligation, not 'procured by the threat or use of force'.[22] However, aggressor states may be bound by peace treaties even if they sign only due to threats carried out in accordance with the UN Charter.[23]

[17] Wolfke (n 15) 97.

[18] Thucydides, *The Complete Writings of Thucydides: The Peloponnesian War* (Random House 1951).

[19] ILC, 'CIL Conclusions' (n 3) 123 [665].

[20] Thus D Bodansky, 'The Legitimacy of International Governance: A Coming Challenge for International Environmental Law?' (1999) 93(3) AJIL 596; M Zürn, 'Global Governance and Legitimacy Problems' (2004) 39(2) Government and Opposition 260; A Buchanan & RO Keohane, 'The Legitimacy of Global Governance Institutions' (2006) 20(4) Ethics and International Affairs 405, 412–14.

[21] N Roughan, 'Sources and the Normativity of International Law: From Validity to Justification' in S Besson & J d'Aspremont (eds), *The Oxford Handbook on the Sources of International Law* (Oxford University Press 2017) 680; O Suttle, 'Rules and Values in International Adjudication: The Case of the WTO Appellate Body' (2019) 68(2) ICLQ 399.

[22] VCLT art 52.

[23] ibid art 75.

States are also subject to some legal obligations without their express consent – such as *jus cogens* norms, 'accepted and recognized by the international community of States as a whole', but not necessarily accepted by every state.[24] Indeed, the number of non-consent-based CIL suggests that state consent is indeed the exception. Consider the weakened persistent-objector rule, third-party effects of treaties giving rise to a general practice, majority voting within treaty bodies, law making by international organizations and international courts, invalid reservations, or the severability doctrine.[25] Sometimes states appear to agree to treaties that crystallise existing CIL, such as *pacta sunt servanda* as recognised in Article 26 of the VCLT.[26] Their consent then does not create new obligations, but the reverse: they consent as a way to recognise and confirm that they regard themselves as already bound. Finally, some CIL norms such as *jus cogens* circumscribe the material contents of the legal obligations states can create through their consent – even retroactively.[27] Indeed, new *jus cogens* norms may in principle even invalidate treaties retroactively. How can such constraints be justified?

So consent plays important roles when PIL makes claims to be obeyed or deferred to.[28] But the mechanism of consent is neither always necessary, nor always sufficient for sovereign states to be under, create, or

[24] ibid art 53; ILC, 'CIL Conclusions' (n 3) Conclusion 8.

[25] A Peters, 'Global Constitutionalism Revisited' (2005) 11 International Legal Theory 39, 51; M Fitzmaurice, 'Third Parties and the Law of Treaties' (2002) 6(1) UNYB 37; J Alvarez, *International Organizations as Law-Makers* (Oxford University Press 2006); I Venzke, *How Interpretation Makes International Law: On Semantic Change and Normative Twists* (Oxford University Press 2012); E Fahey, *The Actors of Postnational Rule-Making: Contemporary Challenges of European and International Law* (Routledge 2017); ILA Committee on Formation of Customary (General) International Law, 'Final Report of the Committee: Statement of Principles Applicable to the Formation of General Customary International Law' (*ILA*, 2000) Principle 10 and its accompanying commentary; ILC, 'CIL Conclusions' (n 3) Conclusion 11(1)(c); ILC, 'Report of the International Law Commission on the Work of Its 59th Session' (7 May–5 June and 9 July–10 August 2007) UN Doc A/62/10, 101; L Helfer, 'Nonconsensual International Lawmaking' (2008) 2008(1) U Ill L Rev 71, 75; R Goodman, 'Human Rights Treaties, Invalid Reservations, and State Consent' 96(3) AJIL 531; C Tomuschat, 'Obligations Arising for States without or against Their Will (Volume 241)' in *Collected Courses of the Hague Academy of International Law* (Brill 1993), 262–64. I owe some examples to an anonymous reviewer.

[26] ILC, 'Fourth Report on the Law of Treaties by Gerald Fitzmaurice, Special Rapporteur' (17 March 1959) UN Doc A/CN.4/120, reproduced in [1959/II] YBILC 37, 42.

[27] VCLT arts 53 & 64.

[28] This is consistent with S Ratner, *The Thin Justice of International Law: A Moral Reckoning of the Law of Nations* (Oxford University Press 2015) 4; T Christiano, 'Is Democratic Legitimacy Possible for International Institutions?' in D Archibugi, M Koenig-Archibugi

avoid, legal obligations. State consent thus seems to create new binding obligations only within some material domain and when some procedural conditions are met. Not all these rules that regulate state consent can exhaustively be based on state consent. A better understanding of the present practice calls for further reflections on the reasons to value state consent, thus regulated, in creating legitimate authority.

3 Why Value State Consent?

The practice and puzzles of state consent sketched above calls for further reflection about the role of state consent, so that we neither dismiss CIL and other PIL norms simply because they are not based on state consent, nor rashly approve the tendency that state consent is 'falling out of favour'.[29] The conditions, limitations and incompleteness of state consent as necessary or sufficient conditions for some of the states' legal obligations may help us identify the justification that such circumscribed state consent provides, to understand why and when international law in general, and CIL in particular, can correctly claim to enjoy legitimate authority.[30] The standards for when CIL is a legitimate authority may be different for states, for judges who interpret and adjudicate international law, and for other 'deference constituencies'.

Such reflections about how well state consent secures certain values may help us assess both criticisms and improvements to the present alleged central role of state consent. On the one hand, the mechanism of state consent may privilege the *status quo* unduly, or give too many actors untrammelled discretionary power to avoid morally required obligations, and block beneficial or urgently needed treaties.[31] On the other hand, improvements will presumably be better specified in light of the reasons we have to value international law, so that we can further fine tune the conditions and exceptions for when state consent creates binding legal obligations – including a better understanding of why and when we have reason to value also the consent of non-democratic states.

& R Marchetti (eds), *Global Democracy Normative and Empirical Perspectives* (Cambridge University Press 2011) 69.

[29] Collins (n 14); Krisch (n 10).

[30] There may be no reason to assume that international legal positivism – understood as a theory of interpretation of given sources – should answer such questions. But theories of international law with more comprehensive objectives might do so.

[31] For example AT Guzman, 'Against Consent' (2012) 52(4) VaJIntlL 747; Christiano (n 28).

Attention to our reasons to value state consent may thus also help us acknowledge certain non-consent-based sources of PIL – be it soft law, lawmaking by international organizations and by international courts – and CIL. Their lack of state consent may be open to benefits but also further risks – risks that may be addressed in light of such a broader understanding. So: why might sovereign states, born free, consent to live in chains? What reasons do they have to consent to treaties in order to publicly acquire or acknowledge an obligation to defer to such norms – to subject themselves to their authority?[32] In general, state consent grants states some *influence over the future* within some policy space that may be of value to them and their citizens for several reasons.

3.1 Non-domination

State consent grants states a domain of protected sovereignty that reduces *domination*: it reduces risks that other actors can arbitrarily determine its options, intentionally or otherwise. Such legal sovereignty of course does not yield perfect protection against domination, as the citizens of Melos realised, and begs important questions about the domains of such sovereignty.

3.2 Some Strategic Control Over the Future

State consent may also increase a state's *control*, to better carry out and adapt the policies its government believes it has reason to pursue. If other actors recognise such consent as a state's attempt to self-bind, the state may secure outcomes otherwise unachievable. The consent must then trigger some new (exclusionary and somewhat content independent) reasons for the state to act otherwise that it has reason to value, and that other actors must understand and respect. Such strategic control is of value only when the state is actually able to identify, assess and select among its options, and when its preferences are not objectionable. Reversely, state consent lacks such value when a state is ignorant of the consequences of alternatives, acts under duress or is unable to reflect

[32] For further discussions see A Buchanan, *Justice, Legitimacy, and Self-Determination: Moral Foundations for International Law* (Oxford University Press 2003) 301; T Christiano, 'Ronald Dworkin, State Consent, and Progressive Cosmopolitanism' in W Waluchow & S Sciaraffa (eds), *The Legacy of Ronald Dworkin* (Oxford University Press 2016) 49.

about the choice[33] – or if the choice has detrimental effects on other parties – for example, if it violates human rights.

3.3 *Predictability*

A state's express consent may increase its future compliance with international law, and hence increase other actors' ability to predict its actions. This process requires a shared understanding that consent imposes legal obligations that exclude or override some other reasons to act. Note that such predictability is only of value if the state's future actions are in fact of value for others. And this may be the case also concerning acts of authoritarian, non-democratic states. And predictability may be enhanced even with some escape clauses for emergencies and exemptions – as long as they cannot be too readily abused. Note that such predictions only work if a state succeeds in conveying its 'intention to abide by a rule'[34] by a signal that convinces other states. The practice of state consent is one way to signal such complex intentions – if the actors know that the consenting state generally respects international law.

3.4 *Status Equality*

A further value of state consent is to express *status equality* among states.[35] So if *some* states enjoy such legal sovereignty within some domain, it is of value for *other* states and their citizens to enjoy the *same* domain for consent. Smaller such domains give rise to two distinct concerns. The state may risk *domination* by other states, and it expresses their relative inferiority. Oppenheim arguably made the latter point thus: 'In entering the Family of Nations a State comes as an equal to equals; it demands a certain consideration to be paid *to its dignity*, the retention of its independence, of its territorial and its personal supremacy.'[36] Note that this value does not require any particular domain of issue areas for binding state consent, as long as all states enjoy the same legal domain.

33 Hart (n 7) 44–45; Christiano (n 28); R Dworkin, 'A New Philosophy for International Law' (2013) 41(1) Phil&PubAff 2, 10.

34 S Besson, *The Morality of Conflict: Reasonable Disagreement and the Law* (Hart 2005) 459.

35 Charter of the United Nations (adopted 26 June 1945, entered into force 24 October 1945) 1 UNTS XVI, 4, art 2(1).

36 L Oppenheim, *International Law – Vol 1: Peace* (8th ed, Longmans 1955) 263 (emphasis added).

3.5 *Some Implications*

One important type of cases where state consent may promote some of the values identified above is when consent helps secure coordination for mutual gain. The requirement of consent may help states negotiate on a somewhat more equal basis when they specify shared objectives and select among available means.

So on the one hand, to require state consent may facilitate a fairer bargaining process, reducing domination.[37] Yet to require unanimity also risks deadlock by states who simply seek a larger share of benefits. There are important coordination challenges: states may agree on overall objectives but disagree about how to specify them and the requisite strategies.[38] Indeed, states often face such two-stage challenges: 'before States can cooperate to enforce an agreement they must bargain to decide which one to implement'.[39] So states' interest in *control* over outcomes may hinder 'global public goods' which they all have an interest in, such as a sustainable environment.[40]

Such benefits and risks may be why member states of the EU agree to (qualified) majority voting for certain issues.[41] Such decision rules may be more appropriate and more likely when states trust that power differentials will not be exploited, and when all expect to often be in the winning coalitions. Similarly, some multilateral environmental treaties and IMO Conventions have secured simplified consent procedures, or developed opt-out clauses etc.[42] Such weaknesses notwithstanding, state consent may sometimes be the best way to manage constrained, 'reasonable' disagreement in 'battle of the sexes' situations. One upshot of these reflections is that the mechanism of state consent is double-edged. It can sometimes promote cooperation on somewhat more equal terms, but it

[37] RD Luce & H Raiffa, *Games and Decisions: Introduction and Critical Survey* (Wiley 1957) ch 5; such cases seem appropriate for the account offered in S Besson, 'State Consent and Disagreement in International Law-Making' (2016) 29(2) LJIL 289, 292.

[38] Besson appears to hold that PIL generally substantially serves to coordinate under circumstances of reasonable disagreement among states, see Besson (n 37); I take it that the cases discussed here are examples of this.

[39] JD Fearon, 'Bargaining, Enforcement, and International Cooperation' 52(2) International Organization 269, 270; A Buchanan, 'Institutional Legitimacy' in D Sobel, P Vallentyne & S Wall (eds), *Oxford Studies in Political Philosophy Volume 4* (Oxford University Press 2018) 57.

[40] Krisch (n 10).

[41] RE Goodin, 'Institutionalizing the Public Interest: The Defense of Deadlock and Beyond' (1996) 90(2) APSR 331 addresses some ways to resolve these.

[42] I am grateful to an anonymous reader for these examples.

can also hinder cooperation, because some states – often sub-state actors within them – insist on agreements that secure them more benefits and less burdens from cooperation.

These brief points have several implications when we turn to consider the legitimate authority of customary international law. The values of state consent draw on some broader account concerning the domain wherein, and conditions under which, state consent is decisive in creating expectations. States' own choice, sufficiently informed and uncoerced, among certain options within some domains, may help states secure some of their appropriate objectives.

The limits of those domains and conditions are *parts* of an account of the value of state consent, not a fundamental challenge to the value of state consent. State consent that contributes in this way to endow treaties with authority is not fundamentally a unilateral act that *expresses* sovereignty, but rather a complex shared practice. As Peters notes, international treaties are thus not simply

> the result of *unilateral decisions (rational choices) to bind oneself*, but [we] can only understand them as commitments towards other actors. The bindingness of a legal instrument (for example a treaty or a pledge not to use nuclear weapons first or to stop nuclear testing) results from the promise given to the other party, and the normative expectations created thereby in the other, and not from a unilateral decision.[43]

Specification of the domain and conditions of state consent helps delineate the substantive contents of state sovereignty in international law, not the other way around.[44] Sovereignty is in part defined as having legal standing to enter into treaties within some domain under certain conditions: 'the sovereignty of the States may be a consequence of these rules, not the rules a consequence of sovereignty'.[45]

Arguments about the domain and conditions for which we have reason to value state consent may help clarify whether the *current* specifications under international law render sovereign states legitimate authorities, and how to change such specifications to enhance the states' legitimate authority.

[43] A Peters, 'Precommitment Theory Applied to International Law: Between Sovereignty and Triviality' (2008) 2008(1) U Ill L Rev 239, 248–49(emphasis added).

[44] J Crawford, *The Creation of States in International Law* (Oxford University Press 2007) 33.

[45] H Kelsen, 'The Principle of Sovereign Equality of States as a Basis for International Organization' (1944) 53(2) Yale LJ 207, 209–10; ibid 100.

Several of these reasons to value state consent also hold for non-democratic states. They – and their populations – may have reason to avoid domination by other states, and their compliance may often but not always be of value also for others.[46] Such commitments increase the likelihood of general compliance and hence are sometimes necessary to ensure the objectives of the treaty. Resolving some such conflicts, for example, to promote human rights, or some forms of trade, also with authoritarian states, may sometimes be of value – also for citizens of those states – and hence legitimate. But the treaties such authoritarian states negotiate may be so unjust as to merely whitewash non-democracies. Consent by non-democratic states may also help address the 'battle of the sexes' situations, to help determine which of several possible institutions that might provide the desired service, should actually be implemented and recognised as authoritative. But the consent requirement does not guarantee a fair domestic allocation of the benefits and burdens – neither in democracies nor especially in authoritarian states.

It is an open question whether these values – of predictability, control, non-domination, and status – can also be secured sufficiently or to some extent through *other* means of international lawmaking that do not rely on state consent, without putting these or other values at risk – or indeed in furtherance of such values. The following sections show that CIL may secure and promote these values, even without state consent.

4 Normative Bases for the Legitimate Authority of Consent and Treaties

This brief sketch has not yet addressed the issue of why and how the mechanism of consent may create a *normative obligation* for states to defer to PIL norms, even if at that time they have countervailing reasons to act otherwise. What are these normative bases that help render PIL legitimate authority for states? We move to that topic now.

It is submitted here that states seek to use consent and promises more generally to create a moral obligation to honour such agreements, to provide assurance among each other. What normative principle would states violate if they fail to act as they have consented to? Consider a specification of the 'do no harm' principle as concerns manipulation, to the effect that we should not frustrate intentionally induced expectations. As background,

[46] *Pace* Besson's claim that 'only democratic States may invoke their consent as a ground not be bound'. Besson (n 37).

first consider an alternative basis, the normative principle of fair play, which seems insufficient to account for this case.

A principle of 'fair play' (or 'fairness') prohibits free riding on others' compliance. As developed by Hart and discussed by Rawls,[47] it holds that we should do our part as the rules of a practice specify when others have already complied with the practice in ways we have benefitted from. The normative obligations triggered by consent and promises might appear to be of this kind, in that breaches violate a principle of fair play. However, it does not seem correct that states' obligations first arise when they have received actual benefits from others' compliance with the practice of promise keeping. Moreover, this account seems insufficient to account for the complex conditions that regulate when state consent to treaties is taken to bind the state. In particular, the principle fails to explain or criticise when and why there are excusing conditions, and the particular scope conditions for binding consent. Such explanations must go beyond simply more careful sociological mapping of the rules of the actual practice, and should instead refer to conditions for, and the domain within which, we have reason to value such a practice of state consent.

An alternative account, developed by Hart, MacCormick, Scanlon and others holds that the normative principle that undergirds promises and contracts is not restricted to existing practices such as the making of binding agreements, but rather concerns manipulation and fidelity. *We should not frustrate intentionally brought about expectations of others about our own conduct.* They suggest that this is a particular case of the more general principle to do no harm. Fulfilment of such promises is 'what we owe to other people when we have led them to form expectations about our future conduct'.[48]

Section 3 above indicates several reasons states may have to deliberately seek to influence others' expectations of their future actions. In particular, we have an interest in constraining our future actions in some ways, in order to have *others* – states, individuals or other actors – restrict their options and act in certain other ways that benefit us. If we are able to impose upon ourselves constraints that others trust, they constrain their actions in ways that increase our ability to predict and pursue policies we prefer. On this account, to lead others to form such expectations without intending to act accordingly would be a form of manipulation of others for the sake of their own interests.

47 HLA Hart, 'Are There Any Natural Rights?' (1955) 64(2) PhilRev 175, 185; Rawls' Principle of Fairness, J Rawls, *A Theory of Justice* (Harvard University Press 1971) 112, 343.

48 Scanlon, 'Promises and Practices' (n 7) 199–201; MacCormick (n 7); Smith (n 2) 263.

The consent mechanism, duly specified and constrained, is one *effective*, *precise* and *valuable* mechanism to create such expectations: 'State consent signals intention to abide by a rule.'[49] This mechanism enables the promisor to convey quite complex intentions quite precisely, with the aim to establish certain expectations in others. The promisor aims to signal that she would regard it as wrong of her not to satisfy these expectations, indeed even a violation of her legal obligations, except under certain sets of conditions.[50]

One upshot of this account is that it underscores that the limits of state sovereignty is not left for an individual state to decide, and particularly not by express or tacit consent. It is PIL that determines the domain within which states can consent to treaties: 'sovereignty seems to amount to a large extent to what legitimate international law says it is, and not the other way around, contrary to what consent-based accounts of sovereignty have long defended'.[51] Also note that the conditions for states to enter into legally binding treaties also reflect other values than honouring expectations created under favourable conditions. On this account there are good reasons to have some conditions and domain constraints on such signals. Hart noted some considerations that restrict the conditions where consent can bind, to ensure that the obligations are ones the agents can regard as worth acquiring. There are only under some such conditions that the possibility to acquire obligations and settle expectations is worth having. We can bring some such conditions to light by answering questions such as 'How important is it to have the selection among these alternatives depend on one's choice? How bad a thing is it to have to choose under these conditions?'[52] We now move to consider such conditions on the procedure and the substantive content of the treaties.

5 Normative Bases for the Authority of Customary International Law

Customary international law may serve at least three important roles relating to the principle of non-manipulation, as applied to PIL. Consider

[49] Besson (n 34) 359; see also 'the Federal Republic had held itself out as so assuming, accepting or recognizing, in such a manner as to cause other States, and in particular Denmark and the Netherlands, to rely on the attitude thus taken up' *North Sea Continental Shelf Cases* 27.

[50] Compare Scanlon, 'The Significance of Choice' (n 7); J Raz, *Morality of Freedom* (Oxford University Press 1986) 176.

[51] Besson (n 37) 305.

[52] Scanlon, 'The Significance of Choice' (n 7) 183.

first constraints on the procedure of consent, and then on the domain within which states may consent to treaties.

5.1 *Procedural Aspects of Becoming Bound by Consenting to Treaties*

States often appear to hold themselves to be obligated by 'pre-existing' norms such as *pacta sunt servanda*, and some other norms recognised in the VCLT, such as fraud or coercion as invalidating consent to be bound.[53] On this account, these norms serve one role of CIL which states have reason to acknowledge. They help delineate when state consent can provide control over own behaviour and the expectations and behaviour of others worth having for a state. States often have good reason to foster expressions of more precise and shared expectations and have an interest in publicly signalling such expectations to others by means of consent to treaties – but only under certain conditions. For instance, states must have information about some alternatives available to them and their likely consequences, for the mechanism of consent to plausibly signal such complex commitments that states have reason to give. In particular, such signalling is usually of no worth if it takes the form of treaties signed under coercion or due to fraud.[54]

Stating such conditions in the VCLT specifies such obligations in ways that are helpful. But these norms cannot easily derive their binding force from the mechanism of state consent – which they help constitute and specify. Indeed, if these norms were only binding among states who consented to them, this would hinder stability and foreseeability. The role of these norms as helping constitute the valuable practice also explain why new states are bound by them: being a sovereign state entails being able to commit to treaties by consent – which is constituted by such complex rules.

Some such conditions may absolve the actor of any obligations. Some excusing conditions identify when it is not wrong to create false expectations. These include when consent does not sufficiently express the interests of the consenter,[55] for example when consent is not voluntary, as when a treaty is signed under duress. Similarly, considerations may excuse the agent if they are unable to reflect sufficiently on alternatives and their consequences, for example due to fraud.[56]

[53] VCLT arts 26, 38, 49, 51–52.
[54] ibid arts 49, 51–2.
[55] Christiano (n 12) 23.
[56] VCLT art 49.

Such lack of deliberation and control among the citizenry would be one reason to be wary of consent by non-democratic states. And this is one reason why it may be appropriate to deny non-democratic governments the ability to bind their successors, for example to repay international loans. However, there may be overriding reasons to still grant such states the authority to enter into certain treaties, based on the value of predictability for others, avoiding domination etc.

I submit that the list of excusing conditions for when treaties are not binding may reflect such complex considerations.[57] The value of honouring expectations may also reasonably be limited under certain drastic, unexpected changes in circumstance – carefully curtailed to prevent abuse and allow credible monitoring.[58] It seems reasonable that there are circumstances where other parties should accept that their expectations may still be broken. Thus, states are not held responsible for otherwise wrongful acts if they are due to *force majeure*, in situations of dire duress, or necessary to safeguard its essential interests[59] – as long as they do not violate peremptory norms. An important issue is who should have the authority to assess such claims of exceptional circumstances, excusing conditions etc., given the risk of abuse by leaving the determinations to the parties of the agreement.

Consider furthermore the particular puzzle of coerced yet binding consent to peace treaties agreed by aggressor states.[60] First of all, the aggressor state's interest in continuing the aggression is not a privilege that the state should be permitted to continue to pursue except when consenting otherwise. And an aggressor state that refuses to consent to a peace treaty has no acceptable reason to do so: that option is not one within the appropriate domain of the mechanism of state consent. To the contrary, all parties, even the aggressor state, have an interest in ending armed conflict at some stage before utter destruction. The aggressor state may have an interest in credibly committing to surrender on some terms – if only to prevent further large-scale demolition of its infrastructure and military by other states. Such considerations counsel that peace treaties signed by aggressor states may be recognised as legally and morally binding even when clearly signed under duress.

[57] Such 'institutionalised' considerations may also reduce the problems of anthropomorphism of the ability of a state to 'will'.

[58] VCLT arts 61–62.

[59] ILC, 'ARSIWA' 23–26.

[60] VCLT art 75.

5.2 Material Aspects of the Domain of Valid Treaties

Treaties are one way to knowingly induce others to form expectations about one's future conduct. The brief overview above indicates that the possibility of entering into binding treaties has value only under certain conditions. Some CIL norms delimit the domain and conditions of state consent to treaties, to help ensure that this practice of creating legal obligations is of value – and hence legitimate. The value of honouring intentionally created expectations is after all only one of several values, and itself only of value in some cases. We may ask how important it is for the legitimate plans of states to create expectations among others about their future behaviour, and (thereby) for them to be able to form expectations about the behaviour of each state.

Thus consent should not be assumed to bind states to clearly objectionable actions – in which states have no legitimate interest – or when they infringe on the interests of third parties, be they states, individuals, or other entities. The claims to honour others' expectations do not outweigh or displace all other values. For instance, expectations that would entail human rights violations would not merit much weight. This concern arguably justifies several constraints on the domains where states may consent to treaties, in the form of peremptory norms of CIL – such as *jus cogens* prohibitions on genocide, torture etc.[61] Just as with the procedural rules, these scope conditions cannot easily themselves be based on state consent for their legitimate authority 'all the way down'.

5.3 Inducing Expectations

A third role of some non-consent-based CIL are as norms that states have an interest to induce and maintain expectations about, but where state consent is an unsuitable mechanism. To not require universal consent reduces the 'transaction costs' of securing general compliance with rules. Moreover, non-consent-based CIL allow states to show that they regard themselves as obligated, and hence that others can be somewhat assured of their future actions – which reduces the commitment problems for some common challenges.

That is: the *same* general normative principle of non-manipulation explains why these particular customs bind states, namely the obligation

[61] VCLT art 53.

to not frustrate intentionally brought about expectations of others about our own conduct. States must take due care to live up to such expectations, and not lead others to form false expectations.[62] Consider an existing practice with public rules which the practitioners regard as creating obligations for them, so that they do wrong if they violate these rules – except in some overriding circumstances. Such rule-guided practices may also serve as signals about complex intentions about one's own future action. The practice may induce others to form expectations about the practitioners' future behaviour, and such expectations may be foreseen and indeed an objective of the participants in the practice. Under such conditions, the same principle on non-manipulation applies to this public practice even though it has not been explicitly consented to. It creates obligations of future compliance among those who uphold the practice.

I submit that states comply with some CIL norms by precisely such practices. Those who have participated in upholding the practice thereby create expectations about their own future actions, and such expectations are part of the rationale of the practice. One aim of CIL norms is to get others to believe that they can expect future behaviour from these parties according to these norms, thus CIL creates and stabilises expectations. This holds true even though states need not explicitly engage the consent mechanism to create such obligations. Why is this, and when might CIL be preferable to consented treaties? On this account, in some cases treaties may be better suited mechanisms for creating such expectations, while in some cases custom may be better – and in yet other cases the two may be equivalent.

There are sometimes reasons to prefer consent-based mechanisms, for example when control over the specifics of the practice is of particular value *and* can be achieved by the mechanism of state consent, such as when the choice is of contested and different value among the parties, or when the expectations and conditions need to be very precise, or when having the decisions be subject to others' discretion is objectionable – *and* where the risk of blocking states is not unreasonable. Cases may include areas when it suffices that a 'club' of states move forward, or when the likelihood of non-consent by any state is small.

[62] This would seem to differ from views that consider CIL based on tacit consent, for example 'As a matter of fact, customary international law-making combines tacit consent in the converging practice of States and explicit dissent in their possibility to object to that practice through a persistent objection'. Besson (n 37) 295.

On the other hand, there are cases where CIL may at least in principle be better than treaties. Some examples are when actual consent is difficult or impossible to secure in advance yet coordination is obviously important for all. Several such cases concern the scope of state sovereignty: the domain of state and diplomatic immunity,[63] and the customs of *pacta sunt servanda* and of how to express the speech act of giving promise in order to engage in the morally binding practice of consent itself indicated above. This is arguably what occurs when states agree to *pacta sunt servanda*: they recognise, acknowledge and specify a norm that they already regard as binding. Other domains of sovereignty where consent is impractical or impossible concern ways to prevent negative impact on other parties of one state's choices. The parties may include states, or citizens of that and other states. Thus, some principle of 'do no harm' has a long pedigree in international law. For some such norms the stability of the international order is arguably at stake. One example is the right to self-defence, where the issue is paramount yet universal consent is improbable. The ICJ notes that 'Article 51 of the [United Nations] Charter is only meaningful on the basis that there is a "natural" or "inherent" right of self-defense, and it is hard to see how this can be other than of a customary nature, even if its present content has been confirmed and influenced by the Charter.'[64]

Another set of cases where relying on a custom may be more beneficial than securing consent to a treaty are those where all parties clearly benefit greatly from having one set of shared practices within some domain,[65] yet where the negotiations about how to distribute benefits and burdens threaten to postpone or even prevent any unanimous treaty. In some such 'battle of the sexes' situations, the veto of any state may block any option. One preferable way to identify and implement one of the several possible solutions may then rather be to follow an established custom – as long as it is within that domain of mutually beneficial alternatives. The selection mechanism is thus to comply with the rules that several states already follow – among several that could have been followed. And once a practice is established, there may be a prima facie case to honour

[63] *Jurisdictional Immunities of the State (Germany v Italy: Greece intervening)* (Judgment) [2012] ICJ Rep 99, 122–23 [55].

[64] *Military and Paramilitary Activities in and against Nicaragua (Nicaragua v USA)* (Merits) [1986] ICJ Rep 14, 98.

[65] Compare the 'core' in game theory.

expectations according to the principle of non-manipulation – and often a duty of fair play as well.[66]

Scanlon proposes a more precise specification of the reliance on customs as a 'Principle of Established Practices', for

> cases . . . in which there is a need for some principle to govern a particular kind of activity, but there are a number of different principles that would do this in a way that no one could reasonably reject. What I will call the Principle of Established Practices holds that in situations of this kind, if one of these (nonrejectable) principles is generally (it need not be unanimously) accepted in a given community, then it is wrong to violate it simply because this suits one's convenience . . . it would be reasonable to reject any principle permitting people to violate one of these established practices whenever they wished to do so or preferred some alternative. It would also be reasonable to reject a principle that would require a practice to be unanimously accepted in order to be binding, since if unanimous agreement were required, practices would be very difficult to establish and the needs they serve would be very likely to go unmet. (It is not necessary to insist on unanimity in order to prevent excessively burdensome practices from being made binding, since the Principle of Established Practices supports only practices that themselves cannot reasonably be rejected.[67]

A note of caution is appropriate. There is no reason to hold that any rule generally followed as custom is normatively acceptable. The 'survival of the fittest' custom may simply mean that those customs survive that the more dominant states have an interest in maintaining. In particular, the emergence and survival of customs does not reliably depend on their fair treatment of all affected parties. One central reason is that not all states, and certainly not all affected individuals, may have been able to contribute equally to develop the custom to ensure it does not impose unacceptable and avoidable burdens. A wide range of criticisms of PIL make this point – including feminist and Third World Approaches to International Law (TWAIL) arguments.[68] This condition may arguably support the

[66] J Bentham, *First Principles Preparatory to Constitutional Code* (Clarendon Press 1989) 97; L Murphy, *What Makes Law: An Introduction to the Philosophy of Law* (Cambridge University Press 2014) 60.

[67] TM Scanlon, *What We Owe to Each Other* (Harvard University Press 1998) 339.

[68] C Chinkin, 'Feminism, Approach to International Law' [2010] MPEPIL; D Otto, 'Feminist Approaches to International Law' in A Orford & F Hoffmann (eds), *The Oxford Handbook of the Theory of International Law* (Oxford University Press 2016); JT Gathii, 'TWAIL: A Brief History of Its Origins, Its Decentralized Network, and a Tentative Bibliography' (2011) 3(1) Trade, Law & Development 26; JD Haskell 'TRAILing TWAIL: Arguments and Blind Spots in Third World Approaches to International Law' (2014) 27(2) CJLJ 383.

specially affected states doctrine, and the requirement of the Conclusions that the CIL practice needs to be widespread, representative, constant and uniform, but not unanimous. A further reason to be wary of customs is that they may not adapt well to changing circumstances.

I submit that this argument supports claims that CIL may create moral obligations to comply for states. Some central cases occur when the norms address issues in ways that most affected parties derive large benefits from, without anyone bearing undue costs; and where prior actual universal consent is impossible or impracticable for various reasons. These norms and conditions will have to be specified and identified in certain ways. The delineation in the Conclusions seem generally consistent with this. The specification of conditions may include:

- When universal consent is *impossible*: that occurs inter alia for the norms that constitute and limit the procedures and domains whereby state consent binds – including those CIL norms that help constitute sovereign statehood; and *pacta sunt servanda*, *jus cogens* limitations etc.
- When universal consent is *impracticable*: in cases where free riding becomes more tempting as more parties join a scheme, or when some parties clearly abuse their power to free ride or to derive undue benefits compared to others.

Such considerations must on the other hand be robust against abuse, for example, when some parties have good reason to not value the alleged benefits secured. This account thus appears to illuminate the 'puzzle' of non-consent-based obligations concerning PIL: certain CIL norms may well bind, though they are not consent based.

5.4 *The Values CIL Secures*

Consider some objections and challenges to this claim, that CIL may be justified on the basis of the same principle of non-manipulation as treaties. One objection is that CIL, thus circumscribed, may not equally well secure the values that the mechanism of state consents, duly circumscribed.

Customary international law which has been in existence for some time prior to the case at hand *reduces* but does certainly not remove the risk of *domination* by some states over others. This is one reason to not recognise 'instant custom'. And this is one reason to have stringent requirements on international courts' determination of new CIL, to reduce the risk of being subject to the broad discretion of international courts in this regard. Judges' good faith references to other cases contribute to reducing such suspicion.

Customary international law does not appear to always give states as much strategic control over the future as the veto power granted them by the consent mechanism. While this is correct, as brought out by TWAIL and feminist critics, this comparative advantage may be limited, and only holds for some CIL norms. Some CIL arguably helps constitute important conditions *for* such control, insofar as CIL (a) helps constitute states and (b) enables states to use consent to enter into binding treaties. Furthermore, the loss of such lack of control has no normative weight not when the discretion lost would anyway only concern others' legitimate policy spaces, that is, when the *jus cogens* norms limit options in unobjectionable ways. The disvalue is even smaller when CIL is binding only on some conditions, and for a range of expected circumstances, but allowing certain exceptions – unexpected very high costs, etc. Finally, less powerful states may not even be able to use the consent mechanism to protect themselves against domination by powerful states – as the Melian dialogue showed.

Customary international law that delineates the scope of what other states may do also enables states to *predict* the future to some greater extent than without such norms – especially if new CIL cannot be introduced suddenly.

Note finally that CIL also preserves the status equality of states, insofar as CIL constitutes and constrains the policy spaces of *all* states equally and thus does not express relative inferiority of some states. However, the criticism of TWAIL and feminist perspectives remains. The domains of equal treatment may favour certain individuals and states more than others, be it the domains of non-interference or free use of the oceans.

Customary international law secures these values more when the processes of identifying and specifying CIL secures broad representation from diverse states, avoids 'instant custom', and when the rules of the practice are clear and not subject to broad discretion by any state.

6 Implications for the Content of CIL

I have suggested that CIL serves several important roles: it delineates some conditions and constraints on both the procedures and the domains for when states' consent bind them. Customary international law is also a means to create expectations among others that states will be legally obligated. I submit that this account supports and helps specify several of the Conclusions regarding the limited role of consent, and the two criteria for CIL – that there must be 'a general practice' which enjoys 'acceptance as law' (*opinio juris*).

6.1 *Is There a Role for 'Tacit Consent'?*

On this account, CIL does not require state consent to be binding. What appears to be required is a weaker form of knowing compliance with the rules of a practice, in the form that a range of states (but not necessarily all) participate in a certain practice. A state that participates in such a practice leads others to expect that it will act in certain ways in the future in ways others want to be assured about. And a state that participates in such a practice should be aware that the practice provides such assurance. Other states may join an existing practice, and thereby signal such commitments – without them having any meaningful consent to give or withhold. An exception may be that persistent objectors to certain rules and practices may thereby prevent such assurances about intentions. This is arguably weaker than 'tacit consent', and it seems that to use the term 'consent' only adds confusion.

6.2 *General Practice*

This account provides a justification and explication of the requirement of a 'general practice' regarding a possible CIL. There is extensive debate on this point. Some urge to replace 'practice' due to conceptual problems[69] and 'determining the existence of practice is far from self-evident'.[70] Indeed, critics argue that international judges exemplify Hart's claim that custom lacks a clear rule of recognition.[71] What is actually practice among states is difficult to discern – and especially in disputes, since parties may point to clusters of states who maintain incompatible practices.

69 GJ Postema, 'Custom, Normative Practice, and the Law' (2012) 62(3) DukeLJ 707; Murphy (n 66) ch 8.

70 A Pellet, 'Article 38' in A Zimmermann & C Tomuschat et al (eds), *The Statute of the International Court of Justice: A Commentary* (Oxford University Press 2006) 750.

71 HLA Hart, *The Concept of Law* (Oxford University Press 1961) 235.

Conclusion 8 maintains that a general though not universal practice suffices – that is, actual consent by all states is not required. But it is important to consider 'the extent to which those States that are particularly involved in the relevant activity or are most likely to be concerned with the alleged rule ("specially affected States") have participated in the practice'.[72] And the practice must be public – known to other states.[73] This is one reason why there can be no 'instant custom', in the literal sense, though a short period may suffice.

All these specifications seem appropriate requirements to create expectations about compliance with the practice in the future, and to reduce the risk that the practice is a mechanism of domination by some states that is detrimental to others. Note that actual consent is not required – it suffices that states have been in a position to react,[74] relying on what it is reasonable to assume regarding whether the state has such knowledge.

I submit that these requirements blunt some criticism against the central role of international judges in determining such a practice. They are often said to exercise extensive discretion – firstly in specifying the criteria of CIL,[75] and then in determining that there is a practice, and which are the rules that govern it.[76] However, the task of the international judges is to determine that the practice is sufficiently general, especially among those states likely to have a stake in the specific rules of the practice. This is certainly not an easy task, especially because the international judges are also called upon to interpret conflicting evidence about a practice. For instance, verbal practice may easily conflict with what states actually do. And the judges of international courts (IC) must decide which instances of conduct

> that are in fact comparable, that is, where the same or similar issues have arisen so that such instances could indeed constitute reliable guides. The Permanent Court of International Justice referred in the Lotus case to 'precedents offering a close analogy to the case under consideration; for it is only from precedents of this nature that the existence of a general

[72] ILC, 'CIL Conclusions' (n 3) 135 [4].

[73] ibid 132 [5].

[74] ibid Conclusion 9.

[75] CJ Tams, 'Meta-Custom and the Court: A Study in Judicial Law-Making' (2015) 14(1) LPICT 51; J d'Aspremont, 'The Four Lives of Customary International Law' (2019) 21(3–4) IntCLRev 229.

[76] F Schauer, 'Pitfalls in the Interpretation of Customary Law' in A Perreau-Saussine & JB Murphy (eds), *The Nature of Customary Law* (Cambridge University Press 2007).

> principle [of customary international law] applicable to the particular case may appear'.[77]

What is thus comparable and analogous is to a great extent a matter of intellectual reconstruction, which leaves much discretion to the IC judges. I submit that this discretion is unavoidable. However, there are ways to reduce the possible damage; firstly, to ensure that the judges reflect a broad range of perspectives and are likely to include the impact of different formulations on different states and populations. The risks are also reduced by the requirement that claims that there is such an (emerging) practice must be made public, especially to those states that may have views. And there must be time for states to formulate opinions about such proposals, and possibly express alternative formulations of the rules.

Another risk stemming from this fluidity is the risk of domination by stronger states – and arguably the international judges they nominate, even when the requirement of generality is satisfied. State consent grants each state a veto, which more powerful states may use to maintain the status quo.[78] Similarly also general principles and CIL that have emerged are likely to promote the interest of strong parties rather than those of weaker states.[79] Thus, some argue that several great powers moved to establish a prohibition against aggressive wars with the Kellogg-Briand /Peace Pact in 1928, precisely at a time when they had finished conquering and had much to gain by preventing other states encroaching on their (new) territories.[80]

These constraints and guides for the discretion of international judges reduce the risk that they exercise undue influence on the development of CIL. However, this is compatible with substantiated concerns that the international judges fail in their tasks. Indeed, some claim there is 'a marked tendency [of the ICJ] to assert the existence of a customary rule more than to prove it'.[81] This seems highly problematic on the account

[77] ILC, 'CIL Conclusions' (n 3) 137 [6].

[78] Goodin (n 41); Guzman (n 31) 754.

[79] E Benvenisti & GW Downs, 'Comment on Nico Krisch, "The Decay of Consent: International Law in an Age of Global Public Goods"' (2014) 108 AJIL Unbound 1.

[80] O Hathaway & SJ Shapiro, *The Internationalists: And Their Plan to Outlaw War* (Allen Lane 2017); O Hathaway & SJ Shapiro, 'What Realists Don't Understand About Law' (*Foreign Policy*, 9 October 2017) <https://bit.ly/3kxeVlf> accessed 1 March 2021.

[81] A Pellet, 'Shaping the Future of International Law: The Role of the World Court in Law-Making' in MH Arsanjani, JK Cogan et al (eds), *Looking to the Future: Essays on International Law in Honor of W Michael Reisman* (Martinus Nijhoff 2011) 1076; S Talmon, 'Determining Customary International Law: The ICJ's Methodology between Induction, Deduction and Assertion' (2015) 26(2) EJIL 417.

explored here, especially for 'emerging' customs.[82] A better response by the international judges would be to ensure that any such claims at least are based on evidence drawn from a range of countries with different legal traditions.

6.3 *Opinio Juris*

The role of *opinio juris* in determining whether a norm is CIL is that states must accept this practice *as law*. That is, the practice in question must be undertaken *with a sense of legal right or obligation*. It is implausible and anthropomorphic to hold that states 'have a sense of' – or that they 'feel' or 'believe' that there is such an obligation. The present account does not require such metaphors and need not refer to mental entities. The main point is rather that the practice must signal to others that the practitioners limit their action and policies because this is what some norms require or prohibit under certain conditions. These norms are thus somewhat content independent and exclusionary – hence enjoy *the sort of authority over the state that law does*. I submit that this provides a helpful explication of accepting a practice '*as law*', or 'conforming to what amounts to a legal obligation'.[83] Evidence of *opinio juris* should thus not focus on psychological effects, but instead consider states' responses to reasons of several kinds. What counts as relevant evidence is that states recognise the legitimate authority of such norms as setting other reasons aside. Such self-constraint 'reflects the existence of a social rule', arguably showing that the actors 'take an internal point of view with respect to that behaviour'.[84] Note that this does not amount to the states actually expressing *consent* to the norm. This behaviour serves to induce expectations among other parties that the practitioners will constrain their future conduct in similar ways. I submit that there are several ways states can send such signals, including several noted in the Conclusions and by ICs: deliberate abstentions, excuses for breaches, etc.

Evidence of the practice may include inaction – but only when clearly deliberate. Conclusion 6–3 mentions that 'deliberate abstention from acting may serve such a role: the State in question needs to be conscious of refraining from acting in a given situation, and it cannot simply be assumed

[82] Lauterpacht (n 14) 31; Brierly (n 14); I owe these references to Collins (n 14).

[83] *North Sea Continental Shelf Cases*.

[84] See D Lefkowitz, '(Dis)solving the Chronological Paradox in Customary International Law: A Hartian Approach' (2008) 21(1) CJLJ 129, 132–34, citing Hart (n 71) 56–57, 101–03 and MacCormick (n 7).

that abstention from acting is deliberate'.[85] Other expressions of state intention may include breaches if they are treated as if they are breaches of apparent legal obligations, and not of etiquette or of mere patterns of behaviour. The relevant state behaviour may include denials of the actions, or arguments concerning excusing conditions, etc. This is in accordance with the Conclusions and the reference to the ICJ's *Nicaragua* judgment:

> instances of State conduct inconsistent with a given rule should generally have been treated as breaches of that rule, not as indications of the recognition of a new rule. If a State acts in a way *prima facie* incompatible with a recognized rule, but defends its conduct by appealing to exceptions or justifications contained within the rule itself, then whether or not the State's conduct is in fact justifiable on that basis, the significance of that attitude is to confirm rather than to weaken the rule.[86]

Evidence would include efforts by states to defend or justify their non-compliance. This indicates that they acknowledge that there is a presumption of deference, violations against which require defence and that such defence may be of the form of plausible specifications and exceptions to the rule or overriding reasons. This account also appears to fit with the Conclusions' discussion of the persistent objector rule:

> the State must express its opposition before a given practice has crystallized into a rule of customary international law, and its position will be best assured if it did so at the earliest possible moment. While the line between objection and violation may not always be an easy one to draw, there is no such thing as a subsequent objector rule: once the rule has come into being, an objection will not avail a State wishing to exempt itself.[87]

Two implications of this are worth noting. This underscores the need for clear statements by those who formulate CIL norms, such as international judges, prior to them being expressed as binding CIL norms. Secondly, new states have no options in this regard – they do not have the possibility to oppose. On this account, that is not an objection to CIL norms being binding, since consent by states is not required to be bound by them.

7 Conclusions: What Is the Added Value of This Account?

The main argument of these reflections is that the reason why CIL can create morally binding legal obligations for states is the same as why

[85] ILC, 'CIL Conclusions' (n 3) 133 [3].
[86] *Military and Paramilitary Activities in and against Nicaragua* [186].
[87] ILC, 'CIL Conclusions' (n 3) 153 [5].

states can do so by consenting to treaties: to honour intentionally created expectations among others about one's future actions. The aim is not to reject several important roles of the mechanism of state consent in current international law, but rather to revise the grounds for its centrality in light of the grounds for valuing such consent. These include the underlying value of fixing expectations and providing assurance of own future conduct. This helps explain why state consent is sometimes but not always appropriate, and neither necessary nor sufficient for a state to create new legal obligations for itself.

States have reasons to value both consent-based obligations, and non-consent based CIL. They are both important signalling mechanisms. This account appears to help resolve several puzzles of the role of state consent. States' consent may sometimes create binding obligations even under conditions that usually are taken to invalidate consent. Aggressor states may be coerced into signing valid peace treaties,[88] because we have good reason to allow states to express such commitment to peace and to create expectations among others about such commitments, to avoid further bloodshed.

I submit that this account also helps justify why states are subject to some legal obligations without their express consent. Some CIL norms are binding in part because they are necessary to constitute state sovereignty and to delimit the domain and conditions for the practice of state consent to establish the legitimate authority of new PIL. On this account, that does not seem paradoxical: states have good reason to foster such expressions of more precise and shared expectations, and have an interest in publicly signalling such expectations to others – even without explicit consent.

On the other hand, states cannot by their consent create legally binding obligations to anything without limits. Some *jus cogens* norms *limit* the material contents of the legal obligations states can create through their consent.[89] States also often appear to hold themselves to be obligated by 'pre-existing' norms – such as some CIL, for example *pacta sunt servanda* as recognised in the VCLT.[90] One main reason is that such limits on the domain of state consent to treaties helps ensure that valid treaties enjoy legitimate authority – *jus cogens* violations are treaty agreements states have no good reason to pursue, and which they have no good objection to

[88] VCLT art 75.
[89] ibid art 53.
[90] ibid art 26.

others violating. Furthermore, CIL may serve to help states pursue other shared objectives, especially when there are difficulties in securing universal consent, and when there is low risk involved – for example, as long as the practice is 'general, meaning that it must be sufficiently widespread and representative'.[91]

Consider in closing concerns that such an account is flawed because it draws on moral premises to account for the legitimate authority of PIL. Such contributions are hence of little use, since moral norms about honouring expectations are too vague or contested. Thus Koskenniemi rejects 'a conception of justice at the root of all customary rules – the principle "legitimate expectations should not be ignored"'.[92] At least two responses are appropriate. Such claims about vagueness and contestedness would seem to be comparative. We would need to hear *other* accounts of the normative grounds for the claim to legitimate authority of PIL – including CIL, which provide a reasonable reconstruction of the practice albeit with critical perspective. We should look closely at such accounts. Secondly, the moral premise used for this account is not a general principle to 'honour legitimate expectations'. Rather, it is more limited: *we should not frustrate intentionally brought about legitimate expectations of others about our own conduct.* It is only legitimate expectations that impose an obligation – where the 'legitimacy' of these expectations is unpacked in light of what we and others have reasons to pursue and expect of others, for example so that expectation of complicity in torture has no standing as an objection to not fulfilling treaty obligations in this regard. Furthermore, states may follow some patterns of behaviour without any interest in bringing about expectations among others about their behaviour. I submit that the practices that contribute to CIL are different: their rationales and justifications require that other parties take the behaviour as evidence that the states will seek to comply with the rules also in the future. Some may further challenge this account because there is no value added by states solemnly agreeing to norms that are morally binding anyway – be it *pacta sunt servanda*, or as Koskeniemmi notes:

> it is really our certainty that genocide or torture is illegal that allows us to understand State behavior and to accept or reject its legal message, not State behavior itself that allows us to understand that these practices are

[91] ILC, 'CIL Conclusions' (n 3) Conclusion 8.

[92] M Koskenniemi, 'The Pull of the Mainstream' (1990) 88(6) MichLRev 1946, 1951.

> prohibited by law. It seems to me that if we are uncertain of the latter fact, then there is really little in this world we can feel confident about.[93]

But Koskenniemi also claims that:

> [a] norm is *jus cogens* . . . not because it was so decreed by God, or because according to this or that theory it is necessary for the survival of the human species. It is *jus cogens* if and inasmuch as, to quote Article 53 of the Vienna Convention on the Law of Treaties, it 'is a norm accepted and recognised by the international community of States as a whole.[94]

One challenge to Koskenniemi's brief account is cases where states claim that they are *recognising* 'pre-existing' *jus cogens* norms that have normative authority prior to or independent of their consent. If they are correct, it is not obvious that it is *only* states' consent that render such a constraint normatively legitimate, which seems to be Koskenniemi's claim. Instead, it seems we need to look further. We need not reject state consent, but combine it with something more, to help explain under what conditions the claims to be legitimate authorities on behalf of CIL and other sources of IL are correct.

I thus submit that some general moral norms can also be *part of* the justification for why *jus cogens* norms are correct in claiming legitimate authority over states – while accepting that state consent is often *also* required. Such moral norms must be specified in order to suit the particular circumstances, for example that the actors are states, with new risks of abuse of rules; and the added value of having such norms be public knowledge. The task, on this view, is to dismiss neither moral principles, nor all roles for state consent, nor all non-consent-based IL, but seek to bring somewhat more order into our considered judgments on these complex issues.

[93] ibid 1952.

[94] M Koskenniemi, 'International Law in a Post-Realist Era' (1995) 16 AustYBIL 1, 3.

7

Custom and the Regulation of 'the Sources of International Law'

DIEGO MEJÍA-LEMOS

> It is the practice of states which demonstrates which sources are acknowledged as giving rise to rules having the force of law ... Article 38 of the Statute of the International Court of Justice ... [which] cannot itself be creative of the legal validity of the sources set out in it ... is, however, ... authoritative generally because it *reflects state practice.*[1]
>
> Article 38(1) of the Statute of the International Court of Justice ... *is regarded as customary international law.*[2]

1 The *Regulation* of Sources of Law

The *law* on the sources of law in international law, if any, appears to be largely neglected by scholarship. So seems to be state practice of *regulation* of the sources of law in international law, even where questions about any legal consequences of such practice are not raised. That these two aspects of lawmaking remain understudied, is, in a way, unsurprising: scholarship has remained divided about the very concept of 'the sources of international law', as evidenced by vexed controversies about their nature.

Article 38(1) of the International Court of Justice (ICJ) Statute[3] almost invariably features in all of these controversies. More importantly, albeit rarely acknowledged in contemporary scholarship, ICJ Statute Article 38(1) is invoked in state practice regarding the sources of law in international law.

[1] RY Jennings & A Watts (eds), *Oppenheim's International Law – Vol 1: Peace* (9th ed, Longmans 1992) 24 [9] (emphasis added).

[2] *Prosecutor v Vlastimir Đorđević* (Appeals Chamber Judgement) IT-05-87/1-A (27 January 2014) [33] fn 117 (emphasis added).

[3] Statute of the International Court of Justice (adopted 26 June 1945, entered into force 24 October 1945) 1 UNTS 993.

Two positions about such state practice can be found among scholars and international courts and tribunals. Some accept that regulation patterns are inferable from such state practice, but stop short of drawing any legal consequences from those patterns. Others go further and argue that such patterns in state practice do have legal consequences, amounting to law in the form of rules, particularly general rules of customary international law (CIL). In this vein, ICJ Statute Article 38(1) is said to reflect such CIL general rules. The former position, which the first epigraph epitomises, has become the standard one. The latter position, of which the second epigraph is illustrative, enjoys support among some leading, mostly early, commentators[4] and, at least, one international court.[5]

'The sources of international law', often used in the plural as a set phrase, is a concept which has constantly evaded precise definition. The multiplicity of meanings attributed to it, as Sur has noted, has resulted in contestations of its pertinence.[6] Kelsen, for instance, observed that it designates not only 'modes' of lawmaking and 'reasons' for the validity of law, but also its 'ultimate fundament'.[7] According to Truyol y Serra, the linkage of these two aspects of lawmaking accounts for various controversies.[8] As Dupuy correctly notes, it ought to be, and has in a way increasingly been, accepted that a source of law is distinct from the law's ultimate basis.[9]

[4] See for instance H Lauterpacht, 'Règles Générales du Droit de la Paix' (1937) 62 RdC 95; A Verdross, 'Les Principes Généraux du Droit dans la Jurisprudence Internationale' (1935) 52 RdC 191.

[5] Namely, the International Criminal Tribunal for the former Yugoslavia's Appeals Chamber's views in *Prosecutor v Đorđević* (n 2).

[6] S Sur, 'La Créativité du Droit International Cours Général de Droit International Public' (2013) 363 RdC 9, 76 ('[t]he critique of the pertinence of the notion of "sources" rests on the multiplicity of its meanings which renders it equivocal and misleading' (*'[l]a critique de la pertinence de la notion de "sources" repose sur la multiplicité de ses sens qui la rend équivoque et trompeuse'*)).

[7] H Kelsen, 'Théorie du Droit International Public' (1953) 84 RdC 1, 119.

[8] A Truyol y Serra, 'Théorie du Droit International Public: Cours Général' (1981) 173 RdC 9, 231 ('the theory of the sources of public international law keeps a close connection with the problem of the fundament of its validity, which explains the divergences which appear there' (*'la théorie des sources du droit international public garde un rapport étroit avec le problème du fondement de sa validité, ce qui explique les divergences qui s'y font jour'*)).

[9] PM Dupuy, 'L'Unité de l'Ordre Juridique International: Cours Général de Droit International Public' (2002) 297 RdC 1, 188 ('[e]veryone seems to agree . . . in theory, to distinguish the source of law from that of its foundation . . . a problem . . . at the edge of legal science' (*'[t]out le monde paraît d'accord . . . en théorie, pour distinguer la source du droit de celle de son fondement . . . un problème . . . aux confins de la science juridique'*)); see also GJH van Hoof, *Rethinking the Sources of International Law* (Kluwer 1983) 71 (casting aside 'the source in the first sense', namely 'the basis of the binding force of international law').

Notwithstanding the consensus reached among scholars about the distinction between the basis of a legal order and lawmaking within that legal order, various disputes about the nature of the sources of international law stemming from the concept's polysemy remain unresolved. As Ago noted, other differences over their nature result from persistent reliance on certain assumptions,[10] and, as Truyol y Serra observed, variations as to those assumptions result in the intractability of related controversies.[11] Some of those assumptions, in turn, may involve a conflation of levels of analysis, an implication to which writers of various schools of thought have drawn attention.[12] Tunkin, for instance, regarded international law as a 'multi-level system'.[13] Abi-Saab and Wood, for their part, rightly warn against such a conflation.[14]

The idea of regulation, as it pertains to the sources of international law, is widely discussed. More broadly, general jurisprudence has also contributed to the understanding of 'regulation' in ways which are apposite to this chapter. Without prejudice to a fuller discussion of its general jurisprudential meaning, which falls outside the scope of this chapter, 'regulation' is used here to designate the making of rules, whether they have attained or not a legal status, or if so, whether they directly govern conduct or not. First, by encompassing rules which arguably cannot, or, if so, have not yet, attained a legal status, regulation gives expression to the common ground among the aforementioned schools of thought, accepting there is state practice on sources of law. Second, the idea of regulation, as opposed to 'norm' in its theoretical sense, is key: while a norm is a rule aiming to guide conduct, other rules may lack such a normative character, and yet still constitute a form of regulation, alongside normative

[10] R Ago, 'Science Juridique et Droit International' (1956) 90 RdC 851, 916 (calling for an analysis of the terms of those problems).

[11] Truyol y Serra (n 8) 231 (noting controversies are 'conditioned by the starting positions of the respective authors' ('*conditionnées par les positions de départ des auteurs respectifs*')).

[12] O de Schutter, 'Les Mots de Droit: Une Grammatologie Critique du Droit International Public' (1990) 6 RQDI 120, 124 (speaking of 'three levels of analysis').

[13] GI Tunkin, 'Politics, Law and Force in the Interstate System' (1989) 219 RdC 227, 259 ('the international community' as 'a subsystem of … the interstate system' which 'is a multi-level system (different levels of actors and different levels of norms)').

[14] G Abi-Saab, 'Cours Général de Droit International Public' (1987) 207 RdC 9, 34 ('it is important to be aware of the level of analysis at which one is situated' ('*il est important d'être conscient du niveau d'analyse auquel on se situe*')); MC Wood, 'Legal Advisers' [2017] MPEPIL [36] (referring to 'the delicate relationship between law and policy in international relations' as an aspect of the work of 'those who advise on matters of public international law'.)

regulation.[15] While a distinction between normative and non-normative regulation may ostensibly overlap with Hart's distinction between primary and secondary rules, a reference to regulation seeks to place emphasis on the *legality* of non-normative legal regulation, as well as on its place within a legal system as *internal* to it. In this vein, it is worth recalling that Hart regarded secondary rules on law ascertainment as non-legal and, ultimately, external to the legal system. Third, the elements of any custom giving rise to such CIL general rules may be better understood. Once the assumption that every custom need derive from the same kind of general practice as that leading to the formation of primary, normative, CIL rules is set aside, any custom giving rise to non-normative rules of CIL, including those on sources of law, can be the object of the same legal scrutiny to which any other custom can be typically subjected. Most notably, any enquiries into such non-normative CIL would not be discarded by any misconception confining CIL to rules of CIL derived from practice consisting in 'physical', as opposed to 'verbal', acts.

The view that there is a phenomenon of regulation of sources of law in international law, and that such regulation is carried out by a 'system of sources' contained within the legal order of international law as a whole, finds some support in international law scholarship. Virally, for instance, considered that legal orders are generally 'self-regulated', including as to their own sources of law. Virally's view that international law, as any legal order, self-regulated its own sources of law was without prejudice to admitting that such autonomy was relative, the legal order of international law being conditioned by the various circumstances within which it operates.[16] Virally's caveat is not contradictory, since it involves a level of analysis other than that of the rules performing self-regulation of the system's sources of law, namely that of the various wider processes within whose framework the legal system operates.

[15] See, generally, J Raz, *The Concept of a Legal System: An Introduction to the Theory of Legal System* (2nd ed, Oxford University Press 1980) 144, 182 (defining law as 'a special social method of regulating human behaviour by guiding it', but noting that 'every legal system . . . contains laws . . . which are not norms').

[16] M Virally, 'Panorama du Droit International Contemporain: Cours Général de Droit International Public' (1983) 183 RdC 9, 167 ('the legal order is a self-regulated system. . . however,. . . it is also conditioned by the particularities, institutional, sociological. . . which explain the specific characteristics of the system of sources of the international legal order' (*'l'ordre juridique est un système autorégulé . . . cependant, . . . il est aussi conditionné par les particularités, institutionnelles, sociologiques . . . qui expliquent les caractères spécifiques du système des sources de l'ordre juridique international*')).

2 Custom as *Source* of Rules Arising out of General Practice on Sources of Law

This section examines the place of custom in the regulation of the sources of international law, with a particular focus on custom's role as source of the law on sources of law, if any, in international law.

The suitability of custom as a source of universal rules has been widely accepted in the literature. An analysis of custom's suitability as a source of universal rules usually involves a comparative analysis, vis-à-vis other sources of law.[17] Such comparative analyses have tended to point out its inherent qualities. For instance, Marek argued that custom's inherent qualities rendered it 'superior' to any treaty as a source of universal rules.[18] Marek characterised this superiority as being a form of 'inherent superiority' or 'superiority of quality', and not a matter of hierarchy among sources of law.[19]

As it relates to general rules regarding the sources of law, on the other hand, the suitability of custom is widely contested. Those who contest the suitability of custom for these particular purposes often deny the possibility of regulation of sources of law by any rule created by one of the regulated sources of law. Jennings and Watts' view, partly quoted in the first epigraph to this chapter, furnishes a typical statement of this denial: 'Article 38 of the Statute of the International Court of Justice . . . cannot itself be creative of the legal validity of the sources set out in it, since it belongs to one of those sources itself.'[20] While Jennings and Watts' denial concerns ICJ Statute Article 38 *qua* treaty only, the view is usually predicated of any other claimed source-based rules on sources, including custom-based ones. This is exemplified by Dinstein's view, for whom reliance on CIL rules on 'how and when custom is brought into being'

[17] Some of those who accept the possibility of legal rules on lawmaking hold the view that such rules may take the form of either CIL or general principles of law. See, for instance, N Arajärvi, *The Changing Nature of Customary International Law: Methods of Interpreting the Concept of Custom in International Criminal Tribunals* (Routledge 2014) 16 ('there are principles of law that ought to be followed in the finding or making of the law – applicable in the customary process as well – which may have crystallised as customary rules in their own right or may exist as general principles of law').

[18] K Marek, 'Le Probleme des Sources du Droit International dans l'Arrêt sur le Plateau Continental de La Mer du Nord' (1970) 6 RBDI 45, 75.

[19] ibid. On the character of hierarchical properties as normative and not formal, see, among others, A Pellet, 'Article 38' in A Zimmermann et al (eds), *The Statute of the International Court of Justice: A Commentary* (2nd ed, Oxford University Press 2012) 846 [284].

[20] Jennings & Watts (n 1) 24 [9].

inherently involves 'a *petitio principii*'.[21] These instances of reluctance to ascribe legality to the regulation of sources of law, which could be collectively called, using Dinstein's term, *petitio principii* objections, are, again, without prejudice to the concomitant acknowledgement of the existence and importance of relevant patterns of regulation of sources of law in general practice.[22]

Leaving aside the *petitio principii* objections, the only major objection to the idea of regulation of sources of law and its character as law, in the form of general rules of CIL, might arise from various forms of scepticism as to the idea of regulation or, where accepted, its legality.[23] This scepticism is not easily amenable to analysis, since it appears to be latent in the respective bodies of scholarship, never being made explicit by virtue of the very view that it would be pointless to engage in any further arguments against the idea of regulation or its legality, if any. The assumed futility of regulation of sources of law or its legality may explain the lack of arguments in the event of a dismissal of a *petitio principii* objection on the part of scholarship underpinned by this assumption: in a way, this assumption implies that the vacuum which would be left if the respective *petitio principii* objection were disproved is one which scholarship based on this presumption has chosen to leave unaddressed. This assumption may underlie the view, expressed by the United Nations' International Law Commission (ILC) Special Rapporteur on CIL identification, Sir Michael Wood, that '[i]t is perhaps unnecessary, at least at this stage, to enter upon the question of the nature of the rules governing the formation and identification of rules of customary international law, for example, whether such rules are themselves part of customary international law'.[24] In support of this proposition, Special Rapporteur Wood quotes Sinclair's view on 'the debate on the nature of some rules of treaty law, particularly *pacta sunt servanda*', to the effect that such an enquiry involved 'doctrinal arguments', ultimately leading the enquirer to 'metaphysical regions'.[25]

[21] Y Dinstein, 'The Interaction between Customary International Law and Treaties' (2007) 322 RdC 295 [67]; which contrasts with the view of L Henkin, 'General Course on Public International Law' (1989) 213 RdC 9.

[22] For a more detailed discussion of various strands of *petitio principii* objections, see DG Mejía-Lemos, 'On Self-Reflectivity, Performativity and Conditions for Existence of Sources of Law in International Law' (2014) 57 GYIL 289.

[23] ibid.

[24] ILC, 'First Report on Formation and Evidence of Customary International Law by Michael Wood, Special Rapporteur' (17 May 2013) UN Doc A/CN.4/663 [38].

[25] ibid [38] fn 85 (quoting I Sinclair, *The Vienna Convention on the Law of Treaties* (2nd ed, Manchester University Press 1984) 2–3).

The remainder of this section proposes to set aside, for the sake of argument, the above *petitio principii* objections, and to focus, instead, on examining patterns of regulation of sources of law as they arise in general practice in which ICJ Statute Article 38(1) is used *outside* ICJ proceedings.[26]

There are two bodies of materials in which ICJ Statute Article 38(1) is used outside ICJ proceedings: decisions of international courts and tribunals and state practice itself. Bearing in mind the difference between these bodies of materials is very significant (a question to which Section 3 returns), and although this section is mainly concerned with selected state practice, it is worth recalling that the place of ICJ Statute Article 38(1) in decisions of international courts and tribunals is widely acknowledged.[27] For instance, Crawford observes that '[ICJ Statute] Article 38(1) has been taken as the standard statement of the so-called "sources" of international law for all international courts and tribunals'.[28] Charney, in a study concerning the proliferation of international courts and tribunals, reached a similar conclusion.[29] He inferred that uniformity among international courts and tribunals regarding the sources of law shows that the proliferation of international courts and tribunals has not eroded 'the international law doctrine of sources'.[30] The aforementioned reliance on ICJ Statute Article 38(1) by contemporary international courts and tribunals gives continuation to the analogous practice of arbitral tribunals constituted prior to the adoption of the ICJ Statute. Those tribunals invoked Article 38 of the Statute of the Permanent Court of International Justice (PCIJ).[31] As Mendelson observes, PCIJ Statute Article 38 had been 'treated as an authoritative list by

[26] MW Janis, 'The Ambiguity of Equity in International Law' (1983) 9 BrookJInt'lL 7, 10 ('article 38 has taken on an importance as a description of the "sources" of international law even outside the confines of the World Court'); JE Noyes, 'The International Tribunal for the Law of the Sea' (1999) 32 CornellInt'lLJ 109, 124 n 79; JA Green, 'Questioning the Peremptory Status of the Prohibition of the Use of Force' (2011) 32 MichJIntlL 215, 220 fn 18.

[27] See, recently, among others, N Grossman, 'Legitimacy and International Adjudicative Bodies' (2009) 41 Geo WashIntlLRev 107, 148 fn 182.

[28] J Crawford, 'Multilateral Rights and Obligations in International Law' (2006) 319 RdC 325, 392.

[29] JI Charney, 'Is International Law Threatened by Multiple International Tribunals?' (1998) 271 RdC 101, 235.

[30] ibid 236.

[31] See also Statute of the Permanent Court of International Justice (adopted 16 December 1920, entered into force 8 October 1921) 6 LNTS 389. Where practice predating the conclusion of the ICJ Statute is involved, Article 38 of the Permanent Court of International Justice (PCIJ) Statute is used for the same purposes.

various arbitral tribunals'.[32] Earlier scholars had also recognised the significance of PCIJ Statute Article 38.[33]

The place of ICJ Statute Article 38(1) in general practice is paramount and more significant than credited in contemporary scholarship. This general practice, whereby states have characterised sources of law through express invocation of, or through statements largely consistent with those contained in, ICJ Statute Article 38(1), is twofold, taking the form of conduct of state organs for international relations, as well as decisions by state judicial organs.

The first category of relevant general practice consists in inter-state arbitration agreements, multilateral treaties beyond matters of dispute settlement, and statements in international organisations, including the United Nations (UN).

A paramount instance of this category is the very adoption of the ICJ Statute. Indeed, it is widely considered that the identity in content between Articles 38 of the PCIJ and ICJ Statutes, except for the opening sentence introduced in the latter, confirms the continuity of the rules stated in both provisions. Furthermore, for several scholars, this continuity evidences that what matters most about the statements contained in Article 38, common to the PCIJ and ICJ Statutes, is not their character as rules *qua* treaty, but their broader place beyond the confines of dispute settlement by the PCIJ and the ICJ, respectively.[34] That this wider significance was attributed to ICJ Statute Article 38 is further confirmed by the fact that proposals to modify its content, in order to account for other categories of acts with purported general lawmaking effects, were unanimously rejected in debates leading to the adoption of the UN Charter,[35] whose preamble expressly states the importance of the 'sources of international law'.[36]

[32] MH Mendelson, 'The Formation of Customary International Law' (1998) 272 RdC 155, 176–7 fn 21.

[33] See, in particular, the arbitral decisions and related arbitration agreements discussed by Verdross (n 4).

[34] B Cheng, *General Principles of Law as Applied by International Courts and Tribunals* (Grotius 1987) 2 (referring to 'alteration' of 'numbering' and 'addition of a few words').

[35] During the UNCIO Conference in San Francisco, in which the UN Charter was drafted, the Philippines' proposal to attribute legislative powers to the UNGA was unanimously rejected. J Castañeda, 'Valeur Juridique des Résolutions des Nations Unies' (1970) 129 RdC 205, 212; G Arangio-Ruíz, 'The Normative Role of the General Assembly of the United Nations and the Declaration of Principles of Friendly Relations' (1972) 137 RdC 419, 447 ('Committee 2 of Commission II (10th meeting) had rejected by 26 votes to 1 the proposal of the Philippines that the Assembly be vested with legislative authority to enact rules of international law').

[36] S Chesterman, 'Reforming the United Nations: Legitimacy, Effectiveness and Power after Iraq' (2006) 10 SYBIL 59, 66.

The reference to ICJ Statute Article 38 in other major multilateral treaties lends additional support to its wider role in the regulation of sources of law. For instance, the reference to ICJ Statute Article 38 in Articles 74(1) and 83(1) of the UN Convention on the Law of the Sea[37] is considered as a general ground for denying the character of equitable principles as legally binding.[38] Other major multilateral treaties, in which no reference to ICJ Statute Article 38(1) is made, are widely regarded as having been negotiated on the understanding that ICJ Statute Article 38(1) underpinned the terms used, as exemplified by Article 42 of the Convention on the Settlement of Investment Disputes between States and Nationals of Other States.[39]

Various states have made multiple statements to the effect that ICJ Statute Article 38(1) sets out the sources of 'positive' international law exhaustively and satisfactorily.[40] Even more pertinently, in some

[37] United Nations Convention on the Law of the Sea (adopted 10 December 1982, entered into force 1 November 1994) 1833 UNTS 397.

[38] A Strati, 'Greece and the Law of the Sea: A Greek Perspective' in A Chircop, A Gerolymatos & JO Iatrides (eds), *The Aegean Sea after the Cold War* (Macmillan 2000) 96 ('reference to Article 38 of the ICJ Statute indicates that an *ex aequo et bono* adjudication of the dispute is excluded' as well as 'an eventual application of equitable principles based on purely subjective appreciations and not on a rule of law').

[39] Convention on the Settlement of Investment Disputes between States and Nationals of Other States (adopted 18 March 1965, entered into force 14 October 1966) 575 UNTS 159; AR Parra, 'The Convention and Centre for Settlement of Investment Disputes' (2014) 374 RdC 313, 380

> [t]he Report of the Executive Directors of the World Bank on the Convention explains that the term 'international law' in the second sentence of Article 42 (1) should be understood in the sense given to it by Article 38 (1) of the Statute of the International Court of Justice', since 'Article 38 (1) of the Statute ... represents an authoritative statement of the sources of international law.

[40] UNGA, 'Review of the Role of the International Court of Justice: Report of the Secretary-General' (15 September 1971) UN Doc A/8382, 24 [61] ('[r]egarding the law applied by the Court, it is the understanding of the Argentine Government that the Court applies *positive* international law as specified in Article 38 of its Statute') (emphasis added); UNGA, 'Review of the Role of the International Court of Justice *(concluded)*' (5 November 1974) UN Doc A/C.6/SR.1492, 166 (containing Brazil's statement that '[t]he sources of international law *were those* listed in Article 38 of the Statute of the International Court of Justice, *and those alone*') (emphasis added); UNGA, 'Review of the Role of the International Court of Justice *(concluded)*' 168 (containing Japan's statement that '[t]he sources of law enumerated in Article 38 of the Statute of the Court were *exhaustive*') (emphasis added); UNGA, 'Review of the Role of the International Court of Justice: Report of the Secretary-General' 24 [63] ('[o]n the question of the law which the Court should apply, the Mexican Ministry of Foreign Affairs on the whole considers Article 38 of the Statute of the Court *satisfactory as it now stands*; it is the ultimate definition of the sources of international law in their most widely recognized gradation') (emphasis added).

instances, states may indicate that ICJ Statute Article 38(1) provides a 'legal basis' for statements about sources of international law. In doing so, states rely on ICJ Statute Article 38(1) as a 'legal basis' for the sources of law, whether seen as a category in whole[41] or with regard to individual sources. Furthermore, states rely on ICJ Statute Article 38(1) in order to deny that a subsidiary source is a proper source of law,[42] or to substantiate their affirmation that individual recognised sources are indeed sources of law proper.[43]

The second category of relevant general practice comprises two forms of state practice, namely decisions of domestic courts and other forms of practice in connection with domestic judicial proceedings. The former subcategory includes decisions constitutive of state practice, capable of giving rise to custom within the meaning of subparagraph (b) of ICJ Statute Article 38(1), by contrast to their other potential role, as a subsidiary means, under subparagraph (d) thereof. The latter subcategory encompasses pleadings by foreign states opposing the execution of arbitral awards before domestic courts of the place where execution is sought.

The authoritativeness of ICJ Statute Article 38(1) is widely affirmed by domestic courts and tribunals in the first subcategory of practice surveyed. For instance, the United States District Court for the Southern District of New York, in *Presbyterian Church of Sudan* v. *Talisman Energy, Inc*, observed that '[t]he Second Circuit has cited Article 38(1)

[41] UNGA, 'Report of the International Court of Justice – 42nd Plenary Meeting' (1 November 2007) UN Doc A/62/PV.42, 16–17 (containing Nicaragua's reference to ICJ Statute Article 38(1) as the legal basis for statements on the sources of international law).

[42] UNGA, 'Report of the International Court of Justice – 39th Plenary Meeting' (27 October 2005) UN Doc A/60/PV.39 (Malaysia stated that: 'Judicial decisions as such are not a source of law, but the dicta by the Court are unanimously considered as the best formulation of the content of international law in force').

[43] ILC, 'Survey on Liability Regimes Relevant to the Topic International Liability for Injurious Consequences Arising Out of Acts Not Prohibited by International Law: Study Prepared by the Secretariat' (23 June 1995) UN Doc A/CN.4/471, 35 [91] fn 119 (referring to Canada's claim against 'claim against the former USSR for damage caused by the crash of the Soviet satellite Cosmos 954 on Canadian territory in January 1978' reproducing Canada's statement to the effect that the principle of 'absolute liability' was a general principle of law within the meaning of Article 38(1)(c), ICJ Statute, and expressly referring to the provision); UN Committee on the Elimination of Racial Discrimination, 'Addendum to the Twelfth Periodic Reports of States Parties Due in 2006: Mozambique' (10 April 2007) UN Doc CERD/C/MOZ/12, (21) [82] (containing Mozambique's reference to ICJ Statute Article 38(1) as the basis for the proposition that custom is a source of international law).

as an authoritative reflection of the sources of international law'.[44] This decision is notable for referring to the character of ICJ Statute Article 38 as a 'reflection' of, as opposed to a provision directly governing, sources of law. Other courts have emphasised the character of ICJ Statute Article 38 as a formulation enjoying authority beyond ICJ proceedings. For example, in *Handelskwekerij GJ Bier BV & Stichting Reinwater* v. *Mines de Potasse d'Alsace SA*, the Amsterdam District Court quoted ICJ Statute Article 38 and held that it 'must be taken as an authoritative formulation of the sources of international law, inside or *outside* the International Court of Justice'.[45]

Some domestic courts go on to indicate that reliance on ICJ Statute Article 38 is necessary, and not merely called for given its authoritativeness. The Argentine Supreme Court of Justice in both *Simon and others* and *Arancibia Clavel*, quoting ICJ Statute Article 38, observed that '[i]t is necessary to determine what are the sources of international law . . . what is provided for by the Statute of the International Court of Justice has to be taken into account'.[46] This stance was confirmed by the Argentine government in a statement at the UN, concerning the place of ICJ Statute Article 38 in its internal judicial practice.[47] Similarly, the Supreme Court of Chile, in *Lauritzen and others* v. *Government of Chile*, invoked ICJ Statute Article 38 in support of its statement that 'customs and treaties figure among the traditional sources, to which may be added principles'.[48] In other cases, such an invocation is stronger, being qualified to the effect that observance of ICJ Statute Article 38 is not only

[44] *Presbyterian Church of Sudan v Talisman Energy, Inc*, 244 F.Supp.2d 289 (SDNY 2003) 289, 304 (citing *Filartiga v Pena-Irala*, 630 F.2d 876 (2d Cir 1980) 881 n8).

[45] *Handelskwekerij GJ Bier BV & Stichting Reinwater v Mines de Potasse d'Alsace SA Handelskwekerij Firma Gebr Strik BV & Handelskwekerij Jac Valstar BV v Mines de Potasse d'Alsace SA* (8 January 1979) District Court of Rotterdam, [1979] ECC 206 [16] (emphasis added).

[46] *Julio Simón et al v Public Prosecutor* (14 June 2005) Supreme Court of Justice of the Argentine Nation, Case No 17.768, 103–4; *Chile v Arancibia Clavel* (24 August 2004) Supreme Court of Justice of the Argentine Nation, Case No 259 [50–51].

[47] UN Committee on the Rights of the Child, 'Consideration of Reports Submitted by States Parties Under Article 8 of the Optional Protocol to the Convention on the Rights of the Child on the Involvement of Children in Armed Conflict: Initial Reports of States Parties Due in 2004: Argentina' (13 November 2007) UN Doc CRC/C/OPAC/ARG/1, 5 [14] (containing Argentina's statement that under 'articles 116 and 117 of the Constitution, the Supreme Court has found that international custom and the general principles of law – the sources of international law in accordance with article 38 of the Statute of the International Court of Justice – are directly incorporated in the legal system').

[48] *Lauritzen et al v Government of Chile* (19 December 1955) Supreme Court of Chile, 52(9–10) RD 444.

necessary, in a conceptual sense, but also legally required. For instance, the Indonesian Constitutional Court, in *Law 27 of 2004 on the Truth and Reconciliation Commission*, considered whether a given alleged general principle of law had been 'created in accordance with the provisions of the Statute of the International Court of Justice regarding the sources of international law'.[49] For similar purposes, Argentina invoked ICJ Statute Article 38(1)(b) before the Court of Cassation of Belgium in *Argentine Republic* v. *NMC Capital*, as a rule of law allegedly breached, in support of one of the grounds for her request for cassation.[50]

Before concluding this succinct survey of state practice, it is worth revisiting Jennings and Watts' discussion of the wider value of ICJ Statute Article 38(1). They reiterate their view that, since '[ICJ Statute] Article 38 . . . cannot be regarded as a necessarily exhaustive statement of the sources of international law for all time . . . [t]hose sources are what the practice of states shows them to be'.[51] And yet, a key aspect of their analysis of the continuing wider relevance of ICJ Statute Article 38(1) lies in '[t]he fact that the International Court of justice, in its numerous judgments and opinions relating to international organisations, has always been able . . . to dispose of the questions arising for decision'.[52] While Jennings and Watts justifiably refer to the practice of the ICJ, since they were concerned with the sufficiency of relying on ICJ Statute Article 38(1) in ICJ proceedings, their reference is notable because it is representative of the tendency to exclusively focus on decisions of international courts and tribunals in spite of general statements to the effect that the primary object of enquiry should be state practice itself. As discussed in Section 3, Jennings and Watts are not alone in their tendency, as the work of earlier scholars who did not raise any *petitio principii* objection to the possibility of CIL on sources of law shows. Indeed, Section 3 shows that practice-based accounts, whether source-based or not, have heretofore tended to overlook state practice itself, given their assumptions regarding state practice, particularly as to decisions of domestic courts.

The character of decisions of domestic courts as general practice has raised various questions, which call for some elucidation of their precise

[49] *Law 27 of 2004 on the Truth and Reconciliation Commission* (2 August 2006) Constitutional Court of the Republic of Indonesia, Perkara No 006/PUU-IV/2006, 5 [131].

[50] *République d'Argentine v NMC Capital LTD* (22 November 2012) Court of Cassation of Belgium, C.11.0688.F.

[51] Jennings & Watts (n 1) 45 [16].

[52] ibid 46 [16].

nature,[53] before turning to the question of the existence of a CIL on sources of law based on states' general practice primarily in the form of decisions domestic courts. It is common to treat selected judicial decisions as 'subsidiary means' under ICJ Statute Article 38(1)(d).[54] This tends to be the case despite their multiple roles.[55] One of those roles is as a form of general practice under ICJ Statute Article 38(1)(b).[56] Lauterpacht had reached the same conclusion regarding PCIJ Statute Article 38.[57] Several scholars likewise accept that these two roles may be concurrently performed.[58]

Leaving aside the dual role a domestic court decision may play under subparagraphs (b) and (d) of ICJ Statute Article 38(1), and focusing on the former role, there is some debate as to whether the two elements of custom within the meaning of subparagraph (b) are present. Whether a decision of a domestic court constitutes practice is a question which partially overlaps with debates over whether practice need consist in physical, as opposed to verbal, acts. Those debates have lost currency, since it has become increasingly uncontroversial to regard verbal acts, including in the form of written statements, as a form of state practice. Indeed, both the ICJ,[59] the

[53] T Giegerich, 'The Case-Law of the European Court of Human Rights on the Immunity of States' in A Peters et al (eds), *Immunities in the Age of Global Constitutionalism* (Brill/Nijhoff 2015) 68 (critiquing their 'ambiguous role' in the 'doctrine of sources').

[54] A Kaczorowska-Ireland, *Public International Law* (5th ed, Routledge 2015) 53 (noting ICJ Statute Article 38(1)(d) 'is not confined to international decisions'). Some wrongly refer to ICJ Statute Article 38(1)(c). See, for example, S Beaulac, 'National Application of International Law: The Statutory Interpretation Perspective' (2003) 41 Can YBIL 225, 239 fn 81 (noting that under ICJ Statute Article 38(1)(c) 'judicial decisions, including those of domestic courts, are a subsidiary source').

[55] See for example M Frankowska, 'The Vienna Convention on the Law of Treaties before United States Courts' (1988) 28 Va J Int'l L 281, 381 (deeming ICJ Statute Article 38 as 'the proper framework' to assess domestic courts' 'functions' but referring to 'article 38(d)' only).

[56] *Jurisdictional Immunities of the State (Germany/Italy, Greece intervening)* (Judgment) [2012] ICJ Rep 131, 132 [72] (relying on '[s]tate practice in the form of the judgments of national courts').

[57] H Lauterpacht, 'Decisions of Municipal Courts as a Source of International Law' (1929) 10 BYBIL 65, 86 (indicating that PCIJ Statute Article 38(2) was where domestic courts decisions found their 'true *sedes materiae* ... in their cumulative effect as international custom').

[58] Mendelson (n 32) 200 ('[d]ecisions of national courts thus perform a dual function'); Arajärvi (n 17) 31 (suggesting that this is the case 'even if overlapping with' each other's function).

[59] *Jurisdictional Immunities of the State* (n 56) 141 [72].

ILC,[60] and some states commenting on the ILC's recent work on CIL identification,[61] have acknowledged that decisions of domestic courts can constitute general practice for the purposes of custom formation and CIL identification. An alternative rationale for the reluctance to accept state practice in the form of domestic courts decisions might lie in the assumption that CIL only encompasses normative regulation. Such an assumption would confine CIL to primary rules, to the exclusion of non-normative regulation, of which secondary rules, including rules on sources of law, are a notable instance. This assumption would translate into a view demanding that all CIL rules derive from the kind of general practice which underlies CIL primary rules, often derived from practice in the form of physical acts. As discussed in Section 1, this assumption results from a misconception requiring all forms of regulation to be normative. The character of decisions of national courts as a form of acceptance as law, or *opinio juris*, on the other hand, has raised less controversy.[62] Some accept their role, but qualify which decisions are more suitable to constitute *opinio juris*.[63]

The question of whether and how the two constitutive elements of custom may be satisfied by a set of statements, including those in domestic court decisions, warrants some further examination. Some scholars have accepted the concurrent character of decisions of national courts as practice and acceptance as law.[64] While the concurrent character of internal judicial

[60] ILC, 'Identification of Customary International Law, Text of the Draft Conclusions Provisionally Adopted by the Drafting Committee' (30 May 2016) UN Doc A/CN.4/L.872, 3 ('[f]orms of evidence of acceptance as law (*opinio juris*) include, but are not limited to: . . . decisions of national courts').

[61] South Korea points to the 'natural [fact] that the form of state practice . . . and the evidence of acceptance as law . . . overlap to a considerable degree, since it most cases acceptance as law should be identified through state behavior or relevant documentation'. Republic of Korea, 'Comments and Observations on the ILC Topic "Identification of Customary International Law"' (*ILC*, 22 December 2017) 2 [3] <https://bit.ly/3r9bZzp> accessed 1 March 2021. Switzerland, for their part, commenting on draft conclusion 11 under the heading 'double-counting', goes on to state that 'the possibility of double counting is accepted by the Swiss authorities, but is not necessarily used' ('*la possibilité du double-comptage est admise par les autorités suisses, mais n'est pas nécessairement utilisée*'). Swiss Confederation, 'La pratique suisse relative à la détermination du droit international coutumier' (*ILC*, 2017) 53 <https://bit.ly/3oVWp7G> accessed 1 March 2021 (internal references omitted).

[62] ibid.

[63] Kaczorowska-Ireland (n 54) 53 (a domestic court decision 'in particular of a highest court of a particular State expresses the *opinio juris* of that State').

[64] R O'Keefe, *International Criminal Law* (Oxford University Press 2015) 110 ('decisions of municipal domestic courts on points of international law . . . constitute . . . state practice and accompanying *opinio juris* on the part of the forum state').

decisions may be contested given its potential for so-called 'double-counting',[65] a set of separate verbal acts cannot be lightly disregarded as establishing both elements of custom. For instance, Argentina's position is apposite, as an example of how a variety of separate statements, including domestic court decisions, may constitute general practice in support of a position and acceptance as law of that position. Indeed, while Argentina's judicial organs engage in actual instances of practice, such as the invocation of ICJ Statute Article 38(1) in decisions of the Argentine Supreme Court, among others, other organs separately issue statements clearly indicating that state's *opinio juris* to the same effect, such as Argentina's unequivocal statements at the UNGA concerning the legal value of ICJ Statute Article 38(1).

3 Customary International Law as *Law* on Sources of Law in International Law: Custom *in Foro* or *in Pays*?

This section examines selected claims of existence of law on sources of law, with a particular focus on major models of CIL rules on sources of law, in international law.

The claim that ICJ Statute Article 38 contains statements regarding CIL rules on sources of law has taken various forms. Some advance the claim unqualifiedly. For instance, Ohlin has recently stated that ICJ Statute Article 38 '*embodies* a customary norm' regarding the sources of international law.[66] He goes on to argue that ICJ Statute Article 38 is such a 'direct statement about the sources of law' that it 'might be the closest thing one could find in any legal system -domestic or international – to a pure rule of recognition'.[67]

Some add that ICJ Article 38, while not directly embodying CIL rules on sources of law, is reflective or declaratory of such CIL rules.[68] While both claims point in the right direction, the view that ICJ Statute Article 38 is reflective, rather than directly constitutive, of CIL is more accurate. Hence, ICJ Statute Article 38 does not in itself 'embody' CIL. As Sur

[65] See Mendelson and Schwebel's critique of the ICJ decision in *Nicaragua*, discussed in M Mendelson, 'The Subjective Element in Customary International Law' (1996) 66 BYBIL 177, 206 fn 196.

[66] JD Ohlin, *The Assault on International Law* (Oxford University Press 2015) 23 (emphasis added).

[67] ibid (adding, for instance, that such a statement cannot be found 'in the US legal system').

[68] B Cheng, *General Principles of Law as Applied by International Courts and Tribunals* (Cambridge University Press 1994) 22.

explains metaphorically, CIL, albeit 'invisible', is reflected in 'mirrors', and yet 'these mirrors are not the rule' of CIL.[69]

The claim that ICJ Statute Article 38(1) has a declaratory or reflective character with respect to sources of law is formulated variously.[70] Some refer to a 'doctrine', but not to rules as such. For example, Dolzer refers to 'the traditionally accepted doctrine of sources, as reflected in the [PCIJ and ICJ] Statutes ... (Article 38)'.[71] Some do refer to rules as being reflected, but do not indicate their legal character. For instance, Tomuschat simply refers to '[t]he rules on law-making, as they are reflected in Article 38(1) of the ICJ Statute'.[72] Other scholars refer to the existence of law and its being declared by ICJ Statute Article 38, without indicating the source of the law declared.[73]

Those who claim that ICJ Statute Article 38 is reflective or declaratory of CIL on the sources of international law may qualify those CIL rules as being of general character. This is illustrated by Abi-Saab, who, noting that ICJ Statute Article 38(1) is commonly perceived to be declaratory of 'general international law' on sources, adds that such general international law corresponds to Hart's 'secondary rules of change'.[74] Some of those who deem ICJ Statute Article 38 as declaratory sometimes hold this claim in relation to propositions regarding specific sub-systems of international law.[75]

The attribution of the character as declaratory or reflective of CIL to ICJ Statute Article 38 is not entirely novel, since this was equally

[69] Sur (n 6) 149.

[70] Debates over ICJ Statute Article 38's character as declaratory of CIL on sources of law are not to be confused with the debate over the character of custom as non-constitutive, but merely 'declaratory', of a form of pre-existing law. For a discussion of the latter debate, which ultimately concerns whether custom is a proper source of law, see P Guggenheim, 'Les Principes de Droit International Public' (1952) 80 RdC 2, 70; Kelsen (n 7) 124. The two debates should be distinguished even if the latter debate arguably had an impact on the drafting of PCIJ Statute Article 38, as Kelsen pointed out.

[71] R Dolzer, 'New Foundations of the Law of Expropriation of Alien Property' (1981) 75 AJIL 553, 556.

[72] C Tomuschat, 'Obligations Arising for States without or against Their Will' (1993) 241 RdC 195, 240.

[73] DC Vanek, 'Is International Law Part of the Law of Canada?' (1950) 8 UTLJ 251, 254 ('although the provisions of that Article relate to a particular court, they are merely declaratory of existing law').

[74] Abi-Saab (n 14) 191.

[75] G Acquaviva & A Whiting, *International Criminal Law: Cases and Commentary* (Oxford University Press 2011) 21 (characterising as 'declaratory of customary international law' Article 38(1)(d) in connection with the proposition that there is no *stare decisis* in international criminal law).

predicated of PCIJ Statute Article 38. Verdross cited approvingly a 1928 arbitral award holding that, in the event of 'silence of the *compromis* on the sources of law, every international arbitral tribunal must apply the rules of the law of nations, taking into account the definition contained in Article 38 of the [PCIJ] Statute'. Verdross implied that custom served as legal basis for findings like this one. In fact, he inferred from the 'long history' of arbitral tribunals' invocation of general principles of law (a source of law already included in PCIJ Statute Article 38) without 'special authorisation', that 'the application of such principles has been sanctioned by international custom'.[76] It is notable that Verdross, unlike Jennings and Watts, did not see any inconsistency in relying on a source of law, such as custom, as basis for the legal character of another source of law, such as general principles of law. Lauterpacht also deemed PCIJ Statute Article 38 as declaratory of 'custom expressed by a long series of conventions and arbitral awards'.[77] Lauterpacht added, with particular reference to PCIJ Statute Article 38(3) (which would become ICJ Statute Article 38(1)(c)), that it was 'purely declaratory' since, prior to the PCIJ Statute, both 'arbitral practice and arbitration agreements' recognised general principles of law.[78]

Various leading authors have more recently noted that declaratory character is attributed to ICJ Statute Article 38. With respect to ICJ Statute Article 38(1)(c), Jennings and Watts, despite their *petitio principii* objection, reported on the 'fact' that 'a number of international tribunals, although not bound by the Statute, have treated that paragraph of Article 38 as declaratory of existing law'.[79] Monaco pointed to the role of PCIJ Statute Article 38 in giving concrete expression to a 'preexisting practice'.[80] Sur, likewise, attributes declaratory character to PCIJ Statute Article 38.[81] Pellet, in his 2012 survey of uses of ICJ Article 38, discusses various international instruments, and implies that some refer indirectly to ICJ Statute Article 38.[82]

76 Verdross (n 4) 199.
77 Lauterpacht (n 4) 164 fn 2.
78 ibid 163–4.
79 Jennings & Watts (n 1) 39 [12].
80 R Monaco, 'Cours Général de Droit International Public' (1968) 125 RdC 93, 188 fn 1.
81 Sur (n 6) 142.
82 Pellet (n 19) 745 [50] fn 77 (discussing, among others, arbitration agreements which refer to Article 33 of the Optional Rules for Arbitrating Disputes between Two States of the Permanent Court of Arbitration).

Some have gone further, holding that ICJ Statute Article 38 codifies the 'sources' of international law,[83] or, more precisely, the CIL rules governing the 'sources' in international law.[84] Supporters of the view that ICJ Statute Article 38 is codificatory include earlier scholars, such as Lauterpacht.[85] Along similar lines, Conforti referred to the role of PCIJ Statute Article 38 as a codification of the 'practice followed by international tribunals'.[86] Lepard, for his part, not only claims that ICJ Statute Article 38 is codificatory, but also attributes to it authoritativeness as a statement of CIL rules on sources of international law directly.[87] Lepard's statement is notable, since most contemporary writers who regard ICJ Statute Article 38 as authoritative fail to indicate whether it is so *qua* treaty or *qua* statement of a separate rule, including any CIL rule.

The foregoing discussion has shown that, in essence, there are two models of CIL on sources of law in scholarship. Before delving into these two models, a discussion of some conceptual underpinnings is warranted. In particular, Bentham's distinction between custom *in foro* and custom *in pays* sheds light on the nature of these two models.[88]

[83] See R Alfert, 'Hostes Humani Generis: An Expanded Notion of US Counterterrorist Legislation' (1992) 6 EmoryInt'lLRev 171, 198 fn 128 (quoting ICJ Statute Article 38 and stating that 'Section 102 of the Restatement (Third) ... also codifies existing sources of international law').

[84] The attribution of codificatory character to ICJ Statute Article 38 is discussed by several authors, including those who approve of this view. See Abi-Saab (n 14) 191; Sur (n 6) 75 ('Article 38 itself is indeed generally regarded as codifying a customary rule' ('*[l]'article 38 lui-même est en effet généralement considéré comme codifiant une règle coutumière*')); Virally (n 16) 167 ('[t]he codification of the system of sources of international law is generally considered as effected by Article 38 of the Statute of the International Court of Justice ... [t]his Article lists three series of sources' ('*[l]a codification du système des sources du droit international est généralement considérée comme effectuée par l'article 38 du Statut de la Cour internationale de Justice ... [c]et article énumère trois séries de sources*')).

[85] See Lauterpacht's statement in his capacity as Special Rapporteur of the ILC, cited in M Lachs, 'Teachings and Teaching of International Law' (1976) 151 RdC 161, 177 fn 3.

[86] B Conforti, 'Cours Général de Droit International Public' (1988) 212 RdC 9, 77.

[87] BD Lepard, *Rethinking Humanitarian Intervention: A Fresh Legal Approach Based on Fundamental Ethical Principles in International Law and World Religions* (Penn Press 2003) 100 ('[t]hese rules regarding the "sources" of international law ... are now codified in Article 38 of the Statute of the International Court of Justice ... often regarded as an authoritative statement of the customary rules regarding the sources of international law').

[88] J Bentham, *A Comment on the Commentaries* (JH Burns & HLA Hart eds, Oxford University Press 1977) 182–4, cited by G Lamond, 'Legal Sources, the Rule of Recognition, and Customary Law' (2014) 59 American Journal of Jurisprudence 25, 43.

This distinction has been recently revisited by Lamond, as part of his critique of Hart's conception of the rule of recognition. Lamond argues that Hart's characterisation of the rule of recognition as a form of 'collective social practice of officials'[89] fails to account for its additional, and more important, character as 'a form of customary law'.[90] Significantly, Lamond advocates the importance of characterising rules on sources of law as customary, not merely as practice-based. While Lamond does not put forward a source-based model of customary rules of recognition, his analysis of the character of the rule of recognition as a form of law standing on an equal footing with other forms of law within a legal system is pertinent.[91]

The following discussion focuses on Lamond's conception of customary rules of recognition, its transferability to an analysis of international lawmaking, and the various aspects of his portrayal of that kind of customary law as internal, systemic and foundational.

The internal character of the rule of recognition is an important aspect, and its denial, particularly where justified by the comparison between games and law, warrants further examination. Lamond contests the relevance of this comparison, which holds that, since players of games are not required to determine the rules of the game as part of the game, those second-order rules are not part of the rules of the game. Instead, Lamond argues, the assumption that game-playing necessarily excludes the creation of rules of game-playing does not hold true with respect to legal systems, which are precisely concerned with a wide range of regulation, 'including crucially the activities of law-identification and law-creation themselves'.[92] Lamond's critique of the widespread reliance on the 'rules of the game' comparison to justify a segregation of the rule of recognition from other rules of law is apposite, in the sense that it reminds that a separation in all respects of secondary rules from primary rules, including as to their making and identification, is mistaken. This, as discussed in Section 1, would be as unjustified as assuming that all regulation need be normative in nature. Indeed, leaving aside functional differentiations, secondary and primary rules may partake in the same properties, as rules of the same legal system, including their source-based creation and identification. This is all the more relevant in international law, given its so-called

[89] ibid 26.
[90] ibid (emphasis omitted).
[91] ibid 31.
[92] ibid 38.

horizontality whereby, among others, even *jus cogens* rules need not 'displace [the] application' of certain non-peremptory rules.[93]

The systemic character Lamond attributes to custom, is also of relevance to international lawmaking. Lamond's systemic account of acceptance aptly introduces the idea of levels of analysis. Indeed, while acceptance may occur at the separate levels of an individual rule and that of the legal system, acceptance ultimately performs the same function, including at the second-order level where a rule of recognition operates.[94] A similar approach is defended by Mendelson in his analysis of the place of consent in the formation of custom. In particular, Mendelson aptly critiques voluntarist theories for importing consent '[a]t the most general, systemic level' into the 'identification-of-sources level'.[95]

The source-based character of a customary rule of recognition is an area where Lamond's model may be of limited relevance, and, in a way, partake in the shortcomings of Hart's conception of the rule of recognition, for the purposes of international lawmaking. For Lamond, the rule of recognition's foundational character does not detract from its place as internal to the legal system. Indeed, he argues, 'the fact that the rule of recognition is the ultimate basis for source-based standards in the system, and does not owe its status to satisfying the criteria in some further standard, does not show that it is not internal to the system of laws'.[96] He appears to accept the idea that the non-application of the standard demanded by the rule of recognition for the creation of custom to the very creation or identification of the rule of recognition is not at odds with the character of the rule of recognition as a customary rule which is internal to the legal system. This seems to be justified by Lamond's apparent view that source-based and non-source-based law are equal parts of a legal system. This view is evidenced by his conception of custom *in foro*. He defines custom *in pays* as 'the custom of non-officials recognized by the law . . . not . . . the custom of the officials themselves'. By contrast, he defines custom *in foro* as 'customary law' which 'rests on being applied in the practice of the courts'. In particular, he lays out four features of custom *in foro*: 'customary legal standards . . . are: (a) authoritative for the courts; (b) not validated by another legal standard; (c) depend for their existence on being applied in the practice

93 *Jurisdictional Immunities of the State* (n 56) 141 [95].
94 Lamond (n 88) 39.
95 Mendelson (n 32) 261–3.
96 Lamond (n 88) 39.

of the courts; and (d) belong to a system of laws'.[97] Nevertheless, establishing a source of law for rules governing sources of law is key to properly determine how such rules may be created, changed or terminated. Lamond himself seems to hint at the importance of characterising a rule as customary, including the rule of recognition, since such an understanding determines '[a]t a practical level, ... how we think they can or cannot be altered'.[98] Yet, it is unclear why understanding the rule of recognition as a form of customary law, without treating it as a form of source-based law, derived from a custom, suffices to determine how that customary law can be changed, let alone how it is created or terminated. As the present author has shown elsewhere with regard to strands of constitutional theories of international lawmaking, theories which do not identify a source of law for rules regulating sources of law are bound to fail in their attempts to properly account for changes of those rules.[99]

It is fitting to now discuss a caveat to the distinction between custom *in foro* and custom *in pays*. Lamond states that '[c]ustomary international law is most similar to the custom of non-officials recognized by the law (custom '*in pays*'), not to the custom of the officials themselves'.[100] This caveat is partly accurate. On one hand, it may misrepresent the dual character of states as both law-addressees (and, in that sense, non-officials) and lawmakers (and, thus, officials, to the extent that they have lawmaking power), a duality encapsulated in Scelle's concept of '*dédoublement fonctionnel*'.[101] On the other hand, Lamond's caveat correctly reminds that custom is a source through which the general practice of subjects of law becomes law (custom *in pays*), independently of the practice international courts and tribunals develop as they settle disputes (akin to a custom *in foro*). Indeed, the 'officialdom' of international courts and tribunals, in their capacity as dispute settlers, is typically limited to the confines of the jurisdiction to which the subjects of law submitting their disputes have consented.

Despite being evidently inconsistent with the tenet of the primacy of state practice, as primary subjects of international law, the large majority of existing theories of CIL on the sources of law are largely modelled after a form of custom *in foro*. As such, those theories seek to establish the existence, scope and content of rules on sources of law without due

97 ibid.
98 ibid 27.
99 Mejía-Lemos (n 22).
100 Lamond (n 88) 43.
101 G Scelle, 'Règles Générales du Droit de la Paix' (1933) RdC 1, 358.

consideration of any relevant general practice of states. Instead, custom is frequently ascertained primarily by reference to decisions of international courts and tribunals. Exceptionally, selected decisions of domestic courts may be examined, provided that they can be regarded as more authoritative than regular national judicial decisions and placed on the same plane as international decisions. This is the model followed by various leading writers supportive of CIL accounts of regulation of sources. In fact, Lauterpacht and Verdross reached their conclusion as to the declaratory status of PCIJ Statute Article 38 solely on the basis of its use by international tribunals other than the PCIJ, without placing the various arbitration agreements underling those treaty-based arbitrations at the centre of their respective claims of existence of CIL then declared by PCIJ Statute Article 38. This model is replicated in more recent accounts which accept the idea of CIL rules on sources of law, as exemplified by Tams' analysis of 'meta-rules' on sources of law, which focuses mainly on ICJ decisions.[102]

By contrast, a model of CIL whereby custom is created through (and ascertained by reference to) state practice proper, is what the notion of custom *in pays* calls for. By means of such general practice, states make determinations as to sources of law in various contexts, whether they engage in lawmaking or in law-identification in connection with dispute settlement proceedings, on the basis of rules which they accept as law. This kind of custom is a model of CIL which is advocated by some scholars, albeit the degrees to which they substantiate their claims varies. Major examples of claims of CIL on sources of law which intend to rely on state practice, but do not fully substantiate those claims by reference to actual instances of state practice, can be found in the work of Henkin. He argued that customary law was a default category including diverse bodies of law which would not necessarily meet the requirements for the existence of custom proper. Nevertheless, and interestingly for the purposes of the present chapter, Henkin claimed that there exists custom regulating the sources of law, and considered that it constituted a form of custom proper, one based on actual general state practice and accepted as law.[103]

[102] CJ Tams, 'Meta-Custom and the Court: A Study in Judicial Law-Making' (2015) 14 LPICT 51.

[103] Henkin (n 21) 54 (arguing that '[t]he norm governing the making of customary law – the requirement of consistent general practice plus *opinio juris* – is . . . developed by custom, by general, repeated practice and acceptance').

4 Conclusions

This chapter has explored various aspects of the idea that there may exist a law on the sources of law, as opposed to a mere theory or doctrine thereof, in the form of CIL. In doing so, the chapter has provided an overview of the existing theories, both in general jurisprudence and international law scholarship, and assessed their limitations and merits.

Section 1, by way of background, has indicated that, in spite of sharing important common ground, as with many other vexed issues in the theory of the sources of international law, there is a controversy as to the idea of regulation of sources of law and the legality of rules on sources of law, if any, among major schools of thought. At the core of debates concerning this idea, it was submitted, is the fact that regulation tends to be conflated with normativity, unjustifiably denying the legality of non-normative regulation.

Section 2, in particular, has shown that the standard position, albeit professing to be practice-based, rejects a source-based account of regulation of sources of law, on grounds of a *petitio principii* objection. It has proposed to set aside, for the sake of argument, any *petitio principii* objection(s), and suggested that the standard account, seemingly assuming the futility of the idea of regulation of sources, has neglected the task of addressing alternative arguments against a source-based account of the regulation of sources of law. In addition, it has examined the idea of custom's inherent features, which make it especially suitable to create general rules of universal scope. Furthermore, it has provided an overview of state practice invoking ICJ Statute Article 38(1) in contexts other than proceedings before the ICJ. It has further shown that there is evidence that this general practice is accepted as law. In addition, it has argued in favour of reaffirming the centrality of state practice itself, including in the form of decisions of domestic courts, as opposed to the typical exclusive reliance on decisions of international courts and tribunals with respect to the regulation of sources of law.

Section 3 has provided an overview of some accounts of CIL on sources of law and has proposed to conceptualise these accounts in terms of two models, along the lines of Bentham's distinction between custom *in foro* and *in pays*, as revisited in recent general jurisprudence literature. In this vein, it has discussed in detail Lamond's recent critique of the rule of recognition which, relying on the distinction between custom *in foro* and custom *in pays*, argues in favour of treating the rule of recognition as a rule of customary law having the same properties as any legal rule of the legal system. Section 3 has argued that, to the extent that this critique is apposite to international law, the insights it contains shed light on the nature of a CIL regulating the sources of law in international law.

To conclude, the chapter suggests that the persistence of custom *in foro* as a model for CIL regulation of the sources of law, a matter calling for further research, may detract from the potential for establishing the existence of a CIL regulating the sources of international law on the solid grounds of proper state general practice and acceptance as law thereof.

8

The ILC's New Way of Codifying International Law, the Motives Behind It, and the Interpretive Approach Best Suited to It

LUIGI CREMA

1 Introduction

Over the past two decades, the International Law Commission (ILC) has taken an original approach to its 'progressive codification' activity.[1] For the most part, in defining international law, the ILC has tended to set aside the attempt to draft articles and pursue binding rules,[2] expressing instead a descriptive conception of its own work, mostly dedicated to the general framework (i.e., sources, interpretation of norms, responsibility), where specialised, codified in written treaties, regimes operate. This course is not necessarily an independent shift by the ILC itself but reflects the expectations of states nowadays with respect to the commission. To ponder the work of the ILC is an exercise in both understanding how the commission composed by independent experts understands its job and understanding how states look to govern the international community. This chapter aims at reflecting on the activity of the ILC and analysing its transformation over the past decades. In particular, it looks at the way it has, in agreement with the international community of states, interpreted its role, in particular of distilling written restatements of customary law, capturing and crystallising the otherwise often murky and erratic international practice.

1 Charter of the United Nations (adopted 26 June 1945, entered into force 24 October 1945) 1 UNTS XVI, art 13(1)(a); UNGA, 'Statute of the International Law Commission' (21 November 1947) UNGA Res 174 (II) (as amended by UNGA Res 485 (V) (12 December 1950), 984 (X) (3 December 1955), 985 (X) (3 December 1955) and 36/39 (18 November 1981)) art 1.

2 P Weil, 'Le droit international en quête de son identité' (1992) 237 RdC 9, 11 ff; see also, with more provocative tones, P Weil, 'Vers une normativité relative en droit international?' (1982) 86 RGDIP 5, 5 ff; M Goldmann, 'Relative Normativity' in J d'Aspremont & S Singh (eds), *Concepts for International Law: Contributions to Disciplinary Thought* (Edward Elgar 2019) 740.

The ILC lately tends to avoid the progressive development of law, rather providing restatements of international practice and scholarly doctrines on given topics. In other words, the ILC looks more and more to the codification of customary rules in written, not binding, form rather than aiming at shaping future practice through new treaties. In recent decades, the ILC has come to rarely draft articles aiming at becoming treaties. It occasionally works with this aim, but the success rate of ILC draft articles turning into a treaty in force has been statistically negligible over the past quarter century. Today, the drafting of written material rules tends to happen on different, bilateral or regional, tables, but not at the ILC.

Sections 2 and 3 of this chapter are dedicated to parsing the activity of the ILC and looking at the contemporary revolution in how it carries out its activity of codification, where the key aspect of the activity of codification is not the creation of treaties, but rather the synthesis of existent practice in order to assist the judicial bodies. Notably, its efforts to create general codifications of law have become outdated. In part, the new course of the ILC is geared toward the creation of guidelines, in part toward the scholarly study of topics of general interest, and in part, finally, toward codifying draft articles aiming at becoming treaties – but without going toward any international conference that intends to negotiate a final text.

All these materials have in common the fact of offering written rules, the binding status of which is not clear, and of creating questions about how to assess their contents. As non-binding restatements of international practice, they (both as guidelines and as articles that do not materialise into a convention) amount to a restatement of practice and are, therefore, open for the assessment of the content of the rule they express as is the case for customary rules. Since they are in written form, in an international law document or a document governed by international law, they call for interpretation using the tools of written international law – Article 31–33 of the Vienna Convention on the Law of Treaties (VCLT), which is, nowadays, used not only to interpret treaties, but also every act of international law.[3] This chapter has several aims. The first is to illustrate the presence and extent of the shift described here, with a look at the factual grounds. The second is to reflect on the reasons for this transformation. The last is to reflect on the interpretive approach

[3] L Crema, *La prassi successiva e l'interpretazione del diritto internazionale scritto* (Giuffré 2017) 3–6.

toward the work of the ILC in defining non-binding (but written) guidelines and articles (that do not become treaties).

In order to do this, the next pages will be dedicated to providing an overview of the work and evolution of the ILC approach to codification and development of international law (Sections 2 and 3), its legality under the UN Charter and the ILC Statute (Section 4), and its possible reasons and purposes (Section 5). The chapter will close with an assessment of its effective impact in the work of international courts and tribunals (Section 6), and explain what are the goals and principles which the ILC should consider in carrying out this new course and the interpretive approach that best suits it.

2 A Brief Survey of the Kind of Activities of the ILC Since the Beginning of Its Work: 1949–2020

Since 1949, when the ILC began its operations, it has addressed many different issues, particularly concerning the sources of international law and the law of international relations. As of 1 July 2020, counting its works on the most-favoured-nation clause (MFN clause) as two separate works, the ILC had completed forty-three topics.[4] Five topics were discontinued or not pursued further.[5] Eight topics are still under consideration.[6]

Looking only at the concluded topics, in sixteen cases, *the ILC approved articles that eventually were brought to a diplomatic conference and culminated in a multilateral treaty*. Some of them are well known: the law of treaties, the 1958 conventions on the law of the sea, the works on the succession of treaties, and many others, up to the works on international criminal law, which resulted in the Rome Statute of 1998.[7] The most recent works of this kind were those dedicated to state immunity, completed in

4 ILC, 'Analytical Guide to the Work of the International Law Commission' (*ILC*, 10 December 2019) <http://legal.un.org/ilc/guide/gfra.shtml> accessed 1 March 2021.

5 Fundamental rights and duties of States; Status, privileges and immunities of international organisations, their officials, experts, *etc*; Right of asylum; Juridical régime of historic waters, including historic bays; shared natural resources (oil and gas).

6 Provisional application of treaties; Peremptory norms of general international law (*jus cogens*); General principles of law; Succession of States in respect of State responsibility; Immunity of State officials from foreign criminal jurisdiction; Protection of the environment in relation to armed conflicts; Protection of the atmosphere; Sea-level rise in relation to international law.

7 Law of the sea – regime of the high seas; Law of the sea – regime of the territorial sea; Diplomatic intercourse and immunities; Consular intercourse and immunities; Special missions; Law of treaties; Succession of States in respect to treaties; Succession of States in respect of matters other than treaties; Representation of States in their relations with

1991, which led to the adoption of the United Nations (UN) Convention on Jurisdictional Immunities of States and their Property, in 2004.

In twelve cases the ILC produced draft articles that *did not later become* (or, have not yet become) *the object of an initiative toward the adoption of a multilateral treaty*.[8] The most famous example is that of the articles on state responsibility for internationally wrongful acts in 2001.[9] The more recently concluded works could, in theory, still become the object of a diplomatic conference to complete a multilateral treaty: the draft articles on prevention and punishment of crimes against humanity were just adopted by the ILC, in 2019, although several states, including Egypt, Russia and Turkey, had already manifested opposition to this project.[10] At the moment, however, these twelve works have never undergone the difficult path of an international diplomatic conference aiming at reaching a treaty. So, while they are formulated in articles, as definitions and obligations, their binding effect has never been crystalised by any binding treaty.

Three topics *produced guidelines or principles*.[11] Except for the 'reservations saga', where the adoption of guidelines was proposed during the

international organizations; Treaties concluded between States and international organizations or between two or more international organizations; Nationality including statelessness; Jurisdictional immunities of States and their property; Draft code of offences against the peace and security of mankind (Part I); Draft code of crimes against the peace and security of mankind (Part II) – including the draft statute for an international criminal court; Law of the non-navigational uses of international watercourses; Question of the protection and inviolability of diplomatic agents and other persons entitled to special protection under international law.

8 For example State Responsibility (2001); Expulsion of Aliens (2014); Diplomatic Protection (2016); Crimes against Humanity (2019).

9 Already since 2007, and then periodically, the United Nations General Assembly (UNGA) leaves open the possibility of convening an international conference with a view to adopting a convention; see UNGA Res 62/61, 'Responsibility of States for Internationally Wrongful Acts' (6 December 2007) UN Doc A/62/446; more recently, UNGA Res 74/180, 'Responsibility of States for Internationally Wrongful Acts' (18 December 2019) UN Doc A/RES/74/180.

10 See the final draft articles in ILC, 'Report of the International Law Commission on the Work of Its 71st Session' (29 April–7 June and 8 July–9 August 2019) UN Doc A/74/10, 10–140.

11 ILC, 'Title and Texts of the Preamble and the Draft Principles on the Allocation of Loss Arising Out of Hazardous Activities Adopted by the Drafting Committee on Second Reading' (1 May–9 June and 3 July–11 August 2006) A/CN.4/L.686 and Corr.1; ILC, 'Guiding Principles Applicable to Unilateral Declarations of States Capable of Creating Legal Obligations, with Commentaries Thereto' [2006/II – Part Two] YBILC 161; ILC, 'Guide to Practice on Reservations to Treaties, with Commentaries' (26 April–3 June and 4 July–12 August 2011) UN Doc A/66/10/Add.1.

extremely lengthy working sessions, for all the other topics, the ILC intended from the beginning to produce this result.

Six topics *culminated in studies*. The first, on the evidence of customary law, led by Manley Hudson in 1950, concludes with a series of recommendations on the publication of state and international practice. The others are more recent and concern the so-called fragmentation of international law, the principle of *aut dedere aut iudicare* and the MFN clause, a highly controversial topic in arbitrational awards on international investments.[12] Two other topics, on subsequent agreements and subsequent practice and on the identification of customary international law, were not discussed by a study group but in the ordinary procedure of work. However, like a study group, they produced a set of *conclusions*.[13]

The six remaining topics are difficult to place in a single category. They include: those on international criminal jurisdiction and on the multilateral treaties concluded under the aegis of the League of Nations, which were structured as legal opinions and lack the depth of a proper study;[14] the works on the soft codification of the Nuremberg principles and on the 'model rules' of arbitration procedure (which, with the proper distinctions, could be grouped with works to establish guidelines);[15] the brief work on the formation process for multilateral treaties; and the earliest study on reservations, which was, *de facto*, rolled into its work on the law of treaties a few years later.[16]

These classifications can be further refined and specified, according to the specific procedure and content adopted for each particular topic,[17] but, for the purpose of this chapter, it is enough to generically differentiate

[12] Ways and Means for Making the Evidence of Customary International Law More Readily Available (1950); Fragmentation of International Law: Difficulties Arising from the Diversification and Expansion of International Law (2006); Obligation to Extradite or Prosecute (*aut dedere aut judicare*) (2014); Most-Favoured-Nation Clause (Part Two) (2015).

[13] Identification of Customary International Law (2015); Subsequent Agreements and Subsequent Practice in Relation to Interpretation of Treaties (2016).

[14] Question of International Criminal Jurisdiction; Extended Participation in General Multilateral Treaties Concluded under the Auspices of the League of Nations.

[15] Formulation of the Nürnberg Principles; Arbitral Procedure.

[16] Review of the Multilateral Treaty-Making Process; Reservations to Multilateral Conventions.

[17] See for example SD Murphy, 'Codification, Progressive Development, or Scholarly Analysis? The Art of Packaging the ILC's Work Product' in M Ragazzi (ed), *The Responsibility of International Organizations: Essays in Memory of Sir Ian Brownlie* (Martinus Nijhoff 2013) 29, 36 ff.

between works dedicated to attempts at codification, and other kinds of works.

At this time, July 2020, the ILC is working on eight topics.[18] The three works on sources are intended to produce soft law; those on the provisional application of treaties are geared toward the formulation of 'guidelines'; those on *jus cogens* and general principles are geared toward 'conclusions'.[19] The three works on the environment are similarly organised: the topic about the protection of the environment during armed conflicts is intended to produce 'draft principles'; the topic on the protection of the atmosphere aims at producing 'draft guidelines'; while the ILC on 21 May 2019 established a study group on sea-level rise in relation to international law.[20] Only two topics are intended to produce articles: the one on the succession of states in respect of state responsibility, and the one on the immunity of state officials from foreign criminal jurisdiction.

3 A Close-Up on the Work of the ILC in the Third Millennium

If we consider only the time period between the year 2000 and today, the numbers are particularly revealing of a shift toward an express intention of the ILC and the UN General Assembly (UNGA) to produce soft law or treatises on international law, rather than draft articles for new multilateral conventions.

Five works adopted guidelines or principles. These included the guiding principles on unilateral acts and on loss from transboundary harm arising out of hazardous activities, both from 2006,[21] as well as the

[18] Provisional application of treaties; Peremptory norms of general international law (*jus cogens*); General principles of law; Immunity of State officials from foreign criminal jurisdiction; Protection of the environment in relation to armed conflicts; Protection of the atmosphere; Sea-level rise in relation to international law; Succession of States in respect of State responsibility.

[19] The work on general principles is leaning in this direction, see ILC, 'Report of the International Law Commission on the Work of Its 69th Session' (1 May–2 June and 3 July–4 August 2017) UN Doc A/72/10 224–25 [4].

[20] ILC, 'Report of the International Law Commission on the Work of Its 71st Session' (29 April–7 June and 8 July–9 August 2019) UN Doc A/74/10, 340–41.

[21] On the *Unilateral acts of States* the ILC adopted ILC, 'Guiding Principles Applicable to Unilateral Declarations of States Capable of Creating Legal Obligations, with Commentaries Thereto' (n 13); ILC, 'Report of the International Law Commission on the Work of Its 58th Session' (1 May–9 June and 3 July–11 August 2006) UN Doc A/61/10; see ILC, 'Title and Texts of the Preamble and the Draft Principles on the Allocation of Loss Arising out of Hazardous Activities Adopted by the Drafting Committee on Second

guidelines on the reservations to treaties, from 2011. Upon close consideration, the (endless) works on reservations, which lasted a full eighteen years, produced something more than a basic set of guidelines, but rather something closer to scholarship: the *Guide to Practice on Reservations to Treaties.*[22] The works on practice and successive agreements and on the identification of customary law resulted in the definitive adoption of 'Conclusions'.[23] Three works were intended from the beginning to be eminently scholarly. They included, first of all, that on the fragmentation of international law, which began in 2000 and was completed in 2006[24]. It contains forty-two final conclusions, and the study group itself, at the close of the working sessions, brought the centrality of the over 250-page overall doctrinal work to attention of the UNGA, on the basis of the conclusions themselves: 'The Study Group stressed the importance of the collective nature of its conclusions. It also emphasized that these conclusions have to be read in connection with the analytical study, finalized by the Chairperson, on which they are based.'[25] Second is that on the *aut dedere aut judicare* principle, completed in 2014, which produced a slim document of less than twenty pages.[26] Last is that on the MFN clause,

Reading' (n 11). While the first half of works on the International Liability for Transboundary Harm ended up in a project of articles – 'Draft articles on Prevention of Transboundary Harm from Hazardous Activities', ILC, Official Records of the General Assembly, 56th Session, Supplement No. 10, UN Doc A/56/10 – in which the UNGA contemplated the possibility of adopting an international convention, about this second part the ILC merely recommended the UNGA to approve the draft principles, and asked states to implement further domestic and international initiatives able to make them effective.

22 ILC, 'Guide to Practice on Reservations to Treaties, with Commentaries' (n 11) which has an introduction and an annex with further conclusions and recommendations.

23 ILC, 'Draft Conclusions on Subsequent Agreements and Subsequent Practice in Relation to the Interpretation of Treaties, with Commentaries' (30 April–1 June and 2 July–10 August 2018) UN Doc A/73/10, reproduced in [2018/II – Part Two] YBILC 11; ILC, 'Draft Conclusions on Identification of Customary International Law, with Commentaries' (30 April–1 June and 2 July–10 August 2018) UN Doc A/73/10, reproduced in [2018/II – Part Two] YBILC 11.

24 ILC, 'Report on Fragmentation of International Law: Difficulties Arising from the Diversification and Expansion of International Law, Finalized by Martti Koskenniemi' (13 April 2006) UN Doc A/CN.4/L.682.

25 ILC, 'Report of the International Law Commission on the Work of Its 58th Session' (1 May–9 June and 3 July–11 August 2006) UN Doc A/61/10, 176 [237].

26 ILC, 'Final Report: Working Group on the Obligation to Extradite or Prosecute (*aut dedere aut judicare*)' (5 May–6 June and 7 July–8 August 2014) UN Doc A/CN.4/L.844; see also UNGA Res 69/118, 'Report of the International Law Commission on the Work of Its 66th Session' (10 December 2014) UN Doc A/RES/69/118 calling for the widest dissemination of the ILC Report.

from 2015.[27] Like the case before, this study group produced a brief document, containing a concise commentary, just over thirty pages long, on the practice of states that followed the ILC's earlier works on the same subject.[28] Even Nolte's work on subsequent practice and agreements began, in 2008, in the form of a study group on 'Treaties over time,' falling *de facto* into the body of work on fragmentation and aiming to complete it with a reflection on the other two parts of Article 31(3) of the 1969 Vienna Convention on the Law of Treaties.[29] However, as noted above with regard to Pellet's work on reservations, Nolte's and Wood's works are short commentaries with sets of conclusions which make them halfway between the guidelines, and the conclusions of scholarly studies. Therefore, even if some of these topics were not discussed by dedicated study groups, a total of six of the ILC's recent works involve studies that are chiefly academic.

Since 2000, only six works culminated in the adoption of draft articles, later approved by the UNGA, but never brought to the preparation of an international convention, nor to the convocation of a diplomatic conference.[30] The last international conventions which were entirely based on the work of the ILC or which greatly benefited from it are the already mentioned 2004 UN Convention on immunity of States (which originated in a topic completed in 1991), and the 1998 ICC Rome Statute (the preparatory works of which relied on the parallel works of the ILC on criminal law).[31] Only *two topics*, diplomatic protection and protection of persons in the event of disasters, culminated in draft articles that are under discussion (and have been for some years) to potentially become an international convention.

[27] Most-Favoured-Nation Clause (Part Two) (67th Session, 2015).

[28] ILC, 'Final Report: Study Group on the Most-Favoured-Nation Clause' (4 May–5 June and 6 July–7 August 2015) UN Doc A/CN.4/L.852.

[29] In 2008 the ILC created a Study Group on *Treaties over Time*; ILC, 'Programme, Procedures and Working Methods of the Commission, and Its Documentation' (1997) reproduced in [1996/II – Part Two] YBILC 84 [351–52]; UNGA Res 63/123, 'Report of the International Law Commission on the Work of Its 60th Session' (11 December 2008) UN Doc A/RES/63/123. In 2012, the ILC then changed the format of the topic during its 64th Session, in 2012.

[30] State responsibility (2001); Responsibility of international organizations (2011); International liability for injurious consequences arising out of acts not prohibited by international law (prevention of transboundary damage from hazardous activities) (2013); Expulsion of aliens (2014); Diplomatic protection (2016); Crimes against Humanity (2019). In all these cases the ILC requested the UNGA to consider the adoption of an international convention.

[31] For a concise summary of the relationship between the ILC and the Rome Statute see Murphy (n 17) 30–1.

As already briefly described above, of the eight topics that are still open and under discussion in July 2020, six are not connected with any plans to draft articles. All works on sources and on the environment are intended to produce soft law (guidelines, principles, of studies with conclusions), and only two of the topics currently under discussion aim at adopting draft articles (whose legal bindingness still needs to be proved through the test of time and of an international convention, or through the test of courts, recognising them as the expression of customary rules).[32]

4 The Legality of the New Path Taken by the Commission

This change of direction by the ILC is striking: the production of draft articles is dwindling. First, as a preliminary observation, it must be noted that, while this ILC approach geared toward academic work and drafting of guidelines is new, it is also legal under the UN framework. Article 1(1) of the 1947 Statute of the International Law Commission provides: 'The International Law Commission shall have for its object the promotion of the progressive development of international law and its codification.' This provision echoes the meaning of 'progressive development of international law' of Article 13 of the UN Charter[33] and seems to extend to *any activity* which aims at developing and codifying international law. It is true that Article 15 of the same statute specifies what is meant by 'progressive development of international law': 'In the following articles the expression "progressive development of international law" is used for convenience as meaning the preparation of draft conventions.'

Other ILC activities, not geared toward the conclusion of international conventions, would appear to be excluded. However, the same provision adds, further down, that: 'the expression "codification of international

[32] Succession of States in respect of State Responsibility; Immunity of State Officials from Foreign Criminal Jurisdiction.

[33] Article 13(1)(a) of the UN Charter: 'The General Assembly shall initiate studies and make recommendations for the purpose of: promoting international co-operation in the political field and encouraging the progressive development of international law and its codification.' On the intertwining of the activity of *codification* and *progressive development* of international law by the ILC see J Sette Câmara, 'The International Law Commission: Discourse on Method' in R Ago (ed), *Le droit international à l'heure de sa codification: études en l'honneur de Roberto Ago*, Vol 1 (Giuffrè 1987) 477–89; Murphy (n 17) 31–32; see also ILC, 'Formation and Evidence of Customary International Law, Elements in the Previous Work of the International Law Commission that Could Be Particularly Relevant to the Topic, Memorandum by the Secretariat' (5 May–7 June and 8 July–9 August 2013) UN Doc A/CN.4/659, 147–48.

law" is used for convenience as meaning the more precise *formulation and systematization of rules of international law*, in fields where there already has been extensive State practice, precedent and doctrine'.[34] Article 20 of the ILC Statute directs the commission to prepare draft articles with a commentary containing reference to precedents and other relevant data, such as treaties, judicial decisions and doctrine. In this way, the statute opens up to any activity characterised by in-depth study of international scholarship and practice, even when it does not result in the elaboration of draft articles, but in the adoption of guidelines, conclusions, principles or mere studies.[35]

While the treaty-oriented work under Article 23 of the commission statute has, in some sense, been shelved because draft articles no longer end up in international conventions, the ILC's work in preparing non-binding guidelines and draft articles ends up exercising the option described by Article 24 to make the evidence of customary law more readily available. Guidelines are technically non-binding, but their importance should not be underestimated. As written summaries of state practice, which look at selected practice and generalise it, the ILC guidelines have potential to be considered as stating binding customary law.

5 Attempts to Uncover the Reasons for the Transformation: The Context of the Fragmentation of International Law

There are many reasons for this evolution, which touch on a variety of different, though interconnected, planes. The first is a sort of renunciation

[34] Statute of the International Court of Justice (adopted 26 June 1945, entered into force 24 October 1945) 1 UNTS 993, art 15 (emphasis added); see also A Tanzi, 'Le forme della codificazione e lo sviluppo progressivo del diritto internazionale' in G Nesi & P Gargiulo (eds), *Luigi Ferrari Bravo: Il diritto internazionale come professione* (Editoriale Scientifica 2015) 152 ff.

[35] In 1996 the ILC Working Group on the Long-Term Programme adopted a set of three criteria in order to select new topics: (a) the topic should reflect the needs of states in respect of the progressive development and codification of international law; (b) the topic should be sufficiently advanced in stage in terms of state practice to permit progressive development and codification; (c) the topic is concrete and feasible for progressive development and codification. ILC Study Group, 'Programme, Procedures and Working Methods of the Commission, and Its Documentation' (n 29) [238]. In 2014 the secretariat proposed a new list of topics, maintaining these criteria: ILC, 'Long-Term Programme of Work: Review of the List of Topics Established in 1996 in the Light of Subsequent Developments, Working Paper Prepared by the Secretariat' (2 May–10 June and 4 July–12 August 2016) UN Doc A/CN.4/679/Add.1.

of the work of imposing solutions on contested topics, instead embracing the work of restating international practice (codification of international law). Any hopes that the ILC would *create* law and propose (and, therefore, impose) it upon states have been extinguished, and the ILC has settled into taking merely descriptive, rather than prescriptive, positions. Using the terminology of the UN Charter, the ILC has taken a step back with regard to *developing* law, settling on its mere *codification*. The decisive event pushing in this direction took place during the long development of the articles on the responsibility of states and its final epilogue. After decades of discussions, James Crawford, pointing to the clashing viewpoints of different governments on the contents of Article 19 of Roberto Ago's 1996 draft articles (responsibility of states for international crimes), eliminated the article itself and moved the draft forward toward its leaner final version.[36]

Another reason is the fragmentation of the international community, and of international law in many of its forms. There are more states and, concomitantly, more state practice, and, therefore, there are more interests to try to converge into a single rule.[37] Moreover, there is a greater number of states aiming at leading the international community: following after the stability of the bipolar phase,[38] and the euphoric moment that followed the fall of the Berlin Wall (during which international law was sometimes framed as the tool of a unipolar world)[39] diminished, their place was taken by a multipolar situation that was, at the very least, much more complex than the previous one,[40] if not actually a full-blown 'international disorder'.[41] Vast international conferences and multilateral treaties became difficult to imagine.

[36] ILC, 'First Report on State Responsibility by Mr James Crawford, Special Rapporteur' (24 April 1998) UN Doc A/CN.4/490 and Add 1–7 [52 ff]; G Arangio-Ruiz, 'Fine prematura del ruolo preminente di studiosi italiani nel progetto di codificazione della responsabilità degli Stati: specie a proposito di crimini internazionali e dei poteri del Consiglio di sicurezza' (1998) 71 RivDirInt 110.

[37] G Abi-Saab, 'La coutume dans tous ses états ou le dilemma du développement du droit international général dans un monde éclaté' in R Ago (ed), *Le Droit international à l'heure de sa codification: études en l'honneur de Roberto Ago* (Giuffrè 1987) 61.

[38] KN Waltz, 'The Stability of a Bipolar World' (1964) 93(3) Daedalus 881.

[39] AM Slaughter Burley, 'International Law and International Relations Theory: A Dual Agenda' (1993) 87 AJIL 205; F Fukuyama, 'The End of History?' (1989) 16 The National Interest 3. Fukuyama later explained that international cooperation, in particular in the EU, represents the real expression of the end of history, absorbing in democratic procedures all previous traditions and disagreements in F Fukuyama, 'The History at the End of History' (*Guardian*, 3 April 2007) <https://bit.ly/2ZEKDpK> accessed 1 March 2021.

[40] M Happold (ed), *International Law in a Multipolar World* (Routledge 2011).

[41] E Di Nolfo, *Il disordine internazionale: Lotte per la supremazia dopo la Guerra fredda* (Bruno Mondadori 2012); Franco Mazzei, *Relazioni Internazionali* (Egea 2016) 1.

Related to this enlargement of the actors playing at the international level is the explosion of legal scholarship, which offers several contexts for proposing diverging interpretations of the law, with an ever-growing number of reviews and specialised publications.[42] On the other hand, international law itself started losing its UN-centred simplicity: specialised international law regimes began to emerge with increasing frequency, with the relative proliferation of courts and tribunals, and the resulting 'judicialisation' of international law.

The recent work of the ILC has been dedicated to help international law to find its centre,[43] fighting back these centrifugal phenomena. The debate on fragmentation of international law began in 1993, when Edith Brown Weiss reflected on the difficult coordination in environmental law due to what she called 'treaty congestion'.[44] It then gained momentum in 1995, when Robert Jennings, former President of the International Court of Justice (ICJ), shifted the attention from the possible clash of treaties to the possible interpretive conflicts between jurisdictions. He publicly warned of the dangers that could potentially flow from the introduction of new international tribunals.[45] It was the time of the creation of ad hoc criminal tribunals, of the Dispute Settlement Body of the World Trade

[42] A Roberts, *Is International Law International?* (Oxford University Press 2017). The topic has often been discussed by Joseph Weiler in several editorials of the *European Journal of International Law* dedicated to the hyper production of contemporary legal scholarship. John Louth tried to catalogue publications about international law in French, German and English, giving up for the enormous number of books and law reviews constantly published: J Louth, 'How Much Public International Law Scholarship Is There?' (*EJILTalk!*, 10 January 2017) <https://bit.ly/3o3pTBq> accessed 1 March 2021. Already in 1987, I Brownlie, 'Problems Concerning the Unity of International Law' in R Ago (ed), *Le Droit international à l'heure de sa codification: études en l'honneur de Roberto Ago* (Giuffrè 1987) 155–56, stressed the expansion and parochialisation of legal scholarship.

[43] This concern emerges clearly in J Crawford, *Chance, Order, Change: The Course of International Law, General Course on Public International Law* (Brill Nijhoff 2014) 308–09.

[44] E Brown Weiss, 'International Environmental Law: Contemporary Issues and the Emergence of a New World Order' (1993) 81 GeoLJ 675, at 697. On a thorough description of the emergence of the issue of fragmentation of international law see T Treves, 'Fragmentation of International Law: The Judicial Perspective' (2007) 23 Comunicazioni e Studi 821.

[45] R Jennings, 'The Proliferation of Adjudicatory Bodies: Dangers and Possible Answers' in L Boisson de Chazournes (ed), *Implications of the Proliferation of International Adjudicatory Bodies for Dispute Resolution* (ASIL Publications 1995) 2, 5–6: '[T]hat is probably the main danger of proliferation, the fragmentation of international law; and by fragmentation I do not mean the very proper local variations for particular purposes. . . . It indicates the tendency of particular tribunals to regard themselves as different, as separate little empires which must as far as possible be augmented.'

Organization, of the Tribunal for the Law of the Sea and so on. How could international jurists respond to a danger of this kind? With 'strong' international law, made up of hierarchies and dogmas?

To a reader in 2020, the solution proffered in the year 2000 by another ICJ president, the French jurist Gilbert Guillaume, to make the ICJ the ultimate guarantor of the coherence of international law, seems somewhat naïve. While Guillaume did not go so far as to imagine the ICJ as a sort of Supreme Court of Cassation of the international legal order (indeed, he observed that appeals and cassation procedures are utilised only very rarely in international law),[46] he did believe that the court at The Hague should be accepted, at least, as a superior court, with the power to receive requests for clarification 'on doubtful or important points of general international law raised in cases before them', following the method of the reference for a preliminary ruling mechanism used by the Court of Justice of the European Union.[47]

The ILC's reaction to each of these evolutions and its response to these underlying issues over the past two decades have amounted to a total departure from the hierarchical approach of Guillaume. The ILC took stock of fragmentation, and, rather than seeing the proliferation of courts and tribunals as a threat, it saw it as an opportunity to deal with the explosion in the number of legal regimes, states and of legal scholarships: the ILC shifted its potential audience from governments gathered in a multilateral diplomatic conference to litigants and adjudicators. It provides them with guidelines dedicated to sources useful for adjudication, with a plausible, legitimate, common interpretive background in a body of expert scholarship useful for *decoding*[48] potentially conflicting interpretations of given rules.[49] It also proposes

[46] HE Judge G Guillaume, 'The Proliferation of International Judicial Bodies: The Outlook for the International Legal Order' (*Speech to the Sixth Committee of the General Assembly of the United Nations*, 27 October 2000) 6 <www.icj-cij.org/public/files/press-releases/1/3001.pdf> accessed 1 March 2021. Then he concludes: 'This would, however, require a powerful political will on the part of States and far reaching changes in the Court, which would need to be given substantial resources. I am not certain whether such a will exists.'

[47] ibid 7.

[48] N Irti, *L'età della decodificazione* (Giuffrè 1978) played on the two possible meanings of the term '*decodificazione*' in Italian: the *dismantling* of the central role of the Italian Civil Code in many special regimes and the *decoding* of a message. Both meanings are well suited to contemporary international law.

[49] International law scholarship has a rather rich scholarship on the so-called soft law. See T Treves, 'International Law: Achievements and Challenges' in J Cardona Llorens (ed), *Cursos Euromediterraneos Bancaja de Derecho Internacional*, Vol 10 (Tirant lo Blanch 2006) 452–70; J d'Aspremont, 'Softness in International Law: A Self-Serving Quest'

(customary – and therefore binding?) restatements of practice about other general issues of international law, leaving it to *those called to adjudicate over a specific dispute* to provide the definitive answer on their legal bindingness.[50]

In order to achieve this, the ILC set about *weakening* general international law, in the philosophical sense that it reflects the thought established by a society that lacks consensus on ultimate values,[51] so to be flexible enough to encompass and serve the new, many, international law regimes. The term 'weak' is used here because the ILC has been characterised by an approach to defining the law that disregards the goal of final approval of strong, binding, treaties; weak because the power of orienting the conduct of states and adjudicators does not come from a command, but from persuasion, that is from the quality of a given study; weak because it assumes that the validity and authority of a rule does not come from the precision and clearness of its content, but rather from its structured interpretation.

First, the ILC affirms the unity of the international system, not as a single set of binding, material rules, but by proposing the formal unity of its rules dedicated to the determination and establishment of international law. It furnishes parties to a dispute and adjudicators with a common legal ground of principles and guidelines to deal with the sources of international law. At the same time, the ILC has overcome the threat of the explosion of legal scholarships in order to propose, with its guidelines and commentaries, the unification of reasoning about the law, by creating a *unique context* for its interpretation: a sort of 'official scholarship'.[52] The ILC's series of works on the sources of international law and the interpretation of written law is very clear on this: it is, quite simply, the attempt to state a single line of orthodoxy on secondary rules

(2008) 19 EJIL 1075; A Pellet, 'Les raisons du développement du *soft law* en droit international: choix ou nécessité?' in P Deumier & JM Sorel (eds), *Regards croisés sur la* soft law *en droit interne, européen et international* (LGDJ 2018) 177–92.

50 The operation that Martti Koskenniemi described as the core of international law, see M Koskenniemi, *From Apology to Utopia: The Structure of the International Legal Argument* (2nd ed, Cambridge University Press 2005) 474 ff.

51 Echoing the term used about postmodern thought by PA Rovatti & G Vattimo (eds), *Il pensiero debole* (Feltrinelli 1983).

52 On this is still relevant what has been observed by PM Dupuy, 'The Danger of Fragmentation or Unification of the International Legal System and the International Court of Justice' (1998–99) 31 NYUJIL&Pol 791; see also Koskenniemi (n 50) 474 ff.; A Pellet & D Müller, 'Article 38' in A Zimmermann & CJ Tams (eds), *The Statute of the International Court of Justice: A Commentary* (3rd ed, Oxford University Press 2019) 914–15.

of international law (according to the Hartian meaning), and to create a line of official scholarship. It both fosters and creates the internal point of view on law and creates an official legal context in which to assess the contents of rules.[53] This official scholarship (a doctrine that distils other doctrine and practice) is: authoritative[54] (because of the credibility and plurality of its source – the ILC of the UN); easily accessible (an easy internet search is all it takes); and open to be used and adopted by anyone involved in a dispute.

Second, the ILC looks at different courts and tribunals as an opportunity to develop international law outside the traditional codifications[55] – every kind of international law, including material law, not just law dedicated to the sources and their interpretation. Their work can turn soft law (both when it is truly soft law and when it comes in the form of draft articles) into customary law, even in the absence of global agreements.

The ILC approach can be summarised, in essence, to be that of experts whose chief aim is to study and summarise, without imposing anything and without even challenging governments, the UNGA or the Sixth Committee to elaborate international agreements. They leave it to counsels and attorneys, who represent states or private parties before the international tribunals to cite the texts they have produced. Above all, their work falls to the hands of judges and arbitrators who, in the chambers of their respective tribunals, decide what to use, keep or reject of what they have produced. It is redundant to observe that often this process is facilitated by the efficient shuttle-service between Geneva and the seats of arbitration or the tribunals serving the commissioners and

[53] HLA Hart, *The Concept of Law* (3rd ed, Oxford University Press 2012) 115–16, 258.

[54] A Pellet, 'L'adaptation du droit international aux besoins changeants de la société internationale' (2007) 329 RdC 9, 42.

[55] The relevance of courts and tribunals in shaping contemporary international law has been abundantly explored. Less attention, however, has been attracted by the ILC. In a collected work expressly dedicated to the new ways of producing international law, C Brölmann & Y Radi (eds), *Research Handbook on the Theory and Practice of International Lawmaking* (Edward Elgar 2016) many areas of international law have been examined such as environmental law and human rights; the creative role of international and domestic courts and tribunals and of monitoring bodies (M Tignino, 'Quasi-Judicial Bodies' 242). The ILC's new role did not attract many comments. The same lack of a specific interest emerges by looking at J d'Aspremont & S Besson (eds), *Oxford Handbook of the Sources of International Law* (Oxford University Press 2017); or at M Goldmann (n 2). On the contrary see S Villalpando, 'Gli strumenti della codificazione del diritto internazionale nell'età della codificazione *light*' in A Annoni, S Forlati & F Salerno (eds), *La codificazione nell'ordinamento internazionale e dell'unione europea* (Editoriale Scientifica 2019) 259.

the former commissioners of the ILC, the *very-visible college* of international lawyers.[56]

In order for something to become law in the new millennium, it does not need to pass through long and fraught negotiations, beholden to political positions that are too far apart and, by this time, nearly irreconcilable. When states and other entities involved in a dispute use the ILC's work product, the third party called upon to adjudicate specific disputes in the concrete can then grant final prescriptive power to an indication contained in a soft-law text or a text that stalled in the draft articles phase.[57] This route is ultimately more practical than reopening long and often fraught negotiations with the over 190 invited states, and faces less risk of compromise, or even failure. Not even references for a preliminary ruling are necessary, as Guillaume had predicted. The authority of law does not come from a multilateral effort, nor from a clear command of a rule, or from a theory of sources, but rather from a shared discourse about law, and a recognised authority charged to settle a dispute.

The success of the 2001 Articles on the Responsibility of States is illustrative and paved the road: if the work is useful and well done, there is an 'audience out there' ready to adopt it and implement it. Crawford and the ILC had put forward not guidelines, but rather articles – but the outcome is analogous – settling for codifying, rather than developing, international law, and leaving the issues of making the rules binding and any potential development of the law to others – particularly international courts and tribunals.

6 A Look at the Practice of International Courts and Tribunals

Under this new approach, draft articles and works of soft law and scholarship naturally flow into the work of international courts and tribunals. Courts and tribunals use some of the articles and conclusions

[56] As opposed to O Schachter, 'The Invisible College of International Lawyers' (1977–78) 72 NWULR 217; about one-third of the ICJ judges have previously been ILC members, compare MJ Aznar & E Methymaki, 'Article 2' in A Zimmermann & CJ Tams (eds), *The Statute of the International Court of Justice: A Commentary* (3rd ed, Oxford University Press 2019) 303.

[57] CM Chinkin, 'The Challenge of Soft Law: Development and Change in International Law' (1989) 38 ICLQ 850, 860, already observed the advantage offered by soft-law codifications, which is not given by the simplicity of its drafting (negotiations are as hard as for treaties), but in avoiding the further complication of the phases of approval ratification and entrance into force of international conventions. Similarly see also Tanzi (n 34) 154–55.

of the ILC as stating customary rules, or as subsidiary means in the sense of 38(1)(d) of the ICJ Statute.[58] They also use the conclusions of the ILC without qualification. In other cases, the ideas of the ILC are cited by the parties, but ignored by the court or tribunal. Leaving aside the briefs submitted by parties, which make references useful to make their cases, but looking only at the reasoning of courts and tribunals themselves, we can find some illustrative decisions.

As far as draft articles are concerned, along with the 2001 articles on the responsibility of states mentioned above (and their 1997 predecessors whose use in the *Gabčíkovo-Nagymaros* case[59] has been already widely commented),[60] we can also look at how the ICJ used the draft articles on diplomatic protection, produced by the ILC in 2007, in the *Diallo* case.[61] In that case, despite the fact that a provision put forward by the ILC drew criticism from some governments (Article 1),[62] the ICJ applied it as an expression of customary law.[63] To determine that something is customary law requires a review of the practice, under which the lack of homogeneity of the practice and lack of consensus among states ordinarily would not have allowed for the formulation of a customary rule. The same draft articles were also cited by an investment tribunal in 2014.[64]

One example of successful regulatory cooperation between the ILC and international tribunals involving soft law is the now consistent case law of investment tribunals with regard to the guiding principles on the unilateral declarations of states capable of creating legal obligations. These have been applied in various cases to interpret unilateral acts, although without

[58] Pellet & Müller (n 52) 914–15.

[59] *Case Concerning the Gabčíkovo-Nagymaros Project (Hungary/Slovakia)* (Judgment) [1997] ICJ Rep 7, 39–41 [50–53].

[60] Pellet & Müller (n 52) 914.

[61] *Ahmadou Sadio Diallo (Republic of Guinea v Democratic Republic of the Congo)* (Preliminary Objections) [2007] ICJ Rep 582 [39].

[62] ILC, 'Comments and Observations Received from Governments' (27 January, 3 & 12 April 2006) UN Doc A/CN.4/561 and Add 1–2, 37–38.

[63] *Ahmadou Sadio Diallo* 582 [39]: 'The Court will recall that under customary international law, as reflected in Article 1 of the draft Articles on Diplomatic Protection of the International Law Commission [...], diplomatic protection consists of the invocation by a State, through diplomatic action or other means of peaceful settlement, of the responsibility of another State for an injury caused by an internationally wrongful act of that State to a natural or legal person that is a national of the former State with a view to the implementation of such responsibility.' The ICJ then did not specify whether Article 11 of the same draft articles reflected customary international law [93].

[64] *Serafín García Armas, Karina García Gruber v Venezuela* (Decision on Jurisdiction of 15 December 2014) PCA Case No 2013-3 [173].

a declaration of customary law status.[65] One International Center for the Settlement of Investment Disputes (ICSID) tribunal, in the case *Total* v. *Argentina*, gave extensive consideration to the principles in question and, while it did not determine that they were customary law, dedicated an in-depth analysis to them, underscoring their relevance even when interpreting 'domestic normative acts relied upon by a foreign private investor'.[66]

Last, if we consider the scholarly activities of the ILC, in a very high number of cases the parties invoked study group reports in their briefs. Even if we only look at the reasoning of the judicial bodies themselves, it is clear that study groups, too, have had an impact on the activities of courts and tribunals. The study on the MFN clause, although brought to a close only recently (2015), has already been referred to extensively. The study was brought to bear, in particular, on the merits of a highly controversial issue, that is, the question of whether or not the MFN clause extends to compromissory clauses, starting with *Maffezini* v. *Spain*.[67]

It is not surprising, therefore, that international investment tribunals immediately latched onto the study and incorporated it into their reasoning. For example, in the *A11Y Ltd* v. *Czech Republic* decision (2017), the tribunal concisely observed: 'The Tribunal is of the view that an MFN clause can, a priori, apply to dispute settlement. The Final Report of the ILC Study Group on the Most-Favoured-Nation clause is instructive in this respect.'[68] In the award *Le Chèque Déjeuner* v. *Hungary*, two key passages of the Tribunal's reasoning on the interpretation of the MFN clause are dedicated entirely to quoting and commenting upon the ILC report.[69] Even the dissenting opinion by Marcelo Kohen attached to the

65 *Mobil Corporation Venezuela et al v Venezuela* (Decision on Jurisdiction of 10 June 2010) ICSID Case No ARB/07/27 [89]; *CEMEX Caracas Investments BV e CEMEX Caracas II Investments BV v Venezuela* (Decision on Jurisdiction of 30 December 2010) ICSID Case No ARB/08/15 [81–82]; *Chevron Corporation and Texaco Petroleum Corporation v The Republic of Ecuador* (Second Partial Award of 30 August 2018) PCA Case No 2009-23 [7.84].

66 *Total SA v Argentine Republic* (Decision on Liability of 27 December 2010) ICSID Case No ARB/04/1 [132], see in general [131–34].

67 *Emilio Agustín Maffezini v Kingdom of Spain* (Award of 25 January 2000) ICSID Case No ARB/97/7; M Paparinskis, 'MFN Clauses and International Dispute Settlement: Moving beyond Maffezini and Plama?' (2011) 26(2) ICSID Review 14.

68 *A11Y Ltd v Czech Republic* (Decision on Jurisdiction of 9 February 2017) ICSID Case No UNCT/15/1 [95–96]; see also [97] which uses the final report of the study group to confirm the proposed interpretation of a clause.

69 *Le Chèque Déjeuner and CD Holding Internationale v Hungary* (Decision on Preliminary Issues of Jurisdiction of 3 March 2016) ICSID Case No ARB/13/35 [165–66] & 209–10.

decision is substantially built around references to the ILC report on the MFN clause.[70]

The study on fragmentation, published in 2006, attracted a great deal of scholarly attention, and a less enthusiastic reception by courts and tribunals. Nonetheless, it is easy to find examples in which they refer to it. In the annulment decision *Tulip* v. *Turkey*, for instance, an ICSID Annulment Committee formulated the proper way that human rights obligations should be integrated into the interpretation of a state contract through extensive reference to the ILC report on fragmentation.[71] Moreover, in the award on jurisdiction of the *RREEF* v. *Spain* case, the tribunal referred extensively to the scholarly work on fragmentation.[72]

Not all the work produced by the ILC in its 'new era' has met with success. One example is its work on reservations, which culminated in 2011, after nearly twenty years, both in a set of guidelines (soft law) and in a thorough scholarly document (the guide). These documents have had practically no impact on international case law. Neither the ICJ nor the investment tribunals have used it, and the Strasbourg Court has only mentioned it in a single case, already eight years old.[73]

The work of the ILC can also have effects that are not as easily detected as the effects of a citation: its influence may remain in the form of an undercurrent, or an international court may prefer to apply customary law as it is described by the ILC without making explicit reference to the work of the ILC itself. Consider, for example, the 2012 case *Habré*, in which the ICJ ruled on the *erga omnes* nature of the convention's obligations forbidding torture. The ICJ did not mention the articles on state responsibility, but only the customary international law on that

[70] *Venezuela US, SRL v Venezuela* (Interim Award on Jurisdiction on the Respondent Objection to Jurisdiction *Ratione Voluntatis* of 26 July 2016) CPA Case No 2013–34, Dissenting Opinion of Professor Marcelo G Kohen.

[71] *Tulip Real Estate and Development Netherlands BV v Turkey* (Decision on Annulment of 30 December 2015) ICSID Case No ARB/11/28 [86–92]. In particular, at [88–89], observed:

> The ILC has discussed Article 31(3)(c) of the VCLT extensively in its Fragmentation Report. In doing so, its Study Group has referred to that provision as a 'master key' to the house of international law. . . . The ILC Study Group has rejected any suggestion that tribunals should restrict themselves to the treaty upon which their jurisdiction is based and which constitutes the treaty under dispute.

[72] *RREEF Infrastructure (GP) Limited and RREEF Pan-European Infrastructure Two Lux Sàrl v Spain* (Decision on Jurisdiction of 6 June 2016) ICSID Case No ARB/13/30 [82].

[73] *Toniolo v San Marino and Italy* ECtHR App No 44853/10 (26 June 2012).

topic.[74] The reasoning, however, clearly reflects the formulation laid out in the ILC's work.

The decision whether or not to make explicit reference to the source of inspiration for a given rule clearly falls to the discretion of the adjudicating body, and reveals that the choice to specify the 'places' in which certain choices are formed and crystallised falls under the policy for legitimising its own work product that a judicial body decides to adopt. At the same time, it also reveals that the influence of the ILC's work cannot be assessed by merely tallying up explicit references, but may also extend beyond them.

7 The 'Principle of Quotability', the Relevance of Official Scholarship and the Importance of an Interpretive Approach Favourable to the *travaux* of the ILC

On the whole, we can conclude that, during this time of transformation of international society, the ILC is orienting its activities toward 'dialogue' with states, other parties and international judicial bodies during a dispute and aims less to elaborate draft conventions. As for the works dedicated to the sources of international law, unity is not reached through an order, nor a shared bedrock of values, but rather through the construction of a common technical language available to international actors and courts, and through reason, which we all still have in common in a fragmented world.

As for the drafting of material rules of international law, the ILC suggests, litigating entities propose, and the courts pick up what they find to be of value and crystallise it into a customary rule.

The ILC's shift from being prescriptive in its work to being scholarly and descriptive, in which the commission decided to address chiefly courts and tribunals instead of elaborating new international conventions, created the need for the commission's activities to attain 'quotable' results. Quotability means generating an expression of the law (in the subtle form of guidelines or the stronger form of draft articles) that provides a third party – a state, a private entity invoking the protection of a treaty, a judge or arbitrator – with a reference which, notwithstanding the fact that it is not necessarily binding, is succinct, clear and immediately applicable.

[74] *Questions Relating to the Obligation to Prosecute or Extradite (Belgium v Senegal)* (Merits) [2012] ICJ Rep 422, 449–50 [68–69].

In light of this, we may draw three final observations. First, even when the ILC does not intend to create draft articles, but aims at articulating soft law, it is important that the commission not fall into overly descriptive passages in an attempt to avoid making choices unsupported by practice, resulting in tools too unwieldy to apply. When it comes to the documents' quotability, the ability to make clear choices in the face of non-homogeneous practice is more important than the exhaustiveness of the studies. It is, above all, in this regard that the activity of the ILC must not spill over into works that fail to take a position on controversial topics. The 2011 *Guide to Practice on Reservations to Treaties*, which has had very little impact so far in international litigation, is illustrative.[75] The more the ILC aims to make its work exhaustive, at the expense of choosing preferable solutions, the more difficult it is for those who adjudicate cases to make use of the conclusions it adopts.

Second, it is important for the ILC to address issues that are relevant on the practical (judicial, especially) plane, and not only those related to the general framework of the sources and their interpretation. Its study of the MFN clause is emblematic here. While its scope was more limited than that of other recently undertaken studies on sources, it had an immediate impact on international arbitral awards because it stepped in to provide order and clarity in an issue on which investment arbitrations had run aground with conflicting solutions. From this point of view, at the risk of making a false prediction, highly practical studies on hotly debated issues seem destined to have a greater future impact than scholarly analysis on, say, general principles of law, which would serve only the function of offering an official context for assessing international law sources.

Third, the existence of ILC quotable guidelines or articles spares adjudicators from the heavy work of demonstrating the existence of widespread practice and *opinio juris* and becomes a practical tool to find a guiding legal principal orienting the decision of the adjudicator, and/or giving legitimacy to it – a reference to an external authority is always more legitimate than taking what would appear to be an arbitrary position by adjudicators.

However, the principle, guideline or draft article can be recalled and applied without an extended analysis of the possible nuances of the text

[75] See, however, M Gervasi, 'The ILC Guide to Practice on Reservations to Treaties Put to the Test in the *Hossam Ezzat* Case before the African Commission on Human and Peoples' Rights' (2019) 102 RivDirInt 109.

only if the litigating parties are not contesting it. In case of disagreement, the customary nature of the non-binding written provision requires the interpreter *not* to start from the text or the object and purpose, *à la* VCLT, but rather from the international practice generating it. Unfortunately, it is not common to find a discussion of the appropriate interpretive method of the non-binding provisions of the ILC in international rulings. In the already mentioned *Diallo* judgment of 2007, an approach keen on customary law would have pushed the ICJ toward an investigation of the *travaux préparatoires* of that provision, that is, the practice analysed by the ILC and the reactions of governments to it. This would have brought to light that the provision was hotly contested and far from being customary. But the ICJ in that case did not follow the rationale behind restatements of customary rules, but merely looked at the text of a rule, as if it were dealing with a conventional rule, binding for the parties, whose text was sufficiently clear. While this attitude can be accepted as an expression of the deciding power of courts, it does not reflect the customary nature of the process leading to it.

9

Beyond Formalism

Reviving the Legacy of Sir Henry Maine for Customary International Law

ANDREAS HADJIGEORGIOU

1 Introduction

Sir Henry Maine is a curious figure.[1] During his time, he was a most famous legal theorist, whose name and fame did not manage to survive the test of time. Nevertheless, his works gave rise to a legacy whose revival can prove invaluable for international law (IL) and, more specifically, customary international law (CIL). This is especially the case as it concerns ontological questions.

While we live in a 'post-ontological' era, 'where the existence of a genuinely legal international order can be safely presumed',[2] not all ontological concerns have disappeared; rather they have shifted. Whereas IL is taken as a 'given', questions still remain about its *genesis* and the place CIL holds within it. Some, for example, deny the existence of CIL as law properly so called, while others urge IL to rid itself of the concept of CIL altogether. Further, this position intertwines with a *formalist* perspective – that is, that law is always the product of *formal design*[3] or *formal ascertainment.*[4]

[1] For an overview of Maine's work and how it affected later generations see A Hadjigeorgiou, 'The Legacy of Sir Henry Maine in the 21st Century' (2020) 34 Noesis 159.

[2] C Pavel and D Lefkowitz, 'Skeptical Challenges to International Law' (2018) 13(8) Philosophy Compass 1, 2.

[3] Austin for example, claimed that law is the product of the sovereign's formal design, shaped out of legislation enforced as commands, and always based upon his own wishes and whims; see J Austin, *Province of Jurisprudence Determined* (John Murray 1832) 6, 18.

[4] Ascertainment holds true whether it is a product of judicial judgment or codification. The Realists for example, claimed that while law is a product of the formal ascertainment of what are otherwise mere customary rules to situations by judges. Of course, it should be mentioned, that most of the Realist schemes still cannot account for international law as

Accordingly, formalism in its moderate form treats formal sources, documents and/or proclamations as 'better' tools for both (a) the preservation of existing rules of CIL[5] and (b) the 'creation' of new legal rules. At its more extreme, formalism purports the view that (c) IL (or even CIL) finds its *genesis* only in formal sources, documents or proclamations.[6] While some formalisation is undeniably helpful and even necessary, we should be more critical of this formalist paradigm. Moreover, these perspectives touch both upon the *genesis* of IL, but also on its *evolution* – that is, how law began and how it ought to be further developed. These positions set the wider themes of the chapter. By reviving the legacy of Sir Henry Maine, it seeks to give a new perspective on the *genesis* of IL as primarily CIL, as well as a new vision of how it should/could be further developed; a vision that goes beyond mere formalism.

2 The Curious Case of Sir Henry Maine

Sir Henry Maine gave jurisprudence a curious spin, one that ended up awarding him the Chair of Jurisprudence in Oxford (a chair later held by Hart and Dworkin). More than that, though, as the University of Oxford's website testifies,[7] the chair was established as an effort to attract Maine to Oxford, while accommodating his 'peculiar genius'.[8] While jurisprudence has always been a discipline built upon the intersection of law and philosophy; Maine redefined it.

His work attacked the philosophical approaches to law of his time. His claim was that they were based upon speculative narratives of how law began; designed to explain domestic legal systems as we experience them

non-law, mainly because such courts lack centralised enforcement and, thus, coercion to back up their decisions; see for example K Llewellyn and A Hoebel, *The Cheyenne Way Conflict and Case Law in Primitive Jurisprudence* (Oxford University Press 1941).

5 The Vienna Convention, the Hague Conventions of 1899 and 1907, as well as the Geneva Conventions, are good examples.

6 This comes in contrast with the more traditional view that CIL (or international law in general) finds its genesis in practices.

7 '[Although] today's worldwide association of Oxford jurisprudence with a philosophical approach to law stems mainly from the appointment of HLA Hart to the chair in 1952. … The Professorship of Jurisprudence was established in 1869 to attract to Oxford Sir Henry Maine, already famous for his Ancient Law and his work in India', see Legal Philosophy in Oxford, 'About Us' <www2.law.ox.ac.uk/jurisprudence/history.htm> accessed on 1 March 2021.

8 This is a phrase used by his successor Pollock, in his inaugural lecture in Oxford, which was devoted to Maine; see F Pollock, *Oxford Lectures and Other Discourses* (Macmillan 1890) 147–68.

in isolation at a given point in time (the famous sovereign-legislative structures). Instead, Maine suggested that any conceptualisation of law should be based upon a solid historical understanding of law's genesis and evolution.

> The mistake which they committed is therefore analogous to the error of one who, in investigating the laws of the material universe, should commence by contemplating the existing physical world as a whole, instead of beginning with the particles which are its simplest ingredients. ... It would seem antecedently that we ought to commence with the simplest social forms in a state as near as possible to their rudimentary condition. *In other words, if we followed the course usual in such inquiries, we should penetrate as far up as we could in the history of primitive societies.*[9]

Hence, Maine's work is not a complete theory of law, but rather blueprints for redefining the way law is philosophically apprehended within jurisprudence, by firmly relating law to its empirical, socio-historical dimensions. Maine's legal history paves the way for something we today coin as *interdisciplinary*. This enquiry led Maine to understand law as an evolutionary phenomenon and this account holds an astounding amount of invaluable observations, which have yet to be applied to the international legal order.

3 The Genesis of (International) Law as Customary (International) Law

Maine's most general theme is that law should not be seen as a static, externally imposed system of commands and/or judgments backed by threats; nor should it be seen as a 'new' nor 'recent' phenomenon. History makes it clear that order and law predate formal organisation, sovereigns or courts. Law's existence stretches from ancient times. Further, even domestically, law began *as custom*.

The simplest truism lies in the fact that later formally ascertained law was itself based upon pre-existing customs, the existence and authority of which was accounted for independently of the persons who came to proclaim them. Even more, the first formal proclamations were not legislative acts, but codifications of *customary law*.[10] Thus, custom is not merely a source of law, it is the first source. From this perspective,

[9] H Maine, *Ancient Law: Its Connection with the Early History of Society and Its Relation to Modern Ideas* (John Murray 1861) 118–19.

[10] Maine rightly points to the XII Tables of Rome as his primary example.

social order is the product of custom, or rather an interconnected network of customary practices, which manifest as one organic whole.[11]

Law, as customary law, is merely one functional subpart of this greater whole. This evolutionary idea was slowly cultivated into *interactionism*.[12] Order and law appear first as custom, which arises freely and unassisted through the simultaneous interactions of various individuals.[13] While law is organically connected to the greater customary network, it is at the same time analytically delineable.[14] Various theorists have made *interactionist* conceptualisations of the international legal order;[15] however the current section would rather build upon this idea using another theme.

As Maine observed, from the beginning of time individuals were not dispersed/unconnected, they were organised. However, they were not organised in societies/communities of individuals as one would expect; rather individuals were organised in societies of institutions, the primary of which was the family. These family institutions were equal units in terms of authority, and the only thing that stood over and above them was customary law – the thing that constituted them. Within the family institution the 'law' was the word of the father, but as Maine wisely reminds us:

> Society in primitive times was not what it is assumed to be at present, a collection of *individuals*. In fact, and in the view of the men who composed it, it was *an aggregation of families*. The contrast may be most forcibly expressed by saying that the *unit* of an ancient society was the Family, of a modern society the Individual. . . . Men are first seen distributed in perfectly insulated groups, held together by obedience to the

[11] Malinowski later came to label this whole as 'culture'; see B Malinowski, *A Scientific Theory of Culture* (The University of North Carolina Press 1944).

[12] Fuller is generally known for paving this way for this idea, although he built a lot upon Maine's work, see L Fuller, 'Human Interaction and the Law' (1969) 14(1) AM J Juris 1; further, Postema is most known for popularising this idea within general jurisprudence, see G Postema, 'Implicit Law' (1994) 13(3) L& Phil 361.

[13] Hayek, another interesting figure within Maine's legacy, describes illuminatingly this process of how customs slowly come to function and come to be understood as law; see F Hayek, *Law, Legislation and Liberty: A New Statement of the Liberal Principles of Justice and Political Economy* (University of Chicago Press 1979).

[14] This claim was first made in such clear terms in B Malinowski, *Crime and Custom in Savage Society* (Kegan Paul 1926).

[15] For an interesting application to international law see J Brunnée & S Toope, *Legitimacy and Legality in International Law: An Interactional Account* (Cambridge University Press 2010). For another interesting application (partly) to international law see W van der Burg, *The Dynamics of Law and Morality: A Pluralist Account of Legal Interactionism* (Ashgate 2014).

> parent. Law is the parent's word, *but it is not yet in the condition of those themistes [judgments of justice/customary law].*[16]

Customary law is, then, law properly so because that is the part of the greater normative system which organises individuals in the institutional units to which they belong; the units that they themselves, others and society at large understands them through. From this perspective, the reason the word of father (within each family institution) is not yet on par with the legality of customary law becomes apparent: it is customary law which dictates that all individuals, in order to be recognised members of the community, must belong to a family unit. Further, not every family unit will qualify. It is, thus, customary law which dictates that all recognised units must be connected through common lineage. It is also customary law which designates the word of the father as an authority within them. This becomes a truism once it is realised that in other societies (customary) law designates the word of the *mother*.[17] As such, without assimilating within our perspective customary law, we are unable to understand a society in the same way that it makes sense of its own self and structure.

This has its own conceptual connection to international and CIL. Whereas looking at CIL from within domestic legal systems, it gives the impression that it is a deficient, problematic or an odd instance of law;[18] through Maine's evolutionary perspective, these characterisations disappear. Law began internationally, in the same way it began domestically, as customary law. Further, in the same way domestically customary law functioned to establish a society of family-institutions (within which the word of the 'father' was law), so did CIL constitute an international society of 'state-institutions' – within which the word of the 'sovereign' is law. Maine was quite aware of this:

> Ancient jurisprudence, if a perhaps deceptive comparison may be employed, may be likened to International Law, filling nothing, as it were, excepting the interstices between the great groups which are the atoms of society. In a community so situated, the legislation of assemblies

[16] Maine (n 9) 126. Emphasis added.

[17] See Malinowski (n 14) 75.

[18] See for example J Goldsmith & E Posner, *The Limits of International Law* (Oxford University Press 2005); A Carty, *The Decay of International Law* (Manchester University Press 1986); A Carty, 'The Need to Be Rid of the Idea of General Customary Law' (2018) 112 AJIL Unbound; J d'Aspremont, 'The Decay of Modern Customary International Law in Spite of Scholarly Heroism' in G Capaldo (ed), *The Global Yearbook of International Law and Jurisprudence 2015* (Oxford University Press 2016).

> and the jurisdiction of Courts reaches only to the heads of families, and to every other individual the rule of conduct is the law of his home, of which his Parent is the legislator.[19]

Moreover, as already noted, customary law also works to establish these atoms. After all, these family-institutions domestically, as these state-institutions internationally, are not entities which exist, or can be understood, independently of rules which first arise customarily. Rather, these state-institutions are *conceptual constructions;* the result of various rules working together. These include rules that states should be attached to a territory, together with rules which define such territories. Rules that dictate that each state should speak with only one voice and that only one voice from within each state can be accepted as authoritative at a time. It also concerns rules which attribute actions done by individuals to a 'state', etc.

Without such common rules to synchronise how and what various individuals see/understand as 'states', there could be no consensus that 'states' exist, let alone a whole international community of states. Further, rules such as these need by definition to be voluntarily accepted, and need to remain unchallenged, in order to operate. It is at such a foundational level that we must primarily situate our conceptualisation of CIL; at the level where a community constitutes itself freely and unassisted. This nicely brings to mind a quote from Philip Allott's 'The Concept of International Law':

> The social function of international law is the same as that of other forms of law. It is a mode of the self-constituting of a society, namely the international society of the whole human race, the society of all societies. Law is a system of legal relations which condition social action to serve the common interest. ... National legal systems (including private international law) are part of the international legal system. International law takes a customary form, in which society orders itself through its experience of self-ordering, and a legislative form (treaties). The state of international law at any time reflects the degree of development of international society.[20]

From this perspective, sovereignty itself is itself constructed through CIL. Maine proposed this conceptualisation as early as 1888, in his posthumous book on *International Law*: 'What really enables states to exercise their Sovereignty in this way is nothing but the legal rule itself.'[21]

[19] Maine (n 9) 167.

[20] P Allott, 'The Concept of International Law' (1999) 10 EJIL 31.

[21] H Maine, *International Law* (John Murray 1890) 65.

This rule can be nothing else but a CIL rule. Maine highlights the primacy we must grant CIL over the state units which are constituted, and regulated, by it. This point of view bears close resemblance to what Kelsen argued about three decades later. It is also a perspective argued by Hart, Maine's successor in Oxford. In the last chapter of his *Concept*, Hart writes:

> For if in fact we find that there exists among states a given form of international authority, the sovereignty of states is to that extent limited, and it has just the extent which the rules allow. . . . Hence we can only know which states are sovereign, and what the extent of their sovereignty is, when we know what the rules are. . . . The question for municipal law is: what is the extent of the supreme legislative authority recognized in this system? For international law it is: what is the maximum area of autonomy which the rules allow to states? . . . [In this way,] there is no way of knowing what sovereignty states have, till we know what the forms of international law are and whether or not they are mere empty forms.[22]

This analysis further highlights that CIL and domestic legal systems, at the most foundational level, are organically connected and work together to bring to life these state-institutions. In the same way individuals in ancient society used custom and customary law to constitute themselves as a society of family-institutions, so have individuals internationally used custom and CIL to constitute themselves as a society of state-institutions – and the two interconnect. State institutions internally came to employ a similar hierarchical structure to what was employed internally by the family institutions, as a prerequisite for participating in this international community.

Thus, the communities which failed to take on this internal hierarchical structure, were historically not understood to be real units of the international community and have failed to contribute to its development. Customary international law dictated a greater vision that each unit had to follow both internally and externally in order to 'count' as a true member of the international community. A unit which did not adhere, would not be coerced, but rather ostracised. Thus, CIL's efficacy rests on the fact that it contains the most agreed upon, and desirable, scheme of international co-existing.

As such, the ontological critiques that CIL has traditionally faced from the perspective of domestic legal systems seem to rest on an ahistorical understanding of the genesis of law. Further, this highlights another

[22] HLA Hart, *The Concept of Law* (2nd ed, Clarendon Press 1994) 224.

interesting argument. Without suggesting that international courts merely interpret and apply existing IL and CIL, to the extent that such courts deal with a pre-existing international community made up (at a minimum) of states, this suggests that an effective CIL is already in operation. It is CIL which (at the most foundational level) constitutes the international society – within which such judgments make sense.

4 The Formalisation of Customary (International) Law

Rather than a special, or a defective, case of law, customary law reveals itself as the most fundamental and primary instance of law. Even the oligarchies, which later came to power, recognised its primacy, since even they only claimed to hold *knowledge* of customary law:

> Before the invention of writing, and during the infancy of the art, an aristocracy invested with judicial privileges formed the only expedient by which accurate preservation of the customs of the race or tribe could be at all approximated to. . . . The epoch of Customary Law, and of its custody by a privileged order, is a very remarkable one. . . . [Nevertheless] what the juristical oligarchy claims is to monopolise the *knowledge* of the laws.[23]

Exactly because this customary organisation was more complex than lay individuals could comprehend, is why oligarchies were vested with such power. As Maine notes, this power was surely abused, but it still did not amount to Austinian command-sovereignty. Nevertheless, because there was abuse, once writing was invented societies wrote down, codified and (thus) formalised first those customary rules which were law. The XII Tables of Rome were Maine's primary example and Hart agreed: 'In Rome, according to tradition, the XII Tables were set up on bronze tablets in the market-place in response to the demands of the Plebeians for publication of an authoritative text of the law. From the meagre evidence available *it seems unlikely that the XII Tables departed much from the traditional customary rules*.'[24] Nevertheless, while this formalisation undeniably had its benefits this had its own adverse effects:

> *When primitive law has once been embodied in a Code, there is an end to what may be called its spontaneous development.* Henceforward the changes effected in it, if effected at all, are effected deliberately and from without. It is impossible to suppose that the customs of any race or tribe remained unaltered during the whole of the long – in some instances the

[23] Maine (n 9) 12. Emphasis added.
[24] Hart (n 22) 292. Emphasis added.

> immense – interval between their declaration by a patriarchal monarch and their publication in writing. . . . It would be unsafe too to affirm that no part of the alteration was effected deliberately. But from the little we know of the progress of law during this period, we are justified in assuming that set purpose had the very smallest share in producing change.[25]

What Maine suggests is that insofar as law was primarily customary, it was continuously changing alongside society, driven by new social needs and a changing environment. That is, spontaneously developing *through practice* and always being 'up-to-date', in the following way. The two primary tools that practitioners use to familiarise someone to a customary practice are examples (of occurrences of the practice) and rules[26] – usually unwritten, that is customary. The two work together. As Wittgenstein reminds us, both rules and examples interrelate to properly triangulate meaning: 'Not only rules, but also examples are needed for establishing a practice. Our rules leave loop-holes open, and the practice has to speak for itself.'[27]

Thus, while rule-governed practices might arise without the use of explicitly formulated rules, rules would still necessarily arise in order to (i) introduce/communicate the practice to others, (ii) settle differences and (iii) better preserve the practice in the participants' collective memory. As such, at a conceptual level, interpreting customary practices is *first* the process of conceptualising rules *out of* an activity, and *second* the process of relating those rules to examples of it as a practice.

Thus, the two, rules and examples, intertwine; however while the rules are customary, examples of the practice take primacy. For a practitioner, the rules one employs in relation to the practice are accurate, and thus acceptable, if they properly explicate at least parts of the practice (i.e., the behaviour of those who engage in it). Nevertheless, whereas the rules remain the same, the practice implicitly grows and changes (even without the awareness of those who engage with it) as it learns to respond better to the same needs, or it begins to respond to new needs.

However, exactly because on the customary level the practice takes the forefront, as the practice grows, existing rules that once 'fitted', slowly begin to seem inaccurate or outdated. From there, new customary rules arise which might describe new or changed parts of the practice, even though the rules themselves might be perceived as 'new (or better)

25 ibid 21. Emphasis added.

26 Hart presented a similar analysis, although he overvalued the independency of rules in relation to examples; see Hart (n 22) 125.

27 L Wittgenstein, *Philosophical Investigations* (Macmillan 1953) [139].

descriptions' of the 'same-old' unchanged practice. The codification and, thus, formalisation of rules, though, severs its relation to the practice and 'freezes' rules in time.

While the practice (or examples of it) might still be used to interpret formalised rules; the evolution of the practice can no longer impact upon the validity of the rules. Whereas at the customary level the practice legitimises the rules, once rules are formalised, the situation reverses. In turn, the formalised rules might stop the customary practice from further evolving and, thus, from better responding to existing or changing needs. The same process applies to the formalisation of CIL. As Thirlway observes:

> The difficulty is of course that customary law develops of its own accord, without there being any need for States to do more than continue their day-to-day relations, whereas a treaty regime can only be changed by deliberate act of the parties. Furthermore, as Professor Baxter has observed, 'The clear formulation of rules in a codification treaty and the assent of a substantial number of States may have the effect of arresting change and flux in the state of customary international law. Although the treaty 'photographs' the state of the law at the time of its entry into force as to individual States, it continues, so long as States remain parties to it, to speak in terms of the present.'[28]

Thirlway goes even further to note that codification might have a halting effect upon the customary practice of even non-parties to the treaty.

> Thus so far as the States non-parties to the treaty are concerned, for whom the codifying treaty is only evidence of the state of customary law at a certain moment in time, a 'photograph' in Prof. Baxter's vivid expression, other evidence, in particular of practice since the treaty, may show that for such States the law has not stood still: but the treaty will remain strong evidence, not easy to controvert, that the law is still as the treaty states it, so that the treaty will undoubtedly have a freezing effect on the customary law even for States non-parties to it.[29]

Even interpretation of codified *customary* rules might completely detach from the underlying practice, as practitioners get overtaken with a textualist outlook. Such a zeal might even alter the underlying practice. On the customary level interpreting rules happens necessarily in relation to the practice which legitimises the rules and, thus, remains embedded

[28] H Thirlway, *International Customary Law and Codification: An Examination of the Continuing Role of Custom in the Present Period of Codification of International Law* (AW Sijthoff 1972) 125.

[29] ibid 126.

within the greater social/cultural whole. The interpretation of codified/ formalised rules, on the other hand, gets overtaken with other things which cannot operate on the customary level.

First, there are the specific words chosen to express the rule, then there is the section in which the rule appears within the overall treaty (or code), as well as the meaning that flows out of a systemic reading of a specific rule with the overall whole. Second, there is the matter of the 'author(s)', their imagined intentions, and an aura of being 'faithful' to that original plan. This could not be truer for IL, where textualist dogmatism is the norm,[30] to the expense of developing competing methods. As Peat and Windsor observe:

> Interpretation in international law has traditionally been understood as a process of assigning meaning to texts with the objective of establishing rights and obligations. . . . As new insights on the practice and process of interpretation have proliferated in other fields, international law and international lawyers have continued to grant an imprimatur to rule-based formalism.[31] . . . [Thus,] the focus on rule-based approaches to interpretation, exemplified by the VCLT, means that international law lags behind other fields in which interpretive issues are examined in a more nuanced and theoretically informed fashion.[32]

Even where the object of interpretation is the codified rules of a customary practice, the sociological roots the content of the rules have with that customary practice (which is itself organically connected to a greater social whole) often get overlooked. This is of course the result of a fierce debate about the formal meaning of the *text*. As Bianchi wisely notes: '[T]he shackles of both formalism and radical critical approaches have scleroticised the debate by focusing on opposite, yet equally sterile, stances that refuse to take duly into account the more sociological aspects of interpretive processes.'[33]Maine's history cautions that while this formalist-culture arose 'normally' in the development of all societies, in most cases its benefits did not outweigh the problems it brought with

[30] See F Zarbiyev, 'A Genealogy of Textualism in Treaty Interpretation' in A Bianchi, D Peat & M Windsor (eds), *Interpretation in International Law* (Oxford University Press 2018) 251.

[31] See D Peat & M Windsor, 'Introduction' in A Bianchi, D Peat & M Windsor (eds), *Interpretation in International Law* (Oxford University Press 2018) 3.

[32] ibid 8.

[33] A Bianchi, 'Textual Interpretation and (International) Law Reading: The Myth of (in) Determinacy and the Genealogy of Meaning' in P Bekker, R Dolzer, M Waibel & D Vagts (eds), *Making Transnational Law Work in the Global Economy: Essays in Honour of Detlev Vagts* (Cambridge University Press 2010) 53.

it. Rather, this formalism imposed a 'staticness' and promoted law's detachment from the greater social whole, which for most societies proved fatal. Only those societies which managed to find ways to continuously alter and evolve their formalised law survived. Thus, Maine focused on those agencies which the 'progressive' societies used to develop their formalised customary law.

Before we say a word about these agencies, this evolutionary outlook challenges us to ponder about law's formalist turn(s). Rather than following the total-formalism domestic legal systems exhibit, the international legal order could follow a more moderate alternative where formalist elements are strategically employed to *supplement,* rather than replace, custom and CIL. By total-formalism I mean a state where (i) codification stops customary law from growing/evolving, (ii) custom is prevented from yielding new legal norms and (iii) from taking away legality from outdated ones.

This can be prevented by following what I shall call a 'strategic-formalisation', which involves a number of interrelated tenets. Despite their deficiencies, custom and CIL are more robust and concrete in producing order and the norms they produce do not suffer from any legitimacy concerns.[34] Further, uncodified CIL can be most advantageous in certain instances[35] and, thus, codification of CIL should be done selectively – primarily in the areas where practices have 'matured' enough and exist in a rather stable environment. Further, these codifications should not be seen as replacements of CIL but as supplements.

This means that codified customary rules should be interpreted closely with the customary practice that underlies them and should be used as aids to properly interpret the practice as well as the function it performs within the greater social whole. It further means that customary practice

[34] Hayek describes the differences between customary and posited/legislated/formally designed rules. He contrasts the two orders that can grow out of each kind of rule as grown versus made order (or also as 'cosmos' and 'taxis'). His most interesting observation is that grown orders can grow larger and accommodate much higher complexity than made orders, making them more valuable for human societies. Further, in the case of customary rules the question 'what makes this legitimately *our* rule' does not arise; see Hayek (n 13) 35.

[35] While space precludes us from dealing further with this, interesting arguments towards this position can be found in the works of Carter who fiercely (and successfully) fought *against* the codification of common law in New York. His claim was that uncodified, customary law can serve society much better than a code, as change happens slowly and robustly while ensuring maximum flexibility. See JC Carter, *The Provinces of the Written and the Unwritten Law* (Banks and Bros 1889); JC Carter, *Law: Its Origin, Growth, and Function* (The Knickerbocker Press 1907).

should be allowed to fill gaps or uncertainties within treaties by producing new customary rules. It also means that we should keep an eye out for the state of the customary practice, and the direction of its development, even after codification. The developments of custom and CIL remain relevant to law even in situations where it is contrary to established law. As Thirlway suggests:

> [W]hen custom *praeter legem* begins, as a result of social development, so to encroach on the existing law's domain, as to verge on the *contra legem*, it can nonetheless be regarded, in the light of social development, as still only *praeter legem*, and as tacit law-making so as to effect a repeal. . . . This argument, it is suggested, remains a correct picture of how custom can develop law beyond, and eventually contrary to, a codifying instrument. . . . It is the increasing number of cases in which the codified law 'does not fit', in which it is natural and proper to apply a different rule, which eventually gives the new rule the status of law enabling it to override the codified law, on the general principle that *lex posterior derogat priori*. . . . Thus there can be little doubt that law deriving from the provisions of a multilateral codifying treaty can be modified by a subsequent general practice constitutive of international custom.[36]

As such, CIL should not only be allowed to exist *next* to formalised versions of itself, but under certain circumstances it might be valuable to allow CIL to exist/develop even *contra* formal law. Custom can not only invalidate existing law, but it might (a) evolve in a different version of itself or (b) create CIL different from what was formally envisioned/agreed. This perspective gives a conceptual and an ontological primacy to CIL. In this way, Maine's perspective forces us to consider as a viable alternative, what Thirlway posited as a prediction:

> [S]o far from supplanting customary law, and reducing its field of operation to a minimum, the codifying of great tracts of international law will, on account of the practical and political difficulties of amending multilateral treaties, whether codifying or otherwise, give over the development of international law almost entirely into the hands of custom, operating upon and beyond the codifying treaties.[37]

This should not be taken to mean that IL should be merely CIL, rather, we should seek to requalify the position CIL holds within the greater matrix of elements which compose IL over and above CIL. This is a viable

[36] Thirlway (n 28) 131–32.
[37] ibid 146.

position because, despite its various other developments, IL still remains primarily CIL. Again, Thirlway points to a similar position:

> [A] 'code' of international law produced in the form of multilateral treaty is, except insofar as it represents or becomes customary law, a code of obligations accepted by the States parties to the treaty, but not law. If the field covered by the treaty were one which was more or less unregulated by custom, and regulated in detail by the treaty, the consequence would be that in that field the only 'law' between the parties would be the single rule '*pacta sunt servanda*'.[38]

In this spirit, the last part of this examination will focus on drafting out some first steps towards reconceptualising the interrelations between certain IL components. The aim will be to place CIL at the forefront and find ways to preserve and supplement its operation rather than replacing it. While formal elements will be strategically employed, this scheme escapes formalism by not aiming to alter (or formalise) the primarily customary nature of the international legal order.

5 The Development of Customary (International) Law

While the formalisation of customary law proved fatal for most societies, Maine focused on those societies that found ways to continuously alter and, thus, 'update' their formalised customary law. Maine calls these agencies of change: 'A general proposition of some value may be advanced with respect to the agencies by which Law is brought into harmony with society. These instrumentalities seem to me to be three in number, Legal Fictions, Equity, and Legislation. Their historical order is that in which I have placed them.'[39] While legislation, as the deliberate making of a rule, would seem to be the most obvious agent of change, it was the last to appear. Each agent drastically altered the legal practice, enabling it to adjust better to the changing social environment it was embedded in. As such, each was a sign of progress and brought law closer to systematisation. We should not be surprised to find both legal fictions and bodies of equity within IL.

While IL surely lacks the kind of legislation that can be found domestically, this clearly signifies that, despite its mainly customary nature, IL is more developed than mere CIL. Of course, exactly because these agents were employed in a state of total-formalism, as a way to override outdated

[38] ibid.
[39] Maine (n 9) 25.

formalised customary law, they produced new formalised rules which did not necessarily correlate with underlying customary practices. Nevertheless, their relationship can still be amended.

5.1 *Legal Fictions*

> I employ the expression 'Legal Fiction' to signify any assumption which conceals, or affects to conceal, the fact that a rule of law has undergone alteration, its letter remaining unchanged, its operation being modified. . . . The *fact* is in both cases that the law has been wholly changed; the *fiction* is that it remains what it always was. . . . The rule of law remains sticking in the system, but it is a mere shell. It has been long ago undermined, and a new rule hides itself under its cover. . . . They satisfy the desire for improvement, which is not quite wanting, at the same time that they do not offend the superstitious disrelish for change which is always present.[40]

In its most basic terms, this process can be termed as (radical) reinterpretation of formal rules, although it could be extended to include evolutive interpretation.[41] In such situations, while the rule formally remains the same, the way it is (re)interpreted reshapes its function. When individuals were confronted with new problems and needs, they threw old rules into previously non-envisioned situations, thus recasting them. Maine points to an interesting example.

As mentioned, ancient society was organised in family-institutions that were connected through common lineage. However, the lineage requirement became too restrictive for an evolving society which was confronted with a new problem: the slow growth of the community. In this scenario the lineage rule was thrown in a new situation and it was recast through a process of legal fiction by reinterpreting it together with another newly arisen concept: adoption. Without the rule ever changing, its operation was drastically altered once common lineage could be established through adoption.

This allowed society to grow out of an outdated formalised customary rule without ever formally changing it. This definitely applies to formalised IL, which evolves implicitly both through the practice of individuals

[40] ibid 26–27.

[41] For discussions on evolutive interpretation see F Pascual-Vives, *Consensus-Based Interpretation of Regional Human Rights Treaties* (Brill Nijhoff 2019) 73, 95; C Djeffal, 'Dynamic and Evolutive Interpretation of the ECHR by Domestic Courts?' in HP Aust & G Nolte (eds), *The Interpretation of International Law by Domestic Courts: Uniformity, Diversity, Convergence* (Oxford University Press 2016) 175.

(at least those who act on behalf of states) and international courts/ tribunals. The ultimate test of whether a specific instance is one of legal fiction or a mistaken interpretation will be the acceptance of the community as a whole – thus, altering CIL. The need for the legal fiction to lead *back* to CIL is especially important in the case of international courts/ tribunals whose judgments in this instance would be *sensu stricto ultra vires*. As Baker notes:

> The problem which arises however is that while neither the ICTY nor ICTR is tasked with 'making' international law, but rather simply applying it, it is inevitable (as legal institutions tasked with the implementation of, at times, ambiguous and general legal rules) that their jurisprudence will, at times, fundamentally reshape the law that they are being asked to apply. . . . [N]ew law often arises, not from lawmaking bodies, but rather from citations of practice where often general and ambiguous rules and statutes are interpreted and put into action.[42]

Further, as it concerns courts/tribunals, at least internationally, legal fiction should not be limited to this radical or evolutive, (re)interpretation of already existing formalised rules, but it should be extended to encompass one more instance. International courts help IL grow not only by reinterpreting and, thus, breathing new life into old rules, but by also establishing new CIL and altogether new rules. While courts cannot account for the entirety of CIL, as some theorists would claim, they do account for a portion of it. This is not necessarily a bad thing.

As for all concepts, CIL does have a 'core of settled meaning', that is rules/practices that are *definitely* law, and a 'penumbra of uncertainty'. Within this penumbra, though, the requirements of CIL identification can be most problematic and perhaps restraining, thus halting the development of law. It is within this penumbra that international courts/ tribunals can best operate to create new CIL through legal fictions. While this process allows room for abuse, there is a safeguard: looking back for community acceptance and CIL-practice.

If we ensure that the decision has been accepted and embedded within CIL practice, then it is irrelevant whether the decision was a process of mere interpretation or legal fictions. In instances of legal fiction an *ultra vires* decision can be legitimised and legalised *ex post facto*, that is through CIL-practice, after it is issued, thus contributing to the growth of CIL. The opposite might also hold true, a decision that is followed by

[42] R Baker, 'Customary International Law in the 21st Century: Old Challenges and New Debates' (2010) 21(1) EJIL 173, 185.

little or no practice, or even uniform but contrary practice, might fail to make IL for the right reasons.

By reconceptualising this process and ensuring that it leads back to CIL, we shorten the gap that exists between legal fictions and the community that has to live by their results. Insofar as the results of these fictions get accepted, they give rise to new practice, which in turn further develops CIL and IL as such.

5.2 *Equity*

> The next instrumentality by which the adaptation of law to social wants is carried on I call Equity, meaning by that word *any body of rules existing by the side of the original civil law, founded on distinct principles and claiming incidentally to supersede the civil law in virtue of a superior sanctity inherent in those principles.* [Equity] differs from the Fictions which in each case preceded it, in that the interference with law is open and avowed. ... On the other hand, it differs from Legislation, the agent of legal improvement which comes after it, in that its claim to authority is grounded, not on the prerogative of any external person or body, not even on that of the magistrate who enunciates it, but on the special nature of its principles, to which it is alleged that all law ought to conform.[43]

Recasting the process of this agent: it speaks of bodies of rules which exist next to settled IL but displace such settled law (and even manage to become law solely/primarily) due to a robust *opinio juris* (even in spite of little state practice), which itself flows out of the normativity generated by its (moral) content. While odd at first sight, once we become accustomed to this idea, we see bodies of 'Equity' all around us. Human rights are a suitable example of this.

Human rights began as a body of formalised (moral) rules enshrined in formal treaties. Nevertheless, and despite little state practice in certain areas, human rights began making claims *as* CIL due to the high *opinio juris* their content amasses. In recognising the need for CIL to develop to include human rights, certain theorists sought to redefine the CIL formation and identification formula which proves to be too rigid to allow CIL to grow in this instance. However, as Baker notes, this was not without its problems:

> At its most extreme, this scholarship argues that international treaties, especially those encompassing human rights obligations, actually generate

[43] Maine (n 9) 28.

> international legal norms, because such conventions are inevitably not simply the codification of existing legal norms but rather the creation of new ones. … This non-traditional scholarship presents a framework which insists that the signing of a convention or treaty by a wide group of countries is, in and of itself, evidence of the creation of new customary legal norms.[44]

The problem Baker describes is a real one. Such a move would bring us closer to total-formalism by detaching CIL completely from the practices which underlie it. This is opposite to the vision the present chapter is suggesting, and Baker seems to agree:

> At their core, these push-backs argue that the reinterpretation of customary international law advocated by the non-traditional scholarship, one which, as has been seen, envisages the transformation of conventional international law into customary international law as a seamless process and minimizes the role of state practice as a key component in customary international law formation, poses a danger to the entire concept of customary international law. The reinterpretation of customary international law advocated by the non- traditional scholarship is, according to those who oppose it, one which seeks to move the sources of customary international law (i.e., state practice and *opinio juris*) away from their 'practice-based' methodological orientation and instead employ methods which are completely normative in nature.[45]

This pitfall can be avoided by recognising, as Maine suggests, that we are confronted with two separate processes. The claims human rights are making within CIL should be neither confused *nor confounded* with traditional CIL formation and identification.[46] Bodies of equity, such as human rights, get grounded as *new* CIL differently than slowly arising practice-based CIL. Unlike traditional CIL, human rights are formally designed, but the moral principles they derive their force from hold such persuasive force, which is capable of overriding the lack of practice.

In this way, Maine's findings highlight the need to conceptualise a new mode of grounding within IL, that of bodies of equity, which run parallel to CIL even if they ultimately seek to be assimilated within it. Creating a separate conceptualisation for the processes of equity allows us to preserve the integrity of CIL and how it has been traditionally perceived, while discerning various other newly arisen normative systems

[44] Baker (n 42) 178.

[45] ibid 183.

[46] Reconciling the two could contribute to the decay of CIL; for such a 'reconciliation' see A Roberts, 'Traditional and Modern Approaches to Customary International Law: A Reconciliation' (2001) AJIL 757.

interrelating with it. This, in turn, reveals new ways of perceiving the international legal community and highlights new possibilities for its development.

Furthermore, the operationalisation of the concept of equity in this context does not stop at human rights but extends beyond it. For example, it could be used to reconceptualise the role and legitimation of international organisations (IOs) within the international legal order.[47] International organisations should then be seen as entities which take abstract values and principles (whether moral or otherwise) and slowly generate concrete bodies of equity, in the form of rules, out of them. Their legitimacy could then be drawn out of these wider values and principles they stand on, as well as out of the relation these values and principles hold with the greater international legal order and the individuals that comprise it, without replacing the concept of CIL.

From this perspective, the legitimacy of IOs is not static, nor uniform, but rather dynamic and dependent upon the wider set of values and principles each operates under. Further, the function of IOs also becomes clearer. By slowly generating rules out of such abstract values/principles, they play a large part in the evolution of IL. This is the case regardless of whether IOs directly create IL through treaties or whether they create bodies of soft law. Both treaties and soft law, in this context, can establish common accepted frameworks which may synchronise state practice and enable new CIL to arise, thus developing IL. Under this vision, IOs, as well as the bodies of equity they produce, do not replace CIL but rather supplement its function and expand upon its operation without necessarily altering IL's primarily customary nature.

6 Conclusion

Looking at the bigger picture Maine paints, we can begin to see how it can benefit the philosophy of CIL and draw some overall conclusions. First, CIL is law properly so, and it has been so since the very beginning, as it has been the case domestically as well – no concerns arise about its ontology. Second, CIL has as tools not only the traditional process of CIL formation, but agents of change such as Legal Fictions and Equity, which aid its evolution into a legal system. Thus, rather than being

[47] For an overview on the legitimacy and legitimation of IOs see J Tallberg & M Zürn, 'The Legitimacy and Legitimation of International Organizations: Introduction and Framework' (2019) 14 RIO 581.

formally 'identified' and 'ascertained', rules get grounded as CIL in a variety of ways, and there is a whole set of intricate tools already in operation which have been hiding in plain sight. In this way, the development of IL has not been so different from that followed by domestic legal systems.

Third, rather than blindly attempting to mimic the total-formalism of domestic legal systems, Maine's perspective highlights other possibilities. While formalism was a necessary evil in the development of domestic legal systems, CIL benefits from a different, more stable, environment; and we should not be so fast to shed or tamper with its customary skin. Rather than replacing customs and CIL with treaties, in their meaningful combination and collaboration we can find better ways to serve society. Maine's legacy can prove to be of invaluable assistance in this task.

Further, Maine's evolutionary narrative speaks of a myriad of under-explored stages in between mere customary law and the current legislative structure of domestic legal systems. The agents of change themselves resemble some of the traits that manifest in different evolutionary stages. This clearly exemplifies that the international legal order is far from the level of mere customary law. Nevertheless, IL is still retaining a primarily customary nature and this might not be such a bad thing.

Maine's legacy paves the way for a different utilisation of CIL within the international legal order, and it is up to theorists to follow in Maine's footsteps and re-conceptualise IL along those lines. Thus, the present chapter suggested some first steps to how such a Mainian reconceptualisation of CIL could look, opening doors for new ideas and debates to take place. At its core, this forgotten legacy gives reasons for international legal theorists to resist the total-formalism so heavily promoted by domestic legal systems and its advocates. Furthermore, Maine's work highlights a new vision where CIL gets supplemented, rather than replaced. In this way, 'strategic-formalisation' can enable us to further develop CIL into a legal system, without necessarily altering IL's primarily customary nature. In turn, this provides some new arguments/positions to old debates.

The present chapter, thus, hopes to be one of the first in a line of papers which seek to revive, refine and apply this lost evolutionary legacy to the international legal order. Maine, and those who followed in his footsteps, present an untapped pool of information, a forgotten school of thought that has never been applied to IL. And this school of thought, as a new way of thinking about law and society, can provide some much-needed theoretical foundation to a decaying CIL. The author is curious to see where this legacy takes us.

10

Enkapsis and the Development of Customary International Law

An Encyclopedic Approach to Inter-legality

ROMEL REGALADO BAGARES*

The jurists are still searching for their concept of law.[1]

To be required to think of law in terms of interconnectedness, among many normativities' 'ins', prevents our search for law from being stuck in one of them or in the other, that is, the *aut-aut* between 'being in' or nothing. Legality again surfaces through the cases as a *continuum*, underlying discrete and separate bodies of law.[2]

1 Introduction

According to Jean d'Aspremont's historiography of the four lives of customary international law (CIL), the 2018 Report of the International Law Commission (ILC) on the identification of CIL has all but solidified the 'formal acceptance' of the proposition that practice and *opinio juris* can be

* I am grateful to Israel Costa, Rudi Hayward, Angela Aguinaldo, Chhaya Bhardwaj and Ruben Alvarado for their comments on an earlier version of this chapter. Special thanks go to DFM Strauss and Alan M Cameron, not only for their comments on the chapter but also for making available to me relevant working drafts of the works by Herman Dooyeweerd referenced here that are still being translated as I write. Moreover, the patient and extensive editing help extended to me by the volume editors beat this essay into a much better shape than what was otherwise possible. All errors point to me.

1 I Kant, as quoted in H Dooyeweerd, *The Encyclopedia of the Science of Law*, Vol 8/1 (RD Knudsen tr & AM Cameron ed, Paideia Press 2012) 89; from the original German, 'Noch suchen die Juristen eine Definition zu ihrem Begriffe vom Recht' in I Kant, *Kritik der reinen Vernunft* (2nd ed, Groszherzog Wilhelm Ernst 1787) 556. I owe the German reference to DFM Strauss.

2 G Palombella, 'Theory, Realities, and Promises of Inter-Legality: A Manifesto' in J Klabbers & G Palombella (eds), *The Challenge of Inter-Legality* (Cambridge University Press 2019) 380.

extracted from the very same acts. With the report, 'practice and *opinio juris* no longer needs to be subject to two distinct tests', and 'practice is no longer restricted to conduct (action or in-action) strictly speaking, but also includes verbal acts and what State officials say, the latter having the potential to be constitutive of both practice and *opinio juris*'.[3] Thus, the ILC unwittingly overturned a ninety-eight-year-old tradition on the roots of CIL in Article 38 of the Statute of the Permanent Court of International Justice and ironically recovered its original unitary form.

But perhaps, because d'Aspremont's essay is essentially a historical reconstruction, he does not offer an account of the philosophical approaches that support the conclusion that CIL is the convergence of state practice and *opinio juris*. In this chapter, I will argue that such an account cannot be divorced from the larger question of an integrating theoretical account of the sources of law itself, of which CIL is but a part. In fact, the question of CIL brings front and centre the question of the concept of law.

Here I turn to the work of the Dutch Christian philosopher Herman Dooyeweerd (1894–1977), former chair of jurisprudence and the history of Dutch law at the Vrije Universiteit Amsterdam (VU), for an integrating theoretical account of custom as a source of international law, based on a systematic concept of law, which he termed the *Encyclopaedie van de Rechtswetenschap* (*Encyclopedia of the Science of Law*). In more than 200 publications, Dooyeweerd fleshed out his own approach to philosophical thought while wrestling with the reigning neo-Kantian legal philosophies of his day. He inaugurated what has been called a 'reformational' philosophical approach, drawing from insights of his predecessor Abraham Kuyper (1837–1920), polymath Dutch statesman, journalist, theologian and founder of the VU Amsterdam. Kuyper had introduced the sociological principle '*souvereiniteit in eigen kring*' (sovereign in its own orbit)[4] to guarantee the independence of various spheres of life from unwelcome state encroachment. Dooyeweered transformed it into an ontological or a 'cosmological' principle for a systematic theoretical account of a universal modal structure of reality.[5]

[3] J d'Aspremont, 'The Four Lives of Customary International Law' (2019) 21 IntCLRev 229.

[4] It is better known via its shorter form 'sphere sovereignty'. René van Woudenberg, 'Theories of Modes of Being (Modalities)' in Philosophical Foundations I Reader, International Masters in Christian Studies of Science and Society Program (Vrije Universitet Amsterdam 2006) 3. Articles compiled in the Reader are not numbered sequentially.

[5] ibid. See also, R. D. Henderson, *Illuminating Law: The Construction of Herman Dooyeweerd's Philosophy, 1918–1928* (PhD thesis, Vrije Universitet Amsterdam, 1994)

His mature system is contained in the three-volume *New Critique of Theoretical Thought*, first published between 1953 and 1958.[6] This was a major revision in English of his Dutch-language *De Wijsbegeerte der Wetsidee* (WdW), which had been published in the 1930s. However, it was in his lesser known *Encyclopedia* – transcripts published by the Student's Council of the VU for use in his jurisprudence and history of law classes – where he first elaborated his philosophical approach.

Dooyeweerd's *Encyclopedia* offers an engaging framework for understanding 'the challenge of inter-legality,' or the question of 'the ways through which legal domains end up overlapping due to the interconnection of substantive, material objects'.[7] In inter-legality, we are confronted with a 'plurality of legalities'[8] even if embodied in a single specimen of law. Here, 'the law surfaces as the composite legal nature of the issue under scrutiny'[9] demonstrating resilient and reflexive 'material interconnectedness'[10] 'among functional fields'.[11] Moreover, this composite question arises from 'the overlapping among regimes and orders',[12] which are also self-referential and coherent in themselves.[13]

In Sections 2–3, I will present key features of Dooyeweerd's systematic theory of law as embodied in his *Encyclopedia*, notably, his theory of the modal aspects and his theory of entities, whose correlation are essential for constructing a comprehensive concept of law. In Sections 4–7, I deploy Dooyeweerd's concept of (legal) 'enkapsis', to show that CIL's various manifestations exhibit the phenomena of inter-legality, and that enkapsis is a promising guide for understanding the phenomena. To that end, I will present an analysis of concrete examples from two interrelated and celebrated international law cases.

131–51. The work referred to here is the self-published book version of Henderson's doctoral dissertation.

[6] H Dooyeweerd, *The Collected Works: A New Critique of Theoretical Thought Series A*, Vols 1–4 (DH Freeman & H De Jongste trs & DFM Strauss ed, first published 1953–58, The Edwin Mellen Press 1997). Vol 4 is a comprehensive index to the first three volumes. The first volume of *A New Critique* is marked as 1/1, the second volume, 1/2, and so on. Paideia Press has since assumed responsibility for the publication of *The Collected Works* (hereinafter *A New Critique*).

[7] J Klabbers & G Palombella, 'Introduction' in J Klabbers & G Palombella (eds), *The Challenge of Inter-Legality* (Cambridge University Press 2019) 1.

[8] Palombella (n 2) 380.

[9] ibid.

[10] ibid 368.

[11] ibid.

[12] ibid.

[13] ibid.

2 Dooyeweerd's Encyclopedic Approach to the Concept of Law

Dooyeweerd asserts that the question of 'legal sources' constitutes 'the key problem for the entire positive science of law as a specific discipline'.[14] Of course many scholars have posed the problem in different ways. Remarking on eight theories of the sources of law in his time, Dooyeweerd concludes that they reveal 'the almost chaotic confusion regarding the meaning in which the phrase "legal source" is employed'.[15] These approaches either explain law by reference to one or other non-legal factors (for example, as a function of history, or of social practices, or of logical concepts, thus obscuring the boundary between law and other spheres of human life) or take the opposite direction, removing law totally from its inner connections with the other spheres of life by positing a transcendent source without any further scientific elaboration.[16] Each is founded on a particular 'cosmonomic idea' or theory of the ordering of reality and its essential elements. Such a 'philosophic ground idea'[17] shapes in profound ways the concept of law and the theory of the sources of law.

Dooyeweerd's 'transcendental critique of theoretical thought' asserts that every scientific endeavour is founded on pre-scientific and pre-theoretical commitments that are in the final analysis religious in nature, because they point to an ultimate conviction about the nature of things.[18] This is the inner connection between theoretical or scientific knowledge and religious conviction.[19] Various scientific disciplines must thus be seen in the context of the whole of human knowledge,[20] whose various areas have 'an inner coherence and are not simply related to each other in

14 This is from a provisional, unpublished and unpaginated draft translation of two monographs strung together, H Dooyeweerd, *Tentative Encyclopedia*, Vol 8/4, to be published by Paideia Press. The intended encyclopedia includes an *Introduction* (Vol 1), *A History of the Concept of Encyclopedia and the Concept of Law* (Vol 2), *The Elementary and Complex Basic Concepts of Law* (Vol 3), *The Typical Basic Concepts of Law and The Theory of the Sources of Law* (Vol 4) and the unfinished *Revised Introduction* (Vol 5). Only the encyclopedia's first volume (see n 1 of this chapter) has been published as part of *The Collected Works*. The others are in varying stages of translation and editing, thus the label 'Tentative' is used for the relevant volumes. The encyclopedia is the 8th volume in the A Series (multiple-volume sets) of *The Collected Works of Herman Dooyeweerd*, hence the labels 8/1 for the first volume, 8/2 for the second volume, and so on.

15 ibid.

16 Dooyeweerd, *Tentative Encyclopedia* (n 14) Vol 8/4.

17 ibid.

18 ibid.

19 ibid.

20 Dooyeweerd, *Encyclopedia* (n 1) Vol 8/1, 11.

an external and arbitrary fashion'.[21] This requires philosophical presuppositions that direct a comprehensive account of the 'mutual relationship and coherence of the jural aspect with the remaining aspects of reality'.[22] Pre-scientific knowing is not invalidated but understood as primary. It enables humans to experience events, acts, things and relations as individual, temporal totalities, their different aspects not separately conceived but encountered in their unbroken and mutual coherence with the whole of reality.[23] In contrast, in theoretical thought, different aspects of reality are analysed and distinguished from one another. The theoretical work of any discipline – the theoretical attitude of knowing, involves the *Gegenstand* relation.[24]

3 The Three Interrelated Pillars of *The Encyclopedia of the Science of Law*

Rejecting an account of the state as the sole lawmaker, Dooyeweerd also proffers a pluralist ontology founded on the philosophical principle of sphere sovereignty as a source of diverse structural-material principles for legal or jural positivisation. Here, there are three interrelated pillars anchored on two horizons of human experience, constituted by his interlocking theory of modal aspects and theory of entities. The first pillar is his modal theory of the jural aspect, which is one of the irreducible yet interconnected universal multidimensional modes or aspects of reality. The second pillar is his theory of entities, which gives rise to law unique to their particular practice (entities as rule complexes, each sovereign in its own orbit, exhibiting a 'differentiated responsibility'[25] and 'distinctive integrity'[26] unique to its nature). The third pillar is the various ways in which entities engage in relations of enkapsis or enkaptic interlacement – resulting in a complex intertwinement of the formal and the material sources of law.

21 ibid.

22 ibid 86.

23 ibid 23.

24 ibid.

25 JW Skillen, *Recharging the American Experiment: Principled Pluralism for Genuine Civic Community* (Baker 1994) 61–82; B Goudzwaard, *A Christian Political Option* (H Praansma tr, Wedge Publishing 1972) 38–39.

26 H van Riessen, *The University and Its Basis* (The ACHEA Press 1997) 5; the 1963 edition of the monograph used the phrase 'sphere sovereignty' but an unlisted editor's flourish replaced it with the phrase 'distinctive integrity' in the 1997 edition.

3.1 The Jural Aspect among the Modal Aspects

In Dooyeweerd's mature systematic philosophy, fifteen universal mutually irreducible but mutually coherent 'modal aspects' of temporal reality occur in the following particular order: numerical, spatial, movement (or kinematic), physical, biological, psychical, logical, historical, lingual (or symbolical), social, economic, aesthetic, jural, moral and the pistical (also referred to as faith or certitudinal aspect). His theory of the modal aspects 'is the distinctive and original element of his philosophical systematics, which includes his legal philosophy'.[27] His general modal theory of these aspects accounts for basic diversity in reality and the unity and coherence that can be found within such diversity. The modal aspects are not specific things but the 'different modes of the universal "how" [that] determine the aspects of our theoretical view of reality'.[28] All things, entities, events and relations function in all of the irreducible, universal aspects. Everything displays all of the aspects in some way.

The *Encyclopedia* as a scientific practice examines the nature of the jural dimension that gives to legal phenomena their jural character,[29] distinguishing the jural aspect from all other aspects of reality, and accounting for the former's internal structure as it is interconnected with those of the other aspects.[30] The jural aspect gives the concrete human laws their inherent legal normativity, with an original meaning – or 'meaning kernel' – for the jural aspect alone (in the same way that the other aspects have a meaning-kernel or nuclear moment proper to each of their spheres, which cannot be defined by any of the other aspects).[31] The meaning-kernel of the jural aspect, according to Dooyeweerd, is 'retribution', which is not to be confused with its criminal law sense. In his sense, retribution is an irreducible mode of balancing and harmonising individual and social interests. It implies 'a standard of proportionality regulating the legal interpretation of social facts and their factual social consequences in order to maintain the juridical balance by a just

[27] AM Cameron, 'Introduction' in Dooyeweerd, *Encyclopedia* (n 1) Vol 8/1, 10. The suite of modal aspects and their particular ordering are provisional, albeit the product of much reflection and analysis.

[28] Dooyeweerd, *A New Critique* (n 6) Vol 1/1, 3.

[29] AM Cameron, 'Dooyeweerd on Law and Morality: Legal Ethics – a Test Case' (1998) 28 VictoriaUnivWelLawRev 263.

[30] Thus, even the Hartian notion of 'ordinary language' is not really ordinary; it is in fact a product of theoretical abstraction, of the *Gegenstand*-relation; see HLA Hart & T Honoré, *Causation in the Law* (2nd ed, Clarendon Press 2002) 2, 29.

[31] Dooyeweerd, *Tentative Encyclopedia* (n 14) Vol 8/3, 3.

reaction, *viz.* the so-called legal consequences of the fact related to a juridical ground'.[32]

This broader idea of retribution 'involves an appeal to all of the modal aspects of reality that precede it in the order of the aspects'.[33] Such an appeal expresses an indissoluble relationship between and among aspects through a series of analogies, as 'no single aspect stands by itself: everyone refers within and beyond itself to all the others'.[34] Yet each has its own unique, undefinable and intuitive core that qualifies its nature and character and directs its full expression in its interlocking coherence with all the other aspects. Jural normativity – 'the perspective of law'[35] – as distinct from other normativities such as economic, social, historical, aesthetic or ethical, can neither be replaced nor erased because it is one of the different interlocking modes of being in reality. But according to the principle of sphere sovereignty, the jural aspect's own meaning-kernel should determine how it uses the analogies from all the other aspects for each concrete situation of jural positivisation.

Dooyeweerd's modal theory provides the building blocks to a full concept of law. Its complex of aspectual analogies or connections pointing backward from the jural aspect – the retrocipations[36] – are a substratum, *constitutive* spheres or aspects, without which the jural aspect and any legal system cannot exist; meanwhile the post-stratum connections pointing forward – the anticipations[37] – are *regulative* in nature,[38] as they deepen the constitutive meaning of the jural aspect by opening-up its ethical (moral) and certitudinal (faith) anticipations in the formative historical process of societal 'disclosure'.[39] So-called primitive societies are 'closed'

[32] Dooyeweerd, *A New Critique* (n 6) Vol 1/2, 129.

[33] AM Cameron, 'Jural Aspect in Dooyeweerd's Philosophy of Law' in C Benge (ed), *In a Reformational Key: Papers Presented for the Life, Work and Vision of Duncan Roper* (Thumbwidth Press 2020) 292.

[34] Dooyeweerd, *A New Critique* (n 6) Vol 1/1, 3, fn 1; this internal interconnectedness from within each modal aspect to all the others is what Dooyeweerd calls 'sphere universality'; see Dooyeweerd, *Encyclopedia* (n 1) Vol 8/1, 123.

[35] Palombella (n 2) 376.

[36] Dooyeweerd, *Encyclopedia* (n 1) Vol 8/1, 103.

[37] ibid.

[38] The distinction made here between the constitutive and the regulative is not Dooyeweerd's, but is a device borrowed from Kant and deployed by some of his interpreters to explain the dynamic interaction between the lower and upper strata of Dooyeweerd's theory of modal aspects; see HJ van Eikema Hommes, *Major Trends in the History of Legal Philosophy* (North Holland 1979) 374–75; DFM Strauss, *Philosophy: Discipline of Disciplines* (Paideia Press 2009) 312–13; and AM Cameron, 'Introduction' in *Encyclopedia* (n 1) Vol 8/1, 8–9.

[39] *Encyclopedia* (n 1) Vol 8/1, 103.

legal systems, valid and working within their own contexts but yet unable to move beyond a most basic system of accountability and punishment, in the absence of disclosed and deepened anticipatory aspects.[40]

This process of disclosure – directed by the certitudinal or faith aspect – may happen for better or for worse, as such leading could also take an 'apostate direction',[41] in which certain aspects of reality are deified and absolutised.[42] Moreover, these analogies are expressed in two correlated grids: of the law or norm side, and subject, or factual side, of reality, such that one is meaningless without the other.[43] Every concrete fact is subject to this cosmic law-ordering – the modal aspects in which those facts function. Such law-ordering on the norm side correlated with the factual side is only discernible in their positivisation in concrete legal phenomena.[44] Yet they are not reducible to each other.[45]

Thus the 'architectonic' modal structure of the jural aspect embodies the following analogies: (numerical) legal unity and multiplicity; (spatial) legal area of validity of legal norms and the juridical place of legal facts, legal subjects, etc; (kinematic) legal constancy and legal dynamism of norms and facts subject to them; (physical) legal force of legal validity and legal causality; (biotic) legal life and competent legal organs; (psychical) ordering legal will and legal will of subjective parties; (logical) legal identity, legal contradiction, legal attribution and imputation; (historical) legal power or legal competence and legal form-giving by competent legal organs; (lingual or symbolical) legal declaration, legal signification and legal interpretation; (social) legal intercourse and correlation of communal and inter-individual or coordinational relationships; (economic) legal economy and equilibrium; (aesthetic) legal harmony and proportionality; (moral) legal morality; and (faith) legal faith or legal conviction.[46] Therefore, the problem

40 ibid 104; in his early philosophy as expressed in the *Encyclopedia*, only the modal retrocipations were called analogies while the forward-looking aspects were called 'modal anticipations'; see Cameron, 'Introduction' in Dooyeweerd, *Encyclopedia* (n 1) Vol 8/1, 103.

41 H Dooyeweerd, *Roots of Western Culture* (J Kraay tr, M Vander Vennen & B Zylstra eds, Paideia Press 2012) 105.

42 ibid.

43 Dooyeweerd, *Tentative Encyclopedia* (n 14) Vol 8/3, 293.

44 Cameron, 'Law and Morality' (n 29) 13.

45 Dooyeweerd, *Tentative Encyclopedia* (n 14) Vol 8/3, 293; in other words, the norm/fact distinction.

46 Eikema Hommes (n 38) 374–75. Eikema Hommes already reflects Dooyeweerd's mature philosophy here.

of 'law-ascertainment'[47] in international law will involve the investigation and application of every analogy involved in the modal structure of the jural aspect.

3.2 Theory of Entities, Enkapsis and the Sources of Law

Dooyeweerd's theory of the modal aspects is interlocked with his theory of entities. The theory of entities deals with how things, events and relationships exhibit typical functions within the modal aspects. Each entity or relationship displays all modal aspects at the same time but there will always be two aspects which will exhibit and define its particular identity. These are the founding and the qualifying functions. The founding function is the aspect qualifying the process of transformation of an entity.[48] The qualifying function is an entity's intrinsic purpose. The intrinsic purpose qualifies the thing's internal structure.[49] The qualifying function is also the 'individual leading function' that plays a role in an entity's internal unfolding process,[50] through which the function acquires 'an internal structural coherence'.[51]

The difference between a modal and entitary perspective is that the latter is focused on the qualifying function of things; the former is not.[52] An entity's qualifying function shows that its identity cannot be understood through the theory of modal aspects but that nevertheless, its structural unity expresses itself in all modal functions.[53] In this way, Dooyeweerd's theory of entities accounts for entitary distinctiveness: family, marriage, church, mosque, temple, corporation, museum, university, a humanitarian NGO, an international organisation or state, each of them imbued with an original material competence, with their own sphere sovereignty. Family or marriage is founded on the biotic aspect but qualified by the ethical aspect; a church, a mosque and a temple are all founded in the historical aspect and all qualified by the faith aspect;

[47] The task of distinguishing law from non-law, in d'Aspremont's terms; J d'Aspremont, *Formalism and the Sources of International Law: A Theory of Ascertainment of Legal Rules* (Oxford University Press 2018) 1.

[48] R Clouser, *The Myth of Religious Neutrality* (University of Notre Dame Press 2005) 263.

[49] R van Woudenberg, 'Theories of Thing-Structures' in *Philosophical Foundations I Reader* (International Masters in Christian Studies of Science and Society Program, VU Amsterdam 2006–7) 6.

[50] Dooyeweerd, *A New Critique* (n 6) Vol 1/3, 59.

[51] van Woudenberg (n 49) 6; Dooyeweerd, *A New Critique* (n 6) Vol 1/3, 90.

[52] ibid.

[53] ibid.

a corporation is founded in the historical aspect but qualified by the economic aspect; a museum, a university or a humanitarian NGO are all founded in the historical aspect but have different qualifying functions: aesthetic for the first, logical for the second and ethical for the third. The UN and the state are founded in the historical aspect but both are qualified by the jural aspect. Each has an intrinsic jural competence as an entity, community or institution. Their legal personality is not dependent on the grant of recognition by the state or any other institution. The radical implications of this differentiated social ontology for international law may be summarised in the following description: '[d]ifferent social relationships have different characters, different kinds of law-making requirements, different foundations'.[54] The structural principles that arise out of differentiated societal entities, spheres, and relations form the building blocks of Dooyeweerd's theory of the sources of law: all law displaying the typical individuality structure of a particular community of inter-individual or inter-communal relationship, in principle falls within the material-jural sphere of competence of such a societal orbit, and is only formally connected (in its genetic form) with spheres of competence of other societal orbits.[55] A legal source is every juridical form in which those organs of a communal or coordinational relationship in the mutual correlation of these communal and coordinational functions, who are competent to form law, positivise legal principles into valid law within a given life context.[56]

Societal structural principles rooted in the differentiated creational order 'lie at the basis of every formation of positive law and it is only these principles that make the latter only possible'.[57] In addition, his theory of entities also accounts for their interrelationships. Here, what Dooyeweerd calls 'enkapsis' comes to the fore. These interlacements are 'free forms of positivisation',[58] owing to their 'typical historical foundation'[59] – or to their development located in the unfolding of the differentiation of society. Enkapsis is the 'complicated manner in which the simple entities are interlaced with each other by the cosmic order of

[54] JW Skillen, 'Development of Calvinistic Political Theory in the Netherlands, with Special Reference to the Thought of Herman Dooyeweerd' (PhD Thesis, Duke University 1973) 388.

[55] Dooyeweerd, *A New Critique* (n 6) Vol 1/3, 670.

[56] Dooyeweerd, *Tentative Encyclopedia* (n 14) Vol 8/4.

[57] Dooyeweerd, *A New Critique* (n 6) Vol 1/3, 669.

[58] ibid.

[59] ibid.

time and through which they are united, in part, within complex structural totalities'.[60]

Enkapsis happens in the mutual intertwinement of differently qualified societal spheres and relationships, which are 'pheno-typical'[61] forms. By this, he means that in these relationships, the inner natures of the societal spheres are not at all obliterated by their particular interlacements. There are different types of enkapsis that are entitary and structural, such as the correlative and the unilateral. In a correlative enkapsis, two structures presuppose each other, as in the case of interlacements between communal and coordinational relationships. A variation of correlative enkapsis is territorial enkapsis, where all differentiated societal structures are territorially bound to the state in whole or in part.[62] Moreover, in concrete expressions – of positivised – law or of formal law proper, there is what may be called 'legal' enkapsis. In other words, positivised laws found in the various spheres of competence are interlinked with one another in complex ways.[63]

A Kelsenian purely formal law in which all positive law is material leads to 'a radical levelling of the material structural differences amongst the various jural norm-systems'.[64] Rather, a material classification of law should be based on the 'typical internal character of the various norm complexes of a legal order'.[65] A formal law must also be distinguished from material competence. Formal law is determined by the different enkaptic relations that happen in the interlacement of different societal structures and relationships.[66] Material competence refers to the invariant structural principles of the various societal relationships that are sovereign in their own spheres; the latter are the material sources of law.[67] One and the same genetic form posivitising jural principles (that is, a formal source of law) may involve an original source of law in one sphere of competence but may be a derived source of law in another sphere.[68] While a formal law is

[60] Dooyeweerd, *Encyclopedia* (n 1) Vol 8/1, 219.

[61] Dooyeweerd, *New Critique* (n 6) Vol 1/3, 664.

[62] ibid 662.

[63] Compare this with what Palombella says of inter-legality: 'Inter-legality . . . starts from the fact that interconnections make up for a kind of *composite law*, one that results out from the contents of separate sources, in a number of recurrent situations', in Palombella (n 2) 375.

[64] Dooyeweerd, *A New Critique* (n 6) Vol 1/3, 204.

[65] ibid 199.

[66] ibid.

[67] ibid.

[68] ibid.

inextricably bound with a law-forming organ, such an organ is interwoven with various material spheres of competence, so that it can never be the sole source of validity of all positive law.[69] Validity and positivity are inextricably connected; there is no juridical validity without positivity, just as there is no positivity without the juridical validity of norms.[70] This is his 'material juridical meaning-theory of validity':[71] 'with its entire sphere-sovereignty every positive legal order rests on the *changing* meaning of those law-spheres lying at the foundation of the jural sphere'.[72]

Transformations in the constitutive spheres lead to corresponding transformations in the positivisation of structural principles. It remains the task of the leading formers of law to be properly guided by faith – by their ultimate commitments – in a way that does not distort or deny the jural limits or boundaries between and among societal spheres and relations.

4 Dooyeweerd's Critique of CIL as an Indirect (Formal) Source of Law

The now familiar two-element test of the crystallisation of customary norms comprising the *opinio* and *longaevus usus* requirements, according to Dooyeweerd, proceeds from the assumption that it is the 'sole indirect mode of legal formation'.[73] But such an approach 'can never qualify custom to become a legal source, because, as we know, a legal source [in the formal sense] is unthinkable without a competent formative legal organ'.[74]

4.1 *The Antinomy of* Opinio *and* Usus

To begin with, there is an inner antinomy to the accepted formula '*opinio* and *usus*', because the former 'concerns a jural anticipation within the psychic sphere', which in the first place 'presupposes the jural', which it then attempts to define.[75] As an earlier and distinct aspect, the psychic aspect cannot define what is normative of the jural aspect, for such would

69 ibid.
70 Dooyeweerd, *Tentative Encyclopedia* (n 14) Vol 8/4.
71 ibid.
72 ibid.
73 ibid.
74 ibid.
75 ibid.

deny the jural aspect its inherent normativity and violate the principle of sphere sovereignty, in which no aspect is reducible to any other aspect. That is, the accepted notion of an *opinio* is an improper understanding of the analogy to the psychic sphere, which precedes and anticipates (points towards) the jural aspect in Dooyeweerd's suite of fifteen modal aspects. Rather, in the unbreakable law-side and factual-side correlation, the analogy to the psychic sphere on the law side is the basic concept of the function of the legal will expressed as 'a legally ordering will of an organ competent to form law'.[76]

On the factual side, the analogy to the psychic aspect is expressed in the 'will-function of a legal subject correlated with the ordering will of a competent organ and capable of accepting jural responsibility and normative accountability for its acts in legal life'.[77] Only a competent organ has the legal power (an analogy to the human formative historical aspect) to positivise structural principles into law. This is an important requirement, given current proposals for deformalisation in law-ascertainment in international law.[78] Law-ascertainment cannot be divorced from the question of who has competence as a legal organ to positivise material-legal principles into law. Thus the work of such a competent organ (itself an analogy to the biotic sphere) should not be confused with the scientific description of norms positivised into law by such competent organ, as in the case of the writings of legal scholars or publicists on CIL.[79] Also, *longaevus usus* is not a requirement for the indirect formation of law, as a rule may develop into CIL within just a brief period of time.[80]

An example is the quick adoption of cruiser rules in naval warfare to submarine warfare, following the experience of World War I. In regard to this, 'a positive piece of the law of nations was formed with regard to the competence to take custody and to bring in with submarines commercial ships, analogous to the existing positive law practice applicable to cruisers'.[81] This came about because of 'a series of legal actions which succeeded each other relatively quickly'.[82] He might be

[76] Dooyeweerd, *Tentative Encyclopedia* (n 14) Vol 8/3 20.
[77] ibid.
[78] As critiqued in chapter 5 of d'Aspremont, *Formalism* (n 47) 118–36.
[79] Dooyeweerd, *Tentative Encyclopedia* (n 14) Vol 8/3, 28; see also d'Aspremont's point on the 'secondary role' of international legal scholars as 'grammarians of formal law-ascertainment who systematize the standards of distinction between law and non-law'; d'Aspremont, *Formalism* (n 47) 209.
[80] Dooyeweerd, *Tentative Encyclopedia* (n 14) Vol 8/3, 28.
[81] ibid Vol 8/4.
[82] ibid.

referring here to Part IV of the Treaty of London of 22 April 1930, which bound submarines to extant rules applicable to surface warships when dealing with merchant ships. According to that treaty provision, surface warships and submarines may not attack a merchant vessel without having first placed passengers, crew and ship's papers in a place of safety. The only exceptions are when the vessel refuses to stop on being summoned, or when it resists a visit or search.[83] Thus, although CIL is an indirect way of forming law, like a treaty, it presupposes the same original competent organ (here, the states in their mutual consent).[84] It was adopted by the major naval powers of the era and many others from their experience of World War I, when submarines were first widely used. However, of forty-nine nations that were parties to the treaty, each of the major powers abrogated the treaty as soon as war broke out again.[85] Here, Dooyeweerd also anticipated by at least three decades the ruling of the *North Sea Continental Shelf* case that widespread and representative adoption of a conventional norm by non-signatory states, even within a short span of time, may transform it into CIL.[86]

Yet, the rise and fall of this legal regime invokes the various analogies in the architectonic modal structure of the jural aspect: in the human formative unfolding process (historical aspect), new rules have to be drafted to apply to a new horrific method of waging war, spurred by technological developments – submarine warfare. The legal life of the treaty, and the CIL on which it was based, proved short-lived (biotic aspect), enjoying a brief legal constancy but eventually losing to the legal dynamism of lawmaking (kinematic aspect) brought about by new historical circumstances, and resulting in the loss of its legal force (physical aspect) in the waters subjected to the legal regime (spatial aspect), as legal subjects – states, who are also legal ordering organs (psychic aspect) – broke faith (analogy to the faith aspect) with it, ceding moral considerations (moral aspect) to the expediency of war.

83 Treaty for the Limitation and Reduction of Naval Armaments (adopted 22 April 1930, entered into force 31 December 1930) part IV, art 22, relating to submarine warfare <https://bit.ly/3roNVJ2> accessed 1 March 2021.

84 Dooyeweerd, *Tentative Encyclopedia* (n 14) Vol 8/4.

85 H Hays Parks 'Making Law of War Treaties: Lessons from Submarine Warfare Regulation' (2000) 75 IntlLStudies 339, 342.

86 *North Sea Continental Shelf Cases (Federal Republic of Germany/Netherlands; Federal Republic of Germany/Denmark)* (Judgment) [1969] ICJ Rep 3.

4.2 A Dooyeweerdian 'Communitarian Semantics'

Secondly, the existence of CIL is determined according to 'other formal sources of knowledge'[87] – in other words, formal knowledge of the practice of states, or of any competent organ for that matter. In principle, formal knowledge of sources would embrace an entire host of indicators, whether written or unwritten, given that CIL is an indirect way of formalising law. It is important that the indicators are traceable to competent organs. This process of law-ascertainment for CIL will then involve the lingual (or symbolical) analogies of *legal declaration*, *legal signification* and *legal interpretation*. The ordering will of competent organs is expressed in a legal declaration – not a social fact. Such declaration may well be a correlation of written and unwritten expression, or by conclusive lawmaking behaviour, *rebus ipsis et factis*.[88] The practice (legal declaration) of competent organs already embodies and implies a belief (by an ordering legal will and accepted as such by the will of other legal subjects) that the rule followed in such practice is legally binding. Thus, it would be circuitous to assert that rules crystallise into CIL through the confluence of *opinio juris* and state practice.[89] The norms embodied in CIL are understood, amplified, communicated, and applied in legal intercourse among legal subjects (analogy to the social aspect).[90] Legal norms do not exist by themselves. In the dynamic process of lawmaking, they are norms of legal intercourse and interaction in inter-individual or inter-communal contexts.[91] Yet their meaningfulness becomes a legal question in any legal dispute, in which case their legal signification will require the legal interpretation by 'law-applying authorities':[92] domestic courts and international tribunals.

In interpreting the legal declaration at issue, courts and tribunals must apply rules of logic in a jural way, considering *legal identity*, *legal contradiction*, *legal attribution* and *imputation*. They also must observe *legal economy* and *legal harmony*, with an opened sense of *legal morality*. Their

[87] Dooyeweerd, *Tentative Encyclopedia* (n 14) Vol 8/4.

[88] Eikema Hommes (n 38) 384.

[89] ibid; thus Dooyeweerd anticipates the ILC's recent turn to a single-element CIL.

[90] ibid.

[91] Eikema Hommes (n 38) 384; thus to speak of law as process, *pace* the New Haven school, is to capture merely the kinematic analogy (legal dynamism) of a jural phenomenon; see R Higgins, *Problems and Process: International Law and How We Use It* (Oxford University Press 1995).

[92] D'Aspremont here uses the phrase in the Hartian sense of a social practice, d'Aspremont (n 47) 52.

legal interpretation of the legal declaration in question will help deepen or otherwise clarify the norms at issue. In time, continued legal intercourse may serve to deepen the international legal order's appreciation and commitment to the norms embodied in the legal declaration, and as interpreted by law-applying authorities, thus resulting in heightened faith or trust in its legitimacy (faith aspect) by legal subjects from various spheres. It is against this backdrop where d'Aspremont's social thesis on the need for a 'communitarian semantics'[93] is better understood: domestic courts and non-state actors generate social practice to illuminate the meaning of the law-ascertainment criteria of the international legal system, thus participating in the reinforcement of the possibility for the international legal system of producing a vocabulary enabling ascertainment of the rules of which it is composed.[94]

4.3 CIL as a Formal Source of Law and the Promise of Pluralist Ontology

Customary international law merely describes the form of a source of law (formal source). The concept 'customary law' itself lacks a juridical delineation that refers to its specific type of positive (jural) material content. What is needed is a granular examination of the material source of norms embodied within the formal source, founded on the modal sphere sovereignty of the jural aspect with its internal connections to the substratum of the preceding modal aspects.[95] But crucially, the material content of valid customary law, as with the material content of all formal sources of law, is also founded upon the multiplicity of the different entities and their enkaptic jural relationships.

This 'thick' account of sources of law amounts to a radical legal pluralism, which implies that the material sources of CIL are not mere invention of states. In their formation of CIL, competent organs ought to recognise the multiple forms of the spheres involved and their respective underlying principles that are each unique. The same rule applies to other formal sources of international law. On the domestic front, there are various normative complexes, the state being only one of them. Each of them has an irreducible material sphere of competence unique to their

[93] ibid 196.

[94] ibid 212.

[95] Dooyeweerd, *Encyclopedia* (n 1) Vol 8/1, 103.

nature, with their own jural sphere sovereignty, and forming a jural unity within a multiplicity of norms.[96] Moreover, if pursued to its logical conclusion, the crystallisation of CIL must be appropriate to the structure and nature of the diversity of spheres, entities and relations. At the very least, on the international level, states or other competent organs should respect their differentiated responsibilities and distinctive integrity in the development of CIL. Palombella would recognise this as a desirable characteristic of the plurality of legalities he writes of with keen approval:

> The plurality of legalities is ensured if law is not monopolized by one single hand, and if it stems from a variety of those capable of triggering the generation of law. Accordingly, rulers (be they sovereign States or omnipotent global regulators) should better be also respectful to a law that is not their own, if the rule of law, not of men, has to thrive. Such premises, then, suggest that the plurality of sources (and one might add, in a wider ultra-state setting, *legalities*) qualifies, in principle, as a legal precondition of non-domination through law and of liberty.[97]

In such theory of inter-legality, the law and liberty of spheres appear to be an external, sociological, explanation. Dooyeweerd's theory of differentiated responsibility with its distinctive integrity, however, leads to a truly radical view of international legal personality, where the normative claims of each sphere are drawn from the givenness of its inner nature. The very idea of the irreducibility and coherence of the modal aspects resists the overreach of one sphere over the others, or the undue dominance of one entity over the others; every sphere or entity is to regard the others' respective differentiated responsibility and distinctive integrity.

5 Inter-legality: Overlapping of Formal and Material Sources in Legal Enkapsis

Thus, legal enkapsis may take place in the international realm between two different genetic forms, or between different formal sources of law. An example is the already well-known intersection between treaty law and CIL demonstrating a 'duality of norms'. It can be the case that a treaty may also embody principles long considered as binding – those longstanding principles of CIL.

96 Dooyeweerd, *Tentative Encyclopedia* (n 14) Vol 8/2, 12.
97 Palombella (n 2) 38.

This has been recognised in *Nicaragua* v. *United States.*[98] Here, the International Court of Justice (ICJ) held that the UN Charter cannot be said to exhaust all principles dealing with the use of force, as the latter is also addressed by CIL, which exists contemporaneously with treaty law – yet the former may also be grafted into the latter by way of codification. A ruling predating the *Nicaragua* case and stating the same principle has been expressed in the Philippine case of *Kuroda* v. *Jalandoni*,[99] which concerned the trial of a Japanese officer for war crimes during World War II. In this case, lawyers for the Japanese officer argued that, under the principle of legality, he could not be tried for war crimes under the Hague Convention on Rules and Regulations covering Land Warfare because the Philippines was not a party to it. However, the Philippine Supreme Court held that while the Philippines was not a party to the Hague Convention, it was nevertheless bound to it because its provisions are also part of CIL, which in turn became domestic law through the Incorporation Clause of the 1935 Philippine Constitution. This analysis is limited only to the level of formal sources.

One illuminating example of the legal enkaptic interlacement of two different material sources in one genetic form of law may be taken from the field of international humanitarian law (IHL). There is a host of treaties embodying the customary practice of protecting religious beliefs and convictions in situations of armed conflicts,[100] which shows how ecclesiastical practice and religious freedom intersect with the sphere that is for the most part the concern of states. Another example is the customary practice of environmental protection, where there is also a host of instruments, declarations, military manuals and pieces of national legislation providing for certain forms of protection for the environment in situations of armed conflict.[101] These examples show the correlation of two distinct interests embodying CIL – the regulation of the means and methods of warfare, with the protection of the environment in times of armed conflict. This illustrates bi-layered legal enkapsis: firstly, the intersection of different formal sources – national

[98] *Military and Paramilitary Activities in and against Nicaragua (Nicaragua v USA)* (Merits) [1986] ICJ Rep 14; see also *North Sea Continental Shelf Cases.*

[99] *Kuroda v Jalandoni* (26 March 1949) Republic of the Philippines Supreme Court, GR No L-2662.

[100] ICRC, 'Practice Relating to Rule 104 Respect for Convictions and Religious Practices' (*ICRC IHL Database*, 2021) <https://bit.ly/3DAOIt8> accessed 1 March 2021.

[101] For example, ICRC, 'Practice Relating to Rule 43 Application of General Principles on the Conduct of Hostilities to the Natural Environment' (*ICRC IHL Database*, 2021) <https://bit.ly/31ei2YG> accessed 1 March 2021.

legislation, treaty law and CIL – and secondly, the meeting of two different material sources providing material-legal principles; that is, environmental protection and the international public regulation of armed conflict in one instrument: treaty law. The norms in question pertain to IHL but also involve norms taken from other spheres; moreover, these latter derived norms do not in any way invalidate the nature of the positive law as IHL.

6 Community Interests in International Law: *South West Africa* and *Barcelona Traction*

South West Africa and *Barcelona Traction* illuminate the reach of the *Encyclopedia of the Science of Law*, not only in understanding the formation of CIL in particular but of the development of international legal processes in general. After ruling in 1962 in the preliminary phase of *South West Africa*[102] that it had jurisdiction to hear the challenges brought by Liberia and Ethiopia against apartheid practiced by South Africa in South West Africa, the ICJ made a surprising turnaround in 1966. There, it dismissed the applications on the ground that the applicants lacked *locus standi*, having possessed no subjective legal right or interest in the subject matter of their claims against South Africa.[103] It held that the applicants have no subjective rights under the concept of the 'sacred trust of civilisation,' as such ground may only be understood within the particular organs and mechanisms established by the League of Nations, which by then were already defunct.

The ICJ's analysis of how the notion of 'sacred trust' was drafted into the legal structure of the mandates is a useful study in how law relates to morality and faith in an analogical way. While agreeing that all states have an interest in seeing the realisation of sacred trust, the ICJ nevertheless held that such a realisation cannot be merely a 'moral or humanitarian ideal';[104] it must assume a particular legal form – a (legal) positivisation – to grant rights and obligations, as for example, the UN trusteeship system or the charter's provisions on non-self-governing territories, which are expressly provided for in relevant texts.[105] Thus,

102 *South West Africa (Liberia v South Africa)* (Preliminary Objections) [1962] ICJ Rep 319.
103 *South West Africa Cases (Second Phase) (Ethiopia v South Africa; Liberia v South Africa)* (Judgment) [1966] ICJ Rep 158 (hereinafter *South West Africa Cases (Second Phase)*).
104 ibid [52].
105 ibid.

it 'must be given form as a juridical regime in the shape of that system'.[106] The ICJ held that in the structure of the mandates there was 'no residual juridical content [that] could, so far as any particular mandate is concerned, operate *per se* to give rise to legal rights and obligations outside the [mandate] system as a whole'.[107]

The mandates provided two modes of rights entitlement of members. The first was the 'conduct' provision in the mandates, pertaining to the mandates as a whole, and the second was the 'special interests' provisions, which were granted to the states as individual members and their nationals.[108] The court held that the applicants founded their claims on the conduct provisions, but this could not be maintained, because the sacred trust as a right was positivised in a different way. The form it had taken meant that individual member states could not, on their own – on the basis of subjective rights not granted by the League's charter – directly intervene in the work of administering the mandatories. This right belonged only to the league's organs under the conduct provisions.

In Dooyeweerd's modal theory, the ethical (moral) aspect stands immediately next or anticipatory to or above the jural aspect; immediately succeeding the ethical aspect is the upper limit of the aspects, the faith or certitudinal aspect. These two latter regulative aspects open up, deepen and disclose a fully orbed meaning of the jural aspect as expressed in concrete legal systems through a developed idea of justice. Thus, here we see how the deepened principles of jural morality may come into being: in the case of apartheid, what would have been relevant is the principle of legal personality as guided by the 'regulative jural principle of the *value of the human being* (*dignitas humana*)',[109] which acquires a significant role in the disclosure or differentiated development of the public spheres of jural freedom of the human personality within the state as well as within the non-political spheres of life.[110] The moral aspect expressed as *dignitas humana* may be incorporated into the jural aspect, not in the original sense but in an analogical manner. Because the jural and the moral constitute distinct aspects that nevertheless cohere with each other, one may not be reduced into the other.[111] Moreover, this legal

[106] ibid.
[107] ibid [54].
[108] ibid.
[109] Strauss (n 38) 571.
[110] ibid 572.
[111] In contrast to Hart's later 'inclusive legal positivism' as discussed in d'Aspremont (n 47) 85; see HLA Hart, *The Concept of Law* (3rd ed, Clarendon Press 2012) 193–212.

use of the idea of sacred trust appeals to notions of the sanctity of faith in the highest ideals of civilisation. In his dissent, Judge Tanaka alludes to its Christian theological roots by saying the principle has been present as far back as Vitoria.[112]

The faith aspect in turn also refers back to, and builds on, the earlier moral aspect, which to begin with, evinces the jural-moral duty not to violate the legal faith concept of sacred trust by causing others injury, and the notion of *dignitas humana* as basis for fundamental equality of races. In fact, there is strong evidence that the mandate system was not the sole juridical expression of such a sacred trust, but is traceable as already well-established in nineteenth-century international law, both as 'consensus of opinion of all civilized states'[113] and as a treaty norm, in particular, as embodied in the General Act of the Berlin Conference of 26 February 1885.[114] The mandates could therefore have also embodied CIL. The *South West Africa Cases* palpably demonstrate a court yet unprepared to recognise an international society's deepened and disclosed understanding of the principle of equality among races as to vest in any state the right – equivalent of an *actio popularis*[115] – to hold South Africa accountable for its practice of what would today be a violation of a *jus cogens* norm.

Four years later in the *Barcelona Traction* case, it would make an about-face, at least with respect to the idea of states being able to make a claim on behalf not just of their particular interests but also in the name of common interests, in the unlikely case of a private commercial dispute.[116] I approach *Barcelona Traction* from two levels. Firstly, there is the question of the diplomatic protection proper and its implications. The ICJ found customary norms for the international legal dispute from municipal law, one traceable to a specific sphere – that of business, where commercial law has developed rules germane to the life-world of

[112] *South West Africa Cases Second Phase*, Dissenting Opinion of Judge Tanaka 265; it might be called today a 'political theology', or perhaps, more accurately, a 'legal theology'; see Antony Anghie's critique of Vitorian thought as 'a particularly insidious justification' of colonialism because it masks itself 'in the language of liberality and even equality' for the conquered natives. A Anghie, *Imperialism, Sovereignty and the Making of International Law* (Cambridge University Press 2008) 28.

[113] In other words, of CIL; see CH Alexandrowicz, 'The Juridical Expression of the Sacred Trust of Civilization' (1971) 65 AJIL 149, 155–59.

[114] ibid.

[115] *South West Africa Cases Second Phase* [88].

[116] *Barcelona Traction, Light & Power Co, Ltd (Belgium v Spain)* [1970] ICJ Rep 3 (hereinafter *Barcelona Traction*).

corporations. It thus provided what may well be a precedent in international law on the separate and distinct legal personality of a corporation from that of its shareholders, as well as on the ascertainment of the nationality of a corporation.[117] It recognised the domain occupied by the corporation as a domestically governed entity, where municipal rules under which it has been created are relevant to the international dispute.[118] Secondly, there is the now famous *obiter dictum* of the ICJ in *Barcelona Traction* pertaining to obligations *erga omnes*, or those 'owed to the international community as a whole'[119] arising from CIL.[120]

7 Legal Enkapsis, Coordinational Interests and the Public-Private Divide in International Law

On the first point, we can speak of enkaptic interlacements between the commercial interest involved in *Barcelona Traction* and international public interest involving states. Indeed, one specific instance of a relevant public interest is that of a state that may have been injured by the failure of another to afford legal protection to the former's nationals. This is separate from the interest of the municipal corporation itself.[121] Here, too, we see how public international law intersects with the realm of private law, in this case, the domestic law of corporations, in a way that might in other circumstances be regarded as being in conflict. This analysis also brings to sharper relief a more nuanced, legal enkaptic treatment of the public-private divide obtaining in the correlation of domestic law-international law in a phenomenon of inter-legality.

Moreover, there is also a retrocipatory connection by international law to the historical and economic aspects, on account of the rapid changes in international commerce, which have transformed and widened the original scope of diplomatic protection 'to municipal institutions, which have transcended frontiers and have begun to exercise considerable

[117] L Jahoon Lee, 'Barcelona Traction in the 21st Century: Revisiting Its Customary and Policy Underpinnings 35 Years Later' (2006) 42 Stan J Intl L 237.

[118] *Barcelona Traction* [38].

[119] ibid.

[120] Such obligations being able to arise both from *jus cogens* and non-peremptory norms. See S Besson, 'Theorizing the Sources of International Law' in S Besson & J Tasioulas (eds), *The Philosophy of International Law* (Oxford University Press, 2010) 174–75.

[121] See Article 33 of ILC, 'Draft Articles on Responsibility of States for Internationally Wrongful Acts with Commentaries' (23 April–1 June and 2 July–10 August 2001) UN Doc A/56/10, reproduced in [2001/II - Part Two] YBILC 31.

influence on international relations'.[122] On the second point, an expanding complexity of international legal processes has led to the deepening of the international legal order's understanding of international law – the *anticipatory analogy* to the moral aspect[123] – where certain violations of CIL now implicate the interest of the international legal order as a whole and not just that of directly affected states. Thus, the ICJ in *Barcelona Traction* recognised the existence of that distinct class of obligations *erga omnes*, which makes 'an essential distinction' 'between the obligations of a State towards the international community as a whole, and those arising vis-a-vis another State in the field of diplomatic protection'.[124] The case demonstrates the reality of a plurality of inter-legalities: (1) the derivation via legal enkapsis of CIL from municipal practice on the legal personality and nationality of corporations, itself sourced from private (corporation) law, which was then (2) applied to a (public) international law dispute involving states; and (3) the diverse conflicting interests involved – of the corporation shareholders as against the corporation itself, of states with conflicting claims to the right to invoke diplomatic protection; and of the international legal order itself, which requires predictability, stability and fairness in the resolution of such conflicting claims.

In Palombella's terms, here we encounter a single specimen of law, CIL, bringing the composite legal nature of a dispute to the surface. The dispute implicates functional fields of law that embody material interconnectedness and at the same time concern overlapping legal regimes and legal orders: (private) commercial law, national law, (public) international law, domestic orders, transnational and international legal orders.[125] Finally, these regimes and orders are self-referential, reflexive, resilient and coherent in themselves.[126] As a retrocipatory analogy to the numerical aspect, these variegated multiplicity of legal interests are woven into a jural unity as coordinated by the enkaptic relations of states in international law as coordinational law. Indeed, *Barcelona Traction* also underlines the need for jural harmonisation of interests implicated in the coordinational relationship of states (the retrocipatory analogy to the aesthetic aspect) in a proportionate manner (retrocipatory analogy to the economic aspect) that any ruling in a legal dispute must consider.

122 *Barcelona Traction* [37].
123 ibid [33–34].
124 ibid.
125 Klabbers & Palombella (n 7) 1.
126 Palombella (n 2) 368.

Jural harmonisation eschews any excessive pursuit of a legal interest over against the others and finds an optimal balance between and among them according to a retributive measure of proportionality.[127] The coordinational relationship between and among states is correlatively enkaptic in nature, as opposed to one involving a part-whole relation characterised by relations of hierarchy and subordination, or of a foundational relation, where one is the basis of another. In coordinational relationships, even where the issues involved pertain to fundamental norms of international law, states never lose their identities as states! This is an essential inference made out of the doctrine of societal sphere sovereignty. The failure to properly understand the distinction between coordinational and communal relations all too often gives rise to unmet, if not unreasonable expectations of what international law can do.[128] It is also at the heart of a proper understanding of the phenomenon of inter-legality as legal enkapsis.

8 Conclusion

Recent codification work of the ILC has devalued the two-factor formula of state practice and *opinio juris* to identify CIL. This gives rise to the question of how to account philosophically for this development. I suggest that such account is properly a question of the concept of law – one often elided, papered over, or otherwise not recognised as a foundational issue, in the continuing debates about the nature of CIL. I have shown that a fruitful alternative approach to understanding CIL is the *Encyclopedia of the Science of Law* developed by Herman Dooyeweerd. It distinguishes the jural aspect from all other aspects of reality, accounting for the former's internal structure as it is interconnected with that of the fourteen other aspects, in ascending (anticipatory and regulative) and descending (retrocipatory and constitutive) analogical relations. Dooyeweerd's approach examines the nature of the jural dimension through three interrelated pillars.

The first pillar is his modal theory of the jural aspect, which is one of the irreducible yet interconnected universal multidimensional modes or

[127] Dooyeweerd, *Tentative Encyclopedia* (n 14) Vol 8/3, 29.

[128] Or for that matter, the stress Palombella places on the distinction between normative claim and compliance in inter-legality, Palombella (n 2) 371; by Dooyeweerd's account, and against Hart, international law is not a primitive system, because the domestic analogy does not apply to the primarily coordinational nature of the international legal order.

aspects of reality, and through which the second and third pillars – entities and enkapsis – are viewed and understood as legal phenomena. The second pillar is his theory of entities, which give rise to pluralistic legal ontologies unique to their particular practice or sphere (entities as rule complexes, each sovereign in its own orbit and exhibiting a differentiated responsibility and differentiated integrity). The third pillar concerns the various ways in which entities and relations engage in enkapsis or enkaptic interlacements, resulting in complex intertwinements of the formal and the material sources of law with profound implications on the private-public (law) distinction. Meanwhile, in 'legal enkapsis' different material sources of law display a mutual interrelationship (enkaptic interlacement) that bind and limit without altogether cancelling one another – a process accounted for by a growing and contemporary movement in legal anthropology as 'inter-legality'. Enkapsis combines the two pillars of his philosophy – the theory of modal aspects and the theory of entities, into a comprehensive and integrative concept of law, thus providing a better systematic and coherent account of inter-legality.

From an encyclopedic modal analysis, there is an inner antinomy to the well-known two-factor formula: the received interpretation of an *opinio* is an analogy to the psychic sphere, which precedes and anticipates (points towards) the jural aspect. The psychic aspect cannot define what is normative of the jural aspect, for such would deny the jural aspect its inherent normativity and violate the principle of sphere sovereignty, in which no aspect is reducible to any other aspect. Rather, *opinio* should be interpreted as the ordering will of a competent organ correlated with the legal will of legal subjects accepting legal responsibility arising from material-legal principles positivised into law by the competent organ. Moreover, this must be seen against the background of the entire constellation of the architectonic modal structure of the jural aspect, in which various analogies come into play in the proper understanding of the making of CIL. Further, I have shown the relevance of legal enkapsis through an examination of CIL as a formal source of law and how it actually weaves together material legal principles in *concreto*. Thus, CIL may be an original source of law in one sphere of competence but may be a derived source of law in another. In other words, its material bases may lie in the particular enkaptic interlacements involved, displaying a multilayered inter-legality of structural-material legal principles. As such, CIL becomes an embodiment of differentiated material legal principles derived from other fields and spheres of law.

Finally, I have demonstrated this phenomenon of differentiated inter-legalities in CIL through concrete examples: in the duality of treaty and CIL norms, IHL, international economic law and state responsibility. Dooyeweerd's theory of the sources of law is a prescient and comprehensive approach to inter-legality in both domestic and international law, in which we are able to account: 'for the very fact that several times *either the norm to be applied in a specific case, and controlling it, derives from a different context and from a different regime of legality, or the norm to be applied results from a concurring/competing legality*'.[129]

[129] Palombella (n 2) 373 (emphasis in the original).

PART III

The Practice of Customary International Law Across Various Fora

Diversity of Approaches and Actors

11

Customary International Law in the Reasoning of International Courts and Tribunals

VLADYSLAV LANOVOY*

1 Introduction

A century ago, Baron Descamps, who presided over the work of the Committee of Jurists that drafted the Statute of the Permanent Court of International Justice (PCIJ), observed that custom has shaped 'the development and establishment of the law of nations'.[1] The continuing relevance of custom as a source of international law is unquestionable to the present day. Despite efforts to codify rules and principles of customary international law (CIL) in multilateral conventions, often initiated by the International Law Commission (ILC), few of these instruments 'have achieved universal or truly broad participation'.[2] Numerous recent decisions of international courts and tribunals confirm that custom is not condemned to disintegrate[3] and certainly does more than simply fill gaps left by the existing treaty regimes, as has been suggested elsewhere.[4] International law has always been and remains principally a customary law.[5]

It is perhaps unsurprising that custom, as a universal unwritten law binding upon sovereign states, has intrigued legal minds over the

* The author would like to thank Heather Clark, Pierre-Marie Dupuy, Iñaki Navarrete-Arechavaleta and Omri Sender for their helpful comments.

1 Advisory Committee of Jurists, *Procès-Verbaux of the Proceedings of the Committee: June 16th–July 24th with Annexes* (Van Langenhuysen Brothers 1920) 322.

2 P Tomka, 'Custom and the International Court of Justice' (2013) 12 LPICT 195, 196.

3 RJ Dupuy, 'Coutume sage et coutume sauvage', *Mélanges offerts à Charles Rousseau: La communauté internationale* (Pedone 1974) 76 ('*condamnée à l'éclatement*').

4 C Chaumont, 'Cours général de droit international public' (1970) 129 RdC 333, 435.

5 S Sur, *La coutume internationale* (Librairies Techniques 1990) 1; O Sender & M Wood, 'Custom's Bright Future: The Continuing Importance of Customary International Law' in CA Bradley (ed), *Custom's Future: International Law in a Changing World* (Cambridge University Press 2016) 360.

centuries, not least because it raises a host of fascinating and challenging theoretical and practical issues relating to the method and process of its formation.[6] To some observers it resembles 'a riddle wrapped in a mystery inside an enigma':[7] how can states act out of a sense of legal obligation in order to create a new customary norm, if the legal obligation does not exist until they have acted?[8] What is the balance of power in the married couple of state practice and *opinio juris sive necessitatis*? How does one go about ascertaining the required generality of practice in order to conclude the existence of custom? What role should be reserved to the practice of specially affected states, and how may these be identified? Many of these issues have been subject of or would merit a treatise on their own but, overall, they are indicative of what is often seen as the rather disorderly and chaotic nature of the process by which unwritten law develops in a horizontal and decentralised system of sovereign states which, whether we like it or not, remain the primary providers of custom.[9]

In 1988, at a colloquium entitled 'Change and Stability in International Law-Making', Jimenez de Aréchaga, the former president of the International Court of Justice (ICJ or the Court), spoke of CIL as being 'spontaneous, unintentional, unconscious in its origin, disorderly, uncertain in its form, slow in its establishment'.[10] Similarly, Henkin described 'the process of making customary law [a]s informal, haphazard, not deliberate, even partly unintentional and fortuitous ... unstructured

[6] For recent inquiries into CIL, see for example M Hakimi, 'Making Sense of Customary International Law' (2020) 118 MichLRev 1487; O Chasapis-Tassinis, 'Customary International Law: Interpretation from Beginning to End' (2020) 31 EJIL 235; J d'Aspremont, 'The Four Lives of Customary International Law' (2019) 21 ICLR 229; L Gradoni, 'Un-Procedural Customary Law' (2019) 10 JIDS 175.

[7] D Bodansky, 'Does Custom Have a Source?' (2014) 108 AJIL Unbound 179.

[8] ibid 182 (presenting this question as the ultimate paradox of CIL understood in line with the traditional methodology underlying its formation and identification).

[9] Dupuy (n 3) 76 ('*les pourvoyeurs principaux du droit coutumier*'); for recent scholarship examining the ways in which other actors, namely international organisations, may directly contribute to the formation of CIL see for example K Daugirdas, 'International Organizations and the Creation of Customary International Law' (2020) 31 EJIL 201; DM DeBartolo, 'Identifying International Organizations' Contributions to Custom' (2014) 108 AJIL Unbound 174; compare ILC Study Group, 'Draft Conclusions on the Identification of Customary International Law' (30 April–1 June and 2 July–10 August 2018) UN Doc A/73/10, reproduced in [2018/II – Part Two] YBILC 11 (hereinafter 'ILC Conclusions') Conclusion 12; see also M Wood, 'Second Report on Identification of Customary International Law' (2014) 2(1) YBILC 163, 183 [45].

[10] See A Cassese & JHH Weiler, *Change and Stability in International Law-Making* (Walter de Gruyter 1988) 1.

and slow'.[11] More recent inquiries into the method and process of CIL have called it 'chaotic, unstructured, and politically charged [in which] the participants make and respond to competing claims on the law as they advance their own agendas',[12] an 'inherently contingent and variable kind of law'[13] or even 'hopelessly indeterminate'.[14] Others have decried custom as being unfit to accompany the rapid pace of developments in international relations nowadays[15] and in a more heterogeneous international community.[16]

Accordingly, no effort has been spared at the international level to analyse the process of custom formation and methodology for its identification.[17] The detailed inquiry into the subject conducted by the ILC under the leadership of Sir Michael Wood is the most recent and authoritative of such efforts.[18] The outcome of its work, in the form of Conclusions on Identification of Customary International Law (ILC Conclusions), sought to provide greater certainty as to the process of identification of CIL and to provide therefore practical guidance to

[11] L Henkin, *How Nations Behave: Law and Foreign Policy* (2nd ed, Columbia University Press 1979) 34.

[12] M Hakimi, 'Custom's Method and Process: Lessons from Humanitarian Law' in CA Bradley (ed), *Custom's Future: International Law in a Changing World* (Cambridge University Press 2016) 149.

[13] Hakimi (n 6) 1487.

[14] J Tasioulas, 'Customary International Law: A Moral Judgment-Based Account' (2014) 108 AJIL Unbound 328, 332.

[15] P Reuter, 'Principes de droit international public' (1961) 103 RdC 425, 466 ('*les règles coutumières ne sont pas adaptées au rythme rapide de l'évolution du monde moderne*'); see also C de Visscher, 'Reflections on the Present Prospects of International Adjudication' (1956) 50 AJIL 467, 472 ('the traditional development of custom is ill suited to the present pace of international relations'); Chaumont (n 4) 434 (describing custom as a craft process, '*le procédé, artisanal sous sa forme ancienne*').

[16] GM Danilenko, *Law-Making in the International Community* (Martinus Nijhoff 1993) xiii.

[17] See for example ILA, Committee on Formation of Customary (General) International Law, 'Final Report of the Committee: Statement of Principles Applicable to the Formation of General Customary International Law' (London Conference, 2000); JM Henckaerts & L Doswald-Beck, *Customary International Humanitarian Law, Vol I (Rules), Vol II (Practice)* (Cambridge University Press 2005); see also IDI, 'The Elaboration of General Multilateral Conventions and of Non-contractual Instruments Having a Normative Function or Objective' (*IDI Resolution*, Session of Cairo, 1987), Conclusions 14, 20 & 22; IDI, 'Problems Arising from a Succession of Codification Conventions on a Particular Subject' (*IDI Resolution*, Session of Lisbon, 1995), Conclusions 2 & 5, 10–13.

[18] ILC Conclusions (n 9); for their endorsement by the UNGA see UNGA Res 73/203, 'Identification of Customary International Law' (11 January 2019) UN Doc A/RES/73/203 [4].

judges and lawyers called to apply such law. Some of the ILC Conclusions will be discussed below.

The focus of this chapter, however, will be on the reasoning of international courts and tribunals and the ways in which they have identified rules of CIL and their content. Four recent studies have already examined various aspects of this practice, with a particular focus on the ICJ. This is to be expected as the Court is the only mechanism of general jurisdiction, has had the greatest number and variety of cases among international courts and tribunals where it has had to ascertain the existence of CIL, and in light of the authority it enjoys as the principal judicial organ of the United Nations. Talmon concludes that beyond inductive or deductive reasoning, the ICJ usually proceeds by asserting the existence of rules of CIL, or combining 'a mixture of induction, deduction and assertion'.[19] Tams describes the role of the Court as clarifying the 'meta-law' on the identification of CIL, and has already identified similar 'argumentative shortcuts' to those that will be addressed in this chapter.[20] Choi and Gulati argue that the ICJ has completely ignored the traditional methodology.[21] Petersen helpfully sets out a detailed classification of the Court's approaches to CIL and factors that shape the ICJ's decision-making in that context.[22] This chapter builds on some of these findings, and its added value is intended to lie in providing an up-to-date analysis of the ICJ's practice as well as expanding the scope of the inquiry beyond the ICJ. In classifying the dominant shortcuts that courts and tribunals have adopted in their reasoning when identifying CIL, this chapter seeks to highlight the systemic issues they may raise in the foreseeable future.

The chapter proceeds as follows. Section 2 briefly sets out the traditional methodology for the identification of CIL as recognised in the jurisprudence of the ICJ and as reaffirmed in the ILC Conclusions. Section 3 analyses the recent practice of international courts and tribunals and specifically their use of a variety of shortcuts for the identification of CIL. Section 4 contains preliminary conclusions as to the challenges that employing such shortcuts in the reasoning of

[19] S Talmon, 'Determining Customary International Law: The ICJ's Methodology between Induction, Deduction and Assertion' (2015) 26 EJIL 417, 441.

[20] CJ Tams, 'Meta-Custom and the Court: A Study in Judicial Law-Making' (2015) 14 LPICT 51, 69–78.

[21] SJ Choi & M Gulati, 'Customary International Law: How Do Courts Do It?' in CA Bradley (ed), *Custom's Future: International Law in a Changing World* (Cambridge University Press 2016) 147.

[22] N Petersen, 'The International Court of Justice and the Judicial Process of Identifying Customary International Law' (2017) 28 EJIL 357.

international courts and tribunals poses to the continuing validity of the methodology for the identification of CIL, the authority of the decisions rendered, and the perception of the role of the international judge not only as an idle scribe of CIL but as a lawmaking agent.

2 The Traditional Methodology for the Identification of CIL

Much ink has been spilled on the methodology for the identification of 'international custom, as evidence of a general practice accepted as law'.[23] This perhaps not fully felicitous wording of Article 38(1)(b) of the Statute of the ICJ,[24] sets out two constituent elements of CIL, namely a general practice and its acceptance as law (also known as *opinio juris sive necessitatis* or *opinio juris*).[25] To borrow the words of one arbitral tribunal, these two elements are the 'guiding beacons' of CIL, a law which is not frozen in time but continues to evolve in accordance with the realities of the international community.[26]

As noted by the ILC, the process of identifying CIL 'is not always susceptible to exact formulations'.[27] Indeed, the end-product of the Commission's inquiry into the subject aimed to set out a 'clear guidance without being overly prescriptive'.[28] The ILC Conclusions and their commentaries contain a wealth of materials on almost every aspect of the two-element methodology, its theoretical and practical application.[29] This chapter does not aim to revisit the methodology for the identification of CIL, which by and large is well-established and accepted by

[23] Statute of the International Court of Justice (adopted 26 June 1945, entered into force 24 October 1945) 1 UNTS 993, art 38(1)(b).

[24] J Crawford, 'Chance, Order, Change: The Course of International Law' (2013) 365 RdC 9, 49–50.

[25] ILC Conclusions (n 9) Conclusion 2; but see P Haggenmacher, 'La doctrine des deux éléments du droit coutumier dans la pratique de la Cour internationale' (1986) 90 RGDIP 5, 31(arguing that at their genesis these two elements formed a single unity: '*les deux "éléments" qu'on se plaît à y discerner se fondent en une unité indistincte*'); see similarly P Guggenheim, 'Les deux éléments de la coutume internationale', *La technique et les principes du droit public: Etudes en l'honneur de Georges Scelle, vol 1* (LGDJ 1950) 275.

[26] *Merrill & Ring Forestry LP v Canada* (Award of 31 March 2010) ICSID Case No UNCT/07/1 [193].

[27] ILC Conclusions (n 9) General Commentary [4].

[28] ibid.

[29] For the assessment of the ILC Conclusions see for example G Nolte, 'How to Identify Customary International Law? On the Outcome of the Work of the International Law Commission (2018)' (2019) 62 JYIL 251.

states,[30] if not 'set in stone'.[31] This chapter only aims to show that the demonstration that this methodology has been followed is often missing in practice and is frequently replaced by shortcuts in the reasoning of international courts and tribunals. It is in this context that it may be worth briefly recalling the gist of the traditional methodology for the identification of CIL, as it will set the scene for the subsequent analysis of international jurisprudence.

The ICJ's *North Sea Continental Shelf* judgment remains a central reference point for any inquiry into the processes of formation and identification of CIL. It represents the fundamental mark that has been left by the Court on 'shaping the meta-law of custom'.[32] In that case, the Court had to determine whether the rule of equidistance, as set out in Article 6 of the 1958 Geneva Convention on the Continental Shelf, was binding on Germany under CIL as Germany was not a party to the Geneva Convention. In holding that this was not the case, the ICJ set out its methodology for the identification of CIL, outlining a range of criteria that may be relevant to that process. The Court held that 'two conditions must be fulfilled', namely the existence of 'a settled practice' as well as 'evidence of a belief that this practice is rendered obligatory by the existence of a rule of law requiring it'.[33] In its more recent jurisprudence, the ICJ has reaffirmed that both elements of custom 'are closely linked'.[34] Thus, in ascertaining the existence of custom, one must look at what states do or do not do, and whether their conduct reflects the sense of a legal obligation. This is the crux of the traditional 'two-element approach', which according to the ILC 'serves to ensure that the exercise of identifying rules of customary international law results in determining only such rules as actually exist'.[35]

[30] Wood (n 9) 169, 171–72 [3(a) & 21]; See also UNGA Res 73/203 (n 4) [4].

[31] Tams (n 20) 60; see *Continental Shelf (Libyan Arab Jamahiriya v Malta)* (Judgment) [1985] ICJ Rep 13, 29 [27]; *Military and Paramilitary Activities in and against Nicaragua (Nicaragua v USA)* (Merits) [1986] ICJ Rep 14, 97 [183]; *Legality of the Threat or Use of Nuclear Weapons* (Advisory Opinion) [1996] ICJ Rep 226, 253–55 [64–73]; *Jurisdictional Immunities of the State (Germany v Italy: Greece intervening)* (Judgment) [2012] ICJ Rep 99, 122–23 [55].

[32] Tams (n 20) 51; J Kammerhofer, 'Uncertainty in the Formal Sources of International Law: Customary International Law and Some of Its Problems' (2004) 15 EJIL 523, 524.

[33] *North Sea Continental Shelf Cases (Federal Republic of Germany v Denmark; Federal Republic of Germany v The Netherlands) (Judgment)* [1969] ICJ Rep 3, 44 [77]; see also *Jurisdictional Immunities of the State* (n 31) 122–23 [55].

[34] *Legal Consequences of the Separation of the Chagos Archipelago from Mauritius in 1965* (Advisory Opinion) [2019] ICJ Rep 95, 131 [149].

[35] ILC Conclusions (n 9) 125, Commentary to Conclusion 2 [1].

As far as the required evidence of each element of custom is concerned, ILC Conclusion 3 illustrates the level of scrutiny that is ordinarily required from an adjudicator pronouncing on the customary nature of a given rule:

Conclusion 3

1. In assessing evidence for the purpose of ascertaining whether there is a general practice and whether that practice is accepted as law (*opinio juris*), regard must be had to the overall context, the nature of the rule and the particular circumstances in which the evidence in question is to be found.
2. Each of the two constituent elements is to be separately ascertained. This requires an assessment of evidence for each element.

Two important aspects follow from this conclusion insofar as the practice of international courts and tribunals in identifying CIL is concerned. First, evidence of practice must be assessed considering the overall context, the nature of the rule and the circumstances in which the evidence is to be found. Second, there should be an independent demonstration of each of the two constituent elements in the reasoning of international courts and tribunals. In other words, two distinct inquiries must be carried out. On the one hand, the adjudicator must be satisfied that the relevant practice exists and is sufficiently widespread, representative and, most importantly, consistent.[36] On the other hand, the adjudicator must ascertain that that practice is accompanied by the sense of legal right or obligation. While this approach is commonly accepted and sound in theory, the actual practice of international courts and tribunals is sometimes a rather different reality.

Judges of international courts and tribunals have been described as 'technician[s] of the application of international law'.[37] But it is no secret that they are much more than that, particularly when it comes to unwritten sources of international law. As the scribes of CIL, seeking to make sense of the unwritten practice of states in the reasoning of their decisions, judges speak with authority and expertise. They are certainly sophisticated scribes and not robots[38] for they do not follow a prescribed form of legal reasoning.

[36] ibid 135, Conclusion 8.

[37] M Bedjaoui, 'L'opportunité dans les décisions de la Cour internationale de Justice' in L Boisson de Chazournes & V Gowlland-Debbas (eds), *The International Legal System in Quest of Equity and Universality* (Kluwer 2001) 563 ('*Le juge international est avant tout le technicien de l'application du droit international*').

[38] ibid 564 ('*en vérité nous sommes loin de la robotisation de "l'office du juge", réduit à un comportement programmé dans l'ordre national, comme dans l'ordre international. Il est même à parier que la "machine à syllogismes", la "machine à dire le droit", la "machine*

It is thus unsurprising that every time an international court or tribunal, and especially the ICJ, renders a judgment or an advisory opinion, there is no shortage of opinions on what the Court did right or wrong (often beside the point of what was actually in dispute). Be that as it may, what a scholar expects from the reasoning in a judicial or arbitral decision is often quite different from what the parties to the case as well as judges, arbitrators or other external observers, including states, consider to be sufficient. In addition, a host of factors, many of which may not be visible to outside observers, influence the content of that reasoning. This may also explain why the content of such reasoning regarding the identification of CIL is so variable across different institutions and even from the same institution over time.

Institutional and practical constraints are particularly evident when a court or tribunal is called to pronounce on the existence and content of CIL. Institutionally, there is an expectation of efficiency and good administration of justice, which would not allow to undertake a comprehensive analysis of the practice and *opinio juris* of almost 200 states in every single case and in respect of every single rule of CIL that the parties may seek to rely on. In many instances, it would be a hopeless or non-manageable exercise; in others, there is simply no need to reinvent the wheel where the rule or principle in question is well-established. Practically, there are also several limitations that may prevent international courts and tribunals from making their legal reasoning and demonstration of CIL more comprehensive and consistent with the traditional two-element methodology, which are often overlooked in the existing scholarship. Three stand out in particular. First, a judgment or an advisory opinion is not an academic exercise; it aims to make the legal reasoning as succinct and clear as possible to dispose of the relevant issues. Second, it is not always feasible to arrive at a comprehensive and/or representative selection of state practice and *opinio juris* in the preparation of a decision. The issue of selectivity and unbalanced representation of practice (either because the practice of many states is simply unavailable, unreported or inaccessible) is often addressed by being less specific in order to secure a more convincing majority or bypass issues that could undermine the logical structure and coherence of a decision as a whole. Some courts and tribunals have expressly acknowledged these concerns as directly

à juger" ne pourra pas voir le jour' ('In truth, we are a long way from the robotisation of the "office of the judge", reduced to a programmed behaviour in the domestic legal order, as well as the international one. It is even a safe bet that the "syllogism machine", the "law-making machine", the "judging machine" will never see the light of day'.)

impacting how they present their reasoning on CIL.[39] The third and final constraint, which applies to judges even more prominently than to academics, is that of language, and with it legal culture, and the influence it has on 'how its speakers conceptualise, and therefore approach, legal reasoning'.[40]

Keeping the above constraints in mind, this chapter will demonstrate that there is a considerable variety of shortcuts in the reasoning of international courts and tribunals. These shortcuts show in turn that the methodology for the identification of CIL, as laid down in *North Sea Continental Shelf*, is often sacrificed for the sake of expediency. While it may be a matter of course in international adjudication, this may, in the long run, raise questions about the continuing validity of that methodology, the role that international judges play not only in the identification but also in the formation of CIL, and the coherence of CIL as a source of law made by states and for states.

3 Shortcuts in the Reasoning of International Courts and Tribunals on CIL

Having recalled the basic tenets of the traditional methodology for the identification of CIL and the challenges faced by international courts and tribunals, this section turns to their actual practice in recent years. It will quickly become apparent that international courts and tribunals have often found shortcuts in their reasoning to sidestep a full-fledged demonstration of the application of that methodology. The logic of 'less is more' is a unifying aspect of many of the decisions analysed below. This chapter will only discuss a few examples of cases without aspiring to be comprehensive. However, the set of cases analysed below is sufficiently representative to show that recourse to these shortcuts is on the rise. It is a phenomenon which is visible both across various international courts and tribunals, and within a single institution, as the example of the ICJ aptly demonstrates.

This review of the recent practice also shows that there is a variety of shortcuts that international courts and tribunals have followed when

39 See for example *Cargill Incorporated v Mexico* (Award of 18 September 2009) ICSID Case No ARB(AF)/05/2 [274] ('The Tribunal acknowledges, however, that surveys of State practice are difficult to undertake and particularly difficult in the case of norms such as "fair and equitable treatment" where developed examples of State practice may not be many or readily accessible').

40 PM Dupuy, 'Introduction to Customary International Law' in PM Dupuy (ed), *Customary International Law* (Elgar 2021) x.

identifying CIL. In this author's view, the following three approaches dominate, with apologies for the somewhat colloquial terminology: (1) 'Check the written materials to find CIL'; (2) 'It is CIL because the ICJ has said so'; and (3) 'It is CIL because the ILC has said so'.

In addition to these three shortcuts which will be analysed in greater detail, there are also other ways of sidestepping the full-fledged demonstration of the traditional methodology.[41] Some of them have already been studied, at least in respect of the ICJ. There are several examples of mere assertions of CIL without any demonstration at all, but this phenomenon is not limited to the ICJ.[42] In some cases, the Court states that it has carefully examined the existing state practice and *opinio juris*, without however making any demonstration thereof.[43] 'Homework done but not demonstrated' so to speak. It is open to question whether these relatively common instances of declaring that a given rule is or is not part of CIL constitute a shortcut to the existing methodology, or rather simply a way of presenting the conclusions without demonstrating the exact elements in support of those conclusions.[44] Either way, these examples are methodologically unsatisfactory, because in law, just like in mathematics, the result, even a correct one, may not always withstand scrutiny without adequate demonstration.

Similarly, on several occasions the ICJ appears to have accepted the existence of an agreement of the parties to a dispute on the CIL status of a given rule as instrumental in reaching its conclusion on the subject, without any additional inquiry into state practice or *opinio juris* beyond those two states.[45] There are instances of other international courts and

41 See for example Petersen (n 22) 368.

42 See for example *Iran v USA* (Award of 2 July 2014) Award No 602-A15(IV)/A24-FT (IUSCT) [283]; *Delimitation of the Maritime Boundary in the Atlantic Ocean (Ghana/Côte d'Ivoire)* (Judgment) [2017] ITLOS Rep 4, 151–52 [558]; *Responsibilities and Obligations of States with Respect to Activities in the Area* (Advisory Opinion) [2011] ITLOS Rep 10, 28 [57].

43 See for example *Arrest Warrant of 11 April 2000 (Democratic Republic of the Congo v Belgium)* (Judgment) [2002] ICJ Rep 3, 24 [58]; *Ahmadou Sadio Diallo (Republic of Guinea v Democratic Republic of the Congo)* (Preliminary Objections) [2007] ICJ Rep 582, 615 [89–90].

44 See O Sender & M Wood, 'The International Court of Justice and Customary International Law: A Reply to Stefan Talmon' [2015] EJIL: Talk! <https://bit.ly/3xKvWOd> (arguing that '[u]nlike induction and deduction, assertion is self-evidently not a methodology for determining the existence of a rule of customary international law. It is essentially a way of drafting a judgment, a way of stating a conclusion familiar to lawyers working in certain national systems').

45 See for example *Territorial and Maritime Dispute (Nicaragua v Colombia)* (Judgment) [2012] ICJ Rep 624, 666 [114–18]; *Continental Shelf (Libyan Arab Jamahiriya/Malta)* 29 [26]; *Maritime Delimitation and Territorial Questions between Qatar and Bahrain (Qatar*

tribunals taking the same shortcut.[46] While such an approach may be justifiable in cases of local or regional custom, it is unclear as to why or how the purported agreement of the parties to a given dispute sheds light on the existence or absence of a particular rule of CIL on a universal scale. Although scholars have considered that this approach may allow the ICJ to signal impartiality due to the institutional constraints it faces,[47] it may equally lead to expansive and not adequately supported conclusions.[48]

Other shortcuts are not sufficiently widespread to merit an in-depth discussion given the limited scope of this chapter. For instance, one decision has been identified where an investor-state arbitral tribunal held that it had to determine the content of a rule of CIL by looking into indirect evidence, such as judicial decisions or scholarly writings, because otherwise it would be compelled to declare *non liquet.*[49] Customary international law thus conceived would be nothing but a means available to the adjudicator to fill the gaps of international law. Be that as it may, what all these and other approaches have in common is that they fuel this and other authors' concerns about departing from any, even if minimal, demonstration of the application of the methodology for the identification of CIL and the impact it may have on the certainty and predictability of international law.

3.1 'Check the Written Materials to Find CIL'

The relationship between treaties and custom is longstanding and intertwined.[50] It is widely accepted that treaties may: (i) reflect pre-existing rules of CIL; (ii) generate a new rule and serve as evidence of the customary character of that rule; or (iii) have a crystallising effect for an emerging rule of

v Bahrain) (Merits) [2001] ICJ Rep 40 [167, 175]; compare *Military and Paramilitary Activities in and against Nicaragua* (n 31) [184] ('the shared view of the Parties as to the content of what they regard as the rule [of CIL] is not enough'); see also Petersen (n 22) 369–72; T Abe, 'ICJ Practice in Determining the Existence of Customary International Law' (2019) 62 JYIL 274.

46 *The Loewen Group Inc and Raymond L Loewen v United States* (Final Award of 26 June 2003) ICSID Case No ARB(AF)/98/3 [129].

47 Petersen (n 22) 369–72.

48 See for example *Certain Activities Carried Out by Nicaragua in the Border Area (Costa Rica v Nicaragua) and Construction of a Road in Costa Rica along the San Juan River (Nicaragua v Costa Rica)* (Judgment) [2015] ICJ Rep 665, 707–08 [106].

49 *Windstream Energy LLC v Canada* (Award of 27 September 2016) UNCITRAL/NAFTA, PCA Case No 2013-22 [351].

50 See for example BB Jia, 'The Relations between Treaties and Custom' (2010) 9 ChinJIntLaw 81; RR Baxter, 'Treaties and Custom' (1970) 129 RdC 27.

CIL.[51] The ICJ has long recognised that 'multilateral conventions may have an important role to play in recording and defining rules deriving from custom, or indeed in developing them'.[52]

At the same time, CIL has an 'existence of its own' even where an identical or similar rule may find expression in a treaty.[53] As such, it is perhaps surprising to see how often international courts and tribunals resort to treaties or other written materials to identify CIL. The practice is particularly prominent in the ICJ's jurisprudence.[54] There are numerous examples in which the Court has, with little or no additional analysis, recognised the customary status of certain treaty provisions.[55] The examples below of two recent decisions rendered by the ICJ and one by an arbitral tribunal demonstrate some of the potential problems with this shortcut. In all three cases, in identifying CIL, recourse was had to written materials, namely treaties that were not even in force between the parties to the dispute, or resolutions of the General Assembly (GA).

In the *Jurisdictional Immunities of the State* case, the Court had to determine whether the so-called territorial tort exception to state immunity existed under CIL.[56] While the Court attempted to demonstrate the application of the two-element methodology in its reasoning, it focused its analysis rather disproportionally on Article 11 of the 1972 European Convention on State Immunity and Article 12 of the 2004 UN Convention on Jurisdictional Immunities of States and Their Property.[57]Having acknowledged that neither convention was actually in force between Germany and Italy, the Court stressed that these instruments were therefore 'relevant only in so far as their provisions and the process of their adoption and implementation shed light on the content of customary international law'.[58] However, the Court appeared

[51] *North Sea Continental Shelf Cases* (n 33) 41–43 [71–74]; see ILC Conclusions (n 9) Conclusion 11.

[52] *Continental Shelf (Libyan Arab Jamahiriya/Malta)* 29–30 [27].

[53] *Military and Paramilitary Activities in and against Nicaragua* 94–96 (n 31) [177–78].

[54] Petersen (n 22) 372–75.

[55] See for example *Armed Activities on the Territory of the Congo (Democratic Republic of the Congo v Uganda)* (Judgment) [2005] ICJ Rep 168, 243 [217]; *Legal Consequences of the Construction of a Wall in the Occupied Palestinian Territories* (Advisory Opinion) [2004] ICJ Rep 136, 172 [89]; *United States Diplomatic and Consular Staff in Tehran (USA v Iran)* (Judgment) [1980] ICJ Rep 3, 24 [45]; *Land, Island and Maritime Frontier Dispute (El Salvador/Honduras: Nicaragua Intervening)* (Judgment) [1992] ICJ Rep 351, 588 [383]; for many other cases proving the point see Tams (n 20) 71–73.

[56] *Jurisdictional Immunities of the State* (n 31) 126–35 [62–79].

[57] ibid 128–30 [66–69].

[58] ibid 128 [66].

to ascribe much weight to these instruments amidst its analysis of other aspects of the relevant state practice, including case law and legislation of various states, as well as in identifying *opinio juris*.[59] It would thus seem that this was a conscious shortcut on the part of the Court in the process of identifying CIL.

Similarly, the *Enrica Lexie* arbitral tribunal recently adopted the same shortcut in examining whether the 'territorial tort' exception to immunity from criminal jurisdiction was recognised under CIL. The tribunal noted that even though national courts in a relatively significant number of states look at the 2004 UN Convention on Jurisdictional Immunities of States and Their Property as a reflection of CIL, the 'states that consider that there is immunity for foreign states before other states' national courts do not accept the provisions of this convention, including Article 12'.[60] It went on, however, to analyse the criteria set out in Article 12 of that convention to conclude that 'even if a "territorial tort" exception were recognised under CIL, the exception would not apply' in the circumstances of that case, as the marines were on board the *Enrica Lexie*, and not on Indian territory.[61] Even though the arbitral tribunal ultimately did not rule on whether such an exception exists under CIL, it is telling that its reasoning relied exclusively on an unratified treaty instrument rather than on any inquiry into the relevant state practice and *opinio juris*.

In the *Chagos* Advisory Opinion, the ICJ had to determine whether the right to self-determination existed as a customary norm at the time of events, that is, in the period between 1965 when the UK excised the Chagos archipelago from Mauritius, then a non-self-governing territory administered by the UK, and 1968 when Mauritius attained independence.[62] In determining whether the right to self-determination was part of CIL at the time, the Court held that 'State practice and *opinio juris* . . . are consolidated and confirmed gradually over time',[63] and highlighted the 'progressive consolidation of the law on self-determination'.[64]

59 ibid 135 [77].

60 *The 'Enrica Lexie' Incident (Italy v India)* (Award of 21 May 2020) PCA Case No 2015–28 [866].

61 ibid [871].

62 *Legal Consequences of the Separation of the Chagos Archipelago from Mauritius in 1965* (n 34) 134–35 [161].

63 ibid 130 [142].

64 ibid 135 [161].

It is noteworthy that in identifying the existence, content and scope of the right to self-determination under CIL, the Court placed much emphasis on the GA resolution 1514 (XV) of 14 December 1960, and the circumstances in which it was adopted.[65] The Court saw a clear correlation between the acceleration of the decolonisation process (with eighteen countries in 1960 and additional twenty-eight non-self-governing territories during the 1960s exercising the right to self-determination) and the adoption of resolution 1514 (XV) which 'clarifie[d] the content and scope' of that right.[66] It considered the adoption of this resolution to be 'a defining moment in the consolidation of State practice on decolonization'.[67] The weight that the Court ascribed to this and other resolutions of the GA in reaching its conclusion on the right to self-determination and its content under CIL[68] was more significant when compared to its earlier jurisprudence, which had taken account of resolutions as evidence of *opinio juris*.[69] It also allowed the Court to effectively dispose of the issue of an allegedly inconsistent practice underlying the obligation incumbent on administering powers to respect the boundaries of the non-self-governing territory.[70] That said, in the particular circumstances of this case, the Court's reliance on the relevant resolutions as a shortcut for identifying CIL might be said to be justified by the conditions in which these resolutions were adopted, their normative value, and the absence of any genuine opposition among states to the existence and content of the right to self-determination.[71]

Beyond these and many other examples of this shortcut to the traditional methodology in practice, one area of increasing interaction between custom and treaty law has been in the context of investor-state arbitration. Several investor-state arbitral tribunals have resisted the temptation of automatically relying on hundreds of bilateral investment treaties (BITs) to inform their task of ascertaining whether certain

[65] ibid 132 [150, 152].
[66] ibid [150].
[67] ibid [150].
[68] ibid 132–33 [151–55].
[69] See for example *Military and Paramilitary Activities in and against Nicaragua* (n 31) 99–100 [188]; *Legality of the Threat or Use of Nuclear Weapons* (n 31) 254–55 [70]; compare *Armed Activities on the Territory of the Congo (Democratic Republic of the Congo v Uganda)* (n 55) 225–26 [161–62].
[70] *Legal Consequences of the Separation of the Chagos Archipelago from Mauritius in 1965* (n 34) 134 [160].
[71] See ibid 132–34 [152–53, 160]; compare *Legality of the Threat or Use of Nuclear Weapons* (n 31) 255 [71] (emphasising that several resolutions under consideration were 'adopted with substantial numbers of negative votes and abstentions').

standards of protection find expression in CIL. For example, in *Glamis Gold*, the tribunal rightly rejected the contention that Article 1105 of the North American Free Trade Agreement (NAFTA) was merely a 'shorthand reference to customary international law',[72] having emphasised that the task of seeking a treaty interpretation of a given standard is fundamentally different from that of ascertaining CIL.[73] The tribunal held that 'arbitral decisions that apply an autonomous standard provide no guidance inasmuch as the entire method of reasoning does not bear on an inquiry into custom'.[74]

As a result, the tribunal rejected the claimant's so-called convergence theory between CIL and specific treaty provisions in BITs, ruling that while 'it is possible that some BITs converge with the requirements established by customary international law; there are, however, numerous BITs that have been interpreted as going beyond customary international law, and thereby requiring more than that to which the NAFTA State Parties have agreed'.[75] Similarly, the *Cargill* tribunal considered that 'significant evidentiary weight should not be afforded to autonomous clauses inasmuch as it could be assumed that such clauses were adopted precisely because they set a standard other than that required by custom'.[76]

Other investor-state tribunals have however reached their conclusions on the content of CIL by relying on specific treaty provisions.[77] The temptation of adjudicators to rely on written materials is strong, particularly where these are the culmination of a codification process or seem to crystallise an emerging rule of CIL.[78] However, investment treaty context is a particularly salient example of an organic mismatch between customary and treaty law. This is the case, for instance, of the evolution of

[72] *Glamis Gold Ltd v United States* (Final Award of 8 June 2009) UNCITRAL/NAFTA<www.italaw.com/sites/default/files/case-documents/ita0378.pdf> [608].

[73] ibid [20].

[74] ibid [608].

[75] ibid [609]; see similarly ILC Conclusions (n 9) Conclusion 11(2).

[76] *Cargill Incorporated v Mexico* [276].

[77] See for example *Mondev International Ltd v United States* (Award of 11 October 2002) ICSID Case No ARB(AF)/99/2 [117, 125]; *CME Czech Republic BV v Czech Republic* (Final Award of 14 March 2003) UNCITRAL [497–98]; *Generation Ukraine Inc v Ukraine* (Final Award of 16 September 2003) ICSID Case No ARB/00/9 [11.3].

[78] See P Tomka, 'Customary International Law in the Jurisprudence of the World Court: The Increasing Relevance of Codification' in L Lijnzaad & Council of Europe (eds), *The Judge and International Custom* (Brill Nijhoff 2016) 2–24.

the minimum standard of protection of aliens and their property, as opposed to the evolution of the standard of fair and equitable treatment in the treaty practices over the last couple of decades.[79] Hasty attempts at converging the two, albeit perhaps desirable in the interest of a greater and more uniform protection to be accorded to investors and investments, are not justifiable through the lenses of a proper methodology for the identification of CIL.[80]

The above examples show how in identifying CIL international courts and tribunals have used written materials, including treaties that are not in force between the parties or GA resolutions. They have done so, at least in part, to circumvent the practical difficulties that may arise in demonstrating the two elements of custom. As such, the existence of codification in a particular area of law allows the courts and tribunals to consider whether the instances of practice support the written rule rather than induce that rule from specific instances of practice. Some authors have seen in such increasing reliance on written law in identifying CIL a departure from 'traditional' towards 'modern' custom, from a predominantly 'inductive' towards a 'deductive' process, from the examination of particular instances of practice towards general statements.[81] While there is nothing per se problematic with such a shortcut,[82] the absence of any detailed discussion on the actual evidence of state practice and *opinio juris* beyond the written materials themselves may lead to unconvincing or incomplete reasoning, which could have been easily remedied with an even minimal attempt at applying the traditional methodology for the identification of CIL.

[79] P Dumberry, 'Has the Fair and Equitable Treatment Standard Become a Rule of Customary International Law?' (2017) 8 JIDS 155 (arguing that the standard of fair and equitable treatment is not part of CIL); see generally M Paparinskis, *The International Minimum Standard and Fair and Equitable Treatment* (Oxford University Press 2013).

[80] In two relatively recent cases, the ICJ has discarded the developments in the context of specific investment treaty provisions as capable of affecting the state of CIL. See for example *Ahmadou Sadio Diallo (Republic of Guinea v Democratic Republic of the Congo)* (n 43) 615 [89–90]; *Obligation to Negotiate Access to the Pacific Ocean (Bolivia v Chile)* (Judgment) [2018] ICJ Rep 507, 559 [162].

[81] A Roberts, 'Traditional and Modern Approaches to Customary International Law: A Reconciliation' (2001) 95 AJIL 757, 758.

[82] See for example GP Buzzini, 'La théorie des sources face au droit international général: Réflexions sur l'émergence du droit objectif dans l'ordre juridique international' (2002) 106 RGDIP 581, 609–12.

3.2 'It Is CIL Because the ICJ Has Said So'

Another frequently used shortcut for identifying CIL is that of relying on previous decisions of the ICJ. This shortcut poses several normative issues.

First, it suggests that the dispute settlement mechanism has adopted a de facto system of binding precedent, whereby earlier decisions constitute authoritative pronouncements on CIL, even if that law may be susceptible to change over time. This is visible, for instance, in *Jones et al* v. *United Kingdom*, where the European Court of Human Rights, when addressing the so-called *jus cogens* exception to state immunity, turned directly to the ICJ judgment in the *Jurisdictional Immunities of the State*, considering it to be 'authoritative as regards the content of customary international law' and that no such exception had yet crystallised in CIL.[83] It did so without any additional demonstration in support of its conclusion. Similarly, in cases where the World Trade Organization (WTO) Appellate Body could identify an earlier decision of the ICJ on a particular rule, it automatically accepted the customary law character thereof.[84] The issue lies in the assumption that the ICJ's decision is dispositive on the question whether or not a given rule is part of CIL.

Second, this shortcut quite often leads to improper generalisations of the scope of earlier judicial pronouncements on CIL. The *Territorial and Maritime Dispute* serves as a perfect example of this phenomenon. In that case, the ICJ recalled its previous jurisprudence, namely *Qatar* v. *Bahrain*, in which it had recognised that the principles of maritime delimitation in Articles 74 and 83 of the UN Convention on the Law of the Sea reflect CIL, and so too does Article 121, paragraphs 1 and 2 thereof.[85] However, in *Qatar* v. *Bahrain*, the Court 'did not specifically address paragraph 3 of Article 121', which qualifies maritime entitlements of a rock as opposed to those of an island. Despite that, the Court merely observed in the *Territorial and Maritime Dispute* that 'the legal régime of islands set out in UNCLOS Article 121 forms an indivisible régime, all of which (as Colombia and Nicaragua recognise) has the status

[83] *Jones et al v United Kingdom* ECtHR App Nos 34356/06 and 40528/06 (14 January 2014) [198] see also [88–94].

[84] See for example WTO, *US – Definitive Safeguard Measures on Imports of Circular Welded Carbon Quality Line Pipe from Korea*, Appellate Body Report (15 February 2002) WT/DS202/AB/R [259].

[85] *Territorial and Maritime Dispute (Nicaragua v Colombia)* (n 45) 674 [139]; see also *Maritime Delimitation and Territorial Questions between Qatar and Bahrain (Qatar v Bahrain)* (n 45) [167] [185] [195].

of customary international law'.[86] This approach is methodologically questionable. The Court makes no attempt at demonstrating the State practice or *opinio juris* in respect of the rule expressed in that treaty provision. Instead, it merely cross-references its earlier judgment, while recognising that that judgment contained no demonstration whatsoever as to the customary law character of the above-mentioned provision.

Perhaps a more worrying example can be found in the *Certain Activities* case, where the Court directly transposed the taxonomy of substantive and procedural obligations from a specific treaty regime as applied in its earlier case law, namely the 1975 Statute on the River Uruguay in the *Pulp Mills* case, to its analysis of the state of CIL in the context of transboundary environmental harm.[87] The Court went on to consider that substantive and procedural obligations with similar content apply as a matter of CIL to any non-industrial activities.[88] It did so without examining in any detail State practice or *opinio juris*.[89] The trend of generalising the scope of previous decisions on CIL is, of course, not limited to the ICJ's practice. For instance, in its 2011 Advisory Opinion, the Seabed Disputes Chamber noted that both the International Tribunal for the Law of the Sea (ITLOS) and the ICJ had considered some of the specific provisions of the Articles on the Responsibility of States for Internationally Wrongful Acts (ARSIWA) as reflecting CIL and appeared to apply that conclusion to the ARSIWA more widely.[90]

Third, the opposite side of this shortcut consists in simply not pronouncing on whether a given rule is part of CIL, in the absence of a pre-existing decision by international courts or tribunals on the subject. In principle, there is nothing improper in refraining from pronouncing on whether a given rule is or is not customary or the scope thereof, particularly when such determination is unnecessary for the court or tribunal to dispose of the issues before it.[91] Indeed, it is in line with the common

[86] *Territorial and Maritime Dispute (Nicaragua v Colombia)* (n 45) 674 [139].

[87] *Certain Activities Carried Out by Nicaragua in the Border Area (Costa Rica v Nicaragua) and Construction of a Road in Costa Rica along the San Juan River (Nicaragua v Costa Rica)* (n 48) 706–07 and 711–12 [104] [118].

[88] ibid 706 [104] ff.

[89] ibid 785, Separate Opinion of Judge Donoghue [10].

[90] *Responsibilities and Obligations of States with Respect to Activities in the Area* 56 [169]; see also *Request for Advisory Opinion Submitted by the Sub-Regional Fisheries Commission* (Advisory Opinion) [2015] ITLOS Rep 4, 44 [144].

[91] There are numerous examples in practice. For some recent ones, see for example *Jadhav (India v Pakistan)* (Judgment) [2019] ICJ Rep 418, 442 [89–90]; *US – Definitive Anti-Dumping*

judicial avoidance techniques and may be justified in the interests of economy of means.[92] However, the absence of an authoritative decision of the ICJ or any other court or tribunal as a reason not to pronounce on the customary law character of a given rule shows a complete misunderstanding insofar as the authority of any judicial or arbitral decision is concerned. A perfect illustration can be found in the *EC – Hormones* Report of the Appellate Body[93] or the subsequent *EC – Biotech* WTO Panel Report,[94] both avoiding pronouncing on the customary law status of the precautionary principle in the absence of an 'authoritative decision by an international court or tribunal which recognises the precautionary principle as a principle of general or customary international law'.[95] Other convincing reasons may certainly explain the reluctance of the WTO Appellate Body and Panel to pronounce on the question whether the precautionary principle is part of CIL. However, it is certainly striking that the basis relied on, first and foremost, is the absence of an authoritative decision by an international court or tribunal recognising the principle as such.

3.3 *'It Is CIL Because the ILC Has Said So'*

Finally, one of the most common shortcuts is to refer to the ILC work as direct evidence of the state of CIL. As noted by the Commission itself, the 'weight to be given to [its] determinations depends, however, on various factors, including the sources relied upon by the Commission, the stage reached in its work, and above all upon States' reception of its output'.[96] Functionally, this shortcut is understandable to the extent that the ILC is tasked with codification and progressive development of international law. In the eyes of international courts and tribunals, the ILC's work is rightly 'most valuable, primarily due to the thoroughness of the

and Countervailing Duties on Certain Products from China, Appellate Body Report (11 March 2011) WT/DS379/AB/R [311]; *The South China Sea Arbitration* (Philippines v China) (Award of 12 July 2016) PCA Case No 2013–19, 471–72 [812].

92 For an interesting categorisation of avoidance techniques in the practice of the ICJ, namely merits-avoidance, issues-avoidance and deferential standards of review see F Fouchard, 'Allowing "Leeway to Expediency, Without Abandoning Principle"? The International Court of Justice's Use of Avoidance Techniques' (2020) 33 LJIL 767.

93 WTO, *EC – Hormones*, Appellate Body Report (16 January 1998) WT/DS26/AB/R [123].

94 WTO, *EC – Measures Affecting the Approval and Marketing of Biotech Products*, Panel Report (21 November 2006) WT/DS291/R, WT/DS292/R, WT/DS293/R [7.88–7.89].

95 ibid [7.88].

96 ILC Conclusions (n 9) 142, Commentary to Part Five [2].

procedures utilized by [it]'.[97] This is particularly the case where a given set of guidelines or articles produced by the ILC is rooted in a thorough survey of state practice and has garnered widespread support among states at the UN Sixth Legal Committee. In such circumstances, it is understandable that there are numerous examples where the ICJ, for instance, has 'referred to provisions of the ILC's codification work as customary with no or little further comment'.[98]

However, at times, the reasoning of international courts and tribunals jumps too quickly to the conclusion that a given ILC end-product reflects the state of CIL. More fundamentally, the reasoning in respect of one particular provision tends to be almost automatically generalised to one or the other provision of the same end-product or, even worse, to the end-product of the ILC as a whole, without any inquiry as to whether that finds support in state practice and *opinio juris*. On many occasions, such generalising techniques may be harmless, but at times they may also forestall the development of the law, which might have purposefully been left in an open-ended texture to be refined by subsequent state practice and *opinio juris*.

For instance, the ICJ has often rubber-stamped statements of the ILC as representative of CIL. It has done so, even when such conclusions were only temporary or provisional, without the final product having been yet adopted. For example, the Court famously did so in the *Gabčíkovo-Nagymaros Project* with respect to the state of necessity, without much of a probing inquiry,[99] even if earlier tribunals had failed to recognise it as a circumstance precluding wrongfulness under CIL.[100] Subsequently, courts and tribunals have simply embraced with approval the ICJ's finding as to the customary law character of what were to become

[97] Tomka (n 2) 202.

[98] ibid 203; see also A Pellet, 'L'adaptation du droit international aux besoins changeants de la société internationale' (2007) 329 RdC 9, 42 (suggesting that the ICJ finds refuge in the ILC's work: '*la Cour s'abrit[e] derrière les travaux de la [CDI] pour établir l'existence d'une règle juridique lorsque ceci lui paraît opportun*' ('the Court takes refuge behind the work of the [ILC] to establish the existence of a legal rule where this seems appropriate')); Talmon (n 19) 437 (presenting the trend as 'outsourcing the inductive process to the Commission').

[99] *Gabčíkovo-Nagymaros Project (Hungary v Slovakia)* (Judgment) [1997] ICJ Rep 7, 39–40 & 46 [50–51, 58]; see also *Difference Relating to Immunity from Legal Process of a Special Rapporteur of the Commission on Human Rights* (Advisory Opinion) [1999] ICJ Rep 62, 87 [62]; *The M/V 'Saiga' (No 2) (Saint Vincent and the Grenadines v Guinea)* (Judgment) [1999] ITLOS Rep 10, 65 [171].

[100] *Rainbow Warrior Affair* (Decision, 30 April 1990) 20 RIAA 215, 254.

Article 25 ARSIWA.[101] In a similar vein of almost blindly approving the work-product of the ILC, the Court in the *Application of the Convention of Genocide* case had recourse by analogy to Article 16 ARSIWA, which it considered to reflect CIL and which informed the Court's analysis whether Serbia breached Article III(e) of the Genocide Convention.[102] In doing so, the Court applied and interpreted restrictively the requirements set out in Article 16 ARSIWA, even if there are serious doubts as to whether some of those requirements adequately reflect the existing state practice and *opinio juris*.[103]

The use of the ILC's work as a reflection of CIL has been part of judicial reasoning for years. It has indeed become a sort of 'ping-pong'[104] or a 'normative Ponzi scheme',[105] whereby the Court heavily draws on and consolidates the work of the Commission, which in turn looks up to the ICJ's case law for authoritative recognition of the rules or principles it seeks to codify. That is understandable on many levels, considering 'a special vantage and authority' that the ILC enjoys as a result of its close relationship with states.[106] Although some have argued that that special position makes 'its pronouncements less tendentious, and more conservative, in character',[107] the reality is that in many areas of international law the ILC is the only mechanism through which the views of states may be directly ascertained and made known in a systematic way. In this sense, the ILC seeks to 'adopt a real-world approach and provide drafts that will hopefully prove useful and acceptable to the international community'.[108] However, more often

[101] *The M/V 'Saiga' (No 2) (Saint Vincent and the Grenadines v Guinea)* (n 99) 56 [133]; *CMS Gas Transmission Company v Argentina* (Award, 12 May 2005) ICSID Case No ARB/01/8 [315]; *Enron Corporation and Ponderosa Assets v Argentina* (Award, 22 May 2007) ICSID Case No ARB/01/3 [303]; *Suez, Sociedad General de Aguas de Barcelona SA and Vivendi Universal SA v Argentina* (Decision on Liability, 30 July 2010) ICSID Case No ARB/03/19 [258].

[102] *Application of the Convention on the Prevention and Punishment of the Crime of Genocide (Bosnia and Herzegovina v Serbia and Montenegro)* (Judgment) [2007] ICJ Rep 43, 217 [420].

[103] See V Lanovoy, *Complicity and Its Limits in the Law of International Responsibility* (Hart 2016) 162–260, 339.

[104] Tams (n 20) 74.

[105] S Villalpando, 'On the International Court of Justice and the Determination of Rules of Law' (2013) 26 LJIL 243, 248.

[106] ET Swaine, 'Identifying Customary International Law: First Thoughts on the ILC's First Steps' (2014) 108 AJIL Unbound 184.

[107] ibid.

[108] M Wood & O Sender, 'Identifying the Rules for Identifying Customary International Law: Response from Michael Wood and Omri Sender' (2014) 108 AJIL Unbound 198.

than not, its drafts are a combination of elements of codification proper and progressive development of international law. This means that a thorough analysis may be required when an international court or tribunal later has to determine whether a given article, guideline, or rule, as presented by the ILC, reflects CIL.

As the examples above (and many more could be cited) demonstrate,[109] the relationship between international courts and tribunals and the ILC has grown increasingly symbiotic over time. One is thus left under the impression that judges do not scratch beneath the surface when making relatively bold pronouncements on rules that until their adoption by the ILC had an uncertain status in international law and were so regarded by states, including in their views as expressed at the UN Sixth Legal Committee. More fundamentally, the tendency to generalise conclusions as to the customary character in respect of one specific provision to other provisions, or to the entirety of projects under consideration, shows the over-reliance by courts and tribunals on the work of the ILC, without always adequately probing into the underlying evidence of state practice and *opinio juris*.

4 Conclusion

This chapter has shown that international courts and tribunals employ various shortcuts to the methodology for CIL identification. In their decisions, international courts and tribunals have often sidestepped an inductive analysis of the two elements, and have found comfort in indirect evidence such as written materials, prior judicial or arbitral decisions, or the work of the ILC. This is telling of the fact that beyond the dichotomy of 'traditional' and 'modern' CIL, as it has been discussed in scholarship, perhaps the time is ripe to speak of 'postmodern' approaches of international courts and tribunals to the identification of CIL. While these approaches do not expressly reject the traditional methodology, the reasoning employed is terser, more assertive, and often fails to provide any demonstration of state practice or *opinio*

[109] See for example *Application of the Convention on the Prevention and Punishment of the Crime of Genocide (Croatia v Serbia)* (Preliminary Objections) [2008] ICJ Rep 412, 459 [127]; *Legal Consequences of the Construction of a Wall in the Occupied Palestinian Territories* 195 [140]; *Land and Maritime Boundary between Cameroon and Nigeria (Cameroon v Nigeria: Equatorial Guinea intervening)* (Judgment) [2002] ICJ Rep 303, 430 [265].

juris, in whichever order or form. Thus, such 'shortcuts are just too appealing not to be taken'.[110]

Of course, some of these shortcuts may be more or less justified in light of various factors, including the particular circumstances of the case, the subject-matter in which such determinations are being made, the level of institutional integration of the dispute settlement mechanism, the authority with which it is endowed, and the considerations of efficiency and economy of means. Incidentally, these approaches may preserve 'the inherently flexible nature of this source of international law'.[111] They may also be instrumental in obviating inherent concerns about selectivity or political expediency when embarking upon a more thorough demonstration of relevant state practice and *opinio juris* in the reasoning of any court or tribunal. As noted by Judge Tomka, former president of the ICJ, 'the Court has never found it necessary to undertake such an inquiry for every rule claimed to be customary in a particular case and instead has made use of the best and most expedient evidence available to determine whether a customary rule of this sort exists'.[112]

However, as the decisions referred to in this chapter show, the fundamental issue is that the legal analysis undertaken by international courts and tribunals too often fails in demonstrating even a minimal inquiry into those material elements of custom. Thus, although in principle many of the shortcuts could be justified in light of the various institutional and practical constraints referred to in the introduction, these shortcuts become a serious issue when they are the sole or the dominant element in the reasoning underlying the identification of CIL.

In the long run, the summary and flexible approach according to which the ICJ and other international courts and tribunals have gone about identifying CIL may lead to systemic issues. This author sees the potential for at least three. First, the more frequent use of shortcuts brings with it an increased risk that conclusions are being reached that are not fully supported by the practice of states and *opinio juris*, thus departing from or undermining the traditional methodology for the identification of CIL.[113]

[110] Tams (n 20) 78.

[111] Wood and Sender (n 108) 197.

[112] Tomka (n 2) 197–98.

[113] J Verhoeven, 'Considérations sur ce qui est commun: Cours général de droit international public' (2008) 334 RdC 9, 115 (arguing that there is no credible alternative to the two-element methodology). For the continuing benefits of the two-element methodology see FL Bordin, 'A Glass Half Full? The Character, Function and Value of the Two-Element Approach to Identifying Customary International Law' (2019) 21 ICLR 283.

Second, and relatedly, judicial declarations of CIL may determine the direction of further development of state practice or, even worse, hamper the development of the law in a given area. The power of the court or tribunal to identify, or not, a given norm as part of CIL has an immeasurable impact on developing or, conversely, arresting 'processes of growth without which the law will be atrophied'.[114] Once an international court or tribunal, particularly the ICJ, declares that a rule is part of CIL, states rarely if ever question the validity of that finding in their subsequent practice.[115] The same holds true for other international courts and tribunals, which rarely if ever question the validity of findings on CIL made by their international peers.[116] Domestic courts follow suit, and their restatements based on the pronouncements made by their international peers become the relevant state practice, thereby generating a vicious circle as far as the development of CIL is concerned.[117] In such circumstances, pronouncements by international courts and tribunals on CIL often are just short of a self-fulfilling prophecy of CIL, and domestic courts simply materialise that prophecy. Third, the increasing use of shortcuts in the identification of CIL may definitively cast doubt on a legal fiction, according to which 'judges merely state, but never create – the law'.[118] This would have important flow-on consequences for the distribution of powers in the existing lawmaking framework in the international legal order, however imperfect and unsatisfactory it may be.

These potential systemic issues are not to be dismissed lightly. At the same time, they are not insurmountable, as there are several examples in the jurisprudence of much more satisfactory efforts, even if perhaps not perfectly comprehensive, at demonstrating the process and the evidence on the basis of which CIL is identified. The ILC Conclusions are certainly

[114] W Jenks, 'The Challenge of Universality' (1959) 53 ASIL PROC 85, 95.

[115] DP O'Connell, *International Law, Vol 1* (2nd ed, Stevens 1970) 32 (speaking of the 'truly astonishing deference' accorded to the ICJ decisions).

[116] A Alvarez-Jiménez, 'Methods for the Identification of Customary International Law in the International Court of Justice's Jurisprudence: 2000–2009' (2011) 60 ICLQ 681, 684.

[117] For the illustration of this phenomenon in respect of Article 16 ARSIWA see for example *Al-Saadoon & Ors v Secretary of State for Defence* (17 March 2015) High Court of England & Wales [2015] EWHC 715 (Admin) [192–98]; *Al-M* (5 November 2003) German Constitutional Court, 2 BvR 1506/03 [47]; for further examples of widespread deference by domestic courts to the findings of their international peers on CIL, subject to a few limited exceptions, see C Ryngaert & D Hora Siccama, 'Ascertaining Customary International Law: An Inquiry into the Methods Used by Domestic Courts' (2018) 65 NILR 1, 17–22; see also C Miles, 'Thoughts on Domestic Adjudication and the Identification and Formation of Customary International Law' (2017) 27 IYIL 133.

[118] Dupuy (n 40) xiii.

a useful reminder for judges and arbitrators to follow in ascertaining CIL.[119] In the interests of legal certainty and predictability, it is hoped that greater methodological rigour and formalism will prevail over the expediency offered by shortcuts in the reasoning of international courts and tribunals on CIL.

[119] For its immediate usefulness in the practice of domestic courts see for example *The Freedom and Justice Party & Ors R (on the Application of) v The Secretary of State for Foreign and Commonwealth Affairs & Anor* [2018] Court of Appeal of England & Wales, EWCA Civ 1719 [18].

12

Eureka! On Courts' Discretion in 'Ascertaining' Rules of Customary International Law

LETIZIA LO GIACCO

1 Introduction

A number of scholarly contributions on the theme have tackled the determination[1] of *rules* of customary international law (CIL) under the umbrella of the *methodological* dualism between induction and deduction.[2] Induction indicates the method of extrapolating a general rule by observing specific instances of practice; deduction is instead the method whereby a specific rule can be inferred from generally accepted rules or principles.[3] 'Filling lacunae' by ascertaining rules of CIL is a canonical example of deduction. Accordingly, two main approaches have been described as underpinning the ascertainment of rules of CIL by interpreters. Pursuant to the former, a rule of CIL may be induced from patterns of state practice and *opinio juris*. This way of ascertaining rules of law proceeds from the observation of empirical facts and, via induction, *finds* rules of customary law which are created by the combination of the two

[1] Preliminarily, 'determination' is used to mirror the terminology adopted in Article 38(1)(d) of the Statute of the International Court of Justice ('judicial decisions ... as subsidiary means for the determination of rules of law'). However, throughout this text, the term 'ascertainment' is used to reflect an approach to legal interpretation in which the interpreter contributes to the construction of the 'object' to interpret. 'Ascertainment' is contrasted with 'identification', used by the ILC, which is arguably underpinned by a competing approach to legal interpretation as a mere *finding* exercise. On the point, see Chapter 2 in this volume.

[2] See, *inter alios*, R Kolb, 'Selected Problems in the Theory of Customary International Law' (2003) 50 NILR 119; S Talmon, 'Determining Customary International Law: The ICJ's Methodology between Induction, Deduction and Assertion' (2015) 26 EJIL 417; A Roberts, 'Traditional and Modern Approaches to Customary International Law: A Reconciliation' (2001) 95 AJIL 757, 758.

[3] Talmon (n 2) 420.

constitutive elements.[4] As such, 'lawyers move behind the law and cannot pretend to lead it'.[5] For the latter, instead, a rule of CIL may be (logically) deduced from the existence of axiomatic rules or principles of international law, for example the principle of sovereign equality between states[6] or the principle of good faith.[7] This way of reasoning is based on the fundamental assumption that international law is a system of rules where claims to the existence of CIL rules draw justification from their coherence with other rules within the system.[8]

However, the methodological dualism between induction and deduction is too ambitious and short-sighted at the same time. It is too ambitious, because it presumes that an extensive review of empirical elements would point to the existence of a legal rule presumably and incontrovertibly existing 'out there', ready to be singled out; and it is too short-sighted, because it disguises – as empirically or logically based – the argumentative nature of claims to existing rules of CIL and the role that judicial discretion plays therein. Interestingly, the methodological oscillation between induction and deduction may be portrayed as a struggle between a historical and a philosophical approach to the identification of rules. While the historical approach (induction) would point to the collection of facts as empirical evidence from which to extract a certain historical narrative, on the other hand the philosophical approach (deduction) would serve as an efficient short-cut to make a logically based descriptive claim of the

[4] The link between the two elements was spelled out by the ICJ in the seminal *North Sea Continental Shelf* cases, in which the court considered that

> [n]ot only must the acts concerned amount to a settled practice, but they must also be such, or be carried out in such a way, as to be evidence of a belief that this practice is rendered obligatory by the existence of a rule of law requiring it. The need for such a belief, ie the existence of a subjective element, is implicit in the very notion of the *opinio juris sive necessitates*. See *North Sea Continental Shelf Cases (Federal Republic of Germany v Denmark; Federal Republic of Germany v The Netherlands)* (Judgment) [1969] ICJ Rep 3 [77].

[5] G Schwarzenberger, 'The Inductive Approach to International Law' (1947) 60 HarvLRev 539, 568.

[6] See for example *Arrest Warrant case (Democratic Republic of the Congo v Belgium)* (Judgment) [2002] ICJ Rep 3 [53–55].

[7] See for example *Gulf of Maine case (Canada/United States of America)* (Judgment) [1984] ICJ Rep 246 [87].

[8] For a critical account of international law as a system, see J d'Aspremont, 'The International Court of Justice and the Irony of System-Design' (2017) 8 JIDS 366.

law.[9] Importantly, both approaches strive to advance claims to scientific truths, thus leaving little space to the contestation of such *findings*.

In light of the foregoing, this chapter has a twofold aim. First, it recalibrates the debate surrounding the ascertainment of CIL towards an argumentative lens. Such a recalibration is conducive to illuminate the element of *discretion* involved in the ascertainment of rules of CIL, which remains controversially clothed in a method-focused debate. Importantly, this implies looking at potential rules of interpretation[10] of CIL not as a method to *find* the law 'out there', but rather as shared arguments to *justify* any claim to existing rules of CIL.

Secondly, this chapter clarifies an irony surrounding the determination of rules of CIL. If, on the one hand, illuminating the element of discretion defeats the idea of an entirely objective reality observable by courts; on the other hand, the authoritative *verbalisation* of such rules by courts is necessary for their materialisation and for their coming to fruition in the legal practice. In the absence of such authoritative verbalisation, there would hardly be any 'rule' of CIL; at best a rough idea of a metaphysical CIL. This is demonstrated by a number of cases[11] in which, where applicable, courts have relied on prior judicial decisions ascertaining rules of CIL or of 'soft law instruments' codifying such rules *qua* written utterances on CIL.

This chapter is divided into four sections followed by a fifth conclusive one. Section 2 takes the cues from the recent work of the International Law Commission on the Identification of Customary International Law and considers the implications of the shift from a methodological to an argumentative lens for such identification. Section 3 presents a perusal of judicial decisions in the context of international criminal law illustrating the range of discretion exercised by judges in appraising evidentiary elements for the purposes of ascertaining rules of CIL. Section 4 reflects upon the role of courts for the materialisation of 'rules' of CIL and the correlated role that past judicial decisions play in the ascertainment of such rules. Finally, Section 5 draws conclusions.

[9] I owe a special acknowledgement to Adeel Hussain for having suggested this parallel of the dialectics between history and philosophy.

[10] These are not necessarily 'legal', but may be 'disciplining', too. On the point see O Fiss, 'Objectivity and Interpretation' (1982) 34 StanLRev 739, 744; J d'Aspremont, 'The Multidimensional Process of Interpretation' in A Bianchi, D Peat and M Windsor (eds), *Interpretation in International Law* (Oxford University Press 2015) 123.

[11] See for instance Chapter 11 by Lanovoy in this volume.

2 Revisiting Old Myths: From Epistemological Methods to Argumentative Strategies

The work of the International Law Commission (ILC) on the identification of CIL[12] intervenes in the debate about the determination of CIL rules by tackling the long-standing question of the '*methodology*' that interpreters '*must*'[13] apply to identify such rules. Indeed, the international law literature has repeatedly emphasised the difficulties linked to the determination of rules of CIL. One of such difficulties rests with the fact that evidence of state practice and of *opinio juris* may be interpreted differently by different courts, may be considered quantitatively insufficient to prove the existence of customary rules or to be regarded as conclusive of such an existence. Different types of practice may be taken into account, as well as different methods may be employed in this identification activity. This point was expressed by Judge Tanaka in his dissenting opinion in the seminal judgment in the *North Sea Continental Shelf* cases:

> To decide whether these two factors [state practice and *opinio juris*] in the formative process of a customary law *exist or not*, is a delicate and difficult matter. The *repetition*, the number of examples of State practice, the *duration* of time required for the generation of customary law *cannot be mathematically and uniformly decided. Each fact requires to be evaluated relatively according to the different occasions and circumstances.*[14]

In the face of such difficulties, the ILC has laid down preliminary conclusions seeking 'to offer *practical* guidance on how the *existence* of rules of customary international law, and their *content*, are to be determined'.[15]

Two points are in order here. First, the ILC conclusions make reference to two types of activities: one ascertaining the existence of a rule of CIL, which, from a formal point of view, was created by state practice and *opinio juris*; the other determining the content of such an identified rule. Although both these activities are interpretive in character, they concern two ontologically different dimensions: that of law-ascertainment and that of

[12] ILC, 'Draft Conclusions on the Identification of Customary International Law' (30 April–1 June and 2 July–10 August 2018) UN Doc A/73/10, reproduced in [2018/II – Part Two] YBILC 11 (ILC Report 2018).

[13] Notably, the ILC Report uses a prescriptive language.

[14] *North Sea Continental Shelf Cases (Federal Republic of Germany/Denmark; Federal Republic of Germany/Netherlands)* (Judgment) [1969] ICJ Rep 3, Dissenting Opinion of Judge Tanaka 175 (emphasis added).

[15] ILC Report 2018 (n 12) General Commentary 2.

content-determination.[16] While the former articulates itself along elements that are constitutive ingredients to a claim to an existing customary rule, the latter typically hinges on interpretive strategies such as the textualist, intentionalist and purposivist.[17] It is germane to acknowledge that while the ascertainment of rules of CIL is ingrained in a vigorous doctrinal convergence towards the two-pronged structure of state practice and *opinio juris*, albeit identifiable via different methods, the content-determination activity appears fuzzier and is indeed a dimension where the exercise of discretion by interpreters is left most unrestrained. This chapter primarily focuses on the law-ascertainment activity.

Secondly, by offering such preliminary conclusions, the ILC seemingly perpetuates two intrinsically entangled myths, namely the myth of a universal methodology to explore and assess state practice[18] and *opinio juris*; and the myth of a hypothetical 'out there' where to identify already existing rules of CIL.[19] The idea of these being myths stems from a sceptical conception of interpretation, defined as an act consisting in ascribing, as a matter of choice, normative meaning to texts as well as in engaging in legal constructions, especially when no text to interpret in the former sense is available. Indeed, legal construction is particularly relevant in the context of ascertaining rules of CIL as, by definition, such rules are unwritten or, *rectius*, 'unexpressed', and are made expressed though the ascription of a normative meaning to empirical facts.[20] Such definition of interpretation may be further reduced by accepting that also

[16] This distinction is drawn from J d'Aspremont (n 10).

[17] ibid 122.

[18] Compare ILC Report 2018, Conclusion 4(2), referring to the practice of international organisations alongside that of states.

[19] These conclusions may arguably be seen as providing a shared methodology (or meta-rules) comparable to that applicable, *mutatis mutandis*, to the interpretation of international treaties, and potentially of legal texts more broadly. See for example *Prosecutor v Nyiramasuhuko et al* (Judgment) ICTR-98-42-A (14 December 2015) [2137]:

> [t]he Appeals Chamber recalls that, while the Statute 'is legally a very different instrument from an international treaty', it is to be interpreted in good faith in accordance with the ordinary meaning to be given to the terms in their context and in the light of its object and purpose, within the meaning of Article 31(1) of the Vienna Convention on the Law of Treaties of 1969, which reflects customary international law.

Prosecutor v Bemba (Trial Judgment) ICC01/05-01/08 (21 March 2016) [75-86]: '[t]he Appeals Chamber clarified that the interpretation of the Statute is governed, first and foremost, by the VCLT, specifically Articles 31 and 32'.

[20] R Guastini, 'A Realist View on Law and Legal Cognition' (2015) 27 Revus 45, 46-48, in particular, Guastini defines 'unexpressed' norms as those 'lack[ing] any official formulation

texts are no more than facts and therefore interpretation is no more than an act of legal construction of facts bearing a normative meaning. As a consequence, law is a set of interpretive practices in which judges play a central role in constructing the object to interpret.

Against this sceptical understanding of interpretation, the *problématique* of reiterating these legendary beliefs essentially rests with the normative view which produces the empirical facts upon which to substantiate the existence of a certain CIL rule. Indeed, state practice and *opinio juris* do not exist, under these labels, in the empirical world out there, but are an interpreter's intellectual construction. As such, they are first identified, selected, assessed and categorised like relevant by the interpreter, as a reflection of his/her normative ideology.[21] In other words, the selection and assessment of practice and *opinio juris* are but the result of an exercise of discretion, which looms in every act of legal interpretation.

The ILC Report does not consider this stage of construction of relevant facts, but rather assumes that state practice and *opinio juris* are given, intelligible to interpreters in equal terms.[22] However, this position has largely displayed its limits,[23] in that legal interpretation entails a subjective choice of the judge between different possible interpretive outcomes and, thus, it cannot be retained watertight to an interpreter's own normative stance vis-à-vis international law as a legal order and its function.[24] Once assumed that interpreters contribute themselves to construct the object of

in the sources of law, not being a plausible meaning of any particular normative sentence'; see also R Guastini, *Interpretare e Argomentare* (Giuffré 2011) 69–70.

21 The concept of 'normative ideology' is to ascribe to Alf Ross, who defined it as the judge's belief about what the law in force is. On the point, A Ross, *A Textbook of International Law: General Part* (first published 1947, Longmans 2013) 83; A Aarnio, *Reason and Authority* (Ashgate 1997) 74; U Bindreiter, 'The Realist Hans Kelsen' in L Duarte d'Almeida, J Gardner & L Green (eds), *Kelsen Revisited: New Essays on the Pure Theory of Law* (Hart 2013) 112.

22 This position itself may be the product of normative stances, postulating that interpretation in international law is an objective exercise in which the interpreter plays a marginal role.

23 G Hernández, 'Interpretation' in J Kammerhöfer & J d'Aspremont (eds), *International Legal Positivism in a Post-Modern World* (Cambridge University Press 2014) 318–19; I Venzke, 'Post-modern Perspectives on Orthodox Positivism' in J Kammerhofer and J d'Aspremont (eds), *International Legal Positivism in a Post-Modern World* (Cambridge University Press 2014) 182.

24 H Lauterpacht, *The Development of International Law by the International Court* (Praeger 1958) 399; D Kennedy, 'The Turn to Interpretation' (1985) 58 SCalLRev 251; G Hernández (n 23) 326; BZ Tamanaha, *Beyond the Formalist-Realist Divide: The Role of Politics in Judging* (Princeton University Press 2010) 6.

interpretation, professing that interpreters operate a *finding* exercise of legal rules appears a commitment of faith more than anything else. As such, questions pertaining to the law-ascertainment and the content-determination of rules of CIL are inescapably accompanied by rival ideologies about the ontology of interpretation in international law and, more broadly, about international law as a legal order.

In light of the foregoing, the ILC conclusions are worthy of reflection beyond the myth's objectivity and 'out-there-ness' in the ascertainment of rules of CIL it seemingly reiterates. Rather, by moving away from understanding law-ascertainment and content-determination as a finding exercise, one could appreciate the ILC draft conclusions as directives constraining the interpreters' range of discretion in the context of justification. In other words, evidence of state practice and *opinio juris* are used to *justify* the claim to existing rules of CIL, *not to find* them. Looking at induction and deduction as argumentative strategies entails that interpreters of international law lay down norm-descriptive statements about the law that require justification in order to be accepted as correct.

The implications of a recalibration from a methodological to an argumentative lens are manifold. First, it entails looking at *opinio juris* and state practice as corroborative or evidentiary elements, rather than truly constitutive or formative ones. Importantly, their persuasive strength rests on the fact that they are traditionally *accepted* as necessary ingredients to a claim to existing rules of CIL. As questions about the existence and content of CIL rules are addressed within an argumentative framework, it follows that, by way of legal justification, these findings need to persuade that they are correct.[25] Secondly, understanding the ascertainment of rules of CIL as a finding exercise rather than an argumentative activity suggests that there is *one* objectively correct rule to which general practice and *opinio juris* point. Conversely, argumentation, as a process of justification, is premised upon the idea that potentially a range of different hypotheses about existing rules of CIL can be justified and regarded as correct in law.[26] By admitting that different

[25] In this context, it is worth observing that the latest ILC report on the identification of CIL acknowledges the necessity of 'a structured and careful process of legal analysis and [that] *evaluation* is required to ensure that a rule of customary international law is properly identified, thus promoting the *credibility* of the particular determination as well as that of customary international law more broadly'. See ILC Report 2018 (n 12) 122, General commentary 2 (emphasis added).

[26] The hypothesis made by a court is authoritative because the court expresses it, not because this is where a convergent practice of the majority of states points to.

simultaneous plausible interpretations of facts and legal rules are possible, the argumentative lens emphasises the subjective element involved in the ascertainment of rules of CIL and, as such, it embraces rather than negating the diverse and competing normative views informing interpretation in international law. Thirdly, a recalibration from a methodological to an argumentative framework entails that criteria (or meta-rules) envisaged as a universal methodological roadmap to the 'identification' of rules of CIL – for example those proposed by the ILC[27] – are instead arguments restraining the *discretion* of interpreters – with special regard to courts – that is, what it can be considered and how much weight shall be given to these elements[28] in determining the existence and the content of rules of CIL.[29] Against this backdrop, the point is not to establish the appropriate method to identify customary international rules existing out there, but rather to establish the range of discretion which a court can possibly exercise in order for the ascertainment of rules of CIL to be reasonable and not to result in arbitrary adjudication.

3 Judicial Discretion in the Ascertainment of CIL: Clues from the Practice

The preceding sections have attempted to problematise the myth of epistemological methods reiterated in the scholarly debate on the determination of rules of CIL. In the wake of this, a twist to an argumentative lens is suggested to illuminate the element of discretion in legal interpretation, typically left in the background. Discretion, in the context of legal interpretation too, is not a concept of easy definition. One tentative definition has been provided by Cass R. Sustein as 'the capacity to exercise official power as one chooses, by reference to such consideration as one wants to consider, weighted as one wants to weight them'.[30] In

[27] ILC Report 2018 (n 12) 122, General commentary 2.

[28] ibid.

[29] This is not to say that the function of such meta-rules could be disentangled further. For instance, in the context of the rules of the Vienna Convention on the Law of Treaties (VCLT), Michael Waibel considers that 'the ILC and the Vienna conference gave limited consideration to the question of why interpretive principles were normatively desirable' except for 'brief references to legal certainty and the need for convergence in treaty interpretation'. See M Waibel, 'Principles of Treaty Interpretation: Developed for and Applied by National Courts', in HP Aust and G Nolte (eds), *The Interpretation of International Law by Domestic Courts: Uniformity, Diversity, Convergence* (Oxford University Press 2016) 12.

[30] CR Sustein, 'Problems with Rules' (1995) 83 CLR 953, 960.

Sustein's view, '[a] legal system cannot avoid some degree of discretion, in the form of power to choose according to one's moral or political convictions. . . . [T]he interpretation of seemingly rigid rules usually allows for discretion. But a legal system can certainly make choices about how much discretion it wants various people to have'.[31]

Typically, in a legal order, courts are afforded some degree of interpretive discretion, enabling judges to make a choice between possible interpretive outcomes. The international legal order is no exception to this. For instance, Article 38(2) of the Statute of the International Court of Justice provides a useful illustration of the discretion vested in the court by state parties, in that it acknowledges the non-prejudiced '*power* of the Court to decide a case *ex aequo et bono*, if the parties agree thereto'. Likewise, in the *Continental Shelf* case, the International Court of Justice (ICJ) expressly recognised its power to discretionary choices: 'when applying positive international law, a court may *choose* among several possible interpretations of the law the one which appears, in the light of the circumstances of the case, to be closest to the requirements of justice'.[32] Indeed, past judicial decisions on points of CIL are a good terrain to explore the way in which courts exercised discretion in the assessment of evidence of state practice and *opinio juris*. Qualities typically associated with rules of CIL such as repetition, generality, uniformity and duration, as well as the weight to allocate to *opinio juris* as compared to state practice were laid down and elaborated in judicial decisions. Arguably, these case-law-based criteria are an expression of *how* discretion is channelled into legal argumentation and enables the exercise of discretion by a judge to appear rationalised, rather than arbitrary, in that they offer a range of arguments that a court may put forward to justify a certain holding.

This section considers some judicial decisions, as well as separate opinions laid down by the International Criminal Tribunal for the Former Yugoslavia (ICTY) established by UN Security Council resolutions under Chapter VII.[33] Looking at these decisions is particularly

[31] ibid.

[32] *Continental Shelf case (Tunisia v Libyan Arab Jamahiriya)* [1982] ICJ Rep 18 [71] (emphasis added); On the point, see M Kotzur, '*Ex aequo et bono*' (2009) MPEPIL.

[33] UNSC Res 827, 'On Establishment of the International Tribunal for Prosecution of Persons Responsible for Serious Violations of International Humanitarian Law Committed in the Territory of the Former Yugoslavia Since 1991' (12 May 1993) UN Doc S/RES/827; for a more comprehensive study on the use of customary international law by the ICTY, and in the area of international criminal law more broadly, see

appropriate for the purposes of this contribution, given the tribunal's mandate to apply rules that had, 'beyond any doubt', crystallised into CIL.[34] The purpose of showcasing these judicial decisions is to illustrate, by reference to practice, the range of approaches exhibited by judges in the ascertainment of rules of CIL. Arguably, such a variation cannot be adequately explained by the methodological dualism between induction and deduction, as the evaluation of evidentiary elements supporting the existence of a rule of CIL is far from incontrovertible. After all, what judges do is to argue in favour of an interpretation rather than another based on certain elements of state practice and *opinio juris*.[35] As such, statements about the existence of a particular rule of CIL are argumentative in nature and seek to persuade a certain audience of their correctness.

In the seminal *Erdemović* case, the ICTY Appeals Chamber was to consider whether, under CIL, duress would allow a complete defence to a soldier charged with the killing of civilians.[36] To this purpose, national courts' decisions and state legislations were examined. Yet, the threshold beyond which such evidence suffices to demonstrate the existence of a rule of CIL lies within the discretion of an interpreter. For instance, the joint separate opinion of Judges McDonald and Judge Vohrah, appended to the judgment is a good illustration of how elements of state practice and *opinio juris* are hardly incontrovertible and can be differently appraised by different interpreters.

> [F]or a rule to pass into customary international law, the International Court of Justice has authoritatively restated in the *North Sea Continental Shelf* cases that there must exist *extensive and uniform state practice* underpinned by *opinio juris sive necessitatis.* To the extent that the domestic decisions and national laws of States relating to the issue of duress as a defence to murder may be regarded as state practice, *it is quite plain that this practice is not at all consistent.*[37]

respectively N Arajärvi, *The Changing Nature of Customary International Law* (Routledge 2014); B Slütter, *Developments in Customary International Law* (Brill 2010).

[34] UNSC, 'Report of the Secretary-General Pursuant to Paragraph 2 of Security Council Resolution 808' (3 May 1993) UN Doc S/25704.

[35] Compare N MacCormick, 'Argumentation and Interpretation in Law' (1995) 9 Argumentation 467, 467: '[interpretation is] a particular form of practical argumentation in law, in which one argues for a particular understanding of authoritative texts or materials as a special kind of (justifying) reason for legal decisions'.

[36] *Prosecutor v Erdemović* (Judgment) IT-96-22-A (7 October 1997) [19]: 'duress *does not afford a complete defence* to a soldier charged with a crime against humanity and/or a war crime involving the killing of innocent human beings'.

[37] ibid [49] (emphasis added).

This holding considered the defence's survey, in its Notice of Appeal, of

> the criminal codes and legislation of *14 civil law jurisdictions* in which necessity or duress is prescribed as a general exculpatory principle applying to all crimes. . . . Indeed, the rejection of duress as a defence to the killing of innocent human beings in the *Stalag Luft III* and the *Feurstein* cases, both before British military tribunals, and in the *Hölzer* case before a Canadian military tribunal, reflects in essence the common law approach.[38]

Judges McDonald and Vohrah finally concluded that '[n]ot only is state practice on the question as to whether duress is a defence to murder *far from consistent,* this practice of States is *not . . . underpinned* by *opinio juris*',[39] since 'the decisions of these tribunals [the post–World War Two military tribunals] or those of other national courts and military tribunals constitute consistent and uniform State practice underpinned by *opinio juris sive necessitates*'.[40]

The approach of Judges McDonald and Vohrah can be contrasted with the declaration of Judge Robinson to the Appeal Judgment in the *Furundžija* case,[41] in which the judge considered that '[a] *global search,* in the sense of an examination of the practice of every state, *has never been a requirement in seeking to ascertain international custom,* because what one is looking for is a *sufficiently widespread practice of states accompanied by opinio juris. . . .* [I]t is accepted that such [*national*] *decisions may, if they are sufficiently uniform, provide evidence of international custom*'.[42]

This strikes a significant discrepancy between the approach of Judges McDonald and Vohrah, in upholding an *extensive* empirical test, as formulated by the ICJ in the cited *North Sea Continental Shelf* cases, for ascertaining the existence of a rule of CIL, and Judge Robinson who instead submitted that a wide ('global') test has never been the requirement, but rather a *sufficiently widespread practice.* The threshold of empirical evidence demanded by the two approaches is expression of the range of discretion available to the interpreter when engaging in the ascertainment of rules of CIL.

[38] ibid [49].
[39] ibid [50] (emphasis added).
[40] ibid [55].
[41] *Prosecutor v Furundžija* (Appeal Judgment) IT-95-17/1-A (21 July 2000) Declaration of Judge Patrick Robinson [12].
[42] ibid (emphasis added).

Moreover, judges have granted a different weight to state practice and *opinio juris* for the purposes of establishing rules of CIL. One such illustration is offered by the *Kupreskić* case[43] in which the ICTY Trial Chamber acknowledged that *opinio juris* may play a primary evidentiary role at the expense of state practice.[44]

> The question nevertheless arises as to whether these provisions [Article 51(6) and Article 52(1) of the First Additional Protocol of 1977], *assuming that they were not declaratory of customary international law, have subsequently been transformed into general rules of international law. . . .* This is however an area where *opinio iuris sive necessitatis* may play a much greater role than *usus*, as a result of the aforementioned Martens Clause. *In the light of the way States and courts have implemented it, this Clause clearly shows that principles of international humanitarian law may emerge through a customary process under the pressure of the demands of humanity or the dictates of public conscience, even where State practice is scant or inconsistent.* The other element, in the form of *opinio necessitatis, crystallising as a result of the imperatives of humanity or public conscience, may turn out to be the decisive element heralding the emergence of a general rule or principle of humanitarian law.*[45]

The ICTY Trial Chamber further elaborated on the formation of a rule of CIL prohibiting reprisals against civilians by reference to 'widespread *opinio necessitatis*' . . . 'confirmed, first of all, by the adoption, by a vast majority, of a Resolution of the UN General Assembly in 1970 which stated that "civilian populations, or individual members thereof, should not be the object of reprisals"' and by the high number of states that have ratified the First Protocol.[46] The reference to manifold instruments such as the above mentioned UN General Assembly (UNGA) resolution of 1970, a Memorandum of the International Committee of the Red Cross (ICRC) of 7 May 1983, the pronouncement of ICTY Trial Chamber I in *Martić*, 'substantially upholding such a rule',[47] shows the intention of the chamber to find ample corroboration to its claim to the existence of a rule of CIL. This overview, in the *Kupreskić* case, finally led the chamber to

43 *Prosecutor v Kupreskić et al* (Trial Judgment) IT-95–16-T (14 January 2000).

44 Notably, a traditional – evidentiary stringent – approach to the identification of rules of customary law, of the type advocated by Judge McDonald and Judge Vohrah in *Erdemović*, is not necessarily conflicting or irreconcilable with the one upheld by the Trial Chamber in *Kupreskić*. Commentators have looked at those as mirroring types of international custom along a sliding scale. See, *inter alios*, P Chiassoni, 'La consuetudine internazionale: una ricognizione analitica' (2014) 43 Ragion pratica 489.

45 *Prosecutor v Kupreskić et al* (n 43) [527] (emphasis added).

46 ibid [532].

47 ibid.

conclude that 'the demands of humanity and the dictates of public conscience, as manifested in *opinio necessitatis*, have by now brought about the *formation* of a customary rule also binding upon those few States that at some stage did not intend to exclude the abstract legal possibility of resorting to the reprisals under discussion'.[48]

In the *Furundžija* case, the ICTY Trial Chamber was to establish the customary character of the prohibition of torture in time of armed conflict. The chamber found that 'the broad convergence of international instruments and international jurisprudence demonstrates that there is now general acceptance of the main elements contained in the definition set out in article 1 of the Torture Convention'.[49] In particular, indication of the customary character of the prohibition of torture in time of armed conflict was inferred from the number of ratification of relevant international treaties, as well as in the lack of opposing claims by states purporting the contrary.[50] This finding was finally sealed by reference to relevant ICJ judicial decisions.[51]

This overview of judicial pronouncements suggests that judges play a fundamental role in the ascertainment of CIL. In particular, judges' verbalisation of 'rules' of CIL in judicial decisions appear a propaedeutic step for making such rules materialise in an authoritative form and bringing them to fruition in legal practice. Courts' engagement in such verbalisation may also be determinant to assess the interpretive steps (meta-rules) claimed to have been adopted for the ascertainment of such

48 ibid [533] (emphasis added).

49 *Prosecutor v Furundžija* (Trial Judgment) IT-95–17/1-T (10 December 1998) [161], the chamber considered this finding 'incontrovertible'; see ibid [139]: 'It therefore seems incontrovertible that torture in time of armed conflict is prohibited by a general rule of international law. In armed conflicts this rule may be applied both as part of international customary law and – if the requisite conditions are met – qua treaty law, the *content* of the prohibition being the same.'

50 ibid [138]: 'the practically universal participation in these treaties shows that all States accept among other things the prohibition of torture. In other words, this participation is highly indicative of the attitude of States to the prohibition of torture'.

51 ibid:

> the International Court of Justice has authoritatively, albeit not with express reference to torture, confirmed this custom-creating process: in the *Nicaragua* case it held that common article 3 of the 1949 Geneva Conventions, which inter alia prohibits torture against persons taking no active part in hostilities, is now well-established as belonging to the corpus of customary international law and is applicable both to international and internal armed conflicts [See *Military and Paramilitary Activities in and against Nicaragua (Nicaragua v United States of America) (Merits)* [1986] ICJ Rep 14, 113–14 [218]].

rules and possibly challenge them. As recalled earlier, judges may engage in the formal ascertainment of rules of CIL, as well as in the determination of their substantive content.[52] While for the former, state practice and *opinio juris* occupy a prominent role in legal argumentation, for the latter courts are seemingly inclined to refer to existing written formulations as bearing normative value. In fact, reference to existing written formulations allows a court to articulate an interpretation of the *content* of existing rules of CIL in a more persuasive way.

4 The Materialisation of 'Unexpressed' Rules and the Role of Past Decisions

Based on the judicial decisions considered thus far, at least two factors have played a role in allowing the interpreter to modulate the range of discretion: first, the threshold of empirical evidence required for a claim to CIL; second, the more or less weight that an interpreter may attribute to state practice and *opinio juris* as evidentiary elements. In addition, one may consider factors which instead appeared to constrain a judicial exercise of discretion. For instance, the following examples show that prior written formulations of unexpressed rules – first and foremost, although not exclusively, judicial decisions – were typically relied upon in international adjudication.

In the recent *Chagos Advisory Opinion*,[53] the ICJ was to determine 'when the *right* to self-determination crystallised as a customary *rule* binding on all States'.[54] After recalling the trite adage that 'custom is constituted through general practice accepted as law', the court turned to the UNGA resolutions to survey the evidence of state practice, which it considers relevant and determinant for sealing the customary nature of the right to self-determination, notably resolutions 637 (VII)/1952, 738 (VIII)/1953, 1188 (XII)/1957 and 1514 (XV)/1960. The court regarded this latter as 'a defining moment in the consolidation on State practice on decolonization' clarifying 'the *content and scope* of the right to self-determination'.[55] In ascertaining the customary character and the

[52] As mentioned earlier, such a *summa divisio* between form and content is maintained by the ILC too, which considers instances in which the existence of a rule of customary international law is agreed but its content is disputed; compare ILC Report 2018 (n 12) 124, General commentary 4.

[53] *Legal Consequences of the Separation of the Chagos Archipelago from Mauritius in 1965* (Advisory Opinion) [2019] ICJ Rep 95.

[54] ibid [148].

[55] ibid [150].

substantive contours of the right to self-determination, the court thus deferred to UNGA resolution 1514/1960 not only as *declaratory* of the existing customary right to self-determination,[56] but also to determine 'the *content* and *scope* of such a right',[57] namely to *interpret* such a right.[58] Unsurprisingly, such material is used by the court to justify the claim of ascertained rules of CIL having a certain meaning.

In the *Rwamakuba* case,[59] the International Criminal Tribunal for Rwanda (ICTR) Appeals Chamber was confronted with the question whether joint criminal enterprise was an existing mode of liability under CIL, whereby conviction of an individual was permissible. The chamber approached the question by reference to state practice and *opinio juris*, but instead of engaging with these elements, it upheld the finding in the *Tadić* Appeals Judgment pursuant to which the participation to a common plan to commit a crime against humanity was criminalised under CIL before 1992.[60] The ICTY Appeals Chamber has placed similar reliance in other cases on proceedings held following World War II, including the proceedings before the International Military Tribunal and before tribunals operating under Allied Control Council Law No 10 ('Control Council Law No 10'), as indicative of principles of CIL at that time.[61]

Similarly, in the *Kayishema & Ruzindana* case, the Appeals Chamber considered the principle of the right to a fair trial as 'part of customary international law ... embodied in several international instruments,

[56] ibid [152].
[57] ibid [150].
[58] See also ibid [146].
[59] *Prosecutor v Rwamakuba* (Decision on Joint Criminal Enterprise) ICTR-98-44-AR72.4 (22 October 2004).
[60] ibid [14]:

> Norms of customary international law are characterized by the two familiar components of state practice and *opinion juris*. In concluding that customary international law permitted a conviction for, *inter alia*, a crime against humanity through participation in a joint criminal enterprise, the *Tadić* Appeals Judgement held that the recognition of that mode of liability in prosecutions for crimes against humanity and war crimes following World War II constituted evidence of these components.

[61] See for example *Prosecutor v Furundžija* (n 49) [195, 211, 217]; *Prosecutor v Duško Tadić* (Appeal Judgement) IT-94-1-A (15 July 1999) [200, 202]; see also *Prosecutor v Milutinović et al* (Decision on Dragoljub Ojdanić's Motion Challenging Jurisdiction – Joint Criminal Enterprise) IT-99-37-AR72 (21 May 2003) Separate Opinion of Judge David Hunt [12] ('It is clear that, notwithstanding the domestic origin of the laws applied in many trials of persons charged with war crimes at that time, the law which was applied must now be regarded as having been accepted as part of customary international law').

including Article 3 common to the Geneva Conventions [See *Čelebeći* Appeal Judgment, §§138 and 139]'.[62] In the *Hadžihasanović et al* case, the ICTY Appeals Chamber considered that 'to hold that a principle was part of customary international law, it has to be satisfied that State practice recognised the principle on the basis of supporting *opinio juris*'.[63] By reference to the ICJ judicial decisions concluded that 'Article 3 common to the Geneva Conventions of 1949, which has long been accepted as having customary status [See *Corfu Channel, Merits, I.C.J. Reports 1949*, p. 22, and *Military and Paramilitary Activities in and against Nicaragua, I.C.J. Reports 1986*, pp. 112 and 114].' In the same case, the Appeals Chamber found 'that the customary international law rule embodied in Article 3(e) is applicable in all situations of armed conflict [international and non-international], and is not limited to occupied territory [*Kordić* Appeals Judgement, §78 ("[t]he prohibition of plunder is general in its application and not limited to occupied territories only")]',[64] and that, as such, 'violations of the prohibition against "plunder of public or private property" under Rule 3(e) entail, under customary law, the individual criminal responsibility of the person breaching the rule'.[65] Similarly, in the *Tadić* Appeal Judgment, the ICTY Appeals Chamber found case law to be reflective of CIL.[66]

At a very first glance, the ascertainment of rules of CIL, more than any other ambit, seems to confirm the tenets of a legal realist approach to law. If law is fact, namely the law which is applied in practice by courts, what else than 'finding' rules of CIL can prove that such rules are brought to 'reality' through judicial pronouncements? Indeed, the ascertainment of 'unwritten law deriving from practice *accepted* as law'[67] entails important juristic and epistemological implications. From a juristic standpoint, the ascertainment of rules of CIL consists in an act of interpretation carrying with itself claims of formal and substantive validity. From an

[62] *Kayishema & Ruzindana* (Appeal Judgement) ICTR-95-1-A (4 December 2001) [51].

[63] *Prosecutor v Hadžihasanović et al* (Decision on Command Responsibility) IT-01-47-AR72 (16 July 2003) [12].

[64] *Prosecutor v Hadžihasanović et al* (Decision of Motions for Acquittal) IT-01-47-73.3 (11 March 2005) [37].

[65] ibid [38]. The same way of argumentation is found in [47–48] of the decision.

[66] *Prosecutor v Tadić* (n 61) [226]: 'The Appeals Chamber considers that the consistency and cogency of the case law and the treaties referred to above, as well as their consonance with the general principles on criminal responsibility laid down both in the Statute and general international criminal law and in national legislation, warrant the conclusion that case law *reflects customary rules of international criminal law*' (emphasis added).

[67] ILC Report 2018 (n 12).

epistemological point of view, the act of ascertainment presupposes that rules of CIL exist 'out there' and that an interpreter may bring them to perceived 'cognition' or to 'reality', hence to fruition of actors in the international legal practice.

In relation to this, two entangled questions are in order. First, what kind of act is the act of ascertaining rules of CIL? It is argued that this is an act of legal construction that is adjudicative, not cognitive, in nature.[68] Second, are interpretive utterances claiming the existence of CIL norm-descriptive or norm-expressing statements? In Alf Ross' view, judicial decisions may be considered as norm-descriptive statements about the law, as opposed to deontic rules, which are norm-expressive statements of the law.[69] More precisely, the written formulation of rules of CIL in judicial decisions provides these rules with an authoritative text constituted by the written utterances of what the court ascertained as existing rules of CIL and what it interpreted as their normative meaning. This owes to, among other things, the nature of international law, and law more generally, as a *learned* profession in which participants – including courts – articulate verbal/written expressions about the formal and substantive validity of the law.[70] Importantly, such verbalisation stems from an evaluative process – entrenched in an exercise of discretion – channelled through the judges' normative ideology[71] about what they believe exists – or should exist – as a matter of legal rules, universally binding *qua* CIL. Within this learned profession, judicial decisions constitute authoritative statements on rules of CIL, embedding a standard of correctness.[72] As such, this actual formulation of rules of CIL in their form and content is necessary in order for 'rules' as such to materialise, as well as to formally and substantively challenge such rules on the basis of a cognised formulation. Even more so, if courts claim to have found rules of CIL based on state practice and *opinio juris*. Whether those verbal

[68] Guastini (n 20) [46]; 'Adjudicative' is the quality of an interpretation consisting in ascribing a certain meaning to the object to be interpreted while discarding other possible ones. Conversely, 'cognitive' indicates the act of clarifying all possible meanings.

[69] A Ross, *On Law and Justice* (University of California Press 1959) 10; A Ross, *On Law and Justice* (JvH Holtermann ed, U Bindreiter tr, Oxford University Press 2019) 18–19; U Bindreiter (n 21) 108; JvH Holtermann, 'A Straw Man Revisited: Resettling the Score between HLA Hart and Scandinavian Legal Realism' (2017) 57 Santa Clara LRev 1, 15–18.

[70] Compare A Carty, 'Scandinavian Realism and Phenomenological Approaches to Statehood and General Custom in International Law' (2003) 14 EJIL 817, 819.

[71] Compare (n 21).

[72] On the expression 'standard of correctness', also reflected in the maxim *jura novit curia*, see J Bell, 'Sources of Law' (2018) 77 CLJ 40.

expressions truly reflect existing law is arguably irrelevant as long as those expressions are accepted as correct.

As such, judicial decisions verbalising rules of CIL fall short to be considered as purely norm-descriptive statements on the law, as they embed the (deontic) expression of rules of CIL. In other words, sentences which formulate unexpressed norms are 'secretely prescriptive',[73] as they pretend to be describing existing law but are actually constructing new rules.

To illustrate this ambiguity, one may refer to the ILC Report on the identification of CIL mentioned above, whose proposed meta-rules are not laid down in a vacuum. Rather, they considerably draw from ICJ pronouncements determining the *qualities* of the constitutive elements of CIL, that is, the criteria necessary to claim the existence of a CIL rule. For instance, in the commentary to Draft Conclusion 2, the ILC maintains the same criteria for the identification of rules of customary law as those established by the ICJ in its judicial decisions:

> (2) A general practice and acceptance of that practice as law (*opinio juris*) are the two constituent elements of customary international law: together they are the essential conditions for the existence of a rule of customary international law. The identification of such a rule thus involves a careful examination of available evidence to establish their presence in any given case. This has been confirmed, inter alia, in the case law of the International Court of Justice, which refers to '*two conditions [that] must be fulfilled* [*North Sea Continental Shelf, Judgment, I.C.J. Reports 1969*, p. 3, at p. 44, para. 77] and has repeatedly laid down that 'the existence of a rule of customary international law requires that there be "*a settled practice*" together *with opinio juris*'.[See, for example, *Jurisdictional Immunities of the* State *(Germany v Italy: Greece intervening), Judgment, I.C.J. Reports 2012*, p. 99, at pp. 122–123, para. 55; *Continental Shelf (Libyan Arab Jamahiriya/Malta), Judgment, I.C.J. Reports 1985*, p. 13, at pp. 29–30, para. 27; and *North Sea Continental Shelf* (see footnote above), at p. 44, para. 77]. To establish that a claim concerning the existence or the content of a rule of customary international law is well-founded thus entails a search for a practice that has gained such acceptance among States that it may be considered to be the expression of a legal right or obligation (namely, that it is required, permitted or prohibited as a matter of law). The test must always be: is there a general practice that is accepted as law?[74]

[73] Guastini (n 20) 51.

[74] ILC Report 2018 (n 12) Conclusion 2, comment 2.

The ample reliance on these judicial decisions suggests that criteria determined therein have been accepted as correct. In particular, criteria such as '*settled* practice' or '*consistent* practice of the *majority* of the States', found in judicial decisions inasmuch in the report of the ILC, stem from the discretion that a court enjoys in the adjudication of legal issues – that is, they are set forth according to the discretion which the court considers it is able to exercise – and have the power to limit or further enlarge the measure of discretion afforded to the judge in later cases. The ILC Report sanctions the criteria relevant for the ascertainment of rules of CIL that have been considered persuasive. Furthermore, the determination by the ILC that the test to ascertain the existence of a rule of CIL '*must always* be: is there general practice accepted as law?' is eloquent for the constraint to interpretive discretion which the ILC conclusions, too, seek to place onto subsequent interpretive authorities.

The spurious nature of judicial decisions ascertaining rules of CIL as merely norm-descriptive statements is further exacerbated by the sceptical understanding of interpretation discussed above, looking at it as an argumentative art rather than an exact science. In fact, courts ascertaining rules of CIL operate an existential interpretation[75] and may not be regarded as performing a merely declaratory function. Although this outlook bears the marks of legal realism,[76] it is not limited to it. Admittedly, even Hans Kelsen argued that 'the function of adjudication is constitutive through and through' and 'the judicial decision is itself an individual legal norm'.[77]

5 Conclusions

Qua unwritten by definition, CIL seems to appertain more to a metaphysical dimension than to the world of reality. In this scenario, the judge seemingly plays an intermediary role between the

[75] The expression 'existential interpretation' is borrowed from D Hollis, 'Sources and Interpretation Theories: An Interdependent Relationship' in J d'Aspremont & S Besson (eds), *The Oxford Handbook of the Sources of International Law* (Oxford University Press 2017); the notion of 'existential interpretation' may be reconciled with a legal realist approach considering the law 'in force' as the one that is considered so by courts; see, *inter alios*, Ross, *On Law and Justice* 1 (n 77) 17–18; Ross, *On Law and Justice* 2 (n 77) note by JvH Holtermann, li–liv.

[76] P Chiassoni, 'Wiener Realism' in L Duarte d'Almeida, J Gardner & L Green (eds), *Kelsen Revisited: New Essays on the Pure Theory of Law* (Hart 2013); SL Paulson, 'Introduction' in SL Paulson & B Litschewski Paulson (eds), *Normativity and Norms: Critical Perspectives on Kelsenian Themes* (Clarendon Press 1998) xliii.

[77] ibid.

metaphysical dimension of intangible CIL and the world of reality in which rules materialise through the pronouncements of the judge. As such, courts may be seen as bringing CIL to real life – as opposed to a metaphysical dimension – drawing from a world of hypothetical rules of CIL. In ascertaining the existence of such rules, and formulating their content,[78] courts lay down written utterances of otherwise unwritten 'law' presumably existing 'out there'. In other words, the route from the metaphysical space to the world of reality channelled by courts enables the materialisation of rules (verbalised in written utterances), the scrutiny of the methods and criteria (meta-rules) used to ascertain such rules, as well as the evaluation of the evidence that a court considered.

Courts are in a special position to pronounce such statements because of the authority typically vested in them within a legal order. As argumentative strategies, induction and deduction enable courts to portray the ascertainment of CIL as an act of *finding*, which does not depend on an exercise of discretion, but rather sets the interpreter in the context of exploring an objective reality. This ascertainment confers to CIL an aura of objectification and divests it of the potential criticism as judge-made law. As such, interpretation – which entails a discretionary choice between possible interpretive outcomes – is *perceived* as an act of cognition rather than adjudication. Discretion not only lies in the power to make such a choice, but also in formulating a hypothesis about a presumably existing rule of CIL, as a reflection of, *inter alia*, the ideal of international legal order that a court seeks to realise, as well as in regarding certain principles of international law as axiomatic. Accordingly, a judge may do away with the principle of sovereign equality between states less easily than – say – with the principle of responsibility to protect, depending on which normative ideology he/she would present as axiomatic.

Against this background, this chapter has revisited the methodological dualism between induction and deduction as applied in the context of the ascertainment of rules of CIL. Revisiting such dualism came with suggesting embracing an argumentative lens. Like shifting lenses may entail empowering or disempowering one's sight, similarly, twisting a methodological focus, which has featured the legal discourse on the identification of CIL, towards an argumentative lens may entail that

[78] A good example of this is provided by the *Arrest Warrant case* (n 6) [61].

elements which previously appeared obfuscated become more candid and vice versa.

It has been contended that while the methodological lens obscures the range of discretion exercised by the court in the ascertainment of rules of CIL, the argumentative lens sheds light on it, insofar as a claim of the existence such rules necessarily entails the selection and assessment of state practice and *opinio juris* which is far from being incontrovertible. The cursory survey of judicial decisions, primarily drawn from the field of international criminal law, has sought to show the different argumentative strategies whereby judges evaluated 'evidentiary elements' (state practice and *opinio juris*). Whether and how judges engage in the argumentative strategies of induction or deduction of existing rules of customary law is after all a discretionary choice. Yet, judicial decisions verbalising rules of CIL are necessary for the materialisation of such unexpressed rules in an authoritative form, as well as for the contestation of such rules, based on the arguably identified form and content. As such, courts play a fundamental role to nurture the myth of rules of CIL as an empirically based discovery rather than a discretion-centred activity.

The ample reference to prior judicial decisions corroborates the fundamental role played by courts in interpreting the world of facts bearing a normative significance ('practice accepted as law') and in verbalising 'rules' of CIL. In other words, courts are in a special position as interpreters, insofar as their pronouncements are understood as authoritative statements on the law embedding a standard of correctness, upon which actors in a legal field can rely, and which seemingly motivates actors to reiterate the myth of rules of CIL existing 'out there'.

13

Identification of and Resort to Customary International Law by the WTO Appellate Body

MARIANA CLARA DE ANDRADE*

1 Introduction

The traditional definition of customary law follows the wording of Article 38 of the Statute of the International Court of Justice (ICJ), which sets forth 'international custom, as evidence of a general practice accepted as law' as a source of international law.[1] This formulation has been read to reflect two elements constituting customary law: (i) a general practice (objective element) which is (ii) accepted as law, the so-called *opinio juris* requirement (subjective element). In its Draft Conclusions on the identification of customary international law (CIL), the International Law Commission (ILC) stated that '[t]o determine the existence and content of a rule of customary international law, it is necessary to ascertain whether there is a general practice that is accepted as law (*opinio juris*)'.[2]

However, while in theory determining the existence of the two constitutive elements of CIL (practice and *opinio juris*) is the accepted

* The author wishes to thank Maurizio Arcari, Gabrielle Marceau and Graham Cook for their invaluable comments on earlier drafts of this chapter, and Paolo Palchetti for very useful discussions on the topic. All errors remain my own. This chapter was drafted in October 2019.

[1] Statute of the International Court of Justice (adopted 26 June 1945, entered into force 24 October 1945) 33 UNTS 993.

[2] Evidence for these two elements can be found through a survey on diplomatic acts and correspondence; public statements made on behalf of states; official publications; government legal opinions; conduct in connection with resolutions adopted by an international organisation or at an intergovernmental conference; treaty provisions; conduct in connection with treaties; executive conduct; legislative and administrative acts; and decisions of national courts. Some forms of evidence may serve for the determination of both elements. ILC, 'Report of the International Law Commission, Seventieth Session' (30 April–1 June and 2 July–10 August 2018) UN Doc A/73/10 ('ILC Draft Conclusions') 117 ff.

methodology for the identification of a customary rule,[3] the practice of international tribunals does not always follow such methodology.[4] Although the ILC conclusions and commentaries provide clarifications on the theoretical underpinnings for the identification of a rule of customary law, in practice the determination of its existence is far less clear. At the same time, international case law can provide great clarification on the existence, content and scope of CIL.

Against this backdrop, this contribution examines the approach followed by the World Trade Organisation's (WTO) Appellate Body (AB) on the identification of and resort to CIL. One should recall that the WTO dispute settlement mechanism (DSM) has one particularity: its jurisdiction is limited to ascertaining violations of WTO law. With this in mind, the aim of this article is twofold: first, to determine how the AB ascertains the existence and content of a customary rule. Second, to examine whether the AB recurs to this source of law for the interpretation of WTO provisions, or whether it directly or indirectly applies CIL.

To this end, Section 2 reviews the rules which have been considered CIL by the AB. It examines the method of identification employed by the adjudicators to qualify a given rule as 'customary'. For the sake of clarity, 'method of identification' is here understood as the approach followed by adjudicators when ascertaining the existence of CIL. Section 2 also analyses the general approach by the AB towards the identification of and reliance on CIL. Section 3 studies the AB's references to CIL in order to determine whether the adjudicators have referred to this source of law for interpretative purposes, or whether they have applied it as more than interpretative tools. While the relevance of the practice of panels is not

[3] For instance, in the recent *Chagos* Advisory Opinion by ICJ, the court stated that the two elements are constitutive of international law and proceeded to ascertain the existence of these two elements with respect to the right to self-determination as a customary norm. *Legal Consequences of the Separation of the Chagos Archipelago from Mauritius in 1965* (Advisory Opinion) [2019] ICJ Rep 95 [149 ff].

[4] In *Chagos Advisory Opinion* it can be said that the ICJ in fact performed a very limited assessment in determining the existence of state practice and *opinio juris*; on this see also S Talmon, 'Determining Customary International Law: The ICJ's Methodology between Induction, Deduction and Assertion' (2015) 26(2) EJIL 417; Choi & Gulatti, in an empirical assessment of the methodology used by international courts for the assessment of CIL, also reach the conclusion that 'international courts do not come anywhere close to engaging in the type of analysis the officially stated two-art rule for the evolution of CIL sets up'. SJ Choi & M Gulati, 'Customary International Law: How Courts Do It?' in CA Bradley (ed), *Custom's Future: International Law in a Changing World* (Cambridge University Press 2016) 146–47.

dismissed, this contribution focuses on reports issued by the AB, as it is the permanent organ of WTO dispute settlement.

2 The AB's Methodology of Identification of CIL

Although the AB's practice reveals reference to several non-WTO sources and concepts of law,[5] only in few instances the adjudicators have declared the customary status of a rule. More specifically, such references cover only two 'areas' of international law: rules governing the law of treaties (described in Section 2.1) and the law of state responsibility (described in Section 2.2).[6] Section 2.3 describes the trends and draws general conclusions on the method employed by the AB, addressing in particular the question of what *it considers* to be CIL.

2.1 Customary Rules on Treaty Interpretation

Article 3.2 of the WTO Dispute Settlement Understanding (DSU) determines that the DSM 'serves to preserve the rights and obligations of Members under the covered agreements, and to clarify the existing provisions of those agreements in accordance with customary rules of interpretation of public international law'. Rules on treaty interpretation, and even more specifically Articles 31, 32 and 33 of the Vienna Convention on the Law of Treaties (VCLT) are the only norms of general international law on the law of treaties that the AB has qualified as customary rules. This is so even though other canons of treaty interpretation can be found in the reports.[7]

[5] For example, the AB has famously invoked multilateral environmental agreements in the *US – Shrimp* dispute. One can also find many references to general principles of procedural law, such as *kompetenz-kompetenz* (WTO, *US – 1916 Act (EC)*, Appellate Body Report (28 August 2000) WT/DS136/AB/R WT/DS162/AB/R 17, fn 30) and *burden of proof* (WTO, *US – Shirts and Blouses*, Appellate Body Report (25 April 1997) WT/DS33/AB/R 14); for a thorough description of the various instances of references to concepts of public international law in WTO case law see G Cook, *A Digest of WTO Jurisprudence on Public International Law Concepts and Principles* (Cambridge University Press 2015).

[6] This conclusion is the result of systematisation of AB reports, according to which the text of all reports to date (as of 19 February 2019) was examined, and references to the term 'customary' were pinpointed and analysed. Multiple references to CIL were found, but only in these two categories of norms the AB has identified the existence of a customary rule.

[7] See for example the reference to *in dubio mitius* in WTO, *EC – Hormones*, Appellate Body Report (16 January 1998) WT/DS26/AB/R 64; For a thorough description of this and other

A possible explanation for this approach is that, in fact, the DSU Article 3.2 reference to 'customary rules of interpretation' was originally intended to refer to the VCLT provisions codifying these customary interpretative guidelines. However, because not all members of the GATT/WTO were parties to the VCLT, the drafters chose to refer to 'customary rules of interpretation of public international law' instead.[8] This shows that from the outset the intention was to resort to the VCLT rules in the interpretation of the agreements. Therefore, the early references by the AB to these rules as those reflected under Article 3.2 of the DSU were but a formality.

Indeed, the rules on treaty interpretation of the VCLT were invoked on the first WTO controversy to reach the appeals stage, the *US – Gasoline* dispute.[9] In this report, the AB held that Article 31 of the VCLT had 'attained the status of customary or general international law'.[10] To ground that statement, the AB inserted a footnote with reference to decisions of the ICJ, European Court of Human Rights and the Inter-American Court of Human Rights, in addition to a few handbooks of international law.[11] It should be recalled that the practice of international courts and tribunals is not the main method for the determination of state practice and *opinio juris*. In fact, as stated by ILC Conclusion 12 on the identification of CIL, 'Decisions of international courts and tribunals, in particular of the International Court of Justice, concerning the existence and content of rules of customary international law are a *subsidiary* means for the determination of such rule.'[12]

While a similar method was employed for Article 32,[13] the AB did not follow the same approach in relation to Article 33.[14] Instead, the adjudicators merely stated the latter was customary law, perhaps because it was

references see M Lennard, 'Navigating by the Stars: Interpreting the WTO Agreements' (2002) 5(1) JIntlEcon 17.

[8] See Negotiating Group on Institutions, 'Meeting of 26 September 1991 – Note by the Secretariat' (18 October 1991) GATT Doc MTN.GNG/IN/1 [3]; Draft Final Act Embodying the Results of the Uruguay Round of Multilateral Trade Negotiations (20 December 1991) GATT Doc MTN.TNC/W/FA ('Draft Final Act').

[9] See WTO, *US – Gasoline*, Panel Report (29 January 1996) WT/DS2/R 33 [6.7].

[10] WTO, *US – Gasoline*, Appellate Body Report (29 April 1996) WT/DS2/AB/R 17.

[11] ibid fn 34.

[12] ILC Draft Conclusions (n 2) Conclusion 12, 121.

[13] WTO, *Japan – Alcoholic Beverages*, Appellate Body Report (4 October 1996) WT/DS8/AB/R 10.

[14] WTO, *Chile – Price Band System*, Appellate Body Report (23 September 2002) WT/DS207/AB/R 22.

already a tautological statement after granting this recognition to Articles 31 and 32.[15]

In subsequent reports, the AB does not seem to have considered it necessary to re-examine the customary value of Articles 31–33 of the VCLT. The adjudicators, including panellists, simply refer authoritatively to these rules, sometimes referencing also DSU Article 3.2. For example, in *US – Carbon Steel*, the AB noted that 'It is well settled in WTO case law that the principles codified in Articles 31 and 32 of the Vienna Convention on the Law of Treaties (the "Vienna Convention") are such customary rules [mentioned in Article 3.2].'[16] In *US – Softwood Lumber IV*, the adjudicators noted that 'As we have observed previously, in accordance with the customary rule of treaty interpretation reflected in Article 33(3) [of the VCLT], the terms of a treaty authenticated in more than one language – like the WTO Agreement – are presumed to have the same meaning in each authentic text.'[17] Therefore, once the customary status has been determined within WTO case law, adjudicators consider it sufficient to refer back to previous adopted reports to make the same claim with respect to the status of a VCLT provision.

The AB's reference to VCLT Article 26 in *Brazil – Desiccated Coconut* corroborates the conclusion that the organ has refrained from declaring other rules on the law of treaties as reflecting CIL. In that dispute, the panel had invoked the principle of non-retroactivity as reflected in Article 28 VCLT as 'an accepted principle of customary international law'.[18] This terminology was not followed by the AB.

The AB case law also features references to non-VCLT rules and principles on treaty interpretation which are *derived* from the provisions in that convention (in particular Article 31). The references to the interpretative principles of effectiveness, systemic integration and *in dubio mitius* are all, in one way or another, connected to VCLT Articles 31 and 32. In other words, this is the legal basis employed by the AB to invoke these interpretative canons. Nonetheless, the AB did not explicitly consider these principles to reflect CIL. For example, in *Japan – Alcoholic*

[15] On the customary status of VCLT Article 33 see A Papaux & R Samson, 'Article 33' in O Corten & P Klein (eds), *The Vienna Convention on the Law of Treaties*, Vol II (Oxford University Press 2011) 868.

[16] WTO, *US – Carbon Steel*, Appellate Body Report (28 November 2002) WT/DS213/AB/R 21 [61].

[17] WTO, *US – Softwood Lumber IV*, Appellate Body Report (19 January 2004) WT/DS257/AB/R [59].

[18] WTO, *Brazil – Desiccated Coconut*, Panel Report (17 October 1996) WT/DS22/R 75 [279].

Beverages II, the AB explicitly invoked the 'principle of effectiveness or *ut res magis valeat quam pereat*', and stated that it was a 'fundamental tenet of treaty interpretation flowing from the general rule of interpretation set out in Article 31'.[19] In *EC and Certain Member States – Large Civil Aircraft*, the AB invoked VCLT Article 31(3)(c) as 'an expression of the "principle of systemic integration"'.[20] Finally, the AB has also referred to the principle of *in dubio mitius*, on a footnote in the *EC – Hormones*[21] and in the *China – Publications and Audiovisual Products* reports.[22] In *EC – Hormones*, the AB cited the 'interpretative principle of *in dubio mitius*', widely recognised in international law as a 'supplementary means of interpretation under VCLT Article 32', and added a quote from an international law handbook with a definition of the principle, in addition to reference to relevant case law (including ICJ, PCIJ and arbitral decisions) as well as other doctrinal works.[23] As opposed to the principles of effectiveness and systemic integration, *in dubio mitius* is not expressly codified in the VCLT. Still, the legal basis indicated by the AB in the *EC – Hormones* report was not entirely detached from the convention.

What is important to remark is that none of these references is considered to reflect CIL, even though they are based on VCLT Articles 31 and 32.

2.2 Customary Rules on State Responsibility

References to general rules on state responsibility appear more frequently in WTO case law since the adoption of the ILC's Articles on Responsibility of States for Internationally Wrongful Acts (ARSIWA) in 2001. Before 2001, the AB mainly resorted to scholarship on the topic.[24] After 2001, the codification of rules on state responsibility by

[19] WTO, *Japan – Alcoholic Beverages II*, Appellate Body Report (4 October 1996) WT/DS8/AB/R 12.

[20] WTO, *EC and Certain Member States – Large Civil Aircraft*, Appellate Body Report (18 May 2011) WT/DS316/AB/R [845].

[21] *EC – Hormones* (n 7) [165].

[22] WTO, *China – Publications and Audiovisual Products*, Appellate Body Report (21 December 2009) WT/DS363/AB/R 166 [144].

[23] *EC – Hormones* (n 7) fn 154.

[24] In *US – Shrimp* (1998) the AB stated that 'The United States, like all other Members of the WTO and of the general community of states, bears responsibility for acts of all its departments of government, including its judiciary.' The assertion was followed by a footnote with a reference to *US – Gasoline* and two handbooks of general international law. WTO, *US – Shrimp*, Appellate Body Report (12 October 1998) WT/DS58/AB/R [129–30].

the ILC left little need for the AB to engage in other methods of identification. Since then, the methodology of reference to these sources of international law in AB reports consists mainly in citing the works of the ILC on state responsibility.

The AB adopted a cautious approach in determining that a rule of state responsibility reflects CIL. The only concept of state responsibility the AB has considered to have attained customary status is the principle of proportionality in the context of countermeasures for wrongful acts.[25] In the *US – Line Pipe* report, adopted in 2002, the AB stated that the ARSIWA was 'not a binding instrument as such', but its Article 51 nevertheless 'sets out a recognized principle of customary international law'.[26]

To support this statement, the AB added a footnote referencing the *Nicaragua* and the *Gabčíkovo-Nagymaros* decisions of the ICJ.[27] Additionally, the AB stated that 'also the United States has acknowledged this principle elsewhere',[28] referencing remarks the United States had made in the commentaries to the works of the ILC in 1997 and its position in proceedings before an arbitral tribunal. The AB, however, did not indicate that this reference to the US's position was reflective of *opinio juris*. Moreover, the AB did not refer to the recognition of the customary status of the principle of proportionality by other states, and the conclusion that Article 51 'sets out a recognized principle of customary international law' is not further explained in the report. Indeed, the ILC commentaries to Article 51 state that '[p]roportionality is a well-established requirement for taking countermeasures, being widely recognized in State practice, doctrine and jurisprudence'.[29] The AB could have

[25] It should be noted that such reference to the principle of proportionality was made in a rather improper manner. Both the *US – Cotton Yarn* and the *US – Line Pipe* reports invoked the principle of proportionality when assessing the limits for the imposition of a safeguard. Interestingly, the rule on proportionality of the ARSIWA deals with the application of countermeasures, not with the question of determination of attributable damage for the purposes of countermeasures (or, in this case, safeguard measures). These are two connected concepts, but which are different in nature. The AB thus imported a concept related to one sphere of state responsibility (countermeasures must be proportionate) to a different one (attribution of serious damage). See A Mitchell, 'Proportionality and Remedies in WTO Disputes' (2006) 17 EJIL 985.

[26] WTO, *US – Line Pipe*, Appellate Body Report (15 February 2002) WT/DS202/AB/R 82 [259].

[27] ibid fn 256.

[28] ibid [259].

[29] ILC, 'Draft Articles on Responsibility of States for Internationally Wrongful Acts with Commentaries' (23 April–1 June and 2 July–10 August 2001) UN Doc A/56/10,

referred to these commentaries as an authoritative source for advancing the customary status of the proportionality principle.

In sum, the method employed by the AB in this case, both in quoting the ICJ case law and the US's position, was to seek purposive legitimation to the conclusion that proportionality reflects CIL. The indication of the US's (the interested party in that dispute in the quality of defendant) position can thus be viewed as a way of ascertaining *opinio juris* to reinforce the reference to proportionality as a customary rule.

References to general rules on attribution and to Article 14 of the ARSIWA are two instances of AB practice that corroborate the organ's reluctance to declare the customary status of general rules on state responsibility. In the case of attribution, in *US – Definitive Anti-Dumping and Countervailing Duties on Certain Products from China (US – AD and CVD (China))*, the AB deliberately avoided taking a position on the status of Article 5 of the ARSIWA as a customary rule. The ARSIWA provision had been invoked by China, the complainant, as a tool for interpreting the term 'public body' in Article 1.1(a)(1)(iv) of the Agreement on Subsidies and Countervailing Measures (ASCM) as a 'relevant rule' under VCLT Article 31(3)(c).[30]

In that dispute, the AB submitted that ARSIWA Article 5 was not binding per se but, insofar as it reflected CIL or general principles, it could be taken into consideration as 'applicable in the relations between the parties' in the terms of Article 31(3)(c).[31] Thus, to assess whether the provisions were 'rules of international law', the AB would have to consider whether they constituted customary law or general principles. Instead, the adjudicators circumvented the question by concluding that, in fact, their interpretation (based on the general rule in VCLT Article 31(1)) of 'public body' in Article 1.1(a)(1)(iv) of the ASCM 'coincide[d] with the essence of Article 5 [of the ILC

reproduced in [2001/II – Part Two] YBILC 31, 134 ('ARSIWA'); the ILC commentaries refer to *Military and Paramilitary Activities in and against Nicaragua (Nicaragua v USA)* (Merits) [1986] ICJ Rep 14 and *Case Concerning the Gabčíkovo-Nagymaros Project (Hungary v Slovakia)* (Judgment) [1997] ICJ Rep 7.

[30] Article 31(3)(c) of the VCLT provides that 'There shall be taken into account, together with the context: . . . (c) any relevant rules of international law applicable in the relations between the parties.'

[31] WTO, *US – AD and CVD (China)*, Appellate Body Report (11 March 2011) WT/DS379/AB/R 119 [308]. The AB also sustained that 'First, the reference to "rules of international law" corresponds to the sources of international law in Article 38(1) of the Statute of the International Court of Justice and thus includes customary rules of international law as well as general principles of law.'

ARSIWA]'.[32] In other words, because the content of the general rule coincided with their interpretation of the WTO provision under scrutiny, it was not necessary to ascertain the customary status of Draft Article 5.[33]

Article 14 of the ARSIWA, on the 'extension in time of the breach of an obligation', was invoked by the European Communities in *EC and Certain Member States – Large Civil Aircraft*. Similarly to the *US – AD and CVD (China)* dispute, there was disagreement between the disputants regarding the status of the rule as customary.[34] In its reasoning and findings, the AB bypassed the discussions on whether Article 14 of the ARSIWA reflected CIL, if it could be considered a customary rule for purposes of interpretation, and whether there is a legal basis for the invocation of this rule in the WTO legal system. Instead, the adjudicators went on to analyse whether ARSIWA Article 14(1) and Article 5 of the ASCM had the same scope, similar to its approach in *US – AD and CVD (China)*.[35] The AB did dismiss the EC's argument, but not based on the allegations that it did not reflect CIL, but because its substance was not relevant to provide support to the interpretation advanced by the European Union.

2.3 The AB's Trends in Ascertaining CIL

Three remarks can be made regarding the methodology employed by the AB when ascertaining the existence of CIL. First, as advanced earlier, there are only two fields of customary law whose existence the organ has explicitly exploited: rules on treaty interpretation and rules on state responsibility. This may be explained because they are not norms of substantive, primary (understood as 'rules that place obligations on States, the violation of which may generate responsibility')[36] nature: they are structural rules which arguably are necessary for the functioning

[32] ibid 120 [310].

[33] ibid [311].

[34] USTR, 'European Communities and Certain Member States – Measures Affecting Trade in Large Civil Aircraft, Appellee Submission of the United States' (30 September 2010) AB-2010–1/DS316 9 [25] <https://bit.ly/3GEIABH> accessed 1 March 2021.

[35] *EC and Certain Member States – Large Civil Aircraft* (n 20) [685–86].

[36] According to Roberto Ago's distinction. See ILC, 'Documents of the 22nd Session Including the Report of the Commission to the General Assembly' (1970) UN Doc A/CN.4/SER.A/1970/Add.1 reproduced in [1970/II] YBILC 306 [66]. The distinction between primary and secondary rules is here used for a better understanding of the different functions of 'structural' 'meta-rules', with the caveat of all the difficulties which come with this distinction.

of any legal system.[37] Moreover, another factor that could explain this choice is that engaging in the two-element methodology for identifying customary rules of primary nature and applying those rules in the WTO DSM would fall outside the jurisdictional scope of WTO adjudication.

The second remark is that the AB seems hesitant to determine the customary status of a rule. It has actively refrained from doing so in at least two cases (general rules on attribution and the relationship between the duration of a conduct and its effects). As described above, in the *US – AD and CVD (China)* and *EC and Certain Member States – Large Civil Aircraft* disputes, there was express disagreement between the parties with respect to the customary status of certain ARSIWA canons, and yet the AB avoided making a finding.

Additionally, the AB followed the same dismissive approach with the precautionary principle in the *EC – Hormones* report. In that dispute, the status of the precautionary principle was challenged by the parties: the EC argued that the precautionary concept reflected a 'general customary rule of international law',[38] while the United States claimed it represented neither a customary rule nor principle, but merely an 'approach'.[39] The AB considered that the question was controversial under international law, and that 'it [was] unnecessary, and probably imprudent, for the Appellate Body in this appeal to take a position on this important, but abstract, question'.[40] The AB concluded only that the precautionary principle 'finds reflection' in Article 5.7 of the Agreement on the Application of Sanitary and Phytosanitary Measures (SPS).[41] In any case, it is relevant to remark that AB's hesitancy to declare the customary status of the precautionary principle is not unique in international adjudication.[42]

Relatedly, the AB's practice also demonstrates that this organ was hesitant in declaring the customary status of a given principle *in particular* when there was a controversy between the parties. The customary status of the treaty interpretation rules in the VCLT is virtually undisputed, and the concept of proportionality is also enshrined in legal logic. Moreover, in these cases, there was no explicit disagreement regarding

37 For a similar take see MF Agius, *Interaction and Delimitation of International Legal Orders* (Brill Nijhoff 2014) 114 ff.

38 *EC – Hormones* (n 7) [16].

39 ibid 17 [43].

40 ibid 45 [123].

41 ibid.

42 M Schröder, 'Precautionary Approach/Principle' [2014] MPEPIL [19–20].

the customary value of these sources of law. In the other cases, there was explicit disagreement, and the AB refrained from taking a position.

The third remark is that the AB does not make a full-blown assessment of *opinio juris* and state practice to ascertain the customary status of a rule. Put differently, the AB does not properly 'identify' the existence of a customary rule, it 'asserts' such existence.[43] In doing so, it relies on codified instruments of international law. In the case of rules of treaty interpretation, it relied on scholarship and decisions from other international law tribunals to state the customary status of Articles 31 and 32 of the VCLT. In the case of rules on state responsibility, it simply stated Article 51 of the ARSIWA reflected a 'principle of customary international law', quoted previous ICJ decisions and referred to the acknowledgement by the United States of this customary status. This methodology hints that the organ was mostly preoccupied with ensuring the acceptance of the legal reasoning by the affected party, rather than determining the customary status of a fundamental principle as a matter of law with legal implications for the WTO legal system. In fact, proceeding with a full-blown query of state practice, *opinio juris* or comparative study of national legal systems for the determination of a customary rule or a general principle seems not only unnecessary but also a potential source of controversy in the context of WTO dispute settlement.[44]

The limits of resorting to CIL in WTO dispute settlement are not evident. In *US – Cotton Yarn*, the AB held that the concept of proportionality was a 'customary principle' of state responsibility that had not been derogated by WTO law. The adjudicators considered that an 'exorbitant derogation from the principle of proportionality . . . could be justified only if the drafters of the [WTO Agreement] had expressly

[43] Merkouris submits that assertion 'is not a valid methodological tool for the determination of either the content of a CIL rule'. P Merkouris, 'Interpreting the Customary Rules on Interpretation' (2017) 19 IntCLRev 126, 138; see also O Sender & M Wood, 'The International Court of Justice and Customary International Law: A Reply to Stefan Talmon' (*EJIL: Talk!*, 30 November 2015) <https://bit.ly/3xKvWOd> accessed 1 March 2021, considering that 'Unlike induction and deduction, assertion is self-evidently not a methodology for determining the existence of a rule of customary international law. It is essentially a way of drafting a judgment, a way of stating a conclusion familiar to lawyers working in certain national systems.'

[44] Note in particular the complaints by the United States according to which the AB has indulged in making findings which are 'unnecessary to resolve the dispute'. See, for instance, 'Statements by the United States at the Meeting of the WTO Dispute Settlement Body' (Geneva, 18 December 2018) <https://bit.ly/3dMTQ2x> accessed 1 March 2021.

provided for it, which is not the case'.[45] Perhaps the determination of the customary status of a rule entails the possibility of fall-back to general international law in the case of a gap in the tool-box of secondary norms of the WTO legal system. This is relevant for the purposes of the distinction between using a non-WTO source of law for interpretative purposes and applying such norm. The next section will address the practical implications of this distinction in light of WTO case law.

3 Use for Interpretation versus Application of CIL: Where Is the Line Drawn by the WTO AB?

World Trade Organisation dispute settlement has limited material jurisdiction, as it can only adjudicate WTO obligations. The difference between the applicable law (understood as the sources to which reference can be made) and the jurisdiction of WTO dispute settlement (understood as the sources which can be enforced) has been intensively debated by the scholarship.[46] It seems well-settled that WTO dispute settlement only has jurisdiction over the so-called WTO covered agreements,[47] while its applicable law can range further than that.[48] Therefore, panel

[45] WTO, *US – Cotton Yarn*, Appellate Body Report (8 October 2001) WT/DS192/AB/R 38 [120].

[46] On this debate, see for example J Pauwelyn, *Conflict of Norms in Public International Law: How WTO Law Relates to Other Rules of International Law* (Cambridge University Press 2003); G Marceau, 'Conflicts of Norms and Conflicts of Jurisdictions: The Relationship between the WTO Agreement and MEAs and Other Treaties' (2001) 35(6) JWT 1081; G Marceau, 'A Call for Coherence in International Law: Praises for the Prohibition against "Clinical Isolation" in WTO Dispute Settlement' (1999) 33(5) JWT 87; L Bartels, 'Applicable Law in WTO Dispute Settlement Proceedings' (2001) 35(3) JWT 499.

[47] The WTO 'covered agreements' are the Agreement establishing the World Trade Organization, the Multilateral Trade Agreements of Annexes 1A, 1B, 1C and 2, and Plurilateral Trade Agreements in Annex 4.

[48] Commenting on the work of the ILC on fragmentation, Marceau observes that part of the controversy on the limits of applicable law is semantic. Her definition of 'applicable law' is the 'law for which a breach can lead to actual remedies', while the conception of the ILC Study Group 'includes all legal rules that are necessary to provide an effective answer to legal issues raised, and it would include procedural-type obligations (like the burden of proof)'. G Marceau, 'Fragmentation in International Law: The Relationship between WTO Law and General International Law – A Few Comments from a WTO Perspective' (2006) 17 FYBIL 6; the present chapter aligns with a broader sense of applicable law – thus, closer to the ILC Study Group's: applicable law here is to be understood as the sources of law that can be used by the DS panels and AB to settle a dispute and interpret the law according to its jurisdictional limitations. See also ILC, 'Report on Fragmentation of International Law: Difficulties Arising from the

and AB reports cannot enforce obligations deriving from external sources.

This section enquires which role the AB has granted to CIL in settling disputes in the multilateral trading system. Section 3.1 proposes a working distinction between the concepts of interpretation and application of law, specifically for the purposes aimed at here, that is, to distinguish between the use of CIL for the interpretation of WTO provisions, as opposed to the application of customary law as a source of rights and obligations. Section 3.2 departs from this definition to examine the instances in which the AB has referred to CIL. The cases in which the AB has resorted to CIL can shed light on understanding the line between interpretation and application of non-WTO law in WTO case law.

3.1 *The Jurisdiction of WTO Dispute Settlement and the Notions of Interpretation and Application of International Law*

Disputes which call into question the use of sources of law outside the jurisdictional limits of a court are controversial because '[t]hey do not fall plainly within the scope of the jurisdictional clause, nor clearly outside it; they straddle the dividing line'.[49] In the context of the WTO, there is no equivalent to Article 38 of the ICJ, enlisting the sources of law that can be invoked. However, Article 3.2 of the DSU determines that the DSM: 'serves to preserve the rights and obligations of Members under the covered agreements, and to clarify the existing provisions of those agreements in accordance with customary rules of interpretation of public international law. Recommendations and rulings of the DSB cannot add to or diminish the rights and obligations provided in the covered agreements.' Article 3.2 of the DSU sets forth an express limitation to WTO adjudication. Applying non-WTO sources of law in the multilateral trading system arguably amounts to 'adding to or diminishing the rights and obligations' of the covered agreements, while using extraneous norms for purposes of interpretation of WTO provisions can serve for the 'clarification of the existing provisions'.[50] Therefore, the distinction

Diversification and Expansion of International Law, Finalized by Martti Koskenniemi' (13 April 2006) UN Doc A/CN.4/L.682, 226–27.

[49] E Cannizzaro & B Bonafé, 'Fragmenting International Law through Compromissory Clauses? Some Remarks on the Decision of the ICJ in the *Oil Platforms* Case' (2005) 16 (3) EJIL 481, 484.

[50] See also D French, 'Treaty Interpretation and the Incorporation of Extraneous Legal Rules' (2006) 55 ICLQ 281.

between interpretation and application of norms can serve as a valuable tool to understand the limits of WTO jurisdiction with respect to CIL.[51]

Distinguishing 'interpretation' and 'application' of norms entails the debate of whether these are two different processes, two processes which are interconnected, or if in fact one cannot draw such a distinction.[52] Gardiner sustains that they reflect a 'natural sequence that is inherent to the process of reading a treaty: first ascribing meaning to its terms and then applying the outcome to a particular situation'.[53] The distinction was discussed during the works of the ILC on the codification of the law of the treaties, in particular in connection to the question of intertemporal law,[54] but the topic was revealed to be highly controversial[55] and any attempt to make a clear-cut distinction was dismissed.[56] The matter was addressed in the document preceding the works of the commission – the Harvard Draft Convention on the Law of Treaties.[57] The following

[51] In the same sense see A Tancredi, 'OMC et coutume(s)' in V Tomkiewicz (ed), *Les sources et les normes dans le droit de l'OMC, Colloque de Nice des 24 et 25 juin 2010* (Pedone 2012) 81, 84.

[52] This problem is normally theorised in the context of issues related to intertemporal law. See for instance J Klabbers, 'Reluctant "*Grundnormen*": Articles 31(3)(C) and 42 of the Vienna Convention on the Law of Treaties and the Fragmentation of International Law' in M Craven, M Fitzmaurice & M Vogiatzi (eds), *Time, History and International Law* (Brill/Nijhoff 2007) 141.

[53] R Gardiner, *Treaty Interpretation* (Oxford University Press 2008) 28. See also A Gourgourinis, 'The Distinction between Interpretation and Application of Norms in International Adjudication' (2011) 2(1) JIDS 36; G Hernández, 'Interpretative Authority and the International Judiciary' in A Bianchi, D Peat & M Windsor (eds), *Interpretation in International Law* (Oxford University Press 2015) 166; P Sands & J Commission, 'Treaty, Custom and Time: Interpretation/Application?' in M Fitzmaurice, O Elias & P Merkouris (eds), *Treaty Interpretation and the Vienna Convention on the Law of the Treaties: 30 Years On* (Martinus Nijhoff 2010) 39.

[54] In 1964 Sir Humphrey Waldock, first Special Rapporteur on the Law of Treaties, suggested draft Article 56 (The Inter-temporal Law), which stated: '1. A treaty is to be interpreted in the light of the law in force at the time when the treaty was drawn up. 2. Subject to paragraph 1, the application of a treaty shall be governed by the rules of international law in force at the time when the treaty is applied'. ILC, 'Third Report on the Law of Treaties by Sir Humphrey Waldock, Special Rapporteur' (3 March, 9 June, 12 June and 7 July 1964) UN Doc A/CN.4/167 reproduced in [1964/II] YBILC 5, 8–9.

[55] See the discussions on Article 56 mentioned in fn 55 of ILC, 'Summary Record of the 729th Meeting' (22 May 1964) UN Doc A/CN.4/SR.729 reproduced in [I/1964] YBILC 34, 34–40.

[56] Gourgourinis (n 53) 32.

[57] Harvard Law School, 'Draft Convention on the Law of Treaties, with Commentary' (1935) 29 AJIL Supp 653, 657–65 ('Harvard Draft Convention'); see further Gardiner (n 53) 27–29; Klabbers (n 52).

distinction is found in the commentaries to the Harvard Draft Convention:

> Interpretation is closely connected with the carrying out of treaties, for before a treaty can be applied in a given set of circumstances it must be determined whether or not it was meant to apply in those circumstances. ... There is, however, a recognized distinction between the two processes. Interpretation is the process of determining the meaning of a text; application is the process of determining the consequences which, according to the text, should follow in a given situation.[58]

The question addressed here is of a slightly different nature. The use of this distinction is intended to clarify the limits of the use of an international source of law for the interpretation of *another* source of law.[59] This being so, the inquiry seeks to clarify the line between using CIL as an interpretative *tool* for the application of another norm, and when this interpretative recourse transfigures into the actual application of that customary rule, which in principle should have only a subsidiary character.[60] In particular, the question here addressed is not related to the interpretation of CIL as such.[61] The above definition can be thus adapted in the following manner: 'The use of a norm for *interpretative purposes* is the process of resorting to an auxiliary source with the aim of determining the meaning of an original norm; *application* of a norm is the process of determining the consequences which, according to its content, should follow in a given situation.' Interpretation is a cognitive process, while application is a practical one. This does not mean the two phases cannot overlap. Overlap may happen when different sources of law are used to interpret an obligation under dispute by an international adjudicator. The end conclusion will thus reflect an intersection between use of sources different than the one originally being 'interpreted' (i.e.,

[58] Harvard Draft Convention (n 57) 938. A very similar definition was given by Judge Ehrlich in his dissenting opinion in the Chorzów Factory case. *Case Concerning the Factory at Chorzów (Germany v Poland)* (Merits) [1928] PCIJ Series A 17, Dissenting Opinion by M Ehrlich 75.

[59] In more detail for the distinction, see M Papadaki, 'Compromissory Clauses as the Gatekeepers of the Law to Be "Used" in the ICJ and the PCIJ' (2014) 5 JIDS 569.

[60] The practical implications that this distinction may entail can be further illustrated by *Oil Platforms (Islamic Republic of Iran v USA)* (Judgment) [2003] ICJ Rep 161.

[61] In fact, because these rules must be identified before being applied, some argue that they cannot be interpreted (or that the process of identification and interpretation is in fact conflated), Gourgourinis (n 53) 36; For an opposing view, see Merkouris (n 43) arguing that interpretation of CIL is the process taking place when a customary rule is resorted to once it has been identified.

a WTO covered agreement term, provision or obligation) – and its final application may be an indirect application of these other sources. Thus, it is of interest whether this final application of the WTO provision entails the incidental application of a non-WTO rule. The practice of the AB may shed some light in the position taken by WTO adjudicators in this sense.

3.2 The AB's Resort to CIL: Interpretation or Application?

As described in Section 2, the AB declared the customary status of rules deriving from outside of the WTO system only in a limited number of instances, and it has refrained from taking a position regarding this status in other instances. The rules the AB considered to reflect customary law are those related to state responsibility and treaty interpretation. Two sets of 'boundaries' can be inferred from the AB's practice described in Section 2. These boundaries seem to ensure that CIL is used solely for interpretative purposes, in detriment of their 'application'.

The first boundary relates to the content of the norm. The AB only declares as customary rules those that are 'structural': meta-norms,[62] such as those related to treaty interpretation, and rules of state responsibility. In particular, rules on treaty interpretation are operational: they lack substantive implications and they relate to the cognitive process of interpreting a norm. Perhaps more crucial is the fact that customary rules on treaty interpretation have been expressly incorporated by the WTO legal system. Although they can be *applied* within the scope of their operational function, they cannot be applied as to add to or diminish the substantive obligations provided for in the WTO Agreements.[63] Because these rules are 'structural' (their role is more procedural or instrumental), they lack substantive content (i.e., they are not 'primary' rules as their content does not prescribe obligations per se)[64] and thus are

[62] The terminology 'meta-norms' is used here as encompassing 'norms governing the existence, applicability, interpretation, suspension and termination of treaty norms' Papadaki (n 59) 580. These rules have also been called 'secondary norms' in Agius (n 37) 57.

[63] See Gourgourinis (n 53) for a useful distinction of application *lato sensu* and *strictu sensu*. See also Judge Bedjaoui's separate opinion in *Case Concerning the Gabčíkovo-Nagymaros Project* considering that '"Interpretation" of a treaty [is] not to be confused with its "revision"' and 'Cautiously take subsequent law into account as an element of interpretation or modification in very special situations', *Case Concerning the Gabčíkovo-Nagymaros Project*, Separate Opinion of Judge Bedjaoui 123–24.

[64] See Agius (n 37).

less likely to 'add to or diminish rights and obligations of WTO members'.[65]

One reason for this approach is that adjudicators may feel that recognising the customary status of a rule with substantive content may give the impression that they are creating substantive obligations or even overriding WTO law. The general reluctance of the AB to refer to non-WTO rules as customary, even when there is ground for doing so, can be regarded as a cautious approach in not overemphasising the role of these sources in the WTO legal system. This possibly explains why the AB granted this status to rules on treaty interpretation and the proportionality principle – as they are operative concepts, and not concepts entailing autonomous substantive obligations. One can infer that this gives more leeway for the AB not to be accused of overstepping its jurisdictional mandate.

The dispute on whether the precautionary principle reflected a customary rule further illustrates this possibility. In *EC – Hormones*, the AB refrained from answering this question, and held that it was 'unnecessary, and probably imprudent, for the Appellate Body in this appeal to take a position on this important, but abstract, question'.[66] It concluded that the precautionary principle found reflection in WTO law, and could not, by itself, override the provisions of the SPS Agreement. Put differently, the AB stated that the principle is incorporated by the SPS, and plays an 'internal' role in the WTO system. Conversely, the adjudicators indicated that an 'extraneous' (i.e., not codified in WTO Agreements) reflection of the precautionary principle has very limited, if any, role in WTO law.

The emphasis that the AB put in the statement that the precautionary principle is part of WTO law can be read as a sign that the adjudicators acknowledged the importance of the concept, but were cautious so as not to overstate – or give the impression that they overstate – its authoritativeness in the WTO legal system. It may be useful to consider that the particularity of the precautionary principle with respect to treaty rules and secondary rules of international law is that the first denotes, at least to some extent, a substantive dimension: even if not consisting of a clear

[65] It is important to stress that this definition is advanced for the sake of methodological clarity and without attempting to exhaust the definition of 'substantive' norms. The distinction between procedural and substantive principles is indisputably blurred. See for example CEM Jervis, 'Jurisdictional Immunities Revisited: An Analysis of the Procedure Substance Distinction in International Law' (2019) 30(1) EJIL 105.

[66] *EC – Hormones* (n 7) [123].

rule of conduct, it nevertheless can be a source of obligations to guiding the conduct of states.[67]

The second, related, 'boundary' that limits the role of customary law in WTO adjudication concerns regarding the way in which the AB employed concepts which it considered having attained this status. The AB's practice has ensured that its reliance on CIL remained subordinated to the prevalence of WTO legal texts.[68] As delineated in Section 3.1, 'application' can be understood as 'the process of determining the consequences which . . . should follow in a given situation'.[69] Accordingly, one can consider that a WTO adjudicator is applying a non-WTO rule to the extent that the findings of violation or non-violation contained in the report ensues from non-WTO language.

In *US – Cotton Yarn*, the AB had to ascertain the meaning of 'serious damage' under Article 6.4 of the Agreement on Textiles in order to determine whether the United States could attribute damage caused by the importation of a certain category of products to one member only and imposing safeguards measures only against that particular country, disregarding proportionality.[70] In *US – Line Pipe*, the AB had to ascertain

[67] Zander argues that the precautionary principle, among other facets, is a 'fundamental principle which obliges governments to act in a precautionary manner'. J Zander, *The Application of the Precautionary Principle in Practice: Comparative Dimensions* (Cambridge University Press 2010) 344; see also L Gradoni, 'Il principio di precauzione nel diritto dell'Organizzazione Mondiale del Commercio' in A Bianchi & M Gestri (eds), *Il principio precauzionale nel diritto internazionale e comunitario* (Giuffrè 2006).

[68] A different situation however is the use of procedural principles. See for example C Brown, 'Inherent Powers in International Adjudication' in CPR Romano, K Alter & Y Shany (eds), *The Oxford Handbook of International Adjudication* (Oxford University Press 2013) 829.

[69] See *Oil Platforms.*

[70] The panel concluded that the United States had not examined the effect of imports from other WTO members individually, inconsistently with its obligations under Article 6.4 of the same agreement. The panel concluded that 'attribution cannot be made only to some of the Members causing damage, it must be made to all such Members'. WTO, *US – Cotton Yarn*, Panel Report (31 May 2001) WT/DS192/R 122 [7.126]. The United States appealed from this finding, arguing that 'Article 6.4 does not deal with "causation"', and that the Panel had 'misunderstood the two distinct concepts of causation and attribution'. WTO, *US – Cotton Yarn*, Appellate Body Report (8 October 2001) WT/DS192/AB/R 25. It is interesting to note that the AB started its analysis by differentiating three different concepts at stake: 'first, causation of serious damage or actual threat thereof by increased imports; second, attribution of that serious damage to the Member(s) the imports from whom contributed to that damage; and third, application of transitional safeguard measures to such Member(s)' *US – Cotton Yarn* 34 [109]. To explain the difference between these concepts, the AB did not revert to general international law, even though it could have been helpful to clarify the issue. To advance the notion of attribution of

the meaning of 'serious injury' that justifies the application of a safeguard measure under Article 5.1 of the Agreement on Safeguards. In both cases, the focus of the interpretation was on the wording of the WTO provisions under scrutiny, and the AB used the principle of proportionality to shed light on and give meaning to specific treaty provisions.

Moreover, neither the principle of proportionality nor the rules on treaty interpretation have an autonomous content or entail legal consequences per se. Rather, by definition, they are operational to interpret other rules of international law. In this sense, both the principle of proportionality and the rules on treaty interpretation must be employed in conjunction with other rules of primary content. It can be concluded that the AB has resorted to (what it declared to reflect) customary law insofar as these concepts were subordinate to the interpretation of WTO provisions.

The principle of good faith could arguably also be considered as having attained the status of a customary rule. However, the AB has declared only VCLT Article 31(1) as a whole to reflect customary law, rather than the concept of good faith as an 'independent' principle. It can be speculated that the AB has only referred to VCLT Articles 31–33 as customary because these provisions are implied in the text of DSU Article 3.2 as the 'customary rules of interpretation of public international law'. Moreover, if good faith were to be declared a customary rule, and not 'just' a principle of treaty interpretation and treaty performance, it could be understood that there are textual grounds to bring claims based on violations of good faith.[71] This could raise criticisms from the membership and amount to accusations that the AB is 'adding to or diminishing rights and obligations of Members'.

Extraneous principles and rules that do not create rights and obligations for WTO members provide safer grounds for the AB not to overstep its jurisdictional mandate. By determining as customary rules norms related only to state responsibility and treaty interpretation (and in the case of the former, even a limited set thereof), the AB ensures that they will remain subordinate to WTO obligations. This approach allows adjudicators to resort to these sources of law for the interpretation of WTO provisions, rather than to create doubts as to whether they are

damage to a member in this report, the adjudicators remained attached to the wording of Article 6.4 of the ATC.

[71] This was discussed in *US – Carbon Steel (India)*, Appellate Body Report (8 December 2014) WT/DS436/AB/R 4.334ff [188–89], and *US – Offset Act (Byrd Amendment)*, Panel Report (16 September 2002) WT/DS217-234/R 7.59ff [314].

being applied, thereby adding to or diminishing rights and obligations contained in the covered agreements.

4 Conclusions

Reference to CIL in the AB case law is very limited, both in scope and in methodology. The AB does not thoroughly follow the two-element approach to identify CIL, and it restricts its resort to this category of norms to codified secondary and meta-norms. Thus, in resorting to these sources the AB does not engage in a query of the constitutive elements for the identification of CIL. Instead, it bases the determination of customary law on reference to authoritative texts such as relevant scholarship, ICJ decisions and ILC commentaries. The very fact that the rules at stake have been codified may be another reason why the AB has referred to them. This gives the adjudicators not only an authoritative source to refer to when invoking such norms, but also allows them to resort to customary law without having to proceed to the identification of these sources.

The AB referred to what could be understood as *opinio juris* only once, when the adjudicators looked for instances outside the WTO system in order to confirm that the United States had recognised the proportionality principle as customary. Yet, the AB did not clarify whether it invoked the United States' position as reflective of *opinio juris*. Moreover, in this case, the United States was the party being 'affected' by the reasoning flowing from resort to this principle. For this reason, reference to its recognition of the rule as customary seems to have been crafted to gauge legitimation for that specific finding.

Moreover, the AB adopts a cautious approach in determining which rules reflect CIL: it has only done so with respect to concepts that are operational and have no autonomous content. In fact, the adjudicators have refrained from determining the customary status of concepts which could be viewed as having autonomous substantive content and of creating rights and obligations not provided by the WTO legal system, such as the precautionary principle. This arguably also contributed to shelter the AB's interpretative practices from claims of judicial activism (at least with respect to references to non-WTO sources of law).

From these considerations, it can be inferred that the AB has not been concerned in giving a contribution to public international law through the identification of customary rules as an authoritative international adjudicative organ. While it seems aware of the need to bridge the relationship between the trade law regime and general international law, its reference to CIL is instrumental and widely attentive to internal legitimacy questions.

14

The Practice of Non-state Armed Groups and the Formation of Customary International Humanitarian Law

Towards Direct Relevance?

ZHUO LIANG

1 Introduction

In orthodox international law, the formation of customary international law (CIL) takes root in the practice and *opinio juris* of states. The prevalence of this doctrine echoes international law's state-centric tradition. The post-war international legal order, however, has deeply changed in many respects. Two of those changes are particularly pertinent to the present topic: first, there has been a proliferation of non-state actors playing an increasingly important role in this legal system; and second, in international humanitarian law (IHL), only since the adoption of the 1949 Geneva Conventions has non-international armed conflict (NIAC), representing the majority of contemporary armed conflicts and involving non-state armed groups (NSAGs), been placed under regular and systematic regulations of international law.[1] Against this background, it is logical to call into question the traditional doctrine as to whether it has or, if not, should have evolved to confer a role upon non-state actors, including NSAGs, in the formative process of CIL.

As shown throughout this chapter, a number of prominent scholars have uttered their approval, with or without substantive reservations, for the proposition that the practice of NSAGs shall be incorporated into, and thus directly relevant to, the formation of customary IHL. This chapter serves as a critical appraisal of this notion. Section 2 reviews

[1] Prior to 1949, states were strongly opposed to any compulsory international regulation of NIAC, accepting only the consensual legal regime of recognition of belligerency; see L Moir, *The Law of Internal Armed Conflict* (Cambridge University Press 2004) 21.

the relevance of the practice of NSAGs to customary IHL under *lex lata*. Section 3 analyses, from a *lex ferenda* perspective, the credibility of the proposed rationales for incorporating the practice of NSAGs. Admitting that this proposition is theoretically possible and, in some ways, desirable, Section 4 turns to examine which types of practice of which armed groups should be potentially absorbed into the corpus of customary IHL. Section 5 zeroes in on the legal implications of effectuating this proposition on the existing frameworks of CIL and IHL.

2 *Lex Lata*

An initial inquiry can be made as to whether the practice of NSAGs has been recognised as an element of CIL under *lex lata*. 'International custom' is defined in Article 38(1)(b) of the Statute of the International Court of Justice (ICJ) as 'evidence of a general practice accepted as law'.[2] The use of words 'general practice' has led some to argue that international custom is not restricted to the practice of states only,[3] as practice may emanate also from non-state actors.[4] While such an interpretation arguably runs against the drafters' intention,[5] it is not ruled out by the textual meaning of the term 'general practice'. For the future purpose at least, this interpretation retains its viability.

At any rate, given this inborn ambiguity of the law in books, international institutions have bred divergent understandings of the relationship between the practice of NSAGs and CIL. The most pertinent and specific elucidation is found in the International Committee of the Red Cross (ICRC)'s *Customary IHL*, in which the ICRC estimated the legal significance of the practice of NSAGs as 'unclear' and classified it under the heading of 'other practice', with a view that such practice may at best

[2] Statute of the International Court of Justice (adopted 26 June 1945, entered into force 24 October 1945) 1 UNTS 993 art 38(1)(b).

[3] RY Jennings & A Watts (eds), *Oppenheim's International Law – Vol 1: Peace* (9th ed, Longmans 1992) 47.

[4] JP Bohoslavsky et al, 'Emerging Customary International Law in Sovereign Debt Governance?' (2014) 9 CMLJ 55, 63.

[5] Karol Wolfke submitted that the original proposal for that provision was based on the 'constant expression of the legal conviction and the needs of nations'; see K Wolfke, *Custom in Present International Law* (2nd ed, Martinus Nijhoff 1993) 3; Robert McCorquodale nevertheless contested that that provision actually 'acknowledges the difference between states and nations . . . [I]t is conceptually coherent to include actions, practices, and views of non-state actors in the determination of "sources"'; see R McCorquodale, 'An Inclusive International Legal System' (2004) 17 LJIL 477, 498.

contain evidence of the acceptance of existing IHL rules.[6] The International Law Commission (ILC), in its comprehensive *Draft Conclusions on Identification of CIL*, asserted that the conduct of non-state actors other than international organisations 'is not practice that contributes to the formation, or expression, of rules of [CIL]',[7] although it 'may have an indirect role in the identification of [CIL], by stimulating or recording the practice and acceptance as law (*opinio juris*) of States and international organizations'.[8]

Hitherto, only a few international institutions have recognised the direct relevance of the practice of NSAGs to the formation of CIL. In the *Tadić* case, the International Criminal Tribunal for the former Yugoslavia (ICTY) considered the practice of NSAGs to be 'instrumental in bringing about the formation of the customary rules at issue'.[9] In the same vein, the International Commission of Inquiry on Darfur observed that many rules of customary IHL originate from the practice of states, international organisations and armed groups.[10] Be that as it may, there is little other support for such a stance.[11] It is also noteworthy that post-*Tadić* ICTY jurisprudence tended to revert to the elements of state practice and *opinio juris*.[12]

It may be concluded that under *lex lata*, only states and international organisations have actually been entrusted with a law-making power.[13] While the practice of NSAGs plays an indirect role in the formation of CIL, its direct relevance to this process has yet been generally recognised. Accordingly, debates over this issue by and large dwell in the domain of *lex ferenda* instead of *lex lata*.

6 JM Henckaerts & L Doswald-Beck, *Customary International Humanitarian Law, Vol I: Rules* (Cambridge University Press 2005) xlii.

7 ILC, 'Draft Conclusions on Subsequent Agreements and Subsequent Practice in Relation to the Interpretation of Treaties, with Commentaries' (30 April–1 June and 2 July–10 August 2018) UN Doc A/73/10, reproduced in [2018/II – Part Two] YBILC 11, 119.

8 ibid 132.

9 *Prosecutor v Duško Tadić a/k/a/ "Dule"* (Decision on the Defence Motion for Interlocutory Appeal on Jurisdiction) IT-94-1-T (2 October 1995) [108].

10 International Commission of Inquiry on Darfur, 'Report of the International Commission of Inquiry on Darfur to the United Nations Secretary-General' (Geneva, 25 January 2005) [156].

11 D Murray, 'How International Humanitarian Law Treaties Bind Non-state Armed Groups' (2015) 20 JC&SL 101, 108.

12 S Sivakumaran, 'Making and Shaping the Law of Armed Conflict' (2018) 71 CLP 118, 145.

13 J d'Aspremont, 'International Law-Making by Non-State Actors: Changing the Model or Putting the Phenomenon into Perspective?' in M Noortmann & C Ryngaert (eds), *Non-State Actor Dynamics in International Law: From Law-Takers to Law-Makers* (Routledge 2010) 187.

3 Rationales for Incorporating the Practice of NSAGs

Scholars advocating the incorporation of the practice of NSAGs into the formation of CIL have commonly built their argumentation upon two grounds, namely, curing the legitimacy deficit of customary rules binding NSAGs and enhancing NSAGs' compliance with IHL.

3.1 The Legitimacy Problem of Customary Rules Binding NSAGs

There is little dispute today that NSAGs are bound by IHL.[14] It is also generally accepted that NSAGs are bound by customary IHL. As the Special Court for Sierra Leone asseverated, '[insurgents] are bound as a matter of international customary law to observe the obligations declared by Common Article 3.'[15] Alleging that NSAGs are bound by CIL, in addition to treaties and their unilateral commitments, substantially expands the ambit of their obligations under IHL[16] and is thus vital for the protection of war victims.

In the eyes of some, the legitimacy of customary rules binding NSAGs is flawed, inasmuch as their formation does not take into account the practice of those actors. As argued, one of the legitimising premises of CIL is that it originates in the actions and beliefs of those whom it later comes to bind.[17] Since CIL binds not only states, clinging to a state-centric notion merely evinces a perceived loss of its democratic legitimacy.[18] In the process of CIL's formation, the unfair lack of the participation of the entities that the law intends to regulate would

[14] However, there has been no consensus on why NSAGs are bound by IHL. It is commonly argued that NSAGs are bound: (1) via the legislative jurisdiction of the state on whose territory they operate; (2) because their members are bound directly by IHL; (3) by virtue of the fact that they exercise de facto governmental functions; (4) through CIL; and (5) because they have consented thereto. For a critical evaluation of these doctrines see for example JK Kleffner, 'The Applicability of International Humanitarian Law to Organized Armed Groups' (2011) 93 IRRC 443, 445–61.

[15] *Prosecutor v Kallon et al* (Decision on Challenge to Jurisdiction: Lomé Accord Amnesty) SCSL-2004-16-AR72(E) (13 March 2004) [47].

[16] M Sassòli, *International Humanitarian Law: Rules, Controversies, and Solutions to Problems Arising in Warfare* (Edward Elgar 2019) 51.

[17] C Ochoa, 'The Individual and Customary International Law Formation' (2007) 48 VaJInt'lL 119, 122; J Klabbers, 'Sources of International Organizations' Law: Reflections on Accountability' in S Besson & J d'Aspremont (eds), *The Oxford Handbook of the Sources of International Law* (Oxford University Press 2017) 997.

[18] T Müller, 'Customary Transnational Law: Attacking the Last Resort of State Sovereignty' (2008) 15 IndJGlobal Legal Studies 19, 40.

severely compromise its legitimacy.[19] The need to cure this legitimacy deficit hence justifies incorporating the practice of non-state actors, such as NSAGs, as an element of CIL.[20]

Indeed, depicting CIL as such a behaviourally self-generated norm-forming process represents the dominant approach, according to which no conceptual obstacle, at first blush, seems to arise for non-state actors to create customary rules for themselves.[21] A closer inspection, however, unveils a major deficiency of this logic chain that is followed by a dramatic corollary: the legitimacy of CIL is fully restored only if all participants of the international legal order, ranging from states to international organisations to individuals, are conferred the capacity to create customary rules for themselves.[22] This theoretical prospect, explicitly noted by a few authors,[23] confuses states which play a cardinal role in international law with others which do not, based on a taken-for-granted equivalence between them. By doing so, it improperly overlooks the built-in but defensible inequality between states and non-state actors before international law.

Such a presupposed equivalence is a fiction. According to Hugh Thirlway, a unique characteristic of states, which bars any non-state actor being promoted to full state rank, is that they best represent the interests and needs of human beings in international society.[24] It is possible that the idea of an entity creating self-governing law fits only the club of sovereign states. Traditional voluntarist approach to international law has confirmed that by virtue of sovereign equality of states, no legal obligations can be imposed on any one of them without its consent.[25] A legitimacy criticism is hence

[19] C Ryngaert, 'Imposing International Duties on Non-State Actors and the Legitimacy of International Law' in M Noortmann & C Ryngaert (eds), *Non-State Actor Dynamics in International Law: From Law-Takers to Law-Makers* (Routledge 2010) 69, 73.

[20] S Sivakumaran, 'Binding Armed Opposition Groups' (2006) 55 ICLQ 369, 374–75.

[21] J d'Aspremont, 'Non-State Actors and the Formation of International Customary Law: Unlearning Some Common Tropes' in S Droubi & J d'Aspremont (eds), *International Organisations, Non-State Actors and the Formation of Customary International Law* (Manchester University Press 2020).

[22] As Hugh Thirlway pointed out, under this approach, no non-state actor shall be excluded from the corpus of law-creators, because doing so would raise just as much of a legitimacy problem; see H Thirlway, 'The Role of Non-State Actors: A Response to Professor Ryngaert' (2017) 64 NILR 141, 149.

[23] See for example M Akehurst, 'Custom as a Source of International Law' (1975) 47 BYBIL 1, 53; DJ Bederman, *Custom as a Source of Law* (Cambridge University Press 2010) 162–63.

[24] Thirlway (n 22) 147.

[25] As the Permanent Court of International Justice declared, '[t]he rules of law binding upon States therefore emanate from their own free will as expressed in conventions or by usages generally accepted as expressing principles of law' see *SS 'Lotus' (France v Turkey)* (Judgment) [1927] PCIJ Series A 10 [44].

devised for addressing the lack of involvement of some states in the formation of CIL.[26] Non-state armed groups and other non-state actors, however, are not sovereign entities, and the principle of voluntarism never precludes the imposition of obligations on them in the absence of their consent.[27] Thus, there is no inherent reason why they cannot be subjected to the will of states in international law.[28] If the creation of CIL should be monopolised by states, even recognising the self-generating nature of this body of law cannot automatically bring out a legitimate appeal for non-state participation. In effect, the theory of legitimacy accommodates the possibility 'for *A* to have legitimate authority over *B* even if *A*'s rule is neither consented to nor democratic'.[29] This modality of legitimacy especially caters to international law which 'does not now enjoy, and is unlikely to achieve in the foreseeable future, a significant grounding either in the consent of its subjects or in democratic law-making processes'.[30]

The ILC's approaches to the role of international organisations in the formation of CIL reveal the intransigence of the state-centred CIL system. In its *Draft Conclusions on Identification of CIL*, the ILC proffered that '[i]n certain cases, the practice of international organizations also contributes to the formation of [CIL].'[31] The ILC foresaw two clear circumstances where such practice arises as an element of CIL: states have transferred exclusive competences to international organisations, or have conferred upon them competences that are functionally equivalent to powers exercised by states.[32] Rossana Deplano argued that the ILC's seemingly ground-breaking conclusion is stealthily anchored in an unspoken premise: international organisations are empowered by states, and their practice can contribute to the formation of CIL only insofar as it is conceived as a surrogate of state

26 See A Roberts, 'Traditional and Modern Approaches to Customary International Law: A Reconciliation' (2001) 95 AJIL 757, 767; JP Kelly, 'Customary International Law in Historical Context: The Exercise of Power without General Acceptance' in BD Lepard (ed), *Reexamining Customary International Law* (Cambridge University Press 2017) 49.

27 Hiemstra H & Nohle E, 'The Role of Non-State Armed Groups in the Development and Interpretation of International Humanitarian Law' (2019) 20 Yearbook of International Humanitarian Law 3, 11.

28 ibid.

29 J Tasioulas, 'The Legitimacy of International Law' in S Besson & J Tasioulas (eds), *The Philosophy of International Law* (Oxford University Press 2010) 101.

30 ibid.

31 ILC Report 2018 (n 7) 119.

32 ibid 131.

practice.[33] To say the least, ILC's work brings to light that contemporary international law offers little ground for elaborating on the contribution to CIL by international organisations as independent actors.[34] In other words, states seem never to have lost, or will lose, monopoly over the creation of CIL by countenancing limited participation of international organisations in this process.

Even if it may be contended that international organisations' capacity to contribute to CIL accords with CIL's character as a set of rules arising from the practice and usage of a distinctive community,[35] their case is not comparable to that of NSAGs. Kristina Daugirdas articulated three reasons justifying why international organisations can directly contribute to CIL: first, the states establishing an international organisation may subjectively intend for that organisation to be able to do so; second, this capacity may be an implied power of the organisation; and third, this capacity may be a byproduct of other features of the organisation, such as international legal personality, the capacity to enter into treaties, incurring responsibility for violations and making claims.[36] None of these is neatly applicable, by analogy, to NSAGs. First and foremost, NSAGs are not created or empowered by states. On the contrary, their presence in the territory is essentially illegal under national laws. Second, NSAGs do not have 'implied powers' – a principle that has no concern with them. Third, NSAGs cannot participate in treaties, and there is no agreement as to whether they can assume direct responsibility under international law.[37] Among all these considerations, the lack of states' empowerment is most fatal. The absence of such a process manifesting states' privilege helps explain why non-state actors other than international organisations are not considered creators of practice that contributes to the formation of CIL.[38]

[33] R Deplano, 'Assessing the Role of Resolutions in the ILC Draft Conclusions on Identification of Customary International Law: Substantive and Methodological Issues' (2017) 14 IOLR 227, 229.

[34] C Brölmann, 'Capturing the Juridical Will of International Organisations' in Droubi S & d'Aspremont J (eds), *International Organisations, Non-State Actors and the Formation of Customary International Law* (Manchester University Press 2020).

[35] K Daugirdas, 'International Organizations and the Creation of Customary International Law' (2020) 31 EJIL 201, 203, 214.

[36] ibid 210.

[37] ILA Committee on Non-State Actors, 'Third Report of the Committee: Non-State Actors' (Washington Conference, 2014) II(1)(b).

[38] SD Murphy, 'Identification of Customary International Law and Other Topics: The Sixty-Seventh Session of the International Law Commission' (2015) 109 AJIL 822, 830.

In sum, although it may be said that the legitimacy of CIL comes from its self-generating character, it is doubtful whether this formula is applicable beyond states and state-empowered entities. At present, 'states always retain the final word' to decide whether to bestow upon non-state actors a law-making power.[39] This is a status quo, and is not bound to suffer from legitimacy flaw if the legal asymmetry between states and non-state actors is not convincingly repudiated.

3.2 *The Sense of Ownership and the Compliance Dynamics*

Moving one step further from the legitimacy criticism, scholars arguing in favour of incorporating the practice of NSAGs put forward an argument concerning compliance. Marco Sassòli questioned how NSAGs could be expected to abide by IHL if they are not involved in the law-making process.[40] Indeed, sometimes NSAGs denied the binding force of IHL norms on them by arguing that they did (and could) not participate in the creation of those norms which is monopolised by states.[41] This was the case with the Fuerzas Armadas Revolucionarias de Colombia, the Frente Farabundo Martí para la Liberación Nacional of El Salvador, and the National Liberation Front of Vietnam.[42] Therefore scholars argued that to overcome this quandary, it is necessary to adopt an ownership approach, whose core message is that engaging NSAGs in the creation of norms vests them with a 'sense of ownership' which would strengthen their incentive for compliance with obligations.[43] On the part of CIL,

[39] J d'Aspremont, 'The Doctrinal Illusion of the Heterogeneity of International Law-Making Processes' in H Ruiz Fabri et al (eds), *Select Proceedings of the European Society of International Law*, Vol 2 (Hart 2010) 301.

[40] M Sassòli, 'Transnational Armed Groups and International Humanitarian Law' (2006) Winter 2006(6) HPCR Occasional Paper Series 1, 40 <https://bit.ly/3oW3F4Y> accessed 1 March 2021.

[41] ICRC, 'Increasing Respect for International Humanitarian Law in Non-international Armed Conflicts' (ICRC 2008) 11 <https://bit.ly/3GK1K9y> accessed 1 March 2021.

[42] S Sivakumaran, 'The Addressees of Common Article 3' in A Clapham et al (eds), *The 1949 Geneva Conventions: A Commentary* (Oxford University Press 2015) 418.

[43] S Rondeau, 'Participation of Armed Groups in the Development of the Law Applicable to Armed Conflicts' (2011) 93 IRRC 649, 654; S Sivakumaran, 'Implementing Humanitarian Norms through Non-State Armed Groups' in H Krieger (ed), *Inducing Compliance with International Humanitarian Law: Lessons from the African Great Lakes Region* (Cambridge University Press 2015) 130; A Bellal & E Heffes, '"Yes, I Do": Binding Armed Non-State Actors to IHL and Human Rights Norms through Their Consent' (2018) 12 HR&ILD 120, 126.

such engagement efforts mean incorporating their practice into the formative process.[44]

This line of reasoning postulates that an actor's compliance can be improved if it feels a sense of ownership of the rules. As Hyeran Jo expounded, '[a] sense of ownership increases the likelihood that rules will take root within a rebel movement and be perceived as meaningful and worthwhile. When rules are internalized in this way, compliant behavior may eventually become a matter of habit ... When this happens, self-implementation and self-policing replace outside supervision.'[45] Notwithstanding the plausibility of such an explanation as it appears, it is doubtful to what extent this ownership approach would work, in the context of custom-making, for NSAGs whose compliance poses a perennial threat to IHL.

The first uncertainty is whether creating a sense of ownership is serviceable enough for fostering compliance. Although the same question can be asked vis-à-vis states, that the compliance mechanisms of NSAGs are more fragile may render the ownership approach particularly feeble. In fact, the ownership consideration is far from the whole picture of the compliance dynamics. Besides the lack of ownership of norms, NSAGs may refuse to observe or implement IHL on various grounds, including strategic military concerns, the likelihood of prosecution, the lack of knowledge of applicable norms and political or religious ideology.[46] More importantly, the sense of ownership arguably stands among the least influential factors affecting NSAGs' behaviour. While it is logically sound for Western scholars that the reluctance to accept IHL norms is due to non-participation in their creation, such a stance is not really expressed by most of NSAGs today.[47] Instead, the ownership argumentation appears only to be retained by some Colombian NSAGs.[48] It is also reported that Geneva Call, in its experience of engaging NSAGs, has not

[44] Sivakumaran (n 20) 375; R Geiss, 'Humanitarian Law Obligations of Organized Armed Groups' in International Institute of Humanitarian Law (ed), *Non-State Actors and International Humanitarian Law: Organized Armed Groups: A Challenge for the 21st Century* (FrancoAngeli 2010) 96.

[45] H Jo, *Compliant Rebels: Rebel Groups and International Law in World Politics* (Cambridge University Press 2015) 255.

[46] A Bellal & S Casey-Maslen, 'Rules of Engagement, Protecting Civilians through Dialogue with Armed Non-State Actors' (Geneva Academy of IHL and Human Rights, 2011) 5–7 <https://bit.ly/3DAwiZK> accessed 1 March 2021.

[47] O Bangerter, 'Reasons Why Armed Groups Choose to Respect International Humanitarian Law or Not' (2011) 93 IRRC 353, 381.

[48] ibid 380–81.

confronted any NSAG citing its exclusion from norm formation as a ground for rejecting the application of humanitarian standards; even many NSAGs which have agreed to adhere to IHL do not raise objections concerning non-participation.[49] Given such a nebulous nexus between the ownership approach and NSAGs' compliance, it might be too exaggerated to suggest that the compliance record of NSAGs would be palpably altered once a sense of ownership is in place, in light of the sundry temptations to ignore the law.

Even if it is acceptable that more engagement and a sense of ownership are better than nothing for cultivating NSAGs' willingness for compliance, another issue that requires careful unpacking is whether such a sentiment can really be aroused in the context of custom-making. Unlike treaty negotiations or issuance of unilateral commitments in which NSAGs may have their voice and (un)acceptance of norms plainly heard, the codification process of customs would foreseeably remain in the hands of expert groups conducting research from a third-party's standpoint. Being remote from that pursuit, NSAGs would stand little chance to express their concerns or mount effective challenges when they have issues. It is thus questionable whether a mere promise to take into account their practice in the codification of CIL, without providing occasions for them to speak their mind, would equip NSAGs with a sense of ownership and induces their adherence to the resultant norms. In fact, criticisms have already been enunciated against the ICRC's study of customary IHL for not being sufficiently reflective of what states truly think and do pursuant to the law.[50] If these criticisms are apposite, to what extent can a sense of ownership be conveyed from the codification of CIL?

It may be argued that to ensure NSAGs' opinions and concerns being genuinely heard and addressed, unprecedented participatory mechanisms are needed. However, there are numerous NSAGs operating in widely scattered areas of the world. Is it physically feasible to come into contact with all, or at least a substantial part of them? If not, should certain NSAGs be selected as 'representatives' getting involved in the

[49] E Decrey Warner et al, 'Armed Non-State Actors and Humanitarian Norms: Lessons from the Geneva Call Experience' in B Perrin (ed), *Modern Warfare: Armed Groups, Private Militaries, Humanitarian Organizations, and the Law* (University of British Columbia Press 2012) 82.

[50] See for example Y Dinstein, 'The ICRC Customary International Humanitarian Law Study' (2006) 36 IsrYBHumRts 1, 6; MN Schmitt, 'The Law of Targeting' in E Wilmshurst & S Breau (eds), *Perspectives on the ICRC Study on Customary International Humanitarian Law* (Cambridge University Press 2007) 134.

codification process? How to then assure that the competence of those who are invited to participate would be recognised by other NSAGs? Moreover, even if participatory mechanisms for NSAGs are adequately devised, they cannot fix the participation and representativeness plights in the long run. Unlike states, NSAGs are often ephemeral. After the close of hostilities, an NSAG may be disbanded or form the legitimate government of a (new) state. Hence, '[t]here remains a risk that even if the armed groups of today contribute to the formation of international law, the armed groups of tomorrow will still not feel any ownership of these norms and will use that as an excuse not to comply with them.'[51]

Hitherto, even though an ownership approach should be adopted for the sake of compliance, constructing the direct relevance between the practice of NSAGs and customary IHL would sit among the most specious propositions for approaching this goal.[52] In fact, there are no statements on the part of NSAGs suggesting that they are aware of the possibility that their acts could contribute to CIL, or that they consent to it.[53] It might eventually become one's own wishful thinking to purport that the compliance predicament could be practically remedied through admitting NSAGs into the formative process of CIL.

4 Scope of Incorporating the Practice of NSAGs

Despite the flaws identified, it is admitted that the proposition of incorporating the practice of NSAGs is still theoretically possible and, in some ways, desirable. Going along with this line of thinking, it has to be decided which types of practice of which NSAGs should be absorbed into the corpus of customary IHL.

4.1 *Scope* Ratione Personae

Non-state armed groups are extremely diverse. They differ in the extent of territorial control, internal structure, capacity to train members, and the

[51] K Fortin, *The Accountability of Armed Groups under Human Rights Law* (Oxford University Press 2017) 328.

[52] The experience of Geneva Call shows that the question of NSAGs' participation in international norm formation appears to be less important than ensuring NSAGs' capability to factually express their adherence to, and ownership of, such norms; see Warner et al (n 49) 82.

[53] A Kleczkowska, 'Searching for Armed Non-State Actors' Role in the Process of Formation of Customary Law' (2019) 19 ICLR 97, 112.

disciplinary or punitive measures that are taken against members.[54] It seems intricate to establish detailed criteria for including some of them while excluding the rest. Pondering over the appropriateness of engaging selected NSAGs only, Marco Sassòli submitted that 'the international community should try to apply all the legal mechanisms suggested to all armed groups.'[55] This view holds up inasmuch as it seems to be the only likely solution in harmony with the legitimacy concern as displayed in Section 3.1, which implies that all non-state actors shall be treated as law-creators because excluding any of them would defeat the argumentation itself.[56] Now that it is insisted that CIL can be legitimately binding only for those whose practice and beliefs are constitutive to its formation, and that it shall bind all NSAGs which are parties to armed conflicts, it would be groundless to disqualify any of them for the purpose of custom-making.

Therefore, since customary IHL applies only in the situations of armed conflict, an NSAG shall be taken into account for the formation of this body of law so long as it can engage in a NIAC.[57] Criteria of a NIAC include 'the intensity of the conflict and the organization of the parties to the conflict'.[58] Accordingly, to be a party to a NIAC and then a prospective candidate for custom-making, an NSAG is required to have 'a sufficient degree of organization' and 'be able to and does conduct, or is otherwise involved, in an armed campaign which reaches the required degree of intensity'.[59]

This approach seems counter-intuitive, as even Al-Qaeda and the Islamic State of Iraq and Syria would attain the law-creator status. It has to be emphasised that an all-inclusive approach for NSAGs per se is not tantamount to indiscriminate incorporation of any sort of their practice. As will be illustrated in Section 4.2 below, the practice should be subject to scrutiny before being utilised as the basis of customary IHL.

4.2 *Scope* Ratione Materiae

The practice of NSAGs consists of various types and forms. They may include, but are not limited to: first, verbal acts, such as codes of conduct,

54 ICRC (n 41) 11.

55 M Sassòli, 'Taking Armed Groups Seriously: Ways to Improve Their Compliance with International Humanitarian Law' (2010) 1 JIHLS 5, 14.

56 Thirlway (n 22) 149.

57 Sassòli (n 55) 14.

58 *Prosecutor v Duško Tadić a/k/a/ "Dule"* (Opinion and Judgment) IT-94-1-T (7 May 1997) [108].

59 D Akande, 'Classification of Armed Conflicts: Relevant Legal Concepts' in E Wilmshurst (ed), *International Law and the Classification of Conflicts* (Oxford University Press 2012) 52.

internal legislations, unilateral commitments, instructions to armed members, special agreements, peace treaties and statements in international fora; and second, physical acts, such as battlefield behaviour, the use of certain weapons and the treatment afforded to different categories of persons.[60]

As with state practice, the practice of NSAGs is innately Janus-faced. It contains both the positive practice of committing to and complying with IHL and the negative acts of disregarding, rejecting and wilfully breaking the rules. As often reported in NIACs, some NSAGs have blatantly denied, in whole or in part, the application of IHL. In the context of custom formation, those persistently defying existing norms and continuing waging their rebellions without any restraints could arguably be labelled as 'persistent objectors'.[61] This reality entails a pressing question: should the anticipated NSAG-contributed customary IHL incorporate both the positive and negative components of their practice? With a view to curbing the implications of the contrary practice of NSAGs, Anthea Roberts and Sandesh Sivakumaran suggested that 'armed groups, acting alone, would not have the power to create a new custom or undermine or change an existing custom.'[62] It is also noteworthy that the ICTY, which affirmed the direct relevance of the practice of NSAGs, has only cited their practice consistent with the objectives of protecting war victims.[63] Nonetheless, the lack of articulated justifications and criteria for doing away with what looks repugnant risks opening the door to arbitrariness and subjectivity.

The imbroglio caused by the negative practice of NSAGs might be defused through the *mutatis mutandis* application of the norms governing custom-making to the case of NSAGs. On one hand, deviation from a rule should generally be treated as 'breaches of that rule, not as indications of the recognition of a new rule'.[64] Therefore, the misdeeds of

[60] A Bellal, P Bongard & E Heffes, 'Research Brief: From Words to Deeds: A Study of Armed Non-State Actors' Practice and Interpretation of International Humanitarian and Human Rights Norms' (Geneva Academy of IHL and Human Rights, December 2019) 4 <https://bit.ly/3lzwCl7> accessed 1 March 2021.

[61] Jo (n 45) 47.

[62] A Roberts & S Sivakumaran, 'Lawmaking by Nonstate Actors: Engaging Armed Groups in the Creation of International Humanitarian Law' (2012) 37 YaleJInt'lL 107, 151.

[63] I Scobbie, 'The Approach to Customary International Law in the Study' in E Wilmshurst & S Breau (eds), *Perspectives on the ICRC Study on Customary International Humanitarian Law* (Cambridge University Press 2007) 46.

[64] *Military and Paramilitary Activities in and against Nicaragua (Nicaragua v USA)* (Merits) [1986] ICJ Rep 14, 98 [186].

NSAGs can seldom result in the emergence of new norms. On the other hand, the formation of CIL demands state practice be 'extensive and virtually uniform'[65] rather than universal, and be generally consistent with, rather than 'in absolutely rigorous conformity with', the rules.[66] While NSAGs have often been demonised as nothing but criminal gangs, some scholars testified that contrary to the public's stereotype, NSAGs have frequently committed to and/or implemented humanitarian norms,[67] and that only a few NSAGs entirely reject the pertinence of IHL.[68] As Raphaël van Steenberghe analysed, 'practice evidences that most of the armed groups being party to an armed conflict are ready to respect IHL . . . [T]he rare official oppositions from armed groups to IHL application do not seem to be sufficiently important [to the formation of CIL rules].'[69] If the empirical evidence as offered is solid, the negative practice of NSAGs may not carry as much weight as it seems to have in determining the contents of CIL norms.

Another mechanism that would function as a powerful filer of practice is *jus cogens* (peremptory norms). One of the legal consequences of *jus cogens* in relation to CIL is that even if constituent elements of CIL are present, a putative customary rule does not come into existence if it conflicts with *jus cogens*.[70] In this sense, there would be no customary rule that may conflict with *jus cogens*. As a logical result, the practice of NSAGs potentially contributing to such a 'rule' would simply play no role in its formation which is forestalled.

This inhibitory effect of *jus cogens* works for those that have persistently objected to an emerging customary rule and maintain their objection after the rule has crystallised. The persistent objector rule does not prevent the emergence of a customary norm of a *jus cogens* character to which one or more states have persistently objected.[71] Likewise, even if

[65] *North Sea Continental Shelf Cases (Federal Republic of Germany/Denmark; Federal Republic of Germany/Netherlands)* (Judgment) [1969] ICJ Rep 3, 43 [74].

[66] *Military and Paramilitary Activities in and against Nicaragua* (n 64) 69 [186].

[67] Sivakumaran (n 43) 125–26; Jo (n 45) 238; Bangerter (n 47) 367.

[68] Bellal & Heffes (n 43) 136.

[69] R van Steenberghe, 'Non-State Actors from the Perspective of the International Committee of the Red Cross' in J d'Aspremont (ed), *Participants in the International Legal System: Multiple Perspectives on Non-State Actors in International Law* (Routledge 2011) 223.

[70] ILC, 'Draft Conclusions on Peremptory Norms of General International Law (*jus cogens*)' (29 April–7 June and 8 July–9 August 2019) UN Doc A/74/10, reproduced in [2019/II – Part Two] YBILC 141, 145, 182.

[71] ibid 185.

an NSAG has persistently maintained its objection to a customary rule of a *jus cogens* character since that rule was in the process of formation, it could not thwart the crystallisation of that rule. In other words, its practice signalling persistent objection would be irrelevant to the formation of such a rule.

Customary IHL contains abundant rules of a *jus cogens* character. In its advisory opinion on the *Legality of the Threat or Use of Nuclear Weapons*, the ICJ described the fundamental rules of IHL as constituting 'intransgressible principles' of CIL.[72] According to the ILC, the intention of the world court was to treat these principles as peremptory.[73] Thus far, it has been widely agreed among scholars that basic rules of IHL have achieved the *jus cogens* status,[74] although there is no consensus as to which basic norms exactly fall into this genre. Also, it has been determined in both international and domestic jurisprudence that IHL rules prohibiting war crimes form part of *jus cogens*.[75] Given the coverage of *jus cogens* in the realm of IHL, it is promising that not much room is left for NSAGs to create customary rules that contravene existing ones, or to maintain objections to them.

With these principles in mind, the implications of the frustrating negative practice of NSAGs should not be overstated. The positive and negative facets of their practice may be weighed together as a whole for determining the contents of customs.

5 Legal Implications of Incorporating the Practice of NSAGs

The proposed direct relevance between the practice of NSAGs and the formation of customary IHL would have legal implications for not only the theory of CIL, but also the contents of IHL. Theoretical and practical difficulties arising therefrom would affect in return the acceptability of this project.

[72] *Legality of the Threat and Use of Nuclear Weapons* (Advisory Opinion) [1996] ICJ Rep 241, 257 [79].

[73] ILC, 'Content of the International Responsibility of a State' (23 April–1 June and 2 July–10 August 2001) UN Doc A/56/10, reproduced in [2001/II – Part Two] YBILC 86, 113.

[74] For enumerations of authors of this view, see R Kolb, *Peremptory International Law* – Jus Cogens: *A General Inventory* (Hart 2015) 81; D Tladi, 'Fourth Report on Peremptory Norms of General International Law (*Jus Cogens*)' (31 January 2019) UN Doc A/CN.4/727 [120].

[75] For international jurisprudence, see *Prosecutor v Kupreskić* (Trial Judgment) IT-95-16-T (14 January 2000) [520]; for cases before domestic courts, see Tladi (n 74) [119].

5.1 Implications on the Structure of CIL

The conceptual distinction between state practice and the practice of NSAGs gives rise to a question: if the practice of NSAGs were to count as an element of CIL, what would the hierarchy between such practice and state practice? Put another way, in determining the contents of norms, would the practice of NSAGs be superior, equal or inferior to state practice be? In fact, this question posits the existence of a unitary body of CIL norms applicable to states and NSAGs alike. A legal pluralist outlook would suggest another way of perceiving the structure of CIL. To address this hierarchy issue, the two scenarios should be examined respectively.

Traditionally, CIL is understood as a unitary legal system. As Daragh Murray maintained, CIL shall 'be regarded as a unitary body of law, binding all entities possessing international legal personality. While elements of the law may be limited *ratione personae*, this does not imply the existence of distinct bodies of customary law relevant to particular categories of entity.'[76] However, the alleged self-generating nature of CIL as noted in Section 3.1 would imply that each and every type of entities which are bound by CIL should be vested with a power to create customary rules for itself. Such a theoretical perspective was envisaged by Anthony Clark Arend: '[i]f, however, the [S]tate were to lose its monopoly in a neomedieval system, ... [t]here could, in fact, be *multiple levels of CIL* ... [A] scholar ... would need to examine the practice of this entire panoply of actors ... [I]t is also possible that there could be rules of CIL that are *binding on some, but not all*, international actors.'[77]

Indeed, if the creators of CIL are no longer to be confined to states, the traditional structure of CIL would be radically stretched. It is conceivable that this body of law is likely, if not bound, to become multi-layered to accommodate multifarious sets of norms created by and applied to different actors.[78] As Jean d'Aspremont wrote, 'if one accepts that non-state actors can contribute to the formation of [CIL] ... the practice of non-state actors can only be germane to the emergence of customary rules whose object is to regulate non-state actors' behaviour.'[79] As to IHL, the expected diversification of CIL, resulted from non-state participation

[76] Murray (n 11) 108.

[77] AC Arend, *Legal Rules and International Society* (Oxford University Press 1999) 176–77 (emphasis added).

[78] Katharine Fortin even asserted that 'different subjects of international law are bound by different norms of CIL' has already become a fact; see Fortin (n 51) 328.

[79] J d'Aspremont, 'Conclusion: Inclusive Law-Making and Law-Enforcement Processes for an Exclusive International Legal System' in J d'Aspremont (ed), *Participants in the*

in custom-making, would engender two main layers of customary norms: (1) norms created by and applicable to states;[80] and (2) norms created by and applicable to NSAGs. In such a double-layered system, the hierarchy problem between state practice and the practice of NSAGs would not arise, because wherever a discrepancy exists between their practices, it can be handily deposited onto two entities' respective exclusive domains of norms whose scopes of application *ratione personae* would not overlap.

In contrast, the hierarchy issue would emerge vis-à-vis the traditional concept of CIL if the practice of NSAGs were to become directly relevant. This is because as long as CIL is considered a unitary system, customary IHL norms binding states and NSAGs alike should be conceptually co-authored by both. In determining the contents of this body of law, the practices of the two entities should be weighed along with one another in a holistic manner. To bridge the potential discrepancies, Anthea Roberts and Sandesh Sivakumaran proposed that states and NSAGs' practices 'need not be treated equally. The centrality of the role of States in international law means that their practice should still be given more weight.'[81] Admittedly, in affirming the direct relevance of the practice of NSAGs, neither the ICTY nor the Darfur Commission pointed to any of such practice that contradicted IHL norms created by states.[82] However, there appears to be a tension between conferring upon NSAGs a custom-making role in the name of legitimacy on one hand and subordinating them to states on the other hand: if CIL's legitimacy – in the proposed meaning of the term – is to be maximised, it is puzzling why states should retain the authority to deplete at will the value of the conduct of other actors. Probably a more sensible approach is to treat, in theory, the practice of state and NSAGs on an equal footing and to determine the superiority between them on a case-by-case basis, in consideration of the specific problem that a norm seeks to address.[83]

International Legal System: Multiple Perspectives on Non-State Actors in International Law (Routledge 2011) 430.

[80] Under this taxonomy, the ICRC's *Customary IHL*, done predominantly based on state practice, would be reclassified as a codification of customary IHL created by and applicable to states, instead of a codification of customary IHL *in toto*.

[81] Roberts & Sivakumaran (n 62) 151.

[82] J Somer, 'Jungle Justice: Passing Sentence on the Equality of Belligerents in Non-International Armed Conflict' (2007) 89 IRRC 655, 662.

[83] Hiemstra (n 27) 26.

5.2 *Implications on the Application and Protective Standards of Customary IHL*

Besides challenging the unitary character of CIL, incorporating the practice of NSAGs would lead to reappraising some crucial aspects of IHL. The most conspicuous is the risk of nullifying the equal application of IHL in NIAC, a principle denoting that IHL 'applies equally to both sides of a conflict'.[84] Apparently, this principle perches at the opposite end of a conceived double-layered system of CIL, in which states and NSAGs are bound by different norms. Two options for assuaging this tension would arise. One is to incorporate the practice of NSAGs into the traditional unitary body of CIL, on account of the importance of equal application. The other option is to close the door for the equal application of IHL in NIAC, with the possibility of the stratification of CIL preserved.

At first glance, the price of taking the latter path seems exorbitant. In fact, however, there is an ongoing debate in academia over whether the principle of equal application should be established in NIAC. Those who contest the applicability of this principle in NIAC first looked for support from the historical origin of this principle. It was argued that the principle of equal application resulted from the separation between *jus ad bellum* (the law governing resorting to force) and *jus in bello* (the law regulating the conduct of war) – a dichotomy that exists only in inter-state conflict.[85] The principle of equal application is a necessity to ensure that the same IHL norms apply to both belligerent states regardless their respective causes for resorting to war. International law, however, does not traditionally regulate the legality of the use of force in internal strife.[86] In other words, there is no *ad bellum/in bello* separation and the resultant theoretical demand for equal application in NIAC. In addition to this argument, it was also noted that the transplant of the equal application from inter-state conflict into NIAC is practically problematic and undesirable, for requiring NSAGs to implement the same obligations as states do is unrealistic, and may result in a high incidence of non-compliance.[87]

[84] C Greenwood, 'The Applicability of International Humanitarian Law and the Law of Neutrality to the Kosovo Campaign' (2002) 78 ILS 35, 40–41.

[85] A Roberts, 'The Equal Application of the Laws of War: A Principle under Pressure' (2008) 90 IRRC 931, 932; M Sassòli, 'Introducing a Sliding-Scale of Obligations to Address the Fundamental Inequality between Armed Groups and States?' (2011) 93 IRRC 426, 427–28.

[86] Y Dinstein, *Non-International Armed Conflicts in International Law* (Cambridge University Press 2014) 4.

[87] Sassòli (n 85) 427; G Blum, 'On a Differential Law of War' (2011) 52 HarvInt'lLJ 163, 172.

Nevertheless, it is the majority view that the principle of equal application is doubtlessly applicable to NIAC.[88] While they did not gainsay the inter-state origin of the equal application, the defenders of this principle warned that abandoning it in NIAC would reduce the incentive of government forces involved to comply with their IHL undertakings, as they would hardly benefit from an asymmetric IHL.[89]

It is not the intention of this chapter to work out a definitive answer for this debate. The suggestion is that there is some room to dispute, in theory, the equal application of IHL in NIAC, at the service of the envisaged customary norms based exclusively on the acts of NSAGs. Be that as it may, this would turn out to be a thankless, if not only dangerous, exercise as it denotes radical deviation from the classical perception of how IHL is applied.[90] It may then be safer to stick to a unitary body of CIL under the co-authorship of states and NSAGs, with the same customs regulating both sides. As can be seen, concerns related to equal application of IHL would restrain the choice of theoretical pathways for those in favour of giving NSAGs a direct role in custom-making.

Another implication that incorporating the practice of NSAGs might have is the risk of regression of IHL, that is, the downgrading of its existing protective standards.[91] While, as analysed in Section 4.2, the negative practice of NSAGs may not have a scathing impact on the formation of CIL, the crux here is that even the acts of NSAGs aimed at regulating their conduct or protecting war victims appear to be more primitive and less humane than states'. For instance, some NSAGs in countries like Sierra Leone, Uganda, Philippines, Nepal and India adopted their codes of conduct based on an instruction of the Chinese People's Liberation Army, with which they share a similar ideology.[92] This instruction encompasses a number of rules of humanitarianism

[88] See Y Sandoz et al (eds), *Commentary on the Additional Protocols of 8 June 1977 to the Geneva Conventions of 12 August 1949* (Martinus Nijhoff 1987) 1345; F Kalshoven & L Zegveld, *Constraints on the Waging of War* (4th ed, Cambridge University Press 2011) 2.

[89] Y Shany, 'A Rebuttal to Marco Sassòli' (2011) 93 IRRC 432, 433.

[90] As Katharine Fortin warned, 'it cannot be right that there could ever be "customary law created by armed groups themselves and only applicable to those groups". To suggest otherwise undermines one of the key principles of international humanitarian law, equality of belligerents'; see Fortin (n 51) 327.

[91] Sassòli (n 40) 41; C Ryngaert, 'Non-State Actors in International Humanitarian Law' in J d'Aspremont (ed), *Participants in the International Legal System: Multiple Perspectives on Non-State Actors in International Law* (Routledge 2011) 289.

[92] Bellal & Heffes (n 43) 127.

such as 'do not hit or swear at people', 'do not take liberties with women' and 'do not maltreat captives'.[93] Notwithstanding such laudable efforts, it is evident that those norms, being oversimplified and crude, would not afford war victims protection as comprehensive as that offered by state-crafted ones. Further examples can be found in the codes of conduct of the Ejército de Liberación Nacional in Colombia, Ejército Zapatista de Liberación Nacional in Mexico, the Sudan People's Liberation Army and the Taliban in Afghanistan. All of those codes contain merely rudimentary or concise rules, and fail to cover many critical aspects of IHL.[94] Should such instruments, reflective of the practice of NSAGs, be taken as a basis for customary IHL, it would be hard to formulate norms reaching the protective standards that have already been achieved in IHL. In effect, this dilemma arises also in relation to the law-making of other non-state actors. As Hilary Charlesworth observed, engaging non-state actors in the creation of CIL 'often has the effect of generating weak norms on a wide variety of topics'.[95]

However, such a pessimistic prospect foretelling the inevitable regression of law is not infallible. It should be equally noted that NSAGs have sometimes embraced more protective rules with obligations whose scopes are wider than those agreed among states. An illustrative example is Geneva Call's Deed of Commitment on landmine ban which has been signed by many NSAGs already.[96] While the Ottawa Convention on anti-personnel landmines, signed among states, prohibits mines that are '*designed to be* exploded by the presence, proximity or contact of a - person',[97] Geneva Call's deed bans mines that have such an effect, whether they are designed for that purpose or not.[98] Furthermore, there are also cases in which unilateral commitments of NSAGs may be

[93] IRRC, 'A Collection of Codes of Conduct Issued by Armed Groups' (2011) 93 IRRC 483, 487.

[94] For the text of these codes, see O Bangerter, *Internal Control: Codes of Conduct within Insurgent Armed Groups* (Small Arms Survey 2012) 85–91, 94–95.

[95] H Charlesworth, 'The Unbearable Lightness of Customary International Law' (1998) 92 ASIL PROC 44, 45.

[96] To date, this document has been signed by fifty-three armed non-state actors; see Geneva Call, 'What We Do' (*Geneva Call*) <https://www.genevacall.org/what-we-do/> accessed 1 March 2021.

[97] Convention on the Prohibition of the Use, Stockpiling, Production and Transfer of Anti-Personnel Mines and on Their Destruction (adopted 18 September 1997, entered into force 1 March 1999) 2056 UNTS 211, art 2(1) (emphasis added).

[98] Geneva Call, 'Deed of Commitment under Geneva Call for Adherence to a Total Ban on Anti-Personnel Mines and for Cooperation in Mine Action', art 1 <https://bit.ly/3DOwhRC> accessed 1 March 2021.

more humane than IHL standards in certain respects. For instance, the Sudan People's Liberation Movement committed to apply the Convention on Certain Conventional Weapons at a time when the convention was applicable to international armed conflicts alone, and the National Transitional Council of Libya issued a communiqué that prohibited the use of anti-vehicle mines and anti-personnel mines during the 2011 civil war in Libya.[99]

These examples illustrate that the alleged regression of IHL may not necessarily be the case, or at least, may not take place in every corner of the law. In certain areas where NSAGs assent to more protection, more progressive norms are in sight. Nevertheless, more empirical studies are needed for judging the exact implications of the practice of NSAGs on the protective standards of customary IHL.

6 Concluding Remarks

Reviewing the seemingly attractive proposal of incorporating the practice of NSAGs into the formation of CIL, this chapter demonstrates that such a concept as it has been explored thus far may not effectively solve as many problems as it may cause. Consequently, while non-state participation in international law-making is often suggested and encouraged, there could be some reasonable hesitation when NSAGs come into sight. It is acknowledged that 'non-state actors' is a designation for entities of diverse origins. A general acceptance of giving a bigger role to them does not naturally guarantee a place for NSAGs. There are good reasons to isolate NSAGs from those non-states entities which are deemed inherently benign (e.g., international organisations, NGOs and judges). What is at the heart of this debate appears not to be the theoretical hurdles for NSAGs to be called law-creators, but the necessity or desirability of moving towards that direction. Indeed, should most NSAGs be able to create exquisite and sophisticated norms and strictly adhere to them, many doubts and objections to their custom-making capacity would fade away.

Such a consequentialist approach is helpful for assuring that international law is evolving on a progressive track. International humanitarian law is a body of law whose implementation greatly depends on voluntary action and goodwill of belligerents.[100] More efforts to engage

[99] Sivakumaran (n 43) 133.

[100] R Kolb & R Hyde, *An Introduction to the International Law of Armed Conflicts* (Hart 2008) 284.

NSAGs are certainly desirable,[101] but law-making represents only one option of engagement. If, through their direct participation in custom-making, NSAGs' compliance records are not expected to be enhanced and/or the application of IHL becomes more uncertain and less protective, it might be hard to convince the mainstream in academia to accept the direct relevance project by hinging on a simplistic call for more inclusiveness with a somewhat hollow legitimacy argumentation. Solutions to the challenges raised during this debate would partially rest with further extensive empirical surveys concerning NSAGs' behaviour. At this stage, it is not unreasonable to stay sceptical about whether such admission of NSAGs marks one of the correct directions of future development for reckoning with the contemporary challenges to IHL.

From a policy-making perspective, it is even more challenging at present to imagine that the direct relevance proposal would be welcomed by states, which are often reluctant to do anything that may legitimise the armed groups with which they are in conflict.[102] In essence, states may have a keen interest in maintaining their exclusive or dominant role in law-making.[103] Even if states, the ICRC or other authorities agree to put this proposition onto the agenda, there would be more questions, beyond what is discussed in this chapter, waiting for answers, such as the difficulty in discerning *opinio juris* of NSAGs as a result of NSAGs' general lack of knowledge of the law.[104] For the sake of theoretical completeness and practical utility, proponents of this project are invited to make further elaborations on it.

101 UNSC 'Report of the Secretary-General on the Protection of Civilians in Armed Conflict' (11 November 2010) UN Doc S/2010/579 [52].
102 Roberts & Sivakumaran (n 62) 135.
103 ibid 133.
104 Bellal & Heffes (n 43) 133.

15

Identifying Custom in Universal Periodic Review Recommendations

FREDERICK COWELL

1 Introduction

In January 2019 the Dominican Republic went before the United Nations (UN) Human Rights Council (HRC) for its review during the third Universal Periodic Review (UPR) cycle. In the report it submitted to the council in advance of their review it was at pains to demonstrate the various legislative measures it had taken in respect of domestic violence.[1] The country had been criticised by NGOs for systemically failing the survivors of domestic violence both in legislative terms – prior to 1997 it was not a crime in the country – and in relation to the training of law enforcement officials.[2] As such the Dominican Republic was keen to demonstrate that, following on from its review in the second UPR cycle in February 2014, it had made changes to the law to reflect the recommendations made to them on the issue of domestic violence by states conducting the review at the HRC.[3] When considering the Dominican Republic's report in 2019 the Australian representative to the HRC expressed concern that some of the domestic legislative reforms did not go far enough, leading it to offer a series of further recommendations on domestic violence and the strengthening of police accountability.[4] Throughout 2019 recommendations were

[1] UN Human Rights Council (HRC), 'National Report Submitted in Accordance with Paragraph 5 of the Annex to Human Rights Council Resolution 16/21: Dominican Republic' (7 November 2018) UN Doc A/HRC/WG.6/32/DOM/1 [50–51].

[2] G Lugo, 'The Dominican Republic's Epidemic of Domestic Violence' (*Guardian*, 23 November 2012) <https://bit.ly/30z5jzW> accessed 1 March 2021; A Moloney, 'Break Silence on 'Terrifying' Femicides in Dominican Republic: Minister' (*Reuters*, 16 July 2017) <https://reut.rs/31TmrkD> accessed 1 March 2021.

[3] HRC, 'Report of the Working Group on the Universal Periodic Review: Dominican Republic' (4 April 2014) UN Doc A/HRC/26/15.

[4] HRC, 'Report of the Working Group on the Universal Periodic Review: Dominican Republic' (18 April 2019) UN Doc A/HRC/41/16 [12, 94.71 & 94.142].

offered to states undergoing the UPR on domestic violence, some going further than the standards set out by the Committee on the Convention of the Elimination of all forms of Discrimination Against Women (CEDAW Committee) others more general in nature, and some building on recommendations offered to states over the previous two review cycles. Universal Periodic Review recommendations are numerous and wide ranging but, when aggregated, can demonstrate certain trends in relation to human rights protection. Although some UPR recommendations are relatively trivial in nature and others concern matters relating to commitments under human rights treaties, there is a large class of recommendations framed in legal language, recommending a specific practice in relation to the protection of human rights to the state under review that is novel or relates to a particular interpretation of a widely acknowledged right. An analysis of these recommendations can show the emergence of customary international human rights law.

The HRC was created by UN General Assembly (GA) in 2006 and the UPR process was one of the most significant features of the new body, which replaced the UN Commission on Human Rights.[5] There has been a wide-ranging debate about the role of GA resolutions in the formation of custom. At the 1945 San Francisco Conference which founded the UN a proposal by the Philippines to give the GA the power to enact rules of international law which would become effective and binding upon members was defeated 26–1. Yet, from the beginning UNGA resolutions were often shaped in a way that suggested that they aimed to have some form of legal effect on states. In 1951 in the *Advisory Opinion on Genocide Reservations* Judge Alverez observed that GA resolutions had 'not yet acquired a binding character' but noted that if resolutions had the support of 'public opinion' they might be recognised as having some form of force over a state.[6] During the 1960s it became clear that certain declarations contained in GA resolutions were treated as quasi-legal statements of authority – in particular Resolution 1514 which called for the end of western colonialism which was often recited in subsequent resolutions.[7] Rosalyn Higgins concluded in

[5] See H Upton, 'The Human Rights Council: First Impressions and Future Challenges' (2007) 7 HRLR 29; N Ghanea 'From UN Commission on Human Rights to UN Human Rights Council: One Step Forwards or Two Steps Sideways' (2006) 55 ICLQ 695.

[6] *Reservations to the Convention on Genocide* (Advisory Opinion) [1951] ICJ Rep 49, Dissenting Opinion of Judge Alvarez 52.

[7] S Bliecher, 'The Legal Significance of Re-citation of General Assembly Resolutions' (1969) 63 AJIL 444.

a 1965 paper that the repeated practice of UN political organs was of 'probative value as customary law'.[8] There are a number of issues that arise with any analysis of the legal status of GA resolutions, such as the status of opposition to resolutions, which makes their customary status contentious.[9] The importance of the debate over custom and UNGA resolutions is that it provides a useful comparison point for understanding how custom can be observed in UPR recommendations.

Understanding the status of UPR recommendations is important in the context of understanding customary international human rights law. Section 2 of this chapter shows that human rights law poses a number of problems for the traditional assumption that custom requires both state practice and *opinio juris*.[10] Due to the way that UPR recommendations shape state behaviour and because of the importance of the review recommendations, the remainder of this chapter argues that UPR recommendations can be a useful means for observing the formation of customary human rights rules. The International Court of Justice (ICJ) has held that certain features of GA resolutions such as the context of their emergence, the language of their substantive provision and the reaction to states can be evidence of a consensus supporting the emergence of a new customary rule.[11] It is possible to trace similar features within a series of UPR recommendations on a particular norm and a framework for analysing UPR recommendations and identifying custom is set out in the final part of this chapter. But as the conclusion goes on to outline this raises wider questions about the rules for identifying custom.

2 Identifying Customary International Human Rights Law

The traditional concept of customary international law (CIL), which the International Law Commission's (ILC) Draft Conclusions adopts, is justified on the basis that the two-element concept is necessary in order to maintain the 'unity and coherence

[8] R Higgins, 'The Development of International Law by the Political Organs of the United Nations' (1965) 59 ASIL PROC 116.

[9] For examples of these issues being raised in the role of the General Assembly see GJ Kerwin, 'The Role of United Nations General Assembly Resolutions in Determining Principles of International Law in United States Courts' (1983) DukeLJ 876.

[10] H Thirlway, 'Human Rights in Customary Law: An Attempt to Define Some of the Issues' (1995) 28 LJIL 495.

[11] M Scharf, *Customary International Law in Times of Fundamental Change: Recognizing Grotian Moments* (Cambridge University Press 2013) 54–56.

of international law'.[12] The idea of different branches of international law having different rules in relation to law formation was rejected by the ILC even though, as Hugh Thirlway notes, there has been a widespread literature arguing that certain fields, such as international human rights law and international criminal law, ought to be treated differently with only the requirement for *opinio juris* to be present.[13] As Jean d'Aspremont also notes, exceptionalist thinking about the role of international human rights law, drawing on the non-reciprocity of rights and the importance of human rights for a constitutional framework of international law, led to a call for the 'argumentative structures of general international law ... not [to] apply' to international human rights law or for them to be in some way 'loosened'.[14] The seeming inflexibility of the rules surrounding custom has led other scholars to argue that the requirements of CIL are actively detrimental for the protection of human rights.[15] There is not really space here to re-examine the different schools of thought in this debate, but there are three important practical issues which arise with any attempt to identify customary international human rights law.

Firstly, the requirement to demonstrate consistency of state practice is hobbled by the basic reality that there are widespread human rights abuses perpetrated by states and human rights practice is often wildly inconsistent.[16] Realist critics, such as Goldsmith and Posner, have explained this by arguing that divergence of practice is simply a reflection of state interest as the 'behavioural regularities' require external incentives, such as coercion from more powerful states.[17] Other realist

[12] ILC, 'Identification of Customary International Law: Text of the Draft Conclusions Provisionally Adopted by the Drafting Committee' (30 May 2016) UN Doc A/CN.4/L.872, 126.

[13] Thirlway (n 10); see also B Lepard, '"Customary International Law: A Third World Perspective": Reflections in Light of an Approach to CIL Based on Fundamental Ethical Principles' (2018) 112 AJIL Unbound 303; there have also been concerns raised that such recognition would further increase the fragmentation of international law. A Cassimatis, 'International Humanitarian Law, International Human Rights Law, and Fragmentation of International Law' (2007) 56 ICLQ 623.

[14] J d'Aspremont, 'Expansion and the Sources of International Human Rights Law' (2016) 46 IsrYBHumRts 223, 224.

[15] I Gunning, 'Modernizing Customary International Law: The Challenge of Human Rights' (1990) 31 VaJIntlL 211.

[16] N Petersen, 'Customary Law Without Custom? Rules, Principles, and the Role of State Practice in International Norm Creation' (2007) 23 AmUIntlLRev 275, 282.

[17] J Goldsmith & E Posner, 'A Theory of Customary International Law' (1999) 66 U Chi L Rev 1113, 1171–72.

critics have taken this further arguing that state interest is in practice reducible to what is required for state survival and as a consequence custom is an inappropriate vehicle for human rights, when compared to treaty law which clearly binds states and defines their obligations.[18] The counter argument to this is that the practice requirement matters less in relation to international human rights law, and, as the ICJ has clarified, the search should be for consistency of practice rather than rigorous conformity.[19] A lot of this argument depends on what is recognised as state practice, as the implementation of rights is different from commitment to the protection of rights.[20] Even though there are potentially good reasons for acknowledging that acceptance of human rights norms through instruments such as GA resolutions is important in altering the normative consensus that leads to the protection of human rights, this leads to uncertainty about what precisely constitutes state practice and where the intention of a state behind a practice can be distinguished from the intention to be bound by that practice.[21]

Secondly, there is genuine debate about the nature of the prohibited practices involved in the protection of human rights, sometimes referred to as the secondary rules problem.[22] D'Amato frames the problem thus: '[w]hat are the parameters of torture? ... Is the battering of wives "torture"? ... what constitutes "inhuman treatment or punishment"?'.[23] The existence of a strong general consensus over particular norms – such as the prohibition of torture – does not necessarily mean clarity over the practical implications of what they entail, even if the customary status of certain rights are citied and recited by courts.[24] For example, Ghana is a party to the International Covenant on Civil and Political Rights (ICCPR) and the Human Rights Committee has since 1994 consistently interpreted the right to privacy under Article 17 as being incompatible

[18] M Beham, *State Interest and the Sources of International Law: Doctrine Morality and Non-Treaty Law* (Routledge 2019) 132–62.

[19] *Military and Paramilitary Activities in and against Nicaragua (Nicaragua v USA)* (Merits) [1986] ICJ Rep 14 [186].

[20] This view was strongly criticised by Anthony D'Amato but mainly in the context of the doctrine of non-intervention's customary status. See A D'Amato, 'Trashing Customary International Law' (1987) 81 AJIL 101, 102.

[21] J Kammerhofer, 'Uncertainty in the Formal Sources of International Law: Customary International Law and Some of Its Problems' (2004) 15 EJIL 523, 530.

[22] M Hakimi, 'Secondary Human Rights Law' (2009) 34 YaleJIntlL 596.

[23] A D'Amato, 'Human Rights as Part of Customary International Law: A Plea for Change of Paradigms' (1995) 25 AJIL 47, 48.

[24] RB Lillich, 'The Growing Importance of Customary International Human Rights' (1995) 25 GaJIntl&CompL 1.

with the criminalisation of same sex relations; yet Ghana not only ignores this but has also rejected UPR recommendations to decriminalise sexual orientation.[25] This speaks to a third related problem in relation to customary international human rights law – the idea that some states do not regard human rights law or human rights practice as creating a legally binding obligation upon them. Even though almost every state in the world is party to at least one legally binding international human rights instrument, mechanisms such as reservations have allowed states to manage the scope of their obligations, and states have used a variety of arguments to maintain they are not bound by treaty obligations in relation to specific rights, relating to practices considered culturally sensitive, or in areas where they have security concerns.[26] The persistent objector doctrine can also perform a similar function in that it allows states to define the limits of what should and what should not be considered human rights.[27]

In an attempt to refocus the debate surrounding the nature of the subjective element of custom, Brian Lepard has argued that a rule or principle ought to be considered customary law if it can be shown that 'states generally believe that it is desirable now or in the near future' to make a 'rule or principle' legally authoritative 'for all members of the global community'.[28] Lepard's argument is that 'state practice is importance of evidence of the belief that a norm should be universally binding' but that that it is not an 'essential independent requirement'; a position criticised by some scholars as fusing the two elements together.[29] Yet, as Lepard goes on to argue, his reformulation clarifies the role of *opinio juris*, because it looks at what should or ought to be binding, rather than what is

[25] This is the view of the HRC contained in *Toonen v Australia* (1994) UN Doc CCPR/C/50/D/488/1992. For the point on Ghana see HRC, 'Report of the Working Group on the Universal Periodic Review: Ghana' (13 December 2018) UN Doc A/HRC/22/6 [126.16, 126.18].

[26] Sonia Cardenas sets out common justifications for non-compliance with human rights obligations in S Cardenas, *Conflict and Compliance: State Responses to International Human Rights Pressure* (University of Pennsylvania Press 2010) 25; see also D Hill, 'Avoiding Obligation: Reservations to Human Rights Treaties' (2016) 60 JConflictResol 1129; E Bates 'Avoiding Legal Obligations Created by Human Rights Treaties' (2008) 57 ICLQ 751.

[27] H Lau, 'Rethinking the Persistent Objector Doctrine in International Human Rights Law' (2005) 6 ChinJIntLaw 495.

[28] B Lepard, 'Toward a New Theory of Customary International Human Rights Law' in B Lepard (ed), *Reexamining Customary International Law* (Cambridge University Press 2017) 262.

[29] Ibid; Mendelson is cautious about 'double counting', see M Mendelson, 'The Formation of Customary International Law' (1999) 272 RDC 155.

or may be perceived as binding.[30] A case study of this approach to custom is the GA resolution containing the Declaration on the Granting of Independence to Colonial Countries and Peoples.[31] This recognised emerging practice from Western states to grant colonial independence and was recognised by many states (particularly those who were newly independent) as having a legal quality to it because it supported the desirable goal of independence, whereas others (European states with colonial territories) were far more reluctant to concede its legal status.[32] Although this is not a formula for replacing the two-element rule – it instead refines how the individual elements are identified and examined – it has come in for criticism as being a form of 'norm entrepreneurship' which dilutes the meaning of custom.[33] Given the competing difficulties that the identification of customary human rights law poses, there is a need not so much for new rules but for a broader consideration of the materials used in the identification of the two elements of custom. An analysis of UPR recommendations, as the remainder of this chapter sets out, provides two clarifying functions for the identification of customary international human rights law. Firstly, it allows for a transparent and more democratic way of measuring the existence of a common consensus on a particular human rights norm. Secondly, the way the UPR process works allows for the contours of any norm to be defined, which is important when that norm is a secondary or interpretative norm about the scope of a particular practice which emerges outside of an agreed codification of a particular right in a treaty or one that is recognised elsewhere as *jus cogens*.

3 UPR Recommendations and Their Effect on State Behaviour

Under UPR rules every UN member has their human rights record reviewed around once every four years – known as UPR cycles.[34] The

[30] Lepard (n 28).

[31] UNGA Res 1514(XV) 'Declaration on the Granting of Independence to Colonial Countries and Peoples' (14 December 1960) UN Doc A/RES/1514(XV).

[32] For an overview of these positions see SP Sinha, 'Perspective of the Newly Independent States on the Binding Quality of International Law' (1965) 14 ICLQ 121; In spite of international opposition Portugal resisted independence for many of its Africa colonies until 1974, see J Miller 'The Politics of Decolonization in Portuguese Africa' (1975) 74 African Affairs 135.

[33] F Tesón, 'Fake Custom' in B Lepard (ed), *Reexamining Customary International Law* (Cambridge University Press 2017) 86.

[34] UNGA Res 60/251 'Resolution Adopted by the General Assembly: 60/251 Human Rights Council' (3 April 2006) UN Doc A/Res/60/251.

review is conducted based on documentary evidence from the state under review, reports from treaty bodies to which the state under review is a party, stakeholder reports from civil society groups in the state under review, international NGOs and other consultative bodies. Every state has participated in the process since its inception in 2006 and the treatment of states as equal peers has been a significant attraction of the process, differentiating it from its predecessor the UN Commission on Human Rights. During the review there is first a documentary review, examining the state under review's performance at treaty bodies, reports from stakeholders, and its own report. Then there is an interactive dialogue between the state under review and other members of the review panel. After that there is the opportunity for all states to issue recommendations to the state under review about changes in domestic law in order to improve their human rights practices. The UPR is a political process and was not intended to be law making but it involves scrutiny and discussion of a state's human rights obligations which leads to it sometimes overlapping with other international legal processes.[35] It was meant to complement and not duplicate the work of treaty bodies and in relation to some treaties the UPR has played a role in reinforcing obligations, by recommendations being cited by treaty bodies as evidence of state practice in relation to a particular norm.[36]

At the time of writing in October 2021 there have been nearly 79,000 recommendations issued to states in the 11 years that the review process has been in operation. Assessing recommendations is difficult because they have no real set form and are constructed by states acting individually rather than collectively or drafting them in concert with others, as is the case with UNGA resolutions. Edward McMahon has devised a system for categorising recommendations based on the nature and quality of action required of a state, ranking them from one to five.[37] Category two recommendations

[35] N Bernaz, 'Reforming the UN Human Rights Protection Procedures: A Legal Perspective on the Establishment of the Universal Periodic Review Mechanism' in K Boyle (ed), *New Institutions for Human Rights Protection* (Oxford University Press 2009) 75.

[36] I Salama, 'Proliferation of Treaty Bodies or Expansion of Protection?' (2011) 105 ASIL PROC 515, 519. For an example of a UPR recommendations being cited by treaty bodies as evidence of state practice see CEDAW Committee, 'Concluding Observations on the Combined Fourth and Fifth Periodic Reports of Maldives' (11 March 2015) UN Doc CEDAW/C/MDV/CO/4–5 [8–9] which directly referred to the Maldives' commitment to remove CEDAW reservations in their first cycle review; HRC, 'Report of the Working Group on the Universal Periodic Review: Maldives' (4 January 2011) UN Doc A/HRC/16/7 [100.1].

[37] E McMahon, 'The Universal Periodic Review: A Work in Progress: An Evaluation of the First Cycle of the New UPR Mechanism of the United Nations Human Rights Council'

concern general comments about what the state under review is currently doing and a request to continue an ongoing course of action. For example a recommendation to Brazil from Senegal during the second review cycle to 'continue fighting violence against women' simply asked the state under review (Brazil) to do nothing beyond what they were currently doing.[38] There has been some criticism of these sorts of recommendation being little more than offerings of praise from the states conducting the review. Sometimes when the state under review was their political ally, states would praise-bargain hoping that favourable recommendations would lead to the state under review affording them similar treatment when it was their turn for review.[39] In 2011, at the end of the first review cycle, a lot of emphasis was placed on the process of following up the implementation of recommendations accepted by states in subsequent review cycles.[40] Follow up can occur in the portion of the review dedicated to interactive dialogue. Sometimes recommendations specifically cross-reference previous commitments; for example, the recommendation issued to India by Botswana during its third cycle review to 'Ratify the Convention against Torture and Other Cruel, Inhuman or Degrading Treatment or Punishment, as previously recommended' was designed to reinforce earlier commitments.[41]

Recommendations in action categories four and five are framed using language which requires positive action on the part of a state, and directly reflects the legal language of a treaty or declaration. Recommendations classed as category five are those using legal verbs such as 'abolish', 'accede', 'adopt', 'amend', 'implement', 'enforce', or 'ratify'.[42] To illustrate this with another example from Brazil in its second cycle review; Spain issued a recommendation to 'adopt Bill No. 2442 in order to guarantee the independence and autonomy of the members of the

(Friedrich Ebert Stiftung, 2012) 18 <http://library.fes.de/pdf-files/bueros/genf/09297.pdf> accessed 1 March 2021.

38 HRC, 'Report of the Working Group on the Universal Periodic Review: Brazil' (9 July 2012) UN Doc A/HRC/21/11 [119.92].

39 A Komanovics, 'The Human Rights Council and the Universal Periodic Review: Is It More Than a Public Relations Exercise' (2012) 150 Studia Iuridica Auctoritate Universitatis Pecs Publicata 119.

40 See UN, 'UN Completes First Review of Human Rights Records of All Member States' (*UN News*, 13 October 2011) <https://news.un.org/en/story/2011/10/391432> accessed 1 March 2021.

41 HRC, 'Report of the Working Group on the Universal Periodic Review: India' (17 July 2017) UN Doc A/HRC/36/10 [161.5].

42 UPR Info, 'UPR Info's Database: Action Category' (UPR Info, 2016) <https://bit.ly/3GNm21E> accessed 1 March 2021.

National Preventive Mechanism, in conformity with Brazil's obligations under OPCAT' which is both precise in its intent and framed with clear instructions to the state party on the course of action to take.[43] After recommendations have been issued it is up to states to either 'Support' (UPR terminology for accept) or classify a reservation as 'Noted' (UPR terminology for reject). There has been some criticism of McMahon's framework as being too narrow, and concern that its focus on the type of action required to implement it obscures the utility of the recommendation for the state under review.[44] Yet, the linguistic framing of recommendations is vital for identifying and distinguishing what could appear to be the language of obligation and commitment from general descriptive language about human rights. Category five recommendations are the recommendations that are most likely to be rejected by the state under review – in the first UPR cycle which ran from 2008 to 2011, 60 per cent of category five recommendations were rejected. In the second cycle, which ran from 2012 to 2016, 55 per cent were rejected.[45] Significantly, in spite of this rejection rate the number of category five recommendations has remained steady over successive review cycles – 35 per cent of all recommendations in the first cycle were category five, in the second cycle it was 37 per cent of recommendations, and of the data available so far for the third cycle, 38 per cent have been category five recommendations. It is, however, important to remember that the categories are analytical tools for understanding the framing of recommendations and not a formal part of the UPR process. Whilst shaping the wording of recommendations, as they author them, states are not necessarily conscious that they are making a recommendation of one particular category or the other. They are best understood as an instrument of measure; ascertaining both the quantity of recommendations and the relative severity of linguistic framing. Moreover, while they may serve as a useful proxy for state intention, they are not always definitive proof of it.

Once accepted, a recommendation does not create an obligation upon the state under review to implement its substance. Recommendations do however affect state behaviour; firstly, the process of follow up, or at least the expectation of follow up, and the deliberative nature of the review process does encourage states to make incremental change to their

[43] HRC, 'Brazil' (n 38) [119.14].

[44] S Gujadhur & M Limon, 'Policy Report: Towards the Third Cycle of the UPR: Stick or Twist' (*Universal Rights Group*, 2016) 31 <https://bit.ly/3ys8FRA> accessed 1 March 2021.

[45] F Cowell, 'Understanding the Legal Status of Universal Periodic Review Recommendations' (2018) 7 CJIL 164.

behaviour in respect to their laws and policies respecting human rights.[46] Jane Cowan and Julie Billard's observation that states under review can treat their review like an 'exam', with state delegations to the UPR concerned about proving they have met minimum standards or demonstrating the implementation of legal reforms, shows that the UPR process can change state behaviour, even if it does not meet some of the loftier objectives about the promotion of dialogue on human rights intended by the UPR's creators.[47] Secondly, in terms of implementation and delivery there is a correlation between states accepting recommendations and implementing changes to their law and policy surrounding human rights in response to those recommendations.[48] Sometimes this relates to a course of action already decided upon by a state party and recommendations help reinforce this course of action.[49] Yet on other occasions there are signs that recommendations act as drivers of reform independently – for example in relation to protection from human trafficking and maternal health there has been some research showing recommendations correlate with the adoption of higher standards on these issues in countries which have accepted recommendations.[50] There was also an upsurge in the number of states signing up to and ratifying treaties in the wake of the first UPR cycle, again seemingly in response to a wave of recommendations in the first cycle relating to treaty provisions.[51]

[46] K Milewicz & R Goodin, 'Deliberative Capacity Building through International Organizations: The Case of the Universal Periodic Review of Human Rights' (2018) 48 BJPolS 513.

[47] J Cowan & J Billaud, 'Between Learning and Schooling: The Politics of Human Rights Monitoring at the Universal Periodic Review' (2015) 36 TWQ 1175, 1179.

[48] Research conducted at the half-way point of the first cycle showed around half of all recommendations had already triggered some kind of action from states. See M White, 'Addressing Human Rights Protection Gaps: Can the Universal Periodic Review Process Live Up to Its Promise?' in J Gomez & R Ramcharan (eds), *The Universal Periodic Review of Southeast Asia* (Palgrave Macmillan 2018) 19.

[49] For an example of research supporting this see G Gunatilleke et al, 'Do Recommendations to the Universal Peer Review Work? Examining Recommendations in UPR's First Two Cycles for Nepal, Sri Lanka and Indonesia' (2016) 2 Journal of Human Rights and Peace Studies 107.

[50] K Gilmore, L Mora, A Barragues et al, 'The Universal Periodic Review: A Platform for Dialogue, Accountability, and Change on Sexual and Reproductive Health and Rights' (2015) 17 HHRJournal 167; K Lerum, K McCurtis, P Saunders et al, 'Using Human Rights to Hold the US Accountable for Its Anti-sex Trafficking Agenda: The Universal Periodic Review and New Directions for US Policy' (2012) 1 Anti-Trafficking Review 80.

[51] UNDP Moldova & the Office of the High Commissioner for Human Rights Chisinau, 'Draft Report: International Conference on Responding to the UPR Recommendations: Challenges, Innovation and Leadership' (UNDP, November 4–5 2011) <www.undp.org/content/dam/rbec/docs/UPR%20Conference.pdf> accessed 1 March 2021.

Regular patterns of state behaviour in accordance with the terms of some GA resolutions has been cited by some scholars as proof of their customary status, even though such behaviour might not be in conformity with all of the terms of a resolution.[52] Regardless of whether states consider the UPR to be a form of ritualised audit or approach the review as an opportunity to advance strategic interests, states' behaviour towards the process indicates that issuing and accepting recommendations carries a degree of importance.[53] A crucial distinction between UPR recommendations and GA resolutions however is that certain resolutions, such as those on outer space or environmental issues, were claimed to create instant custom, without state practice.[54] Some of the most compelling arguments in this debate related to recommendations containing declarations which made normative pronouncements about what the law ought to be in a particular area, and which was then put in a codified text of a resolution and voted on.[55] In 1977 this argument was made by the Group of 77 (a UN grouping principally consisting of newly independent states in Africa and Asia) who contended that a UN resolution on the seabed should be regarded as binding because it represented a true international consensus on what the law ought to be, had been expertly drafted, and the GA resolution containing it passed without any votes in opposition.[56] Universal Periodic Review recommendations differ from GA resolutions as they are drafted by individual states and reflect their own interest and priorities. As Gujadhur and Limon note, one of the

[52] See D Bodansky, 'Customary (and Not So Customary) International Environmental Law' (1995) 3 IndJ Global Legal Studies 105.

[53] J Cowan, 'The Universal Periodic Review as Public Audit Ritual: An Anthropological Perspective on Emerging Practices in the Global Governance of Human Rights' in H Charlesworth & E Larking (eds), *Human Rights and the Universal Periodic Review: Rituals and Ritualism* (Cambridge University Press 2015) 44.

[54] B Cheng, 'United Nations Resolutions on Outer Space: "Instant" International Customary Law' (1965) 5 IJIL 23 who argued that custom could be created if a GA resolution contained *opinio juris*. For a more critical overview see B Krivokapić, 'On the Issue of So-Called "Instant" Customs in International Law' (2017) 9 Acta Universitatis Danubius Administratio 91.

[55] For examples of declarations and custom see S Bleicher, 'The Legal Significance of Re-Citation of General Assembly Resolutions' (1969) 63(3) AJIL 444, 450–51; H Hannum, 'The UDHR in National and International Law' (1998) 3 HHRJournal 144, 148.

[56] The resolution in question was UNGA Res 2749(XXV) 'Declaration of Principles Governing the Sea-Bed and the Ocean Floor, and the Subsoil Thereof, Beyond the Limits of National Jurisdiction' (12 December 1970) UN Doc A/RES/2749(XXV). The incident is described in S Schwebel, 'The Effect of Resolutions of the UN General Assembly on Customary International Law' (1979) 73 ASIL PROC 301.

problems the UPR process faces is the sheer weight of recommendations, many of them of variable quality and relatively poorly constructed.[57] Acceptance and rejection of individual recommendations can mean relatively little and can vary considerably from state to state. It is therefore more important to look at recommendations in aggregate on a particular issue to see the reflection of a normative consensus on any one human rights issue.

4 A Lens through Which to See Custom in UPR Recommendations

Custom's formation is often described as being observed rather than generated. As Anthea Roberts notes, traditionally custom was 'inductive' in that it was derived from an observation of state practice, whereas modern custom is 'deductive' in that is deduced from international instruments, such as declarations and reservation.[58] As Stefan Talmon notes, however, it is incorrect to think of this as a choice between the two methods and at the ICJ there have been situations where it was simply not possible to use an inductive method to identify custom.[59] What is presented here therefore is a deductive framework to use for identifying the emergence of customary human rights norms in the UPR. This framework breaks into three parts and arguably provides greater clarity in the context of the UPR than the two-element approach.

4.1 Acceptance of Recommendations and Practice

Although state practice was historically conceived as the physical acts of states, for example by controlling which ships were allowed into a particular area, there is now a general recognition that verbal acts can in certain circumstances constitute state practice.[60] UPR recommendations are issued through an official process, created by a GA resolution that has a broad-based international acceptance and is treated by human rights treaty bodies as being authoritative evidence of state practice in relation to a particular

57 Gujadhur & Limon (n 44) 4–5.

58 A Roberts, 'Traditional and Modern Approaches to Customary International Law: A Reconciliation' (2001) 95 AJIL 757, 758.

59 S Talmon, 'Determining Customary International Law: The ICJ's Methodology between Induction Deduction and Assertion' (2015) 26 EJIL 417, 422.

60 Kammerhofer (n 21).

norm. Accepted recommendations go beyond mere statements of practice.[61] International decisions – such as a GA resolutions – are exceptional as their institutional provenance means that they are considered indicative of either how states are acting, ought to act or ought not be acting.[62] Conclusion 4 of the ILC's Draft Conclusions on the Identification of Customary International Law makes specific reference to international organisations in the context of state practice, and Draft Conclusion 7 notes that practice includes a 'wide range of forms' including 'resolutions adopted by an international organization'.[63] Strictly speaking recommendations are not resolutions but they are advanced as part of an organisational process and therefore would be analogous to the processes outlined in both the ILC's Draft Proposals and the International Law Association's (ILA) final report.[64] In fact as the ILA's report goes on to note the practice of international tribunals 'is replete with examples of verbal acts being treated as examples of practice' so the concept of practice is viewed in relatively expansive terms.[65]

Yet, this raises the issue of what precise moment in the UPR process – acceptance of a recommendation or implementation of the substance of the recommendation – constitutes state practice. Implementation of a recommendation would demonstrate the existence of a concrete human rights protection within a state and therefore be the physical manifestation of a principle. But, as the ILA notes, 'statements in international organizations and the resolutions these bodies adopt' are more common than 'physical acts, such as arresting people or seizing property' leading to the conclusion that if a claim is publicly communicated it would constitute an act for the purpose of custom.[66] Following UNHRC Resolution 16/21, a state is required to 'clearly communicate to the Council … its positions on all received recommendations' entailing that there is a requirement on states to take a public position in relation

[61] ibid; see also K Wolfke, 'Some Persistent Controversies Regarding Customary International Law' (1993) 24 NYIL 1.

[62] In this sense organisations are acting as conduits of the collective will of states – see for an overview J Odermatt, 'The Development of Customary International Law by International Organizations' (2017) 66 ICLQ 491.

[63] ILC (n 12) Draft Conclusion 7.

[64] See ILA Committee on Formation of Customary (General) International Law, 'Final Report of the Committee: Statement of Principles Applicable to the Formation of General Customary International Law' (ILA, 2000) 14–19 <https://bit.ly/3dU8e9f> accessed 1 March 2021.

[65] ibid.

[66] ibid 15.

to the recommendations they have been offered.[67] Acceptance of a recommendation is therefore made in public, recorded in an official UN document, with an expectation that its terms will be put into practice by a state; thus when a recommendation is accepted, it is state practice. As Malcom Shaw puts it, if practice is considered as simply 'what States actually do', then publicly making a commitment to implement a specified human rights reform and consenting to be examined on progress towards that reform in four years' time, is what states 'do'.[68] Yet, an individual recommendation and acceptance of it by a state under review would not really be sufficient to establish that there was state practice as a recommendation applies to a particular state.[69] Practice, according to the ICJ, needs to be widespread as well as 'sufficiently extensive and convincing' in order for it to be considered the basis of custom.[70] Therefore, multiple accepted recommendations of the category four or five type, which by their nature require a specific course of action on a human rights norm by states, would need to be shown in order to demonstrate a practice.

Even if a chain of accepted recommendations on the same subject can be identified, there are likely to be some rejected recommendations on the same subject. The rejection rate of recommendations in action category five supports the idea that states act with the belief that because of their framing, such commitments are in some way consequential.[71] Yet Elvira Domínguez Redondo notes that this pattern of behaviour can be interpreted narrowly, as simply the state under review 'asserting its reluctance to be monitored by the UPR on the implementation of such a recommendation during its next review'.[72] Therefore, a state may not actually object to the substance of the recommendation but wish to avoid, for a variety of reasons, accepting a UPR recommendation on the subject. The multiplicity of motivations behind rejected recommendations means that they are difficult to read as a conclusive manifestation of the

[67] HRC Res 16/21 'Review of the Work and Functioning of the Human Rights Council' (12 April 2011) UN Doc A/HRC/RES/16/21 [D.16].

[68] M Shaw, *International Law* (7th ed, Cambridge University Press 2014) 53.

[69] Bodansky (n 52).

[70] *Delimitation of the Maritime Boundary in the Gulf of Maine Area (Canada v USA)* (Judgment) [1984] ICJ Rep 299 [111]; on the principle of practice being 'widespread' see *Maritime Delimitation and Territorial Questions between Qatar and Bahrain (Qatar v Bahrain)* (Merits) [2001] ICJ Rep 102 [205].

[71] Cowell (n 45).

[72] E Dominguez-Redondo, 'The Universal Periodic Review: Is There Life beyond Naming and Shaming in Human Rights Implementation?' (2012) 4 NZLRev 673, 701.

persistent objector doctrine.[73] As Joel Trachtman notes, the doctrine only applies 'when the customary rule is in the process of emerging' but that this is a somewhat problematic part of the principle as custom 'is always in a zen-like process of becoming and un-becoming'.[74] As UPR recommendations (as shown below) on the same subject might be accepted in some cases but rejected in others, this means that it is difficult to pinpoint the moment of becoming for a norm. Furthermore, in relation to customary human rights law, the persistent objector rule could mean that a right that ought to be universal is essentially opted out of by a state, although human rights tribunals have rejected this argument where the right is considered *jus cogens*.[75]

Rejected recommendations also do not give much of an insight into the substantive objection to a recommendation. As Lynn Loschin identifies in her four-part model for analysing the persistent objector doctrine in international human rights law, 'the quality and quantity of the State's objection' would be important for validating whether the objection reflects a genuine preference of a state.[76] It is, for example, entirely possible that a recommendation is rejected based on part of its text and not as a reflection of the whole recommendation. Even if a state's rejection of a recommendation is relatively consistent over review cycles, that also may not be grounds for saying that a customary norm should not be universal. As Lepard argues, customary human rights law should be about what rights ought to be protected as a matter of international law, not an assessment of the often-inconsistent nature of state practice.[77] Accepted and rejected recommendations therefore need to be considered in tandem in order to ascertain the nature of a norm which emerges from recommendations, but there would need to be a high number of accepted recommendations which leads onto the next issue – quantification.

[73] In the *Fisheries* case the ICJ held that Norway's consistent objection to an alleged rule surrounding fishing rights meant that it had 'always opposed any attempt' for the 'ten mile rule' for delineating which waters in a bay apply to internal water to apply to the Norwegian coast. *Fisheries Case (UK v Norway)* (Judgment) [1951] ICJ Rep 116, 131.

[74] J Trachtman, 'Persistent Objectors, Cooperation, and the Utility of Customary International Law' (2010) 21 DukeJComp&IntlL 221.

[75] See *Domingues v United States* (Merits) (2002) Inter-American Commission on Human Rights, Report No 62/02, 913; see also H Lau, 'Rethinking the Persistent Objector Doctrine in International Human Rights Law' (2005) 6 CJIL 495.

[76] L Loschin, 'The Persistent Objector and Customary Human Rights Law: A Proposed Analytical Framework' (1996) 2 UCDavisJIntlL&Pol'y 147, 165–66.

[77] See B Lepard, *Customary International Law: A New Theory with Practical Applications* (Cambridge University Press 2010) 113.

4.2 Quantification: Accepted Recommendations Making a Rule?

The ICJ's *Advisory Opinion on Nuclear Weapons* noted that a 'series of [GA] resolutions may show the gradual evolution of the *opinio juris* required for the establishment of a new rule'.[78] Empirical studies on the formation and identification of custom in court briefs and submissions before international tribunals have been relatively inconclusive in establishing trends of how custom is identified, yet this does not mean that thresholds of practice cannot be established.[79] As Christopher Joyner noted in relation to GA resolutions, even though the law making competence of the assembly was qualified, when 'delegates representing almost all the world's national governments cast votes on a resolution, they are in effect providing a common confirmation (or rejection) of the presence and acceptance of that issue in international law'.[80] In the case of UPR recommendations it would mean establishing a common linguistic framing, a common subject matter and a pattern of acceptance from states with a reasonably wide geographic spread – all of which is possible using a database such as UPR Info to track the emergence or existence of such a trend.[81] A constant series of recommendations all aimed at a particular practice, which are accepted and over the course of multiple cycles are adopted by states, could amount to what the ICJ describes as a 'general recognition' that a law or legal obligation is involved.[82] Quantifying recommendations helps to establish to what extent a consensus surrounding a particular norm actually exists, which is important for establishing the existence of practice in the formation of custom.[83] Even adopting a theory of customary international human rights law, of the sort outlined by Lepard, there would need to be some acknowledgement

[78] *Legality of the Threat or Use of Nuclear Weapons* (Advisory Opinion) [1996] ICJ Rep 226 [70].

[79] G Shaffer & T Ginsburg, 'The Empirical Turn in International Legal Scholarship' (2012) 106 AJIL 1, 13.

[80] C Joyner, 'UN General Assembly Resolutions and International Law: Rethinking the Contemporary Dynamics of Norm-Creation' (1981) 11 CalWIntlLJ 445, 460.

[81] UPR Info's mission statement is to 'utilise the United Nations Universal Periodic Review (UPR) to ensure cooperation among all actors . . . implement human rights obligations and commitments' and its database contains all recommendations made to states, UPR Info, 'Database of UPR Recommendations and Voluntary Pledges' (UPR Info Database, 2021) <https://upr-info-database.uwazi.io/> accessed 1 March 2021.

[82] *North Sea Continental Shelf Cases (Federal Republic of Germany/Netherlands; Federal Republic of Germany/Denmark)* (Judgment) [1969] ICJ Rep 3 [74].

[83] N Petersen, 'Customary Law without Custom? Rules, Principles, and the Role of State Practice in International Norm Creation' (2007) 23 AmUIntlLRev 275.

of the scale of moral consensus surrounding a particular norm, to give weight to the claim that it ought to be universal.[84] Because of the nature of recommendations, as outlined in the second section above, it is necessary to trace a particular norm through recommendations and quantify the use of certain words in a series of recommendations on that subject.

A good case study of how this process might work is the prohibition on corporal punishment. According to the Global Initiative to End Corporal Punishment of Children, at the time of writing around 140 states prohibit corporal punishment in the criminal justice system and 132 prohibit it in the education system.[85] There are, however, far fewer states that have prohibited corporal punishment in the home or care system and in total only fifty-six states have a total prohibition on corporal punishment as a matter of law. The European Court of Human Rights has been clear that state sanctioned corporal punishment constitutes inhuman and degrading treatment.[86] An advisory opinion of the Inter-American Court of Human Rights stated that the American Convention on Human Rights required state parties to take 'positive measures . . . to ensure protection of children against mistreatment' especially in 'relations among individuals or with non-governmental entities' but stopped short of formally requiring the prohibition of corporal punishment.[87] Article 19 of the Convention on the Rights of the Child (CRC) requires state parties to take 'appropriate legislative, administrative, social and educational measures to protect the child from all forms of physical or mental violence' which does not explicitly prohibit corporal punishment.[88] In General Comment 1, the Committee on the Rights of the Child noted that in the context of protecting the right to education it had previously made clear in its concluding observations that the use of corporal punishment did 'not respect the inherent dignity of the child nor the strict limits on school discipline' protected in the convention.[89] In General Comment 8 the committee went further, arguing that corporal punishment was incompatible with the requirement to protect children from harm and

[84] Lepard (n 28).

[85] Global Initiative to End Violence against Children, 'Progress' (End Corporal Punishment, 2019) <https://endcorporalpunishment.org/countdown/> accessed 1 March 2021.

[86] *Tyrer v UK* ECtHR, App No 5856/72 (25 April 1978) 2.

[87] *Juridical Status and Human Rights of the Child*, Advisory Opinion OC-17/02, Inter-American Court of Human Rights Series A No 17 (28 August 2002) [87].

[88] Convention on the Rights of the Child (adopted 20 November 1989, entered into force 2 September 1990) 1577 UNTS 3 (CRC), art 19(1).

[89] UNCRC, 'General Comment No 1 (2001), Article 29 (1), The Aims of Education' (17 April 2001) UN Doc CRC/GC/2001/1 [8].

that laws permitting corporal punishment in education needed to be repealed.[90] But crucially it stopped short of recommending the prohibition on corporal punishment in the home.

There have been a large number of UPR recommendations submitted concerning corporal punishment and overall, 58 per cent of them have been accepted. The vast majority of accepted and rejected recommendations are in action category 4 and 5, containing the words 'prohibit', 'end', 'ban' or 'eliminate'. For example, France in its second cycle review accepted a recommendation from Uruguay 'to explicitly ban the corporal punishment of children in all settings, including the family, schools and institutions'.[91] Other recommendations can be more explicit in cross referencing the CRC and existing obligations in international law. For example, Uruguay recommended to Algeria in its second cycle review, after commending it during the interactive dialogue for introducing a prohibition on corporal punishment in schools, that it extend the prohibition to 'home care institutions, penitentiary centres and any other settings, in conformity with Article 19 of CRC'.[92] Other states have, however, been wary of recommendations which include a prohibition that would entail them prohibiting corporal punishment in the home, potentially entailing the introducing of laws which might criminalise parents; Switzerland in the third cycle accepted one recommendation on the prohibition of corporal punishment but rejected another which specifically referenced prohibition 'in all settings, including in the home'.[93] Out of all rejected recommendations referring to corporal punishment, 25 per cent of them are category four or five recommendations referring to the 'home', 'family' or other term referring to prohibition on the domestic sphere.

When analysing recommendations, a basic three-part approach to quantification of recommendations would help identify the emergence of custom. Firstly (as detailed in Figure 15.1) there would need to be a quantification of both the practice, or the noun (i.e., 'corporal punishment') and the verb in connection to the noun (i.e., 'prohibit') because the

[90] UNCRC, 'General Comment No 8 (2006): The Right of the Child to Protection from Corporal Punishment and Other Cruel or Degrading Forms of Punishment (Arts 19; 28, Para 2; and 37, inter alia)' (2 March 2007) UN Doc CRC/C/GC/8 [26].

[91] HRC, 'Report of the Working Group on the Universal Periodic Review: France' (21 March 2013) UN Doc A/HRC/23/3 [120.116].

[92] HRC, 'Report of the Working Group on the Universal Periodic Review: Algeria' (5 July 2012) UN Doc A/HRC/21/13 [129.100].

[93] HRC, 'Report of the Working Group on the Universal Periodic Review: Switzerland' (29 December 2017) UN Doc A/HRC/37/12 [148.61] (offered by Sweden rejected) and [146.103] (offered by Kyrgyzstan accepted).

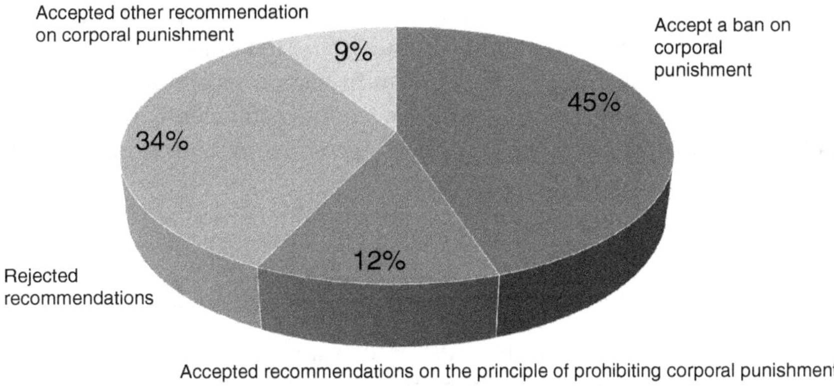

Figure 15.1 Recommendations on banning corporal punishment across UPR cycles to date.

commitment to the 'doing' or 'enacting' of a human rights norm is what differentiates a mere verbal statement from something which can be considered state practice. Given the scale of friendly recommendations and praise bargaining, there needs to be a standard to distinguish accepted recommendations which might be evidence of custom from accepted recommendations which are of largely political significance – hence recommendations looked for as evidence of custom considered would need to be in action categories four and five, as they involve an active commitment from a state party.[94] Although it is conceivable that a state might take action over recommendations in categories one to three, their vague and open-ended wording, which often lacks any clear description of subject matter or action to be undertaken by the state, means that it would be difficult to treat these recommendations as evidence of customary law. Secondly, the framing of rejected recommendations needs to be analysed to see where in the rejected recommendations there appears to be limitations of rights. For example, in the case of corporal punishment the only consistent trend in rejected recommendations on corporal punishment appears to be scepticism about extension of the prohibition to the domestic sphere. This should be read in tandem with other sources on the practice outside the UPR process – such as court decisions – to see if

[94] For detail on the issue of friendly recommendations see C Martin, 'The UPR and Its Impact on the Protection Role of AICHR in Southeast Asia' in J Gomez & R Ramcharan (eds), *The Universal Periodic Review of Southeast Asia* (Palgrave Macmillan 2018); R Terman & E Voeten, 'The Relational Politics of Shame: Evidence from the Universal Periodic Review' (2018) 13 RIO 1.

this would constitute a ground for rejection that indicated a substantive objection to a specific right and hence accepting the limited nature of any customary norm that could be identified in recommendations.[95] Thirdly, the recommendations analysed would need to be sufficiently numerous – in figure 1 above the number of accepted recommendations numbers over 200 – and across more than one cycle and geographic region, to demonstrate evidence of the widespread consensus on a particular issue.

4.3 UPR Recommendations: The Sense of Obligation

The participatory nature of the UPR process arguably makes any consensus identified in accepted recommendations more justifiable on democratic grounds as the basis of a shared belief that a particular principle ought to be binding, in accordance with the interpretation of *opinio juris* set out in the first section of this chapter. All states have participated in at least one UPR review and all states are treated equally before it, in that they all get to be reviewed and can contribute to other states' reviews. Unlike human rights treaty bodies, which subject states to review by panel of experts, the UPR process is genuinely participatory. Nicole Rouhgan's work on the democratic formation of custom attempts to reconcile the way that custom's formation 'falls short of contemporary ideals of democracy' and is characterised by an absence of a mechanism 'to protect formal equality in the development of customary rules'.[96] Emmanuel Voyiakis echoes this criticism, noting how international systems are riven with inequalities, reflecting the interests of powerful states in the formation of custom to the extent that CIL as a concept lacked a firm 'justification for generating rules with normative force' over other states.[97] Most customs, as Anthea Roberts notes, are based on the practice of fewer than a dozen states, meaning that formation of custom skews towards states with power and knowledge of legal formation creating a situation which by default privileges powerful states.[98] In an attempt to re-found an understanding of CIL's formation that is more democratic Roughan argues that it should be

[95] See Loschin (n 75) framework for assessing objections. It is noteworthy that in the case of corporal punishment the CRC expressed some concern about laws criminalising parents in CRC (n 89) [41].

[96] N Rouhgan, 'Democratic Custom v International Customary Law' (2007) 38 VUWLR 403, 409.

[97] E Voyiakis, 'A Disaggregative View of Customary International Law-Making' (2016) 29 LJIL 365.

[98] Roberts (n 58).

'understood at its core to be a matter of social participation'.[99] A series of accepted recommendations would be representative both of a broad commitment on a particular human rights norm from individual states accepting recommendations on that norm, but also would represent a positive statements from the states offering those recommendations on what they believed the law ought to be. But, whilst this would affect the validity of the consensus behind a particular norm, it would not give an insight into the subjective belief that the norm is or ought to be binding.

The process of taking part in the review and being scrutinised on the implementation of accepted recommendations is a form of ongoing interaction, which can build a sense of obligation. Jutta Brunnée and Stephen Toope argue that processes of institutional interaction on the part of a state can build a sense of fidelity to the institution encouraging them to reshape their behaviour so as to create a sense of legality.[100] Their thesis has received criticism from different directions, including claims that it is too reductive about the nature of obligations and fails to really interrogate the nature of international society within which states' values are supposedly shaped.[101] Yet, interaction has instrumental value in showing how the understanding of a norm as obligatory can emerge. As Brunnée and Toope note, within all systems of law (national or international) 'law is constructed through rhetorical activity producing increasingly influential mutual expectations or shared understandings of actors'.[102] Research on the politicised nature of UPR recommendations actually underscores the conclusion that states view the acceptance of recommendations as a process that involves accepting responsibilities.[103] This is because recommendations, when offered in a partisan manner, still appear consequential to the state under review and the overlap between the UPR and other legal processes means that the UPR process itself is seen as important. A reaction to recommendations would need to be actually observed in order to establish that changes were arising

99 Roughan (n 97) 413.

100 J Brunnée & S Toope, *Legitimacy and Legality in International Law: An International Account* (Cambridge University Press 2010) 88.

101 For these critiques see respectively M Koskenniemi, 'The Mystery of Legal Obligation' (2011) 3 International Theory 319; C Reus-Smit, 'Obligation Through Practice' (2011) 3 International Theory 339.

102 J Brunnée & C Toope, 'International Law and Constructivism: Elements of an Interactional Theory of International Law' (2000) 39 ColumJTransnat'lL 19, 65.

103 See R Terman and E Voeten, 'The Relational Politics of Shame: Evidence from the Universal Periodic Review (2018) 13 RIO 1; MH Hong, 'Legal Commitments to United Nations Human Rights Treaties and Higher Monitoring Standards in the Universal Periodic Review' (2018) 17 Journal of Human Rights 660.

in part as a result of interaction with the UPR process, in order to meet the commonly accepted requirements of the subjective element of custom.

One example of such a reaction is child marriage; there have been a few hundred recommendations issued to states in relation to the issue of early forced marriage, 68 per cent of which have been accepted by states across all three cycles. Early forced marriage is prohibited in CEDAW and in the CRC but there is a tension about both the scope of the prohibition and the age of marriage – CEDAW specifies no minimum age of marriage but the CRC implies eighteen.[104] The HRC has interpreted the provisions in the ICCPR on the right to a family in a way which allows for individual states to reach their own conclusion about marriage laws.[105] Recommendations made to Indonesia in their second review cycle to eliminate early marriage prompted the government to investigate the enforcement of marriage laws and to draft a new law raising the age of marriage to eighteen across the country.[106] At their third cycle review they accepted recommendations on the outright prohibition of forced early marriage.[107] Benin accepted recommendations during its second cycle to abolish early marriage and in its third cycle national report detailed measures it had taken to implement new legislation protecting children's rights.[108] In its third cycle review during the interactive dialogue states expressed concern about the persistent prevalence of early forced marriage in spite of changes to the law and in response Benin committed to prosecutions of the perpetrators of forced marriage.[109] In both cases the state undertook actions indicative of a belief they were under an obligation to fulfil the substance of the recommendation. These are just two states

[104] M Freeman, 'Article 16' in M Freeman, C Chinkin & B Rudolf (eds), *The UN Convention on the Elimination of All Forms of Discrimination against Women: A Commentary* (2nd ed, Oxford University Press 2013) 436.

[105] S Joseph & M Castan, *The International Covenant on Civil and Political Rights: Cases, Materials and Commentary* (3rd ed, Oxford University Press 2014) 667.

[106] HRC, 'Report of the Working Group on the Universal Periodic Review: Indonesia' (5 July 2012) UN Doc A/HRC/21/7 [108.124]; HRC, 'National Report Submitted in Accordance with Paragraph 5 of the Annex to Human Rights Council Resolution 16/21: Indonesia' (20 February 2017) UN Doc A/HRC/WG.6/27/IDN/1 [64–66].

[107] HRC, 'Report of the Working Group on the Universal Periodic Review: Indonesia' (14 July 2017) UN Doc A/HRC/36/7 [139.108, 139.128].

[108] HRC, 'Report of the Working Group on the Universal Periodic Review: Benin' (11 December 2012) UN Doc A/HRC/22/9 [108.30, 108.45]; HRC, 'National Report Submitted in Accordance with Paragraph 5 of the Annex to Human Rights Council Resolution 16/21: Benin' (7 August 2017) UN Doc A/HRC/WG.6/28/BEN/1 [25].

[109] HRC, 'Report of the Working Group on the Universal Periodic Review: Benin' (3 January 2018) UN Doc A/HRC/37/10 [86, 112].

and many other states have accepted recommendations on this subject, but these examples serve to illustrate how *opinio juris* can be inferred by looking at a state's subsequent conduct in the UPR process in relation to the recommendation.

5 Conclusion

By way of conclusion, it is worth identifying two potential lines of criticism about the framework advanced here and what it means for the identification of CIL. Firstly it is open in adopting what Noora Arajärvi critically termed the 'paradigm shift' toward the 'demands of humanity' away from the more orthodox position in some of the literature, on the evidence of state practice required for custom to be identified.[110] Fernando Tesón almost pre-empted the argument advanced in the first part of Section 3 with his description of 'the Ad Nauseam Fallacy technique' whereby 'profusely citing nonbinding resolutions' is used to advance a 'sense of normativity' that is not actually present.[111] Yet, this neglects the institutional framework of the UPR described above. As both the ILC and the ILA investigations into the source of custom highlight, interaction with an institution such as the UPR is a key part of what a state 'does' both in terms of the internal procedure and the effect it has on states and in terms of the commitments that states make. This also relates to the sense of obligation. One key criticism of the way that the ICJ has interpreted the legal effect of GA resolutions is that the court has focused more on their binding nature than on the way that they shape legal discourse.[112] Individual UPR recommendations do not bind the states who accept them but collectively a series of accepted recommendations demonstrate the existence of an emerging consensus on a particular norm. This means that a series of recommendations could and, from the perspective of those seeking to defend human rights, probably should, have an authorising effect – in that they identify rights that states need to protect and highlight the legal obligation to protect those rights.[113]

110 N Arajärvi, 'From the "Demands of Humanity": The Formulation of *Opinio Juris* in Decisions of International Criminal Tribunals and the Need for a Renewed Emphasis on State Practice' in B Lepard (ed), *Reexamining Customary International Law* (Cambridge University Press 2017) 190.

111 Tesón (n 33) 93.

112 M Öberg, 'The Legal Effects of Resolutions of the UN Security Council and General Assembly in the Jurisprudence of the ICJ' (2006) 16 EJIL 879.

113 ibid 886.

Secondly this theory involves adopting a constructivist interpretation of both elements of the two-element theory reasoning that state interests are shaped by the social conditions that surround them (in this case the rules of the UPR process).[114] Rationalist and realist critics would probably reject this description of state behaviour, and any analysis of UPR recommendations gravitates heavily towards an empiricist understanding of custom. However, an empiricist understanding of accepted recommendations would allow for the identification of a consensus on a particular norm, and importantly, would provide grounds for establishing a definitive explanation of which rights ought to be protected. The UPR was not meant to be a legal process but its effects have altered the way states act towards certain norms and the recommendations they accept. The mechanism outlined above helps identify where a norm contained in recommendations could have a customary status and addresses some of the criticisms surrounding the identification of customary norms.[115] Overall this theory puts a heavy institutional gloss on the identification of CIL, and questions of the practice and the binding nature of norms are answered technically with reference to the nature of the UPR process. In the context of a process which has mass buy-in from states, with every country in the world being subject to at least one review, a justification for a heavy institutional emphasis on the question of custom can be constructed on the lines that Lepard outlines above as it is possible to discern from the UPR process a strong sense of what rights ought to exist.[116] Whilst challenging some assumptions about what constitutes practice within the existing literature, identifying custom in UPR recommendations can help give coherence to the identification of customary international human rights norms.

[114] E Bates, 'Sophisticated Constructivism in Human Rights Compliance Theory' (2015) 25 EJIL 1169.

[115] See P Staubach, *The Rule of Unwritten International Law: Customary Law, General Principles, and World Order* (Routledge 2018) 79.

[116] Lepard (n 28).

PART IV

Interpretation of Customary International Law

Delineating the Stages in Its Life Cycle

16

Interpreting Customary International Law

You'll Never Walk Alone

PANOS MERKOURIS*

1 Introduction

Oceans of ink have been spilt over both treaty interpretation and customary international law (CIL). Yet the point of convergence between these two areas, that is, CIL interpretation, remains somewhat woefully under-examined. The almost obsessive focus on the formation stage of CIL, with its two elements, state practice and *opinio juris* may have something to do with that. As perhaps does the fact, stemming from the above obsession, that CIL is often cursorily dismissed as not being interpretable. The present contribution aims to question these assumptions, and demonstrate that CIL interpretation is not only plausible, but has been occurring both in international and domestic legal systems. It is a process that is inextricably linked to the life cycle of every rule, irrespective of its source, and it is one that can also breathe life and ensure the relevance of rules across wide swathes of the temporal landscape.

Section 2 will start with an examination of some of the basic objections raised against the interpretability of CIL and will also investigate whether in international law there are other examples of non-written rules that are nonetheless accepted to be interpretable. Section 3 will dive into domestic and international legislation and case-law that evidence that CIL interpretation is actually occurring. Domestic law and case law will also be examined, as we often tend to forget that the interaction between the international and the domestic legal system is not one-way but rather an

* This contribution is based on research conducted in the context of the project 'The Rules of Interpretation of Customary International Law' (TRICI-Law). This project received funding from the European Research Council (ERC) under the European Union's Horizon 2020 Research and Innovation Programme (Grant Agreement No. 759728).

amphidromous one. In fact, domestic legal systems with a rich and much longer tradition than that of international law, may have significant insights to offer in how customary law (both domestic and international) functions. Section 3 will also highlight some key interpretative approaches that seem to emerge from the examined jurisprudence. This will lead us to Section 4, where the outer limits of such an interpretative exercise will be demarcated. As with any interpretation of any rule, so CIL interpretation should not be construed as a *carte blanche* to the judges, that allows then to substitute the states in the creation of norms. This section will focus on these limits, which if exceeded we transgress to judicial lawmaking. Section 5 will offer some concluding thoughts.

2 International Law's Approach to Interpretation of Non-written Rules

The literature on CIL tends to be dominated by inquiries into the formative stage of CIL and/or whether the existing two-element model is a functional one or falls prey to inherent pitfalls. That is not to say that analysis on CIL interpretation is not present, with scholars arguing both against and in favour of CIL's interpretability.[1] Let us, however, examine what the main arguments against the interpretability of CIL are.

Stemming from the doctrinal focus on the two-element approach, an argument often invoked against the interpretability of CIL is that 'content merges with existence', namely that the identification of CIL through

[1] Against, for instance: T Treves, 'Customary International Law' [2006] MPEPIL 1393 [2]; M Bos, *A Methodology of International Law* (Elsevier 1984) 109; VD Degan, *L'interprétation des accords en droit international* (Nijhoff 1963) 162. In favour, for instance: P Merkouris, *Article 31(3)(c) and the Principle of Systemic Integration: Normative Shadows in Plato's Cave* (Brill/Nijhoff 2015) chapter 5; D Alland, 'L' interprétation du droit international public' (2014) 362 RdC 1, 82–88; A Orakhelashvili, *The Interpretation of Acts and Rules in Public International Law* (Oxford University Press 2008) chapter 15; R Kolb, *Interprétation et création du droit international: esquisses d' une herméneutique juridique moderne pour le droit international public* (Bruylant 2006) 219 et seq; A Bleckmann, 'Zur Feststellung und Auslegung von Völkergewohnheitsrecht' (1977) 37 ZaöRV 504. There are also authors who suggest that one can also interpret state practice (see, for instance, O Chasapis Tassinis, 'Customary International Law: Interpretation from Beginning to End' (2020) 31(1) EJIL 235). These authors also accept the interpretability of CIL rule. On the interpretation of CIL versus the interpretation of state practice see Merkouris (n 1); see also in this volume, Chapter 18 by Fortuna. For an excellent presentation on how different understandings of interpretation have different consequences as to the existence, role and content of alleged rules of interpretation see J Kammerhofer, *International Investment Law and Legal Theory* (Cambridge University Press 2021) ch 4.

a strict application of the two-element approach in and of itself satisfies the content-determinative aspect of interpretation, and thus there is no need for interpretation.[2] This approach, however, seems to accept as a given a degree of specificity and precision that even written texts and long-negotiated treaties are incapable of achieving. The requirements of widespread, representative, constant and uniform state practice accompanied by *opinio juris* would never be precise enough to account for newly emerging situations, that in any other case (and especially in the case of written instruments) would be easily addressed through the process of interpretation. Add to that the fact that CIL is often criticised for being vague,[3] and it becomes evident that even more so in the case of CIL interpretation is a *sine qua non*, as it is the only process that allows for lifting this 'penumbra of doubt'.[4] This seems to be summed up by the International Court of Justice (ICJ) itself in the *Gulf of Maine* when it stated that

> [a] body of detailed rules is not to be looked for in customary international law . . . It is therefore unrewarding . . . to look to general international law to provide a readymade set of rules that can be used for solving any delimitation problems that arise. A more useful course is to *seek a better formulation of the fundamental norm*, on which the Parties were fortunate enough to be agreed.[5]

In the same vein, Sur, more recently, in his General Course in the Hague Academy of International also reaffirmed the content-determinative importance of interpretation for CIL when he noted that '[i]nterpretation of customary rules allows the formulation of a statement that specifies their content and meaning'.[6]

The other main strand of objection to the interpretability of CIL is it being non-written. '[T]he irrelevance of linguistic expression excludes

[2] Bos (n 1) 109. Another argument along somewhat similar lines is that there is no exact law-creating moment for CIL (see in this volume Chapter 2 by d'Aspremont). However, the lack of an 'exact' law-creating moment is not the same as that there is no law-creating moment (or at least period). This is very similar to the *sorites* paradox, but even there the *sorites* exists, although we are unclear at which point the individual grains of sand amounted to a *sorites*. On the *sorites* paradox, see D Hyde & D Raffman, 'Sorites Paradox' (*Stanford Encyclopedia of Philosophy*, 26 March 2018) <https://plato.stanford.edu/entries/sorites-paradox/> accessed 1 May 2021.

[3] ILA, 'Final Report of the Committee: Statement of Principles Applicable to the Formation of General Customary International Law' (2000) 69 ILARC 712, 713.

[4] As Hart would call it.

[5] *Delimitation of the Maritime Boundary in the Gulf of Maine Area (Canada v USA)* (Merits) [184] ICJ Rep 246 [111].

[6] S Sur, 'La créativité du droit international' (2013) 363 RdC 9, 294.

interpretation as a necessary operation in order to apply [customary rules].'[7] But is this truly so? This would seem to be based on an understanding of interpretation as entirely based on text. Yet, a simple browsing of Articles 31–33 Vienna Convention on the Law of Treaties (VCLT) reveals a cornucopia of other non-textual elements that exist on par with the text, even more so if one considers the International Law Commission's (ILC) 'crucible approach' to interpretation that these articles reflect. Second, let us consider the following scenario. There are two identical rules at a particular point in time. One is a CIL rule, and the other one is a rule that exists in a codification treaty. The latter rule would be open to interpretation. So the interpreter would be able to refer to the object and purpose, to intention, to other relevant rules and all the other elements enshrined in Articles 31–33 VCLT. The former rule's content, on the other hand, if one accepts the argument that the non-written nature of CIL bars it from being interpretable, would have to be determined solely on the model of state practice and *opinio juris*.[8] The end result being, the written rule having the ability to be further content-determined through the process of interpretation, whereas the CIL rule would not, and situations that could be addressed through the written rule, through a teleological or evolutive interpretation, would remain outside the scope of the CIL rule, despite the fact that our original starting point was that both these rules were identical. This seems to be an illogical result, that militates in favour of the interpretability CIL.

Logical exercises are not the only reason why the linguistic irrelevancy of CIL is not a bar to its interpretability. Interpretation of non-written elements that, nonetheless, create binding rules of international law are *nihil novum sub sole*. Oral treaties, also known as verbal treaties or verbal/oral agreements[9] are one such example. The binding character of oral agreements has been recognized in international jurisprudence, as for instance in *Mavrommatis Jerusalem Concessions*,[10] and did not cause any

[7] Treves (n 1) [2].

[8] Even recourse to the supplementary means of identification would not be an equivalent, unless one tried for instance to induce the teleology of the CIL rule from those supplementary means, in which case again this argues in favour of accepting interpretation of CIL rather than having to engage in such artificial and abuse-prone exercises.

[9] The use of the term agreement is sometimes preferred to avoid the connection with the term treaty as specified in the VCLT, which has as a required element the written form as per Art 2(1)(a) VCLT.

[10] *The Mavrommatis Jerusalem Concessions (Greece v the United Kingdom)* [1925] PCIJ Ser A No 5, 37.

waves during the preparatory work of the VCLT as can also be seen by the final adopted text.[11]

Article 2(1)(a) VCLT defines treaties as 'an international agreement concluded between States *in written form* and governed by international law, whether embodied in a single instrument or in two or more related instruments and whatever its particular designation'.[12] However, that is not to say that the VCLT rejects the potentiality of existence of other types of treaties that do not meet the strict criteria of Article 2(1)(a). So much so in fact, that Article 3 is explicitly devoted to this as it stipulates that the fact that the VCLT 'does not apply to international agreements concluded between States and other subjects of international law or between such other subjects of international law, or to international agreements not in written form' does not affect either the legal force of such agreements or the application to them of customary rules relating to the law of treaties.[13] The reason why the VCLT focused only on written treaties was merely in the interest of clarity and simplicity.[14]

Although the VCLT seems to have taken a rather expansive interpretation of how strict the 'written form' requirement should be, by including even oral agreements that are evidenced in writing, as in the case of an oral agreement that is documented by a third party, which has so been authorized by the parties to the agreement.[15] However, if no such authorized transcription exists, for example as in the case of (video)-taped

[11] ILC, 'Draft Articles on the Law of Treaties with Commentaries' (4 May–19 July 1966) UN Doc A/CN.4/191, reproduced in [1966/II] YBILC 187, 190, Commentary to Draft Article 3, [3]; ILC, 'First Report on the Law of Treaties by Sir Humphrey Waldock, Special Rapporteur' (26 March 1962) UN Doc A/CN.4/144 and Add.1 reproduced in [1962/II] YBILC 27, 35 [2].

[12] Emphasis added.

[13] ILC, 'Draft Articles 1966' (n 11) 189 [7].

[14] ILC, 'Draft Articles on the Law of Treaties' (24 April–29 June 1962) UN Doc A/5209 reproduced in [1962/II] YBILC 161, 163 [10]; K Schmalenbach, 'Article 2' in O Dörr & K Schmalenbach (eds), *Vienna Convention on the Law of Treaties: A Commentary* (Springer 2018) 29, 36 [19]; M Villiger, *Commentary on the 1969 Vienna Convention on the Law of Treaties* (Brill/Nijhoff 2008) 80 [15]; M Fitzmaurice, 'The Identification and Character of Treaties and Treaty Obligations between States in International Law' (2002) 73 BYBIL 141, 149; Y le Bouthillier & J-F Bonin, 'Article 3: Convention of 1969' in O Corten & P Klein (eds), *The Vienna Convention on the Law of Treaties: A Commentary* (Oxford University Press 2011) 66, 71.

[15] P Gautier, 'Article 2: Convention of 1969' in O Corten & P Klein (eds), *The Vienna Convention on the Law of Treaties: A Commentary* (Oxford University Press 2011) 33, 39 [16].

understandings or oral answers to written proposals, these still remain oral agreements.[16]

Oral agreements were more common in the pre-Westphalian era, but have unsurprisingly been on the decline in the last two centuries, not only, as Schmalenbach rightly points out, due to the existence of an obligation to register treaties[17] but also to ensure greater clarity and certainty as to their international obligations.[18] That is not to say that oral agreements do not emerge in international practice, as evidenced by the famous 1919 Ihlen Declaration between the Ministers of Foreign Affairs of Norway and Denmark,[19] and the telephone agreement of 1992 between the prime ministers of Denmark and Finland regarding the Great Belt Bridge.[20]

The customary rules on the law of treaties apply to such oral agreements as long as they are not tied to the written form requirement and, since text is but one of the many elements to be taken into account during interpretation, this would also include the rules of interpretation.[21]

[16] For the VCLT see ILC, 'Report on the Law of Treaties by Mr GG Fitzmaurice' (14 March 1956) UN Doc A/CN.4/101 reproduced in [1956/II] YBILC 104, 117 note 4 (about non-authorised recordings and recordings made with or without the parties' knowledge); United Nations, 'Vienna Conference on the Law of Treaties: 7th Meeting of the Committee of the Whole' (1 April 1968) UN Doc A/CONF.39/C.1/SR.7 [68–69]; for VCLT-II see ILC, 'Second Report on the Question of Treaties Concluded between States and International Organizations or between Two or More International Organizations by Mr Paul Reuter, Special Rapporteur' (15 May 1972) UN Doc A/CN.4/ 271 reproduced in [1972/II] YBILC 75, 81 [35–37].

[17] 1919 Covenant of the League of Nations (adopted 28 June 1919, entered into force 10 January 1920) 225 CTS 188, Art 18; 1945 Charter of the United Nations (adopted 26 June 1945, entered into force 24 October 1945) 1 UNTS XVI, Art 102.

[18] K Schmalenbach, 'Article 3' in O Dörr & K Schmalenbach (eds), *Vienna Convention on the Law of Treaties: A Commentary* (Springer 2018) 55, 57 [5].

[19] M Fitzmaurice & P Merkouris, *Treaties in Motion: The Evolution of Treaties from Formation to Termination* (Cambridge University Press 2020) 48–51; although it has to be noted that whether this was an oral agreement or a set of unilateral acts creating mutually binding international obligations is a topic up for debate; see ILC, 'Summary Record of the 668th Meeting' (26 June 1962) UN Doc A/CN.4/SR.668 [156]; K Widdows, 'On the Form and Distinctive Nature of International Agreements' (1981) 7(1) Australian YBIL 114, 119.

[20] M Koskenniemi, 'Introductory Note: International Court of Justice: Order Discontinuing the Proceedings in *Case Concerning Passage Through the Great Belt (Finland v Denmark)*' (1993) 32 ILM 101, 103 [9]; further examples are provided in Bouthillier & Bonin (n 14), 70–71 [11] and note 27; X Qin, 'Oral International Agreement and China's Relevant Practice' (2005) 4/2 Chinese Journal of International Law 465, 472–76.

[21] Schmalenbach (n 18) 58 [7]; M Herdegen, 'Interpretation in International Law' [2013] MPEPIL 723 [2].

In the same vein, another set of non-written acts that have raised no concerns as to their interpretability are unilateral acts of states capable of creating international obligations. From 1996 to 2006 the ILC worked on the topic of 'Unilateral Acts of States' and their capacity to create binding international obligations. In its Guiding Principle 5, the ILC specified that the form of the declaration, oral or in writing, was immaterial.[22] Thirty years earlier the ICJ had stated the same thing in *Nuclear Tests*; '[w]hether a statement is made orally or in writing makes no essential difference ... *Thus the question of form is not decisive.*'[23] What makes this relevant for the purposes of our analysis is that the ILC also adopted rules of interpretation applicable to such unilateral declarations, again without making any distinction as to whether the declaration is oral or in writing.[24]

As the previous examples demonstrate, interpretation of non-written rules is neither prohibited nor a first for international law. But even the non-written (linguistic irrelevance) objection is not as clear cut as one would think. Alland referring also to Müller and Kolb underscores this point, when he writes that 'it is difficult to think of a custom independently of any linguistic expression, of any "lexical garment", to use [Müller's] wonderful expression. In fact, even if we do not put the customary rule in a codification convention, it must be formulated and, from this formulation, it may appear that we are interpreting linguistic signs expressing a customary rule.'[25] This is also something that we shall see in the next sections being a common pattern in the interpretation of CIL by international and domestic courts.

3 CIL Interpretation in International and Domestic Legal Systems

As shown in the previous section, interpretation of non-written rules is not something that international law is unfamiliar with. But is CIL

[22] ILC, 'Guiding Principles Applicable to Unilateral Declarations of States Capable of Creating Legal Obligations with Commentaries Thereto' (1 May–9 June and 3 July–11 August 2006) UN Doc A/61/10 reproduced in [2006/II – Part Two] YBILC 160, Guiding Principle 5.

[23] *Nuclear Tests (Australia v France)* (Judgment) [1974] ICJ Rep 253 [45] (emphasis added).

[24] ILC (n 22) 173 et seq; Guiding Principle 7.

[25] Alland (n 1) 83 referring to F Müller, *Discours de la méthode juridique* (O Jouanjan tr, Presses Universitaires de France 1996) 171 and R Kolb, *Interprétation et création du droit international: Esquisse d'une herméneutique juridique moderne pour le droit international public* (Bruylant 2006) 221. However, see also Kammerhofer's analysis that CIL 'is not couched in words – *sine letteris*'; Kammerhofer (n 1) 77.

interpretation something that is actually taking place either in the international or domestic legal systems? In order to answer this, we will now turn our attention to the practice of international and domestic courts to examine whether when applying CIL or domestic customary law they engage in a process of interpretation. This issue is also touched upon in a number of other chapters in this volume.[26] To avoid overlap only a few additional cases will be mentioned here, highlighting some common interpretative patterns; the reader however is strongly encouraged to consult those chapters as well in order to get a complete picture of the pervasiveness of CIL interpretation in both the international and domestic legal arena.

3.1 The Interpretability of CIL as Evidenced in Written Instruments

Where one could first look for acknowledgement of the interpretability of CIL is within instruments regulating the judicial process or identifying the sources of applicable domestic or international law. Article 21 of the Rome Statute,[27] for instance, which sets out the law applicable by the International Criminal Court (ICC) makes no distinction between the various sources of law (treaties, custom and general principles). In fact, Article 21(2) clearly spells out that '[t]he Court may apply *principles and rules of law as interpreted in its previous decisions*', while Article 21(3) builds on this uniform approach when it simply refers to '[t]he *application and interpretation of law pursuant to this article*'[28] without finding any reason to suggest that certain types of rules are not open to interpretation and should be approached differently. The ICC has also followed this line of reasoning when it refers to principles and rules as having been interpreted in the ICC's previous judgments.[29]

A more explicit acknowledgement of the interpretability of CIL can also be found in the Statutes of the ICJ and the Permanent Court of International Justice (PCIJ) and their preparatory work. Article 36 of the ICJ Statute, which was almost *verbatim* reproduced from that of the PCIJ Statute, refers to the jurisdiction of the court in all legal disputes concerning 'a. the interpretation of a treaty' and 'b. any question of international law'. One could reasonably arrive at the conclusion that the explicit

[26] See for example in this volume Chapters 16–23.

[27] 1998 Rome Statute of the International Criminal Court (adopted 17 July 1998, entered into force 1 July 2002) 2187 UNTS 3 (hereinafter ICC Statute).

[28] Emphasis added.

[29] *Prosecutor v Jean-Pierre Bemba Gombo* (Pre-Trial Chamber III, Fourth Decision on Victims' Participation) ICC-01/05-01/08-320 (12 December 2006) [15].

avoidance of reference to the word 'interpretation' in sub-paragraph (b), was an intentional one and that this would indicate that the drafters of the PCIJ Statute, the Advisory Committee of Jurists, took a firm position on the matter through this differentiated wording. However, if one looks closely at the *travaux préparatoires* the true reason for this linguistic choice is revealed. What became Article 36 of the PCIJ Statute was based on a draft by Lord Phillimore.[30] While discussing this, another member of the Advisory Committee, Ricci-Busatti, suggested that the proposed version was problematic and should be amended so as to read 'a. the interpretation or application of a treaty; b. *the interpretation or application of a general rule of international law*'.[31] No member raised any objections as to the validity of Ricci-Busatti's proposal;[32] on the contrary some members, such as de la Pradelle and Hagerup, were vocal as to the linguistic defects of Lord Phillimore's version, and the superiority of Ricci-Busatti's proposal.[33] Despite this, the original version remained in place, and the reason was that the language used was copied directly from Article 13 of the Covenant of the League of Nations and the drafters wanted to ensure linguistic continuity as to the expressions used.[34] This notwithstanding, the fact remains that not only interpretation of CIL was actually proposed to be included in the text of the PCIJ Statute, but also it raised no objections from a theoretical standpoint, that is, that CIL is non-interpretable, and its eventual non-inclusion was based solely on linguistic continuity concerns, but not on substantive objections.

The examples offered so far demonstrate that in the statutes of international courts and tribunals and their preparatory work *indicia* can be found that demonstrate that interpretation is a process recognised by the drafters as an inherent element of the application of both conventional and customary rules. Similar evidence can also be traced within constitutions, legislation and codes of domestic legal systems. One point that has to be made here is that in domestic legal systems there is usually one or two caveats often introduced with respect to customary law, be it domestic or international. As with treaty interpretation, interpretation of customary law has certain limits. Although the limits to CIL interpretation will be analysed infra in Section 4, here it is worth noting that an approach that appears with

30 Advisory Committee of Jurists, *Procès Verbaux of the Meetings of the Advisory Committee of Jurists: 16 June–24 July 1920 with Annexes* (van Langenhuysen 1920) 252.

31 ibid 265 & 275 (emphasis added).

32 ibid 283.

33 ibid 284.

34 ibid 264–65 & 283–84.

relative frequency in domestic legal systems is that an interpretation or existence of a customary rule cannot conflict with a written rule of domestic law, and in case of such conflict the written rule prevails.[35] Of import here is that before acknowledging the existence of a conflict between rules, domestic courts always attempt to harmonize the content of the rules through interpretation,[36] a process not unique to domestic courts but equally applied by international courts and recognised by the ILC as well.[37]

Apart from this 'harmonisation through interpretation' that we will see more of in Section 3.2, a more explicit acknowledgement of CIL interpretation can also be seen, for instance, in the case of Article 559(1) of the Greek Code of Civil Procedure. According to that Article '[a]n appeal is allowed only 1) if a rule of substantive law has been violated, which includes the rules of interpretation of legal acts, *regardless of whether this entails a law or custom*, Greek or foreign, of domestic or international law'.[38] This provision and ground of appeal has in fact been interpreted by the Supreme Civil and Criminal Court of Greece in the following manner: 'The legal rule is violated, if it is not applied, . . . as well as if it is applied incorrectly . . . *and the violation is manifested either by false interpretation [misinterpretation]* or by incorrect application.'[39] It is of note that misinterpretation is one of the manifestations of violation of the rule, and neither the Greek Code of Civil Procedure nor the relevant jurisprudence differentiate in their approach on whether the rule is one of written law or a customary rule.[40]

3.2 Patterns of CIL Interpretability in International and Domestic Case Law

Evidence from statutes and domestic pieces of legislation are useful, but not entirely decisive of the ubiquity of CIL interpretation. For this we

[35] See for example Art 2(4) of the Constitution of Kenya.

[36] See below Sections 3.2 and 4.

[37] 'harmonisation through interpretation'; see ILC, 'Report on Fragmentation of International Law: Difficulties Arising from the Diversification and Expansion of International Law, Finalized by Martti Koskenniemi' (1 May–9 June and 3 July–11 August 2006) UN Doc A/CN.4/L.682 [37–43, 88, 229–31, 277 & 411].

[38] Greek Code of Civil Procedure, ΦΕΚ Α 182 19851024, Art 559(1) (author's translation and emphasis added).

[39] *Judgment 7/2006* (23 February 2006) Areios Pagos, Greece, Ολ.ΑΠ 7/2006, referring also to *Judgment 4/2005* (21 April 2005) Areios Pagos, Greece, Ολ.ΑΠ 4/2005.

[40] M Margaritis, 'Article 559' in K Kerameas, D Kondilis & N Nikas, *Interpretation of the Code of Civil Procedure, Vol I, Articles 1–590* (Sakkoulas 2000) 1000; C Apalagaki, *Code of Civil Procedure: Article by Article Interpretation, Articles 1–590* (4th ed, Nomiki Vivliothiki 2016) 1405–09.

shall now turn our attention to case law. The former Chess World Champion Mikhail Botvinik is often credited with the chess aphorism, 'every Russian school boy knows', which is used within chess circles to denote some basic knowledge that everyone has. *Mutatis mutandis* 'every international law student knows' that when talking about CIL two sets of cases are the ones most often used, *Nicaragua* and *North Sea Continental Shelf*, with the latter being the landmark case for the two-element approach of state practice and *opinio juris*. Ironically enough, even in these bastions of the classical two-element approach, one can find references to CIL interpretation. The *Nicaragua* case seems to be open to the interpretability of CIL, when the court opines that '[r]ules which are identical in treaty law and in customary international law are also distinguishable by reference to the methods of interpretation and application'.[41] However, in the *North Sea Continental Shelf* cases this is much more explicit, when Judge Tanaka has the following to say regarding CIL interpretation: 'Customary law, being vague and containing gaps compared with written law, requires precision and completion about its content. This task, in its nature being interpretative, would be incumbent upon the Court. *The method of logical and teleological interpretation can be applied in the case of customary law as in the case of written law*'.[42] Although it is unclear the exact line, if any, drawn by Tanaka between logical and teleological interpretation,[43] the use of 'logical interpretation' is not so foreign. This word may not have found its way in the text of Articles 31–33 VCLT, but it was used in early jurisprudence and in the early codification attempts of the law of treaties and the rules of treaty interpretation. For instance, Fiore's Draft Code suggested that treaty interpretation could be either grammatical or logical, a slightly different structure than that of Tanaka. In the rules of logical interpretation, one could find recourse to, for instance, intention of the parties, context, *contra proferentem*, equity, *ut res magis valeat quam pereat*, systemic/harmonious interpretation and teleology.[44]

41 *Military and Paramilitary Activities in and against Nicaragua (Nicaragua v USA)* (Merits) [1986] ICJ Rep 14 [178].

42 *North Sea Continental Shelf (Germany/Denmark and the Netherlands)* (Judgment) [1969] ICJ Rep [44], Dissenting Opinion of Judge Tanaka, 181 (emphasis added). In the same vein, see also ibid, Dissenting Opinion of Judge Morelli, 200.

43 Or whether they were being used in an interchangeable manner.

44 JW Garner, 'Codification of International Law: Part III – Law of Treaties – Appendix 4: Fiore's Draft Code' (1935) 29 AJIL Supp 1212, 1218–19.

So let us examine if any of these interpretative tools emerge in cases where courts have been called to apply CIL. In Section 2, we discussed Alland's view that CIL is always shrouded in a 'lexical garment'. The practice of courts and tribunals, both international and domestic, seems to utilize this to compensate for the non-existence of a written rule in the case of CIL. Since textual interpretation *stricto sensu* is not possible, what they do is refer to documents which are allegedly reflective of CIL.[45] If one were to try and find an analogy with the rules of treaty interpretation, this would be akin to an application of the principle of systemic integration or *in pari materia* interpretation if the documents referred to were treaties.[46] This attempt at a 'by proxy'/hybrid textual interpretation of CIL is sometimes taken even further, when courts use not only the language of the relevant provision that reflects CIL, but also other provisions of the referred instrument, as a type of context (again by proxy) to determine the meaning of the CIL rule.[47]

However, that is not to say that reference to other treaties, CIL rules or general principles only happens in this context, that is, in a 'by proxy' textual interpretation. There are also several instances where courts and tribunals have interpreted CIL by reference to its normative environment in the traditional 'systemic integration' fashion.[48] The Supreme Court of Italy in *Ferrini* v. *Germany* summarized this very concisely: 'However, it is unquestionably true that *similar criteria [i.e. reference to relevant rules] apply to the interpretation of customary norms*, which like the others *are*

[45] WTO, *EC – Measures Affecting the Approval and Marketing of Biotech Products (EC – Biotech)*, Panel Report (21 November 2006) WT/DS291/R, WT/DS292/R, WT/DS293/R [7.68–7.72] (referring to the VCLT); *Gulf of Maine* (n 5) Dissenting Opinion of Judge Gros [8] (referring to the draft convention produced by the Third United Nations Conference); *The Queen v Alqudsi* (Motion to Quash Indictment and Summons for Declaratory Relief of 27 August 2015) Supreme Court of New South Wales, Australia [2015] NSWSC 1222 [141–42] (referring to the 1970 UNGA Resolution on Friendly Relations Declaration); *Institute of Cetacean Research v Sea Shepherd Conservation Society*, 725 F.3d 940 (9th Cir 2013) [5–6] (referring to the UNCLOS and the High Seas Convention definitions on piracy).

[46] For non-binding instruments (such as declarations or draft treaties) and if one wanted to continue the comparison with the rules of treaty interpretation, these would most likely be qualifiable as supplementary means, unless one argues that under CIL interpretation, the principle of systemic integration has a much wider scope, in which case it would include non-binding instruments as well.

[47] *EC – Biotech* (n 45); for further analysis on this issue see also in this volume Chapter 22 by Ryngaert.

[48] *Continental Shelf (Tunisia/Libya)* (Judgment) [1982] ICJ Rep 18 [38 &70]; *Mondev International Ltd v USA* (Award of 11 October 2002) ICSID Case No ARB(AF)/99/2 [127].

part of a system and therefore may only be correctly understood in relation to other norms that form an integral part of the same legal system.'[49] This interpretative method is often used to ensure that the normative environment is taken into account in order to avoid conflict and ensure 'harmonization through interpretation', as can be easily seen in a string of domestic cases, where state immunity was counter-balanced, for example, with the protection of fundamental human rights/values, and the prohibition of torture.[50]

Another dominant pattern emerging from domestic and international case law is reference to either the *telos* of the rule or its rationale.[51] In *Her Majesty the Queen in Right of Canada* v. *Edelson and others*, for instance, the Supreme Court of Israel was called to identify the content of the CIL rule on state immunity and the criteria to be used in distinguishing between *acta jure imperii* and *acta jure gestionis*. In the *'Comfort Women'* case, the South Koran District Court also had to tackle issues of state immunity but in the context of whether such immunity could be invoked for crimes against humanity committed during World War II. In both cases, the domestic courts relied on the reasons underlying the existence and functioning of the CIL on state immunity in order to come to conclusions as to the content of the rule.[52]

An interesting tendency in CIL interpretation is also that the *telos* referred to is not necessarily that of the CIL rule alone. Sometimes, courts and tribunals based their teleological interpretation of the CIL rule on the *telos* of an entire area of international law.[53] In such instances, such a *lato sensu* teleological interpretation becomes very similar to systemic interpretation.

[49] *Ferrini v Germany* (Appeal Decision of 11 March 2004) Supreme Court of Cassation of Italy, Case No 5044/04 [9.2].

[50] *Her Majesty the Queen in Right of Canada v Edelson and others* (3 June 1997) Supreme Court of Israel PLA 7092/94, 51(1) PD 625 [22]; *Attorney-General v Zaoui and Inspector-General of Intelligence and Security and Human Rights Commission (intervening)* (21 June 2005) Supreme Court of New Zealand [2005] NZSC 38 [32–33]; *A v Swiss Federal Public Prosecutor* (25 July 2012) Swiss Federal Criminal Court, BB.2011.140 [5.4.3].

[51] Depending on the context, these can either both be seen under the umbrella of teleological interpretation, or the former falling under teleological interpretation, while the latter under logical interpretation. For reasons of convenience, for the purposes of the present analysis these will be examined as if forming one and the same pattern.

[52] *Her Majesty the Queen in Right of Canada v Edelson and others* (n 50) [22]; *Case No 2016 Ga-Hap 505092* (8 January 2021) Central District Court of Seoul [3.C.3.7] <https://bit.ly/3f5B7Qz> accessed 1 May 2021 (unofficial translation by Woohee Kim, The Korean Council for Justice and Remembrance for the Issues of Military Sexual Slavery by Japan).

[53] *Prosecutor v Duško Tadić* (Appeal Judgment) IT-94–1-A (15 July 1999) [124]; *Fisheries (UK v Norway)* (Judgment) [1951] ICJ Rep 116, 133.

However, as in treaty interpretation, where various interpretative maxims and approaches not explicitly mentioned in the VCLT are often utilised, these also make their appearance in cases of CIL interpretation. *Ut res magis valeat quam pereat* and *ad absurdum* arguments make regular appearances in the reasoning of courts when they interpret CIL. In *Her Majesty the Queen in Right of Canada* v. *Edelson and others*, the court emphasized that the reason why the purpose criterion was not the appropriate one for distinguishing between *acta jure imperii* and *acta jure gestionis* was that it would end up negating the distinction between private and state acts.[54] In *A* v. *Swiss Federal Public Prosecutor*, the court held that '*it would be both contradictory and futile* if, on the one hand, we affirmed that we wanted to fight against these serious violations of the fundamental values of humanity, and, on the other hand, we allowed a broad interpretation of the rules of functional immunity'.[55] While in the *Sea Shepherd* case the district court did not mince its words on what it thought of a broad interpretation of 'piracy'; '[a]mong *other nonsensical results*, Defendants' interpretation would allow any seaman with a special affinity for a sea creature – say, a tuna – to state a piracy claim against a fisherman'.[56] Other cases have also referred to CIL as being open to evolutive interpretation,[57] or even more dubiously to *in dubio mitius* constructions[58] and presumptions that promote interpretations in favour of internal jurisdiction.[59]

As can be seen from the previous analysis, the examples offered were not meant to be an exhaustive list but rather a demonstration of the occurrence of CIL interpretation across the board and the multifariousness of interpretative tools used, which are, however, familiar from treaty interpretation. It is also of note that several of the cited cases do not use

[54] *Her Majesty the Queen in Right of Canada v Edelson and others* (n 50) [26 & 28].

[55] *A v Swiss Federal Public Prosecutor* (n 50) [5.4.3] (emphasis added).

[56] *Institute of Cetacean Research v Sea Shepherd Conservation Society*, 153 F.Supp.3d 1291 (WD Wash 2015) 1319.

[57] 'Rules developed against the background of a reality which has changed must take on dynamic interpretation which adapts them, in the framework of accepted interpretational rules, to the new reality . . . In the spirit of such interpretation, we shall now proceed to the customary international law dealing with the status of civilians who constitute unlawful combatants'; *Public Committee against Torture in Israel and Palestinian Society for the Protection of Human Rights and the Environment v Israel and ors* (13 December 2006) Supreme Court of Israel, HCJ 769/02 [28]; see in more detail in this volume Chapter 21 by Mileva.

[58] *Institute of Cetacean Research v Sea Shepherd Conservation Society* (n 56) 1319.

[59] *Her Majesty the Queen in Right of Canada v Edelson and others* (n 50) [26 & 28].

just one interpretative method but a number of them, which again also coincides with the ILC's view of interpretation as a holistic exercise.

4 Limits of CIL Interpretation

The fact that CIL is open to interpretation does not mean that judges have a *carte blanche* when engaging in such interpretative exercises. As with interpretation of treaties and of other instruments, so CIL interpretation cannot go beyond certain limits. Certain of these limits are common to all rules irrespective of the source from which they have emerged. It is to these limits that we shall turn our attention.

The first and foremost such limit is a system-oriented one, that is, one that is imposed by the system and its, admittedly limited, hierarchical structure. Any interpretation of a rule cannot be such that it would go against a rule of *jus cogens*.[60] This limit is a very logical one, and stems also from the very definition of *jus cogens* rules, being rules from which no derogation is possible. It is such a fundamental limit that it even found its way into the Institut de Droit International's resolution on 'Intertemporal Law', where it was stated that: 'States and other subjects of international law shall, however, have the power to determine by common consent the temporal sphere of application of norms, . . . subject to any imperative norm of international law which might restrict that power.'[61] Of course, both the cases mentioned in the first footnote to this section and the Institut's resolution were focused on treaties, however the rationale behind the acceptance of *jus cogens* as an interpretative limit is equally applicable to CIL rules and obligations emerging from unilateral acts of states.

This can be seen in the recent works of the ILC, both on 'Identification of CIL' and on '*Jus Cogens*'. With respect to the former, both the commentary to Draft Conclusion 1 and the text of Draft Conclusion 15 made a point of underscoring that these draft conclusions were 'without prejudice to questions of hierarchy among rules of international law,

60 *Application of the Convention on the Prevention and Punishment of the Crime of Genocide (Bosnia and Herzegovina v Serbia and Montenegro)* (Judgment) [2007] ICJ Rep 43, Joint Declaration of Shi and Koroma [2]; *South-West Africa (Second Phase) (Liberia and Ethiopia v South Africa)* (Judgment) [1966] ICJ Rep 6, Dissenting Opinion of Judge Tanaka, 293–95; *Gabčíkovo-Nagymaros Project (Hungary/Slovakia)* (Judgment) [1997] ICJ Rep 7, Separate Opinion of Judge Bedjaoui [6].

61 Institut de Droit International, 'Resolution of 11 August 1975: The Intertemporal Problem in Public International Law' (1975) 56 AIDI 536 [3].

including those concerning peremptory norms of general international law (*jus cogens*)'.[62] This has more recently become even clearer through the conclusions proposed by the Drafting Committee on '*Jus Cogens*'. Draft Conclusion 14 clarifies that with respect to CIL no such rule may come into existence if it conflicts with a peremptory norm of general international law, and 'ceases to exist if and to the extent that it conflicts with a new peremptory norm of general international law'.[63] So Draft Conclusion 14 covers both ends of the spectrum, emergence and termination of CIL rules, but what of its interpretation? Draft Conclusion 20, which deals with the interpretation and application of rules in a manner consistent with peremptory norms of general international law, provides the answer to that: 'Where it appears that there may be a conflict between a peremptory norm of general international law (*jus cogens*) and another rule of international law, the latter is, as far as possible, to be interpreted and applied so as to be consistent with the former.'[64] Of particular note here is that Draft Conclusion 20 makes absolutely no distinction between rules on the basis of their source, but considers that an interpretation that ensures harmony with existing *jus cogens* rules is an interpretative limit for rules irrespective of the type of source from which they emerged.

The second limit is one that derives from the classical distinction between interpretation and revision/modification. In treaty interpretation, for instance, whereas interpretation aims to give flesh to the intention of the parties,[65] revision of a treaty falls outside its outer limits as it changes the content and identity of a rule in ways that could not be arrived at through a normal interpretative exercise. Because revision amounts to creating a new rule, as it exceeds the rule's 'natural limits',[66] interpretation may never amount to a revision of the rule.[67] Treaty revision falls squarely within the exclusive competence of the

[62] ILC, 'Draft Conclusions on Identification of Customary International Law, with Commentaries' (30 April–1 June and 2 July–10 August 2018) UN Doc A/73/10, reproduced in [2018/II – Part Two] YBILC 122, Commentary to Draft Conclusion 1 [5]; Draft Conclusion 15(3); Commentary to Draft Conclusion 15 [10].

[63] ILC, 'Peremptory Norms of General International Law (*jus cogens*): Draft Conclusions' (29 May 2019) UN Doc A/CN.4/L.936, Draft Conclusion 14 (1)–(2).

[64] ibid, Draft Conclusion 20 [10(3), 17(2)].

[65] *Kasikili/Sedudu Island (Botswana/Namibia)* (Judgment) [1999] ICJ Rep 1045, Declaration of Judge Higgins [4].

[66] *Edwards v Attorney-General for Canada* (18 October 1929) Judicial Committee of the Imperial Privy Council [1930] AC 124, 136 per Lord Sankey.

[67] *Gabčíkovo-Nagymaros Project* (n 60) Separate Opinion of Judge Bedjaoui [5]; *Kasikili/Sedudu Island* (n 65) Declaration of Judge Higgins [2]; *Case Concerning a Boundary Dispute between Argentina and Chile Concerning the Frontier Line between Boundary Post*

parties to the treaty (or any body so authorized by the parties), not of the judges. Consequently, an interpretation that would lead to a revision of the rule, would be equivalent to the judges exercising a *pouvoir de légiférer*, a power that they have not been imbued with.[68] As Dupuy very eloquently put it, '[m]emory must remain loyal and not serve to rewrite history; a treaty belongs to its authors and not to the judge'.[69] The ILC also confirmed this recently through Draft Conclusion 7(3) on 'Subsequent Agreements and Subsequent Practice in Relation to Interpretation of Treaties'.[70] According to the ILC, if the limits of interpretation are crossed, then we may be in the realm of treaty modification, although the ILC admitted that the lines may be difficult to draw and was agnostic as to whether modification of a treaty by subsequent practice of the parties was customary law.[71]

This differentiation between the existing rule and its modification/revision seems also to lie at the heart of the *Hadžihasanović* case. The tribunal, on the one hand, felt that there was no sufficient evidence of state practice and *opinio juris* to demonstrate that the existing content of the CIL rule on command responsibility, covered also situations where a change in the command structure had occurred, and therefore that any such reading/interpretation of the rule would amount to an unacceptable and impermissible revision/modification. A number of judges, on the other hand, were of the view that a teleological interpretation of the rule inexorably led to an inclusion of that situation within the regulatory framework of the rule.[72]

The same line in the sand distinction between interpretation and revision/modification seems to be the driving force behind judge ad hoc Kreća's analysis in the *Croatia-Serbia Genocide* case as well. His main objection to certain of the pronouncements of the ICTY and its 'interpretation' of CIL was that the methods used were incoherent and

62 and Mount Fitzroy (Laguna del Desierto) (Argentina v Chile) (1994) 22 UNRIAA 3 [157].

68 *Bayatyan v Armenia* [GC] ECtHR App No 23459/03 (7 July 2011) Dissenting Opinion of Judge Gyulumyan [2]; *Meftah and Others v France* [GC] ECtHR App No 32911/96 (26 July 2002) Concurring Opinion of Judge Lorenzen joined by Judge Hedigan.

69 PM Dupuy, 'Evolutionary Interpretation of Treaties: Between Memory and Prophecy' in E Cannizzaro (ed), *The Law of Treaties beyond the Vienna Convention* (Oxford University Press 2011) 123, 129.

70 ILC, 'Draft Conclusions on Subsequent Agreements and Subsequent Practice in Relation to the Interpretation of Treaties, with Commentaries' [2018/II – Part Two] YBILC 16, 58.

71 ibid 58–59.

72 For a detailed analysis of *Hadžihasanović* see in this volume, Chapter 18 by Fortuna.

subjective, and that the establishment of the content of a CIL rule resembled 'a quasi-customary law exercise based on deductive reasoning driven by meta-legal and extra-legal principles . . . [that] has resulted in judicial law-making through purposive, adventurous interpretation'.[73] Leaving aside that judge ad hoc Kreća also recognises the interpretability of CIL, his objection stems not from the interpretative exercise per se and the use of teleological interpretation, but rather from the fact that such an interpretation is not interpretation in the proper sense, but rather a revision of the rule, which amounts to an exercise by the judges of a *pouvoir de légiférer* (judicial lawmaking). In essence, this objection is an affirmation of the second limit of CIL interpretation, and interpretation in general.

Another limit that needs to be examined in this context is that any interpretation 'can only apply in the observation of the general rule of interpretation laid down in Article 31 of the Vienna Convention on the Law of Treaties'.[74] This was identified by Judge Bedjaoui in the *Gabčíkovo-Nagymaros Project* case in the context of an evolutive interpretation of a written instrument, but it applies equally in the case of CIL. The following cases may help illustrate this point.

On 8 January 2021 the Central District Court of Seoul issued its judgment, now final, regarding compensation of South Korean women, who had been forced into sexual slavery and euphemistically known as 'comfort women', during World War II. A key issue was whether state immunity could be upheld even in cases where grave crimes against humanity had been perpetrated.[75] Although, as analysed above in Section 3, the Central District Court also engaged in a logical and teleological interpretation of CIL, it based part of its reasoning on a somewhat 'systemic-type' of interpretation but of an inward focus, that is, it focused on the potential of harmonization or conflict of an expansive interpretation of state immunity with its domestic constitution. According to it,

> if customary law is applied to exempt the Defendant from jurisdiction even in cases where the Defendant has committed grave crimes against

[73] *Application of the Convention on the Prevention and Punishment of the Crime of Genocide (Croatia v Serbia)* (Merits) [2015] ICJ Rep 3, Separate Opinion of Judge *ad hoc* Kreća [91–92].

[74] *Gabčíkovo-Nagymaros Project* (n 60) Separate Opinion of Judge Bedjaoui, [5].

[75] In detail see E Branca, '"Yet, it moves . . . ": The Dynamic Evolution of State immunity in the "Comfort Women" case' (*EJILTalk!*, 7 April 2021) <https://bit.ly/3GLpkm7> accessed 1 May 2021.

> humanity, *it would be impossible to sanction a State* for violating international conventions that prevent it from committing grave crimes against humanity against citizens of another state, thereby depriving victims of their right of access to courts guaranteed by the Constitution and not providing a remedy for their rights. *Such results are unreasonable and unjust as they are not in accordance with the overall legal order that positions the Constitution as the highest norm.*[76]

Although the first part of this argument shows similarities with an *ut res magis valeat* approach to interpretation, the final part links it to its domestic legal order. Essentially, what the District Court of Seoul focused on was that: (a) an expansive interpretation of state immunity would lead to a non-prosecution of crimes against humanity and (b) such a result would be unreasonable as it would conflict with the right of access to courts guaranteed by the constitution. Consequently, the District Court of Seoul was of the view that a more restrictive interpretation of state immunity was the one that ensured both effectiveness and the harmony among the rules of its domestic legal order. What this boils down to is that the District Court of Seoul, following a mélange of *ut res magis valeat quam pereat* and 'harmonious/systemic interpretation' approaches, interpreted the CIL rule on state immunity in a way that did not allow for its invocation in situations of crimes against humanity. However, the crucial point is that the counterpart to the rule on state immunity against which *ut res magis valeat* and harmonious/systemic interpretation were evaluated were not other rules of international law but rather its own domestic law and in particular its own constitution.

The Supreme Court of Israel in *Her Majesty the Queen in Right of Canada* v. *Edelson and others* when discussing the criteria to be applied in distinguishing between *acta jure imperii* and *acta jure gestionis* also referred to its domestic legal order but with a slight twist compared to the previous case. The Supreme Court, although in earlier paragraphs engaged in a teleological interpretation of the CIL rule, it then felt the need to buttress its findings by reference to its domestic legal order, not as a way to avoid normative conflict, but rather as a way to fill a potential *lacuna*.

> [P]ending the development of a standard international practice regarding this issue, it is inevitable that *each State will apply its own locally accepted criteria in accordance with its existing national jurisprudence* ... It is incumbent upon us to formulate a distinction that accounts for basic

[76] *Case No 2016 Ga-Hap 505092* (n 52) [3.C.3.6] (emphasis added).

> values such as individual rights, equality before the law and the rule of law. This having been said, we will allow the foreign State to realize its sovereign objectives, without subjecting them to judicial review in a foreign state's courts. The balance struck between these conflicting considerations is far from simple and is certainly not immutable. *It would seem that, for the time being, it is sufficient to determine that, when in doubt, we must rule in favor of recognizing internal jurisdiction.* In any case, the tendency should be towards restricting immunity. This is our practice regarding any domestic matter.[77]

A final case that needs to be mentioned in this context is *Sentenza No 238/2014*, where the Italian Constitutional Court had to grapple with the aftermath of the *Jurisdictional Immunities* case.[78] This case is very interesting as the Italian Constitutional Court did not object to the 'interpretation'[79] on jurisdictional immunities adopted by the ICJ as '[i] nternational custom is external to the Italian legal order, and its application by the government and/or the judge, as a result of the referral of Article 10, para 1 of the Constitution, must respect the principle of conformity, ie must follow the interpretation given in its original legal order, that is the international legal order'.[80] What it tried to do was determine whether the interpretation of the CIL rule given by the ICJ could be harmonized with the Italian constitutional order and its fundamental principles.[81] The Constitutional Court came to the conclusion that this was not possible and that therefore the CIL rule as interpreted by the ICJ had not entered the Italian legal order, through Article 10 para 1 of the Italian Constitution, and, thus, did not have any effect therein.[82] The Constitutional Court, then turned its attention to Article 1 of the Law of Adaptation No 848/1957, and declared it unconstitutional, insofar as it concerned the execution of Article 94 of the UN Charter, and that as well exclusively to the extent that it obliged Italian courts to comply with the ICJ judgment in *Jurisdictional Immunities*.[83] The manner in which the Italian Constitutional Court approached the issue of CIL rule on jurisdictional immunities bears

77 *Her Majesty the Queen in Right of Canada v Edelson and others* (n 50) [29–30] (emphasis added).
78 *Jurisdictional Immunities of the State (Germany v Italy: Greece intervening)* [2012] ICJ Rep 99.
79 This is the precise word used by the Italian Constitutional Court throughout its judgment.
80 *Sentenza No 238/2014* (22 October 2014) Italian Constitutional Court [3.1] (unofficial English translation available at <https://bit.ly/322jjT1> accessed 1 May 2021).
81 ibid [3.1 & 3.4].
82 ibid [3.5].
83 ibid [4.1].

similarities both with the *Solange*[84] and *Kadi*[85] cases. With *Solange* in the sense that it determines the applicability of the CIL rule in Italian domestic legal order by applying the 'limit' of the concordance with fundamental principles of the state's own constitutional order,[86] and with *Kadi* in the sense that the Italian Constitutional Court avoided engaging directly with an interpretation of the CIL rule on jurisdictional immunities different from that given by the ICJ, but rather decided to focus on the unconstitutionality of two domestic laws, through which the ICJ judgment and its interpretation would have become effective in the Italian domestic legal order.

The aforementioned three cases are not entirely identical, as they cover a wide spectrum of situations where CIL rules and their interpretation were considered, ranging from an attempt to harmonize the rule with the constitutional order (*Case No 2016 Ga-Hap 505092*), to filling *lacunae* of the CIL rule by reference to the domestic legal order (*Her Majesty the Queen in Right of Canada* v. *Edelson and others*) and including the CIL rule not entering the legal order as it cannot be harmonized with the limit of fundamental constitutional principles (*Sentenza No 238/2014*). These differences aside, a common thread remains an attempt at content-determination[87] of the CIL rule by reference to the state's own domestic legal system. This from an internal, domestic-oriented point of view may not be as problematic,[88] although this is not to say that such an approach is entirely problem-free. This can be seen from the fact that a CIL rule should be interpreted using the rules/methods endemic to that international legal order. While this point was rightly so in *Sentenza No 238/2014* it was not resorted to in the other two cases we discussed. This point also highlights why, from an international perspective, an interpretative approach to CIL focusing only on the domestic legal system of one state

[84] *Solange I* (29 May 1974) BVerfG, 37 BverfGE 291.

[85] *Joined cases C-402/05 P and C-415/05 P, Yassin Abdullah Kadi and Al Barakaat International Foundation v Council of the European Union and Commission of the European Communities* (3 September 2008) CJEU [GC] [2008] ECR I-06351.

[86] For other domestic cases, where similar approaches have been adopted albeit with respect to EU law, see A Peters, 'Let Not Triepel Triumph: How To Make the Best Out of Sentenza No 238 of the Italian Constitutional Court for a Global Legal Order' (*EJILTalk!*, 22 December 2014) <https://bit.ly/3s9sR9F> accessed 1 May 2021.

[87] Somewhat less so in the case of the Italian Constitutional Court, which was very careful in its *Kadi*-inspired approach.

[88] Since most domestic legal systems when referring to customary law (be it domestic or international) will tend to have provisions regulating that such rules should not conflict with written instruments or, of course, their respective constitutions.

raises serious concerns. In all the cases mentioned above, the point being made was an effort to achieve a harmonious interpretation, that by taking into account other relevant rules would ensure that a normative conflict would be avoided. What this amounts to is an attempt at applying the principle of systemic integration in the context of CIL interpretation. However, the system of a CIL rule would refer to international rules (treaties, custom, general principles), but not to domestic rules of a single state. The only potential scenario where domestic rules may come into play is if an argument could be made that these reflected a 'general principle' shared by domestic legal systems. Leaving aside the issues of which domestic legal systems need to be considered,[89] by any stretch of imagination considering just one legal system would not be enough. Ryngaert calls this approach a 'reverse' consistent interpretation, and rightly points out the fact that it is a misapplication or disregard of the interpretative methods of international law.[90] Such an approach, thus, at least from the international perspective, seems to go against the limit of following the rules of interpretation.

As a final thought, it has to be noted that several of the cases cited in this section were also mentioned in Section 3. This is not surprising. In fact, it is demonstrative of why this discussion on CIL interpretation is not only inevitable but quintessential. The same way that the discussion on the rules of treaty interpretation helped and continues to help streamline and clarify the interpretative exercise and led to a common language being used, so can this occur with respect to CIL interpretation.

5 Conclusion

Customary international law is one of the formal sources of international law and plays a pivotal role in the existence and functioning of the international legal system. Although for a rule of CIL to emerge a widespread, representative, constant and virtually uniform state practice is required, accompanied by the requisite *opinio juris*, that does not

[89] ILC, 'Second Report on General Principle of Law, by Marcelo Vázquez-Bermúdez, Special Rapporteur' (9 April 2020) UN Doc A/CN.4/741; A Pellet & D Müller, 'Article 38' in A Zimmermann et al (eds), *The Statute of the International Court of Justice* (3rd ed, Oxford University Press 2019) 819 [251–70 & 296–304].

[90] See in this volume, Chapter 22 by Ryngaert; see also O Ammann, *Domestic Courts and the Interpretation of International Law: Methods and Reasoning Based on the Swiss Example* (Brill 2020) 322; on misinterpretation see in this volume Chapter 3 by Arajärvi.

necessarily mean that CIL is a slow and archaic process, that has been overcome by extensive treaty-making. On the contrary, CIL remains a vital element in the corpus of international law, that is open to refinement, clarification, development and evolution. This process does not happen only through the classical emergence and/or subsequent modification of the rule, but also and perhaps most importantly through the process of interpretation.

In the previous sections what was shown was that not only is CIL interpretable (as are other non-written rules), but also that such an interpretation has and continues to occur with frequency in courts across different international legal regimes and different legal systems. Of course, the variety of interpretative approaches and the differences in the language/terminology used is not something unexpected. After all, if one examines the jurisprudence pre-VCLT, they would reach the same conclusion. But that is why further explorations and increased awareness of CIL interpretation is the key to further clarifying and refining the CIL interpretative process and prompt judicial bodies to be aware of and provide more clearly reasoned explications of the manner in which they interpret CIL.

As Sur very beautifully put it, CIL interpretation and its exploration is vital because whereas treaty interpretation is entropic, '[t]he interpretation of custom is creative or negentropic [i.e., reduces entropy], because it constantly nourishes and updates it [i.e., CIL], softening the distinction between formation and application'.[91] Interpretation has, continues and will always be an integral part of the life cycle of CIL,[92] or in simple terms, CIL will never walk alone.

[91] Sur (n 6) 295.

[92] As of every legal rule for that matter.

17

Practical Reasoning and Interpretation of Customary International Law

KOSTIANTYN GOROBETS

1 Introduction

Interpretability of customary (international) law belongs to the class of jurisprudential problems that entangle and intertwine almost all thorny theoretical and practical issues. It is especially visible against the background of debates around whether customary international law (CIL) can be interpreted, and if so, how this differs from its identification; are there or should there be some rules for CIL interpretation, and what would be the difference between such rules and those guiding interpretation of treaties?

This chapter aims at addressing some of these issues. It seeks to suggest a meaningful way of seeing the process of CIL interpretation through the perspective of practical reasoning. By doing so, it purports to disentangle one of the theoretical knots of CIL interpretation: what is the difference between the identification and interpretation of rules of CIL, considering that both processes concentrate mostly on state practices?[1] For the purposes of this chapter, by 'state practices' I mean a slightly different concept than the one being typically used in international legal scholarship. I defend the view that any practice is normative by definition, otherwise it is not a practice at all. This goes against the commonly accepted view that 'mere' state practices are but collections of actions and fail to constitute a (legal) norm. I use the concept in the plural

[1] This chapter does not address the issue of *opinio juris* and touches upon the legality of customary rules only briefly. It is worth mentioning, nevertheless, that by stating that state practice is of primary interest for interpretation of CIL (and for its identification, too), I endorse the view that the normativity of rules of CIL should be separated from their legality, or legal bindingness. See for example M Mendelson, 'The Formation of Customary International Law' (1998) 272 RdC; M Meguro, 'Distinguishing the Legal Bindingness and Normative Content of Customary International Law' (2017) 6 ESIL Reflections 1.

because the growth of normativity within practical engagements of states is typically dispersed in terms of the subject-matter. Different practical engagements converge into different normative practices, rather than constitute one continuous state practice.

Section 2 addresses the issue of duality of CIL within the doctrine of the container/content distinction, which is of fundamental importance to the theory of sources of international law. Section 3 suggests a view on (state) practices as being inherently normative, which implies the differentiation between tests for normativity and legality when patterns of behaviour are concerned. Section 4 provides a more detailed analysis of customary normativity. The concluding Section 5 highlights the difference in interpretation of state practices depending on their container/content perception and will therefore attempt a differentiation between the interpretation for the purpose of identification and interpretation for the purpose of clarification/application of a rule of CIL.

2 What Is This Thing We Interpret When We Say That We Interpret CIL?

It is at the core of most contemporary doctrines of legal interpretation that interpretation of something is interpretation of *something*. In order to interpret a thing, this thing must already be there, and so its existence, meaning, and function are in principle independent from an act of interpretation. This primary intuition allows to differentiate between interpretation and creation or invention.[2] But it also assumes that locating a thing and interpreting it are two distinct enterprises; identifying a rule of CIL and clarifying its meaning are supposedly not the same.[3] In this regard, legal interpretation is tightly linked to the doctrine of sources of law; interpretation of law presupposes that one knows where to find it and how to identify it amongst other forms of social normativity.

[2] On these and other philosophical and methodological problems of interpretation, see J Dickson, 'Interpretation and Coherence in Legal Reasoning' in EN Zalta (ed), *The Stanford Encyclopedia of Philosophy* (Metaphysics Research Lab, Stanford University, Winter 2016) <https://stanford.io/3mcKaTQ> accessed 1 March 2021.

[3] P Merkouris, 'Interpreting the Customary Rules on Interpretation' (2017) 19 IntCLRev 126. Although this has been a debatable issue in international legal literature, this chapter builds on a presumption that law in general is an intrinsically interpretable enterprise, and therefore it must be proved that CIL cannot be interpreted, rather than vice versa; see, on the inherently interpretative nature of law, HLA Hart, *The Concept of Law* (2nd edn, Oxford University Press 1994) 124–36; R Dworkin, *Law's Empire* (Belknap Press 1986) 45–86.

The doctrine of sources is a groundwork of legal positivism. That a legal order rests on certain sources entails that a specific class of utterances or actions qualify as generating or communicating the law, as long as they match the criteria of validity that emerge from within this legal order. Thus in domestic law we often say that, for instance, statutes or precedents are sources of law in a sense that certain activities of certain bodies (parliament, courts, etc.) within a certain procedure create legal obligations for all or some groups of persons. In international law, it is generally agreed that treaties, customary law, and general principles of law perform that very same function; they create, impose, or generate legal obligations for states.

The qualification of some social facts as matching criteria of validity does not depend on the content of a purported rule or source. As famously framed by HLA Hart, having criteria of validity for sources of law ('rule of recognition') entails that 'members [of social systems] not merely come to accept separate rules piecemeal, but are committed to the acceptance in advance of general classes of rules, marked out by general criteria of validity'.[4] This commitment to accept *in advance* certain classes of rules presupposes that sources of law are merely *containers*, and their *content* does not typically play a role in qualifying a source of law as such.[5] Hence the fundamental postulate of legal positivism is that identifying something as law is separated from assessing its merits.[6]

The container/content duality is of paramount importance for legal interpretation.[7] One may only engage in legal interpretation if one knows

[4] Hart (n 3) 235.

[5] This is without prejudice to the debates around 'inclusive' and 'exclusive' forms of legal positivism. For 'inclusive' legal positivists, certain moral principles may play a role in identifying valid law, which means that law's content may precede its container. See for a general critique of such a view SJ Shapiro, 'On Hart's Way Out' (1998) 4 LEG 469.

[6] This links to the idea of content-independence as being one of the critical features of law within the positivist paradigm (HLA Hart, 'Commands and Authoritative Legal Reasons' in *Essays on Bentham: Jurisprudence and Political Philosophy* (Oxford University Press 1982)). According to Nathan Adams,

> a command can be a content-independent reason only because the command itself is a container. A command is a speech act that has referential content; its content is the act that it refers to. To say that a command is a content-independent reason to obey is to say that its status as a reason to obey depends on features of the *container* (the speech act), not on features of the *content* (what the speech act refers to).

NP Adams, 'In Defense of Content-Independence' (2017) 23 LEG 143, 147 (emphasis added).

[7] For other instances of operationalisation of this dualism see for example J d'Aspremont, 'Softness in International Law: A Self-Serving Quest for New Legal Materials' (2008) 19 EJIL 1075.

that the normative content one wants to clarify, elucidate, or in any other way meaningfully operationalise, is *contained* in a valid source of law. In the case of statutory interpretation, a statute is a container of legal rules one wants to interpret. In the case of treaty law,[8] it is a treaty that is the container, and its provisions form its content. But how about CIL? What is this *thing* that *contains* customary rules? This question has no obvious answer, though it is maintained, by the International Law Commission (ILC) for example, that in case of CIL the content/container differentiation still applies.[9] What, then, is the container one is looking for in order to enquire into the content of a CIL rule?

Apparently, interpretation of CIL is not an interpretation of some texts since it is widely agreed that CIL is an unwritten source of international law. In other words, CIL is not *contained* in any texts. Certainly, it may have some textual *loci* in treaties, judgments, statements by state organs, to mention some. Although true, this does not infringe on the fact that linguistic formulas, or certain articulations of customary rules, are not customary rules *themselves*. They may serve as points of reference, as useful short-hand devices used to communicate and more efficiently engage in the practice that sustains a customary rule, but it would be a mistake to say that a statement of a customary rule by an authority (institutional or academic) is the customary rule itself. In other words, linguistic formulations are but evidences of existence of customary rules, not rules as such. This is true for any type of customary rules, not only legal ones. The same way as judgments merely reflect, articulate, frame customary legal rules that are already *somewhere there* and exist independently of the fact that a court engages them, manuals of English grammar are also but snapshots of the customary rules of language. Neither of these two can be appropriately used as a criterion for maintaining the practices, and it is actually the other way around: we often discard certain articulations of customary rules as outdated or inaccurate

[8] Hereinafter, when invoking treaty law as an example, I mean treaty law within the paradigm of the Vienna Convention on the Law of Treaties (VCLT).

[9] The ILC holds the view that the determination of 'the *"existence and content"* of rules of customary international law reflects the fact that while often the need is to identify both the existence and the content of a rule, in some cases it is accepted that the rule *exists* but its precise *content* is disputed' Report of the International Law Commission Seventieth Session' (30 April–1 June and 2 July–10 August 2018) UN Doc A/73/10, 124 (emphasis added). The differentiation between the *existence* and the *content* of a rule of CIL inevitably implies the container/content duality since there is no other way for treating the ascertainment of the existence of a rule of CIL as an independent mental procedure except for assuming that this rule appears as a container.

on the basis that *this is not how we do it (anymore)*. Therefore, it is a practice itself which is the ultimate criterion of a customary rule, not its certain pronouncement.

Also, it is difficult to see how rules of CIL can be *contained* in intentions or positions of states (regardless of whether we treat these as instances of state practice or of *opinio juris*). That is, interpretation of CIL is not an interpretation of intention or will of a purported author. Unlike treaties, or statutes in domestic law, customary rules cannot be said to have determinate authors. It is a distinct feature of customs that they are matter of what *we do*, not of what one particular member of a community might intend to do on their own.[10] As put by Gerald Postema, 'custom is never reducible to what each participant does or to what each says, or thinks, or believes about what each does'.[11] Thus, even though it may be the case for some customs that they got intentionally sparked by one action of one particular actor,[12] that actor would not, nevertheless, qualify as its 'author'. If their action ever rises to a customary rule, this means that it is *our* rule, not *theirs*. This, once again, is a feature of customary rules generally, not only legal ones, since what separates them from rules being established externally is that customary rules are rules *of* a community, not rules *for* it. They do not get created by someone for the community, rather, they form within the community and define it as such.[13] Identification of an author of a rule only makes sense when a rule was intentionally designed to bind only particular actors (like in the case of agreements, be it a contract in domestic law or a treaty in international law), or when a rule gets imposed by a lawmaker, since in this situation it is necessary to be able to differentiate between a 'genuine' and a 'fake' lawmaker. Neither of the two situations are proper descriptions of the context of customary law creation or appearance. Thus, even though it is at times common, in

[10] Even though it can be argued that the formation of customary rules typically involves only a limited number of states and therefore CIL suffers from a significant democratic deficit (see, for instance A Roberts, 'Traditional and Modern Approaches to Customary International Law: A Reconciliation' (2001) 95 AJIL 757, 767 ff), this does not defy the point that the states which do shape the practice in question cannot be called 'authors' of customary rules.

[11] GJ Postema, 'Custom, Normative Practice, and the Law' (2012) 62 DukeLJ 707, 719.

[12] The 1945 Truman Proclamation on the continental shelf is a classic example in this regard: 1945 US Presidential Proclamation No 2667, 'Policy of the United States with Respect to the Natural Resources of the Subsoil and Sea Bed of the Continental Shelf' 10 Fed Reg 12303 (1945) 13 DSB 485.

[13] This also holds true for regional or even bilateral customary rules.

international law specifically, to design a customary rule consciously, this does not suggest that the interpretation of such a rule, when it comes to its application, would be an interpretation of some intentions, or that these intentions would be the container of rules of CIL.

It appears that interpretation of CIL is first and foremost interpretation of state practice. The same way as we interpret other customary rules, say, rules of language, or rules of etiquette, when we interpret CIL, we enquire into what, how, in which circumstances, and so on, participants of a certain practice do and do not do. In the case of CIL, a state practice is the ultimate point of reference one has when clarifying a particular legal rule. I will further define what I mean by state practices in the next section. For now, it suffices to stress that unlike in the case of statutes or precedents in domestic law, or treaties in international law, state practices are not only the *containers* but also the *content* of rules one wants to interpret. From the perspective of the doctrine of sources of law, customary rules often appear uneasy to deal with, for they are not only a *source* of law, they *are* law themselves.[14] That state practices are both content and containers, however, engenders consequences for what the interpretation of customary rules actually entails.

The content/container dualism of state practices makes them similar to light, as it were, that is, they manifest differently depending on how they are looked at. Light behaves as a wave in one set of conditions of observation, and as particles in another, and as such is, in fact, both.[15] This can also be said about state practices, for when they are interpreted for the purposes of identification of rules of CIL they appear as containers, as something legal obligations are scooped from (see Section 5.1); but when they are interpreted for the purpose of clarifying the meaning of rules of CIL, practices appear as their content, as what the rules *are* content-wise (see Section 5.2). This dualism of state practices creates a confusion as to how these two instances or cases of interpretation differ. If identification and interpretation are, according to the doctrine of sources, different enterprises, how does one tell the difference between the two if both concentrate on state practice?

[14] See for a similar point L Blutman, 'Conceptual Confusion and Methodological Deficiencies: Some Ways That Theories on Customary International Law Fail' (2014) 25 EJIL 529, 532: 'It is misleading to suggest that customary international law is one of the sources of international law. Customary international law forms part of international law. If it is part of international law, then it cannot be its source.'

[15] W Greiner, *Quantum Mechanics: An Introduction* (4th ed, Springer 2001).

Before answering this question, it is necessary to take a closer look at state practices as such, since clarifying their nature is of paramount importance for the further enquiry.

3 State Practices and Normative Deeds

Though it is typically asserted that the concept of *opinio juris* is far more contested than the concept of state practice,[16] the latter also carries many controversies with it. This is partly so due to its container/content duality, but also due to some conceptual assumptions regarding state practices that are deeply rooted in the doctrines of formation and identification of CIL and are constantly replicated in international legal scholarship.

It is a widespread belief, reflected, among other, in the ILC reports and conclusions, and emerging from the famous *North Sea Continental Shelf* judgment, that a general practice that is accepted as law is to be distinguished from mere *usage* or *habit*.[17] To put it in the words of the ILC, 'practice without acceptance as law . . ., even if widespread and consistent, can be no more than *a non-binding usage*'.[18] A characteristic feature of approaching state practice within the doctrine of identification of CIL, defended also by the ILC, is an all-or-nothingness. It appears that there are only two options: either a state practice is accompanied by *opinio juris* and then may, if quantitative and qualitative requirements are met, constitute a rule of CIL, or, if it is not, then there exists no obligation for states to act in a certain manner whatsoever. This view on CIL, which Monica Hakimi labels 'the rulebook conception', assumes that without *opinio juris* state practices are *mere* usages or habits that have no binding force, and that there exist certain clear and formal criteria (i.e., secondary rules) which allow to establish normativity and legality of these practices.[19] This is also articulated by the International Court of Justice (ICJ) that 'many international acts, eg, in the field of ceremonial and

[16] See for example B Cheng, 'Opinio Juris: A Key Concept in International Law That Is Much Misunderstood' in S Yee & W Tieva (eds), *International Law in the Post-Cold War World: Essays in Memory of Li Haopei* (Routledge 2001).

[17] *North Sea Continental Shelf Cases (Federal Republic of Germany/Denmark; Federal Republic of Germany/Netherlands)* (Merits) [1969] ICJ Rep 3 [77].

[18] ILC (n 9) 126 (emphasis added).

[19] M Hakimi, 'Making Sense of Customary International Law' (2020) 118 MichLRev 1487, 1497–504. Hakimi's rejection of the rulebook conception of CIL is resonant with the view advanced here, especially in the context of practical reasoning and normativity of practices, discussed in the next two sections.

protocol, which are performed almost invariably, but which are motivated *only by considerations of courtesy, convenience or tradition*, and not by any sense of legal duty'.[20] It is, therefore, out of paramount importance that 'one must look at what States actually do and seek to determine whether they recognize *an obligation* or *a right* to act in that way'.[21] The position of the ICJ and ILC on this matter clearly opposes legal customary rules and their absence, which is reasonable from the point of view of legal logic. What is disturbing, however, is how state practices are thought of when there is no *opinio juris*. The wording adopted by both institutions not only suggests absence of any obligations within such practices, but also non-normativity of such practices; a view widely supported in the academic literature.[22] *Opinio juris* appears as a magic wand that not only turns the 'raw material' of state practices into a norm, but simultaneously into a *legal* norm.

What seems to be the underlying principle behind such a treatment of state practices rests on two interrelated ideas. First, it is clear that the identification of CIL serves the purpose of establishing the existence of a *legal* obligation binding upon states. When interpreting state practices for this purpose, one therefore asks questions of *legality*, that is, whether there exists a norm that provides for *legal* obligations states must fulfil. What goes alongside it, however, often remains fully or partly unnoticed; namely, that legality is an attribute of a norm,[23] and therefore inquiring into whether there is a legal norm is asking two questions, not one: (1) is there a norm (the question of normativity); (2) if yes, is this norm a legal one (the question of legality)? Importantly, these questions should be answered in this particular order. The question of *normativity*, though, bears entirely different considerations and should be approached with

[20] *North Sea Continental Shelf Cases* (n 17) [77] (emphasis added).

[21] ILC (n 9) 125 (emphasis added).

[22] Michael Akehurst argues that without *opinio juris* there is no way to tell the difference between habitual actions and rule-guided behaviour: M Akehurst, 'Custom as a Source of International Law' (1976) 47 BYBIL 1, 33; Anthea Roberts refers to state practice as the 'raw data', which, taken together with *opinio juris*, must be further tested to see 'if there are any eligible interpretations that adequately explain the raw data of practice', Roberts (n 10) 788; as nicely put by Hugh Thirlway, *opinio juris* is similar to 'the philosopher's stone which transmutes *the inert mass of accumulated usage* into the gold of binding legal rules' H Thirlway, *International Customary Law and Codification* (Sijthoff 1972) 47 (emphasis added); see also Blutman (n 14) 535 ff.

[23] This does not imply that everything that can, in some legal order, qualify as law is by necessity normative. In any legal order there are laws which are not norms (e.g., declarations or recommendations); J Raz, *The Concept of a Legal System* (2nd ed, Oxford University Press 1980) 168 ff.

a distinct methodology and conceptual framework, than the question of legality.[24]

The language adopted by the ILC and the ICJ, however, makes it seem as if deciding on the legality of certain practices is fundamentally the same as deciding on their normativity; when a practice does not meet the threshold of legality, it is a habit or a usage that creates no obligation or a right, which is basically tantamount to the absence of a norm altogether. This brings the second assumption into play, namely, that state practices are often taken as certain collections of individual actions of states, collections that may or may not feature some pattern (actions that are 'performed almost invariably' – as if their performance is a matter of (in) variability, rather than following certain normative consideration). It is thus claimed that 'the requirement that the practice be consistent means that where the relevant acts are divergent to the extent that *no pattern of behaviour can be discerned, no general practice* (and thus no corresponding rule of customary international law) can be said to exist'.[25]

The focus on (in)variability and patterns of behaviour that is so explicit in the reasoning of the ILC and the ICJ seems to neglect the idea that the existence of an observable pattern of conduct is not a relevant marker of there being a practice. Invariability of some actions, even when absolutely consistent, may or may not be evidence of a practice, because it is not the invariability or consistency of actions that matters, but the meaning these actions have for those engaged in them. It is a well-known example by HLA Hart that for an external observer all more or less consistent regularities of behaviour look the same in terms of people doing certain things in certain circumstances. However, that some people go to a cinema once a week does not mean that there is a normative consideration to that effect, that is, that it is somehow socially expected or required from them to go to a cinema once a week.[26] On the other hand, that all people lie from time to time (some people more often than others) does not deny the existence of a normative consideration that one must not lie. Thus, that some people go to a cinema once a week is a *regularity of behaviour*, but not a *practice*. The only way to differentiate between people engaging in a practice and people simply acting uniformly is to adopt what HLA Hart calls 'the internal point of view'; practices, unlike mere regularities or patterns of behaviour, feature

[24] See Section 5, below.
[25] ILC (n 9) 137 (emphasis added).
[26] Hart (n 3) 10–11.

a critical reflective attitude towards actions, which entails their inherently normative nature.[27] So, let us take a closer look at the concept of practice.

Practices, unlike mere regularities of behaviour (like that some people happen to go to the cinema once a week), are of normative nature. In ordinary life, it can be said that at the moment a person steps into a practice, they are expected to accept certain deeds that infiltrate and govern this practice, give it shape, and make it meaningful for the participants. A simple test to be used to determine whether a regularity of behaviour is a practice is whether one may fail in performing or not performing certain actions. This is typically ascertained either through existing mutual expectations that deeds of practice are and will be followed, or through criticism explicated when these deeds are ignored, this criticism being an aspect of the practice concerned.[28] For people who happened to go to a cinema once a week, it is not a failure not to go there this week, but go twice the next one instead; no one's expectations are failed to be met, and no criticism would follow. At the same time, lying to people does usually constitute a failure to meet certain expectations, even when no criticism follows (not all lies get discovered, after all). This latter point also relates to other actions rendered prohibited in the context of existing practices, for example, tortures. Such actions are sometimes colloquially referred to as 'practices', but even there we can only meaningfully speak of them as 'practices' if there exist normative considerations that somehow make tortures meaningful for those engaged in them (e.g., various utilitarian 'ticking-bomb scenarios'). Existence of conflicting normative expectations within the domain of the same practice is not at all uncommon, given how much these expectations may depend on underlying reasons (see the next section). This is why some practices may feature uncertainty as to what constitutes a failure in following it.[29]

[27] ibid 56–57; compare SJ Shapiro, *Legality* (Harvard University Press 2011) 102–5.

[28] Note that expectations and criticism are themselves aspects of a practice, not something to be *added* to a practice to make it normative, as the two-element theory of customary norms suggests; Postema (n 11); GJ Postema, 'Custom in International Law: A Normative Practice Account' in A Perreau-Saussine & JB Murphy (eds), *The Nature of Customary Law: Legal, Historical, and Philosophical Perspectives* (Cambridge University Press 2007).

[29] It is also worth noting the problem of individuation of practices, which I do not touch upon in this chapter. Still, an argument can be made that prohibitive customary rules (such as prohibition of lying, or prohibition of torture, mentioned in the main text) are not independent practices, meaningful in their own right, but rather parts of more complex and intricate practices that govern the ways in which we deem it appropriate or inappropriate to treat our fellow human beings. On the problem of individuation in legal theory in general, see Raz (n 23), 70–92.

The difference between the two examples given above is that there is nothing to be failed in the context of going or not going to the cinema; there are no deeds flowing through the conduct of going to a cinema with a certain regularity, and therefore there is no practice, regardless of the fact that for an external observer this could be the most consistent pattern of behaviour by these people they can observe. In the latter example with lying or torturing, though, there is a certain standard embedded into behaviour, a standard that constitutes a deed that generates certain expectations that other participants of a practice would follow this deed. What differentiates practices from regularities of behaviour, therefore, is the existence of deeds as certain standards that get learned and adopted by the participants of a practice and generate expectations regarding other participants.[30] Practices, in such a way, are inherently normative, because the mere existence of deeds as standards constitutes an independent reason for acting in one way and not in another. As emphasised by Gerald Postema,

> [Customs] are not (merely) *patterns* of behavior; rather they set *standards for* behavior, standards of correct and incorrect behavior, and thus purport to guide that behavior and provide bases for its assessment. Thus, mere regularities of behavior taken alone – the *usus* or 'state practice' of international law discourse – not only fail to constitute customs of international law, they fail to constitute customs of any sort, including those of 'comity', because they fail to constitute norms.[31]

From this perspective, customary rules do not and cannot exist separately or detached from practices that sustain them. Besides, that there is a practice, and not just a regularity of behaviour, means that there is a norm that shapes this practice. In other words, to say that there exists a state practice on a certain matter *already* entails saying that there is a norm on this matter, and n-I. For this reason, it is not entirely accurate to ascertain that when a certain practice fails to qualify as a rule of CIL, there is no moral or social obligation in general binding upon states that flows from the deeds and mutual expectation of participants of such a practice.

This view on state practice was particularly endorsed by the International Law Association (ILA) in its 'Statements of Principles

[30] As famously marked by Lon Fuller, 'customary law arises . . . out of situations of human interaction where each participant guides himself by an anticipation of what the other will do and will expect him to do' LL Fuller, *Anatomy of the Law* (Praeger 1968) 73.

[31] Postema (n 28) 285.

Applicable to Formation of General Customary International Law', where it claims that:

> 'a rule of customary international law is one which is created and sustained by the constant and uniform practice of States and other subjects of international law in or impinging upon their international legal relations, in circumstances which give rise to a legitimate expectation of similar conduct in the future'.[32]

To recapitulate, there are two fundamental considerations flowing from the view expressed above. First, practices (any practices, not just state practices) are inherently normative, otherwise they are not practices at all. The normativity of practices is determined by the character of deeds framing them and by the function these practices perform, as well as by the meaning they have for participants. According to Gerald Postema, the normativity of practices is ascertainable first and foremost from the perspective of those participating in them:

> Those who participate in a custom's practice undertake commitments (a) to judge certain performances as appropriate or correct and others as mistaken; (b) to act when the occasion arises in accord with these judgments; (c) to challenge conduct that falls short of these judgments; and (d) to recognize appeals to the judgments as vindications of their actions or valid criticisms of them.[33]

Second, the content and meaning of customary rules can be (and usually is) determined without necessarily assessing the character and nature of the normative claims they exhibit (moral, legal, etc.). Hence, practices always create obligations and endow those participating in them with rights. This does not mean that these obligations and rights are of *legal* nature, but it is important to bear in mind that absence of *opinio juris* does not signify absence of *any* obligation.

With an image of state practice as inherently normative, we may now take a further step and try to clarify how such practice can be reconstructed for the purposes of interpretation. What does the normativity of practice look like and what are the interpretative beacons one may use in order to clarify its meaning?

[32] ILA Committee on Formation of Customary (General) International Law, 'Final Report of the Committee: Statement of Principles Applicable to the Formation of General Customary International Law' (ILA, 2000) 1, 8 <https://bit.ly/3dU8e9f> accessed 1 March 2020.

[33] Postema (n 11) 719; it is important to notice that these commitments are not steps or stages of integration into practice; all of them are intertwined and none of them can be detached from the rest (I am grateful to André de Hoogh for drawing my attention to this).

4 Practice as Network of Reasons

In the previous section, I endorsed the conception that practices are inherently normative, and that getting involved in a practice means accepting and following certain normative standards that are embodied in it and are inseparable from deeds penetrating and shaping it. This view entails, among other things, that practices are sustained by mutual expectations of participants and by more or less implicit normative standards that one in principle is able to fail to meet. Importantly, such character of practices makes them normative, and this normativity may, under certain circumstances, qualify as legal. This characteristic of practices is by and large generic and applies to state practices as well.

Normativity, according to a dominant view, reflects a special ability of law and other social practices to provide those participating in them with reasons for action.[34] In other words, practices, such as state practices, are normative in a sense that for those who participate in them the mere fact that they do so is a reason for acting and reacting to the actions of other participants in a certain way. This reason-giving function of practices, in their normative manifestation (i.e., from the internal point of view), entails that they require meaningful participation, and this meaningfulness comprises of participants' ability to recognise and react to actions of others in a way that is intelligible for the rest of the participants. This is precisely why, even when states do not explicate their position regarding actions of other states, this may still contribute to formation of a new, or sustaining an existing, practice. Even an absence of reaction may, under certain circumstances, get deciphered by other participants of a practice meaningfully either as endorsement or at least as acquiescence.

For such meaningful participation, states must consider practice not only as a reason, but as a *network of reasons*. It is almost never the case that a practice can in one way or another be boiled down to one standalone reason that states ought to comply with, for each practice gets its function, meaning, and normative significance in a wider context of related activities.[35] In fact, especially when we look at a broader scope of social practices, even the simplest ones (such as the practice of eating

[34] See generally S Bertea & G Pavlakos (eds), *New Essays on the Normativity of Law* (Hart 2011); S Delacroix, 'Hart's and Kelsen's Concepts of Normativity Contrasted' (2004) 17 Ratio Juris 501; N Gur, *Legal Directives and Practical Reasons* (Oxford University Press 2018); J Kaplan, 'Attitude and the Normativity of Law' (2017) 36 L&Phil 469; J Raz, *Practical Reason and Norms* (2nd ed, Oxford University Press 1999).

[35] See for an in-depth elaboration on this point V Rodriguez-Blanco, *Law and Authority under the Guise of the Good* (Hart 2016).

with a fork and a knife) are only meaningful when taken in the context of a much wider set of considerations which justify the existence of these practices and shape their content. Because of this, the precise normative boundaries of practices may be difficult to define. But what is more fundamental for the purposes of interpretation and for the purposes of identification of a state practice is that reasons comprising a practice vary in nature, function, and strength.

One of the most popular and influential explanations of normativity, developed by Joseph Raz, suggests that even though norms are reasons for actions, not all reasons are norms.[36] A reason for action, according to his latest definition, is 'a consideration that renders its [i.e., an action's] choice intelligible, and counts in its favor'.[37] Reasons as such do not give rise to obligations, but it is nevertheless a basic moral principle that one ought to act according to an optimal balance of reasons one has, all things considered. This equally applies to states, since it is almost never disputed that they are morally accountable agents (were they not, it would have been impossible to defend even a proposition that international law has any function or basis for existence whatsoever). In international relations, states claim reasons for their actions all the time, and some of them are norms. Michael Akehurst, in his influential article on custom as a source of international law, refers to an example of states using white paper for diplomatic correspondence to advance his argument that habits do not create rules of law.[38] And indeed, that states almost unanimously use white paper only shows that they do so for a widely shared reason, a reason which, nevertheless, is not a norm. If not all reasons are norms, how is it possible to mark a class of reasons that *are* norms?

Joseph Raz's solution to the problem of norms being linguistically inseparable from the rest of the reasons[39] suggests that there must be some other

[36] See for an in-depth discussion of reasons and norms Raz (n 34) chapters 1–3.

[37] J Raz, 'The Problem of Authority: Revisiting the Service Conception' (2006) 90 MinnLRev 1003, 1006.

[38] Akehurst (n 22) 33–34. In fact, this argument is not particularly convincing in the light of the concept endorsed in the previous section; habits not only fail to create legal obligation, they are in principle unable to create *any* obligation. Overall, this example suggests that Akehurst advances the same conception adopted by the ILC when absence of legal obligation gets contextually equated to an absence of any obligation at all. Thus, though making a valid claim that *opinio juris* helps to distinguish legal obligations from non-legal obligations, he seems to suggest that non-legal obligations are essentially no different from the absence of an obligation as such. This view, however practical it may be, creates a distorted image of normativity of an international order.

[39] Both norms and ordinary reasons may be appropriately expressed in 'ought-statements', and therefore purely linguistic analysis is irrelevant for determining the features of

criteria according to which we could differentiate between 'mere' reasons and norms. Norms are second-order pre-emptive reasons,[40] and because of this they play a drastically different role in practical reasoning as compared to ordinary first-order reasons.[41] Norms, just like other second-order reasons, are reasons to act or to refrain from acting on some first-order reasons. For example, states may share a wide set of reasons for not using armed force in international relations, and the norm of international law that prohibits the use of force is a second-order reason for acting on all those reasons. But also, and probably most importantly, the existence of a norm prohibiting the use of force is a reason for *not* acting on certain other first-order reasons. The mere fact of such a prohibition implies that states may not act for reasons that count in favour of using force against other states. In such a way, norms are second-order reasons in the sense that they *reinforce* some first-order reasons and *exclude* some other first-order reasons. What this means is that not only are norms reasons for actions they prescribe, but they are also reasons for disregarding reasons for non-compliance.[42] For example, diplomatic immunity is a norm precisely because it is *both* a reason for states to refrain from subjecting diplomats to their jurisdiction, *and* a reason for disregarding any other reasons for acting otherwise, no matter how weighty these may be, such as in the cases when diplomats cause lethal accidents or interfere in the internal affairs of the receiving state.[43] This pre-emptive character is what differentiates norms from other reasons for action.

normativity. Linguistically, there is no difference between a statement 'You ought to go outside and enjoy the sun' and a statement 'You ought to drive no faster than 60 km/h in an inhabited area.' Yet it is prima facie clear that the former is a statement of a 'mere' reason, whereas the latter is a statement of a norm.

[40] The concept of pre-emptive reasons is highly debated. See for instance L Alexander, 'Law and Exclusionary Reasons' (1990) 18 Philosophical Topics 5; S Darwall, 'Authority and Reasons: Exclusionary and Second-Personal' (2010) 120 Ethics 257; N Gur, 'Are Legal Rules Content-Independent Reasons?' (2011) 5 Problema 175; MS Moore, 'Authority, Law, and Razian Reasons' (1988) 62 SCalLRev 827. It is beyond the scope of this chapter to engage in the debate on this matter. Suffice to say that the idea of pre-emption seems promising in explaining the role norms play in practical reasoning, however it is disputable whether pre-emption is a binary or a discrete quality of norms.

[41] Promises, voluntary commitments, orders and commands, and some others are second-order reasons, but they are not norms. See J Raz, 'Promises and Obligations' in PMS Hacker and J Raz (eds), *Law, Morality, and Society: Essays in Honor of H. L. A. Hart* (Clarendon Press 1977). For the sake of clarity, whenever a second-order reason is mentioned, it purports a norm.

[42] Raz (n 34) 58–59.

[43] *Case Concerning United States Diplomatic and Consular Staff in Tehran (United States of America v Iran)* (Merits) [1980] ICJ Rep 3 [83–87].

Practices are networks of both second-order reasons, that is, norms, and first-order reasons. This allows for complex and often multidimensional justificatory strategies for one or other course of behaviour.[44] Apart from this, however, this reflects a feature of norms not only being embedded into practices, but also being virtually inseparable from them. Norms, as intrinsically interwoven into practices, do not 'hang in the air' or exist in some metaphysical space, and their justification, therefore, is shaped by, and depends on, a wider network of reasons employed within a certain practice. Norms may be justified in a number of ways; as time- and labour-saving devices, as error-eliminating devices, that is, those subjected to such norms use them as shortcuts in practical reasoning so that if a norm gets accepted it is not necessary anymore to figure out each time an optimal balance of reasons to act upon. Some other norms are justified by recourse to an authority, that is, acceptance of a norm comes as a result of acceptance of authorities issuing them. These (and many more) methods of justification of norms may overlap and supplement each other; in fact, most of the norms by which people are bound have more than just one justification.[45]

In such a way, practices, such as state practice, explicate their normativity as tightly intertwined networks of first- and second-order reasons. Seen as such, their interpretation therefore relates to discovering the interconnection between these two classes of reasons, assessing their balance, and unveiling them in justifications employed by states or implied in their actions.

5 Asking the Right Questions: Re-approaching the Content/Container Duality

Thus far this chapter explored the features and intrinsic qualities of (state) practices as *the thing* being interpreted within the process of legal interpretation. Now it is time to take this a step further and take a look at this interpretation anew. If state practices are networks

[44] From this perspective, Martti Koskenniemi's idea of the sliding scale between apolitical and utopian line of argument, from the perspective of practical reasoning, is merely an interplay between first- and second-order reasons used for justification of a state's behaviour. See M Koskenniemi, *From Apology to Utopia: The Structure of International Legal Argument* (2nd ed, Cambridge University Press 2006); M Hakimi also points out that CIL does not always operate as a set of rules, and may feature inconstancies and contingencies, Hakimi (n 19) 1516.

[45] Raz (n 34) 74.

of first- and second-order reasons within which states form, manifest, and explicate expectations regarding the actions of other states, how does this affect the nature of state practices for the purposes of legal interpretation? How are these networks of reasons interpreted when looked at as containers, and when looked at as contents?

The theory of normativity as a special case of practical reasoning offers an illuminating perspective on interpretation of state practice as network of reasons. Most importantly, it allows to clearly differentiate two instances of interpretation: interpretation of state practice for the purpose of identification of a rule of CIL, and interpretation for the purposes of clarification of its normative content.

5.1 *Interpretation as Identification*

The formation of a norm is a process of conversion of reasons and expectations, and it may not always be possible to draw straight lines between a stage when states act for a widely shared reason and do not explicate any expectations, a stage practice emerges, and a stage when it has fully developed. Sometimes, articulation of reasons is enough to generate expectations that these reasons would be followed and other reasons would be excluded, which exhibits a practice being formed (e.g., Truman proclamation on continental shelf). At other times, conversion of reasons into norms does not happen because of difficulties associated with balancing them in a most appropriate way, which causes uncertainties and disagreements as to whether a practice has emerged (e.g., uncertainties in regard of the right to unilateral secession). Yet some features of practical reasoning exploited by actors serve as beacons of there to be or not to be a norm and whether it may qualify as a legal one. Thus, when states' actions are looked at with the purpose of enquiring whether a new rule of CIL has emerged, the network of reasons appears as a purported *container*, and what states do and how they react to what other states do get assessed within a logic of sources of law. This, first and foremost, affects the questions through which the interpretation of states' actions is carried out:

(1) do states act for the first-order reasons only, and is there therefore only a semblance of a practice ('pattern' or 'regularity of behaviour')?
(2) or do states act for a second-order reason (i.e., norm), and is there therefore a formed practice, where participants exhibit expectations about reasons being followed or excluded, and shape their conduct based on these expectations?

(3) if the latter, then is this second-order reason acted upon and articulated as a part of a wider network of legally relevant reasons, that is, does it conform to certain conventional criteria of validity of custom as *legal* custom?[46]

Questions (1)–(2) inquire into the existence of a second-order reason that states use as a justification for their action. There is a big difference between justification based on first-order reasons and justification based on second-order reasons, that is, norms. Justification based on first-order reasons does not purport any expectations from other actors and such justification may, as a matter of fact, be implicit and not designed as foreseeing, or matching, such expectations. This, however, is a much rarer situation than it may appear. In today's world, states are much more often acting within practices than they used to, even when it relates to their internal affairs, and therefore justifications, even when implied, are typically met with expectations from other actors. Hence, it is normal that first-order reasons-based justifications are usually addressed to states' actions in their domestic realm, though even there second-order reasons embedded into state practices play a more and more significant role.[47]

The existence of a norm manifests in a reason that has a pre-emptive function, that is, a reason that counts for not acting on, and not using as a justification some other reasons. Not only does this mean that certain reasons cannot be legitimately acted upon, but it also entails that other states expect these reasons to be excluded and react accordingly when they are not. This, however, does not in and of itself mean that a norm embedded into a practice is a *legal* norm. There may exist mutual expectations as to what reasons may or may not be acted on, and what

[46] *Opinio juris* is such a criterion, for it is a matter of *practice* of international law to use it as a threshold for assessing legal validity of customary rules. Yet it is worth stressing that *opinio juris* is not an element of a customary legal rule, but rather a conventional criterion, according to which the legal relevance of a certain practice is assessed. See, for the same line of argument, Postema (n 11); Postema (n 28).

[47] Similarly, private actions by persons may not constitute any practices, if they do not purport any sort of expectations from other persons. States, too, within the doctrine of sovereignty, may organise their internal life according to considerations that do not and are not purported to create any expectations for other states. Gradually, however, this may change, when even internal affairs of a state create expectations for other states. For instance, as the recent situation with Poland suggests, it may be said that there is a gradual movement towards operationalising the practices of the Rule of Law as generating political and even legal expectations. See European Commission, 'Commission Recommendation Regarding the Rule of Law in Poland' C(2016) 5703 final.

kind of second-order reason bridges them, even when these expectations do not have a manifestly legal character. International relations of states are by and large governed by such second-order reasons, which means that state practices (and hence also norms) are virtually omnipresent.[48]

The first two questions, in such a way, are asked in order to determine the reasons-made boundaries of a container of a customary rule. The third question is quite different, though. It aims at establishing whether this container meets the requirements of validity set by a legal order. It is beyond the scope of this chapter to discuss the intricacies of legality of state practices, if only because they do not, in principle, contribute to the process of interpretation of rules of CIL. The dimension of the legality of customary rules, as was suggested in Section 2, is typically of little relevance to the determination of their content. Let us therefore shift to a different mode of interpretation: that aimed at clarification of the content of customary rules.

5.2 *Interpretation as Clarification*

A more specific, and more legally charged instance of interpretation of state practices is, certainly, interpretation for the purposes of clarification of the normative content of a rule of CIL. This instance of interpretation, however, tends to adopt a view of state practices as the content of rules, rather than their containers. This, though, does not change the nature of state practices as networks of reasons, and therefore the questions through which interpretation proceeds are again addressed to these networks, but these are very different questions:

(1) what first-order reasons does a rule of CIL exclude, that is, what reasons states may not legitimately invoke as justification for their actions within a given practice?

[48] This should not come as a surprise since practices are shadows of interactions. This obviously goes against the Lotus principle that 'rules of law binding upon States therefore emanate from their own free will as expressed in conventions or by usages generally accepted as expressing principles of law and established in order to regulate the relations between these co-existing independent communities or with a view to the achievement of common aims. *Restrictions upon the independence of States cannot therefore be presumed.*' *SS 'Lotus' (France v Turkey)* (Judgment) [1927] PCIJ Series A 10 [44] (emphasis added); human interactions are almost always practice-based and, consequently, normative. It is not that easy to think of an example of human interaction that does not presuppose any mutual expectations and normative deeds. The same applies equally to states, since their interaction is but a species of human interaction; it may be almost impossible to single out states' actions in international realm that are not *ab initio* met with deeds-based normative expectations from other states.

(2) what first-order reasons does a rule of CIL reinforce, that is, what first-order reasons does this norm account for, how does it balance them, and whether this balance corresponds to expectations of those involved in a practice?

Let us address the first question. Since exclusion is of crucial importance for differentiating norms from other reasons, interpretation of rules of CIL is primarily concerned with what reasons get excluded by a rule that is being interpreted. For example, is it meaningful within existing state practices to ascertain that a cyber-operation as a single 'hostile' act employed by one state against another constitutes an armed conflict within the meaning of customary rules of international humanitarian law (IHL)?[49] To translate this into the language of practical reasoning, may a state justify the reasons for its act of cyber warfare as *not* being excluded by the norms of IHL? This question can only be answered by looking at how states accommodate a new reason into existing deeds; whether they discursively assess cyber warfare as an instance of an armed conflict, or as something separate, probably creating an independent deed. By its very nature, exclusion is the function of a norm that renders acting on certain reasons as violation of this norm, and therefore when a new reason emerges from within a practice (a practice of modern warfare, in this example), it is a matter of whether states accommodate this new reason within existing normative deeds, or whether they exclude it from practice and prevent it from becoming its deed. This process of accommodation or rejection typically manifests in how states react to a new reason being invoked as a justification for an action within an existing practice.

Where the first question addresses the external boundaries of a practice, that is, the issues of what kind of reasons count as parts of a practice and what kind of reasons are excluded from it, the second question offers a different perspective. It relates to the justification of norms, briefly touched upon in the previous section. Norms, including legal norms, are typically justified as accounting for a certain balance of the first-order reasons that render a practice intelligible. From this perspective, norms always serve a purpose of simplifying or optimising participants' compliance with these first-order reasons.[50] Interpretation, therefore, may not only address the issues of exclusion of some reasons,

[49] ICRC, 'International Humanitarian Law and the Challenges of Contemporary Armed Conflicts' (ICRC, 2011) 31IC/11/5.1.2, 36–37.

[50] See J Raz, *The Morality of Freedom* (Oxford University Press 1986) 40 ff.

but also the issues of reassessing or even reshaping the balance of reasons that are included in practice. Thus, it is a matter of interpretation to inquire whether a rule of CIL adequately reflects and accounts for underlying reasons that shape a practice and guide a state's actions.[51] If, for example, the principle of equidistance as a method of delimitation of continental shelves does not properly account for the reasons that comprise the practice of the use of continental shelf, there may exist a need to rebalance these reasons according to a more fundamental principle.[52] Such a rebalancing, though made within a wider normative framework of equity, does affect the balance of reasons represented by the equidistance rule; some of the reasons it accounts for are now weightier.

These two questions, though different from those discussed in the previous subsection, build on them. It is in the foundations of legal interpretation to enquire into what considerations and in which particular manner legal norms account for, since it is the core function of legal norms to improve or simplify people's compliance with reasons. And since in the case of customary rules their content and container are one and the same thing, their interpretation ultimately entails clarifying the boundaries of practices. The need for this clarification reflects that it is in the nature of practices to evolve. The normative deeds comprising the inherent normative standard of a practice are typically on the move; not only do they depend on what participants in practices do, but also on how they react to actions. Thus, those engaged in practices constantly accommodate or reject new reasons that may or may not affect the perception of the normative standard, and this is exactly why interpretation of customary rules is essentially an inquiry into the dynamics of practical reasoning implied within a practice.

It is, therefore, not only *possible* that rules of CIL allow for evolutive interpretation, it is *essential*, since it follows directly from the way practices operate and develop. It should be noted, however, that evolutive interpretation in the case of treaties is not the same as in the case of CIL.[53] For interpretation of treaties, evolutive interpretation generally relates to the phenomenon that when treaty text remains the same, its meaning is

[51] This may be taken in a shape of the object-and-purpose strategy of interpretation which, though emerging in the treaty law, may also be used for interpretation of CIL. See P Merkouris, *Article 31(3)(C) VCLT and the Principle of Systemic Integration: Normative Shadows in Plato's Cave* (Brill Nijhoff 2015) 263–69.

[52] *North Sea Continental Shelf Cases* (n 17) [88–99].

[53] I am grateful to Prof Adil Haque for drawing my attention to this issue.

altered in the course of time.[54] It is argued that evolutive interpretation of treaties is justified when there is evidence that the parties intended, from the outset, that their treaty would be capable of evolving over time, that it can remain effective or relevant in the face of changing conditions.[55] It is, therefore, essential that evolutive interpretation of treaties is based on the provision of Article 31(1) of the VCLT, according to which 'a treaty shall be interpreted . . . in the light of its object and purpose'. When a rule of CIL is in question, though, it seems not entirely accurate to speak of its object and purpose, since rules of CIL cannot be always traced back to some shared intentions (as argued in Section 2), their object and purpose are far less clear and determined than in the case of treaties. In the case of treaties, their object and purpose may be an *explanandum* for the purposes of interpretation, but in the case of rules of CIL, they rather appear as *explanans*. In other words, an object and purpose of a customary rule may well be the end point of interpretation rather than its starting point. For this reason, evolutive interpretation of the rules of CIL relates more to the function a certain practice performs and to the meaning its practice has in a wider context of states' activities. Such an evolutive interpretation, then, focuses on re-evaluating the balance of reasons reflected in a norm, adjusting it to the developing patterns of practice itself.[56] Every instance of interpretation of a rule of CIL is therefore a snapshot of the balance of reasons currently accepted within a practice. However, since practices are dynamic entities, so are the norms which define them and are sustained by them.

To summarise, the interpretation of state practices as normative networks of reasons takes different shape depending on how they are looked at. If a state practice is approached as a container and is thus investigated for the purposes of identification of a rule of CIL, the main strategy of interpretation will consist in assessing whether states act for a second-order reason (a norm, in this context) and whether it meets the threshold of legal validity. When a state practice is addressed as content, the interpretative strategy will primarily entail determination of those

[54] C Djeffal, *Static and Evolutive Treaty Interpretation: A Functional Reconstruction* (Cambridge University Press 2016) 19; from this perspective, evolutive interpretation relates to the establishment of a change in a treaty without its modification. J Arato, 'Subsequent Practice and Evolutive Interpretation: Techniques of Treaty Interpretation over Time and Their Diverse Consequences' (2010) 9 LPICT 443, 456 ff.

[55] M Fitzmaurice, 'Dynamic (Evolutive) Interpretation of Treaties, Part I' (2008) HYIL 101, 153.

[56] See generally on the idea of rebalancing reasons SR Perry, 'Second-Order Reasons, Uncertainty and Legal Theory' (1989) 62 SCalLRev 913.

reasons a rule of CIL excludes and assessment of whether those reasons it accounts for are properly balanced.

6 Conclusions

It is in the core of the idea of CIL that it manifests in a peculiar duality; it is a source of international law, and at the same time it is international law as such. By blurring the line between container and content, which is essential for the conventional doctrine of sources, CIL challenges the process of its interpretation too. State practices, which appear as both containers and content of rules of CIL, are subject to interpretation from two different positions – when a new rule is identified, and when an existing rule is clarified. This creates confusions as to how to separate these two instances of interpretation.

This chapter endorses the view on state practices as inherently normative networks of reasons. Approached as such, state practice manifests as comprising of deeds and reasons, the latter existing on two different levels. The normativity of a state practice is explained through there being second-order pre-emptive reasons, that is, norms that bridge a variety of first-order reasons, balancing and mutually rendering them meaningful. The interpretation of these norms embedded into state practices entails discovering connections between different groups and levels of reasons. The interpretation for the purpose of identification of a rule of CIL is primarily concerned with a question of whether there is a second-order reason that systematises expectations and critical stances of states, and whether this second-order reason qualifies as a legal one. The interpretation for the purposes of clarification, in turn, focuses on what reasons a rule of CIL excludes, and what reasons it balances, how well this balance reflects the actual weight of the first-order reasons, and how to ensure that newly formed reasons are properly assessed and accommodated within practice, or get excluded from it.

Such an approach to state practice and interpretation of CIL allows one to distinguish different interpretative stages of a lifecycle of state practice, as well as to conceptualise state practice as a normative network of reasons.

18

Different Strings of the Same Harp

Interpretation of Rules of Customary International Law, Their Identification and Treaty Interpretation

MARINA FORTUNA*

1 Introduction

At the heart of all knowledge lies *difference* – the ability to distinguish one concept from another one.[1] From Heraclitus to Derrida and Deleuze, philosophers have grappled with issues of identity and difference and, though not settling on a *single* truth, have equipped humanity with a conceptual toolbox to categorise human experience.[2] Differentiation between concepts and their objects is as important in law as it is in other disciplines and is one of the fundamental instruments in the toolbox of legal scholars in their pursuit to understand the workings of law.

Considering this, the present chapter is a reflection in broad brushstrokes on the differences between three interconnected judicial operations: interpretation of customary rules, identification of customary rules and treaty interpretation. While identification of customary rules and treaty interpretation have been explored comprehensively, interpretation of customary rules is a recent addition to the thread of under-researched and complex topics in international law. Until recently hardly anybody throughout the existence of international law has ever asked

* The author expresses her gratitude to Professor Panos Merkouris, Professor André de Hoogh, Dr Noora Arajärvi, Dr Sotirios-Ioannis Lekkas and Mr Alexandros-Catalin Bakos for their valuable suggestions and comments offered during the different stages of writing. This chapter is based on research conducted in the context of the project 'The Rules of Interpretation of Customary International Law' ('TRICI-Law'). This project received funding from the European Research Council ('ERC') under the European Union's Horizon 2020 Research and Innovation Programme (Grant Agreement No. 759728).

[1] VW Cisney, 'Differential Ontology' (*Internet Encyclopedia of Philosophy*, 2013) <www.iep.utm.edu/diff-ont/> accessed 1 March 2021.

[2] ibid.

whether customary international law (CIL) could be or had been interpreted. Today, when the question has been asked, the community of international lawyers faces a difficult task. The difficulty of this task owes, firstly, to the lack of agreement among scholars on the meaning of the concept of interpretation, a notion which is used in legal scholarship with various meanings. Interpretation is perceived both in its hermeneutic dimension (as the determination of the meaning of and the intention behind an act/words/behaviour), but also as a wider concept including within it legal construction. Secondly, hardly any theoretical account of CIL can coherently explain what it is, how it emerges and how it develops, thus, occupying a sort of *sui generis* space among other sources. Thirdly, interpretation of customary rules seems to be difficult to distinguish, both in theory and in practice, from identification of customary rules and treaty interpretation, which owes largely to the first two reasons.

Interpretation of customary rules is not always appropriately distinguished from identification of customary rules because (1) customary rules are perceived as being equivalent to elements of custom (state practice and *opinio juris*) and (2) because, according to some scholars, there is an inherent element of interpretation in identification. This linguistic similarity, instead of leading to more clarity, contributes to a greater confusion between the two types of judicial acts.

The difference between interpretation of customary rules and treaty interpretation is another issue which is addressed in this chapter. Unlike the distinction between interpretation of customary rules and their identification, the potential confusion is not linked so much to terminology, as it is to practice. The fact that interpretation of customary rules and treaty interpretation are two different judicial acts (just like customary rules and treaty rules are two different sources of law) has been overlooked in some cases. Two examples are given where international judges engaged in an act of treaty interpretation to clarify the content of customary rules. This non-recognition of the distinction between the two may lead either to a misapplication of the law or to solutions which do not accurately reflect the content of customary rules.

The working definition adopted in this chapter of interpretation of customary rules is 'the act of determining/construing the content of customary rules the existence of which is unchallenged'. This definition is inspired from a preliminary analysis of the case law on the subject and on the definition of interpretation of customary rules in the meaning used by Merkouris and Orakhelashvili (see Section 1(b)). Both legal scholars conducted an inquiry into the case law of international courts and tribunals and observed that, firstly, judges do not only gather state practice and *opinio juris* in order to determine the content of customary rules and secondly, that judges use methods of treaty interpretation or similar methods to establish the substance of customary rules. The fact that judges themselves refer to this latter process as interpretation and given the similarity (and sometimes even identity) of the methods used with those employed in treaty interpretation these two scholars settled on the notion 'interpretation of customary rules' as the best description for this process.

This chapter encourages further scholarly reflection on the distinction, both in theory and in practice, between these different judicial acts. While all three make up a kind of unity (especially in legal practice) and as strings of a harp work together to build the content and further the evolution of the content of CIL, they remain distinct and should be, according to this author, recognised as such.

The chapter is structured along three main sections. Section 1 provides a contextual background by addressing the concept of interpretation and the arguments supporting the amenability of customary rules to interpretation. It is followed by Section 2, which examines the differences between interpretation of customary rules and their identification (in particular, interpretation in identification) and Section 3, which focuses on the distinction between interpretation of customary rules and treaty interpretation.

2 Interpretation of Customary Rules: The Concept

This section seeks to unravel the meaning of the concept of interpretation of customary rules, while at the same time demonstrating why interpretation of customary rules is not a contradiction in terms. The section starts off by describing the concept of interpretation of customary rules in legal scholarship (Section 2.1) and the arguments against the interpretability of customary rules (Section 2.2). It is followed by the argument concerning the reasons why customary rules are amenable to interpretation (Section 2.3) and the working definition of interpretation of customary rules (Section 2.4).

2.1 The Concept of Interpretation of Customary Rules in Legal Scholarship

Judging by reference to the hundreds of years of international law's existence, the concept of interpretation of customary rules is quite novel. Arguably the first legal scholar who discussed interpretation of

CIL was Charles de Visscher. In *Problemes d'Interpretation Judiciaire en Droit International Public* de Visscher examined two dimensions of interpretation with respect to custom: interpretation as part of the customary process of law creation and interpretation of customary rules proper.[3] As part of the development/formation of customary rules interpretation was perceived by de Visscher as a value judgement on the content of a customary rule made by a relevant agent subsequently to the observation of patterns of repeated state practice. These patterns of facts were to be evaluated in light of moral and social imperatives.[4] In contrast, interpretation of customary rules was seen as an act of judicial elaboration or, more precisely, the adaptation of general customary norms to particular situations[5] that marked the transition from the abstract norm to the concrete norm.[6] De Visscher believed that there are two types of customary rules: customs, the essential components of which make up a hard core and, thus, are rarely, if ever, subject to dispute, and customs in the case of which a dispute may arise around its nucleus, where a fringe of indeterminacy always remained.[7] The subject was taken over by Sur who, in line with the views expressed by de Visscher, advanced a tripartite classification of interpretation in relation to international custom: (1) interpretation that establishes the existence of a customary rule, (2) interpretation that establishes the content of a customary rule and (3) interpretation that establishes the scope of a customary rule.[8] For both scholars, interpretation was indispensable to all stages of the existence and development of custom. This position on the omnipresence of interpretation in the life of custom taken as a whole is

[3] C de Visscher, *Problemes d'Interpretation judiciaire en droit international public* (Pedone 1963) 221 et seq.

[4] ibid 221.

[5] ibid 235–36.

[6] ibid 236. On the difference between a general norm and a particular norm and an abstract versus a concrete norm see M Gaetano, 'Cours general de droit international public' (1956) 89 RDC 439, 475–76. He argues that norms are either general or particular depending on the subjects of the rule – if a subject is individualised then it is a particular rule, when the subject is general then the rule can apply to anyone (the subjects of law to whom it applies are not determined individually). The second subdivision is in abstract and concrete. The concrete rule is specific, whereas the abstract rule is capable of operating in relation to an unlimited number of factual situations. General rules are usually, according to Gaetano, abstract rules, whereas particular rules can be either abstract or concrete/specific; see also JP Jacqué, 'Acte et norme en droit international public' (1991) 227 RDC 387.

[7] ibid 236.

[8] S Sur, *L'interpretation en droit international public* (Librairie Générale de droit et de jurisprudence 1974) 190 ff. He reiterated his position in S Sur, 'La créativité du droit international cours général de droit international public' (2013) 363 RDC 18, 295–96.

shared today by contemporary scholars like Alland and Tassinis (see Section 2).[9]

Around the same time that Sur wrote on the subject of interpretation of customary law Bleckmann, a German legal scholar, published a paper on the identification and interpretation of CIL. According to Bleckmann, customary rules were to be determined by induction – the abstract legal principle being derived from practice – and applied to new factual situations by deduction, which could involve the interpretation of the abstract legal principle.[10] Considering this, customary rules, as abstract legal principles, were subject to grammatical, systemic and teleological interpretation.[11] In support of this position Capotorti, in his 1994 general course at the Hague Academy of International Law, stated that rules of interpretation enshrined in the Vienna Convention on the Law of Treaties (VCLT) which have a customary basis also regulate the interpretation of international custom and that of other sources of law.[12] More recently, somewhat similar was made by Merkouris and Orakhelashvili.[13] Both Merkouris and Orakhelashvili conducted an analysis into the case law of international courts and tribunals and have revealed a plethora of cases where judges either use the notion of interpretation with respect to customary rules, or without doing so, employ methods from treaty interpretation.[14] This led them to

[9] O Chasapis Tassinis, 'Customary International Law: Interpretation from Beginning to End' (2020) 31 EJIL 235; D Alland, 'L'interprétation du droit international public' (2013) 362 RDC 45, 85.

[10] A Bleckmann, 'Zur Feststellung und Auslegung von Völkergewohnheitsrecht' (1977) 37 ZaöRV 505.

[11] ibid 526.

[12] F Capotorti, 'Cours général de droit international public' (1994) 248 RDC 17, 121.

[13] P Merkouris, 'Interpreting the Customary Rules of Interpretation' (2017) 19 Int CL Rev 127, 134–7; P Merkouris, *Article 31(3)(c) VCLT and the Principle of Systemic Integration: Normative Shadows in Plato's Cave* (Brill 2015) 231–300; A Orakhelashvili, *The Interpretation of Acts and Rules in Public International Law* (Oxford University Press 2008) 496.

[14] Other examples include: *Obligations Concerning Negotiations Relating to Cessation of the Nuclear Arms Race and to Nuclear Disarmament (Marshall Islands v United Kingdom)* (Preliminary Objections) [2016] ICJ Rep 833, Dissenting Opinion of Judge Trindade [70]; *Questions Relating to the Obligation to Prosecute or Extradite (Belgium v Senegal)* (Merits) [2012] ICJ Rep 422, Declaration of Judge Donogue [21]; *Case Concerning Pulp Mills on the River Uruguay (Argentina v Uruguay)* (Merits) [2010] ICJ Rep 14 [216]; *'ARA Libertad' (Argentina v Ghana)* (Provisional Measures) [2012] ITLOS Rep 363, Joint Separate Opinion of Judges Wolrfum and Cot [7]; 'Interpretation' was also a term used during the preparation of the ILC Draft Conclusions on the identification of CIL. For instance, 'interpretation' was referred to by Mathias Forteau, who affirmed that the European Court of Human Rights has given 'a slightly different interpretation of the customary *law* applicable to immunity'. Besides reference to interpretation of customary

conclude that interpretation of CIL is not only possible, but actually happens in practice. Since judges used the term 'interpretation' with respect to the determination of the content of customary rules in a way that is different from inquiring into state practice and *opinio juris* and due to the obvious similarities with treaty interpretation, both scholars reached the conclusion that the process of content determination of previously established customary rules is none other than an interpretative act. Thus, the definition advanced by Orakhelashvili (probably induced from the plethora of practice) is that interpretation of customary rules refers to the clarification of 'the modes and details of applicability of customary rules to specific situations to which they are designed to apply due to their general scope'.[15]

law, some ILC members have referred to interpretation of customary *rules.* Marie G Jacobsson made a comment with respect to the practice of the European Union – 'if an international court found that the European Union's interpretation of *a rule* of customary international law in an area where it had exclusive competence accurately reflected customary international law, it would be difficult to maintain that the practice did not amount to State practice.' In addition, Mahmoud D Hmoud called for a clarification of the situations when acts of the state (especially decisions of national courts) are either samples of state practice (otherwise said, 'raw material' for the purposes of identification of CIL) or show the *interpretation* given by the state to a particular *rule* of CIL. Outside of any reference to the practice of international courts and tribunals, 'interpretation' was mentioned by the representative of Slovenia, Ernest Petric, who contended that 'unless codified, customary international law was unwritten law, and the consequences of that fact in terms of its identification and interpretation should also be considered'. His comment is important because it seems to imply that identification and interpretation are two different processes, since they are mentioned separately. Finally, Georg Nolte, when emphasising the interaction between CIL and the general principles of law, noted that 'it was thus conceivable for a customary *rule* to be *interpreted* in the light of a recognized general principle'. See ILC, 'Provisional Summary Record of the 3338th Meeting' (2 May 2017) UN Doc A/CN.4/SR.3338, 5; ILC, 'Summary Record of the 3150th Meeting' (26 July 2012) UN Doc A/CN.4/SR.3150, 154 [64]; ILC, 'Summary Record of the 3184th Meeting' (23 July 2013) UN Doc A/CN.4/SR.3184 [53]; ILC, 'Provisional Summary Record of the 3225th Meeting' (18 September 2014) UN Doc A/CN.4/SR.3225, 7; ILC, Summary Record of the 3183rd Meeting' (19 July 2013) UN Doc A/CN.4/SR.3183 92 [14], 93 [21]; see also ILC, 'Identification of Customary International Law: Comments and Observations received from Governments, Comments and Observations by the Kingdom of the Netherlands submitted on 23 January 2018' (14 February 2018) UN Doc A/CN.4/716 [5]; Advisory Committee on Issues of Public International Law, 'Advisory Report on the Identification of Customary International Law' (Advisory Report No 29, 2017) 4–5 <https://bit.ly/3Dx6tcX> accessed 1 March 2021.

15 Orakhelashvili (n 13) 496; Another important contribution concerning the topic was written by Staubach. See PG Staubach, *The Rule of Unwritten International Law: Customary Law, General Principles, and World Order* (Routledge 2018); see also D Hollis, 'Interpretation' in J d'Aspremont & S Singth, *Concepts for International Law: Contributions to Disciplinary Thought* (Edward Elgar 2019) 559–60.

2.2 Arguments against the Amenability of Customary Rules to Interpretation

Two main arguments have been forwarded against the amenability of CIL to interpretation.[16] Firstly, it has been argued that the identification of customary rules is the only operation which establishes its content and, thus, any form of clarification of a customary rule would require a new stage of identification and, secondly, that the object of interpretation can only be written law and, since customary rules are unwritten, they cannot be subject to interpretation.[17] These two arguments depend on (1) the understanding of what customary law is and (2) the definition given to interpretation. Essentially, a new cycle of identification is required each and every time only if international custom is equivalent to its constituent elements. Moreover, interpretation is only confined to written rules depending on the definition of interpretation one adopts.

2.3 Reasons in Favour of the Amenability of Customary Rules to Interpretation

2.3.1 Customary Rules Distinguished from Elements of Custom

To address the first argument against the interpretability of CIL, a distinction is made between customary rules and elements of custom.

According to Article 38(1)(b) of the Statute of the International Court of Justice (ICJ), CIL is one of the sources of law to be applied by the ICJ. In conformity with the provisions of this article, CIL is 'general practice accepted as law', which, according to the case law of the ICJ, is comprised of two elements: state practice and *opinio juris*.[18] Nonetheless, it is not its only meaning. Even a cursory glance at the discussions surrounding the

[16] M Herdegen, 'Interpretation in International Law' [2013] MPEPIL 723 [61]; T Treves, 'Customary International Law' [2006] MPEPIL 1393; Maarten Bos, *A Methodology of International Law* (North-Holland 1984) 108; R Bernhardt, 'Interpretation in International Law' in R Bernhardt & RL Bindschedler (eds), *Encyclopedia of Public International Law – Vol II* (North-Holland 1992) 1417.

[17] A Gourgourinis, 'The Distinction Between Interpretation and Application of Norms in International Adjudication' (2011) 2(1) JIDS 31, 36.

[18] North Sea Continental Shelf cases (Federal Republic of Germany v Denmark; Federal Republic of Germany v Netherlands) (Judgment) [1969] ICJ Rep 3 [77]; see also SS 'Lotus' (France v Turkey) (Judgment) [1927] PCIJ Series A 10, 28; Asylum Case (Colombia v Peru) (Counter-claims) [1950] ICJ Rep 266, 276–77; for an analysis of the evolution of the elements of custom see J D'Aspremont, 'The Four Lives of Customary International Law' (2019) 21 International Community Law Review 229.

conclusion of the Statute of the Permanent Court of International Justice reveals that 'custom' is also another name for the process of law development. In the words of the chairman of the Drafting Committee, '[custom] is a very natural and extremely reliable method of development, since it results entirely from the constant expression of the legal convictions and of the needs of the nations in their mutual intercourse'.[19] Thus, one should distinguish between custom as the process and custom as the product of this process.[20]

At the same time, custom is also the name for the legal norm derived from general practice accepted as law. This meaning of custom is important to emphasise as some legal scholars oppose the possibility of interpretation of customary rules by reducing custom to its constituent elements. For instance, Bos rejects the amenability of CIL to interpretation on the basis that the content of custom is determined simultaneously with its existence.[21] But this argument would only hold true if custom was identical to its elements. That this is not the case is evidenced, firstly, by the language employed by the International Law Commission (ILC) in its recent Draft Conclusions on the identification of CIL[22] and, secondly, confirmed by the opinions of established international legal scholars, theorists of law and by the ICJ itself (see Section 2).

In its conclusions on identification of international custom the ILC has implicitly supported the division between constituent elements of custom and customary rules when it defined CIL as 'unwritten law *deriving from* practice accepted as law'. This implies that customar (the rule itself) is not equivalent to state practice, as the act of

19 Advisory Committee of Jurists, *Procès Verbaux of the Meetings of the Advisory Committee of Jurists: 16 June–24 July 1920 with Annexes* (van Langenhuysen 1920) 322; M Byers, *Custom, Power and the Power of Rules* (Cambridge University Press 2009) 129 ff; H Kelsen, *General Theory of Law and State* (first published 1949, Transaction Publishers 2006) 34.

20 'Customary International Law is the product of an age-old and worldwide and highly efficient system of law-making in which the subjects of the law make the law unconsciously and in which the common interest of society is secreted silently and organically', P Allott, 'Interpretation: An Exact Art' in A Bianchi, D Peat & M Windsor (eds) *Interpretation in International Law* (Oxford University Press 2015) 373, 385. Of course whether CIL is indeed made unconsciously can be subject to debate, as it may contradict existence of the element of *opinio juris.*

21 Gourgourinis (n 17) 31; Bos (n 16).

22 ILC, 'Draft Conclusions on identification of customary international law, with commentaries' (30 April–1 June and 2 July–10 August 2018) UN Doc A/73/10, reproduced in [2018/II – Part Two] YBILC 123.

deriving means obtaining something from something else – if there is identity between two things, then one cannot derive something from itself; in other words, the act of deriving requires for two *different* things to be present. What follows logically is the lack of identity between the unwritten rule of customary law and its elements (state practice and *opinio juris*).

Turning to legal scholarship, influential scholars such as de Visscher and Sur, who (while considering interpretation omnipresent in the life cycle of CIL – a point we shall return to later in the chapter) explicitly talked about 'interpretation *de la regle*'.[23] In a similar vein, Kelsen, in his discussion of custom as a source of law made the observation that 'such is the nature of those particular facts which together constitute the existence of the "custom", '*creating the general rule*'.[24] Needless to say, judgments of international courts and tribunals frequently refer to 'customary *rules*',[25] thus confirming the distinction between customary norms and state practice with *opinio juris*.[26] This distinction between state practice and *opinio juris* as elements of custom and customary rules is aptly portrayed in this volume by Gorobets with the container versus content metaphor.[27] Slightly adapting the original metaphor, it is possible to argue that the elements of custom are the containers, whereas the customary norms are the content,[28] similarly to the distinction in treaty law between the treaty as *instrumentum* and the norms contained in the treaty.[29]

2.3.2 Interpretation in Public International Law as Applicative Construction

The second criticism against the amenability of CIL to interpretation rests implicitly on each author's understanding of the term 'interpretation'.

[23] De Visscher (n 3); Sur, *L'interpretation en droit international public* (n 8).

[24] Kelsen (n 19) 34.

[25] Indicatively *North Sea Continental Shelf* [60, 62, 74, 76]; *Jurisdictional Immunities of the State (Germany v Italy)* (Judgment) [2012] ICJ Rep 99 [52, 93].

[26] There may of course be other arguments supporting this distinction. For instance, if custom was treated in international law merely as patterns of behaviour accepted as law, they would have been applied by way of precedent and not in the capacity of self-standing rules.

[27] See Chapter 17 by Gorobets in this volume.

[28] Although I do not necessarily agree that it is the container that needs to be interpreted for the purposes of content, but rather the content itself.

[29] Jacqué (n 6) 38586.

Black's Law Dictionary defines interpretation as 'the process of determining what something, esp. the law or a legal document, means; the ascertainment of meaning to be given to words or other manifestations of intention'.[30] This definition is different from the ordinary meaning of interpretation/to interpret as 'the way in which someone explains or understands an event, information, someone's actions etc',[31] 'to explain or tell the meaning of' or 'to conceive in light of individual belief, judgment, or circumstance',[32] 'an explanation or opinion of what something is'.[33] While the general notion of interpretation is tied to meaning,[34] which can be the meaning of any object that is meaningful, legal interpretation necessarily requires (as per its definition) that the object is a law or a legal document (and the words contained in it) or, in any event, a manifestation of a (legal) intention (it is presumed that the dictionary referred not to just any intention but legal intention), as an intention to enter/create legal relations/to produce legal consequences. While philosophers still debate on the meaning of interpretation and the space that intention occupies in it,[35] for the purposes of this inquiry it suffices to say that legal dictionaries are reflections of a certain consensus within the epistemic community/interpretative community in the discipline. Therefore, in law interpretation is generally tied to some kind of manifestation of intention and is an act which unravels this intention.

Zooming into the discipline of public international law (PIL), the prototype of interpretation is interpretation of treaties, especially since the VCLT, which codified the rules of treaty interpretation. In an illuminating account of what interpretation is for the community of international lawyers, Kammerhofer noted that, as opposed to interpretation, strictly speaking, in PIL interpretation is the name for 'an applicative

30 BA Garner (ed), *Black's Law Dictionary* (9th ed, WEST 2009).

31 Longman Dictionary, 'Interpretation' <www.ldoceonline.com/dictionary/interpretation> (accessed 15 November 2020).

32 Merriam Webster Dictionary, 'Interpreting' <www.merriam-webster.com/dictionary/interpreting> (accessed 15 November 2020).

33 Cambridge Dictionary, 'Interpretation' <https://bit.ly/3F8jevF> accessed 15 November 2020.

34 Endicott distinguishes between three types of meaning: the meaning of the object, what the author means by the object (meaning that) and what the object means to the interpreter (meaning for). See TAO Endicott, 'Putting Interpretation in Its Place' (1994) 13 L& Phil 451, 454.

35 Endicott (n 34); A Marmor, 'Meaning and Interpretation' in K Ziegler (ed), *Interpretation and Legal Theory* (Bloomsbury 2005); see also the distinction between interpretative and non-interpretative doctrines in A Barak, *Purposive Interpretation in Law* (Princeton University Press 2005).

construction of the law's meaning',[36] which involves both the extraction of legal meaning, but also 'the concretisation of abstract general norms in individual instances'.[37] While in *some* domestic legal systems a distinction is made between interpretation, as clarification of semantic meaning of legal texts, and construction, as the judicial activity of determining a rule's scope of application and the resolution of gaps and contradictions,[38] this distinction was intentionally dismissed upon the drafting of the first Draft Convention on the law of treaties and, subsequently, of the VCLT.[39] Compared to the general legal definition offered by *Black's Law Dictionary*, the definition of interpretation contained in the VCLT (as an authoritative document on the matter) is considerably wider and goes beyond the mere determination of intention and, therefore, it is reasonable to assume that the meaning in which judges use 'interpretation' is also wider than the stricter meaning of interpretation in law more generally. Thus, interpretation of customary rules is not a contradiction in terms or a misconception even if the analysis performed for the purpose to determine a rule's content disregards intention and focuses on other reference points within the parameters of the

[36] J Kammerhofer, 'Taking the Rules of Interpretation Seriously, but Not Literally: A Theoretical Reconstruction of the Orthodox Dogma' (2017) 86 Nord J Intl L 125, 131.

[37] ibid. It should be noted here that interpretation is also closely linked to norms of conflict resolution. See ILC, 'Report of the Study Group, Fragmentation of International Law: Difficulties Arising from the Diversification and Expansion of International Law: Conclusions' (18 July 2006) UN Doc A/CN. 4/L.702 [26, 67, 83, 412].

[38] LB Solum, 'The Interpretation-Construction Distinction' (2010) 27 Const Comment 95, 95–98.

[39] The argument used by the Harvard Research Group (the soundness of which is open to debate) was that there was no difference in kind, but rather in degree between the two operations. Harvard Law School, 'Draft Convention on the Law of Treaties, With Commentary' (1935) 29 AJIL Supp 653, 939; see also T Yu, *Interpretation of Treaties* (Columbia University Press 1927) 40–43, fn 3. The drafters of the VCLT have maintained the inclusion of the notion of construction within the concept of interpretation. The term construction was only mentioned in the ILC reports by reference to priority in conflicting treaties 'the Commission recognized that there is always a preliminary question of construction of the two treaties in order to determine the extent of their incompatibility and the intentions of the parties with respect to the maintenance in force of the earlier treaty'. ILC, 'Documents of the Sixteenth Session Including the Report of the Commission to the General Assembly' (1964) UN Doc A/CN.4/SER.A/1964/ADD.1 reproduced in [1964/II] YBILC 35; On the reasons why the drafters of the VCLT opted for a holistic method for interpretation (which encompasses methods that do not fall under the narrow understanding of interpretation) see R Bachand, 'L'interprétation en droit international: une analyse par les contraintes' (2007) Société européenne de droit international <https://esil-sedi.eu/wp-content/uploads/2018/04/Bachand.pdf> accessed 1 March 2021.

language of our discipline. Similarly to treaties, customary rules can be interpreted in the sense of construing their content on the basis of considerations such as teleology, the interconnectedness of norms in the system of law etc. and, thus, interpretation of customary rules is not a contradiction in terms.

2.4 *Interpretation of Customary Rules: A Definition*

Considering the aforementioned, the working definition of interpretation of customary rules is 'the act of determining/construing the content of customary rules the existence of which is unchallenged'. This is the definition which, as previously demonstrated, makes sense from a theoretical standpoint, but also best describes the instances of judicial practice in which the content of customary rules is determined differently than by looking at state practice and *opinio juris*.

3 Interpretation of Customary Rules versus Identification of Customary Rules

Having in mind the definition given to interpretation of customary rules, this contribution now turns to discussing the differences between interpretation of customary rules and their identification.

According to Merkouris, CIL identification is both a process of law-ascertainment and a process of content determination.[40] By examining evidence of state practice and *opinio juris* it seeks to determine whether a customary rule exists and what its content is. Similar to identification, interpretation of CIL is also a process of content determination. However, it is a process of content determination that takes place only after the customary rule has been first identified. This relationship between the two processes can be seen as mirroring (to a certain degree) what happens in treaty law. Firstly, the judge finds the relevant applicable rule (which, strictly speaking, is an act of law-ascertainment), which already has a content embodied in the text, and only then the adjudicator can proceed to the interpretation of the rule.

It is quite common to refer to the judicial act which happens at the stage of identification of a customary rule as interpretation. The term is used in four situations: to describe the conglomerate of state practice and

[40] Merkouris, 'Interpreting the Customary Rules of Interpretation' (n 13) 134–37.

opinio juris,[41] to refer to the process of evaluating the mass of state practice and *opinio juris*,[42] to derive/infer the relevant customary rule from the mass of state practice[43] or to connote the analysis of a singular sample of state practice and the motivation behind it.

Firstly, unlike the somewhat ideal (and sterile) model which allegedly describes the process of identification of customary rules by way of spotting samples of state practice, identification of customary rules is argued to be rarely just about discretionary data collection and, more often than not, as involving some form of interpretation.[44]

Secondly, interpretation is deemed necessary in situations where there is inconsistent state practice and *opinio juris*.[45] Such a problem occurs when there are simultaneously examples of state practice supporting the fact that a customary rule has emerged and equally compelling examples of contrary behaviour on behalf of other states. An example given in this sense is the prohibition of torture.[46] On the one hand, some states do not engage in acts of torture, whereas, on the other hand, there are examples of states that torture individuals and do so without protest from third states. In such a case, the argument goes, there are two possible interpretations of state practice: (1) torture is permitted and (2) torture is prohibited,[47] and the decision should ultimately be made on the basis of considerations of morality as an implementation of the Rawlsian theory of reflective equilibrium.[48]

Thirdly, there is also some measure of interpretation at the stage of deriving norms from patterns of state practice as 'the same set of data can support indefinite series of statements as to what the content of the law is'.[49] This is connected to the previous use of 'interpretation' with the difference that in this case it is argued that interpretation is always present, even if there is no inconsistent practice as such. In this case,

[41] Chasapis Tassinis (n 9) 242–44.

[42] A Roberts, 'Traditional and Modern Approaches to Customary International Law: A Reconciliation' (2001) 95 AJIL 757; N Banteka, 'A Theory of Constructive Interpretation for Customary International Law Identification' (2018) 39(3) Mich J Intl L 301.

[43] Chasapis Tassinis (n 9) 241–42.

[44] ibid 242–44.

[45] Roberts (n 42) 781.

[46] ibid 781.

[47] Yet, it ignores the third possibility: that there is neither a prohibition, nor a permission to torture.

[48] Roberts (n 42) 781.

[49] Chasapis Tassinis (n 9) 242.

'interpretation' means 'formulations of logical propositions describing the norm that we might infer from such conduct'.[50]

Finally, 'interpretation' is used as a synonym for the process of assessing the motivation of a state behind a specific behaviour, such as allowing another state's warship to enter its port without authorisation.[51] Such an interpretative act then contributes to the understanding of whether *opinio juris*, understood as a collective agreement on a rule, as opposed to the singular motivation of each state, is present. Yet the analysis, as opposed to the first case, is made at the level of a singular specimen of practice, not at the level of the whole *mass* of state practice.

Qualitatively these types of 'interpretation' are different from interpretation of customary rules. Firstly, they are different by reference to their object as they concern the elements of custom, as opposed to the customary rule itself. Secondly, all of them are concerned with what is not yet law and, therefore, do not squarely fit into the notion of legal interpretation. For instance, interpretation in describing state practice and *opinio juris* is a form of perceptual evaluation,[52] and focuses on the cognitive dimension (understanding) as opposed to legal interpretation. What is labelled as interpretation in the case of inconsistent state practice is, although similar to legal interpretation (in the sense that it requires a judgment/decision to be made on alternative propositions), primarily a process of law-ascertainment and not an interpretation of a law the existence of which was previously acknowledged. Additionally, the act itself is more an exercise in judging than it is in interpretation, understood in its legal sense. The same can be said of 'interpretation' at the stage of deriving a customary norm from legal practice. Finally, the assessment of the motivation behind an instance of state practice, while similar to interpretation in the sense of an act concerned with deciphering legal intention, is, again, part of an exercise in law-ascertainment, as opposed to legal interpretation, because it is an interpretation of the meaning of facts and not of the meaning of existing law.

Even if these acts could be described as interpretative in nature by reference to the ordinary meaning of interpretation (which is also very general), it is still more beneficial to have them distinguished terminologically. Using interpretation at both stages may create confusion and already does, given the complex nature of CIL, which balances between

50 ibid.

51 M Koskenniemi, *From Apology to Utopia: The Structure of International Legal Argument* (Cambridge University Press 2005) 435.

52 J Searle, *The Construction of Social Reality* (Free Press 1995) 133–34.

fact and law. Since the VCLT already codifies (implicitly) an authoritative meaning of interpretation, using it with the same meaning with respect to rules of CIL will contribute to linguistic consistency within the discipline. In other words, since the meaning of interpretation, as derived from its use with respect to sources of international law other than CIL, is both interpretation understood strictly and construction, it is better to confine the notion of 'interpretation of CIL' to the posterior content determination of customary rules in a way that mirrors treaty interpretation and brings more unity to the system as a whole.

Another argument in favour of using the notion of interpretation only with respect to the content determination of customary rules (as opposed to the evaluation of state practice and *opinio juris*) is the difference in the aims of the two judicial acts. The initial content determination process seeks to find the customary rule itself and initially determine its content – to make the inductive generalisation out of a collection of state practice, which, even if requiring some kind of interpretative reasoning as method, does not undermine the fact that it is an exercise of law-ascertainment. The subsequent act of content determination is concerned not with law-ascertainment, but rather with construing the relevant norm in a way that contributes to the solution of a dispute. Thus, it is the position of this author that the different aims of the two judicial acts should be reflected in the name of these processes. This is best done by confining the notion of interpretation solely to the subsequent act of content determination.

4 Interpretation of Customary Rules versus Treaty Interpretation

Another difference worth reflecting upon is the one between interpretation of customary rules and treaty interpretation. Both Merkouris and Orakhelashvili noticed a similarity in the methods that different judges or different international courts used when determining the content of a rule past the identification stage.[53] For instance, judges have referenced the technique of interpretation by reference to ordinary meaning in *Hadzihasanović*.[54] Two legal issues were raised in this decision: (1) whether

[53] Compare (n 26).

[54] *Prosecutor v Hadzihasanović, Mehmed Alagic and Amir Kubura* (Decision on Interlocutory Appeal Challenging Jurisdiction in Relation to Command Responsibility) IT-01-47-AR72 (16 July 2003).

the principle of command responsibility applicable to international armed conflict is also applicable to non-international armed conflict and (2) whether a superior can be punished under the principle of command responsibility for acts committed by subordinates prior to the assumption of command. Having found no specific state practice and *opinio juris* on the principle of command responsibility for acts committed in *non-international* armed conflict, the tribunal argued that 'where a principle can be shown to have been so established [on the basis of state practice and *opinio juris*], it is not an objection to the application of the principle to a particular situation to say that the situation is new if it reasonably falls within the application of the principle'.[55] The interesting part was that in order to support this argument, the Appeals Chamber of the ICTY relied on the prohibitions contained in common Article 3 of the Geneva Conventions and reasoned that 'in the absence of anything to the contrary, it is the task of a court to interpret the underlying State practice and *opinio juris* . . . as bearing its *normal meaning* that military organization implies responsible command and that responsible command in turn implies command responsibility'.[56] Leaving aside the convoluted language and possible concerns regarding the strength of the court's argument, in order to make the argument concerning the meaning of a previously established customary rule, the court borrows the language of treaty interpretation and although it mentions state practice and opinio juris, it actually mentions the preexistent rule.

In the *Orić* case, where the *ratio decidendi* in *Hadzihasanović* was the object of contention,[57] Judge Schomburg, as one of the dissenting judges, argued that the customary principle of command responsibility must be interpreted by giving 'consideration to the *purpose* of a superior's obligation to effectively make his subordinates criminally accountable for breaches of the law of armed conflict'.[58] He then emphasised that 'considering thus the *purpose* of superior responsibility, it is arbitrary – and contrary to the *spirit* of international humanitarian law – to require for a superior's individual criminal responsibility that the subordinate's conduct took place only when he was placed under the superior's effective control'.[59]

In *Furundžija*[60] the court faced a question concerning the definition of rape and the forms of behaviour that fall under this offence (in particular,

[55] ibid [12].
[56] ibid [17].
[57] *Prosecutor v Naser Orić* (Appeals Chamber Judgment) IT-03–68-A (3 July 2008).
[58] ibid, Dissenting Opinion of Judge Schomburg [16] (emphasis added).
[59] ibid [17] (emphasis added).
[60] *Prosecutor v Anto Furundzija* (Judgment) IT-95–17/1-T (10 December 1998).

whether oral penetration can qualify as rape). The Trial Chamber, firstly, stated that the prohibition of rape in armed conflict has evolved into a norm of CIL,[61] yet found that international law (either treaty or custom) contains no definition of rape.[62] Then, it scrutinised national legislation and found major discrepancies between the criminal laws of various countries as to the definition of rape and whether oral penetration qualifies as rape or a different type of sexual assault.[63] Lastly, it resorted to the principle of respect for human dignity to interpret the crime of rape. The Trial Chamber noted 'it is consonant with this principle [principle of protection of human dignity] that such an extremely serious sexual outrage as forced oral penetration should be classified as rape'.[64] As the statement reveals, the Trial Chamber did not *apply* the principle of protection of human dignity to the case directly,[65] but it determined the definition of rape in consonance with this principle.[66] This example can be taken as a form of interpretation similar to systemic interpretation in treaty interpretation.

What runs like a red thread through these examples are the arguments typically resorted to for the purposes of treaty interpretation (it would not be far-fetched even to argue that judges apply the same interpretative techniques by analogy). Depending on the interpretative method used, some cases raise important questions concerning the relationship between interpretation of customary rules and treaty interpretation. For example, in the previously mentioned *Hadzihasanović* case one of the Appeal Chamber judges appended a dissenting opinion where he noted that 'any interpretation [of the customary rule] can be made by reference to the object and purpose of the provisions laying down the doctrine'.[67] By the same token, in the *North Sea Continental Shelf* case, in his dissenting opinion, Judge Sørensen observed:

> If the provisions of a given convention are recognized as generally accepted rules of law, this is likely to have an important bearing upon any problem of interpretation which may arise. In the absence of

[61] ibid [168].
[62] ibid [174].
[63] ibid [178–82].
[64] ibid [183] (emphasis added).
[65] On the differences between 'interpretation' and 'application' see Gourgourinis (n 17).
[66] For a different opinion see N Arajärvi, *The Changing Nature of Customary International Law: Methods of Interpreting the Concept of Custom in International Criminal Tribunals* (Routledge 2014).
[67] *Prosecutor v Hadzihasanović*, Dissenting Opinion Judge Shahabudeen [11]. Judge Shahabudeen refers to the provisions of Additional Protocol I to the Geneva Conventions.

> a convention of this nature, any question as to the exact scope and implications of a customary rule must be answered on the basis of a detailed analysis of the State practice out of which the customary rule has emerged. If, on the other hand, the provisions of the convention serve as evidence of generally accepted rules of law, it is legitimate, or even necessary, to have recourse to ordinary principles of treaty interpretation, including, if the circumstances so require, an examination of *travaux preparatoires.*[68]

In legal scholarship these and other similar examples have been frowned upon either as a failure to distinguish between treaty interpretation and identification of custom[69] or as a disregard for the fact that customary rules possess an independent rationale and should be assessed by reference to it, rather than by reference to a treaty's object and purpose.[70] The main point behind these criticisms is the need to keep interpretation (or identification) of customary rules separate from treaty interpretation. The danger is that using reference points related to the treaty counterpart of the customary rule may lead to a misapplication of the law — to the application of a treaty rule which is not clearly established as a customary rule or the usage of considerations which are related to the treaty, but not, as such, connected to the customary rule.

According to this author, the answer should be nuanced depending on the type of customary rule involved — a question which ties to the relationship between customary rules and treaty rules more generally. Generally speaking, the relationship between custom and treaties is a multifaceted one. On the one hand, treaties may codify, crystallise or lead to the creation of customary rules. On the other hand, treaties may be used to confirm the existence of a customary rule in the process of identification. According to the empirical study conducted by Choi and Gulati, treaties are the dominant form of evidence in the ascertainment of customary rules.[71] Not only the existence, but also the content of customary rules may be determined by reference to treaty provisions, which includes the situation when the content of a customary rule is determined posterior to the acknowledgement of its existence. Otherwise said,

[68] *North Sea Continental Shelf Cases*, Dissenting Opinion Judge Sørensen [13].

[69] See B Schlütter, *Developments in Customary International Law: Theory and the Practice of the International Court of Justice and the International Ad Hoc Criminal Tribunals for Rwanda and Yugoslavia* (Martinus Nijhoff 2010) 254–59.

[70] See Orakhelashvili (n 13).

[71] See SJ Choi and M Gulati, 'Customary International Law: How Do Courts Do It?' in CA Bradley (ed), *Custom's Future: International Law in a Changing World* (Cambridge University Press 2016) 117.

treaties can be an important reference point in the interpretation of customary rules. According to the ICJ itself, 'multilateral conventions may have an important role to play in recording and *defining* rules deriving from custom'.[72] In a similar vein to what Bleckmann (one of the forerunners of the concept of interpretation of customary rules) argued with respect to using state documents for the purposes of grammatical interpretation of custom, treaties can be used to define concepts contained in CIL, when their meaning is disputed. Moreover, just as customary rules have been used for the purposes of treaty interpretation under Article 31(3)(c), treaties (and general principles of law) can be used for interpreting customary rules as a form of systemic interpretation. For the purposes of interpretation of customary rules, judges may use both codification treaties which contain provisions with content similar to that of the customary rule or on the same subject matter, or, equally, treaties that are neither codifications of customary rules, nor belong to a different (albeit, possibly related) subject matter. A relevant example in this sense is Judge Guillaume's suggestion in the *Advisory Opinion on Nuclear Weapons* that rules of *jus ad bellum* may aid the clarification of the rules of the *jus in bello*. However, the problem arises at the level of argumentative reference points such as the ordinary meaning of terms, context, *travaux preparatoires*, intention of the parties or object and purpose and the answer as to whether each one of these reference points may be used for the purpose of a customary rule's content determination should depend on the type of customary rule involved. As rightfully pointed out by Judge Jennings in his Dissenting Opinion to the *Nicaragua* case:

> [t]o indulge the treaty interpretation process, in order to determine the content of a posited customary rule, must raise a suspicion that it is in reality the treaty itself that is being applied under another name. Of course this way of going about things may be justified where the treaty text was, from the beginning, designed to be a codification of custom; or where the treaty is itself the origin of a customary law rule.[73]

When a treaty is a codification of customary rules, either completely or preponderantly, it could be imagined that the judge heavily relies on the text of the treaty, since having a text as a reference point allows for a more

[72] *Case Concerning the Continental Shelf (Libyan Arab Jamahiriya v Malta)* (Judgment) [1985] ICJ Rep 13 [27].

[73] *Military and Paramilitary Activities in and Against Nicaragua (Nicaragua v United States)* (Merits) [1986] ICJ Rep 14, Dissenting Opinion of Judge Jennings, 532–33.

straightforward interpretation of a rule, which might be more acceptable to the subjects of law because of its predictability (achieved through the written/codified nature of the rule). However, ideally, this should only be permissible provided that there are no indications that the customary rule has evolved posterior to its codification.[74] In the case of crystallised rules or rules which passed into CIL from treaties the same considerations apply.

With regard to other reference points, such as context or *travaux preparatoires*, matters are slightly different. For instance, in the case of a customary rule codified in a treaty a contextual interpretation may use the context of the treaty if other rules are also a codification of CIL. It is more likely to admit an interpretation which uses the context of the treaty as a reference point in customary rules crystallised or which evolved into a rule of custom from a treaty, as the treaty serves as their springboard. Also, it is doubtful whether it is possible to use the context of the treaty (especially other provisions of the same treaty) when the customary rules (either codified, crystallised or evolved from a treaty) do not form an organic unity or unity of origin with the other provisions. Such a unity may be created by the fact that two norms belong to the same sub-branch of international law. A multilateral treaty which contains provisions from different fields of international law and which does not contain other customary rules except the one which is under scrutiny will be an unlikely candidate as a reference point for interpreting the customary rule in question. This is unless these other types of rules are used as a form of systemic interpretation justified by the fact that they are somehow related to the dispute and, thus, to the customary rule which is interpreted.

Travaux preparatoires may be used for the purposes of analysing the content of customary rules crystallised from or evolved from treaties as they may aid in determining the precise meaning and, thus, scope of a customary rule, again, unless there is evidence that the content of the customary rule has changed through time. As for object and purpose, the treaty's rationale can hardly be a valid reference point, unless the treaty as a whole is a codification and there is some kind of organic unity in its provisions. This is because the object and purpose of the treaty may be much wider than the subject matter to which the customary rule refers to. For instance, the object and purpose of a regional treaty between a handful of states which declares in the Preamble that its aim is the

[74] A D'Amato, 'Trashing Customary International Law' (1987) 81(1) AJIL 101, 103–05; BB Jia, 'The Relations between Treaties and Custom' (2010) 9 Chin J Int Law 81, 92.

maintenance of friendly relations between the parties can hardly be used as an interpretative reference point to interpret a customary rule on environmental protection (even if it has emerged from this treaty) as it does not aid in clarifying the content of this rule. In any event, automatic application of reference points from treaties to CIL is not advised and alertness should always be present when a treaty is used to aid the interpretation of customary rules.

5 Conclusion

This chapter was a reflection on the differences between, on the one hand, interpretation of customary rules and their identification, and interpretation of customary rules and treaty interpretation, on the other. Section 2 examined the concept of interpretation of customary rules by firstly distinguishing between elements of custom and customary rules proper and, secondly, by presenting the different meanings that the term interpretation may have. While the general definition of interpretation is 'understanding', the legal definition is limited to the determination of meaning of words or other manifestations of intention. Even more importantly, in PIL the term 'interpretation' is not limited to its hermeneutical dimension but can better be described as a form of applicative construction.

Section 3 examined the difference between interpretation of customary rules and their identification. Firstly, there is a difference in the object of the analysis and, secondly, there is a qualitative difference in the process, which, while possible to be regarded as 'interpretation' in its ordinary meaning, does not fall within the notion of 'legal interpretation'.

Section 4 discussed the differences between interpretation of customary rules and treaty interpretation. While the methods of interpretation may be similar, using reference points from treaty interpretation will not always be a sensible solution and judges should remain alert to the differences between the two sources of law.

Taking the points made in this chapter as a whole, the crux of the matter is that the processes that have been analysed are part of the same palette that judges use when giving a solution on a case. Nonetheless, these operations are in meaningful ways different from each other, just like different strings of the same harp, and it is important to remain alert to these differences, both in theory and in practice.

19

Customary International Law

Identification versus Interpretation

RICCARDO DI MARCO

1 Introduction

When dealing with a difficult issue such as the theory of interpretation,[1] the first obstacle to be faced concerns the nature of the object under examination: is interpretation relevant to a point of law or not?[2] Each doctrinal orientation would give a different answer. Some scholars consider that interpretation is an intellectual operation;[3] others define interpretation as a creative activity;[4] still others argue that interpretation is a linguistic issue, maybe even a methodological one, but, in any case, not a legal matter.[5] On the contrary, some scholars incorporate the study of interpretation into positive law:[6] by perceiving the legal

[1] A complete bibliography on legal interpretation is almost impossible to collect, since it has been studied extensively throughout time. Hence, only those which seem most useful to understand the current problems will be indicated below: E Betti, *Interpretazione della legge e degli atti giuridici* (Giuffrè 1949); S Pugliatti, *Conoscenza e diritto* (Giuffrè 1961); HLA Hart, *The Concept of Law* (Clarendon Press 1963); G Tarello, *Diritto, enunciati, usi: Studi di teoria e metateoria del diritto* (il Mulino 1974); N Bobbio, *Per un lessico di teoria generale del diritto* (CEDAM 1975); G Tarello, *L'interpretazione della legge* (Giuffrè 1980); E Betti, *Teoria generale dell'interpretazione* (Giuffrè 1990); H Kelsen, *On the Theory of Interpretation* (Cambridge University Press 1990); R Guastini, *Le fonti del diritto e l'interpretazione* (Giuffrè 1993); F Modugno, *Interpretazione giuridica* (CEDAM 2012).

[2] Interpretation is a human activity which goes well beyond the boundaries of law. Any human activity can be the object of interpretation, from music to language to paintings to dreams, from scientific theories to archaeological remains. A theory of legal interpretation should rest, therefore, on a general theory of interpretation.

[3] S Romano, *Frammenti di un dizionario giuridico* (Giuffrè 1947).

[4] 'The interpretation by the law-applying organ is always authentic. It creates law.' H Kelsen, *Pure Theory of Law* (University of California Press 1967) 354.

[5] See M Heidegger, *Being and Time* (Harper & Row ed 1962); HG Gadamer, *Truth and Method* (Bloomsbury Academic 2013).

[6] See N Bobbio, *Il positivismo giuridico* (Giappichelli Editore 1996).

character of the object, they act on the ground of the so-called rules of interpretation.[7] It is impossible to give an exhaustive picture of such a debate in only a few lines.[8] I will confine myself to note that international law writers consider the matter under a different light compared to scholars of other juridical systems. In fact, with respect to public international law, a clear position has already been taken: I refer to the Vienna Convention on the Law of Treaties (VCLT)[9] that, while codifying the law of treaties,[10] included certain *rules* of interpretation.[11] Even though sometimes slightly modified, these rules of interpretation have been constantly applied by international tribunals. Internationalists, usually hindered by the soft formalism of the international legal order, in this matter enjoy a privileged position.

To interpret a rule means to seek and understand its exact meaning, and, as a consequence, to clarify its scope, in order to be able to correctly apply it to the material case. In fact, since a rule is susceptible to different applications – because of its character of generality and abstractness – that content must be specified from time to time for the particular case. To determine the meaning of a rule, thus, the interpreter must accomplish a task of cognition (or recognition). This creative activity also raises practical issues: to which types of rules can interpretation be applied? Which theoretical-methodological tools should the interpreter use? With regard to customary rules, is it possible to separate the two distinct processes of identification and interpretation?

[7] R Quadri, *Diritto internazionale pubblico* (Priulla 1960).

[8] For a complete overview on this topic see N Bobbio, *Giusnaturalismo e positivismo giuridico* (Editori Laterza 2011).

[9] Vienna Convention on the Law of Treaties (adopted 23 May 1969, entered into force 27 January 1980) 1155 UNTS 331 (VCLT).

[10] See among others F Capotorti, *Il diritto dei trattati secondo la Convenzione di Vienna: studio introduttivo al volume Convenzione di Vienna sul diritto dei trattati* (CEDAM 1969); R Ago, 'Droit des traités à la lumière de la Convention de Vienne' (1971) 134 RdC 297; G Gaja, 'Trattati internazionali' in *Digesto delle Discipline Pubblicistiche*, Vol XV (UTET 1988) 344.

[11] On treaty interpretation, *ex multis*, see D Anzilotti, 'Efficacia ed interpretazione dei trattati' (1912) Rivista di diritto internazionale 520; H Lauterpacht, 'Les travaux préparatoires et l'interprétation des traités' (1934) 48 RdC 709; C De Visscher, 'Remarques sur l'interprétation dite textuelle des traites internationaux' (1959) 6 Nederlands Tijdschrift voor Internationaal Recht 383; V Degan, *L'interprétation des accords en droit international* (Martinus Nijhoff 1963); MK Yasseen, 'L'interprétation des traités d'après la convention de Vienne sur le droit des traités' (1976) 151 RdC 1; M Fitzmaurice, O Elias & P Merkouris (eds), *Treaty Interpretation and the Vienna Convention on the Law of the Treaties: 30 Years On* (Martinus Nijhoff 2010).

Bearing in mind the horizontal nature of the international legal system[12] as well as the important role played by customary rules in public international law, it is worth considering the following question: is it possible to apply to custom the international rules of interpretation (that, on their turn, are customary too)? In other words, is it possible to interpret customary international law (CIL) or can it only be identified? Hence, how can internationalists distinguish interpretation from identification with respect to customary rules? Has the International Court of Justice (ICJ or 'the Court') provided some methodological tools in this regard?

The recent codification promoted by the United Nations, in relation to the identification of customary rules,[13] has prompted the author to reflect about such questions.[14] At the end of its work, the International Law

[12] As far as the main subject of this chapter is concerned, it is worth mentioning that the role of interpretation is closely related to the legal system taken into consideration. The more homogeneous it is, consisting of harmonised rules, written and adapted to the system in its entirety, the more the role of the interpreter tends to be marginal. On the contrary, if these rules are few, poorly coordinated and moreover unwritten, the interpretative activity is of fundamental importance and covers a very wide scope. The international legal system undoubtedly falls into this second category. In this system, in fact, the interpretative function is not centralised: the power to interpret belongs to all subjects of the international community. This has inevitably led to a fragmentation of the methods of interpretation, which, although jointly established between the states, are optionally applicable and, thus, extremely uncertain.

[13] ILC, 'Report of the International Law Commission on the Work of its 70th Session' (30 April–1 June and 2 July–10 August 2018) UN Doc A/73/10.

[14] The doctrine on the subject under examination is very broad considering that every book of public international law dedicates at least one chapter to CIL. However, for an exhaustive overview of the relevant doctrine, the following should be consulted: H Kelsen, 'Théorie du droit international coutumier' (1939) 1 Revue internationale de la théorie du droit 253; N Bobbio, *La consuetudine come fatto normativo* (Giappichelli 1942); R Ago, *Scienza giuridica e diritto internazionale* (Giuffrè 1950); G Barile, *Diritto internazionale e diritto interno* (Giuffrè 1957); LM Bentivoglio, *La funzione interpretativa nell'ordinamento internazionale* (Giuffrè 1958); P Ziccardi 'Consuetudine (diritto internazionale)', *Enciclopedia del diritto IX* (1961) 476; N Bobbio, 'Consuetudine (teoria generale)' (1962) IX *Enciclopedia del diritto* 426; C de Visscher, *Problèmes d'interprétation judiciaire en droit international public* (Pedone 1963); G Tunkin, *Droit international public: problèmes théoriques* (Pedone 1965); N Bobbio, 'Fatto normativo' (1967) XVI *Enciclopedia del diritto* (1967) 988; G Morelli, 'A proposito di norme internazionali cogenti' (1968) 51 Rivista di diritto internazionale 108; RR Baxter, 'Treaties and Custom' (1970) 129 RdC 31; A D'Amato, *The Concept of Custom in International Law* (Cornell University Press 1971); RJ Dupuy, 'Coutume sage et coutume sauvage' in C Rousseau (ed), *Mélanges offerts à Charles Rousseau: la communauté internationale* (A Pedone 1974) 75; S Sur, *L'interprétation en droit international public* (LGDJ 1974); G Arangio-Ruiz, 'Consuetudine internazionale', *Enciclopedia Giuridica* VIII (1988); L Condorelli, 'Consuetudine internazionale' in *Digesto delle discipline pubblicistiche,*

Commission (ILC) reached highly practical draft conclusions.[15] Indeed, pointing out that the determination of the existence of a customary rule and of its content would be simultaneous processes,[16] the ILC seemed not to have independently dealt with the content-ascertainment issue of CIL, nor with the similarly interesting topic of its meaning-determination. Namely, whether a particular unwritten rule could be interpreted (even or exclusively?) after its identification. It is also worth noting that the relation between customary rules and rules of interpretation – the latter being usually considered relevant only for written rules – has been scarcely investigated in international legal literature.

In this chapter I shall draw a schematisation of the differences (many) and similarities (very few) between the processes of identification and interpretation of an international rule: in particular CIL.[17] By following

Vol III (UTET 1989) 490; R Kolb, *Interprétation et création du droit international* (Bruylant Editions 2006); G Arangio-Ruiz, 'Customary Law: A Few More Thoughts on the Theory of "Spontaneous International" Custom' in J Salmon (ed), *Droit du pouvoir, pouvoir du droit: mélanges offerts à Jean Salmon* (Bruylant 2007) 93; A Orakhelashvili, *The Interpretation of Acts and Rules in Public International Law* (Oxford University Press 2008); D Alland, 'L'interprétation du droit international public' (2014) 362 RdC 41; P Merkouris, *Article 31(3)(c) VCLT and the Principle of Systemic Integration: Normative Shadows in Plato's Cave* (Brill Nijhoff 2015); S Talmon, 'Determining Customary International Law: The ICJ's Methodology between Induction, Deduction and Assertion' (2015) 26(2) EJIL 417; A Gianelli, 'Consuetudine (diritto internazionale)', *Treccani* (2017) <https://bit.ly/3F1QjcG> accessed 18 December 2021.

15 Both the conclusions and the commentaries aim to offer practical guidance on how the existence (or non-existence) of rules of CIL is to be established. In the end, the ILC, while able to avoid some of the theoretical debates connected with the formation of CIL given its focus on identification, has recognised that in practice the formation and identification cannot be distinguished. See ILC, 'Summary Record of the 3151st Meeting' (27 July 2012) UN Doc A/CN.4/SR.3151, 168[52] (Nolte); ILC, 'Summary Record of the 3183rd Meeting' (19 July 2013) UN Doc A/CN.4/3183, 92[18] (Hmoud); ILC, 'Summary Record of the 3185th Meeting' (24 July 2013) UN Doc A/CN.4/3185, 103[14] (Singh).

16 Broadly speaking, the UN General Assembly has finally accepted that: 'To determine the existence and content of a rule of particular customary international law, it is necessary to ascertain whether there is a general practice among the States concerned that is accepted by them as law (*opinio juris*) among themselves.' See ILC, 'Draft Conclusions on the Identification of Customary International Law' (30 April–1 June and 2 July–10 August 2018) UN Doc A/73/10, reproduced in [2018/II – Part Two] YBILC 11, Conclusion 16 [65].

17 One caveat is in order. The following presentation is a synthesis. Within the confines of this chapter, it is not possible to deal with the very large topic of interpretation of CIL as a – logically and practically – distinct moment from its identification. My intention is to highlight the relevance of this subject and, for this reason, I would like to lay the foundations for solving (or, at least, try to solve) some questions I will illustrate. I will simply provide a summary of certain critiques that have been expressed with regard to the interpretability of CIL combined with some attempts to solve this debate.

a positivist approach – which reflects, at the same time, the reality of the social phenomenon to which international law refers and its historical evolution – I will try to take into account the close connection with the dynamics of international relations, proper to the relationship between the international community and the law which regulates it. This chapter will therefore aim to present international law as it results from the practice of international actors on the one hand and, on the other, as it is interpreted by international jurisdictions, in particular by the ICJ.

My argument is developed in two parts. After providing a plausible definition of interpretation in international law, I will investigate – by taking as main example the *Jurisdictional Immunities of the State* case – both legal and logical differences between the two distinct moments of identification and interpretation of a customary rule.

2 A Fundamental Preliminary Definition

The interpretation of international law in general[18] poses a multitude of challenges:[19] one of these is that its rules are often extremely indeterminate. In fact, sometimes they are unwritten,[20] like CIL. Unwritten rules present, especially in public international law, a peculiar issue of interpretation. There is no text and, despite this, they would appear to be constantly interpreted. In fact, the very fact that the customary rule is not written, makes this rule even more subject to a heterogenesis of meanings. It is therefore very difficult not to ask the fundamental question: is CIL subject to the interpretative rules of international law? And by consequence, in practice, are customary rules interpreted or are they only identified? It should also be noted that interpretation, being a ubiquitous and helpful activity for the intricate nature of the discipline of international law, can potentially produce conflicts between rules too. Yet even if it is taken as a ubiquitous activity, it does not mean that interpretation is a homogeneous and unitary phenomenon. According to the interpretative process, judges interpret the rule which they are

18 For a detailed analysis, see for instance: LM Bentivoglio, 'Interpretazione delle norme internazionali', *Enciclopedia del diritto XXII* (1972) 310; Bentivoglio (n 14); H Lauterpacht, *The Development of International Law by the International Court* (Stevens & Sons 1958); de Visscher (n 14); Sur (n 14); Kolb (n 14); Alland (n 14); Orakhelashvili (n 14); Merkouris (n 14).

19 See E Betti, *Problematica del diritto internazionale* (Giuffrè 1956).

20 See P Ziccardi, 'La consuetudine internazionale nella teoria delle fonti giuridiche' (1958) 10 Comunicazioni e studi 190.

empowered to apply, with a view to determining (or creating, according to a Kelsenian account[21]) the normative guideline for the case of which they are seized. This activity consists in an interpretation for meaning-determination purposes, which is surely not an activity reserved only to the judges. In fact, any professional dealing with international law will undertake this operation.[22] Nevertheless, it is within the context of adjudication that the interpretative activity is the most visible. Excluding those who in no way allow customary law to be interpreted, I now refer to those who argue that the interpretation of a custom is contextual to its identification. The main point to be made here is that our understanding of interpretation of a customary rule should not be limited to its identification process. This particular distinction between the content-ascertainment process and the scope-determination process of a customary rule is, in my opinion, essential to understand the concept and the practice of interpretation as well as the general concept of law. Mainstream studies of interpretation in international law look almost exclusively at the content-determination of a customary rule. However, what allows a rule to be applied involves an act of interpretation. When applying a custom, the judge, the practitioner, or the academic necessarily try to clarify the meaning of some pre-existing – thus, already identified – customary international rules.[23] Hence, to fully understand the distinction – in my

[21] See Kelsen (n 4).

[22] No authority in the international legal system has been able to legitimise itself as a monopolistic interpretative entity for international legal rules. Neither the establishment of a world court nor the Institut de Droit international, intended to mirror '*the legal conscience of the civilized world*', came to balance the lack of a supreme guardian of the interpretative activity in the community of international lawyers. Interpretative power in international law has accordingly persisted extremely scattered. Today, this activity is diffused between domestic and international courts, universal and regional codifying bodies as well as prominent and creative minds affiliated with prestigious research institutions, which clash with one another for authority and persuasiveness in the interpretative activity.

[23] See Kelsen (n 4): 'there also exists an interpretation of the norms created by international treaties or of the norms of general international law created by custom, if these norms are to be applied in a concrete case by a government or an international or national court or an administrative organ'; see also *Delimitation of the Maritime Boundary in the Gulf of Maine Area (Canada v USA)* (Judgment) [1984] ICJ Rep 246. That dispute did not concern the existence of the customary rule in question, on which both the parties involved and, above all, the whole international community '*agreed*', but rather a clearer determination ('*better formulation*') of its content. In addition, Judge Gros, in his dissenting opinion, maintained that the ICJ a few years earlier had proceeded to interpret general international law concerning the delimitation of the continental shelf, whose existence was not questioned, pursuant to the provisions of the draft convention provided by the Third United Nations Conference on the Law of the Sea. This, exclusively

opinion not only terminological – between identification and interpretation that I will try to outline in this chapter, it seems appropriate first to define what is meant by interpretation of a rule: ascertainment of content or determination of meaning? If the scholarly debate does not preliminarily agree on the definition to give to the interpretative activity, it seems useless to carry on.[24] This is precisely the point that deserves a preliminary, more careful reflection. If by interpretation we mean determination of content, it seems natural to affirm that the interpretative process of a customary rule is absorbed in its identification process and that, by consequence, it takes place at the same time as the ascertainment of its existence. If, on the contrary, we define interpretation as the operation by which the meaning of a legal provision is reconstructed, in order to understand its scope, it would seem logical to maintain that such activity is carried out at a different time from that of its identification. As a result, if the second definition of interpretation is accepted, it would appear that the answer to this question does not raise too many difficulties and that it is therefore possible to clearly distinguish between the activity of identification and that of interpretation.

3 Identification versus Interpretation

First of all, it is necessary to provide some tools in order to deal with the peculiar distinction between 'identification' and 'interpretation' of a rule in general, and, in particular, of a customary rule.[25] With respect to customary

in order to clarify the content of the customary rule taken into account: 'The Court had already, in February 1982, revised the 1969 Judgment so far as delimitation of the continental shelf was concerned, by interpreting customary law in accordance with the known provisions of the draft convention produced by the Third United Nations Conference'. *Delimitation of the Maritime Boundary in the Gulf of Maine Area*, Dissenting Opinion of Judge Gros 360, 365 [8]. Hence, by admitting that identification and interpretation of a customary rule are two distinguished operations and therefore not always contextual, once the existence of a customary rule is ascertained, the interpreter will be able to analyse its content.

24

> We all have a world of things inside ourselves and each one of us has his own private world. How can we understand each other if the words I use have the sense and the value that I expect them to have, but whoever is listening to me inevitably thinks that those same words have a different sense and value, because of the private world he has inside himself, too.

L Pirandello, *Six Characters in Search of an Author* (Mineola 2000).

25 According to some scholars, treaty interpretation and customary interpretation are two clearly distinct operations since they refer to two different sources of international law. See Judge Shahabuddeen who, in his dissenting opinion in the Advisory Opinion on the *Nuclear*

rules, in fact, the confusion between the two concepts is at the root of numerous misunderstandings and essential divergences. As far as treaty law is concerned, interpretation and identification are two, clearly separate, processes. Treaties are generally easy to identify and in most cases, once their identification is completed, it is possible to interpret their content with ease. Instead, when dealing with unwritten rules, specifically with customary rules, this distinction does not seem to be so evident. In this case, the analysis seems to concern two groups of elements: those relevant to the emersion process of the rule (state practice and *opinio juris*), on one side and the written and/or verbal formulations of the rule (generally retrospective, but sometimes programmatic or even concomitant) defined by a number of actors (judges, diplomatic chancelleries, scholars, etc.), that spare no efforts to express with words the customary rule, on the other.[26]

Both identification and interpretation processes have been the object of formalisation by international legal scholars. International lawyers have long attempted to balance the uncertainty of the meaning of rules through a definition of the techniques and methods of the interpretative process. The process of such formalisation has not followed the same path for interpretation and identification, the two concepts being substantially distinct. With regard to interpretation, scholars have tried to delineate its criteria, finding a compromise between intentional, purposive and textual methods. On the one hand, the VCLT can be seen as the epitome of this effort to delineate the techniques of interpretation.[27] On the other hand, as

Weapons case, stated that: 'the purpose of the Martens Clause was confined to supplying a humanitarian standard by which to interpret separately existing rules of conventional or CIL on the subject of the conduct of hostilities'. *Legality of the Threat or Use of Nuclear Weapons* (Advisory Opinion) [1996] ICJ Rep 375, Dissenting Opinion of Judge Shahabuddeen.

26 When the judges deal with a customary rule, they are naturally led to take into consideration and try to coordinate the different formulations (juridical, diplomatic, etc.) of such rule. At least this seems to be the process followed. Written formulations helped to clarify the meaning of certain customary rules and to consolidate it in the international system. The meaning of certain customary rules defined over the years – such as, for example, those establishing territorial sovereignty, freedom of the high seas, the relative effect of treaties or the immunities – has been subject to a perceptible interpretative work frequently accompanied by a harmonising effort of the '*auctoritas*' – doctrinal or jurisdictional – which expressed case-by-case the meaning of those customary rules.

27 The debate on the delineation of the most appropriate method of interpretation in international law can be traced back to Grotius, the upholder of the subjective method, which was later opposed by Vattel, proponent of the objective method. In H Grotius, *De iure belli ac pacis* (1625) Grotius entirely dedicated Chapter XV of Book II to public conventions and, starting from the Roman jurists, used Ulpian as the main source for his examination. One of the chapters of Vattel's *Droit des gens* which received much acclamation as well as many criticisms during the eighteenth and nineteenth centuries

to identification, recent works of the ILC on 'identification of customary international law' can be considered the embodiment of such an attempt to formalise the recognition methods of customary law. The suggested dichotomy implies a practical discrepancy between interpretation and identification,[28] each of these processes accomplishing a peculiar operation. The former seeks to explicate the meaning of rules with a view to establishing the standard of conduct, hence, the scope of the rule. The latter intends to determine how a given rule is a part of the international legal order. This means that interpretation is supposed to define meanings and standards of behaviour, while identification is meant to build a double architecture of ascertainment that differentiates law and non-law. Consequently, as far as both customary and treaty rules are concerned, while 'identification' seems to be an intellectual phenomenon, 'interpretation' appears a purely legal operation. More precisely, the first seems to consist in 'representing' a rule, the second in 'building it'[29] or, to put it in another way, to rebuild it on the basis of certain legal methods.[30]

is certainly the one dealing with the problem of treaty interpretation. Here, Vattel explained why legal doctrine should lay down general criteria for interpreting international rules. According to the Swiss jurist, the interpretative rules – recognised through natural law – are, in fact, those '*capables de répandre la lumière sur ce qui est obscur*'. It does not seem bizarre to try to find interpretative methods of customary rules in other generally recognised interpretative rules. One could, for example, apply rules of legal interpretation developed in Roman law (as internationalists did with respect to treaty law). Legal interpretation, indeed, still remains a logical operation. Notably, this operation is guided by logical rules as well as by very general criteria that can be deduced from the nature and the character of the legal system. Perhaps the internationalist doctrinal tradition can be helpful today, especially on this, still '*obscure*', matter.

28 Judge Morelli, in his dissenting opinion in the *North Sea Continental Shelf* case, affirmed the need to clarify (i.e., to interpret) the content of a customary rule even after its existence has been ascertained: 'Once the existence of a rule of general international law which confers certain rights over the continental shelf on various States considered individually is admitted, the necessity must be recognised for such a rule to determine the subject-matter of the rights it confers'. *North Sea Continental Shelf Cases (Federal Republic of Germany/Netherlands; Federal Republic of Germany/Denmark)* (Judgment) [1969] ICJ Rep 3, Dissenting Opinion of Judge Morelli 198.

29 This operation is usually accomplished with the aim of obtaining a certain form of understanding of the rule. See M Klatt, *Making the Law Explicit: The Normativity of Legal Argumentation* (Oxford University Press 2008).

30 As is well known, the three articles relating to the interpretation of treaties between states enshrined in the VCLT, have been subsequently reproduced as they stand in the Vienna Convention on the Law of Treaties between States and International Organizations or between International Organizations (adopted 21 March 1986, not yet in force) 25 ILM 543. It is usually believed that these principles of interpretation are of general application and that they can be used to interpret not only the treaties but also other sources of law, such as unilateral declarations, Security Council resolutions, or even contracts between

Nevertheless, it seems likewise appropriate to admit that both processes of interpretation and identification of a customary rule can share some comparable characteristics. Such similar features may justify the fact that – with respect to customary law – they are often confused one for the other. The difficulty in categorising them and, by consequence, in denying the possibility to interpret the *ius non scriptum*,[31] is also intensified by the fact that in practice, according to many authors, they may be performed at the same time.[32] Nonetheless, by accepting the abovementioned conceptual dissimilarities between the two operations, it seems difficult to argue that the process of identification of a rule is indistinguishable from the one of its interpretation, even in the case of an unwritten rule.[33] It is true that, in the case of a written rule, the determination of its content is clearer. That is evident. However, it is also true that although a written rule has (apparently) a clear content, this should be interpreted in the subsequent moment of the rule application. And the same operation, in my view, takes place with reference to customary rules too. These, in fact, once identified, have a (more or less) clear content. Afterwards, at the moment of the application to the

domestic entities and states (see *Eurotunnel, Channel Tunnel Group Limited and France-Manche S A v Secretary of Transport of the United Kingdom and Secretary of Transport of France* (Partial Award) (2007) PCA Case No 2003–06); therefore, it would seem natural to apply – *mutatis mutandis* – these general criteria of interpretation (which, in turn, are customary) to customary international rules: 'The method of logical and teleological interpretation can be applied in the case of customary law as in the case of written law.' *North Sea Continental Shelf cases*, Dissenting Opinion of Judge Tanaka 172; see also Kolb (n 14); Orakhelashvili (n 14); Merkouris (n 14).

31 See Quadri (n 7); Bentivoglio (n 14); Degan (n 11); T Treves 'Customary International Law' [2006] MPEPIL 1393.

32 According to some authors, the interpretative process of the custom is absorbed by the process of its identification. See in more detail: G Barile, *I principi fondamentali della comunità statale ed il coordinamento tra sistemi* (CEDAM 1969); R Monaco 'Interpretazione', *Enciclopedia Giuridica VIII* (1988); M Herdegen 'Interpretation in International Law' [2013] MPEPIL.

33 In more than one case, the ICJ explicitly mentioned the possibility to interpret a customary rule without having made any allusion to its identification process. With regard to state responsibility, for example, in the *Nicaragua* case, the ICJ declared that it was possible to distinguish treaty law and customary international law 'by reference to the methods of interpretation and application'. It is also worth noting that, in this landmark case, the Court had no difficulties to closely correlate the two moments of interpretation and application of a rule. In so doing, the Court seemed to acknowledge that, as stated in the present chapter, identification and interpretation seems not to happen simultaneously, in reverse of what can occur with respect to the interpretation and application processes. *Military and Paramilitary Activities in and against Nicaragua (Nicaragua v USA)* (Merits) [1986] ICJ Rep 14 [178].

particular case, this (the content) needs to be interpreted in order to exactly understand the scope of the rule. Consequently, to deny the possibility that such an operation is also applicable to customary rules would be detrimental to the correct and consistent application of the whole international law. This point of view intends, in fact, to assure the maintenance of a reasonable (logical and juridical) flexibility in the application of rules in general. Hence, in the application of customary rules too.

In order to better understand my perspective, I will refer to the 'dynamic' of customary rules. Such a 'dynamic' is obviously tied to the existence of the rule (formation and identification), but it can also involve the interpretation of the same (i.e., meaning and scope determination aimed at the rule application). In my opinion, those two 'dynamics' operate in a totally independent way to one another. In fact, they refer to two distinct operations: one thing is to investigate the dynamic of the existence of a customary rule (identification), and another is to analyse – once dealing with an already consolidated customary rule – the dynamic of its application, hence, its scope (interpretation).[34] Although in legal literature it is widely considered that the only logical path to follow is: first, identification (thus, the simultaneous interpretation); second, application of a customary rule, from my point of view, it would seem difficult

[34] Indeed, since customary law produces rules not formulated in a text, it often happens that the evidence of the two constitutive elements of a customary rule is theoretically and logically confused with the interpretation of a customary rule properly understood (unwritten). Nonetheless, it appears logical to distinguish these two operations too, since they refer to two distinct objects and to two distinct stages towards the application of a customary rule. Hence, bearing in mind the before-mentioned 'dynamic', customary rules interpretation should be also clearly distinguished from the process aimed at proving both its existence and content, through an examination of practice and *opinio juris*. While the 'examination' moment of practice and *opinio juris* can also take place when a customary rule is not yet born – and it exclusively refers to the two constitutive elements of a customary rule, not to the rule itself – the interpretative moment of a customary rule can only take place once its identification process (ascertainment of existence and content) has been completed. By consequence, once a customary rule has been identified, the clarification of its meaning will be a matter of interpretation. In this sense, the interpretative activity of CIL can be possible only with regard to an existing customary rule. More accurately and in short, the interpretative moment of a customary rule should be clearly distinguished from the evaluation moment of practice and *opinio juris*. Thus, it seems logical to argue that a customary rule, as distinct from each of its two constitutive elements, can be expressed verbally as well as in a written way. Therefore, since all customary rules are verbally expressible and since any verbal concept can be interpreted, customary rules should also be interpretable. However, this argument, although abstractly logical, needs to be practically proved.

to deny that identification and interpretation take place in two distinct moment of the 'dynamics' of a customary rule. As a result, after the customary rule formation, by means of both a consistent and general international practice by states and a subjective acceptance of the practice as binding by the international community, once the rule is identified (i.e., its existence and its content are ascertained) – through an evaluation of its two constitutive elements – this can be applied to a particular case only after a preliminary interpretative operation. An important premise must be made to fully understand this point of view: by interpreting a customary rule I explicitly refer to an already identified rule, properly understood (i.e., unwritten) and not to its constitutive elements, nor to its written reformulation.

Its existence being totally uncontested, I will take as a main example the customary rule of state immunity in order to investigate whether and to what extent this distinction occurred in practice by exploring the thin border between rule modification (related to the dynamic of its existence) and rule interpretation (related to the dynamic of its application). The practical relevance of this matter has been particularly evident with regard to the *Jurisdictional Immunities of the State* case.[35] The object of the litigation dealt with '*the scope and extent*' of the customary rule, whose existence was recognised by Italy as well as by Germany, regarding foreign states' immunity from civil jurisdiction. Indeed, both parties admitted 'that States are generally entitled to immunity in respect of *acta jure imperii*',[36] but they disagreed on the scope of such a norm. Italy invoked the application of the so-called tort exception – that is, the absence of immunity in case of actions having caused death, personal injury or damages in the territory of the host state – also in relation to *acta jure imperii*. On the contrary, Germany – by giving a different interpretation of such rule, that is, by considering that this particular case did not fall within the rule's scope – denied the application of such an exception of the customary international rule. The ICJ itself stated that the parties' agreement on the existence and/or the content of a rule would not, after establishing the existence of this international custom (i.e., identifying it), exempt it from making its own evaluation on the scope and extension of state immunity (i.e., to make its own interpretation).[37] Hence,

[35] *Jurisdictional Immunities of the State (Germany v Italy: Greece intervening)* (Judgment) [2012] ICJ Rep 99.

[36] ibid [61].

[37] ibid [55]: 'the Court must determine, in accordance with Article 38 (1) (b) of its Statute, the existence of "international custom as evidence of a general practice accepted as law" conferring immunity on States and, if so, what is the scope and extent of that immunity'.

in order to decide this case, did the court interpret or identify the customary rule under consideration? More generally, when a judge deals with a modification of a customary rule, does he identify the rule or does he interpret it? Both stances could be convincingly supported.[38] Nevertheless, in the *Jurisdictional Immunities of the State* case, by ruling upon the so-called tort exception, the ICJ seemed to confine its assignment to the identification of the existence of an exception from the general rule and, thus, stated the inexistence of such exception. However, the Court could have operated in a different manner. In fact, as asserted in the judgment, the ICJ task could also have been understood as an interpretation of the customary rule under consideration.[39] Without searching for the two constitutive elements of the customary rule on state immunity, aimed at confirming or not the existence of the tort exception, the ICJ could have interpreted the customary rule on state immunity – already identified and uncontested by the parties – in order to establish the scope of the same: that is, whether and to what extent it could have been applied to this specific case. As mentioned above, since examining state practice and *opinio juris* reveals the existence and the content of the rule and does not explain whether this rule is applicable or not to the particular case, in order to apply a rule to a specific case, it seems crucial to investigate the scope and the extent of the same (to interpret it), and not anymore its existence (to identify it).[40] In fact, any operation by which a rule is applied requires a prior interpretative activity. The application to a particular case of a general and abstract rule, logically implies the determination of its meaning too. Without such operation, it would not be even possible to understand all the legal consequences resulting in that particular case. In other words, the problem of legal

[38] On the difficulty to discern these two performable logical operations by the ICJ see Gianelli (n 14).

[39] In its jurisprudence, the Court itself stated very clearly that interpreting customary rules is one of its tasks. 'The Court is of the opinion that, for the purpose of interpreting the general rule of international law concerning diplomatic protection, which is its task, it has no need to determine the meaning of the term interests in the conventional rules, in other words to determine whether by this term the conventional rules refer to rights rather than simple interests'. *Barcelona Traction, Light and Power Company, Limited (Belgium v Spain)* (Judgment) [1970] ICJ Rep 3 [54]. Furthermore, even after an international case law short examination, it is possible to observe the ICJ interpretative activity with respect to various areas of CIL, namely: law of the sea, state responsibility, international humanitarian law, diplomatic protection, state immunity, etc.; see *North Sea Continental Shelf*; *Military and Paramilitary Activities in and against Nicaragua*; *Nuclear Weapons Advisory Opinion*; *Barcelona Traction*; *Jurisdictional Immunities of the State.*

[40] Indeed, the main task of the judge is to investigate the legal meaning of the applicable rule and the scope of its application.

interpretation cannot be circumvented since it is always indispensable (and propaedeutic) for the rule application. Therefore, by taking the *Jurisdictional Immunities of the State* case as main example, my purpose is to highlight how in practice identification and interpretation processes can both be easily performable and, by consequence, often confused. This case is particularly relevant for my argument since here it is evident how thin the line between the two operations can be, one related to the 'dynamic' of a rule existence, and the other related to the 'dynamic' of a rule application.

The logical correlation between the two moments of interpretation and application, with respect to customary rules too, can also be grasped by observing the conduct of the actors obliged to comply with the customary rule provision: the states. The customary rule, already identified, conditions their behaviour through an intellectual operation (interpretation) intended to clarify the correct meaning in the specific case. This means that customary rules would require the state whether it is or not in the situation (the particular case) provided for by the rule itself.[41] This intellectual operation – aimed at verifying whether in a particular case the conditions provided by the customary rule are satisfied – can, indeed, determine state observance of customary provisions. It can also lead to a conflict of evaluations between two or more states,[42] to a rule infringement,[43] possibly also to an impartial, third-party evaluation.[44] The spontaneous observance, the impartial evaluation as well as the enforcement of a customary rule, all belong to the application of CIL. The practical implication is the safeguard of a reasonable flexibility in the process of customary rule application. In fact, excluding any interpretative activity with reference to custom would

41 In fact, it would seem that the states belonging to the international community are constantly interpreting customary international rules in order to act (or, at least, try to act) according to their provisions.

42 Take the case where two or more states offer a different interpretation of a customary rule. Besides the above-mentioned case on state immunity, in practice there has been a distorted interpretation of the rule of *uti possidetis* too. In the *Land, Island and Maritime Frontier Dispute* case, both El Salvador and Honduras recognised the existence and the applicability of the customary rule of *uti possidetis* to their border dispute; however, at the same time, they both contested the scope of this custom, due to their behavior. See *Land, Island and Maritime Frontier Dispute (El Salvador/Honduras: Nicaragua intervening)* (Judgment) [1992] ICJ Rep 351.

43 That is, every case in which a state breaches a customary rule.

44 This is the case where two or more states resort to an international jurisdiction to determine the exact meaning of a customary rule. See the *Barcelona Traction* case where the ICJ, by rejecting Belgium's claim based on its interpretation of diplomatic protection – and after including the interpretation of general international rules among its tasks – seems to have applied to that particular case a different interpretation of that customary rule.

artificially restrict the interpreter's necessary task.[45] Hence, in the application of a well-established custom, the legal operator must take into account the content of the rule in order to understand its meaning (interpretation).[46] This, of course, without affecting its content (established at the time of identification) by modifying it.

At the end of this short analysis, it should also be emphasised that this practical and theoretical distinction raises the question of the admissibility of analogy[47] or restrictive[48] interpretation of customary rules too. Indeed, one should not wonder what and how the international community

[45] One example of the practical relevance of this matter can be found when the interpreter is bound to apply a customary rule to a situation which has no precedents. See L Gradoni, 'Consuetudine internazionale e caso inconsueto' (2012) 95(3) Rivista di diritto internazionale 704.

[46] As a consequence, once the existence of a customary rule is not called into question, the interpreter, in order to clarify its meaning, should only investigate the content of this rule and not its constitutive elements. This is what Judge Morelli argued in his dissenting opinion in the *North Sea Continental Shelf* case. Moreover, in applying the already existing rule, the Court has frequently proceeded to the determination, more or less exact, of its meaning. An evidence of this eventuality can be found in the ICJ Advisory Opinion in the *Chagos* case. The ICJ, after maintaining that the General Assembly confirmed on several occasions the existence of the customary rule on self-determination, stated that only after UNGA Res 1514(XV) 'Declaration on the Granting of Independence to Colonial Countries and Peoples' (14 December 1960) UN Doc A/RES/1514(XV) 'the content and scope of the right to self-determination' was clarified: namely the customary rule to self-determination was interpreted. The ICJ seemed also to distinguish the moment of birth of the customary rule concerning the right to self-determination from the moment of clarification of its content. By ascertaining the customary character of the right to self-determination, the Court referred to UNGA Res 1514(XV), not only to interpret this customary rule, but also as evidence of an already existing custom in question. This means that, according to the Court, a customary rule can also be interpreted after its formation/identification process. See *Legal Consequences of the Separation of the Chagos Archipelago from Mauritius in 1965* (Advisory Opinion) [2019] ICJ Rep 95 [150].

[47] Customary rules are applicable through an analogical interpretation. As known, analogy is a form of extensive interpretation, which consists in applying a rule to a case which it does not provide for, but whose essential characteristics are similar to those of the particular case. In the area of CIL, the use of analogy makes sense only with respect to new cases. Consider both the application of maritime navigation customary rules to air navigation and the application of air navigation rules to cosmic navigation.

[48] As far as a particular (or regional) custom is concerned, for example in the *Asylum* case, the ICJ apparently operated a restrictive interpretation of the so-called American customary international law on political asylum. In this judgment, the Court sought to balance the claim of sovereignty of Colombia versus the right of political asylum of a Peruvian political leader. The Court resolved the question by giving greater weight to the claim of sovereignty, as embodied in the prohibition of intervention. For that reason, according to Sir Hersch Lauterpacht : 'the Judgment provides an example of a restrictive interpretation of an alleged particular, or regional, custom by reference to what the Court

members would have decided in a specific matter by going to investigate the constitutive elements of a customary rule, such as state judgments, domestic laws or diplomatic notes. In the search for the meaning of the prescription of the customary rule, it would not seem to be relevant, nor it would seem to lead to any reliable result in the interpretation of the rule itself. On the contrary, this is an evaluation on whether the content of the customary rule (established through the identification process) can be applied to the new particular case too, for example, through its analogy with the hypotheses regulated by the customary rules in question. This will widen, narrow down or otherwise correct the scope of the rule already formed for the generality of the affiliates.

4 Concluding Observations

To differentiate the two operations of identification and interpretation is essential to correctly determine the scope of a rule. This is true for a written rule and, in my view, is even more true for an unwritten rule. For a written rule it can be considered that, exactly because it is written, it is relatively simple to separate its content-ascertainment moment from that of its meaning and scope-determination. By contrast, for an unwritten rule – and in particular, for a customary rule – this may not be evident. As is well known, in a legal system as little organised as the international one, given the importance of customary rules as well as the lack of specific bodies for the formation and manifestation of collective will – and therefore for the formation and manifestation of law – the need to distinguish these two operations seems even more important.

Hence, this distinction is evident for both categories of rules (treaty and customary), being, even if at times confusing, two operations logically and chronologically clearly divergent. As I tried to highlight with respect to the *Jurisdictional Immunities of the State* case, the interpretative activity takes place at a time subsequent to that of the identification of the content. That is, when the rule is applied to the particular case. In fact, for customary rules, as well as for treaty rules, the search for the scope is an indispensable operation, accomplished after the identification and preliminary to that of the application of the rule to the particular case. In other words, it is the application of the rule to a particular case that, indeed, forces the legal practitioner to interpret its content. The

considered to be general principles of international law'. H Lauterpacht, *The Development of International Law by the International Court* (Stevens & Sons 1958) 382.

interpretative activity, thus understood, is therefore inherent to the moment of the rule application to the particular case. If this were not the case, there would never be a problem of interpretation, neither with regard to treaty rules nor with regard to customary rules. This would be the same as arguing that any content of a law is so clear and so specific that it is able to precisely reproduce every case that will occur in the future.[49] A rule will never be so clear as to be directly applied to a particular case without further logical steps. Furthermore, to support the assimilation of the interpretative process of a customary rule to its identifying process would lead to the paradoxical scenario in which a customary rule would require to be identified each and every time it needs to be applied.[50] This begs the question of whether a customary rule can be interpreted.[51] Consequently, according to such an approach, whenever a dispute concerning a customary rule is brought before a judge, he should constantly – by making reference to both state practice and *opinio juris* – take into account the existence, development and manifestation of customary rules. According to such a perspective, a judge should identify the customary rule each time he applies it to the particular case. In a similar conception there would exist an infinity of customary rules, all different from each other but each of them extremely specific and very particular, being applicable to only one specific case: the one in which it was identified. This would defeat the very function of having a rule and it would no longer be useful to have a system composed of general and abstract rules. It seems extremely difficult to argue that a previously established customary rule could be applied to new cases falling within its scope, regardless of the general principles of interpretation. Such a theoretical approach would seem to conform to the logical requirements of the whole dynamic of customary rule.

However, several doubts remain. For example, how did the international actors deal with the issue of the interpretation of CIL? Has it been differently addressed in the various cases? According to the ICJ, what would it mean to interpret a customary rule? Has the Court

[49] Clearly no rule, nor state practice or *opinio juris* will ever be so specific as to provide concrete solutions to the application of a customary rule in any imaginable particular situation. No rules (although written) have such degree of specificity.

[50] See P Merkouris, 'Interpreting the Customary Rules on Interpretation' (2017) 19 IntCLRev 126.

[51] In logic, begging the question defines the sophism that occurs when an argument's premises assume the truth of the conclusion, in lieu of supporting it. It recalls both the Aristotelian αἰτεῖσθαι τὸ ἐν ἀρχῇ and the Latin expression *petitio principi*.

provided the theoretical-methodological tools needed to interpret a customary rule? And to distinguish the two logical operations of interpretation and identification? What are the principles established in this regard by the ICJ? As pointed out before, in the *Jurisdictional Immunities of the State* case the Court could have interpreted the customary rule on state immunity? Or it could exclusively have identified it? Both stances could be convincingly supported. Further study and analysis of the topic might try to answer some of these questions.

20

'And in the Darkness Bind Them'

Hand-Waving, Bootstrapping, and the Interpretation of Customary International Law after *Chagos*[*]

JOHN R. MORSS AND EMILY FORBES

1 Introduction

The essential role of interpretation in relation to national statutes has, especially in common law jurisdictions, given rise to a complex apparatus of guidelines, axioms and indeed further statutes ('Interpretation Acts'). Somewhat by analogy or by extension, the interpretation of international conventions (treaties) has long been recognised as itself both complex and immanent to the process of application of treaties, not least when the effect of a treaty is in dispute. It is true that despite well over a century of international jurisprudence on the interpretation of treaties, including the development of the Vienna Convention on the Law of Treaties (VCLT) itself, complexities and unresolved difficulties remain in that sphere.[1] However the processes of disciplined interpretation of written statements of law, whether municipal (national) or international, and the problems that arise therefrom, are at least familiar.

The role of interpretation in the second of the sources of public international law – 'international custom, as evidence of a general practice accepted as law' – is much less familiar. Scholarship in this area is just beginning.[2] It has been proposed that interpretation in this

* Thanks are due to Helmut Aust, Gleider Hernández, Jörg Kammerhofer, Panos Merkouris, Marko Milanovic and Sundhya Pahuja.

1 P Merkouris, 'Treaty Interpretation and Its Rules: Of Motion through Time, "Time-Will" and "Time-Bubbles"' in M Fitzmaurice and P Merkouris (eds), *Treaties in Motion* (Cambridge University Press 2020) 121; J Crawford, *Brownlie's Principles of Public International Law* (9th ed, Oxford University Press 2019) 369.

2 Merkouris (n 1); See Chapter 22 by Ryngaert in this volume; P Staubach, 'The Interpretation of Unwritten International Law by Domestic Judges' in HP Aust and

context is of most significance in the application of customary international law (CIL) to new situations, rather than in its initial discernment as such. Without disputing the relative importance of interpretation in the application of CIL, vis-à-vis interpretation in other aspects of the technique of CIL, it may still prove of value to widen the scope of enquiry in that respect. There is thus room for the view that interpretation is intrinsic to the definition, articulation and implementation of CIL just as it is for the law of treaties, for 'general principles', for teachings of the publicists or for previous decisions of international tribunals; and indeed for considerations *ex aequo et bono*.[3] Interpretation may of course be applicable in somewhat different ways to these various genres of 'source' (by which term they are collectively and colloquially known) in international law.[4] Put this way, interpretation is ubiquitous; and while this is itself significant, care must also be taken to distinguish modes or genres of interpretation. To draw attention to a role for interpretation in relation to CIL is thus only a very preliminary step, as is of course recognised by scholars.[5]

In this chapter we argue that some of the most important aspects of the role of interpretation in the context of CIL can be expressed in the following way: namely to claim at least for the sake of argument that the most characteristic phrase concerning CIL in the discourse of public international law is the phrase '*this may represent customary international law*'.

G Nolte (eds), *The Interpretation of International Law by Domestic Courts: Uniformity, Diversity, Convergence* (Oxford University Press 2016) 113.

3 Every genre of international law recognised by the Statute of the International Court of Justice is by definition distinct in its *modus operandi*. Thus the *ex aequo et bono* of Article 38(2) works in a very different way from sources indicated in Article 38(1); and publicists' contributions work very differently from judicial decisions, both of which are located within Article 38(1)(d). *Ex aequo et bono* may in any event be considered to lie outside sources proper; Crawford (n 1) 41.

4 Ryngaert (n 2).

5 Merkouris (n 1). It is self-evident that any reference to 'principles' or 'doctrines' in relation to CIL, immediately raises questions of the role of interpretation whether the reference is to an aspect of the customary form or to 'the doctrine of CIL' as a whole. Respectively, KJ Heller, 'Specially-Affected States and the Formation of Custom' (2018) 112 AJIL 191; BS Chimni, 'Customary International Law: A Third World Perspective' (2018) 112 AJIL 1, 43; some 'doctrines' that may hint at international customary status, perhaps of a regional nature ('regional understandings'), find their way into treaties. Thus the reference to a version of the Monroe Doctrine in Article 21 of the Covenant of the League of Nations: JP Scarfi, 'Denaturalizing the Monroe Doctrine: The Rise of Latin American Legal Anti-Imperialism in the Face of the Modern US and Hemispheric Redefinition of the Monroe Doctrine' (2020) LJIL 541, 551.

It is the word 'may' on which we lay emphasis. This hypothetical or tentative assertion of the existence and validity of a particular CIL, is intrinsically interpretive. What we will argue is that this hypothetical or tentative gesture, thought of as a species of interpretation, takes us to the heart of CIL. In other words, what is central to any statement about CIL is the attribution of the possibility of customary justification for some conduct or prohibition, irrespective of whether this has ever been or will ever be, tested.[6] Despite the gravity of the rights and obligations connected with the norm thus speculated upon, there is a certain archness to the trope. The kind of uncertainty thereby conjured is a kind of uncertainty quite different to what one finds with other genres of source. A wished-for consensus of the most qualified publicists or of judicial decisions, on a particular point, might expose uncertainty of a somewhat humble variety and one that is in essence empirical. A survey of relevantly common municipal regulation, entered into in the spirit of the *Barcelona Traction* dispute, would be uncertain in somewhat the same manner, as of research. To refer in an open-ended manner to the possibility of there existing a presently unknown, written agreement between sovereigns would seem absurdly speculative yet this is only the case because treaty making has become a public affair. In principle all such hypothesised sources might be enquired into with a reasonable expectation of establishing either their existence or non-existence. Often CIL will be sought out in a similarly empirical manner yet the gesture seems intrinsic to this source of norms in a way unmatched by the other sources. This gesture, almost a gesture to a higher realm of the transcendent, might be said to locate CIL in some grey zone between *lex lata* and *lex ferenda*: a zone we might call *lex hypothetica*.[7]

Approached in this somewhat sceptical manner, the essence of CIL seems to be 'bindingness' (legal obligation) combined with opacity – what might be called 'blindingness' – because the transparency that comes with treaties (albeit, only since the mid-twentieth century) is necessarily absent. Accountability might be said to be dramatically

[6] On emerging CIL regulating state conduct over human rights obligations see EJ Criddle and E Fox-Decent, 'Mandatory Multilateralism' (2019) 113 AJIL 272, 285. On emerging CIL regulating state conduct over climate change mitigation and response see B Mayer, 'Climate Assessment as an Emerging Obligation under Customary International Law' (2019) 68 ICLQ 271. These claims are of methodological interest irrespective of their substantive merits or persuasiveness.

[7] Alongside a number of important distinctions, this appeal to the vocabulary of modal logic is also to be seen in speculative claims concerning the peremptory norm as discussed below.

lacking.[8] The combination of these two factors might be referred to by borrowing, with apologies and with some poetic license, the words of J. R. R. Tolkien: 'And in the darkness bind them.' Only retrospectively and vicariously, that is to say in the decisions or advisory opinions of tribunals, is CIL endowed with a measure of transparency. This takes place by means of the 'translation' of the CIL into written form. Thus CIL, which is defined as unwritten, paradoxically only has normative force when it is written. Up until that point at least it is something of a will o' the wisp. The process seems a little like the recognition of states under the declarative mode, or like the announced discovery of a common law principle or a maxim of equity: more alchemy than chemistry or, to adjust the metaphor, more priestly than Priestley. A qualitative change takes place, a transubstantiation or saltation.[9] Correspondingly, the circularity in argument or 'bootstrapping' aspect seems problematic as one intangible step leads on to another. Of course the enigmatic if not paradoxical character of CIL is widely recognised, for example in the arcane form of the persistent objector to an emerging customary norm.[10] Here a sovereign is held retrospectively to have been sufficiently cognizant of an emerging customary norm as between relevant sovereigns, of which that sovereign is one, that the sovereign's historical protests constitute a kind of negative prescription by means of which his or her putative obligations are nullified. Given the relationships between prescription in the international law of territory and the common law principle of adverse possession, the persistent objector would seem to be claiming something like an 'adverse immunity'.[11]

Further below, we will frame and motivate our comments on the role of interpretation in CIL by means of an enquiry into the role played by CIL in

[8] In this connection note should be taken of the Appeals Chamber of the International Criminal Court declaring an end to a CIL of head of state immunity, an example surely of the consequences and risks of poor accountability. See Dapo Akande, 'ICC Appeals Chamber Holds that Heads of State Have No Immunity under Customary International Law Before International Tribunals' (*EJIL: Talk!*, 6 May 2019) <https://bit.ly/3F8lRO2> accessed 1 March 2021.

[9] On the trigonometrically 'tangent'-like form of time understood within international law see JR Morss, 'Riddle of the Sands: Time, Power and Legitimacy in International Law' in P Singh & B Mayer (eds), *Critical International Law: Post-realism, Post-colonialism, and Transnationalism* (Oxford University Press 2014) 53, 71.

[10] JR Morss, 'Book Review: *Brownlie's Principles of Public International Law* by James Crawford and *International Law* by Gleider Hernández' (2020) 21(1) MJIL 1.

[11] As Hohfeld would observe, an immunity in one party connotes a corresponding disability in another; JR Morss, 'Cutting Global Justice Down to Size? Rights, Vulnerabilities, Immunities, Communities' (2019) 40(30) Liverpool LR 179, 200.

the *Chagos Advisory Opinion*.[12] On 25 February 2019 the International Court of Justice (ICJ) handed down its Advisory Opinion in relation to the continuing administration by the UK of the Chagos Archipelago in the Indian Ocean. In exerting control over the territory, which prior to the independence of Mauritius was part of that non-self-governing entity, the UK had forcibly transferred its population. A population of Chagossians had been dispossessed by the British government and its military in the 1960s, and relocated to mainland Mauritius, giving rise to various deleterious consequences for that population both material and affective.[13] The UK had undertaken to 'return' the Chagos Archipelago to Mauritius if and when it was no longer needed for defence purposes.[14] Subsequent General Assembly resolutions consistently condemned the continuing administration of the Chagos Archipelago by the UK.[15] While at pains to avoid the appearance of treating the question before it as a dispute between two parties, namely Mauritius and the UK, the majority clearly endorsed the postcolonialist argument that was proposed on behalf of Mauritius and also on behalf of many other states contributing to the proceedings.[16] Thus the process of decolonisation was found not to have been 'lawfully completed' in 1968 when Mauritius acceded to independence.[17] Merits of arguments submitted to the court will not be rehearsed or evaluated.[18] This Advisory Opinion has

[12] UNGA Res 71/292 'Request for an Advisory Opinion of the International Court of Justice on the Legal Consequences of the Separation of the Chagos Archipelago from Mauritius in 1965' (22 June 2017) UN Doc A/71/PV.88; *Legal Consequences of the Separation of the Chagos Archipelago from Mauritius in 1965* (Advisory Opinion) [2019] ICJ Rep 95 (*Chagos Advisory Opinion*).

[13] E Forbes & JR Morss, 'Peoplehood Obscured? The Normative Status of Self-Determination after the Chagos Advisory Opinion' (2020) 46(3) Monash University Law Review 145–68; J Trinidad, *Self-Determination in Disputed Colonial Territories* (Cambridge University Press 2018) 83.

[14] This statement was made in the course of the Lancaster House Agreement in 1965 between Mauritian and British officials, prior to the independence of a truncated Mauritius: *Chagos Advisory Opinion* [108].

[15] See for example UNGA Res 2066 'Question of Mauritius' (16 December 1965) UN Doc A/RES/2066(XX).

[16] S Allen, 'Self-Determination, the Chagos Archipelago Advisory Opinion and the Chagossians' (2020) 69 ICLQ 203; FL Bordin, 'Reckoning with British Colonialism' (2019) 78 CLJ 253; J Klabbers, 'Shrinking Self-Determination: The Chagos Opinion of the International Court of Justice' (2019) 8(2) ESIL Reflections 1 <https://bit.ly/3GPgTX5> accessed 1 March 2021; M Milanovic, 'ICJ Delivers Chagos Advisory Opinion, UK Loses Badly (*EJIL: Talk!*, 25 February 2019) <https://bit.ly/3FdrXNq> accessed 1 March 2021.

[17] *Chagos Advisory Opinion* [183].

[18] It may be that an argument based on estoppel or prescription would trump any argument based on CIL. As noted above, the UK assured the government of Mauritius in the 1960s

already generated considerable commentary and debate in relation to the continuing administration by the UK of the Chagos Archipelago.[19]

Customary international law plays an important role in the *Chagos* opinion. Has *Chagos* advanced our understanding of CIL? Has it 'developed' CIL? Has it clarified the relationships between CIL and such denizens of international law as the peremptory norm, obligations *erga omnes*, the technique of *uti possidetis juris*, the general principle of international law or the inexorable (e.g. anticolonial) trend of modern history recognised as a matter of fact by the court? Has it 'stabilise[d] history' as, it has been suggested, was the aspiration behind the UN Charter itself?[20] In other words what, against the background of our observations above, does *Chagos* tell us about the role of interpretation in CIL? Before engaging with this question however, some wider questions need to be addressed.

2 On Structure, Depth and Explanation in International Legal Discourse

There is no a priori reason to treat interpretation as so intimately connected to written text that norms based on unwritten conduct fall outside of its scope. Certainly the academic disciplines of hermeneutics and other interpretive techniques evolved from practices of the glossing of written texts, namely texts of Holy Writ.[21] That history clings to the techniques in ways that we sometimes notice and sometimes do not notice, just as international law as a whole is contaminated but not entirely determined by the colonial oppression inflicted on the globe by the hegemonic princes of past centuries.[22] And just as hermeneutics has

that Chagos would be 'returned' in due course, thus defining the UK occupation as illicit or at least irregular and based on the legal fiction of the sovereign consent of Mauritius, a consent that, even if valid in the past, has been withdrawn by the sovereign in question. Alternatively, as observed by Cançado Trindade J in his Separate Opinion the UK had in the context of denying the need for any report to the Human Rights Committee described BIOT (British Indian Ocean Territory) as having no population; in which case a claim based on *terra nullius* might have been open to Mauritius: *Chagos Advisory Opinion*, Separate Opinion of Judge Cançado Trindade, 22 [64].

19 T Frost & CRG Murray, 'Homeland: Reconceptualising the Chagossians' Litigation' (2020) 40(4) OJLS 764.

20 PM Dupuy, 'Intergenerational Reflections on International Law' (*EJIL: Talk!*, January 2020) <https://bit.ly/3sbh9M1> accessed 1 March 2021.

21 MJ Inwood, 'Hermeneutics' in T Honderich (ed), *The Oxford Companion to Philosophy* (Oxford University Press 1995) 353.

22 Compare A Anghie, 'On Critique and the Other' in A Orford (ed), *International Law and its Others* (Cambridge University Press 2006) 389.

no intrinsic, constrained identity with particular texts in that sense, being relevant to a variety of profane as well as religious writings (and to non-Christian as well as Christian religious materials, it goes without saying), interpretation has no intrinsic constrained identity with the printed word in any language. Not to recognise this would be among other things to entirely misunderstand Derrida's dictum (or was it a *ratio*?) to the effect that 'there is nothing outside the text'. What 'text' meant for Derrida was not restricted to cold print on the page, as in the myth of 'black letter law' so derided by critical writers in legal theory; and without neglecting the significance of the challenge made by Derrida to hermeneutics, to phenomenology, and to other brands of interpretive discipline, his point ranged more widely. To approach this point from another direction, the science or discipline of semiotics is patently concerned with meaning-making well beyond the written (or indeed the spoken) word. Famously Roland Barthes analysed dress codes.[23] Semiotics in that respect is cognate with structuralist anthropology from Levi-Strauss to Margaret Strathern and hence with structuralism in general.[24]

2.1 *Bootstrapping and Hand-Waving*

Interpretation thus includes any appeal to particular frameworks of meaning beyond the specific text, conduct or pattern that is observed. Across the many forms and disciplines of interpretation, it can be generally said that coherence is a significant virtue. By the application of meaning systems, propositions gain a kind of validity from that coherence independently of other forms of legitimation. Coherence becomes a kind of authority.[25] However, to develop an argument based primarily on coherence might in some circumstances be unkindly referred to as 'bootstrapping'. To attempt to lift oneself up by one's own bootstraps is a telling metaphor. It is of course the reflexivity that is the problem. As Archimedes noticed, an external point of leverage is called for by the aid of which the lifting becomes possible. Again, if one's bootstraps are sufficiently robust and the boots themselves of the correct size, an external agent standing on *terra firma* may well be able to lift one up in such a manner, however undignified that would be.

[23] F Dosse, *History of Structuralism Vol 1: The Rising Sign, 1945–1966* (University of Minnesota Press 1997) 75.

[24] JR Morss 'Description Without Apology? On Structures, Signs and Subjectivity in International Legal Scholarship' (2018) 58 IJIL 235.

[25] S Wolfram, 'Coherence Theory of Truth' in T Honderich (ed), *The Oxford Companion to Philosophy* (Oxford University Press 1995) 140.

Coherence is not to be lightly dismissed. After all, any use of logic or of mathematics involves reliance on a system of coherence, and is usually not considered the worse for that. But neither logic nor mathematics is self-executing. In a context relevant to the discussion below, it has been claimed that the principle of *uti possedetis* according to which administrative boundaries of the colonial power are retained by new neighbours after independence, is 'logically connected with the phenomenon of the obtaining of independence, wherever it occurs'.[26] Just as the application of mathematics or logic can lead the scholar astray at times, without it always being obvious exactly when the wrong step was taken or the wrong connection made, so the cumulative construction of claims about the conduct of international entities as generating normativity – the bread and butter of CIL as usually understood – may risk the inevitable fate of a house of cards. It is merely high school level physics to learn how error estimates accumulate in the laboratory, such that a modest error range on each of two or three independent parameters (temperature, weight and so forth) may accumulate to a hefty 'known unknown' when those readings are combined in sequence. If the discourse of CIL involves a sequence of 'ifs' and 'maybes', as is surely so often the case, then it may be a tottering tower of claims that is constructed. If apples and oranges are on occasion pressed into service, so to speak – so that what is being built comprises somewhat different elements – the fragility is again manifest. A telling analogy is the conceit of the chain of counterfactuals across history, so that the retrospective adjustment of one event suggests consequences which themselves serve to generate further and equally fictitious consequences. Historian Niall Ferguson has attempted such a conceit.[27] 'Hand-waving' refers to the argumentative practice of deliberately indicating that one is evading difficult questions or traversing fragile steps of a thesis. In combination these discursive gestures or techniques have a tendency to generate conclusions that leap well ahead of any substantive basis in interconnected claims either empirical, conceptual or legal. To change the metaphor yet again, the conclusions thus arrived at may appear somewhat like the rabbit produced from the hat of the conjuror. If that comparison is in any way apt, then there would be cause for concern.

Before exploring this idea further, other distinctions between CIL and other genres of international norm should be considered. The unwritten

[26] *Case Concerning the Frontier Dispute (Burkina Faso v Republic of Mali)* (Judgment) [1986] ICJ Rep 554 [20].

[27] N Ferguson (ed), *Virtual History: Alternatives and Counterfactuals* (Picador 1997).

aspect of CIL is often considered its essential characteristic. But it is only in contrast to international treaties or 'conventions' that the unwritten aspect of CIL seems to be noteworthy in the context of the sources of international law. Treaties are written documents, signed by representatives of polities. 'General principles' of international law are not, as such, reduced to writing. The most canonical examples of such principles, at least in terms of the jurisprudence of the ICJ, consist of the appeal to common practices among relevant States vis-à-vis their national legal frameworks on the status of corporate entities. The fact that these national laws (in Belgium, Spain and so on) are themselves, and in a variety of languages, written law in a very traditional sense, does not affect the conclusion that the general principle abstracted from them in the case of the *Barcelona Traction*, is not itself written. The status of so-called principles of international law in a wider sense (beyond the definition in Article 38(1)(c)) is problematical in any event. Text-book writers have been trying to tie down such generic principles for several centuries.

One extreme example – extreme in its scale and self-confidence, and perhaps in its practical import – is the encyclopaedic package of claims made on behalf of the International Committee of the Red Cross (ICRC) concerning regulation of armed conflict in the form of international humanitarian law.[28] That project has given rise to extensive online resources that attempt to maintain and update a body of knowledge on both conduct-based ('objective') and *opinio*-based ('subjective') grounds for the identification of CIL. While the specialised focus of those claims takes the ICRC exercise outside the substantive scope of this chapter, it might be borne in mind as a marker for the potential scope of an industry of speculation relating to CIL.

Optimism is one might say 'in the DNA' of the ICRC, given its Sisyphus-like exertions in the face of human conflict. What this chapter is concerned with is a more general process. It is the *Chagos Advisory Opinion* as paradigm for the discerning of 'general' CIL, that is, rules of CIL valid for all states as such.[29] A familiar example of such a general or pan-state CIL would be immunity from prosecution of heads of state.[30] Such rules must be distinguished from rules *jus cogens* that are asserted,

[28] JM Henckaerts & L Doswald-Beck, *Customary International Humanitarian Law* (Cambridge University Press 2005).

[29] ILC, 'Third Report on Identification of Customary International Law by Michael Wood, Special Rapporteur' (27 March 2015) UN Doc A/CN.4/682 [80].

[30] G Hernández, *International Law* (Oxford University Press 2019) 234.

on grounds other than customary observance, to have peremptory force as such. At this point it could be observed that one of the points of contact between the norm *jus cogens* (the peremptory norm) and CIL is precisely in this modality of the hopeful hypothetical.[31] The substance of posited norms *jus cogens* is typically weighty in an ethical sense, as compared to the typical CIL on boundaries or access to fish, but while they diverge in various other ways these two challenging forms of international norm do seem to share this gesture; and of course, self-determination as a putative CIL does indeed involve weighty ethical issues. What will be suggested here is that the step by which a general rule of CIL is identified in the *Chagos Advisory Opinion* comprises an extrapolation from at best a combination of majoritarian avowal on behalf of sovereigns, and the sovereign ratification of international instruments. As we shall see, the gap between 'ought' and 'is' is bridged by a mixture of hand-waving and bootstrapping even if the expressed view of the majority of the bench is much more restrained in this regard than some of the separate opinions.

2.2 Alternative Reference Classes for Customary International Law

The reference class of the term CIL can be defined in a wide variety of ways. One alternative is of extreme breadth but little precision. As James Crawford indicates, in the tradition of Ian Brownlie and others, the practice of states understood most generally can be what is indicated.[32] Without neglecting the essential distinction between CIL and mere comity or courtesy, a distinction that goes back at least to the beginning of the nineteenth century,[33] it is still the case that customary forms of international law represent a kind of oceanic backdrop for much that is more narrow, more technical or more specified in terms of the conduct and the expectations of parties. Thus in what might be called the Brownlie-Crawford approach, attention is paid to what are taken to be deeper and slower-moving features of the international legal landscape, generative of 'principles'. This is an extensive rather than an intensive approach to what might loosely be termed custom-based conduct. It is exemplified by the observation that 'the state is itself a customary law phenomenon'.[34] This recognition does not claim that all such conduct is CIL in a substantive,

[31] On the promissory aspect of international law see Dupuy (n 20).

[32] Crawford (n 1) 21.

[33] The distinction was observed as being already a century old, and in that respect attributable to Lord Stowell when discussed in *The Paquete Habana*, 175 US 677 (1900) 677.

[34] Crawford (n 1) 44.

dispute-resolving sense. It is in some ways a Kelsenian argument, pointing to an infrastructure of norms that might be said to be logically necessary in order for substantive CIL to exist and function. That is to say, these oceanic customs are understood as disconnected from the CIL that according to the jurisprudence of the ICJ, is provided in Article 38 (1)(b). Nor is it claimed in any systematic way that such background customs constitute necessary appurtenances of states. In other words there is something of a policy-oriented positivism in operation here: 'this is what states do'.[35]

As suggested in the preceding, a reference class for CIL may be the class of incidents of statehood. This 'ontological' variety of the sense of custom at the international level, tied to the definition of statehood in recursive ways, has an extensive lineage even if its inadequacies are patent. Clearly the reference class of customs that apply to all states, whether or not that relationship is thought of as involving inherence, is an important variety of reference class. So as well as the background or process-oriented framework, we have the statehood-intrinsic (or ontological) and the statehood-generic as additional, distinct but overlapping reference classes. Specially affected states as constituting the relevant set might be thought of as yet another option; and the admittedly old-fashioned view that hegemonic or elite states play a special role in generating and legitimising CIL, might be further added.[36] Finally, reference to CIL may narrowly refer to a CIL that has been found by an appropriate tribunal – and this really means the ICJ – to meet its technical and forensic requirements, as famously laid out for example in the *North Sea Continental Shelf Cases.* That is to say, CIL may refer specifically and narrowly to legal obligations discerned by the ICJ (or similar) in dispute resolution or in the context of advisory opinions. This narrowly defined category would correspond to an approach to the notion of peremptory norms on the basis of accepting only those norms that the ICJ has in fact identified as having *jus cogens* status.[37]

3 Interpretation in *Chagos:* A Customary International Law of Self-Determination?

So what of the *Chagos Advisory Opinion*? In the opinion crafted by the majority, considerable reliance is placed on CIL.[38] It could be said to be the

35 R Higgins, *The Development of International Law Through the Political Organs of the United Nations* (Oxford University Press 1963).
36 See Chimni (n 5); Heller (n 5).
37 For a rigorous analysis see Hernández (n 30) 66.
38 *Chagos Advisory Opinion* [142].

most significant basis for the outcome, always granted the overriding role of the UN Charter. The latter of course refers to the 'self-determination of peoples' but without much clarity.[39] In the *Chagos Advisory Opinion*, the right to self-determination is defined as CIL and moreover, one that is 'binding on all States'.[40] Respect for such a right 'is an obligation *erga omnes*'.[41] On that basis, the majority finds that the territorial integrity of a former non-self-governing territory is violated if part of that territory is excised from the territory of the newly independent entity.[42]

It should be noted that the majority is at pains to emphasise its restrained approach in contrast to the enthusiastic and even crusading, *ex cathedra* values-based approach advocated by the Separate Opinion of Judge Cançado Trindade. The majority emphasises its continuity of approach with previous findings and opinions of the ICJ. If anything the majority presents itself, if only strategically, as conservative and cautious. Thus in its *Chagos Advisory Opinion* the majority of the ICJ bench carried out an exercise in the interpretation of CIL in the context of the self-determination of peoples and of the administration of non-self-governing territories in terms of Chapter XI of the UN Charter. However politically welcome the outcome in respect of a snub for a former colonial power, and ipso facto a snub for that power's powerful client, the United States in this case (since the United States had leased the Diego Garcia location as a naval base), the reasoning of the court in terms of its reliance on CIL stands in need of interrogation.[43]

In the *Chagos Advisory Opinion* it appears that the court provided an object lesson in the ascertainment and application of CIL in twenty-first century international law. While insisting that the ascertainment of the content of the putative rule of CIL (the 'what') as well as the ascertainment of the chronology of its coming into effect (the 'when') are exercises limited to the specific customary rule in question, more general methodological assertions can certainly be identified. The unpacking of the putative

[39] '[T]he principle of equal rights and self-determination of peoples' is referred to in connection with the Purposes of the United Nations at Article 1(2) yet self-determination is not in itself one of the Principles of the UN which focus on the peaceful co-existence and internal autonomy of member states (Article 2).

[40] *Chagos Advisory Opinion* [148].

[41] ibid [180].

[42] ibid [160].

[43] The circumstances of the French Overseas Department of Mayotte with respect to Comoros, are in some respects comparable to Chagos. See M Hébié, 'Was There Something Missing in the Decolonization Process in Africa? The Territorial Dimension' (2015) 28 LJIL 529, 547.

customary rule and the closely related investigation of its provenance are anchored to previous findings of the court in relation to quite different kinds of CIL such as the allocation of access to offshore resources among adjacent coastal states. The parameters of difference are such matters as human rights norms versus access to resources norms; but also, pan-state norms versus 'regional' or 'specially affected state' norms. Although the court's primary steps in enquiring into a putatively salient customary rule in this context may be said to be formal ones, to the extent that finding the relevant and adequate combination of conduct and *opinio juris* is a formal exercise, the investigation into the content and thus the consequences or effects of the customary rule is unambiguously a matter of interpretation. (In any event form and content are intermingled, if not circular, in the context of CIL.) The extent to which 'reading up' of the CIL takes place – the widening and the increased weighting of the obligations which are said to flow from it – is perhaps much greater than would usually be the case, for example with another *North Sea Continental Shelf* situation. An advisory opinion is indeed more appropriate to such an expansive exercise than a dispute between states. The CIL that is examined in the *Chagos Advisory Opinion*, with its UN Charter connections, its General Assembly contributions and its world-historical resonances, might be said with some justification to be *sui generis*. But the building of the edifice of the CIL of the decolonising of non-self-governing territories is still remarkable. The method of interpretation employed by the court enables it to successively unpack this CIL into what one might describe as an articulated and systematic project management scheme governing the decolonising process as generic historical transition. It is such a process, read by the ICJ majority into the combined effect of the UN Charter and Resolutions of the General Assembly, that according to the bench was applicable to the case of the Chagos Archipelago but manifestly dishonoured by successive UK governments.

According to the majority, a right to self-determination based on CIL may be discerned, crucially one that was in existence before the time at which the UK government purported to excise the Chagos Archipelago.[44] The court saw it as its task to ascertain 'when the [right to self-determination] crystallised as a customary rule binding on all States'.[45]

[44] Also crucially, not 'Chagos for the Chagossians' but 'Mauritius (including Chagos) for the Mauritians (including the Chagossians)'. See JR Morss, 'Mars for the Martians? On the Obsolescence of Self-Determination' in FR Tesón (ed), *The Theory of Self-Determination* (Cambridge University Press 2016) 184.

[45] *Chagos Advisory Opinion* [148]; also see Sir Michael Wood's observation on 'General' Customary International Law, that is rules of CIL valid for all states: M Wood (n 29) [80].

In this light, General Assembly Resolution 1514 (XV) of 1960, the Declaration on the Granting of Independence to Colonial Countries and Peoples, was 'a defining moment in the consolidation of State practice on decolonization'; it 'clarifies the content and scope of the right to self-determination'.[46] It has the character of a declaration of a right to self-determination as 'a customary norm'.[47] This right to self-determination is a 'basic principle of international law' and 'its normative character under customary international law' was also confirmed by General Assembly Resolution 2625 (XXV) of 1970, to which was annexed the Declaration on Principles of International Law concerning Friendly Relations and Co-operation among States in accordance with the Charter of the United Nations.[48]

Moreover, a right to the territorial integrity of a non-self-governing territory is *itself* a customary law.[49] In this context the court observed, in a methodological vein, that 'State practice and *opinio juris* ... are consolidated and confirmed gradually over time'.[50] Thus it is proper for the court to consider 'the evolution of the law of self-determination' since Resolution 1514.[51] But 'confirmed gradually' seems odd, as does the language of 'evolution'. How can 'confirming' be gradual? Perhaps it might be said that, as observed by Criddle and Fox-Decent, *evidence* going to the identification of a rule of CIL may be said to accumulate. Thus in the context of a posited rule of CIL requiring state cooperation over human rights breaches, '[a]s evidence of state practice and *opinio juris* continues to accumulate in the future [the existence of such a rule of customary international law] may eventually become the prevailing view'.[52] Now despite the attractiveness of this innocent-looking proposal, complexities still arise in this formulation. As discussed above, a postulated customary norm is not amenable to empirical investigation and the accumulation of data in the way that other forms of source may perhaps be. Common strategies in municipal law across the globe might well accumulate in a factual sense, thus building up the argument for a 'general principle' à la *Barcelona Traction* should a suitable international dispute

46 *Chagos Advisory Opinion* [150].

47 ibid [152]. This view had been expressed trenchantly as early as 1963 by Rosalyn Higgins (n 35) 100.

48 *Chagos Advisory Opinion* [155].

49 ibid [160].

50 ibid [142].

51 ibid.

52 Criddle & Fox-Decent (n 6) 285.

arise. Despite their subsidiary status, judicial decisions or the writings of the publicists might accumulate across time in relevantly patterned ways, to which international tribunals may well pay attention. Suitably trained agents might keep track of such data. Nor would processes of interpretation be entirely absent from the epistemological projects involved, for the categorisation of a second or subsequent statute, judicial finding or scholarly conclusion as adding weight to a first rather than starting its own pile, must always involve interpretation.

Yet, CIL just does not seem amenable to such scientistic accretion of data. Especially in the domain of the *opinio*, where the data would have to take the form of evidence of obligations understood by sovereigns as binding, the customary norm must first be postulated and in effect promulgated in order for the data to be defined. There is a circularity here which the discerning of other forms of international norm can evade. It is true of course that the doctrine of 'intertemporal law' requires retrospective assessments of international norms, that is to say ascertainments of applicable norms from a previous era.[53] Various sources of international law and various forms of evidence for them might be investigated in that historical mode. Quite deliberately, and in effect as a 'legal fiction', the bench transports itself as in a time machine to that past era in a quasi-archaeological investigation. The 'synchronic' findings, such as the conclusions on legitimate modes of acquisition of territory in the late nineteenth century, may subsequently be drawn on by scholars interested in defining 'diachronic' trends across historical time in relation to such norms. But that would be an entirely separate and so to speak parasitic exercise. The application of intertemporal law does not yield knowledge in the diachronic domain. The time machine travels strictly between 'then' and 'now', it does not traverse the times before or between. Nor does it generate comparisons even between 'then' and 'now'; the 'now' is no more than a launching pad for the shuttle which returns to base after its sample of the core. This methodology for dispute resolution does not seek to trace longitudinal patterns, developments or 'evolution'. It does of course involve a leap of the institutional imagination but that leap is strictly constrained; it is not a leap of faith.

The term 'evolution' therefore does not assist. The term is a flexible one, as it has been across many disciplines and several centuries.[54] But it

[53] *Western Sahara* (Advisory Opinion) [1975] ICJ Rep 12 [55–57].

[54] JR Morss, *The Biologising of Childhood: Developmental Psychology and the Darwinian Myth* (Erlbaum 1990).

certainly connotes gradual improvement in a manner that is in some sense natural and certainly not the direct result of human agency, even if the Darwinian model of natural selection is closely modelled on the systematic interventions of the breeder of domesticated animals, that persistent objector to the customary reign of Mother Nature. In an otherwise carefully crafted opinion, the term may be readily excused. It is perhaps a harmless nod to the grand historical narrative of the postcolonial. Yet the implication that the customary form of international legal norm is in some sense a natural emanation, deserves a little more investigation. It is of course straightforward to connect such an appeal to the natural law tendencies of some of the world's most influential jurists. A progressivist and even triumphalist tone is not difficult to discern. But this attitude would seem to have a particular connection with CIL if that variety of norm is thought of as the expression of an organic and inarticulate global conscience of mankind, growing or unfolding, slowly yet inexorably, across time.[55] And of course such treatment would be interpretation, indeed.

Finally, the implications of the *Chagos Advisory Opinion* for other putative customary norms should be briefly discussed. The principle of *uti possidetis juris* in international dispute resolution has famously been applied in postcolonial Africa in treating as default international boundaries between newly independent states, the administrative boundaries drawn up by former colonial sovereigns. As with any reference to a 'principle' of international law, the question must always be put as to what kind of source such a posited norm may be. The claim that *uti possidetis* has customary status is questionable.[56] It seems to exist in that penumbra of the quasi-customary along with procedural norms of wider significance such as *pacta sunt servanda*. In any event to the extent *uti possidetis* represents the dead hand of colonialism, the *Chagos Advisory Opinion* represents if anything the revenge of the principle. Here, the colonial boundary manifested by the inclusion of the Chagos Archipelago into a larger Mauritius entity by France, is now relied upon to the detriment of the residual administrative power (the UK), so that it is hoist by its own imperialist petard.[57] Of course any reference

[55] The '*opinio juris communis*' promulgated by Cançado Trindade J seems to derive only from scholarly writings of Bin Cheng. *Chagos Advisory Opinion* (n 12) (Separate Opinion of Judge Cançado Trindade) 22 [87].

[56] S Lalonde, *Determining Boundaries in a Conflicted World: The Role of Uti Possidetis* (McGill-Queen's University Press 2002) 131.

[57] *Chagos Advisory Opinion* [27].

to *uti possidetis* raises questions of self-determination.[58] The formula is in effect an alternative to self-determination and consigns the latter to the 'too hard' basket, in favour of 'nation building'.[59] To the extent self-determination is coterminous with peoplehood, peoplehood is recognised as flowing across national borders so that pluri-peoplehood within one territory is implicit, typically in the form of one or more minority populations. If two or more peoples are clearly identified within one state territory, then territorial integrity might become a burden rather than a virtue from the point of view of the self-determination of 'peoples'.[60] Thus the key finding in the *Chagos Advisory Opinion* that territorial integrity of a non-self-governing territory is the essence of the CIL of self-determination in decolonisation, serves to undermine self-determination in favour of territorial integrity.[61] There still does not seem to be a substantive contribution from CIL to the vital question of 'what is a people?'[62]

In a methodological sense, the account now provided by the ICJ of the international legal norms governing self-determination constitutes primarily an act of interpretation of CIL. Disappointing or not in its achievements in that regard, it is a reminder of the significance of such

[58] Lalonde (n 56) 239.

[59] *Case Concerning the Frontier Dispute* (n 27).

[60] In Chapter XI of the UN Charter (Declaration Regarding Non-Self-Governing Territories) the chapeau for Article 73 speaks of 'territories whose peoples' while Article 73(b) talks of 'the particular circumstances of *each territory and its peoples*' [emphasis added]. The latter phrase is also employed in the corresponding article under Chapter XII (International Trusteeship System), viz art 76(b). The difference may be subtle yet the second formulation, unlike the first, expressly indicates the possibility of pluri-peoplehood, consistent with the harsh territoriality, entirely at odds with the principle of self-determination, conveyed by *uti possedetis*. The term 'self-determination' is not employed in either of these chapters.

[61] Trinidad (n 13).

[62] A Badiou et al, *What Is a People?* (Columbia University Press 2016); Forbes & Morss (n 13); JR Morss, 'Pluralism, Peoplehood and Political Theology in International Legal Scholarship' (2018) 27(1) GLR 77. Whether or not the conceptual circularity is to be attributed to inadequacies in CIL, it has been correctly observed by David Miller that '[t]o confine the right of self-determination to existing *states* is effectively to say that only those who have already achieved self-determination are entitled to exercise it'. D Miller, *Is Self-Determination a Dangerous Illusion?* (Polity Press 2020) 7. Comparing such historic and primarily European nations (well-deserved self-determination achieved) with the populations of administered territories elsewhere (self-determination a distracting pipe dream under *uti possedetis*) indeed reveals a striking manifestation of imperialism (ibid 8). The UN Charter might be said to encapsulate this worldview. Also it is of interest that self-determination is erased in two ways here: as already achieved at the centre and as a false hope at the margins.

interpretive processes. Customary norms of international law weigh heavy on minority populations and there is no route to resolving such injustice save through interpretation of those norms in a variety of senses of 'interpretation'. Paradoxically again, it may be that interpretation in CIL turns out to be even more important than it is in its familiar 'comfort zone' of treaties.

4 Conclusion

Sceptical remarks have been made above concerning the rhetorical devices employed in the discourse of CIL. Especially in the writings of commentators, one of the myriad ways in which interpretation is thus involved is in the ubiquity of the proposal that such-and-such a conduct or prohibition 'may be' CIL or 'may be emerging' as such. This mode of speculation has been said above to be of the essence of what CIL means in the public international law of the present era. Opacity and regulation sit uncomfortably together either at the municipal or the international level. At the municipal level democratic arrangements, however fragile and imperfect, play an important role in battling the forces of obscurantism. At the international level the barriers to transparency must be dismantled by eminent jurists, assisted by commentators. To express it generously, the goal of hermeneutics is interpretation in the interest of enlightenment. That goal is an honourable one and therefore the systematic investigation of the role played by interpretation in the theory and practice of CIL is essential. International law like all law in the real world is made and remade by humans, albeit in complex ways; and binding in darkness belongs only in fantasy fiction.

PART V

Customary International Law in the Practice of Domestic Courts

What Lessons for International Law?

21

The Role of Domestic Courts in the Interpretation of Customary International Law

How Can We Learn from Domestic Interpretive Practices?

NINA MILEVA[*]

1 Introduction

The role of domestic courts in the development of rules of international law is an area of research that has received increased scholarly interest in the past decade. Within the formal framework of sources, domestic courts can contribute to the development of international law in broadly three ways: as an expression of state practice or *opinio juris* for the purpose of customary international law (CIL),[1] as a contribution to general principles of law,[2] or as relevant subsequent practice for the purposes of treaty interpretation.[3] Moreover, scholars have also identified a role for domestic courts beyond the framework of sources, pointing to further contributions of domestic courts to the development of international law. For instance, using the analytical lens of 'domestic courts as agents of development of international law' a symposium hosted by the *Leiden Journal of International Law* demonstrated that while domestic courts may have a limited impact on the development of international law within the

[*] This contribution is based on research conducted in the context of the project 'The Rules of Interpretation of Customary International Law' ('TRICI-Law'). This project received funding from the European Research Council ('ERC') under the European Union's Horizon 2020 Research and Innovation Programme (Grant Agreement No. 759728).

[1] ILC, 'Draft Conclusions on Identification of Customary International Law, with Commentaries' (30 April–1 June and 2 July–10 August 2018) UN Doc A/73/10, reproduced in [2018/II - Part Two] YBILC 11.

[2] As defined by Article 38(1)(c) of the Statute of the International Court of Justice (adopted 26 June 1945, entered into force 24 October 1945) 1 UNTS 993.

[3] As defined by Article 31(3)(b) of the Vienna Convention on the Law of Treaties (adopted 23 May 1969, entered into force 27 January 1980) 1155 UNTS 331.

regime of sources, they can still exercise an informal influence; particularly so if their pronouncements are taken up and validated or endorsed by other actors.[4] Similarly, the analytical framework of a 'cycle of contestation and deference' tells us that contestations by domestic courts in cases where they engage with international law can provoke an international reaction or adjustment of the law in response to the contestation.[5]

This chapter examines the contribution that domestic courts may have in the development of rules or guidelines for the interpretation of CIL. The examination is motivated by three considerations. Firstly, unlike in the case of treaties whose interpretation is guided by Article 31 of the Vienna Convention on the Law of Treaties (VCLT) and its customary counterparts, presently we do not have clear rules or guidelines for the interpretation of CIL. In fact, as other chapters in this volume demonstrate, legal scholarship is currently still discussing whether custom as a source of law can be subject to interpretation, and if so, what are apposite methods for its interpretation. While at present little is certain, it has been argued persuasively that custom and treaties cannot always be subject to the same methods of interpretation.[6] Thus, we cannot simply transplant the methodology of treaty interpretation onto custom wholesale, and it might even be the case that custom requires a methodology of its own. Secondly, scholarship on the role of domestic courts in the development of international law has persuasively demonstrated that domestic courts can contribute to international law both formally and informally, especially in areas where there are lacunae or the law is yet to be developed. Thus, the practice of domestic courts with respect to the interpretation of custom may prove a valuable source in our study and understanding of this developing field. Finally, by turning to domestic courts we open the door to a wealth of cases which can provide us with examples and insight into the interpretation of custom. Depending on the legal system in place, domestic courts may be faced with the task of interpreting not only CIL but also domestic custom. Thus, domestic

[4] A Tzanakopoulos & CJ Tams, 'Introduction: Domestic Courts as Agents of Development of International Law' (2013) 26 LJIL 531, 538.

[5] M Steinbruck Platiše, 'The Development of the Immunities of International Organisations in Response to Domestic Contestations' in M Kanetake & A Nollkaemper (eds), *The Rule of Law at the National and International Levels: Contestations and Deference* (Hart 2016) 67.

[6] See P Merkouris, *Article 31(3)(c) VCLT and the Principle of Systemic Integration: Normative Shadows in Plato's Cave* (Brill 2015) 232–69; See Chapter 18 by Fortuna in this volume.

courts may be uniquely positioned to provide insight into the methodology of interpreting custom as a source of law.

With these three considerations in mind, the chapter poses the question: how can interpretive methodologies employed by domestic courts inform the development of rules or guidelines for the interpretation of CIL? The chapter is organised along three substantive sections. Section 2 provides an overview of the current academic discourse with respect to CIL interpretation, and briefly introduces the interpretation of CIL as conceptualised by this chapter. Section 3 turns to the contribution of domestic courts to the development of international law, and maps the existing scholarship on the topic. Section 4 contains the operative contribution of the chapter, and begins with an overview of five domestic cases which contain examples of domestic courts interpreting customary law. It then provides some preliminary observations organised along two lines of inquiry: (i) how can we learn from domestic interpretive practices? and (ii) why should we learn from them? The observations provided in this chapter are part of the author's ongoing doctoral research focused on the interpretability of CIL and the role of domestic courts in this process. In light of this, the findings presented in it will evolve and be updated with further research.

Before continuing with the chapter, a point of terminology is in order. This chapter uses the terms 'rules' and 'guidelines' for CIL interpretation broadly and interchangeably. This is because currently there is no set terminology which denotes the parameters according to which CIL is interpreted by relevant actors. One of the main objectives of the TRICI-Law project (of which the present author is a member) is to demonstrate the interpretability of CIL and to identify the parameters which guide the process. Therefore, the chapter presently does not take a position on the nature of these parameters, and the jury is still out on the final appropriate terminology.

2 CIL Interpretation

Before delving into an analysis of the ways in which international law may learn from domestic courts' practice for the purpose of CIL interpretation, a few paragraphs must be dedicated to the interpretability of CIL and the current scholarly debates surrounding it. A detailed discussion of the interpretation of CIL is beyond the scope of this chapter and is addressed more elaborately elsewhere in this volume.[7] This section is

[7] See Chapters 16–18 in this volume.

only intended to briefly map the current state of the scholarly discourse, and to show the reader what is the thing that we speak of when we speak of CIL interpretation throughout the chapter.

Unlike treaties, whose interpretation is guided by the VCLT and its customary counterparts, CIL's interpretation remains a mercurial process whose functioning is both questioned and unregulated. Claims against the interpretability of CIL are broadly organised along two lines: firstly, it is argued that CIL's unwritten character excludes the need for its interpretation. Here, the argument is that even though language is necessary to communicate the content of customary rules, expression through language is not an indispensable element of CIL rules. This irrelevance of linguistic expression excludes interpretation as a necessary operation in order to apply CIL rules.[8] Secondly, it is argued that CIL cannot be subject to interpretation because if an attempt is made to interpret an unwritten source such as CIL the interpretative reasoning will inevitably need to refer back to the elements of the lawmaking process and as such be circular.[9] In a similar vein, it is posited that CIL rules do not require interpretation because the mere process of their identification delineates their content as well.[10]

The argument that CIL is not subject to interpretation because it is unwritten is problematic. It is not entirely clear why the absence of a written textual manifestation in the context of CIL rules would imply that a CIL rule should not be subject to interpretation. An absence of a written manifestation merely means that a rule is not codified; it does not however deprive this rule of other forms of linguistic expression (e.g., oral expression) or of content, and subsequently of the need to clarify this content for the purpose of application in a given legal and factual context. Furthermore, in international law there is no universal approach which dictates that the unwritten character of a particular source precludes it from interpretation. For instance, as has been established by the International Law Commission (ILC) in its 'Guiding Principles Applicable to Unilateral Declarations of State',[11] unilateral declarations,

[8] T Treves, 'Customary International Law' [2006] MPEPIL 1393 [1.2].

[9] A Gourgourinis, 'The Distinction between Interpretation and Application of Norms in International Adjudication' (2011) 2(1) JIDS 31, 56.

[10] M Bos, *A Methodology of International Law* (Elsevier 1984) 109; see also J d'Aspremont, 'The Multidimensional Process of Interpretation' in A Bianchi, D Peat & M Windsor (eds), *Interpretation in International Law* (Oxford University Press 2015) 111, 118.

[11] ILC, 'Guiding Principles Applicable to Unilateral Declarations of States Capable of Creating Legal Obligations, with Commentaries Thereto' (2006) UN Doc A/61/10, reproduced in [2006/II – Part Two] YBILC 161.

which may be formulated orally,[12] are subject to interpretation if their content is unclear.[13] Similarly, with respect to general principles of international law, which are also themselves unwritten,[14] scholars seem to acknowledge, albeit in a more limited manner, that this source of law may be subject to interpretation.[15] Therefore, it cannot be concluded that the unwritten character of CIL automatically implies that this source of law is not subject to interpretation. Moreover, it is reasonable to observe that unwritten sources, as opposed to written ones, contain a higher degree of vagueness as a result of their unwritten character. This certainly seems to be the case with CIL, where scholars often point to this source's inherent abstractness.[16] This would in turn imply that unwritten sources, rather than not being subject to interpretation, require precisely the exercise of interpretation in order to grasp their otherwise elusive content.

Turning to the second line of argument, it must be observed that this claim is negated by the practice of international courts which regularly engage in CIL interpretation as separate from its identification. For instance, in *Mondev International Ltd* v. *United States of America*, the Arbitral Tribunal observed that: 'the question is not that of a failure to show opinio juris or to amass sufficient evidence demonstrating it. The question rather is: what is the content of customary international law providing for fair and equitable treatment and full protection and security in investment treaties?'[17] The tribunal then proceeded to interpret the customary rule of fair and equitable treatment.[18] Similarly, in its judgment in the *Frontier Dispute* case which dealt with the customary principle of *uti possidetis*, the

[12] ibid 163, Guiding Principle 5.

[13] ibid 164, Guiding Principle 7.

[14] A Pellet & D Müller, 'Article 38' in A Zimmermann & CJ Tams (eds), *The Statute of the International Court of Justice: A Commentary* (Oxford University Press 2019) 924 [255].

[15] See indicatively PG Staubach, *The Rule of Unwritten International Law: Customary Law, General Principles, and World Order* (Routledge 2018) 155–99; MC Bassiouni, 'A Functional Approach to General Principles of International Law' (1990) 11 Mich J Intl L 767, 771.

[16] ILA Committee on Formation of Customary (General) International Law, 'Final Report of the Committee: Statement of Principles Applicable to the Formation of General Customary International Law' (*ILA*, 2000) 2 <https://bit.ly/3yMGuwT> accessed 1 March 2021; F Schauer, 'Pitfalls in the Interpretation of Customary Law' in A Perreau-Saussine & JB Murphy (eds), *The Nature of Customary Law: Legal, Historical and Philosophical Perspectives* (Cambridge University Press 2007) 13; Merkouris (n 6) 233.

[17] *Mondev International Ltd v United States of America* (Award of 11 October 2002) ICSID Case No ARB(AF)/99/2 [113].

[18] ibid [114–16].

International Court of Justice (ICJ), after briefly pointing to the 'elements of *uti possidetis*',[19] turned to an interpretation of the principle for the purposes of the case at hand.[20] In addition to these examples which illustrate a clear distinction between identification and interpretation, courts more generally and regularly engage in the interpretation of CIL. Examples are replete from the dockets of the ICJ,[21] the International Tribunal for the Former Yugoslavia (ICTY),[22] and the World Trade Organization Appellate Body (WTO AB)[23] to name a few.

Beyond the identification of examples where judges engage in the interpretation of CIL, accounting for the process of CIL interpretation bears a lot of theoretical relevance as well. In the absence of an interpretative process, there is no explanation about what happens to a CIL rule after it has been identified. Namely, once a rule of CIL is identified for the first time through an assessment of state practice and *opinio juris*, its existence is not restricted to the case where it was identified for the first time, but is rather a continuous one. When the same rule is invoked in subsequent cases before the same or a different judicial body, the judicial body does not usually go into the exercise of re-establishing that the rule in question is a customary one.[24] Instead, the rule is interpreted within the given legal and factual context of the case at hand. In this sense, interpretation accounts for the CIL rule after its identification and before its application in a subsequent case. Arguing that CIL is not subject to interpretation thus fails to account for the continued existence and operation of a CIL rule after its first identification, and rather operates from the paradoxical premise that a rule of CIL should be identified each and every time anew.

19 *Case concerning the Frontier Dispute (Burkina Faso v Republic of Mali)* (Judgment) [1986] ICJ Rep 554 [22].

20 ibid [23]; that this is an interpretive exercise is evident in the reference to the 'purpose' of *uti possidetis*, and the 'essence of the principle'.

21 *Military and Paramilitary Activities in and against Nicaragua (Nicaragua v USA)* (Merits) [1986] ICJ Rep 14 [178]; *North Sea Continental Shelf cases (Federal Republic of Germany v Denmark; Federal Republic of Germany v Netherlands*) (Judgment) [1969] ICJ Rep 3, Dissenting Opinion of Judge Tanaka, 181; *Case concerning the Arrest Warrant of 11 April 2000 (Democratic Republic of the Congo v Belgium)* (Judgment) [2002] ICJ Rep 3 [53–54].

22 *Prosecutor v Enver Hadzihasanovic, Mehmed Alagic and Amir Kubura* (Decision on Interlocutory Appeal challenging Jurisdiction in Relation to Command Responsibility) IT-01-47-AR72 (16 July 2003) Partial Dissenting Opinion of Judge Shahabuddeen [9–10].

23 WTO, *EC – Approval and Marketing of Biotech Products – Reports of the Panel* (29 September 2006) WT/DS291/R [7.68–7.72].

24 Merkouris (n 6) 241.

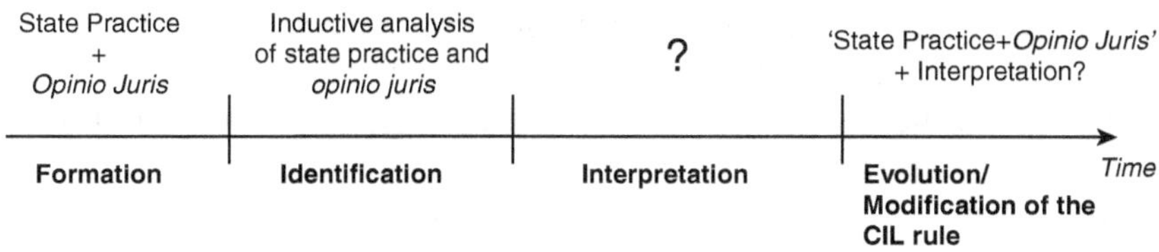

Figure 21.1 The CIL timeline

This chapter accounts for the process of CIL interpretation through the illustrative tool of a 'CIL timeline' (Figure 21.1).[25] The CIL timeline begins with the formation of a customary rule through the constitutive elements of state practice and *opinio juris*. The rule is then identified by an inductive analysis of these two elements. The reasoning in this stage includes the evaluation of evidence of practice and *opinio juris* and provides an answer to the question: does a customary rule exist? The outcome here is a binary one, in the sense that the answer will either be 'yes, a customary rule exists' or 'no, a customary rule does not exist'. This reasoning however does not provide an answer to the question 'is this customary rule applicable to the case at hand, and if yes, how is it applicable?'. This question is answered at the later stage of the CIL timeline, that is, at the stage of interpretation.

It is important to note that a form of interpretation may also be said to take place at the stage of identification. However, at this stage the relevant authority does not interpret a customary rule (as this rule has not been identified yet) but rather interprets the evidence of state practice and *opinio juris* in order to evaluate them and ascertain whether a rule has been formed. This distinction is particularly important, because although some authors have used the term 'interpretation'[26] for the reasoning that takes place at the stage of identification, this may not be considered as interpretation *stricto sensu*.[27] This is because the exercise of weighing and measuring

[25] For a discussion of CIL interpretation by reference to the 'CIL Timeline' see also N Mileva & M Fortuna, 'Emerging Voices: The Case for CIL Interpretation – An Argument from Theory and an Argument from Practice' (*Opinio Juris*, 23 August 2019) <https://bit.ly/3yGm7BD> accessed 1 March 2021.

[26] See for instance N Banteka, 'A Theory of Constructive Interpretation for Customary International Law Identification' (2018) 39(3) MichJIntlL 301, 304; DB Hollis, 'The Existential Function of Interpretation in International Law' in A Bianchi, D Peat & M Windsor (eds), *Interpretation in International Law* (Oxford University Press 2015) 78, 79; A Roberts, 'Traditional and Modern Approaches to Customary International Law: A Reconciliation' (2001) 95 AJIL 757, 781.

[27] P Merkouris, 'Interpreting the Customary Rules on Interpretation' (2017) 19 ICLR 126, 138–9.

evidence of practice and *opinio juris* in order to discover whether they can be counted for the purpose of establishing a CIL rule is not the same as applying and interpreting the CIL rule to the legal and factual context of a case. The former is an exercise of evaluating evidence; the latter is an exercise of applying a formulated legal rule to a particular context of a case. In the former we ask questions such as: 'does this piece of (state) behavior count as practice or *opinio juris*?', 'is this practice sufficiently widespread?', 'does this piece of evidence constitute a manifestation of *opinio juris*?', 'does this collection of practice and *opinio juris* point towards the existence of a rule?', etc. In the latter we ask questions such as 'is this CIL rule applicable to the factual context of the present case?', 'how does this CIL rule play out in the present context?', 'what is the specific content of this general CIL rule?', etc. Thus, while the exercise of CIL identification may in fact also contain interpretative reasoning, this is not the same type of interpretation as the one exercised over an already identified CIL rule.

Even if one would concede that in the phase of interpretation the relevant interpreter may rely on some of the evidence of state practice or *opinio juris* from the phase of identification, this would still not constitute a counterargument to the overall claim that CIL rules are in fact interpretable.[28] This is because, in this scenario, for the lack of a better analogy, this interpretative behaviour could be likened to how sometimes in the interpretation of a treaty interpreters may rely on the preparatory texts to elucidate intent, object and purpose, etc. Thus, an interpreter of a CIL rule might look back at evidence of state practice or *opinio juris* in the course of their interpretation of the rule, to answer some questions such as 'what prompted the formation of this customary rule?', 'what is the aim to be achieved with this rule?', or 'can we discern specific sub-elements of this rule if we look back to past behavior?'.

Once a rule is identified by a relevant authority, every subsequent invocation of that rule in following cases is not an exercise of re-identification but rather of application and interpretation. The reasoning employed at the stage of interpretation is concerned with the determination of the content of the CIL rule and how this rule applies to the case at hand. Unlike the binary outcome of the identification stage, this reasoning may have a variety of outcomes depending on the rule being interpreted and the legal and factual circumstances it is being interpreted in.

[28] This is also the argument forwarded by Gourgourinis (n 9) 56, according to which an attempt at interpretation of a CIL rule would be circular because it would inevitably end up back at an evaluation of the elements.

By distinguishing the two stages in this way, the CIL timeline illustrates the fact that the interpretation of a CIL rule is a process which manifests in a different and separate way from identification, a process which is subject to a separate (and perhaps unique) methodology, and a process which merits its own separate study (Figure 21.1).

In its 2016 Preliminary Report, the Study Group on Content and Evolution of the Rules of Interpretation flagged CIL interpretation as a relevant topic of exploration.[29] Building on this recommendation, and observing the existing gap posed by the lack of guidelines for CIL interpretation, this chapter now turns to its central discussion on how domestic interpretive practice may be instructive to the development of rules or guidelines for CIL interpretation in international law.

3 The Role of Domestic Courts in the Development of International Law

For the purposes of this section, the role of domestic courts in the development of international law is examined along two broad lines of inquiry: the contribution of domestic courts to international law within the framework of sources (Section 3.1), and the informal contribution of domestic courts to international law beyond or outside the framework of sources (Section 3.2). The distinction of formal versus informal contribution employed in this section is used broadly and without prejudice to the more focused discussion on formalism and the sources of international law.[30] The distinction is drawn with the aim of juxtaposing on the one hand the contribution of domestic courts to the development of international law primarily from within the framework of sources, and on the other hand the contribution of domestic courts to the development of international law beyond the framework of sources and in informal ways.

3.1 Domestic Courts within the Framework of Sources

Within the formal framework of sources, domestic courts can contribute to the development of international law in broadly three ways. Firstly, domestic judicial practice can contribute to the formation of

[29] ILA, 'Preliminary Report of the Study Group on the Content and Evolution of the Rules of Interpretation' (*ILA*, 7–11 August 2016) 9 <https://bit.ly/3q5oWbi> accessed 1 March 2021.

[30] See here notably J d'Aspremont, *Formalism and the Sources of International Law* (Oxford University Press 2011).

a rule of CIL. Here, the decisions of a domestic court may be considered as evidence of state practice[31] or *opinio juris*[32] and thus count towards the formation of CIL. Secondly, decisions of domestic courts may be taken into account in the determination of general principles of international law as set out in Article 38(1)(c) of the ICJ Statute.[33] Finally, domestic court decisions as a form of state practice may be considered as 'subsequent practice' in the sense of Article 31(3)(b) of the VCLT and as such contribute towards the agreed interpretation of a treaty.[34] Some authors have argued that a fourth way in which domestic courts' practice can contribute to the development of international law from within the framework of sources is as subsidiary means for the determination of rules of law within the meaning of Article 38(1)(d) of the ICJ Statute.[35] This, however, greatly depends on one's reading of Article 38. The most recent commentary to the ICJ Statute for instance takes the view that, in spite of alternative readings, Article 38(1)(d) does not include the decisions of domestic courts in its reference to 'judicial decisions'.[36]

While it may seem that domestic court practice has various 'points of entry' in the formal development of international law, it must be observed that their contribution within this framework is fairly limited. Namely, although domestic court practice may feature in the formation of CIL or general principles, or the interpretation of treaties, their conduct can only meaningfully contribute to the development of international law if it is shared by other domestic courts across a multitude of states. For instance, for the purpose of CIL, the conduct of one single state is not sufficient to create a customary rule. Similarly, for the purpose of general principles, the implied threshold is that these principles are shared across most (if

[31] ILC (n 1) 133, Conclusion 6 with commentary.

[32] ibid 140, Conclusion 10 with commentary.

[33] Pellet &Müller (n 14) 925–31; Tzanakopoulos & Tams (n 4) 537.

[34] ILC, 'Draft Conclusions on Subsequent Agreements and Subsequent Practice in Relation to the Interpretation of Treaties, with Commentaries' (30 April–1 June and 2 July–10 August 2018) UN Doc A/73/10, reproduced in [2018/II – Part Two] YBILC 11, 37, Conclusion 5 with commentary.

[35] R Higgins, *Problems and Process: International Law and How We Use It* (Oxford University Press 1995) 208–09; A Tzanakopoulos & E Methymaki, 'Sources and the Enforcement of International Law: Domestic Courts – Another Brick in the Wall?' in S Besson & J d'Aspremont (eds), *The Oxford Handbook of the Sources of International Law* (Oxford University Press 2017) 813; A Roberts & S Sivakumaran, 'The Theory and Reality of the Sources on International Law' in M Evans (ed), *International Law* (Oxford University Press 2018) 89, 99.

[36] Pellet &Müller (n 14) 954 [323].

not all) nations.[37] Thus, while domestic courts are featured in the doctrine of sources and into processes of treaty interpretation, they are formally treated just like one organ of one state and this significantly limits their formal impact on the development of international law.[38] In light of this, scholars increasingly examine the role of domestic courts in the development of international law beyond the formal framework of sources. It is to this body of scholarship that we now turn.

3.2 Domestic Courts beyond the Framework of Sources

In studying the contribution of domestic courts to the development of international law, scholars have pointed to the need to look beyond the traditionally formal approach of the framework of sources and widen the lens of inquiry in order to fully grasp their role.[39] What this seems to signify is that scholars retain the framework of sources as a departing point in their analysis, but identify that in practice domestic courts contribute to the development of international law much more significantly.[40] For instance, in her development of the concept of comparative international law, Anthea Roberts identifies a so-called duality of domestic courts in their interaction with international law. In this framework the role of domestic courts under international law is split between on the one hand law creation and on the other law enforcement.[41] In order to demonstrate this duality, Roberts relies on the theory of sources, but argues that domestic court decisions actually have a far greater effect on international law than what is envisaged by the sources doctrine.[42] She points to examples from the law on state immunity and human rights law where domestic judges have contributed to the progressive development of international law,[43] observing that international law does not only percolate down from the international to the domestic sphere, but also bubbles up in the opposite direction. 'In this process, national court decisions play a crucial role in developing international law, particularly in areas that tend to be tested by

[37] See for example the Trial Chamber's reasoning on this in *Prosecutor v Anto Furundzija* (Judgment) IT-95-17/1-T (10 December 1998) [178].

[38] Tzanakopoulos & Tams (n 4) 538.

[39] Roberts & Sivakumaran (n 35) 89.

[40] Tzanakopoulos & Tams (n 4) 536; Roberts & Sivakumaran (n 35) 100–15.

[41] A Roberts, 'Comparative International Law? The Role of National Courts in Creating and Enforcing International Law' (2011) 60 ICLQ 57, 61.

[42] ibid 63.

[43] ibid 69–70.

domestic courts.'[44] A similar analysis can be found in the description of a so-called feedback loop between domestic courts and international law, which describes the interaction by observing that 'domestic courts are at once organs of the state, and thus potential international law-makers, and judicial institutions applying and thus enforcing the law'.[45] This indicates that domestic courts do not only passively implement international law but also, through their practice, contribute to the development of the law as well. Thus, in the case of CIL interpretation, domestic courts' interpretive practice may be instructive both in the initial phase when rules are yet to be identified or developed, and in the subsequent process where domestic courts will be one of the actors implementing the developed rules. This potential feedback loop in CIL interpretation will be further discussed in Section 4 below.

In the analytical framework of a 'cycle of contestation and deference' domestic contestations of international law may invite procedural or substantive changes, and international law may respond by paying deference to domestic systems and adjusting accordingly.[46] Within this cycle, domestic courts are one of the relevant domestic actors which have the power to invite changes on the international level through their practice of applying and interpreting international law.[47] For instance, Kanetake argues that beyond the traditional modes of interaction between domestic courts and international law provided for in the sources doctrine, domestic courts may contribute to international law through so-called normative or conceptual points of connection.[48] Normative points of connection occur in instances of inter-judicial communication across national courts of different states, when domestic courts refer to each other's decisions. In these instances, the communication 'may create norms which are yet to become part of formal international law but which affect the way international organisations and international judicial institutions render their decisions'.[49] This observation is particularly relevant for our present inquiry, because it demonstrates that the interpretive methodologies of

[44] ibid.

[45] Tzanakopoulos & Methymaki (n 35) 820.

[46] M Kanetake & A Nollkaemper, 'The International Rule of Law in the Cycle of Contestations and Deference' in M Kanetake & A Nollkaemper (eds), *The Rule of Law at the National and International Levels: Contestations and Deference* (Hart 2016) 445.

[47] M Kanetake, 'The Interfaces Between the National and International Rule of Law: A Framework Paper' in M Kanetake & A Nollkaemper (eds), *The Rule of Law at the National and International Levels: Contestations and Deference* (Hart 2016) 13, 24–26.

[48] ibid 28–30.

[49] ibid 28.

domestic courts, if shared or communicated across courts of various states, may contribute to the development of rules for CIL interpretation on the international level. Conceptual points of connection concern the translation of national law and domestic decisions into international law by analogy. Kanetake observes that analogical reasoning is widely used in judicial practices, and offers as an example the translation of domestic law and practices into international law by means of legal transplants.[50] The conceptual points of connection inform our inquiry by demonstrating that the interpretive practices of a domestic court may, where relevant, be transplanted to the international level for the purposes of CIL interpretation. Arguing along similar lines, Nollkaemper observes that domestic courts may contribute to the normative development of international law through their acceptance or not of pronouncements by international courts. Here, the fate of pronouncements by international courts depends on their acceptance and recognition by other actors, and domestic courts are one of the actors that play this role.[51] For the purpose of our present inquiry this points to a potential 'conversation among courts' (to use Nollkaemper's terminology) both at the stage of identification or development of rules for CIL interpretation, and at a later stage when these rules are more established. Namely, domestic courts may already be confirming existing pronouncements by international courts when it comes to the interpretation of CIL – thereby adding to a body of domestic jurisprudence from which to draw at the stage of identifying rules of interpretation; and they may continue to participate in this 'conversation' after clear rules or guidelines for CIL interpretation are identified or developed.

4 The Role of Domestic Courts in the Development of Rules for CIL Interpretation

Having examined the role of domestic courts in the development of international law both within the framework of source and beyond it, we now turn to the operative portion of this chapter. What the above examination demonstrates is that there is ample scholarship to draw

[50] ibid; see also JB Wiener, 'Something Borrowed for Something Blue: Legal Transplants and the Evolution of Global Environmental Law' (2001) 27 Ecology LQ 1295; A Dolidze, 'Bridging Comparative and International Law: Amicus Curiae Participation as a Vertical Legal Transplant' (2016) 26 (4) EJIL 851.

[51] A Nollkaemper, 'Conversations among Courts: Domestic and International Adjudicators' in CPR Romano, KJ Alter & Y Shany (eds), *The Oxford Handbook of International Adjudication* (Oxford University Press 2013) 524, 539–40.

from when examining the relationship between domestic courts and international law. However, as the reader might have already noticed, the majority of scholarship focuses on the potential contribution of domestic courts in the form of substantive legal analysis and content. Conversely, what seems to be lacking is an account of the ways in which the interpretive methodologies of domestic courts may contribute to the development of interpretive methodologies in international law. In this section, we will first examine several cases where domestic courts engaged with CIL or domestic custom, with a particular focus on the methods of interpretation they employed, and, where available, the rationale behind that methodological choice (Section 4.1). Then, the section will lay out a set of preliminary observations on how these examples by domestic courts may contribute to the development of rules for CIL interpretation in international law along two lines of inquiry: how can we learn from domestic interpretive practices? (Section 4.2) and why should we learn from them? (Section 4.3).

4.1 Some Examples from Domestic Courts

This section contains examples of domestic courts interpreting CIL and domestic custom. The cases were found in cooperation with national research teams in various jurisdictions, as part of an ongoing research cooperation between these teams and the TRICI-Law project.[52]

4.1.1 Domestic Courts Interpreting CIL

We begin our analysis with the case of *Public Committee against Torture in Israel and Palestinian Society for the Protection of Human Rights and the Environment* v. *Israel and ors*, brought before the Israel Supreme court. Of the cases examined in this section this is the only case where a domestic court engages in the interpretation of CIL, as opposed to the other cases which are all examples of domestic courts interpreting domestic custom. It is for this reason that the case is catalogued under its own sub-heading.

In this case, the core question put before the court was whether the policy of targeted killings employed by Israel against members of Palestinian 'terrorist' organisations was legal under international law. Overall, the court found that it cannot be determined in advance that every targeted killing is either permissible or prohibited according to CIL.

[52] For more information see <https://trici-law.com/research/domestic/>.

Rather, the legality of each individual targeted killing is to be decided according to its particular circumstances.[53]

The court began its analysis by observing that the 'geometric location of our issue is in customary international law dealing with armed conflict'.[54] This is relevant because, as we will see in the subsequent analysis, the court took the text of Article 51(3) of *Protocol Additional to the Geneva Conventions of 12 August 1949* (AP I) as a verbatim statement of the relevant CIL rule, and applied it to the case not as a treaty provision but as a rule of CIL. This was done because (i) Israel is not party to AP I, and (ii) even if it was, 'the international law entrenched in international conventions which is not part of CIL is not part of the internal law of the State of Israel'.[55] Thus, although the court made constant reference to the wording of Article 51(3), when doing so it was not interpreting a treaty provision but was interpreting the customary rule reflected in that provision.

The court first went through the categories of 'combatants' and 'civilians' as defined by CIL, to conclude that members of 'terrorist' organisations do not belong to either of these categories. Instead, the court turned to the category of 'civilian taking direct part in hostilities' as the more apposite description.[56] Next, relying on 'extensive literature on the subject' the court found that presently the category of 'unlawful combatants' proposed by the Israeli state is not recognised in CIL. However, the court continued, 'new reality at times requires new interpretation. Rules developed against the background of a reality which has changed must take on dynamic interpretation which adapts them, in the framework of accepted interpretational rules, to the new reality.'[57] With this statement the court introduced in no uncertain terms the possibility, and indeed its intention, to interpret the customary rule pertaining to civilians taking direct part in hostilities evolutively.[58] The relevant customary rule was identified by reference to Article 51(3) of AP I which states that 'Civilians shall enjoy the protection afforded by this section, unless and for such time as they

[53] *Public Committee against Torture in Israel and Palestinian Society for the Protection of Human Rights and the Environment v Israel and ors* (13 December 2006) Supreme Court of Israel, HCJ 769/02 [60].
[54] ibid [19].
[55] ibid.
[56] ibid [24–26].
[57] ibid [28].
[58] For a discussion on evolutive interpretation see E Bjorge, *The Evolutionary Interpretation of Treaties* (Oxford University Press 2014); N Mileva & M Fortuna, 'Environmental Protection as an Object of and Tool for Evolutionary Interpretation' in G Abi-Saab et al (eds), *Evolutionary Interpretation and International Law* (Hart 2020) 123.

take a direct part in hostilities.' This formulation was found by the court to express CIL in its entirety.[59] From here the court embarked on an assessment of what it observed to be the three constitutive parts of this customary rule: (i) taking part in 'hostilities', (ii) taking 'direct' part and (iii) 'for such time'.[60]

With regard to the definition of 'hostilities' the court relied on a Commentary on the Additional Protocols by the Red Cross to observe that hostilities are acts which by nature and objective are intended to cause damage to the army. Next, the court expanded this definition by stating that '[i]t seems that acts which by nature and objective are intended to cause damage to civilians should be added to that definition'.[61] Reading this passage alone, it may seem unclear how the court arrived at the finding that acts which are intended to cause damage to civilians should be added to the definition of hostilities. In the passage itself the court relied on a scholarly analysis but did not elaborate on this reference. However, reading this passage in the context of the court's earlier statement, it becomes evident that here the court is 'updating' the definition of 'hostilities' to correspond to the new factual reality of the conflict, or, in other words, is interpreting the customary concept of hostilities evolutively.

Turning next to the definition of 'direct', the court catalogued commentaries, scholarly work, and judgments of international tribunals to conclude that there is no uniform definition of direct participation in hostilities. 'In that state of affairs, and without a comprehensive and agreed upon customary standard, there is no escaping going case by case, while narrowing the area of disagreement'.[62] In order to find an appropriate definition of 'direct' for the context of justified targeted killings the court examined the objective to be achieved with the interpretive exercise:

> On the one hand, the desire to protect innocent civilians leads, in the hard cases, to a narrow interpretation of the term 'direct' part in hostilities. . . . On the other hand, it can be said that the desire to protect combatants and the desire to protect innocent civilians leads, in the hard cases, to a wide interpretation of the 'direct' character of the hostilities, as thus civilians are encouraged to stay away from the hostilities to the extent possible.[63]

[59] *Public Committee against Torture in Israel and Palestinian Society for the Protection of Human Rights and the Environment v Israel and ors* [30].
[60] ibid [32].
[61] ibid [33].
[62] ibid [34].
[63] ibid [35].

On this reasoning, the court opted for a wider interpretation, and enumerated a wide spectrum of behavior that should be considered 'direct' participation.[64] Similarly, turning to the definition of 'for such time', the court found that there is currently no consensus on the meaning and thus it must be examined on a case-by-case basis. For the case of targeted killings, the court identified four general principles that should be borne in mind in the assessment.[65]

This case is a rich and complex example of the interpretation of CIL by a domestic court. Overall, three observations can be made. Firstly, the court took a treaty rule as the codified version of a CIL rule, and used this text for its subsequent interpretation. While this conflation of a customary rule with its codified counterpart may be considered problematic because it opens a discussion on the relationship between CIL and treaties, it may also be argued that in doing this the court engaged in systemic interpretation of CIL. Namely, when the content of a CIL rule is examined by reference to its codified counterpart, this is done because the two rules are taken as relevant to each other due to their identical content. Thus, what is in fact happening is that the CIL rule is interpreted by taking into account the treaty rule that codifies it, or in other words is interpreted according to the principle of systemic integration.[66] Secondly, it seems that two interpretative methodologies may be discerned in the court's reasoning. Overall, the court interpreted the customary rule on direct participation in hostilities evolutively, by adding new modalities of behavior which should be considered as coming under the scope of the rule in light of the new factual situation of the conflict. Moreover, the court elaborated new standards which should be considered when assessing whether a civilian is taking direct participation in hostilities for the purposes of deciding whether they can legitimately be a target of targeted killings. However, while the court interpreted the overall customary rule evolutively, in its interpretation of the individual elements of the rule it also engaged in teleological interpretation. In particular, when assessing the element of 'direct' the court inquired what objective is to be achieved with the rule, and opted for a wider interpretation in order to ensure the protection of combatants and innocent civilians and to encourage civilians to stay away from the hostilities. Finally, in the

[64] ibid [35–37].
[65] ibid [39–40].
[66] Merkouris (n 6) 264–65.

grander scheme of things, the court's reliance on evolutive interpretation might make us wonder about the role of interpretation in the life of a CIL rule. What we can see in this case is that through evolutive interpretation the court ended up 'updating' and specifying the content of the customary rule in question, thus arguably transforming it for those who may rely on it in the future. This raises the question as to what is the role of evolutive interpretation in the modification of existing CIL rules, and how does this method of interpretation play into our understanding of the genesis and continued existence of customary rules. While this discussion is presently beyond the scope of this chapter, it is certainly an interesting avenue for further research.

4.1.2 Teleological Interpretation of Domestic Custom

The next case considered in this section is *TC1.6p.7613* argued before the Veles Court of First Instance in North Macedonia. The case is an example of a domestic court interpreting a domestic customary rule. In this case, the court was asked to review a penalty stipulated in a written agreement between the plaintiff and respondent. Namely, the two had concluded an agreement regulating the payment of penalties which might arise in the case of non-compliance with two previously concluded sales contracts (agreement). The agreement was governed by the 'Law of Obligations', which is a law governing contracts and damages in the area of civil law in the Macedonian legal system. Pursuant to this law, all legal agreements between parties need to comply with the constitution, the laws and good customs.[67] Furthermore, legal agreements which do not comply with the constitution, the laws and good customs are considered null and void.[68] Thus, in this case the court had to evaluate whether the penalty for breach of contract stipulated in the agreement between the parties was in keeping with, among others, customary law.

It is important to note that in the Macedonian law of obligations custom has a secondary role behind the constitution and other written rules, and is only considered in cases where the written law is silent or

[67] Article 3 of the 'Law of Obligations' reads: 'The parties engaged in legal transactions are free to regulate their obligation relations in accordance with the Constitution, laws, and good customs and usages'; Article 15(1) of the 'Law of Obligations' reads: 'The participants of obligational relations have a duty to observe the good business customs in their legal relations' *Law of Obligations*, Official Gazette of R Macedonia No 18 of 5 March 2001 (the law has not been translated in English, and this is an unofficial translation of the relevant provision by the author) <https://bit.ly/3mOqrZU> accessed 1 March 2021.

[68] Article 95 of the 'Law of Obligations' (n 67).

there is a gap.[69] In light of this, in *TC1.6p.7613* the court considered customary law only briefly, and ultimately made its decision on a combined consideration of written law and customary rules. Nonetheless, in doing so, the court made some observations with respect to the interpretation of custom. Notably, the court observed as follows:

> In circumstances when we are dealing with a contractual penalty, that penalty needs to remain within the limits of the good business customs and serve the purpose of strengthening the discipline of the parties in their timely fulfillment of contractual obligations, and not to serve as a source of unjust enrichment contrary to the principles of conscientiousness and honesty. This is because the objective of a contractual penalty does not allow for the penalty to be excessive and disproportionate to the obligation for whose protection it is stipulated.[70]

In this case, there was no rule applicable to the situation which stipulated the specific amount that a contractual penalty can reach. Instead, the court only identified the general rule that 'a penalty should be in keeping with good business customs'. Subsequently, the court examined this general rule by reference to the objective of such rules and the purposes they are supposed to serve. In other words, it seems that here the court engaged in teleological interpretation of the customary rule. It is difficult to gauge why the court opted for teleological interpretation as the relevant method for the interpretation of custom, and more research needs to be conducted to find whether this is an isolated choice or a consistent trait of this particular legal system. Nonetheless, a few initial questions come to mind: is teleological interpretation an apposite method when it comes to customary law? How can we assess the object and purpose of a customary rule if we bear in mind that it is a rule which usually emerges gradually and in a decentralised manner?

4.1.3 Evolutive Interpretation of Domestic Custom

The final three cases examined in this section all come from the domestic courts of Kenya, and are examples of domestic courts interpreting domestic customary law. In the case of *Mary Rono* v. *Jane Rono & another* the Court of Appeal was asked to review a judgment of the High Court of Kenya related to the distribution of inheritance. In the disputed decision, the High

[69] G Galev & J Dabovikj-Anastasovska, *Obligaciono Pravo* (3rd ed, University of St. Cyril and Methodius Skopje 2012) 32–33.

[70] *TC1.6p.7613* (2013) Veles Court of First Instance, North Macedonia, 21 (unofficial translation of the original passage by the author).

Court arrived at a distribution of the inheritance based on both customary law and statutory laws on succession.[71] Namely, the High Court found that according to the relevant customary law the distribution of inheritance was by reference to the house of each wife irrespective of the number of children, and that daughters received no inheritance. On the other hand, taking statutory law and the will of the parties in consideration, the High Court found that the daughters should also be entitled to a share of the inheritance. However, because they are likely to marry, they were apportioned a lower share of the inheritance than the male children.[72]

In its review of this judgment, the Court of Appeal considered both customary law and statutory law, as well as relevant international law.[73] While the court eventually made its decision primarily on the basis of the written law, it nonetheless dedicated considerable space in the judgment on the interpretation of African customary law. 'The manner in which courts apply the law in this country is spelt out in section 3 of the Judicature Act Chapter 8, Laws of Kenya. The application of African Customary Laws takes pride of place in section 3(2) but is circumscribed thus: " . . . so far as it is applicable and is not repugnant to justice and morality or inconsistent with any written law . . . ".'[74] Having outlined this, the Court of Appeal went on to discuss whether the customary rules on distribution of inheritance could be considered 'repugnant to justice and morality'. In particular, the court considered the prohibition on discrimination contained in Kenya's constitution,[75] and the international human rights treaties and CIL applicable in Kenya,[76] as indicators of what might be considered for the purposes of the repugnancy test. Two observations can be made concerning the interpretation of the court in this case. First, when assessing whether the customary rules on distribution of inheritance might be considered discriminatory according to prevalent rules of non-discrimination from both Kenyan and international law, the court was arguably engaging in systemic interpretation of those customary rules. In this sense, the court was interpreting the customary rules in the context of the overall legal system that they are operating in and with reference to other legal rules that the customary rules coexist with. Secondly, the 'repugnant to justice and

[71] *Mary Rono v Jane Rono & Another* (29 April 2005) Kenyan Court of Appeal at Eldoret, Civil Appeal No 66 of 2002, 4.

[72] ibid.

[73] ibid 7.

[74] ibid.

[75] ibid 7–8.

[76] ibid 8.

morality' caveat to the application of African customary law is a very interesting provision of the Kenyan Judicature Act.[77] What this caveat implies is that African customary law is applicable insofar as it is not repugnant to justice and morality. Thus, by consequence, every rule of African customary law when invoked needs to be assessed against the justice and morality standards prevalent in Kenyan society. What this in essence means is that when an African customary law comes before a Kenyan court it will need to be assessed in light of the justice and morality standards prevalent in Kenyan society at that point in time. If those standards change or evolve with time, the customary rule will need to evolve with them or fall into disuse. Thus, this provision of the Kenyan constitution is in fact allowing for the evolutive interpretation of African customary law.

This conclusion is also supported by the reasoning of the High Court of Kenya in the case of *Katet Nchoe and Nalangu Sekut* v. *Republic*. In this case, the High Court of Kenya was asked to review a 10-year prison sentence handed down by a lower criminal court for the crime of manslaughter. The crime occurred during a procedure of female genital mutilation (FGM) which went wrong and resulted in the death of a 16-year-old girl. Counsel for the appellants argued that the prison sentence was harsh and excessive, and stressed that the offence for which the appellants were charged, convicted, and sentenced arose out of an old customary practice of circumcision.[78] The court accepted that this is indeed an old customary practice, and proceeded in the following manner:

> Section 3 of the Judicature Act . . . enjoins the High Court . . . to apply customary law where such custom is not repugnant to justice and morality. The repugnancy clause evokes a lot of anger and discussion among students of law, whose justice, and whose morality, I do not think it is the justice of the colonialist, or the judge or the court. It is the justice of all the surrounding circumstances of the custom in point. There is no more justice in this custom if ever there was any. . . .

[77] The full provision reads:

> The High Court, the Court of Appeal and all subordinate courts shall be guided by African customary law in civil cases in which one or more of the parties is subject to it or affected by it, so far as it is applicable and is not repugnant to justice and morality or inconsistent with any written law, and shall decide all such cases according to substantial justice without undue regard to technicalities of procedure and without undue delay'.

Judicature Act, 2012 rev KLR CAP 8, 5 <https://bit.ly/2YLRay8> accessed 1 March 2021.

[78] *Katet Nchoe & Another v Republic* (11 February 2011) High Court of Kenya, Criminal Appeal No 115 of 2010, 3.

> . . . In our case, female genital mutilation is certainly harmful to the physical and no doubt the psychological and sound well-being of the victim. . . . That kind of custom could truly be well discarded and buried in the annuals of history.[79]

On this reasoning, the High Court upheld the decision to sentence the two appellants, but lowered their sentence to two years and mandated subsequent seminars on the eradication of FGM for both.[80]

Yet another case where a court relied on evolutive interpretation in their assessment of customary law is the case of *Martha Wanjiru Kimata & another* v. *Dorcas Wanjiru & another*. However, unlike in *Mary Rono* and *Katet Nchoe*, here the court did not have to evaluate the custom in question against the repugnancy clause, but resorted to evolutive interpretation in light of another line of reasoning. In this case, the High Court of Kenya was asked to consider which member(s) of family have the right to make decisions concerning a person's burial. The court found that the law applicable to a burial decision is customary law.[81] The court then went on to observe: 'Customary law like all laws is dynamic. It is especially so because it is not codified. Its application is left to the good sense of the judges who are called to apply it. It is worded the way it is to allow the consideration of individual circumstances of each case.'[82] It seems that here the High Court opted for an evolutive interpretation of custom because of the nature of custom as a source of law. Namely, in the words of the court, custom is like all laws dynamic, but especially so because it is not codified. This is an interesting observation which seems to imply that because of its unwritten character customary law is a good candidate for evolutive interpretation. In other words, the method of evolutive interpretation seems to be particularly apposite for a source like custom which is both unwritten, and, because of its unwritten character, dynamic and able to evolve together with the community it stems from.

4.2 How Can We Learn from Domestic Interpretive Practices?

We must always be careful not to draw too grand a conclusion from a small sample of cases, and it is in this spirit that these findings, however interesting, remain preliminary. Nonetheless, it emerges from a reading of the

[79] ibid 4.
[80] ibid 5.
[81] *Martha Wanjiru Kimata & another v Dorcas Wanjiru & Another* (24 February 2015) High Court of Kenya, Civil Appeal No 94 of 2014, 5.
[82] ibid.

above cases that across varied jurisdictions judges seem to arrive at similar choices with respect to interpretive methodologies in the case of customary law. Moreover, there seems to be no prima facie difference between the methods of interpretation that domestic courts employ when interpreting domestic custom and when interpreting CIL. It transpires from the above cases that when dealing with custom judges may refer to the object and purpose of the customary rule, thus engaging in teleological interpretation. This raises the question of how might we assess the object and purpose of customary rules, and where do we turn for evidence of this? Furthermore, it seems that judges may interpret customary rules by reference to their codified counterparts, or by assessing them in the context of other rules of the legal system to which they belong, thus engaging in systemic interpretation. Finally, it emerges from the above cases that judges may resort to evolutive interpretation in their assessment of a customary rule, in order to 'update' the rule in light of new factual or legal considerations. This last observation in particular opens the questions of what the role of interpretation in the life of a CIL rule is, and how interpretation plays into our understanding of the genesis and continued existence of this source of law.

So, observing these few examples from cases and bearing in mind the role of domestic courts in the development of international law analysed in Section 3 above, we ask once again: how can the interpretive practices of domestic court contribute to the development of rules or guidelines for the interpretation of CIL? It is this author's view that the role of domestic courts envisaged by the formal framework of sources of international law does not fully grasp the contribution that domestic courts can have in the development of international law. Rather, in order to fully utilise the lessons that domestic courts have to offer, an informal line of influence must be accounted for as well. It is important to clarify that this chapter does not advocate for a complete departure from the framework of sources. Much like the scholarship discussed in Section 3, this chapter proposes that an adequate approach includes the sources framework as a point of departure and builds a broader framework of analysis from there. Thus, beginning with the framework of sources, the interpretive methodologies of domestic courts may contribute to the development of rules for the interpretation of CIL in the following ways. Firstly, the interpretive methodologies of domestic courts may contribute to customary rules of interpretation of CIL, as evidence of state practice. If an interpretive methodology can be identified across domestic courts when they interpret customary law, this may point to the existence of a customary rule(s) for the interpretation of CIL. Secondly, the interpretive methodologies of domestic courts, if shared across the domestic courts of a majority (if not all) of states, may contribute to the identification of general principles of interpretation of customary law. However, a study of domestic court practice for the purpose of identifying general principles of interpretation raises both practical[83] and theoretical[84] problems, and this must be taken in account in future research on the subject. Finally, and depending on one's reading of Article 38(1)(d) of the ICJ Statute, the decisions of domestic courts may be considered as subsidiary means for determining the rules for CIL interpretation. However, as already mentioned in Section 3 above, scholarly views as to the inclusion of domestic court practice in the reference to 'judicial decisions' in Article 38(1)(d) are divided.

Looking beyond the framework of sources, the 'cycle of contestation and deference' framework tells us that the practice of domestic courts may also contribute to the development of international law through normative or conceptual points of connection.[85] Namely, with respect to normative points of connection which occur in instances of inter-judicial communication across national courts of different states, it is argued that they may create norms which, although not yet part of formal international law, affect the ways in which international judicial institutions render their decisions. What this means for our present inquiry is that interpretive methodologies of domestic courts, if shared or communicated across courts of various states, may informally contribute to the way CIL is interpreted by international judicial institutions by generating norms of interpretation that will be picked up by international judges. Furthermore, conceptual points of connection occur when domestic legal concepts are analogised into international law. In this context, interpretive methodologies of domestic judges may be introduced into international law or practice through means of analogy. Normative and conceptual points of connection differ from the influence of domestic courts described through the framework of sources because they account for the potential influence of domestic judicial practice on the development of international law even when this judicial practice would not otherwise qualify as evidence of CIL or general principles. What is meant here is simply that while for the purpose of a customary rule or general principle of interpretation to be extrapolated from the practice of domestic courts this practice would have

[83] Can we truly examine the practice of the domestic courts of most (or all) states in order to identify universally shared principles?

[84] Can we identify general principles of interpretation, and if so, how will this exercise differ from an identification of customary rules of interpretation?

[85] Kanetake (n 47).

to meet the standards of widespread, uniform and representative, in the context of normative or conceptual points of connection it seems that this threshold is lower. In light of this, as an analytical framework, they capture the informal ways in which domestic court practice may be taken in consideration by international judges or practitioners, and can register instances where only a handful of domestic courts or even one single domestic court has exerted a significant influence on the development of international law. In this sense, this framework allows the researcher to examine the influence of domestic courts through a wider lens.

4.3 Why Should We Learn from Domestic Interpretive Practices?

In this author's view, there are three reasons why international law should learn from domestic law for the purpose of CIL interpretation.

Firstly, because the interpretation of CIL is currently an under-examined and unregulated sphere of international law. As demonstrated by Section 2, international legal theory and practice presently offer little discussion and guidance on the issue of CIL interpretation, and there are no uniform guidelines for the process of CIL interpretation. Such an existing gap in international law may be considered to legitimately invite contributions from domestic law. For instance, scholars observe that national court decisions play a crucial role in developing international law in areas of the law that tend to come before domestic courts,[86] or in instances where there is a need to plug legal gaps in international law.[87] Similarly, domestic courts are crucial in the normative development of international law insofar as they can confirm or not pronouncements by international courts.[88] Furthermore, learning from existing legal practices and approaches in domestic law for the purpose of CIL interpretation provides the benefit of already developed knowledge and practice. Seen as we are still only at the beginning of studying and developing the rules that guide the interpretation of CIL, interpretive practices of domestic courts which have dealt with the interpretation of custom offer the opportunity to benefit from the experience of already developed practices. Moreover, existing scholarship demonstrates that international law is already in fact to a great extent relying on interpretive canons

[86] See Steinbruck Platiše (n 5); Roberts (n 26).

[87] H van der Wilt, 'National Law: A Small but Neat Utensil in the Toolbox of International Criminal Tribunals' (2010) 10 Int CLR 209, 241.

[88] See Nollkaemper (n 51).

which originate in or are derived from domestic legal systems.[89] While interpretive canons originating in domestic legal systems have so far contributed primarily to the exercise of treaty interpretation, there is no reason why domestic interpretive practices, where relevant, should not be considered instructive to the development of rules or guidelines for CIL interpretation as well.

Secondly, because domestic courts are increasingly engaging with CIL in their proceedings, and there is an ever-growing pool of relevant interpretive practice which can contribute to the development of rules or guidelines for CIL interpretation. On this point, In his contribution to a recently published casebook on international law in domestic courts, Jorian Hamster demonstrates that a variety of domestic courts across different states engage in the application and interpretation of CIL.[90] Moreover, when domestic courts are faced with the need to ascertain or interpret CIL, they often turn to international case law or international legal scholars for guidance.[91] This shows us that the interaction between the two legal orders for the purpose of CIL interpretation is already taking place, and accentuates the need to study these avenues of mutual learning further.

Finally, because by learning from domestic practices for the purpose of CIL interpretation, international law can then provide domestic judges with various familiar tools for their further engagement with CIL in the domestic context. If we consider the cyclical interaction between domestic and international law, we will recall that the two legal orders interact both in the domestic-to-international and in the international-to-domestic directions. In particular, here it would be useful to recall the feedback loop which tells us that domestic courts are both contributors to the development of international law in their various roles in (and beyond) the framework of sources, as well as judicial institutions which apply and enforce international law. What this means in our present context is that

[89] J Klingler, Y Parkhomenko & C Salonidis (eds), *Between the Lines of the Vienna Convention? Canons and Other Principles of Interpretation in Public International Law* (Kluwer Law International 2019); see in particular M Waibel, 'The Origins of Interpretive Canons in Domestic Legal Systems' in J Klingler, Y Parkhomenko & C Salonidis (eds), *Between the Lines of the Vienna Convention? Canons and Other Principles of Interpretation in Public International Law* (Kluwer Law International 2019) 25–46.

[90] J Hamster, 'Customary International Law' in A Nollkaemper & A Reinisch (eds), *International Law in Domestic Courts: A Casebook* (Oxford University Press 2018) 243; see also C Ryngaert & D Hora Siccama, 'Ascertaining Customary International Law: An Inquiry into the Methods Used by Domestic Courts' (2018) 65 NILR 1, 3–4; see also Chapter 22 by Ryngaert in this volume.

[91] Hamster (n 90) 245–46.

if domestic interpretive practices feed the development of rules for CIL interpretation in international law, the developed rules for interpretation will then find their way back to domestic courts in future cases where those courts will again be faced with the task to apply and interpret CIL. The benefit of this cycle is twofold. Firstly, it is beneficial for future domestic judicial practice, because it will provide domestic judges with a familiar and coherent blueprint which they can refer to when they need to interpret CIL in future cases. Secondly, it is indirectly beneficial for the further development of international law; since domestic judicial practice can be a source of international law, by providing domestic judges with familiar and coherent guidelines for CIL interpretation we ensure that subsequent domestic case law can contribute to international law in a coherent manner. Thus, learning from domestic practices promotes the achievement of an integrated system of international law which remains closely related to and aware of domestic law.

5 Concluding Remarks

Domestic courts have the potential to contribute significantly in the development of rules or guidelines for the interpretation of CIL. Scholars have demonstrated that domestic courts are in fact often faced with the task to apply and interpret CIL, and thus yield relevant practice from which we may learn in the study of CIL interpretation. Moreover, a brief survey of some domestic practice indicates that domestic courts employ a variety of methods to interpret customary law, and there is a lot to learn from and examine in these methodological choices.

This chapter began with the question: how can interpretive methodologies employed by domestic courts inform the development of rules or guidelines for the interpretation of CIL? It examined the general scholarship on the role of domestic courts in the development of international law, and applied these findings particularly to the potential contribution of interpretive methodologies of domestic courts to the development of interpretive methodologies in international law. By examining five cases from various jurisdictions the chapter observed that in the interpretation of custom domestic courts may employ teleological, systemic or evolutive interpretation. While this is a restricted sample and no grand conclusions may be reached yet, these cases open many interesting questions about the nature of customary law interpretation and the role of interpretation in the genesis and continued existence of customary rules.

Bearing this in mind, the chapter laid out some preliminary observations along two lines of inquiry: (i) how can we learn from domestic interpretive practices? and (ii) why should we learn from them? With respect to the first question, it was observed that in order to adequately study the contribution of domestic courts' practice to the identification and development of rules for the interpretation of CIL we should depart from the role of domestic courts within the sources framework and build a broader framework of analysis from there. Thus, additional informal normative and conceptual points of interaction need to be considered in order to register and account for all the ways in which domestic interpretive practices can inform our inquiry. In answering the second question, the chapter submitted three reasons why we should look to domestic practice. Firstly, because the interpretation of CIL is currently an under-examined and unregulated sphere of international law, and this kind of 'gap' legitimately invites contributions from domestic practice. Secondly, because domestic courts are frequently engaging with customary law, and this provides a growing pool of relevant interpretive practice which can be instructive to the development of rules for CIL interpretation in international law. Finally, because by learning from domestic practices for the purpose of CIL interpretation, international law can provide domestic judges with various familiar tools for their further engagement with CIL in the domestic context. This is beneficial both for domestic judicial practice and for the further development of international law.

Overall, the chapter found that this is an area of research which raises various relevant questions, and thus invites substantive further investigation.

22

Customary International Law Interpretation

The Role of Domestic Courts

CEDRIC RYNGAERT

1 Introduction

The TRICI-Law project observes that 'in the study of customary international law (CIL) there is a critical gap in understanding how CIL can be applied in individual cases once it has been formed'. The project then sets for itself the goal to uncover rules of interpretation of CIL. In the words of the project, if such rules were to exist, CIL need not be induced (ascertained) each and every time, by reference to state practice and *opinio juris* or asserted by judges.

This chapter attempts to narrow the gap in understanding how CIL is applied and interpreted by domestic courts. Domestic courts are important agents of international legal development,[1] and they contribute to the entrenchment of the rule of international law, including CIL.[2] Accordingly, a study of the interpretation of CIL cannot do without an analysis of domestic court practices.

The contribution opens with a critical reflection on the proposed doctrinal shift from mere CIL ascertainment to interpretation of more or less stabilised CIL norms (Section 2). As domestic courts tend to apply pre-existing CIL rather than ascertain CIL *de novo*,[3] the author sees a window of opportunity for CIL interpretation. He then goes on to ascertain whether domestic courts also use this window in practice. He does so by analysing a large data set of domestic court decisions

[1] A Tzanakopoulos & CJ Tams, 'Introduction: Domestic Courts as Agents of Development of International Law' (2013) 26 LJIL 531.

[2] A Nollkaemper, *National Courts and the International Rule of Law* (Oxford University Press 2012).

[3] CMJ Ryngaert & DW Hora Siccama, 'Ascertaining Customary International Law: An Inquiry into the Methods Used by Domestic Courts' (2018) 65 NILR 1.

(Section 3). The empirical analysis yields a number of 'true positives' which suggest that, in admittedly rare cases, domestic courts genuinely interpret relatively stable, pre-existing CIL norms, in particular in the area of international immunities. These courts appear to use methods of interpretation that reflect those used for treaty interpretation, notably systemic interpretation and interpretation taking into account subsequent practice.

2 From CIL Ascertainment to Interpretation

The quest for rules governing the interpretation of norms of international law other than treaty-based norms is not new. Reference can notably be made to the interpretation of the text of resolutions of the United Nations Security Council (UNSC).[4] The Advocate General advising the Dutch Supreme Court, for instance, recently opined that 'while Article 31 VCLT did strictly speaking not apply to a resolution of the UN Security Council, its rule of interpretation can be considered as a rule of customary international law'.[5] The reasoning appears to be that, precisely because Article 31 of the Vienna Convention on the Law of Treaties (VCLT) is of a customary nature, it can also be applied to the interpretation of sources of international law other than treaty law, such as UNSC

[4] For example *State of the Netherlands v [respondent] et al* (14 December 2012) Supreme Court of the Netherlands, AG Advisory Opinion, 11/03521 [3.7.2]; in a most recent case decided by the Dutch Supreme Court the Advocate General (AG),who advises the Court also applied Article 31(1) VCLT to the term 'asset freeze' as it featured in a UN Security Council resolution (Libya sanctions), emphasising the ordinary meaning of the notion of 'asset freeze' *Palladyne International Asset Management BV v Upper Brook (I) Limited* (12 October 2018) Supreme Court of the Netherlands, AG Advisory Opinion, 17/03964 [3.13]; while the court itself did not cite Article 31(1) VCLT and reached another conclusion than the AG regarding the meaning of an asset freeze, it drew attention to the objective of the resolution, *Palladyne International Asset Management BV v Upper Brook (I) Limited* (18 January 2019) Supreme Court of the Netherlands, 17/03964 [3.6.3] ('*Ook zou een beperkte uitleg afbreuk kunnen doen aan het doel van de resoluties om de tegoeden ten goede te laten komen aan de bevolking van Libië.*'). Thus, the court implicitly applied Article 31(1) VCLT which counsels both textual and teleological interpretation ('A treaty shall be interpreted in good faith in accordance with the ordinary meaning to be given to the terms of the treaty in their context and in the light of its object and purpose.').

[5] *Palladyne International Asset Management BV v Upper Brook (I) Limited*, AG Advisory Opinion [3.5] (author's translation); *State of the Netherlands v [respondent] et al* fn 23 ('*De uitlegregels van verdragen gelden ook voor besluiten van internationale organisaties, hoewel het WVV daarop strikt genomen geen betrekking heeft. Art. 31 WVV kan echter worden gezien als een regel van internationaal gewoonterecht*'); see A Orakhelashvili, 'The Acts of the Security Council: Meaning and Standards of Review' (2007) 11 UNYB 149, 153, 157; MC Wood, 'The Interpretation of Security Council Resolutions' (1998) 2 UNYB 73.

resolutions. If that is the case, nothing stands in the way of applying the rules of interpretation laid down in Article 31 VCLT to CIL as well.

This line of argumentation is not necessarily convincing, however. There may be little doubt regarding the customary character of Article 31 VCLT,[6] but that does not make the rules of interpretation laid down in that provision applicable to sources of international law other than the treaties which the VCLT is supposed to govern.[7] In fact, that the relevant rules of Article 31 VCLT are customary means, in the first place, that they can be applied to other treaties that are not governed by the VCLT, for example, because they predate the entry into force of the VCLT in 1980, because the state party to the relevant treaty has not ratified the VCLT, or because the treaty does not fall within the scope of the VCLT (for instance because it has been concluded in oral form, or between states and other subjects of international law, or between such other subjects *inter se*).[8] After all, Article 31(1) VCLT specifically stipulates that '[a] treaty shall be interpreted in good faith'.[9] If that rule has customary character, the parallel customary rule should also state 'a treaty shall be interpreted in good faith'.

[6] See O Dörr, 'Article 31. General Rule of Interpretation' in O Dörr & K Schmalenbach (eds), *Vienna Convention on the Law of Treaties: A Commentary* (Springer 2012) 521 [6] with references to relevant case law of the ICJ and other international dispute-settlement bodies.

[7] Similar confusion may perhaps surround the binding character of customary international norms for subjects *other than states*, such as international organisations or other non-state actors. The argument would then go that, because a particular norm is of a CIL character, that law is necessarily binding on other subjects of international law, or at the very least on intergovernmental organisations (which happen to typically consist of states). See regarding international organisations N Blokker, 'International Organizations and Customary International Law: Is the International Law Commission Taking International Organizations Seriously?' (2017) 14(1) IOLR 1 [3] (submitting that 'in the areas in which powers have been given to international organizations, it is increasingly recognized that these organizations are bound by the relevant rules of customary international law that are applicable in these areas'); see regarding non-state armed (opposition) groups: S Sivakumaran, 'Binding Armed Opposition Groups' (2006) 55(2) ICLQ 369 (discussing the explanation of the binding character of international humanitarian law (IHL) for non-state armed groups in the context of IHL being, at least in part, customary in nature, although in the end considering the state's ability to legislate on behalf of all its individuals to be the best explanation).

[8] Article 2(a) VCLT ('"treaty" means an international agreement concluded between States in written form'). Note that there is a 1986 Vienna Convention on the Law of Treaties between States and International Organizations or Between International Organizations (not yet in force), which in Articles 31–33 restates the corresponding articles of the 1969 VCLT.

[9] Emphasis added.

Nevertheless, this does not mean that Article 31 VCLT has no relevance for the interpretation of norms from other sources of international law. It may have such relevance, as a material source of inspiration, or via reasoning by analogy. In all likelihood, the VCLT rules of interpretation should not be transposed lock-stock-and-barrel to the interpretation of norms derived from other sources of international law, to paraphrase Arnold McNair's warning in the International Court of Justice (ICJ) *South West Africa* advisory opinion not to simply import domestic law institutions into international law.[10] Rather, when considering transposition, one may have to bear in mind the special features of other sources of international law compared to treaty law. Thus, Sir Michael Wood has sympathy for interpreters' reliance on Article 31 VCLT when interpreting UNSC resolutions, but, given the more political nature of this source of law, invites the interpreter to pay specific attention to the circumstances in which the resolution has been adopted as well as the context of the UN Charter.[11]

That the rules of interpretation devised for treaties can apply *mutatis mutandis* to UNSC resolutions is in any event understandable to the extent that a binding UNSC resolution is, just like a treaty, a written source of international law. Moreover, UNSC resolutions find their legal basis in a treaty (the UN Charter).[12] It is less self-evident to apply Article 31 VCLT, with the necessary modifications or not, to the interpretation of CIL norms. Unlike a treaty or a UNSC resolution, CIL is an unwritten source of international law, and it does not, at least not formally, find its legal basis in a treaty. The material source of CIL may sometimes be a treaty, for example, because subsequent to the adoption of a treaty norm, state practice and *opinio juris* converge on the content of that norm, but at the end of the day, for its legal existence the customary norm is not dependent

[10] *International Status of South West Africa* (Advisory Opinion) [1950] ICJ Rep 146, Separate Opinion of Judge McNair, 148.

[11] MC Wood, 'The Interpretation of Security Council Resolutions, Revisited' (2017) 20 UNYB 1.

[12] Compare Charter of the United Nations (adopted 26 June 1945, entered into force 24 October 1945) 1 UNTS XVI 40, art 25 UN Charter ('The Members of the United Nations agree to accept and carry out the decisions of the Security Council in accordance with the present Charter'). In fact, in the context of Article 103 of the UN Charter ('In the event of a conflict between the obligations of the Members of the United Nations under the present Charter and their obligations under any other international agreement, their obligations under the present Charter shall prevail'), legal obligations under the charter are considered as largely synonymous with legal obligations under UNSC resolutions; see for example S Kitharidis, 'The Power of Article 103 of the UN Charter on Treaty Obligations' (2016) 20 IP 111.

on the treaty norm.[13] Because CIL is an unwritten, flexible and protean source of international law, it does not easily lend itself to the transposition of rules of treaty interpretation. What is more, the question may arise whether rules of interpretation of customary law norms serve any purpose at all, as CIL is – at least potentially – in a state of constant flux. Interpretation of norms only makes sense if those norms have a stable existence. In the classic understanding of ascertainment and identification of norms of CIL, legal authorities (law-applying or law-ascertainment agencies) always have to revisit the very existence of customary norms *de novo*. Although unlikely, it is after all not impossible that customary norms change or form almost overnight (instant custom).[14]

This also appears to follow from the very text of Article 38(1)(b) of the ICJ Statute, which provides that the ICJ (and courts more generally one may well posit) 'shall apply' … 'international custom, as evidence of a general practice accepted as law'. Pursuant to this provision, courts apply a customary norm as soon as they have established its evidence-based existence, without any need for interpretation *stricto sensu*. This process may perhaps appear interpretative, in that judges interpret evidentiary materials placed before them with the aim of distilling customary norms from those materials. But such interpretation takes place only in an evidentiary rather than normative sense. Judges do not interpret previously crystallised norms by analogy with Article 31 VCLT; they simply ascertain the law. Thus, Merkouris observes that judges do 'not interpret State practice, they evaluate it, they examine its gravity for the purpose of determining the existence or not of CIL', whereas 'interpretation of CIL requires an already existing CIL rule'.[15]

[13] For instance, when the treaty norm disappears, for example because the treaty is terminated, the customary norm can survive. Admittedly, a relatively stronger argument can be made for reliance on VCLT rules of treaty interpretation, or any rules of interpretation for that matter, in case of parallel existence of a customary norm with the same content, and in particular in case of that customary norm having been developed on the basis of the treaty norm: in case of parallelism, the customary norm is likely to be more stable, as it mirrors the treaty norm. See in this respect also the ICJ's reference to interpretation of CIL in *Military and Paramilitary Activities in and against Nicaragua (Nicaragua v USA)* (Merits) [1949] ICJ Rep 14 [178] ('Rules which are identical in treaty law and in customary international law are also distinguishable by reference to the methods of interpretation and application').

[14] See on instant custom regarding the use of force for example B Langille, 'It's "Instant Custom": How the Bush Doctrine Became Law after the Terrorist Attacks of September 11, 2001' (2003) 26 BC Int'l & Comp L Rev 145, 145–56.

[15] P Merkouris, 'Interpreting the Customary Rules on Interpretation' (2017) 19 Int CL Rev 126, 138.

This process of CIL ascertainment or identification has been the subject of many studies, most recently by the International Law Commission (ILC).[16] In a previous publication with a co-author, this author systematised and categorised the variegated CIL ascertainment techniques used by *domestic courts*.[17] Triggered by Stefan Talmon's earlier finding that, 'when determining the rules of customary international law, the ICJ does not use one single methodology but, instead, uses a mixture of induction, deduction and assertion',[18] it was examined whether similar processes could be witnessed in domestic courts. An analysis of a large number of recent domestic court cases bore out that this is indeed the case. Domestic courts do not normally identify CIL norms on the basis of the textbook method of ascertaining a general practice accepted as law. Rather, they tend to outsource the determination of custom to treaties, non-binding documents, doctrine or international judicial practice. Sometimes, these courts simply assert, without citing persuasive practice, the existence of a customary norm.

While, in principle, 'other authorities' only have evidentiary value that should be weighted with other materials which more inductively evidence (or not) the existence of a particular customary norm, one cannot escape the impression that domestic courts are simply giving effect to, or applying pre-existing customary norms, that is, norms which have been identified earlier. But if that is true, there is in principle room for the development of rules of interpretation. As Merkouris observed: '[O]nce CIL has been identified as having been formed, its continued manifestation and application in a particular case will be dependent on the deductive process of interpretation. In this manner, interpretation focuses on how the rule is to be understood and applied after the rule has come into existence and for its duration.'[19] If domestic courts are in

[16] ILC, 'Draft conclusions on identification of customary international law, with commentaries' (30 April–1 June and 2 July–10 August 2018) UN Doc A/73/10, reproduced in [2018/II – Part Two] YBILC.

[17] Ryngaert & Hora Siccama (n 3).

[18] S Talmon, 'Determining Customary International Law: the ICJ's Methodology between Induction, Deduction and Assertion' (2015) 26 EJIL 417.

[19] Merkouris (n 15) 136; see also P Merkouris, *Article 31(3)(c) VCLT and the Principle of Systemic Integration: Normative Shadows in Plato's Cave* (Brill 2015) 241–42

> [A] rule of customary international law, once identified by an international court or tribunal, does not cease to exist. When the same or a different judicial body attempts to apply the same rule in a different case, it usually does not go on about re-establishing that the rule in question is customary international law. It considers it as a given, but this does not imply that it

fact interpreting customary norms when applying them in given cases, our earlier publication's lament that domestic courts failed to engage in a serious CIL ascertainment process (which includes parsing all available materials),[20] loses some of its force. Indeed, assuming that customary norms existentially stabilise at one point, after which they are simply interpreted, there is no need for an elaborate process of identifying a customary norm *de novo*. Instead, courts may satisfy themselves with reaffirming the existence of the norm – presumably established by other law-ascertainment agencies at an earlier stage without subsequently being challenged – and instead concentrate on how to interpret the norm in a manner similar to how treaty interpretation takes place. Specific CIL rules of interpretation that are autonomous from the VCLT rules of interpretation can, in principle, develop via the regular customary process, through concurrent state practice and *opinio juris*.[21] Merkouris has argued that such rules already exist, and that they themselves are amenable to interpretation.[22]

3 The Practice of Domestic Courts Interpreting CIL

The author's earlier research on how domestic courts found and applied customary norms was conducted through the lens of ascertainment. The current contribution, revisits relevant court decisions with a view to understanding more in-depth how domestic courts engage in CIL *interpretation*.

Oxford University Press's database International Law in Domestic Courts (ILDC) was used as the main resource to find relevant domestic court decisions. 'Interpretation' was used as the search term, combined with the generic subject 'Sources, foundations and principles of international law'. The headnote of the search results subsequently indicates

can immediately apply it either. In this context, between the identification of a customary rule and its application at a later date and in a different case there is an intermediate stage; that of interpretation of the rule by the later court or tribunal.

20 Ryngaert & Hora Siccama (n 3) 23.

21 See Merkouris (n 15) 141 ('[T]here are rules that guide the process of interpretation of CIL, although these will be, by virtue of the nature of CIL, different than those of treaties'), also citing *North Sea Continental Shelf cases (Federal Republic of Germany v Denmark; Federal Republic of Germany v Netherlands)* (Judgment) [1969] ICJ Rep 3, Dissenting Opinion of Judge Tanaka, 181.

22 Merkouris (n 15) 142–54 (discussing notably the customary law counterparts of Article 31(3)(a) and (b), and Article 32 VCLT).

whether CIL was relevant to the domestic court decision.[23] Also, ILDC marks the search term – in this case 'interpretation' – in the summary and text of the decision, which greatly facilitated the research.[24] Methodologically, a discourse analysis of written texts (judgments) was carried out;[25] the research analysed to what extent domestic courts *explicitly* used the term 'interpretation' when applying CIL.[26] Such an analysis has its limitations in that it may discount practices of courts implicitly interpreting customary norms. Accordingly, it also included references to interpretation by the ILDC commentators directly commenting on the judgments. However, the emphasis does not lie on what courts *may have meant* when applying customary norms, but primarily on what they did *in fact*: did they consciously consider customary norms to be amenable to interpretation?

The search yielded a number of domestic court decisions which featured both 'customary international law' and 'interpretation'. However, not all of these results pertain to the interpretation of CIL norms proper. Such results are 'false positives'.[27] A first category of false positives comprises those decisions in which domestic courts *erroneously* use the term 'interpretation', when they in fact meant something else, in particular *ascertainment*. A second category of false positive comprises those decisions in which courts do engage in interpretation, but not of CIL, but rather of domestic (statutory) law, although *in light of* CIL.

23 Somewhat confusingly, ILDC also uses the term 'subject(s)' in this regard.

24 In the earlier publication in NILR, we also consulted Cambridge University Press's *International Law Reports* (ILR). *International Law Reports*, however, is less user-friendly than ILDC, at least in the version I had access to via my institution. It was not possible to combine the search words 'interpretation' and 'customary international law', and unlike ILDC, the ILR application did not mark the term 'interpretation' in the summary or text of the decision. It was considered to be too time-intensive to copy, case-by-case, all decisions relevant to customary international law (e.g. to Word), and then apply a search for 'interpretation'.

25 See on discourse analysis at length: TA van Dijk, *Handbook of Discourse Analysis* (Academic Press 1985). Discourse analysis has been developed and applied mainly in linguistics, semiotics and psychology.

26 Obviously, the English term interpretation is not as such used in non-English-speaking jurisdiction. However, ILDC uploads official English translations of foreign-language judgments, translates relevant parts, and/or states in the headnote's 'Held' (H) sections the key holdings in English.

27 The term 'false positives' has its origins in medical research, where it refers to errors in test results, which indicate that a disease is present which in reality is not; compare TR Dresselhaus, J Luck & JW Peabody, 'The Ethical Problem of False Positives: A Prospective Evaluation of Physician Reporting in the Medical Record' (2002) 28 J Med Ethics 291.

These two categories of false positives are briefly discussed in Section 3.1. Subsequently, Section 3.2 proceeds to the core analysis of *true positives*, that is, decisions in which courts genuinely interpret CIL norms.

3.1 False Positives

A number of domestic court decisions in which courts profess to *interpret* CIL are in fact examples of CIL *ascertainment*. These cases are false positives as they pertain to the identification of the very existence of a customary norm rather than its subsequent interpretation. For example, in the US Court of Appeals (Second Circuit) judgment in *Kiobel*, Leval, J., concurring, criticises the majority's holding that corporate liability does not exist under CIL,[28] on the following grounds: 'The majority's interpretation of international law, which accords to corporations a free pass to act in contravention of international law's norms, conflicts with the humanitarian objectives of that body of law.'[29] What the majority in fact did in *Kiobel* was *ascertaining the very existence* of a customary norm providing for liability of corporations for violations of international law, rather than 'interpreting (the body of) international law'. Another example is the following characterisation by the US Court of Appeals (11th Circuit) of the difficulties of determining offences that violate CIL under the Offences Clause of the US Constitution (such as offences of drug trafficking):

> The determination of what offenses violate customary international law . . . is no simple task. Customary international law is discerned from myriad decisions made in numerous and varied international and domestic arenas. Furthermore, the relevant evidence of customary international law is widely dispersed and generally unfamiliar to lawyers and judges. These difficulties are compounded by the fact that customary international law – as the term itself implies – is created by the general customs and practices of nations and therefore does not stem from any single, definitive, readily-identifiable source. All of these characteristics give the body of customary international law a soft indeterminate character that is subject to creative *interpretation*.[30]

Here, the court refers to *evidentiary* interpretation, that is, the process of parsing state practice with a view to *ascertaining* CIL. It does *not* refer to

[28] *Kiobel v Royal Dutch Petroleum Co*, 621 F.3d 111 (2d Cir 2010) [58].
[29] ibid 155.
[30] *US v Bellaizac-Hurtado*, 700 F.3d 1245 (11th Cir 2012) 1253, citing *Flores v Southern Peru Copper Corp*, 414 F.3d 233 (2d Cir 2003) 247–49 (citations and references omitted) (emphasis added).

the interpretation of customary norms that have already come into existence.

A final example is the US trial court judgment in *Talisman*, where the court held that 'interpretations of [customary] international law [the law of nations] of the Supreme Court and Second Circuit are binding upon this Court'.[31] This case also concerned the question of whether corporations may be liable for international law violations, which, as pointed out above, is a matter of ascertainment rather than interpretation of international law. This lower court simply wanted to say that, on the basis of *stare decisis*, it has little agency in *ascertaining* CIL.[32] Of course, this need not totally exclude its *interpretation of* this law subsequent to its ascertainment – an issue which the court however did not address.

The search also yielded a relatively large number of potentially relevant cases that pertained to *statutory* interpretation in light of CIL. These cases are false positives as well, in that they are instances of 'consistent interpretation', that is, interpretation of domestic law in light of international law,[33] rather than interpretation of CIL proper. For instance, the Supreme Court of Appeal of South Africa held that '[w]hen interpreting legislation, the courts had to prefer a reasonable interpretation that was consistent with international law [including CIL] over any alternative inconsistent interpretation'.[34] Another example is the Italian Supreme Court's interpretation of a provision in the Italian criminal code in light of CIL on the prevention of terrorism.[35] Also included in this category

[31] *Presbyterian Church of Sudan v Talisman Energy, Inc*, 244 F.Supp.2d 289 (SDNY 2003) 308.

[32] See its reference to *United States v Smith*, 18 US 153 (1820), quoted in *Filartiga v Pena-Irala*, 630 F.2d 876 (2nd Cir 1980) 880 (the law of nations may be ascertained by consulting, inter alia, 'judicial decisions recognising and enforcing [international law]').

[33] G Betlem & A Nollkaemper, 'Giving Effect to Public International Law and European Community Law before Domestic Courts: A Comparative Analysis of the Practice of Consistent Interpretation' (2003) 14 EJIL 569. In the US, this is known as the *Charming Betsy* canon of statutory construction. *Murray v The Schooner Charming Betsy*, 6 US 64 (1804).

[34] *The Minister of Justice and Constitutional Development v The Southern African Litigation Centre* (867/15) (15 March 2016) South African Supreme Court of Appeal, ZASCA 17 [62].

[35] *Public Prosecutor at the Tribunal of Brescia v Elvis and el Mahdi* (9 October 2015) Supreme Court of Cassation of Italy, No 40699, ILDC 2565. The decision pertained to the question whether the expression 'enlistment for conducting acts of violence for terrorist purposes' in Article 270-quater of the Criminal Code (Italy), when interpreted in the light of international law, referred not only to the formal joining of armed forces, but also to the formal recruitment of enlisted persons in military or paramilitary terrorist networks.

are a large number of immunity cases from Anglo-Saxon jurisdictions (such as the USA, UK, Canada), which have adopted specific immunity legislation, and whose courts go on to interpret such legislation in light of customary immunity rules.[36] In the end, however, all these decisions, while interesting in their own right, *do not interpret customary international law*, but rather *statutory law*, unless it happens that, when interpreting statutory law, they also explicitly interpret rather than merely apply CIL.

Somewhere on a continuum between false and true positives are instances of 'reverse' consistent interpretation. Reverse consistent interpretation can be defined as interpretation of CIL in light of domestic law, meaning that in case of various possible interpretations of a norm, the interpretation that is most consistent with domestic law should be chosen. An Israeli judgment can serve as an example. In a case on the scope of state immunity from jurisdiction, the Supreme Court of Israel held that '[a]mong various possible alternatives offered by customary international law, an Israeli court should have chosen the alternative most consistent with the basic values of Israeli law, which, in the present context, favoured the restriction of state immunity'.[37] While the Israeli court appears to be interpreting CIL, using the method of systemic interpretation, it does so in a very insulated and parochial manner, by paying heed to the values of the domestic legal system rather than to 'the relevant rules of international law'.[38] Following Odile

36 For example *Kazemi Estate v Islamic Republic of Iran* (10 October 2014) Supreme Court of Canada, Case No 35034, 2014 SCC 62; *Most Rev Pedro D Arigo, et al v Scott H Swift, et al* (16 September 2014) Republic of the Philippines Supreme Court, GR No 206510 (the latter court in fact applying the US Foreign Sovereign Immunities Act).

37 *Her Majesty the Queen in Right of Canada v Edelson* (3 June 1997) Supreme Court of Israel, PLA 7092/94 [23].

38 That is, the formulation of the principle of systemic interpretation of treaties in Article 31(3)(c) VCLT, which could arguably be applied *mutatis mutandis* to the CIL. The ILDC commentator to the Israeli case pointed out that the Supreme Court also 'determined the content of the international law principles', but also that it did not clearly distinguish this process from 'their implementation in domestic law'. *Her Majesty the Queen in Right of Canada v Edelson,* Commentary E Peled, ILDC 577 [A2]; see the same court for a similar approach to CIL interpretation, having both international and domestic elements: *Public Committee v Israel* (13 December 2006) Supreme Court of Israel, HCJ 769/02, Commentary E Peled, ILDC 597 [A2] ('as President Barak indicated elsewhere in the decision, his interpretative approach (to the concept of 'direct participation in hostilities' under customary international law was mandated ... by the reality of Israel's struggle against terrorism in particular'); *Public Committee v Israel,* Commentary E Peled, ILDC 597 [A3] ('parts of the Israeli public who might regard the decision as excessively burdening the fight against terrorism may have been the intended addressees of ... parts of the judgment'). This case is analysed in more depth in Chapter 21 by Mileva.

Ammann, such an interpretative approach can be considered as disregarding or misapplying the interpretative methods of international law, and thus lacking quality and legality.[39] Interpretation requires international interaction,[40] that is, paying attention to how other states apply and interpret customary norms. Accordingly, instances of reverse consistent interpretation can largely be considered as false positives.

3.2 True Positives

The research did not just yield decisions in which domestic courts did *not* engage in CIL interpretation proper. In some cases, domestic courts appear to truly *interpret* CIL norms. These are the 'true positives' in which we are interested. They demonstrate that domestic courts assume that they *can* interpret CIL norms,[41] even if they have not given much thought to the doctrinal underpinnings or normative consequences of CIL interpretation.

Most relevant domestic court decisions relate to *immunities*. This is not surprising as (1) immunities are normally invoked before *domestic courts* and (2) the law of immunities, in particular the immunities of states and their officials, is one of the few fields of international law that is largely governed by CIL.[42] As pointed out above, in Anglo-Saxon jurisdictions, international immunities tend to be laid down in statutes, as result of which statutory law – possibly interpreted in light of CIL – will be applied. However, in other jurisdictions, for example on the European

[39] O Ammann, *Domestic Courts and the Interpretation of International Law: Methods and Reasoning Based on the Swiss Example* (Brill 2020) 322.

[40] ibid 282 (warning for domestic courts' self-serving interpretations and stating that 'this risk must be mitigated if States are to interact on a level playing field'). Parochialism is one of the major ills plaguing domestic courts' identification and interpretation of CIL: 'courts tend to predominantly (or even solely) refer to their own State's practice and *opinio juris* and to their own case law, in lieu of establishing the existence of the constitutive elements of CIL or the meaning of a customary norm on the international plane'.

[41] This finding is highly significant, as it proves that customary norms *can* be interpreted by domestic courts. Merkouris calls such decisions 'black swans', which disprove the statement that 'no swan can have any other colour other than white' Merkouris (n 15) 143. Applied to CIL interpretation by domestic courts, this means that it suffices to identify one instance of a domestic court interpreting CIL to disprove the statement that CIL is not, and cannot be, interpreted by domestic courts. In fact, there is more than one instance.

[42] See also Ammann (n 39) 302 (concluding her analysis of the application of customary international law by Swiss domestic courts as follows: 'Common features include the fact that CIL is seldom mentioned, and that, when it is, it is often in cases dealing with the law of immunities').

continent, immunities are directly derived from (customary) international law, possibly via a *renvoi* provision in domestic legislation.[43]

For analytical and pedagogical purposes, these decisions are clustered into three theoretical categories. These categories have been generated inductively through coding, conceptualising and analysing the available data (the court decisions referencing interpretation). In social science, such an approach would be termed 'grounded theory research'.[44] As the coding exercise is carried out by human beings, the data may obviously feed into different categories.[45] However, the generic categories offered here may have particular expository power in that they are also transferable to CIL interpretation by law-interpreting agencies other than domestic courts, for example international courts. They allow us to zoom out of the particular context in which domestic courts apply and interpret law, and to reflect at a more abstract level on the practice of CIL interpretation.

The following analytical categories will be successively discussed: (3.2.1) autonomous CIL interpretation, (3.2.2) deference to CIL interpretation by other (international) courts and (3.2.3) interpreting CIL norms laid down in authoritative (written) documents. In the discussion, particular attention is paid to the *method* of interpretation applied by the court.

3.2.1 Autonomous CIL Interpretation

The research yielded a number of decisions in which domestic courts appeared to interpret CIL relatively autonomously, that is, without (explicitly) taking their cue from international courts' interpretations, or from written documents purportedly codifying CIL. Most of these decisions pertain to the immunity *ratione materiae* of state officials from foreign criminal jurisdiction, which has not been codified, at least not until recently,[46] and regarding which international courts have given

[43] For example Article 13a of the Dutch *Wet Algemene Bepalingen* ('Act on General Provisions'), which provides (in old Dutch) that '*[d]e regtsmagt van den regter en de uitvoerbaarheid van regterlijke vonnissen en van authentieke akten worden beperkt door de uitzonderingen in het volkenregt erkend*' ('The jurisdiction of the judge and the execution of court judgments and authentic acts are limited by the exceptions recognized in public international law').

[44] I have also applied this approach in Ryngaert & Hora Siccama (n 3) 3–5, where grounded theory is explained in greater detail.

[45] The coding has been done by me and a research assistant.

[46] See the ongoing work of the ILC on the 'Immunity of state officials from foreign criminal jurisdiction' (since 2007), details of which are available at <http://legal.un.org/ilc/guide/4_2.shtml>.

little to no guidance. A Swiss, US and Italian case were considered to be relevant.

In *A* v. *Swiss Federal Public Prosecutor*, the Swiss Federal Criminal Court *interpreted* the customary norms on state official immunity *ratione materiae* (functional immunity) as follows, in a case concerning the claimed immunity of a former defence minister of a foreign state regarding a charge of war crime:

> It remained to be decided whether A's residual immunity *ratione materiae* covered acts performed while in office, and whether it trumped the necessity of establishing his responsibility for alleged grave human rights violations. In light of . . . developments, it was not clear that this immunity should prevail, as serious crimes against humanity, including torture, were prohibited by customary international law. The Swiss legislature's commitment to repressing *ius cogens* violations was an additional reason for denying A immunity *ratione materiae*, as it would be contradictory to express such a commitment while giving a broad *interpretation* to this immunity.[47]

Arguably, the Swiss court assumed that a state official's immunity *ratione materiae* for official acts had already crystallised as a customary norm and thus had a relatively stable existence.[48] What mattered now, was how to *understand and apply* the norm in respect of *jus cogens* violations. This is an *interpretative* exercise that mirrors the interpretative rule enshrined in Article 31(3)(c) VCLT, pursuant to which '[t]here shall be taken into account, together with the context . . . any relevant rules of international law applicable in the relations between the parties'.

A practice of *interpreting* functional immunity in respect of *jus cogens* violations can also be gleaned from the judgment of the US Court of Appeals for the Fourth Circuit in *Yousuf* v. *Samantar*, which concerned the same question of whether a high-ranking government official was

[47] *A v Swiss Federal Public Prosecutor* (25 July 2012) Swiss Federal Criminal Court, BB.2011.140 [5.4.3] (emphasis added). In the original French version:

> *Or, il serait à la fois contradictoire et vain si, d'un côté, on affirmait vouloir lutter contre ces violations graves aux valeurs fondamentales de l'humanité, et, d'un autre côté, l'on admettait une interprétation large des règles de l'immunité fonctionnelle (*ratione materiae*) pouvant bénéficier aux anciens potentats ou officiels dont le résultat concret empêcherait,* ab initio, *toute ouverture d'enquête.*

[48] See also ILC, 'Report of the International Law Commission: Sixty-ninth session' (1 May–2 June and 3 July–4 August 2017) UN Doc A/72/10 175–76, Article 5 ('State officials acting as such enjoy immunity *ratione materiae* from the exercise of foreign criminal jurisdiction').

immune from suit under head-of-state immunity or foreign official immunity for *jus cogens* violations, even if the acts had been performed in the defendant's official capacity.[49] The case had been remanded by the US Supreme Court, which had held that the Foreign Sovereign Immunities Act did *not* govern a claim of immunity by a foreign official.[50] On remand, the Court of Appeals held that the common law, which included CIL, governed such a claim,[51] and it went on to (arguably) *interpret* functional immunity, holding that '[t]here has been an increasing trend in international law to abrogate foreign official immunity for individuals who commit acts, otherwise attributable to the State, that violate *jus cogens* norms – i.e., they commit international crimes or human rights violations'.[52] Admittedly, the court itself did not use the term interpretation, but the ILDC commentator conspicuously did, not only in the analysis of the judgment, but also in the Held section which is supposed to simply restate the court's reasoning.

There is obviously a fine distinction with *law ascertainment* here, as it could as well be argued that whether immunity *ratione materiae* extends to international crimes is itself amenable to customary law *formation*: can sufficient state practice be identified to buttress the crystallisation of a customary law exception to the immunity *ratione materiae* of state officials?[53] However, both courts embraced a deductive approach[54] which emphasises the relationship of immunity with *jus cogens* norms. Such an approach can be termed 'interpretative', as it gives meaning to an established customary norm in the specific milieu of international crimes. The fact that a court may also cite other state practice (other domestic court decisions)[55] does not necessarily render the process one of customary law ascertainment, as such practice may well qualify as subsequent practice in the application of the customary norm which establishes the agreement of states regarding its *interpretation*, to paraphrase Article 31(3)(b) VCLT. Specifically regarding the purported immunity 'exception' for *jus cogens* violations, the systemic integration-based technique of interpretation may also be of particular relevance, that

[49] *Yousuf v Samantar*, 699 F.3d 763 (4th Cir 2012).
[50] *Samantar v Yousuf*, 560 US 305 (2010).
[51] *Yousuf v Samantar* [7].
[52] ibid [33].
[53] SD Murphy, 'Immunity *Ratione Materiae* of State Officials from Foreign Criminal Jurisdiction: Where is the State Practice in Support of Exceptions?' (2018) 112 AJIL Unbound 4–8.
[54] See also Merkouris (n 15) 135–36.
[55] See notably *Yousuf v Samantar* [34].

is, the interpretation of a customary norm in light of 'any relevant rules of international law applicable in the relations between the [states]', to paraphrase Article 31(3)(c) VCLT; *jus cogens* norms qualify as such rules.[56]

The fine line between law ascertainment and interpretation is also apparent in another functional immunity case, *Abu Omar*, before the Italian Court of Cassation. In this case, which pertained to the question of whether, under CIL, state officials who had participated in an extraordinary rendition operation enjoyed functional immunity from the criminal jurisdiction of a foreign state, the court decided as follows:

> The problem … consists of checking whether there effectively exists a customary law regulation under international law that also guarantees criminal immunity to the individual-entity of a sovereign state, even when it does not involve Diplomatic and/or Consular officials and high appointments of state.
>
> On this point, jurisprudence is divided, because alongside those authorities that recognise the existence of a customary law regulation of this kind, there are others that recognise this only in respect of the activities authorised by the foreign country where these take place, while there are still others that maintain that the benefit of immunity is recognised according to specific regulations only to certain categories of entities in exercising the functions that are typical of their office.
>
> This Court believes that this last *interpretation* is the more correct one, because it takes into account the developments in international relations, which as already stated, the *Nato [London] Convention* [Agreement between the Parties to the North Atlantic Treaty regarding the Status of their Forces] and the *[Vienna Convention on Consular Relations]* are valid examples.[57]

At first sight, in this case, the Italian court appears to ascertain the very existence of a customary norm on functional immunity ('checking whether there effectively exists a customary law regulation'). However,

[56] This is not the place to engage at length with the relationship between *jus cogens* and immunity, which has spawned a cottage industry of its own. See for relevant doctrine inter alia: T Weatherall, 'Jus Cogens and Sovereign Immunity: Reconciling Divergence in Contemporary Jurisprudence' (2015) 46 Georget J Int Law 1151–212; AJ Colangelo, 'Jurisdiction, Immunity, Legality, and Jus Cogens' (2013) 14 ChJIL 53–92; see also ILC, 'Text of the draft articles on immunity of State officials from foreign criminal jurisdiction provisionally adopted so far by the Commission' (2017) UN Doc A/72/10 175–76, Article 7(1) ('Immunity *ratione materiae* from the exercise of foreign criminal jurisdiction shall not apply in respect of the following crimes under international law').

[57] *'Abu Omar' case, General Prosecutor at the Court of Appeals of Milan v Adler* (29th November 2012) Court of Cassation of Italy, No 46340/2012 [23.7] (interpretation emphasised).

the court's use of the term 'interpretation' is not necessarily misguided, as what the court may actually be doing is to *interpret the scope* of functional immunity, without casting doubt on the principled customary existence of functional immunity (the 'core norm'). The judgment could be read as affirming the principled existence of customary functional immunity, while denying its blanket application to all categories of state entities exercising official functions. To reach the conclusion that functional immunity under customary law 'only' applies to certain categories, the court appears to have recourse to contextual interpretation, when it states that it 'takes into account the developments in international relations'.

Finally, there is a decision by the Belgian Court of Cassation with respect to immunity from execution, which is particularly relevant from a conceptual perspective. In this decision, the court held as follows:

> *Il ne résulte pas de [l'article 38, § 1er, b), du Statut de la Cour internationale de Justice] que le juge étatique qui identifie et interprète une règle coutumière internationale est tenu de constater, dans sa décision, l'existence d'une pratique générale, admise par une majorité des États, qui soit à l'origine de cette règle coutumière.*[58]

What the court states here is that domestic courts identifying *and* interpreting a CIL norm are not required to establish the existence of a general practice accepted by a majority of states which is at the origin of the CIL norm. As the court uses the terms 'identifying' and 'interpreting', it is apparent that the court is not conflating law ascertainment and law interpretation. Arguably, the court uses the term 'interpretation' in response to the applicant's subsidiary argument that the lower court:

> *[N]e justifie pas légalement sa décision en rendant applicable aux comptes d'ambassade la règle ne impediatur legatio,* à supposer celle-ci établie, *sans constater d'abord qu'une majorité des États admet que la règle ne impediatur legatio consacre également une immunité d'exécution diplomatique autonome des comptes d'ambassade (violation de la règle coutumière internationale ne impediatur legatio).*[59]

58 'It does not result from Article 38(1)(b) ICJ Statute that the domestic judge who identifies and *interprets* a rule of customary international law is obliged to establish in his decision the existence of a general practice admitted by a majority of States, which is at the origin of this customary rule' [author's own translation] *NML Capital Ltd v République d'Argentine* (11 December 2014) Court of Cassation of Belgium, C.13.0537 (emphasis added).

59 '[D]oes not legally justify its decision by applying to embassy accounts the rule of *ne impediatur legatio*, assuming it were established, without first ascertaining that a majority of States admit that the rule of *ne impediatur legatio* also establishes an autonomous diplomatic immunity from execution of embassy accounts (violation of customary international law rule of *ne impediatur legatio*)' [author's own translation] *NML*

Thus, the applicant assumes, *arguendo*, that the CIL norm *ne impediatur legatio* has already crystallised,[60] and then proceeds to argue that the majority of states still need to accept that this norm also provides for autonomous diplomatic immunity from execution of embassy bank accounts.[61] The Court of Cassation rejects this argument. While in the context of law identification, this holding may possibly be problematic,[62]

Capital Ltd v République d'Argentine (emphasis added). The applicant's primary argument was that the Court of Appeal had wrongly introduced the doctrine of *stare decisis* through the backdoor, by relying on a judgment of the Court of Cassation of 22 November 2012 in the same case the court held: '*En vertu de la règle coutumière internationale* ne impediatur legatio, *suivant laquelle le fonctionnement de la mission diplomatique ne peut être entravé, l'ensemble des biens de cette mission qui servent à son fonctionnement bénéficie d'une immunité d'exécution autonome, se superposant à celle de l'État accréditant*' ('By virtue of the customary international law rule *ne impediatur legatio*, according to which the functioning of the diplomatic mission cannot be hindered, all the property of this mission which is used for its functioning enjoys autonomous immunity from autonomous execution, superimposed on that of the sending State' (author's own translation).

60 Articles 22(3) and 25 of the Vienna Convention on Diplomatic Relations (VCDR) could be considered to have codified some specific aspects of the CIL norm of *ne impediatur legatio*. Article 22(3) VCDR provides that '[t]he premises of the mission, their furnishings and other property thereon and the means of transport of the mission shall be immune from search, requisition, attachment or execution', while Article 25 VCDR provides that '[t]he receiving State shall accord full facilities for the performance of the functions of the mission'. In the judgment of *République d'Argentine v NML Capital LTD* (22 November 2012) Court of Cassation of Belgium, C.11.0688.F held that *'[l]'arrêt, qui, sans constater que les sommes saisies étaient affectées à d'autres fins que le fonctionnement de la mission diplomatique de la demanderesse, décide que la renonciation générale contenue dans les actes susmentionnés s'étend aux biens de cette mission diplomatique, y compris ses comptes bancaires, sans qu'il soit besoin d'une renonciation expresse et spéciale en ce qui concerne ces biens'* ('[t]he judgment, which, without finding that the sums seized were allocated for purposes other than the operation of the plaintiff's diplomatic mission, decides that the general waiver contained in the aforementioned acts extends to the property of this diplomatic mission, including its bank accounts, without the need for an express and special waiver in respect of such property') violates both the VCDR provisions and the CIL norm of *ne impediatur legatio*.

61 This is particularly relevant for the question whether a general waiver of immunity from execution by a foreign state also extends to embassy bank accounts. If diplomatic property were to have an autonomous status pursuant to the rule of *ne impediatur legatio*, a waiver that specifically applies to such property would be required. For a discussion regarding the Belgian context see S Duquet & J Wouters, 'De (on)beslagbaarheid van bankrekeningen van buitenlandse ambassades' (2015) 16 Rechtskundig Weekblad nr 38, 1483–99.

62 *North Sea Continental Shelf cases* [74] ('State practice, including that of States whose interests are specially affected, should have been both extensive and virtually uniform in the sense of the provision invoked; and should moreover have occurred in such a way as to show a general recognition that a rule of law or legal obligation is involved.'); A Henriksen, *International Law* (Oxford University Press 2017) 26 ('While unanimity is not required, practice should include the majority of states.'). That being said, neither

it is far less so in the context of law interpretation insofar as the core CIL norm has already crystallised and no proof of existence needs to be adduced. The Court of Cassation ultimately does not state what rules govern the interpretation of CIL norms (the principle of *ne impediatur legatio* in particular), nor does the lower court.[63]

3.2.2 Deference to CIL Interpretation by International Courts

In Conclusion 13(1) of its draft conclusions on identification of CIL, the ILC states that '[d]ecisions of international courts and tribunals, in particular of the International Court of Justice, concerning the existence and content of rules of customary international law are a subsidiary means for the determination of such rules'.[64] And indeed, domestic courts tend to look to international courts for guidance when ascertaining international law.[65] However, they may also refer and defer to international courts which have *interpreted* CIL. Such domestic court decisions are relevant in that they confirm the methodological validity of interpreting CIL.

Three decisions with respect to the immunity of states, the scope of which the ICJ clarified in *Jurisdictional Immunities of the State*,[66] stand out. In *Simoncioni*, the Italian Constitutional Court cited the '*interpretation* by the ICJ of the customary rule on state immunity for acts *iure*

the ICJ nor the ILC technically require acceptance by the *majority* of states; see ILC, 'Draft conclusions on identification of customary international law, with commentaries' (n 16) 136 [3]

> The requirement that the practice be 'widespread and representative' does not lend itself to exact formulations, as circumstances may vary greatly from one case to another . . . [U]niversal participation is not required: it is not necessary to show that all States have participated in the practice in question. The participating States should include those that had an opportunity or possibility of applying the alleged rule. It is important that such States are representative, which needs to be assessed in light of all the circumstances, including the various interests at stake and/or the various geographical regions.

[63] The lower court's decision has not been made public (Court of Appeals Brussels, judgment of 28 June 2013), but it was summarised in the Court of Cassation's 2014 judgment. In *République d'Argentine v NML Capital LTD*, the Court of Cassation did not elaborate either on its methods to ascertain or interpret the CIL norm.

[64] ILC, 'Draft conclusions on identification of customary international law, with commentaries' (n 16).

[65] Ryngaert & Hora Siccama (n 3) 17–21.

[66] *Jurisdictional Immunities of the State (Germany v Italy: Greece intervening)* (Judgment) [2012] ICJ Rep 99.

imperii' in *Jurisdictional Immunities of the State*.[67] By the same token, in *Alessi*, the Florence Court of First Instance held that the Italian court is not permitted 'an *interpretation* of the binding, inescapable validity of the *jus cogens* rules of international law, the area in which the International Court of Justice has absolute and exclusive jurisdiction'.[68] In the context of state immunity from execution, a commentator commenting on a decision of the German Federal Court of Justice somewhat similarly pointed out that the distinction between state property used for sovereign purposes and property not so used 'corresponded to the *interpretation* of customary international law on immunity from enforcement given by the International Court of Justice ('ICJ') in *Jurisdictional Immunities*'.[69]

That the ICJ interpreted customary law in *Jurisdictional Immunities of the State* is *itself* an interpretation by domestic courts, for that matter. Indeed, in *Jurisdictional Immunities of the State* the ICJ did not explicitly use the term 'interpretation' in the context of immunities under CIL. Still, the judgment contains indications that the ICJ did actually *interpret* rather than ascertain CIL on immunities, in line with how the aforementioned domestic courts construed the ICJ's judgment. First, with respect to immunity from jurisdiction, the ICJ stated in respect of Article 12 of the UN Convention on Jurisdictional Immunities that '[n]o state questioned this *interpretation*',[70] that is, the interpretation that military activities are not covered by the territorial tort exception. While it may appear that the ICJ interpreted the convention and thus simply applied rules of treaty interpretation – in this case having recourse to the *travaux préparatoires* of the convention per Article 32 VCLT – it bears emphasis that the convention had not yet entered into force. The territorial tort exception being of customary law character,[71] the ICJ may instead have

67 *Simoncioni and ors v Germany and President of the Council of Ministers of the Italian Republic* (intervening) (22 October 2014) Constitutional Court of Italy, Judgment No 238/2014 [3.1] (emphasis added).

68 *Alessi and ors v Germany and Presidency of the Council of Ministers of the Italian Republic* (intervening) (21 January 2014) Florence, Italy, Court of First Instance, Order No 85/2014 [18] (emphasis added).

69 *Greece v A* (25 June 2014) Federal Court of Justice of Germany, BGH Urteil vom 25.06.2014 – VII ZB 24/13, Analysis by L Manthey, ILDC 2388 [A3] (emphasis added). The court itself however did *not* refer to interpretation and limited itself to stating as follows: 'In German practice, the cultural institutions of foreign states were considered immune from enforcement. The promotion of culture and research by a foreign state formed part of its sovereign functions' *Greece v A* [14].

70 *Jurisdictional Immunities of the State* [69] (emphasis added).

71 ibid [77–78].

interpreted the *CIL* equivalent of the conventional exception. The stabilised 'core' customary norm is that immunity in principle does not extend to territorial torts, whereas interpretation of that norm may yield the identification of the limited circumstances in which immunity *does* extend to territorial torts. Second, with respect to state immunity from execution, the ICJ may have used the term 'find',[72] which may suggest ascertainment rather than interpretation of the law,[73] but it is of note that 'find' has other meanings too. The most relevant are 'to discover' and 'to determine and make a statement about',[74] the latter approximating the meaning of 'to interpret' as 'to conceive in the light of individual belief, judgment, or circumstance'.[75] Accordingly, what the ICJ possibly did was to interpret a core customary norm on state immunity from execution on the basis of 'subsequent practice in the application of the [customary norm] which establishes the agreement of [states] regarding its interpretation', to paraphrase Article 31(3)(b) VCLT. Besides, the customary norm on state immunity could also be interpreted in light of international human rights law, in particular creditors' rights to a remedy and to property.[76] Such an interpretation would give effect to the CIL equivalent of Article 31(3)(c) VCLT. Arguably, the relevant core customary norm is that state immunity from execution is not absolute, but relative. Under what precise circumstances state immunity does not apply will then be amenable to *interpretation*.[77]

[72] ibid [118] ('it suffices for the Court to find that there is at least one condition that has to be satisfied before any measure of constraint may be taken against property belonging to a foreign State').

[73] Especially in combination with the ICJ's identification of state practice (four judgments of national Supreme Courts) ibid [118] which cites: *Philippine Embassy Bank Account Case* (14 December 1977) German Constitutional Court, 46 BVerfGE 342; *Kingdom of Spain v Société X* (30 April 1986) Swiss Federal Tribunal, 43 Annuaire suisse de droit international 158; *Alcom Ltd v Republic of Colombia* (12 April 1984) UK House of Lords, 1 AC 580; *Abbott v Republic of South Africa* (1 July 1992) Spanish Constitutional Court, 44 Revista española de derecho internacional 565.

[74] Merriam-Webster Dictionary online.

[75] ibid.

[76] C Ryngaert, 'Embassy Bank Accounts and State Immunity from Execution: Doing Justice to the Financial Interests of Creditors' (2013) 26 LJIL 73; C Ryngaert, 'Immunity from Execution and Diplomatic Property' in T Ruys, N Angelet & L Ferro (eds), *The Cambridge Handbook of Immunities and International Law* (Cambridge University Press 2019) 285.

[77] These circumstances may have been specified in Article 19 of the UN Convention on the Jurisdictional Immunities of States and their Properties, but it is of note that in *Jurisdictional Immunities of the State* the ICJ considered 'that it is unnecessary for purposes of the present case for it to decide whether all aspects of Article 19 reflect current customary international law' *Jurisdictional Immunities of the State* (n 67) [118].

3.2.3 Interpreting CIL Norms Laid Down in Authoritative (Written) Documents

A third category is made up of those decisions that indirectly interpret CIL norms by interpreting the written documents in which they have been laid down. Insofar as CIL is laid down in an authoritative written text, courts will be more likely to have recourse to customary law *interpretation* than to customary law *ascertainment*, as supposedly the norm has already crystallised, black-on-white. It is the very codification of customary law which gives this body of law a more stable existence and shifts the focus to subsequent interpretation. Methodologically speaking, reliance on codification treaties to understand the meaning of CIL rules is a form of systemic interpretation mirroring the interpretative rule laid down in Article 31(3)(c) VCLT, the written text being a 'relevant rule of international law'.[78]

The most obvious written documents serving such a purpose are treaties. Thus, it is no surprise that the ICJ relied on, and arguably *interpreted* Article 12 of the UN Convention on Jurisdictional Immunities as CIL, as discussed in Section 3.2.2. Another example is offered by US courts' reliance on the UN Convention on the Law of the Sea (UNCLOS), to which the US is not a party, for purposes of applying parallel CIL of the sea with the same content.[79] The application of such CIL also has an interpretative dimension, as is borne out by the *Sea*

Arguably, the core customary norm can be found in the first sentence of Article 19: 'No post-judgment measures of constraint, such as attachment, arrest or execution, against property of a State may be taken in connection with a proceeding before a court of another State unless and except to the extent that . . .', with the precise exceptions and circumstances being a matter of interpretation. Thus, the ICJ's finding [118]

> that there is at least one condition that has to be satisfied before any measure of constraint may be taken against property belonging to a foreign State: that the property in question must be in use for an activity not pursuing government non-commercial purposes, or that the State which owns the property has expressly consented to the taking of a measure of constraint, or that that State has allocated the property in question for the satisfaction of a judicial claim

can be considered as the interpretation or further refinement of the relative character of the core customary norm on state immunity from execution.

78 Merkouris (n 15) 272.

79 *US v Beyle*, 782 F.3d 159 (4th Cir. 2015) 169 [33] (holding that widespread acceptance of the UNCLOS provided support for its status as an accurate reflection of customary international law); *Institute of Cetacean Research v Sea Shepherd Conservation Soc*, 725 F.3d 940 (9th Cir 2013); see on the interpretation of treaty rules and CIL rules with the same content also Merkouris (n 15) 246.

Shepherd case. In this case, the US Court of Appeals for the Ninth Circuit interpreted the 'private ends' requirement of piracy by taking the UNCLOS definition of piracy (Article 101 UNCLOS) as the starting point for its investigation of whether 'private ends' include those pursued on personal, moral or philosophical grounds, such as the NGO Sea Shepherd's professed environmental goals.[80] The court held as follows: 'Belgian courts, perhaps the only ones to have previously considered the issue, have held that environmental activism qualifies as a private end.... This *interpretation* is "entitled to considerable weight"'.[81] What the court was in fact doing was to *interpret* the 'private ends' variant of the *CIL* definition of piracy, which just happens to be codified in UNCLOS. The interpretative rule applied by the court was arguably the one based on subsequent practice, echoing Article 31(3)(b) VCLT.[82]

The shift from ascertainment to interpretation, facilitated by CIL having been laid down in a written document, may not be limited to situations of CIL norms codified in a *treaty*. It may also extend to situations of such norms being derived from *authoritative*, although *non-binding* written documents. An example of a court apparently *interpreting* CIL laid down in such a document is the Haifa District Court (Israel), which held that the non-binding San Remo Manual on International Law applicable to Armed Conflicts at Sea (1990)[83] was recognised as reflecting CIL, and thus that the authority for confiscating a vessel, at issue in the case, derived from CIL.[84] The court then proceeded to find that most states required legal adjudication for an act of confiscating a vessel and also required a speedy court procedure,[85]

80 *Institute of Cetacean Research v Sea Shepherd Conservation Soc.*

81 ibid [6] (emphasis added), citing *Castle John v NV Mabeco* (19 December 1986) Court of Cassation of Belgium, 77 ILR 537.

82 For a similar evolving or dynamic interpretation of CIL, although not as explicit: *SRYYY v Minister for Immigration and Multicultural and Indigenous Affairs* (17 March 2005) Federal Court of Australia, [2005] FCAFC 42 [66] ('The reference in Article 1F(a) of the Refugee Convention to "international instruments drawn up" clearly embraced the Rome Statute [of the International Criminal Court] ... This was because the Rome Statute was expressive of customary international law.'); *SRYYY v Minister for Immigration and Multicultural and Indigenous Affairs*, Commentary J Navidi, ILDC 981 [A3] (the judgment 'accepts the dynamic nature and evolution of customary international criminal law by leaving it open to the decision maker to select an instrument appropriate to the circumstances of the case').

83 L Doswald-Beck (ed), *San Remo Manual on International Law Applicable to Armed Conflicts at Sea* (Grotius Publications, Cambridge University Press 1995).

84 *Israel v 'Estelle'* (31 August 2014) Haifa, Israel, District Court, Claim In Rem 26861–08–13 [42–43].

85 ibid [48–49].

thereby apparently *interpreting* the provisions of the San Remo Manual on prize law (which do not set forth a court procedure) by resorting to subsequent practice. Admittedly, the court itself did not use the term interpretation, but the ILDC commentator did, observing, in addition, that 'any maritime court would have to address the potential impact of human rights law on the *interpretation* of the right to capture blockade-runners under traditional prize law' (thus favouring systemic interpretation taking into account other norms of international law).[86] The Israeli Court decision suggests that law interpreters may consider CIL norms that have been laid down in authoritative non-binding documents to lead a relatively stable existence, and thus to be amenable to interpretation.[87]

4 Concluding Observations

By and large, domestic courts, just like international courts, hew to the fiction that they find, identify or ascertain CIL. Earlier research has demonstrated that domestic courts have only limited agency in identifying CIL.[88] Instead, they tend to simply apply pre-existing CIL. However, when domestic courts apply such CIL, they may also interpret and develop CIL, as any application of law, almost out of necessity, also involves a measure of interpretation and legal development.[89] This contribution supports the TRICI project's methodological premise that CIL norms, just like treaty norms, *can* be interpreted. Interpretation will notably take place after a 'core' CIL norm has crystallised and stabilised,

[86] ibid, Commentary D Markowicz, ILDC 2299 [A6] (emphasis added).

[87] Compare *Re Víctor Raúl Pinto, Re, Pinto (Víctor Raúl) v Relatives of Tomás Rojas* (13 March 2007) Supreme Court of Chile, Case No 3125–04. While neither this court nor the ILDC commentator use the term interpretation, the court arguably engages in the interpretation of CIL. The judgment considers the 1950 Nuremberg Principles, which (at least according to the court) provide for the state duty to prosecute crimes against humanity, to reflect customary international law [29]. Subsequently, it arguably goes on to interpret this customary duty in light of a later treaty development, namely Article 6(5) of Additional Protocol II to the Geneva Conventions, which calls on states parties to grant as broad an amnesty as possible [20–21]; *Re Víctor Raúl Pinto, Re, Pinto (Víctor Raúl) v Relatives of Tomás Rojas*, Commentary X Fuentes, ILDC 1093 [A6] ('the Supreme Court had to reconcile Article 6(5) of Protocol II with its own interpretation of the customary law status of the duty to prosecute involved in the concept of crimes against humanity').

[88] Ryngaert & Hora Siccama (n 3).

[89] See on the link between application, interpretation and development of international law by domestic courts: A Tzanakopoulos, 'Domestic Courts in International Law: The International Judicial Function of National Courts' (2011) 34 Loy LA Int'l & Comp L 135.

after which the penumbra of that rule – its precise scope, its exceptions – are amenable to mechanisms of interpretation.

This chapter has analysed a large dataset of domestic court decisions relevant to CIL, and found that, indeed, domestic courts at times engage in CIL interpretation, even if they largely refrain from using that term. Domestic courts may interpret CIL autonomously, may defer to and validate international courts' CIL interpretations, or they interpret written documents, such as treaties, codifying CIL norms. Such practices bear out that domestic courts may consider some core CIL norms to be relatively stable and amenable to further refinement through interpretation.

When interpreting CIL, domestic courts appear to resort mainly to systemic interpretation and interpretation on the basis of subsequent state practice. This reflects earlier findings by Panos Merkouris with respect to CIL interpretation by international courts.[90] In particular, domestic courts apply by analogy the canons of construction laid down in Article 31(3)(b) VCLT ('any subsequent practice in the application of the treaty which establishes the agreement of the parties regarding its interpretation'), and Article 31(3)(c) ('any relevant rules of international law applicable in the relations between the parties'). The analysis of state practice under the CIL equivalent of Article 31(3)(b) VCLT tends to be cursory, however. As Odile Ammann has pointed out, mainly in respect of CIL ascertainment, domestic courts tend to refer to their own practice or the practice of their own state, a process which she characterises as self-referentiality and circularity.[91] Cast in terms of interpretation, such a process may take the form of 'reverse consistent interpretation': domestic courts may choose this interpretation of a CIL norm which is mostly in line with domestic law and practice.[92]

In future cases, domestic courts deciding cases on the basis of CIL may in any event want to be more explicit regarding whether they engage in *de novo* CIL norm-identification or rather in the interpretation of pre-existing and stabilised customary norms. In case of interpretation, they may want to improve the methodological quality of their reasoning by

[90] Compare Merkouris (n 15) 264–68 (arguing that international judges prefer 'to employ teleological and systemic interpretation instead, which are more easily distinguishable from the process of formation of customary international law' and discounting textual interpretation as well as interpretation based on the intention of the parties).

[91] Ammann (n 39) 243–45.

[92] *Her Majesty the Queen in Right of Canada v Edelson* [23].

pinpointing the canon of construction which they apply (e.g., systemic interpretation; interpretation on the basis of subsequent practice). Finally, in the case of both CIL identification and interpretation, they should make sure that they rely on sufficient international (including foreign) legal practice, in keeping with the methodological requirements of CIL identification and interpretation.

23

The Relevance of Customary International Law in the Domestic Legal Order of a Federal State

GERHARD HOOGERS

1 Introduction

Although the relevance of treaty law has grown over time in international law, customary rules remain an important source of law in international relations. An underdeveloped theme when studying customary norms is the use of customary international law (CIL) within domestic legal orders. Especially in federal states, where the composing parts of the polity are sometimes seen as 'remnants' of or reminiscent to sovereign states, rules pertaining to the relationship between states within the field of international law might also prove useful for regulating the behaviour of states that share at least some of the characteristics of sovereign entities but have entered into compacts merging them into greater and tighter-knit polities. For a constitutional court in a federal state, such norms therefore might be a useful tool in solving disputes between the states or between the federation and the states. They might also be useful in regulating treaty practices in federations where there exists a possibility of interstate treaties. Yet, this ambiguity (is the legal order that unites the states and the federation through the federal constitution all-encompassing, or does it leave room for the use of non-domestic norms?) concerning the relationship between partners in a federal makeup can also be shown in the way in which domestic courts make use of these norms. It is seldom completely clear-cut whether a court actually does use a rule of CIL in its original meaning.

In this chapter, I will try to shed some light on the way in which rules of CIL have been used within the domestic legal order for regulating the relations between the states of both federal entities in Germany and Austria. Other federal states might have been used instead of these two countries. The reason for choosing Germany and Austria is that in the former an extensive debate has been held on the question whether the German states that entered into the federal compact of 1871 could still be described as states despite the fact that they had lost their independent status under international law.[1] This debate created an intellectual and legal atmosphere in which the statehood of the German regional entities remained relevant, even after the end of the German empire in 1918 – and thus the idea that the rules pertaining to the relationship between states, that is, international law, could still be relevant as well. Austria only became a federal state in 1920, after the demise of the Habsburg empire and thus more or less followed the ideas and conceptions already developed in Germany. Moreover, in both Germany and Austria, domestic interstate law is primarily created through treaties, which also points in the direction of an interesting analogy to international law.

As will be demonstrated, rules of CIL have (arguably) shown to be useful, especially when it comes to disputes between two or more states. As stated above, the use of these norms does raise important questions concerning the nature of federal legal orders, however. Are the component parts of a federal state still 'states' in an international law sense of the word? If so, how much legal manoeuvring space exists to make use of norms of international law to regulate their relations? What is the legal justification, if any, for the 'domestic' use of norms originating under international law? These questions, and the ambiguous unease they provoke in domestic courts, will be dealt with in the following paragraphs.

In the next section, the focus will be laid on the way in which in the Weimar Republic rules of CIL were used to solve disputes between German states. This will be done through an analysis of the case law of the special court constituted under the 1919 German constitution to deal with such legal questions, the Staatsgerichtshof für das deutsche Reich (RStGH). In the third section, the focus will be on the post-war case law of the Federal Constitutional Court, the Bundesverfassungsgericht (BVerfG). The question will be analysed how the case law of the BVerfG has built upon the foundations laid in the 1920s by its Weimar predecessor. The fourth section deals with the situation in Austria: interestingly enough, the Austrian constitution (the Bundes-Verfassungsgesetz, B-VG) contains an article explicitly acknowledging the existence and the relevance of international law within the domestic legal order to regulate interstate and

[1] An illuminating analysis of this German debate can be found in M Duchateau, *Het Europees Parlement als transnationale volksvertegenwoordiging* (Subreeks Grondslagen van de EU ed, Kluwer 2014) 302–27.

federal-state relations, Article 15a B-VG. This article and its practical use under the Austrian constitution will be scrutinised. Finally, some conclusions will be drawn and some light will be shed on the question whether or not courts are using norms of CIL, or are merely using them as a source of inspiration to develop unwritten principles of federal law.

2 The Use of CIL in the Republic of Weimar

After the fall of the monarchy in Germany in November 1918, the new republican government organised elections for a federal constituent assembly, which assembled for the first time on 6 February 1919 in the Thuringian city of Weimar.[2] Over the following months, it elaborated a new constitution for the German Reich that introduced general suffrage for men and women, a catalogue of fundamental rights, a full parliamentary system and a strong, directly elected federal president with far-reaching powers. The constitution was enacted on 11 August 1919. The Reich constitution (often described as the 'Weimar' constitution because it was created there)[3] maintained the existing makeup of the German state as a federation, but it contained many characteristics that strengthened the role of the central authorities. Notable among those were the fact that the new Reich government would be dependent on the confidence of the majority of the directly elected Federal Diet,[4] representing the whole of the German nation and that the new Reich president was also elected by the whole nation,[5] but it was also visible in the division of powers between the federation and the states: compared to Bismarck's 1871 constitution, the legislative and executive powers of the federation were visibly strengthened.

Among the 'federal' innovations of the Weimar constitution we also find the introduction of a new federal court, the so-called Staatsgerichtshof für das deutsche Reich (Federal State Court, RStGH) a specialised court to deal with disputes of a federal nature. Article 19 of the constitution described its legal powers. The RStGH was empowered to settle disputes of a public law

[2] E Zweigert (intr), *Die Verfassung des Deutschen Reichs vom 11. August 1919* (J Bensheimer 1919) 8.

[3] For similar reasons, the 1919 Bavarian constitution is often referred to as the 'Bamberg' constitution.

[4] Verfassung des Deutschen Reichs vom 11 August 1919, RGBl 1919, S 1383, art 54. In this chapter, the standard German abbreviation RV, for Reichsverfassung (Federal Constitution) will be used to refer to articles of this constitution.

[5] ibid art 41.

nature within one of the German states, between two or more states or between the Reich and one or more states, insofar as no other court was created to deal with any of these issues.[6] It was originally envisioned as being an adjacent court to the proposed Federal Administrative Court, the Reichsverwaltungsgericht. This, however, was never actually created, which led to the situation that the court became permanently organised along the lines originally meant as a temporal solution: it was an ad hoc court, annexed to the Reichsgericht. Its president was the president of the Reichsgericht itself, and it consisted of six other members: three judges of the Reichsgericht, one judge from the Oberverwaltungsgericht of the state of Prussia, one judge from the Verwaltungsgerichtshof of the state of Bavaria and one judge from the Oberverwaltungsgericht of the state of Saxony.[7] Thus, the RStGH was a mixture of 'ordinary' and administrative judges.

Although case law concerning constitutional disputes within a state formed the bulk of the activities of the RStGH (the majority of the German states, including the largest and most populous of them all, Prussia, did not create their own constitutional courts), it did decide a number of interesting cases concerning disputes between different states. And it was especially in this field that the court used norms of CIL to settle these disputes, insofar as the domestic legal order did not provide sufficiently clear or relevant norms. The basis of the use of customary norms was found in Article 4 RV. This article stated: '*Die allgemein anerkannten Regeln des Völkerrechts gelten als bindende Bestandteile des deutschen Reichsrechts.*'[8] This article was a novelty in German constitutional law: under the old constitution of 1871, international law was solely seen as the law between states: for the citizens of Germany, it formed *a res inter alios acta*. That changed because of Article 4 of the new 1919 constitution: for the first time, norms of international law became part of the domestic legal order, binding public bodies and citizens alike and gaining relevance before the

[6] Thus, when a German state created its own specialised constitutional court the RStGH could only decide legal cases within that state for which this state court had no competence. Any federal dispute brought under the competence of another federal court by the federal legislator limited the competence of the RStGH as well. The constitutionality of state acts, for instance, was brought under the competence of the Reichsgericht and the Reichsfinanzgericht (for tax and budgetary acts) respectively and could therefore not be decided by the RStGH.

[7] Reichsgesetz vom 9 Juli 1921 (Federal Act of 9 July 1921) RGBl 1921, S 905.

[8] 'The generally acknowledged rules of international law are binding norms of German federal law.'

German courts.[9] It was never entirely clear which norms of international law were covered by Article 4: only norms of CIL, or also treaty norms? Those acknowledging that treaty law could be covered by Article 4 RV mostly accepted that the criterion for 'acknowledgement' by Germany entailed the ratification of the treaty through a federal act, as provided for by Article 45 (3) RV.[10] Those denying it mostly adhered to the idea that Article 45 (3) RV itself regulated the transformation of treaty norms into the German legal order. Since according to both theories Article 4 RV regulated the transformation of customary norms and according to both theories the internal hierarchical status of all international norms was that of a federal act, the question did not have huge practical relevance.[11] Being on a par with federal acts, customary norms of international law took precedence over earlier federal acts on the basis of the *lex posterior* rule and took precedence over all state law (including constitutional state law) on the basis of the *lex superior* rule.[12]

The RStGH never chose sides in the debate on the specific relationship between Article 4 and Article 45 (3) RV. In four of the cases it decided on disputes between two or more of Germany's states it made use of Article 4 RV to settle the case in a legally binding matter. The first of those was a dispute between Prussia and Bremen concerning a 1904 treaty between

9

> *Das ist eine Neuerung, deren Tragweite nicht unterschätzt werden darf. Die deutschen Gerichte werden auf Grund des Artikels 4 nicht nur ... Akten der deutschen Gerichtsbarkeit gegen fremde Staaten in direkter Anwendung völkerrechtlicher Normen für unzulässig erklären, sie werden etwa auch Klagen von Einzelpersonen ... die sich auf das Völkerrecht und seine Quellen (etwa auf die Haager Konferenzbeschlüsse), stützen, zulassen müssen.*
>
> That is a new development of which the relevance can hardly be overestimated. The German courts will not only declare acts under German jurisdiction against foreign powers unlawful when directly applying rules of international law, they will also have to allow standing to individual complaints founded in international law and its sources, such as the decisions of the conference of the Hague.

G Anschütz, *Die Verfassung des deutschen Reichs vom 11. August 1919. Ein Kommentar für Wissenschaft und Praxis* (4th ed, Stilke 1924) 47 (unofficial translation by the author).

10 '*Bündnisse und Verträge mit fremden Staaten, die sich auf Gegenstände der Reichsgesetzgebung bestehen, bedürfen der Zustimmung des Reichstags*' ('Alliances and treaties with foreign powers concerning matters of federal legislation can only be entered upon with the prior assent of the federal diet'). Unofficial translation by the author.

11 Anschütz (n 9) 49.

12 ibid 50.

the two states on the legal and economic status of Bremerhaven. Bremen claimed before the RStGH that this treaty had a very negative impact on the Bremen economy because it was heavily written in favour of Prussia's interests in the region. Under the circumstances of the old Reich this could perhaps be justified, Bremen claimed, because under the old constitution Prussia had been more than a *primus inter pares*.[13] But under the new 1919 constitution this had changed and Prussia had become nothing more than just the largest of the German states. Thus, the 1904 treaty should not be used under the same circumstances as before the war, Bremen argued before the court. The second one decided by the RStGH concerned a dispute between Baden on the one hand and Württemberg and Prussia (for its Hohenzollern territories bordering Baden and Württemberg) on the other concerning the use of water rights from the river Danube. The third one was a case concerning Bremen on the one hand and Prussia, Brunswick and Thuringia on the other hand concerning the pollution of the river Weser by potassium mines in the latter states, forcing Bremen to halt the use of the river as a source of drinking water. The fourth and final case in which the RStGH used Article 4 RV was a dispute between the states of Lübeck and Mecklenburg-Strelitz on fishing rights in the Lübecker Bucht, a part of the (German) Baltic Sea.[14]

The second decision mentioned above is a good example of the way in which the RStGH made use of Article 4 of the 1919 constitution in all four of these cases and is therefore worthwhile looking into in some more detail. The case centred around the fact that water from the Danube leaked away on the territory of Baden, ending up in the small Badener river Aach. This river was an important source of drinking water in parts

[13] The 1871 Reich constitution gave Prussia in many respects a superior status over other states. The king of Prussia was the principal monarch of Germany and *qualitate qua* German Emperor; the ministers in the government of Prussia were *qualitate qua* the ministers of the Reich, although they were in that capacity referred to as *Staatssekretäre*, state secretaries; the Reich chancellor was also the prime minister of Prussia and in the Bundesrat, the Reich assembly representing the interests of the states, Prussia had a blocking veto. All that was no longer the case under the 1919 republican constitution. The governments of the Reich and Prussia became completely separated and within the Reichsrat, the successor to the old Bundesrat, Prussia had only 2/5th of the votes. Moreover, half of those Prussian votes were not cast by the government of the state of Prussia, but by the executives of the Prussian provinces, who voted independently from the state government, RV, arts 61, 63.

[14] See G Hoogers & G Karapetian, 'Federal Disputes in the German Reich under the Weimar Constitution: Lessons in Dispute Settlement for the Kingdom of the Netherlands' (2018) 12(3) Vienna Journal on International Constitutional Law 257.

of Baden, and the Badener authorities had a keen interest in the continuation of this leakage. This, however, led to measurable lower levels in the Danube during periods of lesser rainfall. Both Württemberg and the Hohenzollern province of Prussia used the Danube for drinking water and industrial purposes too. They claimed that Baden strengthened the natural seepage through lack of confining measures on the banks of the river and even through active measures, thereby infringing on the rights of both states. They brought a case before the RStGH in order to compel Baden to desist from any further measure that would strengthen the natural seepage of the Danube waters. The RStGH gave its decision on 18 June 1927.[15] The court concludes in a preliminary remark that the conflict is not of a private law, but of a public law nature, since the conflict deals with the way in which the three states conduct their water policies: and those powers were not conferred to the federation by the Reich constitution, Thus, the conflict was of an interstate, public law nature, making it one of the types of dispute for which the Staatsgerichtshof enjoyed competence under Article 19 RV. The court further concludes that neither federal law nor Badener law can be used as a legal basis for settling the claim, an analysis that leads to one of the key paragraphs of the decision.

When neither federal nor state law is available, the court must make use of other sources of law to settle the dispute, since there can be no gap in the legal order (*Rechtslücke*), the court states.[16] Only international law can play that part. It can be used in the interstate relations within Germany, albeit in a limited way. For although the relationship between the German states is primarily regulated and structured through the federal constitution, the Reich never intended to create an all-encompassing order. Fundamentally, the German states are still (sovereign) states, albeit with a limited sovereignty. Article 5 RV states that the state powers are enacted through state organs on the basis of the state

[15] H Lammers & W Simons (eds), *Die Rechtsprechung des Staatsgerichtshofes für das Deutsche Reich und des Reichsgerichts auf Grund von Artikel 13 Abs 2 der Reichsverfassung* (Berlin 1927) vol 1(37), 178.

[16] The RStGH does not argue that rules of CIL are a prime source of law for German courts in this respect. The fundamental rule is that the relations between the federation and the Ctates, as well as the interstate relations, are regulated by domestic federal law: '*In erster Linie regeln sich die gegenseitigen Rechtsbeziehungen der deutschen Staaten nach der Reichsverfassung und den auf ihrer Grundlage erlassenen Reichsgesetzen*' ('Primarily, the legal relations between the German states are regulated by the federal Constitution and the federal acts promulgated on the basis thereof'), Lammers & Simons (n 15), 185. Unofficial translation by the author.

constitutions. Articles 6 frth. RV regulate the legislative powers of the federation in such a way that the states enjoy all legislative competences unless and insofar the federal legislator has been made competent. Insofar as the states have retained legislative competences, they also have the right to enter into treaties with foreign powers (Article 78 (2) RV). Thus, there is a clear basis, through the whole structure of the federal makeup of the 1919 constitution and through Article 4 RV itself, to make international law applicable on the interstate relations of the German states.[17]

From this, the court draws some important conclusions. It claims that international law, in its more recent developments, has strengthened the idea that states are limited in their sovereignty because they belong to an international order of states. It follows that there exists a general (unwritten)

17 *Kann die Entscheidung demnach weder dem Reichsrecht noch dem Landesrecht entnommen werden, so kommt nur noch zwischenstaatliches, d.h. Völkerrecht in Frage. Seine Anwendbarkeit im Verhältniss der deutschen Länder zueinander ist anzuerkennen, wenngleich in beschränktem Maße. In erster Linie regeln sich die gegenseitigen Rechtsbeziehungen der deutschen Staaten nach der Reichsverfassung und den auf ihrer Grundlage erlassenen Reichsgesetzen. Diese Regelung ist aber unvollständig.... Die historische Stellung der Länder als selbständiger Staaten ist ... bis heute bestehen geblieben.... Soweit sich die Länder danach als selbständige Staaten betätigen können, auf den Gebieten also, die ihrer Gesetzgebungsgewalt unterliegen ... regeln sich ihre Rechtsbeziehungen zueinander nach Völkerrecht, d.h. nach den in Artikel 4 RVerf. genannten allgemein anerkannten Regeln des Völkerrechts, die als bindende Bestandteile des deutschen Reichsrechts gelten.*

(Should both federal law and state law be incapable of providing a decision, then only interstate law, i.e. international law, can be used. Its applicability is to be acknowledged in the relationship of the German states to one another, albeit in a limited manner. Primarily, the legal relations between the German states are regulated by the federal Constitution and the federal acts promulgated on the basis thereof. This is an incomplete legal order, however. Up until the present, the historical position of the German states as autonomous entities has been maintained. Insofar as the states can act in an autonomous manner, in those areas where they enjoy legislative powers, their interstate relations are regulated by international law, i.e. according to the generally acknowledged norms of international law mentioned in art. 4 of the federal constitution, which operate as binding norms of German federal law.)

Lammers & Simons (n 15), unofficial translation by the author; See also H Schneider & W Schaumann, 'Verträge zwischen Gliedstaaten im Bundesstaat' (1961) 19 Veröffentlichungen der Vereinigung der Deutschen Staatsrechtslehrer 122; H Bauer, *Die Bundestreue: Zugleich ein Beitrag zur Dogmatik des Bundesstaatsrechts und zur Rechtsverhältnislehre* (Mohr Siebeck 1992) 95–6.

principle of mutual respect and good neighbourliness and a duty of non-harm. Within the German legal order, this is even more the case: the preamble of the 1919 constitution states that it originates from the unity of the German nation itself, with the aim to promote the inner peace of Germany. The constitution also creates through Article 110 (2) the right to equal treatment in every German state for all German citizens. From this it follows, the RStGH argues, that every German state has a duty to act in such a manner as not to infringe upon the rights and interests of Germans in other states unless this is absolutely necessary. The sovereignty of the German states on their own territory is therefore even more limited than the limitations that would follow from the aforementioned general principle of international law, because the German states form a legal community that is more close-knit than an ordinary international one.[18]

18 *Die Sätze des Völkerrechts in seiner neueren Entwicklung beruhen wesentlich auf dem Gedanken einer Einschränkung der Gebietshoheit der einzelnen Staaten durch ihre Zugehörigkeit zur Völkerrechtsgemeinschaft. Aus ihr wird eine Pflicht der Staaten zur gegenseitigen Achtung und Rücksichtnahme hergeleitet, eine Pflicht, einander nicht zu verletzen. Noch enger als diese allgemeine Völkergemeinschaft ist die Gemeinschaft in der die deutschen Länder als Glieder des deutschen Reichs zueinander stehen. Die Verfassung vom 11. August 1919 beruht nach ihrem Vorspruch auf der Einigung des deutschen Volkes in seinen Stämmen und will seinem inneren Frieden dienen. Sie gibt in Artikel 110 Abs. 2 jedem Deutschen in jedem Lande des Reichs die gleichen Rechte und Pflichten wie die Angehörigen des Landes selbst.... So gelangt man im Verhältnis der deutschen Länder zueinander zu einer stärkeren Einschränkung des Grundsatzes der Gebietshoheit, als wenn sich zwei völlig fremde Staaten gegenüberstehen.... Daraus ergeben sich Verpflichtungen der einzelnen deutschen Staaten zueinander, die sich, wenigstens in gleichem Maße, aus dem für alle Staaten geltenden Völkerrecht nicht herleiten lassen.*

(The recent development of international law is fundamentally based upon the idea that the territorial sovereignty of individual states is limited by the fact that they belong to the international community. From this concept stems the duty of states to respect and acknowledge each other, a duty to refrain from reciprocal harm. Far more closely knit is the community in which the German states are bound as members of the German Reich. The preamble of the Constitution of 11 August 1919 makes clear that it is based upon the unity of the German people in its geographical diversity and the promotion of its inner peace. It grants in article 110 par. 2 every German in every state of the Reich the same rights and duties as the inhabitants of that state itself. From this it follows that the territorial sovereignty of the German states in their interstate relations are more limited than would have been the case if it were two completely independent states. And from that, it follows that they have obligations to each other that cannot be discerned in the same way from international law itself.)

Lammers & Simons (n 15) 186, unofficial translation by the author; Bauer (n 17) 96.

The use of CIL by the RStGH is therefore of a somewhat ambiguous nature. On the one hand, the court fully recognises that Article 4 of the federal constitution regulates the domestic force of (customary) international norms. It acknowledges that the principle of friendly co-existence and non-harm to other states is a norm that is valid, applicable and enforceable within the domestic legal order of Germany. On the other hand, however, the court clearly accepts the idea that because of the fact that the relationship between the German states is not primarily of an international legal character, it is primarily domestic, federal law that regulates interstate relations. Furthermore, customary international norms have a different, and more material content than they would have in the international legal order. One could perhaps argue (although the Staatsgerichtshof is silent on the matter) that Article 4 RV not only transforms norms of CIL into German law but also – dependent on the norm – adapts their content to make them better suited for domestic use.

3 The Use of CIL in the Federal Republic of Germany

This ambiguity has not been clearly solved in the post-war legal order of the Grundgesetz either. One of the very first decisions the Bundesverfassungsgericht gave after its inception was the so-called Südweststaatentscheidung of 23 October 1951.[19] Although the new federal constitutional court had far more powers than the ones given to the RStGH, public law disputes between the federation and one or more states and between two or more states are enumerated among them.[20] In that sense, the RStGH is a clear legal predecessor of the BVerfG. The Südweststaatentscheidung originated in an agreement between France and the United States of July 1945 to demarcate their respective zones of occupation in the southwest of Germany along the federal highway (*Reichsautobahn*) Karlsruhe-Ulm-Stuttgart. This divided the existing territories of the old states of Württemberg and Baden (and the Prussian province of Hohenzollern-Sigmaringen) between the French and American zones of responsibility. The American military authorities created in their zone of occupation the new state of Württemberg-Baden; the French created two new states, Baden and Württemberg-Hohenzollern.

[19] Bundesverfassungsgericht (Entscheidung vom 23 Oktober 1951) BVerfGE 1, 14.

[20] Grundgesetz für die Bundesrepublik Deutschland vom 23 Mai 1949, BGBl 1949, S 1, Art 93.1(4).

These three states enacted their respective state constitutions on 28 November 1946,[21] 18 May 1947[22] and 22 May 1947.[23] All three states became part of the Federal Republic of Germany; their State Diets enacted the Basic Law on 18 and 21 May 1949 respectively. Almost immediately after the creation of the three states in the southwest it became clear that they were not only artificial creations, which bore no resemblance to the old territorial divisions in the region, but that they were all three too small to function properly in the new makeup of the Federal Republic of Germany. Especially Württemberg-Hohenzollern was a reminder of the Kleinstaaterei that was already partially abolished by the 1919 constitution (which had enabled the federal lawgiver to act on these matters in Article 18 RV, resulting in the creation of the state of Thuringia), but had for the rest completely disappeared under the post-1945 allied occupation.[24] Despite pressure from the allied authorities and negotiations in the summer of 1948, no solution had yet been found when the Basic Law entered into force on 23 May 1949. The Basic Law did, however, contain a special provision for the reshaping of the south-west in Article 118. This article created a more expedient regulation for the possible merger of the three south-western states compared to the

[21] Verfassung des Landes Württemberg-Baden vom 28 November 1946, RegBl 1946, S 277.

[22] Verfassung des Landes Württemberg-Hohenzollern vom 18 Mai 1947, RegBl 1947, S 1.

[23] Verfassung des Landes Baden vom 22 Mai 1947, GVBl 1947, S 129.

[24] Thuringia was created through the Federal Act of 1 May 1920 through the unification of the former states of Saxony-Weimar-Eisenach, Saxony-Meiningen, Saxony-Altenburg, Saxony-Gotha, Schwarzburg-Rudofstadt, Schwarzburg-Sondershausen and the People's State of Reuss, itself a 1919 merger of the old principalities of Reuss-Older Line and Reuss-Younger Line. The Free State of Saxony-Coburg, however, did not join Thuringia but chose to become part of Bavaria in 1920. The post-war cleanup of 1945–49 was far more rigorous: the very small states of Schaumburg-Lippe and Lippe-Detmold disappeared, and so did the slightly bigger states of Oldenburg, Brunswick and Anhalt. Mecklenburg-Strelitz and Mecklenburg-Schwerin had already been merged into Mecklenburg by Federal Act in 1934, Lübeck had been merged with Prussia in 1937. The only small states remaining in the post-war legal order were the old Hanseatic republics of Bremen and Hamburg and the newly created territory of Berlin, which never became fully part of either the Federal Republic of Germany nor the German Democratic Republic because of the special rights of the four allied powers in the city. The most dramatic change was of course the abolition of Prussia by the Allied Control Council in 1947, by far the largest state of Germany. Parts of its former territory are now in Russia and Poland; other parts of Prussia are now the territory of Berlin (a full state since 1990), Brandenburg and Schleswig-Holstein and parts of Mecklenburg-West Pomerania, Saxony-Anhalt, Thuringia, Lower Saxony, North Rhine-Westphalia, Rhineland-Palatinate, Hesse and Baden-Württemberg respectively.

'normal' procedure for the creation or dissolution of a state of Article 29 GG. In all three states a referendum was held (on 24 September 1950) about the question whether or not they should merge into a new Südweststaat. In Württemberg and in the old Hohenzollern lands a vast majority wanted the merger: but in Baden, a clear majority wanted the old state of Baden back, while in the old Badener parts of Württemberg-Baden a significant part of the voters (over 40 per cent) wanted this as well.

Since the three states could not come to an agreement, the federal legislator decided to act unilaterally through Article 118 of the Basic Law. One of the two federal acts published jointly on 4 May 1951 was an act that prolonged the tenure of the existing state diets of Baden and Württemberg-Hohenzollern until the day the state constitutions would be abolished because of the creation of the new state of Baden-Württemberg. This was deemed necessary because their tenure would end before this date and new elections for state diets that would only exist for a couple of weeks were seen as useless and onerous.

Both Baden and Württemberg-Hohenzollern had come to the same conclusion, however. They both started a procedure to amend their state constitutions in order to extend the tenure of their respective diets. Both state constitutions made a plebiscite compulsory for amending the state constitution; both plebiscites were planned for 8 May 1951. Thus, it could be argued, the federal legislator had regulated a matter that fell within the constitutional autonomy of the states. The government of Baden decided to bring the matter before the newly created Bundesverfassungsgericht. Baden not only claimed that this federal act violated the constitutional autonomy of the state, but it also claimed that the other federal act of 4 May 1951 (which regulated the merger of Baden, Württemberg-Hohenzollern and Württemberg-Baden into Baden-Württemberg) was unconstitutional as well, because the Badeners had clearly voted through the referendum in September 1950 that they wanted their old Baden back, not a new Baden-Württemberg. The federal constitutional court sided with the state government of Baden insofar as the federal act prolonging the tenure of the state diets was concerned. It concluded that since the Basic Law was founded upon the principle of democracy, the federal legislator could not interfere unilaterally with the tenure of a state diet in bypassing the constitution that the people of that state have given themselves democratically.[25]

[25] BVerfGE 1, 14, Rn 81–83.

With regard to the second act, the one creating Baden-Württemberg, the situation was different. Article 118 (2) of the Basic Law regulated that the creation of the new Südweststaat was only possible under the guarantee of a mandate of the people. The federal legislator therefore regulated that a referendum was to be held that asked two questions: do you want the new Baden-Württemberg? Or do you want the existing state of Baden? (or in Württemberg-Baden and Württemberg-Hohenzollern: do you want a state of Württemberg, including Württemberg-Hohenzollern?). Baden claimed that this infringed upon the rights to self-determination of the people of Baden because it was not possible for the Badeners to recreate the old pre-1945 state of Baden, although the majority of the Badeners had chosen that option in the 1950 referendum. The Baden state government defended the existence of this right to self-determination partially on the basis of Article 25 of the Basic Law, the successor to the old Article 4 RV. The main difference between the two articles is that Article 25 GG not only states that the general norms of international law are part of the federal legal order, but it also states that these norms create rights and obligations for the inhabitants of the federal republic and that they take precedence over federal acts and state law.[26] Baden claimed that because of Article 25 GG, the general norm of the right to self-determination took precedence over said federal act. The BVerfG denied this claim: it stated, following the reasoning of the RStGH in the Danube decision of 1927, that (customary) rules of international law could only play a part in interstate relations, not in the constitutional relation between the federation and the states.[27]

[26] '*Die allgemeinen Regeln des Völkerrechtes sind Bestandteil des Bundesrechtes. Sie gehen den Gesetzen vor und erzeugen Rechte und Pflichten unmittelbar für die Bewohner des Bundesgebietes*' ('The general norms of international law are part of the federal law. They take precedence over acts of the federal diet and directly create rights and obligations for the inhabitants of the federal territory'). Unofficial translation by the author.

[27]
> *Ferner soll § 10 unvereinbar sein mit einer durch Artikel 25 GG in Bezug genommenen allgemeinen Regel des Völkerrechts, nach der kein Staat gegen den Willen seines Volkes zur Aufgabe seiner Existenz und zum Eingehen in einen anderen Staat gezwungen werden könne.... Jedenfalls könnte ein das Verhältnis von Staaten zu einander regelnder Völkerrechtssatz innerhalb des Bundesstaates nur im Verhältnis von Land zu Land und im Bereich ihrer rechtlichen Gleichordnung angewendet werden (vgl. Entscheidung des RStGH vom 18. Juni 1927, 7/25, Lammers-Simons I S. 185 ff. u. ö.), nicht dagegen auf das Überordnungsverhältnis von Bund und Land; dieses Verhältnis wird durch die bundesstaatliche Rechtsordnung bestimmt. Bei der Neugliederung – sowohl*

The question which role – if any – CIL as transformed by Article 25 of the Basic Law *did* play in the interstate relations within Germany was decided by the federal constitutional court in a later decision, the *Coburg* decision.[28] The case arose from a dispute between the cities of Coburg and Neustadt bei Coburg and the State of Bavaria. Saxony-Coburg, as has been stated above, was one of the Thuringian states. But while all the others had merged into the state of Thuringia by the Federal Act of 1 May 1920, Coburg (including the smaller city of Neustadt bei Coburg) had been merged with Bavaria through a state treaty (*Staatsvertrag*) between the two states of 24 February 1920.[29] One of the clauses of this treaty between the states of Bavaria and Saxony-Coburg had been that Neustadt bei Coburg would be and remain a separate municipality under its own jurisdiction within Bavaria. Through the state decree on the new territorial division of Bavaria of 27 December 1971,[30] Neustadt bei Coburg had been

> *nach Artikel 29 wie nach Artikel 118 GG – handelt es sich aber nicht nur um das gegenseitige Verhältnis der beteiligten Länder untereinander, sondern zugleich auch um das Verhältnis zwischen Bund und Ländern. Das Bundesrecht, insbesondere das Grundgesetz hat diese Rechtsbeziehungen wie dargelegt, geregelt. Für die Anwendung völkerrechtlicher Normen, die durch Artikel 25 GG Bundesrecht geworden sind, ist damit kein Raum mehr.*
>
> (Further it is claimed that par. 10 is incompatible with the general norm of international law, acknowledged by article 25 of the Basic Law, according to which no state can be forced to give up its own existence and be merged with another state against the will of its own people. In any case, an international norm regulating the interstate relations can only be applicable within a federal state for true state to state relations in the field of their legal equality (see decision of the RStGH of 18 June 1927, 7/25, Lammers-Simons I p. 185 fth.), but not in the hierarchical relationship of federation and state: this is exclusively regulated by the federal legal order. When it comes to the reconstruction of the federal territory – both when applying article 29 or article 118 of the Basic Law – not just the relationship of the relevant states to each other, but also the relationship of the federation to the states is touched upon. Federal law, and especially the Basic Law, has regulated that relationship as is. There is therefore no room for the application of international norms that have become federal law through article 25 of the Basic Law.)

BVerfGE 1, 14, Rn 134, unofficial translation by the author. Interesting, of course, is the fact that the RStGH had said nothing about the question whether or not CIL could play a part in the regulation of federal-state relations; it was simply not part of the 1927 dispute decision.

28 Bundesverfassungsgericht (Entscheidung vom 30 Januar 1973) BVerfGE 34, 216.

29 Staatsvertrag zwischen den Freistaaten Bayern und Coburg vom 20 Februar 1920, GVBl 1920, S 335.

30 Verordnung vom 27 Dezember 1971 zur Neugliederung Bayerns in Landkreise und kreisfreie Städte GVBl 1971, S 495.

made a part of the district (*Kreis*) of Coburg. Both the cities of Coburg and Neustadt bei Coburg claimed that this decree violated the clause of the 1920 treaty that guaranteed Neustadt bei Coburg the right to remain its own district (*kreisfreier Stadt*) and in doing so also violated the 1946 Bavarian constitution, which stated in Article 182 that earlier state treaties to which Bavaria was a party would remain in force. As legal successors of the state of Saxony-Coburg, both municipalities invoked the right before the Bundesverfassungsgericht to represent the interests of the erstwhile state, which could no longer act and speak for itself. Coburg and Neustadt bei Coburg claimed that Bavaria acted in bad faith in invoking the customary rule of *clausula rebus sic stantibus* to terminate the 1920 state treaty: they stated that the circumstances since 1920 had not changed so much that it would entitle Bavaria to unilaterally abolish the guarantee given to Neustadt bei Coburg.

The court rejects the claim of Coburg and Neustadt bei Coburg. The BVerfG acknowledges the right of the two municipalities to speak on behalf of the no longer existing Free State of Saxony-Coburg.[31] It also rules that the state treaty of 1920 was still valid; the federal constitutional court underlines that the 1920 state treaty guarantees the city of Neustadt bei Coburg an autonomous existence without subordination to a district authority.[32] But, the Bundesverfassungsgericht argues, the *clausula rebus sic stantibus* does come into play, because the circumstances in Germany and Bavaria in 1971 differ vastly from those in 1920. It is, the court claims, as a rule regulating the behaviour of German states towards each other, an unwritten part of the German federal constitutional law. It is therefore not a rule of CIL transformed by Article 25 of the Basic Law. The BVerfG acknowledges that under the 1919 constitution the RStGH had ruled that norms of CIL could play a part in interstate relations, but under the Basic Law there is no longer any room for such rules: all norms regulating the federal makeup of Germany are German, domestic rules of constitutional law.[33] Bavaria is therefore entitled to unilaterally change the status of Neustadt bei Coburg, despite the 1920 treaty.

[31] BVerfGE 34, 216, Rn 43.
[32] ibid Rn 46–49.
[33] ibid Rn 53. Unofficial translation by the author.

> *Die* clausula rebus sic stantibus *ist ungeschriebener Bestandteil des Bundesverfassungsrechts. Das innere Verhältnis des Bundesstaats, d. h. sowohl die staatsrechtlichen Beziehungen zwischen Bund und Ländern als auch die staatsrechtlichen Beziehungen zwischen den Gliedern des Bundesstaats, den*

So far, so good: in the post-war makeup of Germany there is no longer any place for rules of CIL to solve disputes between German states, although materially speaking the unwritten rules of German constitutional law that oblige the state organs to *Bundestreue* towards one another are basically the same as the rules of CIL invoked by the RStGH in the 1920s. Or is there? For the categorical denial of the relevance of rules of customary law in the *Coburg* decision did not hold for long. In its *Grundlagenvertrag* decision of 31 July 1973[34] the BVerfG cast serious doubt on the steadfastness of its

Ländern der Bundesrepublik Deutschland, werden nach dem Recht des Grundgesetzes ausschließlich durch das geltende Bundesverfassungsrecht bestimmt. Insoweit ist kein Raum für die Anwendung von Völkerrecht. . . . Artikel 25 GG bestimmt zwar allgemein etwas über das Verhältnis von Völkerrecht zu innerstaatlichem Recht, bietet aber keinen Ansatz, die verfassungsrechtliche Regelung der Beziehungen zwischen den Ländern, die sich aus ihrer gliedstaatlichen Stellung im Bundesstaat ergeben, zu modifizieren oder zu ergänzen. . . . Heute ist das Verhältnis der Länder im Bundesstaat zueinander lückenlos durch das Bundesverfassungsrecht geregelt, teils durch ausdrückliche Regelungen im Grundgesetz, teils durch den vom Bundesverfassungsgericht entwickelten Grundsatz des bundesfreundlichen Verhaltens; dieser Grundsatz verpflichtet im Kern jedes Land, bei der Inanspruchnahme seiner Rechte die gebotene Rücksicht auf die Interessen der anderen Länder und des Bundes zu nehmen und nicht auf Durchsetzung rechtlich eingeräumter Positionen zu dringen, die elementare Interessen eines anderen Landes schwerwiegend beeinträchtigen. In diesem verfassungsrechtlichen Grundsatz wurzelt systematisch der ungeschriebene Satz von der clausula rebus sic stantibus, *der auf staatsvertragliche Beziehungen zwischen den Gliedern der Bundesrepublik Deutschland einwirkt.*

(The *clausula rebus sic stantibus* is an unwritten part of the federal constitutional order. The inner relation of the federation, i.e. both the legal relations of the federation to the states and the legal relations between the members of the federation, the states of the federal republic of Germany, are governed exclusively by the federal constitutional law as regulated by the Basic Law. There is therefore no room for the application of international law. Article 25 of the Basic Law does generally regulate aspects of the relationship between international and domestic law, but offers no ground for the assumption that it would modify or enhance the constitutional framework regulating the interstate relations originating in their membership of the federation. Presently, the relationship of the states to each other is governed exclusively by the federal constitutional legal order, in part through explicit norms in the Basic Law, and in part through the concept of federal loyalty developed by the Federal Constitutional Court; this latter concept obliges every state not to pursue or force through its own interests to the detriment of other states or seriously harming the fundamental interests of other states. In this fundamental constitutional norm originates the unwritten principle of the *clausula rebus sic stantibus*, which influences the legal relations of the members of the Federal Republic of Germany to each other.)

[34] BVerfGE 36, 1.

recent convictions. The constitutional court had to decide on the constitutionality of the Federal Act ratifying the treaty between the Federal Republic of Germany (FRG) and the German Democratic Republic (GDR) of 21 December 1972. The treaty regulated the relations between the two German states and their respective citizens. The government of Bavaria claimed that this treaty (and therefore the act ratifying it) was unconstitutional because it violated the reunification duty that the Basic Law dictated to all (West-)German authorities.

The BVerfG ruled that it did not, and in its reasoning it developed the famous thesis that the German Reich had not disappeared in 1945, but continued to exist. Because the Reich has no state authorities of its own, the FRG can act on its behalf, at least on its own territory. Because of that, the Federal Republic shared an identity with the German Reich for its own territory and the Germans living there; FRG and German Reich are therefore not identical, but they are partly so (*teilidentisch*).[35] Because of the continued existence of the Reich that was created in 1871, the GDR is not a separate country. Like the Federal Republic, the GDR also belongs to the German Reich and continues to be *teilidentisch* with it, at least until the German question has been definitively solved.[36] This treaty is therefore a treaty under international law, the BVerfG argues, because under international law, both the FRG and the GDR are states; but that does not mean that this treaty creates a situation where both German states are subjects of international law per se. From the perspective of the FRG, the GDR is not a foreign country and the *Grundlagen* treaty does not change that. After laying the groundworks, the court continues in stating that even within a federal constitutional framework like the German one, international law plays a part in regulating the interstate relations; it is therefore perfectly conceivable that the same is true for the *inter se* relations of the two German states.[37] As the quote from the decision

[35] ibid Rn 78–79.

[36] ibid Rn 79. The question was legally solved in 1990 through the two-plus-four treaty between the two German states and the four allied powers, ending their last occupation rights and laying the groundwork for the recreated states on the territory of the GDR to join the Federal Republic, ending the German partition.

[37] ibid Rn 89. Unofficial translation by the author.

> *Der Vertrag hat also einen* Doppel*charakter; er ist seiner Art nach ein völkerrechtlicher Vertrag, seinem spezifischen Inhalt nach ein Vertrag, der vor allem inter-se-Beziehungen regelt. Inter-se-Beziehungen in einem völkerrechtlichen Vertrag zu regeln, kann vor allem dann nötig sein, wenn eine staatsrechtliche Ordnung, wie hier wegen der Desorganisation des Gesamtstaats, fehlt. Selbst im Bundesstaat bemessen sich, falls eine*

shows clearly, the BVerfG explicitly mentions the 1927 *Danube* decision of the RStGH to show that there *is* in fact room for the use of customary international norms within the German legal order, although it had explicitly rejected this only a few months earlier. Since this decision of the summer of 1973, the BVerfG has not ruled on the use of CIL; its most recent decision, therefore, does seem to acknowledge the idea that the case law of the RStGH still has relevance today. And even if one would stick with the *Coburg* decision, materially speaking the same norms are applied: and the RStGH itself had already felt entitled to interpret customary norms in such a way that they would 'fit' within a domestic legal order with its own characteristics. The question if the relations between the German states are regulated by transformed customary norms of international law or by unwritten rules of German constitutional law falling under the scope of *Bundestreue* is therefore mostly academic in nature. Still, the final word – for now – from Germany's highest court seems to be to underline the idea that CIL might have its part to play in regulating the relations between the German states.

4 The Use of CIL in the Republic of Austria

The Austrian federal constitution, the Bundes-Verfassungsgesetz[38] or B-VG of 1920 contains a separate clause on the position of CIL within

Regelung in der Bundesverfassung fehlt, die Beziehungen zwischen den Gliedstaaten nach den Regeln des Völkerrechts (vgl. die Entscheidung des Staatsgerichtshofs für das Deutsche Reich, Lammers-Simons, 1, 178 ff., 207 ff.; dazu die Fortentwicklung nach dem Recht des Grundgesetzes (. . .)): Unrichtig ist also die Auffassung, jedes "Zwei-Staaten-Modell" sei mit der grundgesetzlichen Ordnung unvereinbar.

(The treaty therefore has a dual character: it has the character of an international treaty, more specifically, a treaty regulating inter se relations. Regulating inter se relations in an international treaty may be mostly needed, when a constitutional regulation is lacking, in this case because of the fact that the overarching state is disorganised. Even within a federation the relations between the member states may be regulated by norms of international law, when no domestic rules are available (cf. the decision of the Staatsgerichtshof für das deutsche Reich, Lammers-Simons 1, 178 fth., 207 fth. and the further development of this principle under the Basic Law). The point of view that every 'two state model' is contrary to the federal legal order is therefore wrong.)

[38] One of the peculiarities of the constitutional system of Austria is that its constitutional law is not laid down in one or a few central documents, as is the case in most states with a written constitution. Instead, there is a central document, the aforementioned B-VG, but the B-VG allows the federal legislator in Article 44 to create constitutional law outside

the Austrian domestic legal order. Article 9 (1) B-VG is more or less a copy of Article 4 RV.[39] The Austrian doctrine is not quite clear on the exact hierarchical positions of these customary rules of international law within the Austrian legal order. The majority position seems to be that Article 9 B-VG contributes to these norms a position equivocal to the one explicitly provided for by Article 25 GG: superior to ordinary acts, but inferior to federal constitutional law.[40] It has never played a large part within the domestic legal order of Austria, however.

This has a lot to do with the introduction of another provision into the constitution. This article, Article 15a, was introduced in the B-VG in 1974.[41] It regulates primarily that the federation and the states can enter into treaties with one another on matters of common competence. On the side of the federation, the federal government or a federal minister shall be competent to enter into the treaty; if matters of a legislative nature are regulated by the treaty, it shall need the approval by the federal legislator (1). Interstate treaties are only possible with regard to matters pertaining to the competences of the states themselves; they shall be brought to the attention of the federal government (2). For both treaties between the federation and one or more states and interstate treaties, the fundamentals of international treaty law shall be applicable. For interstate treaties, this applicability can be overruled by corresponding constitutional state acts of the states involved regulating otherwise (3).[42]

of the B-VG itself by enacting legislation through the same procedure as the one prescribed for amending the B-VG. And since this is in most cases a rather easy procedure (a 2/3rd majority of the votes in the federal diet in one reading, half the members present), this has led to a number of federal constitutional acts (Bundesverfassungsgesetze, or BVG) with the same rank as the B-VG itself, and a couple of hundred constitutional articles in ordinary acts (Bundesverfassungsbestimmungen), also of the same rank as the B-VG itself. This has made the Austrian constitution a massive and very complicated structure, since all the BVG and the Verfassungsbestimmungen in ordinary acts cannot just enhance the B-VG itself, but also amend or contravene it. The norms regulating the topic of this article are all regulated in the B-VG, however.

39 '*Die allgemein anerkannten Regeln des Völkerrechtes gelten als Bestandteile des Bundesrechtes*' ('The generally acknowledged norms of international law form part of the federal legal order'). Unofficial translation by the author.

40 T Öhlinger & H Eberhard, *Verfassungsrecht* (12th rev ed, Facultas 2019) 80.

41 *Bundes-Verfassungsgesetznovelle* vom 30 Juli 1974, BGBl nr 444/1974.

42 Artikel 15a

(1) *Bund und Länder können untereinander Vereinbarungen über Angelegenheiten ihres jeweiligen Wirkungsbereiches schließen. Der Abschluss solcher Vereinbarungen namens des Bundes obliegt je nach dem Gegenstand der Bundesregierung oder den Bundesministern. Vereinbarungen, die auch die Organe der Bundesgesetzgebung binden sollen, dürfen nur von der Bundesregierung mit Genehmigung des*

The new Article 15a was introduced into the federal constitution because of the lack of clarity with regard to the norms applicable on treaties and on interstate and federal-state relations within the Austrian legal order.[43] There was never any doubt as to the nature of these kinds of treaties: they are as such not of an international, but of a domestic nature.[44] Article 15a under 3 B-VG therefore transforms the fundamental principles of international treaty law into Austrian constitutional law and the article prescribes the use of these norms for all treaties between the federation and one or more states and between two or more states – with the exception of a regulation through corresponding constitutional state acts for the latter. Where both the 1919 Federal Constitution and the 1949 Basic Law are silent on the subject and the relevant German courts have never unequivocally stated that, indeed, norms of international law can and must be used *as such* within the domestic legal order, the Austrian constitutional legislator has taken

Nationalrates abgeschlossen werden, wobei Artikel 50 Abs. 3 auf solche Beschlüsse des Nationalrates sinngemäß anzuwenden ist; sie sind im Bundesgesetzblatt kundzumachen.

(2) *Vereinbarungen der Länder untereinander können nur über Angelegenheiten ihres selbständigen Wirkungsbereiches getroffen werden und sind der Bundesregierung unverzüglich zur Kenntnis zu bringen.*

(3) *Die Grundsätze des völkerrechtlichen Vertragsrechtes sind auf Vereinbarungen im Sinne des Abs. 1 anzuwenden. Das Gleiche gilt auch für Vereinbarungen im Sinne des Abs. 2, soweit nicht durch übereinstimmende Verfassungsgesetze der betreffenden Länder anderes bestimmt ist.*

(1) The federation and the Land can conclude agreements between themselves concerning matters of their current scope of competence. The conclusion of such agreements on the part of the federation requires, depending upon the subject matter, the countersignature of the Federal Government or the Federal Minister. Agreements which are also to bind the organs of the Federal legislation, may be concluded by the Federal Government only with the consent of the National Council, in which case Article 50, Paragraph (3) is to be applied correspondingly to such resolutions; they are to be promulgated in the Bundesgesetzblatt.

(2) Agreements between the Länder can only be made concerning matters within their independent field of competence and must be brought to the knowledge of the Federal Government without delay.

(3) The principles of the International Law of Treaties are to be applied to the agreement in the sense of Paragraph (1) of this Article. The same applies to agreements in the sense of Paragraph (2), insofar as it is not determined otherwise through harmonised Constitutional laws of the concerned Länder.) (Unofficial translation by the author.)

[43] T Öhlinger, *Die Anwendung des Völkerrechts auf Verträge im Bundesstaat* (Braumüller 1982) 12.

[44] ibid 12–13.

sides. It has deemed all generally applicable norms of international treaty law such 'fundamental principles'.[45] This means that – generally speaking – the norms laid down in the Vienna Convention on the Law of Treaties (VCLT) are the ones applicable within the domestic legal order of Austria as well for the creation, interpretation and termination of treaties and the settling of disputes arising from them. The norms of the VCLT are for the most part codifications of existing rules of CIL. Both the constitutional legislator itself[46] and the Austrian constitutional court (Verfassungsgerichtshof, VfGH)[47] have ruled that the convention norms should be applied to domestic treaties in the sense of Article 15a under 3 B-VG.

The 1998 decision by the VfGH is the only one in which a clear ruling is given on the application of the VCLT itself on domestic treaties. The case involved a treaty between the federation and the state of Vienna, however. Since Austria is a party to the VCLT, it can be argued that the treaty itself is applicable to the federal authorities, and therefore is applicable to a treaty between the federation and a state. But is the VCLT *itself* applicable to interstate treaties as well? This is somewhat questionable – the Austrian states[48] are not themselves parties to the VCLT, and the fact that the contents of the convention are transformed through Article 15a under 1 B-VG does not necessarily mean that the VCLT as such is transformed as well: the fact that the states are allowed to digress from it through state constitutional acts of their own also suggests that this might not be a straightforward situation. It could therefore perhaps be argued that on an interstate level, the VCLT norms are applicable in their 'older guise' as rules of CIL. The difference is, of course, highly theoretical. Only when a case is decided by the constitutional court about a pure interstate treaty (of which there are not many in Austria) will we perhaps know for sure what the formal status of these rules within the Austrian legal order is. So far, this has not happened. What *is* clear, however, is that Austria unequivocally chooses norms of an international nature, whose origins are undoubtedly customary in nature, to regulate interstate relations, showing the usefulness of these norms for that purpose.

45 ibid 14–15.

46 ibid 21.

47 *Verfassungsgerichtshof* (Entscheidung vom 15 Oktober 1998) VfSlg 15.309/1998.

48 The Republic of Austria comprises of nine States: Burgenland, Carinthia, Lower Austria, Salzburg, Styria, Tyrol, Upper Austria, Vienna and Vorarlberg.

5 Conclusion

This article has focused on the use of norms of CIL for the regulation of interstate relations in two states with a federal constitutional makeup, the FRG and the Republic of Austria. In Germany, the possibility of the use of CIL became relevant after the Great War, with the introduction of the new republican constitution in August 1919. One of the novelties of this new constitution was its Article 4, which regulated that general rules of international law (and therefore norms of CIL) were a binding part of German federal law. The newly minted Staatsgerichtshof für das deutsche Reich, whose main task it was to solve public law disputes of a federal nature, was quick to acknowledge the possibilities of this new provision in the constitution. In a number of cases on disputes between German states in the 1920s, it argued that when domestic constitutional norms did not provide a reasonable settlement, rules of CIL could be used via the way of Article 4 *RV* to solve the issue. The court did, however, interpret these norms so as to fit into a domestic legal order, which raises the question whether the *RStGH* used 'real' norms of CIL – or merely saw them as a source of inspiration to draw up what are in fact unwritten norms of constitutional law.

This ambiguity concerning the use of customary norms survived the German apocalypse of 1945. The post-war Bundesverfassungsgericht is partly the legal successor to the old Staatsgerichtshof. In three of its cases, it dealt with the question whether rules of CIL could play a part within the domestic legal order of Germany. An analysis of these cases shows that there is no clear-cut answer to the question whether the BVerfG acknowledges an independent role for customary norms in the German federal makeup.

Like Germany, Austria too has a constitutional norm transforming customary international norms into the domestic legal order. This article is no longer relevant for the questions dealt with in this chapter however, since the Austrian constitution also contains a specific norm dealing with the relevance of international law for interstate relations. Article 15a B-VG under 3 states since 1974 that rules of international law are relevant for the creation, interpretation and termination of treaties between the Austrian federation and one or more states and between two or more states. They can also be used to solve federal-state and interstate disputes. In the latter cases, the states party can decide to create differing norms through mutual constitutional state acts. The article was introduced into the Austrian constitution precisely to terminate the debate that is so topical in Germany: whether there is an actual role for international law in the regulation of interstate and federal-state relations. The Austrian constitution explicitly affirms this concept. The only remaining unclarity is if these norms are simply those of the Vienna convention or if they are of a customary nature. Since the Austrian states are not themselves parties to the Vienna convention, the latter might be the case. The Austrian VfGH has so far not ruled on this question.

The example of these two countries shows that international law norms can play a limited, but useful role within the domestic legal order of a federal state. Whereas in Germany an ambiguity has continued to exist on the question whether such norms, especially if they are of a customary nature, are valid as such within the domestic legal order of Germany or if they merely provide material inspiration for the development of unwritten domestic norms, such as federal loyalty, in Austria the constitutional legislator has been quite clear. Both federal-state and interstate relations in Austria are regulated by international norms, although these legal relations themselves are clearly domestic. Especially the VCLT is a relevant source of law in this respect. The ambiguity in Austria is of a different nature: it is not entirely clear whether the VCLT itself or materially similar norms of a customary nature are applicable in interstate relations, because the nine Austrian states are themselves not party to the convention. Despite this slight ambiguity, the introduction of a new article into the Basic Law along the lines of Article 15a B-VG, but instead focusing on rules of customary law, would seem a good idea to end the continuing vagueness in Germany resulting from the hesitant case law of the relevant German courts since the 1920s.

BIBLIOGRAPHY

Books and Chapters in Edited Volumes

Aarnio A, *Reason and Authority* (Ashgate 1997)

Abi-Saab G, 'La coutume dans tous ses états ou le dilemma du développement du droit international général dans un monde éclaté' in Ago R (ed), *Le Droit international à l'heure de sa codification: études en l'honneur de Roberto Ago* (Giuffrè 1987) 61

Achour YB, *Le Rôle des Civilisations dans le Système International (Droit et Relations Internationales)* (Editions Bruylant/Editions de l'Université des Bruxelles 2003)

Acquaviva G & Whiting A, *International Criminal Law: Cases and Commentary* (Oxford University Press 2011)

Agius MF, *Interaction and Delimitation of International Legal Orders* (Brill Nijhoff 2014)

Ago R, *Scienza giuridica e diritto internazionale* (Giuffrè 1950)

Akande D, 'Classification of Armed Conflicts: Relevant Legal Concepts' in Wilmshurst E (ed), *International Law and the Classification of Conflicts* (Oxford University Press 2012) 52

Allott P, 'Interpretation: An Exact Art' in Bianchi A, Peat D and Windsor M (eds), *Interpretation in International Law* (Oxford University Press 2015) 373

American Law Institute, *Restatement of the Law: The Foreign Relations of the United States*, Vol 1 (American Law Institute Publishers 1987)

Ammann O, *Domestic Courts and the Interpretation of International Law: Methods and Reasoning Based on the Swiss Example* (Brill 2020)

Anghie A, 'On Critique and the Other' in Orford A (ed), *International Law and its Others* (Cambridge University Press 2006) 389

Anghie A, *Imperialism, Sovereignty and the Making of International Law* (Cambridge University Press 2008)

Anschütz G, *Die Verfassung des deutschen Reichs vom 11 August 1919: Ein Kommentar für Wissenschaft und Praxis* (4th ed, Stilke 1924)

Anzilotti D, *Scritti di diritto internazionale pubblico* (Cedan Padova 1956–7)

Apalagaki Ch, *Code of Civil Procedure: Article by Article Interpretation, Articles 1–590* (4th ed, Nomiki Vivliothiki 2016) 1405

Arajärvi N, *The Changing Nature of Customary International Law: Methods of Interpreting the Concept of Custom in International Criminal Tribunals* (Routledge 2014)

Arajärvi N, 'From the "Demands of Humanity": The Formulation of *Opinio Juris* in Decisions of International Criminal Tribunals and the Need for a Renewed Emphasis on State Practice' in Lepard B (ed), *Reexamining Customary International Law* (Cambridge University Press 2017) 190

Arangio-Ruiz G, 'Customary Law: A Few More Thoughts on the Theory of "Spontaneous International" Custom' in Salmon J (ed), *Droit du pouvoir, pouvoir du droit: mélanges offerts à Jean Salmon* (Bruylant 2007) 93

Arend AC, *Legal Rules and International Society* (Oxford University Press 1999)

Arendt H, *The Human Condition* (2nd ed, University of Chicago Press 1998)

Austin J, *Province of Jurisprudence Determined* (John Murray 1832)

Aznar MJ & Methymaki E, 'Article 2' in Zimmermann A & Tams CJ (eds), *The Statute of the International Court of Justice: A Commentary* (3rd ed, Oxford University Press 2019) 303

Badiou A et al, *What Is a People?* (Columbia University Press 2016)

Bangerter O, *Internal Control: Codes of Conduct within Insurgent Armed Groups* (Small Arms Survey 2012)

Barak A, *Purposive Interpretation in Law* (Princeton University Press 2005)

Barile G, *Diritto internazionale e diritto interno* (Giuffrè 1957)

Barile G, *I principi fondamentali della comunità statale ed il coordinamento tra sistemi* (CEDAM 1969)

Barthes R, *L'aventure sémiologique* (Seuil 1985)

Bassiouni MC, 'Advancing the Responsibility to Protect Through International Criminal Justice' in Cooper RH & Voïnov Kohler J (eds), *Responsibility to Protect: The Global Moral Compact for the 21st Century* (Palgrave Macmillan 2009) 31

Bassiouni MC, 'Revisiting the Architecture of Crimes Against Humanity: Almost a Century in the Making, with Gaps and Ambiguities Remaining – the Need for a Specialized Convention' in Sadat LN (ed), *Forging a Convention for Crimes Against Humanity* (Cambridge University Press 2011) 43

Bauer H, *Die Bundestreue. Zugleich ein Beitrag zur Dogmatik des Bundesstaatsrechts und zur Rechtsverhältnislehre* (Mohr Siebeck 1992)

Bederman DJ, *Custom as a Source of Law* (Cambridge University Press 2010)

Bedjaoui M, 'L'opportunité dans les décisions de la Cour internationale de Justice' in Boisson de Chazournes L & Gowlland-Debbas V (eds), *The International Legal System in Quest of Equity and Universality* (Kluwer 2001) 563

Beham M, *State Interest and the Sources of International Law. Doctrine, Morality, and Non-Treaty Law* (Routledge 2018)

Beham M, Fink M & Janik R, *Völkerrecht verstehen* (Facultas 2015)

Bentham J, *First Principles Preparatory to Constitutional Code* (Clarendon Press 1989)

Bentivoglio LM, *La funzione interpretativa nell'ordinamento internazionale* (Giuffrè 1958)

Bernaz N, 'Reforming the UN Human Rights Protection Procedures: A Legal Perspective on the Establishment of the Universal Periodic Review Mechanism' in Boyle K (ed), *New Institutions for Human Rights Protection* (Oxford University Press 2009) 75

Bertea S & Pavlakos G (eds), *New Essays on the Normativity of Law* (Hart 2011)

Besson S, *The Morality of Conflict: Reasonable Disagreement and the Law* (Hart 2005)

Betti E, *L'interpretazione della legge e degli atti giuridici* (Giuffrè 1949)

Betti E, *Problematica del diritto internazionale* (Giuffrè 1956)

Betti E, *Teoria generale dell'interpretazione* (Giuffrè 1990)

Bianchi A, 'Textual Interpretation and (International) Law Reading: The Myth of (in) Determinacy and the Genealogy of Meaning' in Bekker P, Dolzer R, Waibel M and Vagts D (eds), *Making Transnational Law Work in the Global Economy: Essays in Honour of Detlev Vagts* (Cambridge University Press 2010) 53

Bianchi A, Peat D & Windsor M (eds), *Interpretation in International Law* (Oxford University Press 2015)

Bindreiter U, 'The Realist Hans Kelsen' in Duarte d'Almeida L, Gardner J & Green L (eds), *Kelsen Revisited: New Essays on the Pure Theory of Law* (Hart 2013) 112

Bjorge E, *The Evolutionary Interpretation of Treaties* (Oxford University Press 2014)

Bobbio N, *La consuetudine come fatto normativo* (Giappichelli 1942)

Bobbio N, *Per un lessico di teoria generale del diritto* (CEDAM 1975)

Bobbio N, *Il positivismo giuridico* (Giappichelli Editore 1996)

Bobbio N, *Giusnaturalismo e positivismo giuridico* (Editori Laterza 2011)

Bos M, *A Methodology of International Law* (Elsevier Science 1984)

Bradley CA, 'Customary International Law Adjudication as Common Law Adjudication' in Bradley CA (ed), *Custom's Future: International Law in a Changing World* (Cambridge University Press 2016) 34

Brie S, *Die Lehre vom Gewohnheitsrecht: Eine historisch-dogmatische Untersuchung* (Marcus 1899)

Brierly JL, 'The Basis of Obligation in International Law' in Lauterpacht H & Waldock CHM (eds), *The Basis of Obligation in International Law and Other Papers by the Late James Leslie Brierly* (Clarendon Press 1958)

Brierly JL, *The Law of Nations: An Introduction to the International Law of Peace* (Humphrey Waldock ed, 6th ed, Clarendon Press 1963)

Brölmann C & Radi Y (eds), *Research Handbook on the Theory and Practice of International Lawmaking* (Edward Elgar 2016)

Brölmann C, 'Capturing the Juridical Will of International Organisations' in Droubi S & d'Aspremont J (eds), *International Organisations, Non-State*

Actors and the Formation of Customary International Law (Manchester University Press 2020) 42.

Brown C, 'Inherent Powers in International Adjudication' in Romano CPR, Alter K & Shany Y (eds), *The Oxford Handbook of International Adjudication* (Oxford University Press 2013) 829

Brownlie I, 'Problems Concerning the Unity of International Law' in Ago R (ed), *Le droit international à l'heure de sa codification: études en l'honneur de Roberto Ago* (Giuffrè 1987) 155

Brunnée J & Toope S, *Legitimacy and Legality in International Law: An Interactional Account* (Cambridge University Press 2010)

Brunnée J & Toope S, 'Constructivism and International Law' in Dunoff JL & Pollack MA (eds), *Interdisciplinary Perspectives on International Law and International Relations: The State of the Art* (Cambridge University Press 2012) 119

Buchanan A, *Justice, Legitimacy, and Self-Determination: Moral Foundations for International Law* (Oxford University Press 2003)

Buchanan A, 'Institutional Legitimacy' in Sobel D, Vallentyne P & Wall S (eds), *Oxford Studies in Political Philosophy Volume 4* (Oxford University Press 2018) 57

Burgstaller M, *Theories of Compliance with International Law* (Martinus Nijhoff 2005)

Burns JH & Hart HLA (eds.), *A Comment on the Commentaries and a Fragment on Government: The Collected Works of Jeremy Bentham* (Oxford University Press 2008)

Byers M, *Custom, Power and the Power of Rules: International Relations and Customary International Law* (Cambridge University Press 1999)

Cameron AM, 'Jural Aspect in Dooyeweerd's Philosophy of Law' in Benge C (ed), *In a Reformational Key: Papers presented for the Life, Work and Vision of Duncan Roper* (Thumbwidth Press 2020) 292

Capotorti F, *Il diritto dei trattati secondo la Convenzione di Vienna: studio introduttivo al volume Convenzione di Vienna sul diritto dei trattati* (CEDAM 1969)

Cardenas S, *Conflict and Compliance: State Responses to International Human Rights Pressure* (University of Pennsylvania Press 2010)

Carter JC, *The Provinces of the Written and the Unwritten Law* (Banks & Bros 1889)

Carter JC, *Law: It's Origin, Growth, and Function* (The Knickerbocker Press 1907)

Carty A, *The Philosophy of International Law* (Edinburgh University Press 2007)

Carty A, *The Decay of International Law: A Reappraisal of the Limits of Legal Imagination in International Affairs* (Manchester University Press 2019)

Cassese A, *International Law* (2nd ed, Oxford University Press 2005)

Cassese A, 'For an Enhanced Role of *Jus Cogens*' in Cassese A (ed), *Realizing Utopia: The Future of International Law* (Oxford University Press 2012) 158

Cassese A & Weiler JHH, *Change and Stability in International Law-Making* (Walter de Gruyter 1988)

Cheng B, 'Custom: The Future of General State Practice in a Divided World' in St John Macdonald R & Johnston DM (eds), *The Structure and Process of International Law: Essays in Legal Philosophy Doctrine and Theory* (Martinus Nijhoff 1983) 513

Cheng B, *General Principles of Law as Applied by International Courts and Tribunals* (Grotius 1987)

Chiassoni P, 'Wiener Realism' in Duarte d'Almeida L, Gardner J & Green L (eds), *Kelsen Revisited: New Essays on the Pure Theory of Law* (Hart 2013)

Choi SJ & Gulati M, 'Customary International Law: How Do Courts Do It?' in Bradley CA (ed), *Custom's Future. International Law in a Changing World* (Cambridge University Press 2016) 117

Christiano T, 'Is Democratic Legitimacy Possible for International Institutions?' in Archibugi D, Koenig-Archibugi M & Marchetti R (eds), *Global Democracy Normative and Empirical Perspectives* (Cambridge University Press 2011) 69

Christiano T, 'Climate Change and State Consent' in Moss J (ed), *Climate Change and Justice* (Cambridge University Press 2015) 17

Christiano T, 'Ronald Dworkin, State Consent, and Progressive Cosmopolitanism' in Waluchow W & Sciaraffa S (eds), *The Legacy of Ronald Dworkin* (Oxford University Press 2016) 49

Clouser R, *The Myth of Religious Neutrality* (University of Notre Dame Press 2005)

Cohen HG, 'Theorizing Precedent in International Law' in Bianchi A, Peat D & Windsor M (eds), *Interpretation in International Law* (Oxford University Press 2015) 268

Cohen J, *An Introduction to the Philosophy of Induction and Probability* (Clarendon Press 1989)

Collins R, 'Consent, Obligation and the Legitimate Authority of International Law' in Capps P & Olsen HP (eds), *Legal Authority Beyond the State* (Cambridge University Press 2018) 206

Condorelli L, 'Customary International Law: The Yesterday, Today, and Tomorrow of General International Law' in Cassese A (ed), *Realizing Utopia: The Future of International Law* (Oxford University Press 2012) 148

Cook G, *A Digest of WTO Jurisprudence on Public International Law Concepts and Principles* (Cambridge University Press 2015)

Corten O, *Méthodologie du droit international public* (Editions de l'Université Libre de Bruxelles 2009)

Cotterrell R, 'Why Must Legal Ideas Be Interpreted Sociologically?' in Del Mar M & Giudice M (eds), *Legal Theory and the Social Sciences Vol II* (Routledge 2010) 101

Cowan J, 'The Universal Periodic Review as Public Audit Ritual: An Anthropological Perspective on Emerging Practices in the Global Governance of Human Rights' in Charlesworth H &Larking E (eds), *Human Rights and the*

Universal Periodic Review: Rituals and Ritualism (Cambridge University Press 2015) 44

Craven M, 'The Invention of a Tradition: Westlake, The Berlin Conference and the Historicisation of International Law' in Nuzzo L & Vec M, *Constructing International Law: The Birth of a Discipline* (Klostermann 2012) 4

Crawford J, *The Creation of States in International Law* (Oxford University Press 2007)

Crawford J, *Chance, Order, Change: The Course of International Law, General Course of Public International Law* (Brill 2014)

Crawford J, *Brownlie's Principles of Public International Law* (9th ed, Oxford University Press 2019) 369

Crema L, *La prassi successiva e l'interpretazione del diritto internazionale scritto* (Giuffré 2017)

D'Amato A, *The Concept of Custom in International Law* (Cornell University Press 1971)

D'Aspremont J, 'Conclusion: Inclusive Law-Making and Law-Enforcement Processes for an Exclusive International Legal System' in d'Aspremont J (ed), *Participants in the International Legal System: Multiple Perspectives on Non-State Actors in International Law* (Routledge 2011) 425

D'Aspremont J, 'Current Theorizations about the Treaty in International Law' in Hollis D (ed), *The Oxford Guide to Treaties* (2nd ed, Oxford University Press 2020) 46

D'Aspremont J, 'International Law-Making by Non-State Actors: Changing the Model or Putting the Phenomenon into Perspective?' in Noortmann M & Ryngaert C (eds), *Non-State Actor Dynamics in International Law: From Law-Takers to Law-Makers* (Routledge 2010) 158

D'Aspremont J, 'Non-State Actors and the Formation of International Customary Law: Unlearning Some Common Tropes' in Droubi S & d'Aspremont J (eds), *International Organisations, Non-State Actors and the Formation of Customary International Law* (Manchester University Press 2020) 166

D'Aspremont J, 'The Doctrinal Illusion of the Heterogeneity of International Law-Making Processes' in Ruiz Fabri H et al (eds), *Select Proceedings of the European Society of International Law*, vol 2 (Hart 2010) 297

D'Aspremont J, 'The Multidimensional Process of Interpretation: Content-Determination and Law-Ascertainment Distinguished' in Bianchi A, Peat D, & Windsor M (eds), *Interpretation in International Law* (Oxford University Press 2015) 111

D'Aspremont J, *Formalism and the Sources of International Law: A Theory of the Ascertainment of Legal Rules* (Oxford University Press 2011)

D'Aspremont J, *International Law as a Belief System* (Cambridge University Press 2017)

D'Aspremont J, *The Discourse on Customary International Law* (Oxford University Press 2021)

D'Aspremont J & Besson S (eds), *Oxford Handbook of the Sources of International Law* (Oxford University Press 2017)

Danilenko GM, *Law-Making in the International Community* (Martinus Nijhoff 1993)

De Certeau M, *L'écriture de l'histoire* (Gallimard 1975)

De Visscher C, *Problèmes d'interprétation judiciaire en droit international public* (Pedone 1963)

De Visscher C, *Theory and Reality in Public International Law. Revised Edition* (Princeton University Press 1968)

Decrey Warner E et al, 'Armed Non-State Actors and Humanitarian Norms: Lessons from the Geneva Call Experience' in Perrin B (ed), *Modern Warfare: Armed Groups, Private Militaries, Humanitarian Organizations, and the Law* (UBC Press 2012) 73

Degan V, *L' interprétation des accords en droit international* (Martinus Nijhoff 1963)

Derrida J, *De la Grammatologie* (Editions de Minuit 1967)

Derrida J, *L'écriture et la différence* (Editions du Seuil 1967)

Di Nolfo E, *Il disordine internazionale. Lotte per la supremazia dopo la Guerra fredda* (Bruno Mondadori 2012)

Dinstein Y, *Non-International Armed Conflicts in International Law* (Cambridge University Press 2014)

Dixon M, *Textbook on International Law* (7th ed, Oxford University Press 2013)

Djeffal C, 'Dynamic and Evolutive Interpretation of the ECHR by Domestic Courts?' in Aust HP & Nolte G (eds), *The Interpretation of International Law by Domestic Courts: Uniformity, Diversity, Convergence* (Oxford University Press 2016) 175

Djeffal C, *Static and Evolutive Treaty Interpretation: A Functional Reconstruction* (Cambridge University Press 2016)

Dooyeweerd H, *The Collected Works: A New Critique of Theoretical Thought Series A*, Vols 1–4 (Freeman DH & De Jongste H trs, Strauss DFM ed, first published 1953–1958, The Edwin Mellen Press 1997)

Dooyeweerd H, *Roots of Western Culture* (Kraay J tr, Vander Vennen M & Zylstra B eds, Paideia Press 2012)

Dooyeweerd H, *The Encyclopedia of the Science of Law*, Vol 8/1 (RD Knudsen tr & AM Cameron ed, Paideia Press 2012)

Dörr O, 'Article 31' in Dörr O & Schmalenbach K (eds), *Vienna Convention on the Law of Treaties: A Commentary* (2012 Springer) 521

Dosse F, *History of Structuralism Vol 1: The Rising Sign, 1945–1966* (University of Minnesota Press 1997)

Doswald-Beck L (ed), *San Remo Manual on International Law Applicable to Armed Conflicts at Sea* (Grotius Publications, Cambridge University Press 1995)

Droubi S, 'Opinio Juris: Between Mental States and Institutional Objects' in Droubi S and D'Aspremont J (eds), *International Organizations, Non-State Actors and the Formation of Customary International Law, Melland Schill Perspectives on International Law* (Manchester University Press 2020) 62

Droubi S & d'Aspremont J (eds), *International Organizations, Non-State Actors, and the Formation of Customary International Law, Melland Schill Perspectives on International Law* (Manchester University Press 2020)

Dupuy PM, 'Evolutionary Interpretation of Treaties: Between Memory and Prophecy' in E Cannizzaro (ed), *The Law of Treaties Beyond the Vienna Convention* (Oxford University Press 2011) 123

Dupuy PM, 'Introduction to Customary International Law' in Dupuy PM (ed), *Customary International Law* (Elgar 2021) 1

Dupuy RJ, 'Coutume sage et coutume sauvage' in Rousseau C (ed), *Mélanges offerts à Charles Rousseau: la communauté internationale* (Pedone 1974) 75

Dworkin R, *Law' s Empire* (Harvard University Press 1986)

Fahey E, *The Actors of Postnational Rule-Making: Contemporary Challenges of European and International Law* (Routledge 2017)

Ferguson N (ed), *Virtual History: Alternatives and Counterfactuals* (Picador 1997)

Fitzmaurice M & Merkouris P, *Treaties in Motion: The Evolution of Treaties from Formation to Termination* (Cambridge University Press 2020)

Fitzmaurice M, Elias O & Merkouris P, *Treaty Interpretation and the Vienna Convention on the Law of the Treaties: 30 Years On* (Brill/Nijhoff 2010)

Fortin K, *The Accountability of Armed Groups under Human Rights Law* (Oxford University Press 2017)

Frankel J, *National Interest* (Macmillan 1970)

Freeman M, 'Article 16' in Freeman M, Chinkin C & Rudolf B (eds), *The UN Convention on the Elimination of All forms of Discrimination Against Women: A Commentary* (2nd ed, Oxford University Press 2013) 436

Fuller LL, *Anatomy of the Law* (Praeger 1968)

Gadamer HG, *Truth and Method* (Bloomsbury Academic 2013)

Galev G & Dabovikj-Anastasovska J, *Obligaciono Pravo* (3rd ed, University of St Cyril and Methodius Skopje 2012)

Gallant K, *The Principle of Legality in International and Comparative Criminal Law* (Cambridge University Press 2008)

Gardiner R, *Treaty Interpretation* (Oxford University Press 2008)

Garner BA (ed), *Black's Law Dictionary* (9th ed, WEST 2009)

Gautier P, 'Article 2 – Convention of 1969' in O Corten & P Klein (eds), *The Vienna Convention on the Law of Treaties: A Commentary* (Oxford University Press 2011) 33

Geiss R, 'Humanitarian Law Obligations of Organized Armed Groups' in International Institute of Humanitarian Law (ed), *Non-State Actors and*

International Humanitarian Law: Organized Armed Groups: A Challenge for the 21st Century (FrancoAngeli 2010) 93

Gentili A, *On the Law of War* (Rolfe JC tr, Clarendon Press 1933)

Giegerich T, 'The Case-Law of the European Court of Human Rights on the Immunity of States' in Peters A et al (eds), *Immunities in the Age of Global Constitutionalism* (Brill Nijhoff 2015) 68

Goldmann M, 'Relative Normativity' in d'Aspremont J & Singh S (eds), *Concepts for International Law: Contributions to Disciplinary Thought* (Edward Elgar 2019) 740

Goldsmith JL & Posner EA, *The Limits of International Law* (Oxford University Press 2005)

Goudzwaard B, *A Christian Political Option* (Praansma H tr, Wedge Publishing 1972)

Gradoni L, 'Il principio di precauzione nel diritto dell'Organizzazione Mondiale del Commercio' in Bianchi A & Gestri M (eds), *Il principio precauzionale nel diritto internazionale e comunitario* (Giuffrè 2006) 147

Grotius H, *De iure belli ac pacis* (1625)

Guastini R, *Interpretare e argomentare* (Giuffré 2011)

Guastini R, *Le fonti del diritto e l'interpretazione* (Giuffrè 1993)

Guggenheim P, '*Les deux elements de la coutume en droit international*', in Scelle G & Bastid S (eds), *La technique et les principes du droit public : études en l'honneur de Georges Scelle* (LGDJ 1950) 275

Günther H, *Zur Entstehung von Völkergewohnheitsrecht* (Duncker & Humblot 1970)

Gur N, *Legal Directives and Practical Reasons* (Oxford University Press 2018)

Guzman AT & Hsiang J, 'Reinvigorating Customary International Law' in Bradley CA (ed), *Custom's Future: International Law in a Changing World* (Cambridge University Press 2016) 275

Habermas J, *The Philosophical Discourse of Modernity. Twelve Lectures* (Lawrence F tr, Polity Press 1987)

Hakimi M, 'Custom's Method and Process: Lessons from Humanitarian Law' in Bradley CA (ed), *Custom's Future: International Law in a Changing World* (Cambridge University Press 2016) 149

Hamster J, 'Customary International Law' in Nollkaemper A & Reinisch A (eds), *International Law in Domestic Courts. A Casebook* (Oxford University Press 2018) 243

Happold M (ed), *International Law in a Multipolar World* (Routledge 2011)

Hart HLA, *The Concept of Law* (Oxford University Press 1961)

Hart HLA, *The Concept of Law* (Clarendon Press 1963)

Hart HLA, *Punishment and responsibility: Essays in the Philosophy of Law* (Oxford University Press 1968)

Hart HLA, 'Commands and Authoritative Legal Reasons' in *Essays on Bentham: Jurisprudence and Political Philosophy* (Oxford University Press 1982)

Hart HLA, *The Concept of Law* (2nd ed, Clarendon Press 1994)
Hart HLA, *The Concept of Law* (3rd ed, Clarendon Press 2012)
Hart HLA & Honoré T, *Causation in the Law* (2nd ed, Clarendon Press 2002)
Hathaway O & Shapiro SJ, *The Internationalists: And Their Plan to Outlaw War* (Allen Lane 2017)
Hayek G, *Law, Legislation and Liberty: A New Statement of the Liberal Principles of Justice and Political Economy* (University of Chicago Press 1979)
Heidegger M, *Being and Time* (Harper & Row Edition 1962)
Henderson Roger, *Illuminating Law: The Construction of Herman Dooyeweerd's Philosophy, 1918–1928* (PhD thesis, Vrije Universitet Amsterdam 1994)
Henckaerts JM & Doswald-Beck L, *Customary International Humanitarian Law* (Cambridge University Press 2005)
Henkin L, *How Nations Behave: Law and Foreign Policy* (2nd ed, Columbia University Press 1979)
Henriksen A, *International Law* (Oxford University Press 2017)
Hernández G, 'Interpretation' in Kammerhofer J & d'Aspremont J (eds), *International Legal Positivism in a Post-Modern World* (Cambridge University Press 2014) 318
Hernández G, 'Interpretative Authority and the International Judiciary' in Bianchi A, Peat D & Windsor M (eds), *Interpretation in International Law* (Oxford University Press 2015) 166
Hernández G, *International Law* (Oxford University Press 2019)
Higgins R, *The Development of International Law Through the Political Organs of the United Nations* (Oxford University Press 1963)
Higgins R, *Problems and Process: International Law and How we Use It* (Oxford University Press 1995)
Hollis D, 'Sources and Interpretation Theories: An Interdependent Relationship' in d'Aspremont J & Besson S (eds), *The Oxford Handbook of the Sources of International Law* (Oxford University Press 2017) 422
Hollis D, 'Interpretation' in d'Aspremont J & Singth S, *Concepts for International Law. Contributions to Disciplinary Thought* (Edward Elgar 2019) 559
Hollis DB, 'The Existential Function of Interpretation in International Law' in Bianchi A, Peat D & Windsor M (eds), *Interpretation in International Law* (Oxford University Press 2015) 78
Hume D, *A Treatise of Human Nature* (first published 1739, Clarendon Press 1960)
Imbert PH, 'L'Utilisation des droits de l'homme dans les relations internationales' in Société Française pour le Droit International (ed), *Colloque de Strasbourg. La Protection des Droits de l'Homme et l'Évolution du Droit International* (Pedone 1998) 282
Inwood MJ, 'Hermeneutics' in Honderich T (ed), *The Oxford Companion to Philosophy* (Oxford University Press 1995) 353

Irti N, *L'età della decodificazione* (Giuffrè 1978)

Jellinek G, *Allgemeine Staatslehre* (3rd ed, O Häring 1914)

Jennings R, 'The Proliferation of Adjudicatory Bodies: Dangers and Possible Answers' in Boisson De Chazournes L (ed), *Implications of the Proliferation of International Adjudicatory Bodies for Dispute Resolution* (ASIL Publications 1995) 2

Jennings RY & Watts A (eds), *Oppenheim's International Law – Vol 1: Peace* (9th ed, Longmans 1992)

Jevons SW, *Elementary Lessons in Logic: Deductive and Inductive* (Macmillan 1948)

Jo H, *Compliant Rebels: Rebel Groups and International Law in World Politics* (Cambridge University Press 2015)

Joseph S & Castan M, *The International Covenant on Civil and Political Rights: Cases, Materials and Commentary* (3rd ed, Oxford University Press 2014)

Kaczorowska-Ireland A, *Public International Law* (5th ed, Routledge 2015)

Kadens E, 'Custom's Past' in Bradley CA (ed), *Custom's Future: International Law in a Changing World* (Cambridge University Press 2016) 11

Kalshoven F & Zegveld L, *Constraints on the Waging of War* (4th ed, Cambridge University Press 2011)

Kammerhofer J, *Uncertainty in International Law: A Kelsenian Perspective* (Routledge 2010)

Kammerhofer J, 'Orthodox Generalists and Political Activists in International Legal Scholarship' in Happold M (ed), *International Law in a Multipolar World* (Routledge 2011) 138

Kammerhofer J, 'International Legal Positivism' in Hoffmann F & Orford A (eds), *The Oxford Handbook of the Theory of International Law* (Oxford University Press 2016) 407

Kammerhofer J, 'Sources in Legal Positivist Theories: The Pure Theory's Structural Analysis of the Law' in Besson S & d'Aspremont J (eds), *The Oxford Handbook of the Sources of International Law* (Oxford University Press 2017) 343

Kammerhofer J, 'International Legal Positivist Research Methods' in Deplano R & Tsagourias N (eds), *Research Methods in International Law: A Handbook* (Edward Elgar 2021) 95

Kammerhofer J, *International Investment Law and Legal Theory* (Cambridge University Press 2021)

Kanetake M & Nollkaemper A, 'The International Rule of Law in the Cycle of Contestations and Deference' in Kanetake M & Nollkaemper A (eds), *The Rule of Law at the National and International Levels: Contestations and Deference* (Hart Publishing 2016) 445

Kanetake M, 'The Interfaces Between the National and International Rule of Law: A Framework Paper' in Kanetake M & Nollkaemper A (eds), *The Rule of Law at the National and International Levels: Contestations and Deference* (Hart 2016) 13

Kant I, *Kritik der Reinen Vernunft* (2nd ed, Groszherzog Wilhelm Ernst, 1787)

Kant I, *Die Metaphysik der Sitten. Erster Theil. Metaphysische Anfangsgründe der Rechtslehre* (2nd ed, Friedrich Nicolovius 1798)

Kedar N, 'The Political Origins of the Modern Legal Paradoxes' in Perez O & Teubner G (eds), *Paradoxes and Inconsistencies in the Law* (Hart 2006) 112

Kelly JP, 'Customary International Law in Historical Context: The Exercise of Power without General Acceptance' in Lepard BD (ed), *Reexamining Customary International Law* (Cambridge University Press 2017) 47

Kelsen H, *General Theory of Law and State* (Harvard University Press 1945)

Kelsen H, *Principles of International Law* (Rinehart 1952)

Kelsen H, *Reine Rechtslehre* (2nd ed, Deuticke 1960)

Kelsen H, *Pure Theory of Law* (Knight M tr, 2nd ed, University of California Press 1967)

Kelsen H, *Essays in Legal and Moral Philosophy* (D Reidel 1973)

Kelsen H, *On the Theory of Interpretation* (Cambridge University Press 1990)

Kennedy D, *A World of Struggle: How Power, Law, and Expertise Shape Global Political Economy* (Princeton University Press 2016)

Kingsbury B & Straumann B (eds), *The Roman Foundations of the Law of Nations* (Cambridge University Press 2011)

Klabbers J, 'Reluctant "*Grundnormen*": Articles 31(3)(c) and 42 of the Vienna Convention on the Law of Treaties and the Fragmentation of International Law' in Craven M, Fitzmaurice M & Vogiatzi M (eds), *Time, History and International Law* (Nijhoff 2007) 141

Klabbers J, 'Sources of International Organizations' Law: Reflections on Accountability' in Besson S & d'Aspremont J (eds), *The Oxford Handbook of the Sources of International Law* (Oxford University Press 2017) 987

Klabbers J & Palombella G, 'Introduction' in Klabbers J & Palombella G (eds), *The Challenge of Inter-Legality* (Cambridge University Press 2019) 1

Klatt M, *Making the Law Explicit: The Normativity of Legal Argumentation* (Oxford University Press 2008)

Kolb R, *Interprétation et création du droit international* (Editions Bruylant 2006)

Kolb R, *Interprétation et création du droit international: esquisses d' une herméneutique juridique moderne pour le droit international public* (Bruylant 2006)

Kolb R, *Interprétation et création du droit international: Esquisse d'une herméneutique juridique moderne pour le droit international public* (Bruylant 2006)

Kolb R, *Peremptory International Law –* Jus Cogens*: A General Inventory* (Hart 2015)

Kolb R & Hyde R, *An Introduction to the International Law of Armed Conflicts* (Hart 2008)

Koskenniemi M, *From Apology to Utopia: The Structure of the International Legal Argument* (2nd ed, Cambridge University Press 2005)

Koskenniemi M, 'The Place of Law in Collective Security' in M Koskenniemi M (ed), *The Politics of International Law* (Hart 2011) 79

Koskenniemi M, 'Epilogue' in Werner W et al (eds), *The Law of International Lawyers: Reading Martti Koskenniemi* (Cambridge University Press 2017) 406

Krygier M, 'The Concept of Law and Social Theory' in Del Mar M & Giudice M (eds), *Legal Theory and the Social Sciences* (Routledge 2010) 7

Lalonde S, *Determining Boundaries in a Conflicted World: The Role of* Uti Possidetis (McGill-Queen's University Press 2002)

Lammers H & Simons W (eds), *Die Rechtsprechung des Staatsgerichtshofes für das Deutsche Reich und des Reichsgerichts auf Grund von Article 13 Abs. 2 der Reichsverfassung* (Vol 1(37) Stilke 1927)

Lanovoy V, *Complicity and Its Limits in the Law of International Responsibility* (Hart 2016)

Latour B, *An Inquiry into Modes of Existence. An Anthropology of the Moderns* (Catherine Porter tr, Harvard University Press 2013)

Lauterpacht H, *The Development of International Law by the International Court* (Stevens & Sons 1958)

Lawrence T, *The Principles of International Law* (7th ed, Heath & Co 1923)

Le Bouthillier Y & Bonin J-F, 'Article 3 – Convention of 1969' in O Corten & P Klein (eds), *The Vienna Convention on the Law of Treaties: A Commentary* (Oxford University Press 2011) 66

Lefkowitz D, 'The Legitimacy of International Law' in Held D & Maffettone P (eds), *Global Political Theory* (Polity 2016) 98

Lepard B, 'Customary International Law as a Dynamic Process' in Bradley CA (ed), *Custom's Future: International Law in a Changing World* (Cambridge University Press 2016) 62

Lepard B, 'Toward a New Theory of Customary International Human Rights Law' in Lepard B (ed), *Reexamining Customary International Law* (Cambridge University Press 2017) 262

Lepard BD, *Rethinking Humanitarian Intervention: A Fresh Legal Approach Based on Fundamental Ethical Principles in International Law and World Religions* (Penn Press 2003)

Lepard BD, *Customary International Law: A New Theory with Practical Applications* (Cambridge University Press 2010)

Llewellyn K & Hoebel A, *The Cheyenne Way Conflict and Case Law in Primitive Jurisprudence* (University of Oklahoma Press 1941)

Locke J, *Two Treatise of Government* (first published 1690, The New English Library 1963)

Luce RD & Raiffa H, *Games and Decisions: Introduction and Critical Survey* (Wiley 1957)

Lyotard JF, *La condition postmoderne* (Editions de Minuit 1979)

MacCormick N, *Legal Reasoning and Legal Theory* (Clarendon Press 1978)

Maine H, *Ancient Law: Its Connection with the Early History of Society and its Relation to Modern Ideas* (John Murray 1861)

Maine H, *International Law* (John Murray 1890)

Malinowski B, *Crime and Custom in Savage Society* (Keagan Paul 1926)

Malinowski B, *A Scientific Theory of Culture* (University of North Carolina Press 1944)

Margaritis M, 'Article 559' in K Kerameas, D Kondilis & N Nikas, *Interpretation of the Code of Civil Procedure, Vol I, Articles 1–590* (Sakkoulas 2000) 1000

Marmor A, 'Meaning and Interpretation' in Ziegler K (ed), *Interpretation and Legal Theory* (Bloomsbury 2005) 9

Martin C, 'The UPR and Its Impact on the Protection Role of AICHR in Southeast Asia' in Gomez J & Ramcharan R (eds), *The Universal Periodic Review of Southeast Asia* (Palgrave Macmillan 2018) 201

Mazzei F, *Relazioni internazionali* (Egea 2016)

McCraw B, 'Appeal to Ignorance' in Arp R, Barbone S & Bruce M (eds), *Bad Arguments:100 of the Most Important Fallacies in Western Philosophy* (Wiley Blackwell 2019) 106

McCrudden C, 'Legal Research and the Social Sciences' in Del Mar M & Giudice M (eds), *Legal Theory and the Social Sciences Vol II* (Routledge 2010) 633

Meguro M, 'Customary International Law and Non-State Actors: Between Anthropomorphism and Artificial Unity' in Droubi S and d'Aspremont J (eds), *International Organizations Non-State Actors, and the Formation of Customary International Law, Melland Schill Perspectives on International Law* (Manchester University Press 2020)

Merkouris P, *Article 31(3)(c) VCLT and the Principle of Systemic Integration: Normative Shadows in Plato's Cave* (Brill Nijhoff 2015)

Merkouris P, 'Treaty Interpretation and its Rules: Of Motion Through Time, "Time-Will" and "Time-Bubbles"' in Fitzmaurice M & Merkouris P (eds), *Treaties in Motion* (Cambridge University Press 2020) 121

Mileva N & Fortuna M, 'Environmental Protection as an Object of and Tool for Evolutionary Interpretation' in Abi-Saab G et al (eds), *Evolutionary Interpretation and International Law* (Hart 2020) 123

Mill JS, *Philosophy of Scientific Method* (Hafner 1950)

Miller D, *Is Self-Determination a Dangerous Illusion?* (Polity Press 2020)

Minto W, *Logic Inductive and Deductive* (John Murray 1915)

Modugno F, *Interpretazione giuridica* (CEDAM 2012)

Moir L, *The Law of Internal Armed Conflict* (Cambridge University Press 2004)

Morgenthau HJ & Thompson KW, *Politics Among Nations. The Struggle for Power and Peace* (6th ed, Alfred A Knopf 1985)

Morss JR, *The Biologising of Childhood: Developmental Psychology and the Darwinian Myth* (Erlbaum 1990)

Morss JR, 'Riddle of the Sands: Time, Power and Legitimacy in International Law' in Singh P & Mayer B (eds), *Critical International Law: Post-realism, Post-colonialism, and Transnationalism* (Oxford University Press 2014) 53

Morss JR, 'Mars for the Martians? On the Obsolescence of Self-Determination' in Tesón FR (ed), *The Theory of Self-Determination* (Cambridge University Press 2016) 184

Müller F, *Discours de la méthode juridique* (O Jouanjan tr, Presses Universitaires de France 1996)

Murphy L, *What Makes Law: An Introduction to the Philosophy of Law* (Cambridge University Press 2014)

Murphy SD, 'Codification, Progressive Development, or Scholarly Analysis? The Art of Packaging the ILC's Work Product' in Ragazzi M (ed), *The Responsibility of International Organizations: Essays in Memory of Sir Ian Brownlie* (Martinus Nijhoff 2013) 29

Nollkaemper A, *National Courts and the International Rule of Law* (Oxford University Press 2012)

Nollkaemper N, 'Conversations among Courts: Domestic and International Adjudicators' in Romano CPR, Alter K & Shany Y (eds), *The Oxford Handbook of International Adjudication* (Oxford University Press 2013) 524

O'Connell DP, *International Law, Vol 1* (2nd ed, Stevens 1970)

O'Keefe R, *International Criminal Law* (Oxford University Press 2015)

Oeser E, *Evolution and Constitution: The Evolutionary Self-Construction of Law* (Kluwer Academic Publishers 2003)

Ohlin JD, *The Assault on International Law* (Oxford University Press 2015)

Öhlinger T, *Die Anwendung des Völkerrechts auf Verträge im Bundesstaat* (Braumüller 1982)

Öhlinger T & Eberhard H, *Verfassungsrecht* (12th rev ed, Facultas 2019)

Onuf N, *World of Our Making: Rules and Rule in Social Theory and International Relations* (USC Press 1989)

Oppenheim L, *International Law – Vol 1: Peace* (8th ed, Longmans 1955)

Orakhelashvili A, *The Interpretation of Acts and Rules in Public International Law* (Oxford University Press 2008)

Orford A, 'International Law and the Limits of History' in Werner W et al (eds), *The Law of International Lawyers: Reading Martti Koskenniemi* (Cambridge University Press 2015) 297

Otto D, 'Feminist Approaches to International Law' in Orford A & Hoffmann F (eds), *The Oxford Handbook of the Theory of International Law* (Oxford University Press 2016) 488

Pagden A & Lawrence J (eds), *Vitoria: Political Writings* (Cambridge University Press 1991)

Pahuja S, 'Decolonization and the Eventness of International Law' in Johns F, Joyce R & Pahuja S (eds), *Events: The Force of International Law* (Routledge 2011) 91

Palombella G, 'Theory, Realities, and Promises of Inter-Legality, A Manifesto' in Klabbers J & Palombella G (eds), *The Challenge of Inter-Legality* (Cambridge University Press 2019) 380

Paparinskis M, *The International Minimum Standard and Fair and Equitable Treatment* (Oxford University Press 2013)

Papaux A & Samson R, 'Article 33' in Corten O & Klein P (eds), *The Vienna Convention on the Law of Treaties* (Oxford University Press 2011) 868

Pascual-Vives F, *Consensus-Based Interpretation of Regional Human Rights Treaties* (Brill Nijhoff 2019)

Paulson SL, 'Introduction' in Paulson SL & Litschewski Paulson B (eds), *Normativity and Norms: Critical Perspectives on Kelsenian Themes* (Clarendon Press 1998) xliii

Pauwelyn J, *Conflict of Norms in Public International Law: How WTO Law Relates to Other Rules of International Law* (Cambridge University Press 2003)

Peat D & Windsor M, 'Introduction' in Bianchi A, Peat D & Windsor M (eds), *Interpretation in International Law* (Oxford University Press 2018) 3

Pellet A, 'Article 38' in Zimmermann A et al (eds), *The Statute of the International Court of Justice: A Commentary* (Oxford University Press 2006) 750

Pellet A, 'Shaping the Future of International Law: The Role of the World Court in Law-Making' in Arsanjani MH et al (eds), *Looking to the Future: Essays on International Law in Honor of W Michael Reisman* (Brill/Nijhoff 2011) 1065

Pellet A, 'Article 38' in Zimmermann A et al (eds), *The Statute of the International Court of Justice: A Commentary* (2nd ed, Oxford University Press 2012) 731

Pellet A, 'Les raisons du développement du *soft law* en droit international: choix ou nécessité?' in Deumier P & Sorel JM (eds), *Regards croisés sur la* soft law *en droit interne, européen et international* (LGDJ 2018) 177

Pellet A & Müller D, 'Article 38' in Zimmermann A et al (eds), *The Statute of the International Court of Justice: A Commentary* (3rd ed, Oxford University Press 2019) 914

Petersen N, 'The Role of Consent and Uncertainty in the Formation of Customary International Law', in Lepard BD (ed), *Reexamining Customary International Law* (Cambridge University Press 2017) 111

Piggott L, 'The "Bush Doctrine" and the Use of Force in International Law' in Morgan MJ (ed), *The Impact of 9/11 and the New Legal Landscape: The Day that Changed Everything?* (Palgrave Macmillan 2009) 241

Pirandello L, *Six Characters in Search of an Author* (Mineola 2000)

Pollock F, *Oxford Lectures and Other Discourses* (Macmillan 1890)

Postema GJ, 'Custom in International Law: A Normative Practice Account' in Perreau-Saussine A & Murphy JB (eds), *The Nature of Customary Law: Legal, Historical, and Philosophical Perspectives* (Cambridge University Press 2007) 279

Postema G, 'Conformity, Custom, and Congruence: Rethinking the Efficacy of Law' in Kramer MH, Grant C, Colburn B & Hatzistavrou A (eds), *The Legacy of HLA Hart: Legal, Political and Moral Philosophy* (Oxford University Press 2008) 45

Pugliatti S, *Conoscenza e diritto* (Giuffrè 1961)

Quadri R, *Diritto internazionale pubblico* (Priulla 1960)

Ratner S, *The Thin Justice of International Law: A Moral Reckoning of the Law of Nations* (Oxford University Press 2015)

Rauter T, *Judicial Practice, Customary International Criminal Law and Nullum Crimen Sine Lege* (Springer 2017)

Rawls J, *A Theory of Justice* (Harvard University Press 1971)

Raz J, 'Promises and Obligations' in Raz J & Hacker PMS (eds), *Law, Morality and Society: Essays in Honour of HLA Hart* (Oxford University Press 1977) 223

Raz J, *The Concept of a Legal System: An Introduction to the Theory of Legal System* (2nd ed, Oxford University Press 1980)

Raz J, *Morality of Freedom* (Oxford University Press 1986)

Raz J, *Practical Reason and Norms* (2nd ed, Oxford University Press 1999)

Raz J, *The Authority of Law. Essays on Law and Morality* (2nd ed, Oxford University Press 2009)

Ricoeur P, *La mémoire, l'histoire, l'oubli* (Seuil 2000)

Roberts A & Sivakumaran S, 'The Theory and Reality of the Sources on International Law' in Evans M (ed), *International Law* (Oxford University Press 2018) 89

Roberts A, *Is International Law International?* (Oxford University Press 2017)

Rockmore T, 'Hegel' in Tucker A (eds), *A Companion to the Philosophy of History and Historiography* (Wiley-Blackwell 2011) 468

Rodriguez-Blanco V, *Law and Authority under the Guise of the Good* (Hart 2016)

Romano S, *Frammenti di un dizionario giuridico* (Giuffrè 1947)

Ross A, *On Law and Justice* (University of California Press 1959)

Ross A, *A Textbook of International Law: General Part* (first published 1947, Longmans 2013)

Ross A, *On Law and Justice* (Holtermann JvH ed, Bindreiter U tr, Oxford University Press 2019)

Roughan N, 'Sources and the Normativity of International Law: From Validity to Justification' in Besson S & d'Aspremont J (eds), *The Oxford Handbook on the Sources of International Law* (Oxford University Press 2017) 680

Rovatti PA & Vattimo G (eds), *Il pensiero debole* (Feltrinelli 1983)

Ryngaert C, 'Imposing International Duties on Non-State Actors and the Legitimacy of International Law' in Noortmann M & Ryngaert C (eds),

Non-State Actor Dynamics in International Law: From Law-Takers to Law-Makers (Routledge 2010) 69

Ryngaert C, 'Non-State Actors in International Humanitarian Law' in d'Aspremont J (ed), *Participants in the International Legal System: Multiple Perspectives on Non-State Actors in International Law* (Routledge 2011) 284

Ryngaert C, 'Immunity from Execution and Diplomatic Property' in Ruys T, Angelet N & Ferro L (eds), *The Cambridge Handbook of Immunities and International Law* (Cambridge University Press 2019) 285

Samuel G, 'Is Law Really a Social Science? A View from Comparative Law' in Del Mar M & Giudice M (eds), *Legal Theory and the Social Sciences Vol II* (Routledge 2010) 178

Sandoz Y et al (eds), *Commentary on the Additional Protocols of 8 June 1977 to the Geneva Conventions of 12 August 1949* (Martinus Nijhoff 1987)

Sands P & Commission J, 'Treaty, Custom and Time: Interpretation/Application?' in Fitzmaurice M, Elias O & Merkouris P (eds), *Treaty Interpretation and the Vienna Convention on the Law of the Treaties: 30 Years On* (Brill/Nijhoff 2010) 39

Sassòli M, *International Humanitarian Law: Rules, Controversies, and Solutions to Problems Arising in Warfare* (Edward Elgar 2019)

Scanlon TM, *What We Owe to Each Other* (Harvard University Press 1998)

Scelle G, 'Essai sur les sources formelles du droit international' in Appleton C (ed), *Recueil Recueil d'études sur les sources du droit en l'honneur de François Gény. Tome III. Les sources des diverses branches du droit* (Sirey 1934) 400

Scharf M, *Customary International Law in Times of Fundamental Change: Recognizing Grotian Moments* (Cambridge University Press 2013)

Schauer F, 'Pitfalls in the Interpretation of Customary Law' in Perreau-Saussine A & Murphy JB (eds), *The Nature of Customary Law: Legal, Historical and Philosophical Perspectives* (Cambridge University Press 2007) 13

Schlütter B, *Developments in Customary International Law: Theory and the Practice of the International Court of Justice and the International Ad Hoc Criminal Tribunals for Rwanda and Yugoslavia* (Martinus Nijhoff 2010)

Schmalenbach K, 'Article 2' in O Dörr & K Schmalenbach (eds), *Vienna Convention on the Law of Treaties: A Commentary* (Springer 2018) 29

Schmalenbach K, 'Article 3' in O Dörr & K Schmalenbach (eds), *Vienna Convention on the Law of Treaties: A Commentary* (Springer 2018) 55

Schmitt C, *Der Begriff des Politischen: Text von 1932 mit einem Vorwort und drei Corollarien* (Duncker & Humblot 1963)

Schmitt C, *Der Begriff des Politischen* (first published 1932, 7th ed, Duncker & Humblot 1991)

Schmitt MN, 'The Law of Targeting' in Wilmshurst E & Breau S (eds), *Perspectives on the ICRC Study on Customary International Humanitarian Law* (Cambridge University Press 2007) 131

Schwarzenberger G, *The Inductive Approach to International Law* (Oceana Publications 1965)

Scobbie I, 'The Approach to Customary International Law in the Study' in Wilmshurst E & Breau S (eds), *Perspectives on the ICRC Study on Customary International Humanitarian Law* (Cambridge University Press 2007) 15

Searle J, *Speech Acts: An Essay in the Philosophy of Language* (Cambridge University Press 1969)

Searle J, *The Construction of Social Reality* (The Free Press 1995)

Seibert-Fohr A, 'Modern Concepts of Customary International Law as a Manifestation of a Value-Based International Order' in Zimmermann A & Hofmann R (eds), *Unity and Diversity in International Law* (Duncker & Humblot 2006) 257

Sender O & Wood M, 'Custom's Bright Future: The Continuing Importance of Customary International Law' in Bradley CA (ed), *Custom's Future: International Law in a Changing World* (Cambridge University Press 2016) 360

Sender O & Wood M, 'The Emergence of Customary International Law: Between Theory and Practice' in Brölmann C & Radi Y (eds), *Handbook on the Theory and Practice of International Lawmaking* (Edward Elgar 2016) 133

Shapiro SJ, *Legality* (Harvard University Press 2011)

Shaw M, *International Law* (7th ed, Cambridge University Press 2014)

Shaw M, *International Law* (8th ed, Cambridge University Press 2017)

Simma B, *Das Reziprozitätselement in der Entstehung des Völkergewohnheitsrechts* (Wilhelm Fink 1970)

Simma B, *Das Reziprozitätselement im Zustandekommen völkerrechtlicher Verträge* (Duncker & Humblot 1972)

Sinclair I, *The Vienna Convention on the Law of Treaties* (2nd ed, Manchester University Press 1984)

Sivakumaran S, 'Implementing Humanitarian Norms through Non-State Armed Groups' in Krieger H (ed), *Inducing Compliance with International Humanitarian Law: Lessons from the African Great Lakes Region* (Cambridge University Press 2015) 125

Sivakumaran S, 'The Addressees of Common Article 3' in Clapham A et al (eds), *The 1949 Geneva Conventions: A Commentary* (Oxford University Press 2015) 415

Skillen JW, *Recharging the American Experiment: Principled Pluralism for Genuine Civic Community* (Baker 1994)

Sloterdijk P, *Critique of Cynical Reason* (University of Minnesota Press 1987)

Slütter B, *Developments in Customary International Law* (Brill 2010)

Smith A, 'Of Contract' in Meek RL, Raphael DD & Stein PG (eds), *Lectures on Jurisprudence* (Oxford University Press 1978) 176

Staubach P, *The Rule of Unwritten International Law: Customary Law, General Principles, and World Order* (Routledge 2018)

Steinberg RH, 'Wanted – Dead or Alive: Realism in International Law' in Dunoff JL & Pollack MA (eds), *Interdisciplinary Perspectives on International Law and International Relations* (Cambridge University Press 2013) 146

Steinbruck Platiše M, 'The Development of the Immunities of International Organisations in Response to Domestic Contestations' in Kanetake M & Nollkaemper A (eds), *The Rule of Law at the National and International Levels: Contestations and Deference* (Hart 2016) 67

Strati A, 'Greece and the Law of the Sea: A Greek Perspective' in Chircop A, Gerolymatos A & Iatrides JO (eds), *The Aegean Sea after the Cold War* (Macmillan 2000) 96

Strauss DFM, *Philosophy: Discipline of Disciplines* (Paideia Press 2009)

Strupp K, *Elements du droit international public* (Rousseau & Co 1927)

Suárez F, *De legibus ac Deo legislatore* (first published 1612, Williams GL et al tr 1944)

Suárez F, *The Laws and God the Lawgiver* (Naples 1612)

Sur S, *L'interprétation en droit international public* (LGDJ 1974)

Sur S, *La coutume internationale* (Librairies Techniques 1990)

Tamanaha BZ, *Beyond the Formalist-Realist Divide: The Role of Politics in Judging* (Princeton University Press 2010)

Tancredi A, 'OMC et coutume(s)' in Tomkiewicz V (ed), *Les sources et les normes dans le droit de l'OMC, Colloque de Nice des 24 et 25 juin 2010* (Pedone 2012) 81

Tanzi A, 'Le forme della codificazione e lo sviluppo progressivo del diritto internazionale' in Nesi G & Gargiulo P (eds), *Luigi Ferrari Bravo: Il diritto internazionale come professione* (Editoriale Scientifica 2015) 152

Tarello G, *Diritto, enunciati, usi: Studi di teoria e metateoria del diritto* (il Mulino 1974)

Tarello G, *L'interpretazione della legge* (Giuffrè 1980)

Tasioulas J, 'The Legitimacy of International Law' in Besson S & Tasioulas J (eds), *The Philosophy of International Law* (Oxford University Press 2010) 101

Tasioulas J, 'Custom, *Jus Cogens*, and Human Rights', in Bradley CA (ed), *Custom's Future: International Law in a Changing World* (Cambridge University Press 2016) 95

Tesón F, 'Fake Custom' in Lepard B (ed), *Reexamining Customary International Law* (Cambridge University Press 2017) 86

Thirlway H, *International Customary Law and Codification: An Examination of the Continuing Role of Custom in the Present Period of Codification of International Law* (AW Sijthoff 1972)

Thirlway H, *The Sources of International Law* (2nd ed, Oxford University Press 2019)

Thucydides, *The Complete Writings of Thucydides: The Peloponnesian War* (Random House 1951)

Tomka P, 'Customary International Law in the Jurisprudence of the World Court: The Increasing Relevance of Codification' in Lijnzaad L & Council of Europe (eds), *The Judge and International Custom* (Brill Nijhoff 2016) 2

Trachtman J, 'The Growing Obsolescence of Customary International Law' in Bradley CA (ed), *Custom's Future: International Law in a Changing World* (Cambridge University Press 2016) 172

Treves T, 'International Law: Achievements and Challenges' in Cardona Llorens J (ed), *Cursos Euromediterraneos Bancaja de Derecho Internacional*, Vol 10 (Tirant lo Blanch 2006) 452

Triepel H, *Völkerrecht und Landesrecht* (Scientia Verlag 1899)

Trinidad J, *Self-Determination in Disputed Colonial Territories* (Cambridge University Press 2018) 83

Tunkin G, *Droit international public: problémes théoriques* (Pedone 1965)

Tunkin GI, *Theory of International Law* (Harvard University Press 1974)

Tzanakopoulos A & Methymaki E, 'Sources and the Enforcement of International Law: Domestic Courts-Another Brick in the Wall?' in Besson S & d'Aspremont J (eds), *The Oxford Handbook of the Sources of International Law* (Oxford University Press 2017) 813

Unger R, *The Critical Legal Studies Movement. Another Time. A Greater Task* (Verso 2015)

Van der Burg W, *The Dynamics of Law and Morality: A Pluralist Account of Legal Interactionism* (Ashgate 2014)

Van Dijk TA, *Handbook of Discourse Analysis* (Academic Press 1985)

Van Eikema Hommes HJ, *Major Trends in the History of Legal Philosophy* (North Holland 1979)

Van Hoof GJH, *Rethinking the Sources of International Law* (Kluwer 1983)

Van Riessen H, *The University and its Basis* (The ACHEA Press 1997)

Van Steenberghe R, 'Non-State Actors from the Perspective of the International Committee of the Red Cross' in d'Aspremont J (ed), *Participants in the International Legal System: Multiple Perspectives on Non-State Actors in International Law* (Routledge 2011) 204

Van Woudenberg, R 'Theories of Thing-Structures' in *Philosophical Foundations I Reader* (International Masters in Christian Studies of Science and Society Program, VU Amsterdam 2006–7) 6

Van Woudenberg, R, 'Theories of Modes of Being (Modalities)' *in Philosophical Foundations I Reader* (International Masters in Christian Studies of Science and Society Program, VU Amsterdam 2006) 3

Vattel E, *Le droit des gens* (1758)

Venzke I, *How Interpretation Makes International Law: On Semantic Change and Normative Twists* (Oxford University Press 2012)

Venzke I, 'Post-modern Perspectives on Orthodox Positivism' in Kammerhofer J & d'Aspremont J (eds), *International Legal Positivism in a Post-Modern World* (Cambridge University Press 2014) 182

Verosta S, *Theorie und Realität von Bündnissen: Heinrich Lammasch, Karl Renner und Der Zweibund (1897–1914)* (Europa Verlag 1971)

Villalpando S, 'Gli strumenti della codificazione del diritto internazionale nell'età della codificazione *light*', in Annoni A, Forlati S & Salerno F (eds), *La codificazione nell'ordinamento internazionale e dell'unione europea* (Editoriale Scientifica 2019) 259

Villiger M, *Customary International Law and Treaties: A Manual on the Theory and Practice of the Interrelation of Sources* (2nd ed, Kluwer Law International 1997)

Villiger M, *Commentary on the 1969 Vienna Convention on the Law of Treaties* (Brill/Nijhoff 2008)

Virally M, 'The Sources of International Law', in Sorensen M (ed) *Manual of Public International Law* (St Martin's Press 1968) 116

Waibel M, 'Principles of Treaty Interpretation: Developed for and Applied by National Courts', in Aust HP & Nolte G (eds), *The Interpretation of International Law by Domestic Courts: Uniformity, Diversity, Convergence* (Oxford University Press 2016) 12

Waibel M, 'The Origins of Interpretive Canons in Domestic Legal Systems' in Klingler J, Parkhomenko Y & Salonidis C (eds), *Between the Lines of the Vienna Convention? Canons and Other Principles of Interpretation in Public International Law* (Kluwer Law International BV 2019) 25

Waltz KN, *Theory of International Politics* (Addison Wesley 1979)

Westlake J, *International Law* (The University Press 1904)

White H, *Tropics of Discourses: Essays in Cultural Criticism* (The Johns Hopkins University Press 1986)

White M, 'Addressing Human Rights Protection Gaps: Can the Universal Periodic Review Process Live Up to Its Promise?' in Gomez J & Ramcharan R (eds) *The Universal Periodic Review of Southeast Asia* (Palgrave Macmillan 2018) 19

Willke W, 'The Autopoietic Theory of Law: Autonomy of Law and Contextual Transfer' in Amselek P & MacCormick N (eds), *Controversies About Law's Ontology* (Edinburgh University Press 1991) 108

Winter SL, *A Clearing in the Forest: Law, Life and Mind* (The University of Chicago Press 2001)

Wittgenstein L, *Philosophical Investigations* (Macmillan 1953)

Wolfke K, *Custom in Present International Law* (2nd ed, Martinus Nijhoff 1993)

Wolfram S, 'Coherence Theory of Truth' in Honderich T (ed), *The Oxford Companion to Philosophy* (Oxford University Press 1995) 140

Yu T, *Interpretation of Treaties* (Columbia University Press 1927)

Zander J, *The Application of the Precautionary Principle in Practice: Comparative Dimensions* (Cambridge University Press 2010)

Zarbiyev F, 'A Genealogy of Textualism in Treaty Interpretation' in Bianchi A, Peat D & Windsor M (eds), *Interpretation in International Law* (Oxford University Press 2018) 251

Zemanek K, 'What is State Practice and Who Makes It?' in Beyerlin U et al (eds), *Recht zwischen Umbruch und Bewahrung: Völkerrecht, Europarecht, Staatsrecht: Festschrift für Rudolf Bernhardt* (Springer 1995) 289

Zweigert E, 'Introduction' in *Die Verfassung des Deutschen Reichs vom 11 August 1919* (J Bensheimer 1919)

Articles

Abe T, 'ICJ Practice in Determining the Existence of Customary International Law' (2019) 62 JYIL 274

Abi-Saab G, 'Cours Général de Droit International Public' (1987) 207 RdC 9

Adams NP, 'In Defense of Content-Independence' (2017) 23 LEG 143

Adler J, 'Belief and Negation' (2000) 20(3) Informal Logic 207

Ago R, 'Science Juridique et Droit International' (1956) 90 RdC 851

Ago R, 'Positive Law and International Law' (1957) 51 AJIL 691

Ago R, 'Droit des traités à la lumière de la Convention de Vienne' (1971) 134 RdC 297

Akehurst M, 'Custom as a Source of International Law' (1975) 47 BYBIL 1

Alexander L, 'Law and Exclusionary Reasons' (1990) 18 Philosophical Topics 5

Alexandrowicz CH, 'The Juridical Expression of the Sacred Trust of Civilization' (1971) 65 AJIL 149

Alfert R, '*Hostes Humani Generis*: An Expanded Notion of US Counterterrorist Legislation' (1992) 6 EmoryInt'lLRev 171

Alland D, 'L'interprétation du droit international public' (2014) 362 RdC 41

Allen S, 'Self-determination, the Chagos Archipelago Advisory Opinion and the Chagossians' (2020) 69 ICLQ 203

Alvarez-Jiménez A, 'Methods for the Identification of Customary International Law in the International Court of Justice's Jurisprudence: 2000–2009' (2011) 60 ICLQ 681

Anzilotti D, 'Efficacia ed interpretazione dei trattati' (1912) Rivista di diritto internazionale 520

Arajärvi N, 'The Requisite Rigour in the Identification of Customary International Law: A Look at the Reports of the Special Rapporteur of the International Law Commission' (2017) 19(1) ICLR 9

Arangio-Ruíz G, 'The Normative Role of the General Assembly of the United Nations and the Declaration of Principles of Friendly Relations' (1972) 137 RdC 419

Arangio-Ruiz G, 'Consuetudine internazionale' (1988) VIII Enciclopedia Giuridica 1

Arangio-Ruiz G, 'Fine prematura del ruolo preminente di studiosi italiani nel progetto di codificazione della responsabilità degli Stati: specie a proposito di crimini internazionali e dei poteri del Consiglio di sicurezza' (1998) 71 RivDirInt 110

Arato J, 'Subsequent Practice and Evolutive Interpretation: Techniques of Treaty Interpretation over Time and Their Diverse Consequences' (2010) 9 LPICT 443

Badar ME, 'Just Convict Everyone! Joint Perpetration from Tadić to Stakić and Back Again' (2006) 6 Int CLR 293

Baker R, 'Customary International Law in the 21st Century: Old Challenges and New Debates' (2010) 21(1) EJIL 173

Bangerter O, 'Reasons Why Armed Groups Choose to Respect International Humanitarian Law or Not' (2011) 93 IRRC 353

Banteka N, 'A Theory of Constructive Interpretation for Customary International Law Identification' (2018) 39(3) MichJIntlL 301

Bartels L, 'Applicable Law in WTO Dispute Settlement Proceedings' (2001) 35(3) JWT 499

Bassiouni MC, 'A Functional Approach to General Principles of International Law' (1990) 11 MichJIntlL 767

Bates E, 'Avoiding Legal Obligations Created by Human Rights Treaties' (2008) 57 ICLQ 751

Bates E, 'Sophisticated Constructivism in Human Rights Compliance Theory' (2015) 25 EJIL 1169

Baxter RR, 'Treaties and Custom' (1970) 129 RdC 27

Beaulac S, 'National Application of International Law: The Statutory Interpretation Perspective' (2003) 41 CanYBIL 225

Bell J, 'Sources of Law' (2018) 77 CLJ 40

Bellal A & Heffes E, '"Yes, I Do": Binding Armed Non-State Actors to IHL and Human Rights Norms through their Consent' (2018) 12(1) HR&ILD 120

Bellinger III JB & Haynes II WJ, 'A US Government Response to the International Committee of the Red Cross Study Customary International Humanitarian Law' (2007) 89 IRRC 443

Bentivoglio LM, 'Interpretazione delle norme internazionali' (1972) XXII Enciclopedia del diritto 310

Benvenisti E & Downs GW, 'Comment on Nico Krisch, "The Decay of Consent: International Law in an Age of Global Public Goods"' (2014) 108 AJIL Unbound 1

Bernhardt R, 'Interpretation in International Law' (1992) II Encyclopedia of Public International Law 1417

Besson S, 'State Consent and Disagreement in International Law-Making' (2016) 29(2)LJIL 289

Betlem G & Nollkaemper A, 'Giving Effect to Public International Law and European Community Law before Domestic Courts: A Comparative Analysis of the Practice of Consistent Interpretation' (2003) 14 EJIL 569

Bleckmann A, 'Zur Feststellung und Auslegung von Völkergewohnheitsrecht' (1977) 37 ZaöRV 504

Bleicher S, 'The Legal Significance of Re-Citation of General Assembly Resolutions' (1969) 63 AJIL 444

Blokker N, 'International Organizations and Customary International Law: Is the International Law Commission Taking International Organizations Seriously?' (2017) 14(1)IOLR 1

Blum G, 'On a Differential Law of War' (2011) 52 HarvInt'lLJ 163

Blutman L, 'Conceptual Confusion and Methodological Deficiencies: Some Ways that Theories on Customary International Law Fail' (2014) 25 (2) EJIL 529

Bobbio N, 'Consuetudine (teoria generale)' (1962) IX Enciclopedia del diritto 426

Bobbio N, 'Fatto normativo' (1967) XVI Enciclopedia del diritto 988

Bodansky D, 'Customary (and Not So Customary) International Environmental Law' (1995) 3 Global Legal Studies Journal 105

Bodansky D, 'The Legitimacy of International Governance: A Coming Challenge for International Environmental Law?' (1999) 93(3)AJIL 596

Bodansky D, 'Does Custom Have a Source?' (2014) 108 AJIL Unbound 179

Bohoslavsky JP et al, 'Emerging Customary International Law in Sovereign Debt Governance?' (2014) 9 CMLJ 55

Bordin FL, 'A Glass Half Full? The Character, Function and Value of the Two-Element Approach to Identifying Customary International Law' (2019) 21 ICLR 283

Bordin FL, 'Reckoning with British Colonialism' (2019) 78 CLJ 253

Brown Weiss E, 'International Environmental Law: Contemporary Issues and the Emergence of a New World Order' (1993) 81 GeoLJ 675

Brunnée J & Toope C, 'International Law and Constructivism: Elements of an Interactional Theory of International Law (2000) 39 ColumJTransnat'lL 19

Buchanan A & Keohane RO, 'The Legitimacy of Global Governance Institutions' (2006) 20(4) Ethics and International Affairs 405

Buzzini GP, 'La théorie des sources face au droit international général: Réflexions sur l'émergence du droit objectif dans l'ordre juridique international' (2002) 106 RGDIP 581

Cameron AM, 'Dooyeweerd on Law and Morality: Legal Ethics – a Test Case' (1998) 28 Victoria UnivWelLawRev 263

Cannizzaro E and Bonafé B, 'Fragmenting International Law through compromissory clauses? Some remarks on the decision of the ICJ in the Oil Platforms case' (2005) 16(3)EJIL 481

Capotorti F, 'Cours général de droit international public' (1994) 248 RdC 17

Carty A, 'Scandinavian Realism and Phenomenological Approaches to Statehood and General Custom in International Law' (2003) 14 EJIL 817

Carty A, 'The Need to be Rid of the Idea of General Customary Law' (2018) AJIL Unbound 319

Cassese A, 'The Proper Limits of Individual Responsibility under the Doctrine of Joint Criminal Enterprise' (2007) 5 JICJ 109

Cassimatis A, 'International Humanitarian Law, International Human Rights Law, and Fragmentation of International Law' (2007) 56 ICLQ 623

Castañeda J, 'Valeur Juridique des Résolutions des Nations Unies' (1970) 129 RdC 205

Charlesworth H, 'Customary International Law and the Nicaragua Case' (1984–87) 11 Aust YBIL 9

Charlesworth H, 'The Unbearable Lightness of Customary International Law' (1998) 92 ASIL Proc 44

Charney JI, 'Is International Law Threatened by Multiple International Tribunals?' (1998) 271 RdC 101

Chasapis Tassinis O, 'Customary International Law: Interpretation from Beginning to End' (2020) 31 EJIL 235

Chaumont S, 'Cours général de droit international public' (1970) 129 RdC 333

Cheng B, 'United Nations Resolutions on Outer Space: "Instant" International Customary Law' (1965) 5 IJIL 23

Chesterman S, 'Reforming the United Nations: Legitimacy, Effectiveness and Power After Iraq' (2006) 10 SYBIL 59

Chiassoni P, 'La consuetudine internazionale: una ricognizione analitica' (2014) 43 Ragion pratica 489

Chimni BS, 'Customary International Law: A Third World Perspective' (2018) 112 AJIL 1

Chinkin C, 'Feminism, Approach to International Law' [2010] MPEPIL 701

Chinkin CM, 'The Challenge of Soft Law: Development and Change in International Law' (1989) 38 ICLQ 850

Cohan JA, 'The Bush Doctrine and the Emerging Norm of Anticipatory Self-Defense in Customary International Law' (2003) 15(2)PaceInt'lLRev 283

Colangelo AJ, 'Jurisdiction, Immunity, Legality, and Jus Cogens' (2013) 14 ChJIL 53

Condorelli L, 'Consuetudine internazionale' (1989) III Digesto delle discipline pubblicistiche 490

Conforti B, 'Cours général de droit international public' (1988) 212 RdC 9

Cowan J and Billaud J, 'Between Learning and Schooling: The Politics of Human Rights Monitoring at the Universal Periodic Review' (2015) 36 TWQ 1175

Cowell F, 'Understanding the Legal Status of Universal Periodic Review Recommendations' (2018) 7 CJIL 164

Crawford J, 'Multilateral Rights and Obligations in International Law' (2006) 319 RdC 325

Crawford J, 'Chance, Order, Change: The Course of International Law' (2013) 365 RdC 9

Criddle EJ and Fox-Decent E, 'Mandatory Multilateralism' (2019) 113 AJIL 272

D'Amato A, 'Treaties as a Source of General Rules of International Law' (1962) 3 HarvInt'lLJ 1

D'Amato A, 'The Neo-Positivist Concept of International Law' 59 AJIL (1965) 321

D'Amato A, 'Trashing Customary International Law' (1987) 81 AJIL 101

D'Amato A, 'Human Rights as Part of Customary International Law: A Plea for Change of Paradigms' (1995) 25 AJIL 47

D'Aspremont J, 'The Foundations of the International Legal Order' (2007) 18 FYBIL 219

D'Aspremont J, 'Softness in International Law: A Self-Serving Quest' (2008) 19 EJIL 1075

D'Aspremont J, 'The Idea of "Rules" in the Sources of International Law' (2014) 84 BYBIL 103

D'Aspremont J, 'The Decay of Modern Customary International Law in Spite of Scholarly Heroism' (2015) 15(1) The Global Community Yearbook of International Law and Jurisprudence 9

D'Aspremont J, 'Expansion and the Sources of International Human Rights Law' (2016) 46 IsrYBHumRts 223

D'Aspremont J, 'The International Court of Justice and the Irony of System-Design' (2017) 8 JIDS 366

D'Aspremont J, 'The Four Lives of Customary International Law' (2019) 21 IntCLRev 229

Darwall S, 'Authority and Reasons: Exclusionary and Second-Personal' (2010) 120 Ethics 257

Daugirdas K, 'International Organizations and the Creation of Customary International Law' (2020) 31 EJIL 201

David SL, 'A Foul Immigration Policy: US Misinterpretation of the Non-refoulement Obligation under the Convention against Torture' (2003) 19 NYLSchJHumRts 769

De Burca G, 'Internalization of International Law by the CJEU and the US Supreme Court' (2015) 13(4) IntJConstL 987

De Schutter O, 'Les mots de droit: une grammatologie critique du droit international public' (1990) 6 RQDI 120

De Visscher C, 'Reflections on the Present Prospects of International Adjudication' (1956) 50 AJIL 467

De Visscher C, 'Remarques sur l'interprétation dite textuelle des traités internationaux' (1959) Nederlands Tijdschrift voor Internationaal Recht 383

De Wet E, 'The Prohibition of Torture as an International Norm of jus cogens and Its Implications for National and Customary Law' (2004) 15(1)EJIL 97

DeBartolo DM, 'Identifying International Organizations' Contributions to Custom' (2014) 108 AJIL Unbound 174

Delacroix S, 'Hart's and Kelsen's Concepts of Normativity Contrasted' (2004) 17 Ratio Juris 501

Deplano R, 'Assessing the Role of Resolutions in the ILC Draft Conclusions on Identification of Customary International Law: Substantive and Methodological Issues' (2017) 14 (2)IOLR 227

Derrida J, 'Force de Loi: le 'fondement mystique de l'autorité' (1990) 11 CardozoLRev 920

Dinstein Y, 'The ICRC Customary International Humanitarian Law Study' (2006) 36 IsrYBHumRts 1

Dinstein Y, 'The Interaction between Customary International Law and Treaties' (2007) 322 RdC 295

Dolidze A, 'Bridging Comparative and International Law: *Amicus Curiae* Participation as a Vertical Legal Transplant' (2016) 26 (4)EJIL 851

Dolzer R, 'New Foundations of the Law of Expropriation of Alien Property' (1981) 75 AJIL 553

Dominguez-Redondo E, 'The Universal Periodic Review: Is There Life Beyond Naming and Shaming in Human Rights Implementation?' (2012) 4 NZLRev 673

Dresselhaus TR, Luck J and Peabody JW, 'The Ethical Problem of False Positives: A Prospective Evaluation of Physician Reporting in the Medical Record' (2002) 28 J Med Ethics 291

Dumberry P, 'Has the Fair and Equitable Treatment Standard Become a Rule of Customary International Law?' (2017) 8 JIDS 155

Dupuy PM, 'The Danger of Fragmentation or Unification of the International Legal System and the International Court of Justice' (1998-99) 31 NYUJIL&Pol 791

Dupuy PM, 'L'unité de l'ordre juridique international: cours général de droit international public' (2002) 297 RdC 1

Duquet S and Wouters J, 'De (on)beslagbaarheid van bankrekeningen van buiten-landse ambassades' (2015) 16(38)Rechtskundig Weekblad 1483

Dworkin R, 'A New Philosophy for International Law' (2013) 41(1)Phil&PubAff 2

Endicott TAO, 'Putting Interpretation in Its Place' (1994) 13 L&Phil 451

Fearon JD, 'Bargaining, Enforcement, and International Cooperation' 52(2) IO 269

Fiss O, 'Objectivity and Interpretation' (1982) 34 StanLRev 739

Fitzmaurice M, 'The Identification and Character of Treaties and Treaty Obligations Between States in International Law' (2002) 73 BYBIL 141

Fitzmaurice M, 'Third Parties and the Law of Treaties' (2002) 6(1) UNYB 37

Fitzmaurice M, 'Dynamic (Evolutive) Interpretation of Treaties, Part I' (2008) HYIL 101

Forbes E & Morss JR, 'Peoplehood Obscured? The Normative Status of Self-Determination after the Chagos Advisory Opinion' (2020) 46(3)Monash University Law Review 145

Forteau M, 'A New "Baxter Paradox"? Does the Work of the ILC on Matters Already Governed by Multilateral Treaties Necessarily Constitute a Dead End? Some Observations on the ILC Draft Articles on the Expulsion of Aliens' (2016) HarvHumRtsJ 1

Fouchard F, 'Allowing "Leeway to Expediency, Without Abandoning Principle"? The International Court of Justice's Use of Avoidance Techniques' (2020) 33 LJIL 767

Frankowska M, 'The Vienna Convention on the Law of Treaties before United States Courts' (1988) 28 VaJInt'lL 281

French D, 'Treaty Interpretation and the Incorporation of Extraneous Legal Rules' (2006) 55 ICLQ 281

Frost T and Murray CRG, 'Homeland: Reconceptualising the Chagossians' Litigation' (2020) 40(4)OJLS 764

Fukuyama F, 'The End of History?' (1989) 16 The National Interest 3

Fuller L, 'Human Interaction and the Law' (1969) 14(1)AmJJuris 1

Gaetano M, 'Cours General de Droit International Public' (1956) 89 RdC 439

Gaja G, 'Trattati internazionali' (1988) XV Digesto delle Discipline Pubblicistiche 344

Garner JW, 'Codification of International Law: Part III – Law of Treaties – Appendix 4: Fiore's Draft Code' (1935) 29 AJIL Supp 1212

Gathii JT, 'TWAIL: A Brief History of Its Origins, Its Decentralized Network, and a Tentative Bibliography' (2011) 3(1) Trade, Law & Development 26

Ghanea N 'From UN Commission on Human Rights to UN Human Rights Council: One Step Forwards or Two Steps Sideways' (2006) 55 ICLQ 695

Gilmore K, Mora L, Barragues A & Mikkelsen I, 'The Universal Periodic Review: A Platform for Dialogue, Accountability, and Change on Sexual and Reproductive Health and Rights' (2015) 17 HHR Journal 167

Goldsmith J and Posner E, 'A Theory of Customary International Law' (1999) 66 UChiLRev 1113

Goodin RE, 'Institutionalizing the Public Interest: The Defense of Deadlock and Beyond' (1996) 90 (2)APSR 331

Goodman R, 'Human Rights Treaties, Invalid Reservations, and State Consent' 96(3) AJIL 531

Gouldner AW, 'The Norm of Reciprocity: A Preliminary Statement' (1960) 25(2) AmerSociolRev 161

Gourgourinis A, 'The Distinction between Interpretation and Application of Norms in International Adjudication' (2011) 2(1) JIDS 31

Gradoni L, 'Consuetudine internazionale e caso inconsueto' (2012) Rivista di diritto internazionale 704

Gradoni L, 'Un-Procedural Customary Law' (2019) 10 JIDS 175

Green JA, 'Questioning the Peremptory Status of the Prohibition of the Use of Force' (2011) 32 MichJIntlL 215

Greenwood C, 'The Applicability of International Humanitarian Law and the Law of Neutrality to the Kosovo Campaign' (2002) 78 ILS 35
Grossman N, 'Legitimacy and International Adjudicative Bodies' (2009) 41 GeoWashIntlLRev 107
Guastini R, 'A Realist View on Law and Legal Cognition' (2015) 27 Revus 45
Guggenheim P, 'Les principes de droit international public' (1952) 80 RdC 2
Gunatilleke G et al, 'Do Recommendations to the Universal Peer Review Work? Examining Recommendations in UPR's First Two Cycles for Nepal, Sri Lanka and Indonesia' (2016) 2 Journal of Human Rights and Peace Studies 107
Gunning I, 'Modernizing Customary International Law: The Challenge of Human Rights' (1990) 31 VaJInt'lL 211
Gur N, 'Are Legal Rules Content-Independent Reasons?' (2011) 5 Problema 175
Guzman AT, 'Against Consent' (2012) 52(4) VaJInt'lL 747
Haan V, 'The Development of the Concept of Joint Criminal Enterprise at the International Criminal Tribunal for the Former Yugoslavia' (2005) 5 IntCLR 167
Hadjigeorgiou A, 'The Legacy of Sir Henry Maine in the 21st Century' (2020) 34 Noesis 159
Hafner G, 'Some Thoughts on the State-Oriented and Individual-Oriented Approaches in International Law' (2009) 14 ARIEL 27
Haggenmacher J, 'La doctrine des deux éléments du droit coutumier dans la pratique de la Cour internationale' (1986) 90 RGDIP 5
Hakimi M, 'Secondary Human Rights Law' (2009) 34 YaleJInt'lL 596
Hakimi M, 'The Work of International Law' (2017) 58 HarvInt'lLJ 1
Hakimi M, 'Making Sense of Customary International Law' (2020) 118 MichLRev 1487
Hannum H, 'The UDHR in National and International Law' (1998) 3 HHR Journal 144
Hart HLA, 'Are There Any Natural Rights?' (1955) 64(2) PhilRev 175
Harvard Law School, 'Draft Convention on the Law of Treaties, With Commentary' (1935) 29 AJIL Supp 653
Haskell JD, 'TRAIL-ing TWAIL: Arguments and Blind Spots in Third World Approaches to International Law' (2014) 27(2) CJLJ 383
Hays Parks H, 'Making Law of War Treaties: Lessons from Submarine Warfare Regulation' (2000) 75 IntlLStudies 339
Hébié M, 'Was There Something Missing in the Decolonization Process in Africa? The Territorial Dimension' (2015) 28 LJIL 529
Helfer L, 'Nonconsensual International Lawmaking' (2008) 2008(1) UIllLRev 71
Helfer LR and Wuerth IB, 'Customary International Law: An Instrument Choice Perspective' (2016) 37(4) MichJIntlL 563
Heller KJ, 'Specially-Affected States and the Formation of Custom' (2018) 112 AJIL 191
Henkin L, 'General Course on Public International Law' (1989) 213 RdC 9

Herdegen M, 'Interpretation in International Law' [2013] MPEPIL 723

Hiemstra H & Nohle E, 'The Role of Non-State Armed Groups in the Development and Interpretation of International Humanitarian Law' (2019) 20 Yearbook of International Humanitarian Law 3

Higgins R 'The Development of International Law by the Political Organs of the United Nations' (1965) 59 Proceedings of the American Society of International Law at Its Annual Meeting 116

Hill D, 'Avoiding obligation: Reservations to Human Rights Treaties' (2016) 60 Journal of Conflict Resolution 1129

Holtermann JvH, 'A Straw Man Revisited: Resettling the Score Between HLA Hart and Scandinavian Legal Realism' (2017) 57 Santa Clara LRev 1

Hong MH, 'Legal Commitments to United Nations Human Rights Treaties and Higher Monitoring Standards in the Universal Periodic Review' (2018) 17 Journal of Human Rights 660

Hoogers G & Karapetian G, 'Federal Disputes in the German Reich under the Weimar Constitution: Lessons in Dispute Settlement for the Kingdom of the Netherlands' (2018) 12 (3)Vienna Journal on International Constitutional Law 257

IRRC, 'A Collection of Codes of Conduct Issued by Armed Groups' (2011) 93 IRRC 483

Jacqué JP, 'Acte et norme en droit international public' (1991) 227 RdC 387

Jahoon Lee L, 'Barcelona Traction in the 21st Century: Revisiting its Customary and Policy Underpinnings 35 years Later' (2006) 42 StanJIntlL 237

Janis MW, 'The Ambiguity of Equity in International Law' (1983) 9 BrookJInt'lL 7

Jenks W, 'The Challenge of Universality' (1959) 53 ASIL Proc 85

Jervis CEM, 'Jurisdictional Immunities Revisited: An Analysis of the Procedure Substance Distinction in International Law' (2019) 30(1) EJIL 105

Jia BB, 'The Relations Between Treaties and Custom' (2010) 9 ChinJIntLaw 81

Joyner C, 'UN General Assembly Resolutions and International Law: Rethinking the Contemporary Dynamics of Norm-Creation' (1981) 11 CalWInt'lLJ 445

Joyner DH, 'Why I Stopped Believing in Customary International Law' (2019) 9 Asian JIL 31

Kammerhofer J, 'Uncertainty in the Formal Sources of International Law: Customary International Law and Some of its Problems' (2004) 15 EJIL 523

Kammerhofer J, 'Gaps, the Nuclear Weapons Advisory Opinion and the Structure of International Legal Argument between Theory and Practice' (2010) 80 BYBIL 333

Kammerhofer J, 'Taking the Rules of Interpretation Seriously, but not Literally? A Theoretical Reconstruction of Orthodox Dogma' (2017) 86 NordJIntlL 125

Kaplan J, 'Attitude and the Normativity of Law' (2017) 36 L&Phil 469

Karnavas MG, 'Joint Criminal Enterprise at the ECCC: A Critical Analysis of the Pre-Trial Chamber's Decision against the Application of JCE III and Two Divergent Commentaries on the Same' (2010) 21 Crim LF 445

Kelsen H, 'Théorie du Droit International Coutumier' (1939) 1 Revue Internationale de Theorie du Droit 253

Kelsen H, 'The Principle of Sovereign Equality of States as a Basis for International Organization' (1944) 53(2) Yale LJ 207

Kelsen H, 'Théorie du droit international public' (1953) 84 RdC 1

Kennedy D, 'The Turn to Interpretation' (1985) 58 S CalLRev 251

Kerwin GJ, 'The Role of United Nations General Assembly Resolutions in Determining Principles of International Law in United States Courts' (1983) Duke LJ 876

Kirgis F, 'Custom on a Sliding Scale' (1987) 81 AJIL 146

Kitharidis S, 'The Power of Article 103 of the UN Charter on Treaty Obligations' (2016) 20 IP 111

Klabbers J, 'Shrinking Self-Determination: The Chagos Opinion of the International Court of Justice' (2019) 8(2) ESIL Reflections <https://bit.ly/3GPgTX5>

Kleczkowska A, 'Searching for Armed Non-State Actors' Role in the Process of Formation of Customary Law' (2019) 19 ICLR 97

Kleffner JK, 'The Applicability of International Humanitarian Law to Organized Armed Groups' (2011) 93 IRRC 443

Kleinlein T, 'International Legal Thought: Creation of a Tradition and the Potential of Disciplinary Self-Reflection' (2016) 16(1) The Global Community: Yearbook of International Law and Jurisprudence 811

Kolb R, 'Selected Problems in the Theory of Customary International Law' (2003) 50 NILR 119

Kolodny N & Wallace RJ, 'Promises and Practices Revisited' (2005) 31(2) Phil&PubAff 119

Komanovics A, 'The Human Rights Council and the Universal Periodic Review: Is it More Than a Public Relations Exercise?' (2012) 150 Studia Iuridica Auctoritate Universitatis Pecs Publicata 119

Koskenniemi M, 'The Pull of the Mainstream' (1990) 88(6)MichLRev 1946

Koskenniemi M, 'Introductory Note: International Court of Justice: Order Discontinuing the Proceedings in *Case Concerning Passage Through the Great Belt (Finland v Denmark)*' (1993) 32 ILM 101

Koskenniemi M, 'International Law in a Post-Realist Era' (1995) 16 Aust YBIL 1

Koskenniemi M, 'The Politics of International Law: 20 Years Later' (2009) 20 EJIL 7

Koskenniemi M, 'The Mystery of Legal Obligation' (2011) 3 International Theory 319

Kotzur M, '*Ex aequo et bono*' [2009] MPEPIL 1402

Krisch N, 'International Law in Times of Hegemony: Unequal Power and the Shaping of the International Legal Order' 16(3) EJIL (2005) 369

Krisch N, 'The Decay of Consent: International Law in an Age of Global Public Goods' (2014) 108(1) AJIL 1

Kritsiotis D, 'Reappraising Policy Objections to Humanitarian Intervention' (1998) 19(4) MichJIntlL 1005

Krivokapić B, 'On the Issue of So-Called "Instant" Customs in International Law' (2017) 9 Acta Universitatis Danubius. Administratio 91

Lachs M, 'Teachings and Teaching of International Law' (1976) 151 RdC 161

Lamond G, 'Legal Sources, the Rule of Recognition, and Customary Law' (2014) 59 American Journal of Jurisprudence 25

Langille B, 'It's "Instant Custom": How the Bush Doctrine Became Law after the Terrorist Attacks of September 11, 2001' (2003) 26 BC Int'l&CompLRev 145

Lau H, 'Rethinking the Persistent Objector Doctrine in International Human Rights Law' (2005) 6 ChinJIntLaw 495

Lauterpacht H, 'Decisions of Municipal Courts as a Source of International Law' (1929) 10 BYBIL 65

Lauterpacht H, 'The Nature of International Law and General Jurisprudence' (1932) 37 Economica 301

Lauterpacht H, 'Les travaux préparatoires et l'interprétation des traités' (1934) 48 RdC 709

Lauterpacht H, 'Règles générales du droit de la paix' (1937) 62 RdC 95

Lefkowitz D, '(Dis)solving the Chronological Paradox in Customary International Law: A Hartian Approach' (2008) 21(1) CJLJ 129

Lennard M, 'Navigating by the Stars: Interpreting the WTO Agreements' (2002) 5 (1) JIntlEconL 17

Lepard B, '"Customary International Law: A Third World Perspective": Reflections in Light of an Approach to CIL Based on Fundamental Ethical Principles' (2018) 112 AJIL Unbound 303

Lerum K, McCurtis K, Saunders P & Wahab S, 'Using Human Rights to Hold the US Accountable for its Anti-Sex Trafficking Agenda: The Universal Periodic Review and New Directions for US Policy' (2012) 1 Anti-Trafficking Review 80

Lillich RB, 'The Growing Importance of Customary International Human Rights' (1995) 25 Ga JInt'l&CompL 1

Lippold M, 'Reflections on Custom Critique and on Functional Equivalents in the Work of Jean d'Aspremont' (2019) 21 IntCLRev 257

Loschin L, 'The Persistent Objector and Customary Human Rights Law: A Proposed Analytical Framework' (1996) 2 UCDavis JInt'l L&Pol'y 147

MacCormick N, 'Voluntary Obligations and Normative Powers I' (1972) 46 Proceedings of the Aristotelian Society 59

MacCormick N, 'Argumentation and Interpretation in Law' (1995) 9 Argumentation 467

Marceau G, 'A Call for Coherence in International Law: Praises for the Prohibition Against "Clinical Isolation" in WTO Dispute Settlement' (1999) 33(5) JWT 87

Marceau G, 'Conflicts of Norms and Conflicts of Jurisdictions: The Relationship between the WTO Agreement and MEAs and Other Treaties' (2001) 35(6) JWT 1081

Marceau G, 'Fragmentation in International Law: The Relationship between WTO Law and General International Law – A Few Comments from a WTO Perspective' (2006) 17 FYBIL 6

Mayer B, 'Climate Assessment as an Emerging Obligation Under Customary International Law' (2019) 68 ICLQ 271

Marek K, 'Le probleme des sources du droit international dans l'arrêt sur le plateau continental de la mer du nord' (1970) 6 RBDI 45

McCorquodale R, 'An Inclusive International Legal System' (2004) 17 LJIL 477

McFarland S & Mathews M, 'Who Cares About Human Rights?' (2005) 26(3) Political Psychology 365

Meguro M, 'Distinguishing the Legal Bindingness and Normative Content of Customary International Law' (2017) 6(11) ESIL Reflections <https://esil-sedi.eu/post_name-1149/>

Meijers H, 'How is International Law Made? The Stages of Growth of International Law and the Use of Its Customary Rules' (1978) 9 NYIL 1

Mejía-Lemos DG, 'On Self-Reflectivity, Performativity and Conditions for Existence of Sources of Law in International Law' (2014) 57 GYIL 289

Mendelson M, 'The Subjective Element in Customary International Law' (1995) 66 BYBIL 177

Mendelson M, 'The Formation of Customary International Law' (1999) 272 RdC 155

Merkouris P, 'Interpreting the Customary Rules on Interpretation' (2017) 19 ICLR 126

Miles C, 'Thoughts on Domestic Adjudication and the Identification and Formation of Customary International Law' (2017) 27 IYIL 163

Milewicz K & Goodin R, 'Deliberative Capacity Building through International Organizations: The Case of the Universal Periodic Review of Human Rights' (2018) 48 BJPolS 513

Monaco R, 'Cours général de droit international public' (1968) 125 RdC 93

Monaco R, 'Interpretazione' (1988) VIII Enciclopedia Giuridica 2 Moore MS, 'Authority, Law, and Razian Reasons' (1988) 62 S CalLRev 827

Morelli G, 'A proposito di norme internazionali cogenti' (1968) Rivista di diritto internazionale 108

Morgenthau HJ, 'The Twilight of International Morality' (1948) 58(2) Ethics 79

Morss JR 'Description Without Apology? On Structures, Signs and Subjectivity in International Legal Scholarship' (2018) 58 IJIL 235

Morss JR, 'Pluralism, Peoplehood and Political Theology in International Legal Scholarship' (2018) 27(1) GLR 77

Morss JR, 'Cutting Global Justice Down to Size? Rights, Vulnerabilities, Immunities, Communities' (2019) 40(30) Liverpool LR 179

Morss JR, 'Book Review: *Brownlie's Principles of Public International Law* by James Crawford and *International Law* by Gleider Hernández' (2020) 21(1) MJIL 1

Müller T, 'Customary Transnational Law: Attacking the Last Resort of State Sovereignty' (2008) 15 IndJ Global Legal Studies 19

Murphy SD, 'Identification of Customary International Law and Other Topics: The Sixty-Seventh Session of the International Law Commission' (2015) 109 AJIL 822

Murphy SD, 'Immunity *Ratione Materiae* of State Officials from Foreign Criminal Jurisdiction: Where is the State Practice in Support of Exceptions?' (2018) 112 AJIL Unbound 4

Murray D, 'How International Humanitarian Law Treaties Bind Non-State Armed Groups' (2015) 20 JC&SL 101

Nolte G, 'How to Identify Customary International Law? On the Outcome of the Work of the International Law Commission (2018)' (2019) 62 JYIL 251

Norman G and Trachtman JP, 'The Customary International Law Game' (2005) 99 (3) AJIL 541

Norton PM, 'A Law of the Future or a Law of the Past? Modern Tribunals and the International Law of Expropriation' (1991) 85 AJIL 474

Nouwen SMH, 'Return to Sender: Let the International Court of Justice Justify or Qualify International-Criminal-Court Exceptionalism Regarding Personal Immunities' (2019) 78(3) CLJ 596

Noyes JE, 'The International Tribunal for the Law of the Sea' (1999) 32 Cornell Int'lLJ 109

Öberg M, 'The Legal Effects of Resolutions of the UN Security Council and General Assembly in the Jurisprudence of the ICJ' (2006) 16 EJIL 879

Ochoa C, 'The Individual and Customary International Law Formation' (2007) 48 VaJInt'lL 119

Odermatt J, 'The Development of Customary International Law by International Organizations' (2017) 66 ICLQ 491

Ohlin JD, 'Three Conceptual Problems with the Doctrine of Joint Criminal Enterprise' (2007) 5 JICJ 69

Omorogbe EY, 'The Crisis of International Criminal Law in Africa: A Regional Regime in Response?' (2019) 66(2) NILR 287

Onuf N, 'The Constitution of International Society' (1994) 5 EJIL 1

Orakhelashvili A, 'The Acts of the Security Council: Meaning and Standards of Review' (2007) 11 UNYB 149

Orford A, 'On International Legal Method' (2013) 1 London Review of International Law 166

Papadaki M, 'Compromissory Clauses as the Gatekeepers of the Law to be "Used" in the ICJ and the PCIJ' (2014) 5 JIDS 569

Paparinskis M, 'MFN Clauses and International Dispute Settlement: Moving beyond Maffezini and Plama?' (2011) 26(2) ICSID Review 14

Parfitt R, 'The Spectre of Sources' (2014) 25 EJIL 297

Parra AR, 'The Convention and Centre for Settlement of Investment Disputes' (2014) 374 RdC 313

Paulus AL and Simma B, 'The Responsibility of Individuals for Human Rights Abuses in Internal Conflicts: A Positivist View' (1999) 93(2) AJIL 302

Paust JJ, 'The Complex Nature, Sources and Evidences of Customary Human Rights' (1995/1996) 25 GaJInt'l&CompL 147

Pavel C and Lefkowitz D, 'Skeptical Challenges to International Law' (2018) 13(8) Philosophy Compass 1

Pellet A, 'The Normative Dilemma: Will and Consent in International Law-Making' (1989) 12 Aust YBIL 22

Pellet A, 'L'adaptation du droit international aux besoins changeants de la société internationale' (2007) 329 RdC 9

Perry SR, 'Second-Order Reasons, Uncertainty and Legal Theory' (1989) 62 SCalLRev 913

Peters A, 'Global Constitutionalism Revisited' (2005) 11 International Legal Theory 39

Peters A, 'Precommitment Theory Applied to International Law: Between Sovereignty and Triviality' (2008) 2008(1) UIllLRev 239

Petersen N, 'Customary Law Without Custom? Rules, Principles, and the Role of State Practice in International Norm Creation' (2007) 32 AmUInt'lLRev 275

Petersen N, 'The International Court of Justice and the Judicial Process of Identifying Customary International Law' (2017) 28(2)EJIL 357

Pillai P, 'The African Union, the International Criminal Court, and the International Court of Justice: At the Fault Lines of International Accountability' (2018) 22(10) ASIL Insights <https://bit.ly/3te9eOs>

Posner E, 'Do States Have a Moral Obligation to Obey International Law?' (2003) 55(5) Stan L Rev 1901

Posner R, 'A Theory of Negligence' (1972) 1 JLS 32

Postema G, 'Implicit Law' (1994) 13(3)L&Phil 361

Postema GJ, 'Custom, Normative Practice, and the Law' (2012) 62(3) Duke LJ 707

Qin X, 'Oral International Agreement and China's Relevant Practice' (2005) 4(2) Chinese Journal of International Law 465

Quane H, 'Silence in International Law' (2014) 84(1) BYBIL 240

Raz J, 'The Problem of Authority: Revisiting the Service Conception' (2006) 90 MinnLRev 1003

Reus-Smit C, 'Obligation through Practice' (2011) 3 International Theory 339

Reuter P, 'Principes de droit international public' (1961) 103 RdC 425

Ritchie AD, 'Scientific Method in Social Studies' (1945) 20 Philosophy 3

Roberts A, 'Traditional and Modern Approaches to Customary International Law: A Reconciliation' (2001) 95 AJIL 757

Roberts R, 'The Equal Application of the Laws of War: A Principle under Pressure' (2008) 90 IRRC 931

Roberts A, 'Comparative International Law? The Role of National Courts in Creating and Enforcing International Law' (2011) 60 ICLQ 57

Roberts A & Sivakumaran S, 'Lawmaking by Nonstate Actors: Engaging Armed Groups in the Creation of International Humanitarian Law' (2012) 37 YaleJInt'lL 107

Rondeau S, 'Participation of Armed Groups in the Development of the Law Applicable to Armed Conflicts' (2011) 93 IRRC 649

Rouhgan N, 'Democratic Custom v International Customary Law' (2007) 38 VUWLR 403

Rouillard LPF, 'Misinterpreting the Prohibition of Torture Under International Law: The Office of Legal Counsel Memorandum' (2005) 21(1) AmUInt'lLRev 9

Ryngaert C, 'Embassy Bank Accounts and State Immunity from Execution: Doing Justice to the Financial Interests of Creditors' (2013) 26 LJIL 73

Ryngaert C & Hora Siccama D, 'Ascertaining Customary International Law: An Inquiry into the Methods Used by Domestic Courts' (2018) 65 NILR 1

SáCouto S, Sadat LN & Viseur Sellers P, 'Collective Criminality and Sexual Violence: Fixing a Failed Approach' (2020) 33(1) LJIL 207

Salama I, 'Proliferation of Treaty Bodies or Expansion of Protection?' (2011) 105 ASIL Proc 515

Sassòli M, 'Transnational Armed Groups and International Humanitarian Law' (2006) Winter 2006(6) HPCR Occasional Paper Series 1 <https://bit.ly/3oW3F4Y>

Sassòli M, 'Taking Armed Groups Seriously: Ways to Improve their Compliance with International Humanitarian Law' (2010) 1 JIHLS 5

Sassòli M, 'Introducing a Sliding-Scale of Obligations to Address the Fundamental Inequality between Armed Groups and States?' (2011) 93 IRRC 426

Scanlon TM, 'The Significance of Choice' (1986) 7 The Tanner Lectures on Human Values 149

Scanlon TM, 'Promises and Practices' (1990) 19(3) Phil&PubAff 199

Scarfi JP, 'Denaturalizing the Monroe Doctrine: The Rise of Latin American Legal Anti-Imperialism in the Face of the Modern US and Hemispheric Redefinition of the Monroe Doctrine' (2020) 33(3) LJIL 541

Scelle G, 'Règles générales du droit de la paix' (1933) RdC 1

Schachter O, 'The Invisible College of International Lawyers' (1977–1978) 72 NWULR 217

Schneider H & Schaumann W, 'Verträge zwischen Gliedstaaten im Bundesstaat' (1961) 19 Veröffentlichungen der Vereinigung der Deutschen Staatsrechtslehrer 122

Schröder M, 'Precautionary Approach/Principle' [2014] MPEPIL 1603

Schrödinger E, 'Die gegenwärtige Situation in der Quantenmechanik' (1935) 23 (49)Die Naturwissenschaften 807

Schwarzenberger G, 'The Inductive Approach to International Law' (1947) 60 HarvLRev 539

Schwebel S, 'The Effect of Resolutions of the UN General Assembly on Customary International Law' (1979) 73 ASIL Proc 301

Shaffer G & Ginsburg T, 'The Empirical Turn in International Legal Scholarship' (2012) 106 AJIL 1

Shany Y, 'A Rebuttal to Marco Sassòli' (2011) 93 IRRC 432

Shany Y, 'Assessing the Effectiveness of International Courts: A Goal-Based Approach' (2012) 106(2) AJIL 225

Shapiro SJ, 'On Hart's Way Out' (1998) 4 LEG 469

Sinha SP, 'Perspective of the Newly Independent States on the Binding Quality of International Law' (1965) 14 ICLQ 121

Sivakumaran S, 'Binding Armed Opposition Groups' (2006) 55(2) ICLQ 369

Sivakumaran S, 'Making and Shaping the Law of Armed Conflict' (2018) 71 CLP 118

Slaughter Burley AM, 'International Law and International Relations Theory: A Dual Agenda' (1993) 87 AJIL 205

Solum B, 'The Interpretation-Construction Distinction' (2010) 27 Const Comment 95

Somek A, 'Kelsen Lives' (2007) 18(3) EJIL 409

Somek A, 'From the Rule of Law to the Constitutionalist Makeover: Changing European Conceptions of Public International Law' (2011) 18(4) Constellations 576

Somer J, 'Jungle Justice: Passing Sentence on the Equality of Belligerents in Non-International Armed Conflict' (2007) 89 IRRC 655

Stern B, 'Custom at the Heart of International Law' (2001) 11DukeJComp&Int'lL 89

Sur S, 'La créativité du droit international cours général de droit international public' (2013) 363 RdC 18

Sur S, 'La créativité du droit international' (2013) 363 RdC 9

Sustein CR, 'Problems with Rules' (1995) 83 CLR 953

Suttle O, 'Rules and Values in International Adjudication: The Case of the WTO Appellate Body' (2019) 68(2) ICLQ 399

Swaine ET, 'Identifying Customary International Law: First Thoughts on the ILC's First Steps' (2014) 108 AJIL Unbound 184

Tallberg J & Zürn M, 'The Legitimacy and Legitimation of International Organizations: Introduction and Framework' (2019) 14 The Review of International Organizations 581

Talmon S, 'Determining Customary International Law: The ICJ's Methodology between Induction, Deduction and Assertion' (2015) 26(2) EJIL 417

Tams CJ, 'Meta-Custom and the Court: A Study in Judicial Law-Making' (2015) 14 LPICT 51

Tasioulas J, '*Opinio Juris* and the Genesis of Custom: A Solution to the "Paradox"' (2007) 26 Aust YBIL 199

Tasioulas J, 'Customary International Law: A Moral Judgment-Based Account' (2014) 108 AJIL Unbound 328

Terman R & Voeten E, 'The Relational Politics of Shame: Evidence from the Universal Periodic Review (2018) 13 The Review of International Organizations 1

Thirlway H, 'Human Rights in Customary Law: An Attempt to Define Some of the Issues' (1995) 28 LJIL 495

Thirlway H, 'Professor Baxter's Legacy: Still Paradoxical?' (2017) 6(3) ESIL Reflections <https://esil-sedi.eu/post_name-121/>

Thirlway H, 'The Role of Non-State Actors: A Response to Professor Ryngaert' (2017) 64 NILR 141

Tladi D, 'The International Law Commission's Recent Work on Exceptions to Immunity: Charting the Course for a Brave New World in International Law?' (2019) 32 NJIL 169

Tomka P, 'Custom and the International Court of Justice' (2013) 12 LPICT 195

Tomuschat C, 'Obligations Arising for States Without or Against Their Will' (1993) 241 RdC 195

Trachtman J, 'Persistent Objectors, Cooperation, and the Utility of Customary International Law' (2010) 21 DukeJComp&Int'lL 221

Treves T, 'Customary International Law' [2006] MPEPIL 1393

Treves T, 'Fragmentation of International Law: The Judicial Perspective' (2007) 23 Comunicazioni e Studi 821

Trimble PR, 'The Supreme Court and International Law: The Demise of Restatement Section 403' (1995) 89(1) AJIL 53

Truyol y Serra A, 'Théorie du Droit International Public: Cours Général' (1981) 173 RdC 9

Tunkin GI, 'Politics, Law and Force in the Interstate System' (1989) 219 RdC 227

Tzanakopoulos A, 'Domestic Courts in International Law: The International Judicial Function of National Courts' (2011) 34 LoyLAInt'l&CompLRev 135

Tzanakopoulos A & Tams CJ, 'Introduction: Domestic Courts as Agents of Development of International Law' (2013) 26 LJIL 531

Upton H 'The Human Rights Council: First Impressions and Future Challenges' (2007) 7 HRLR 29

Van der Wilt H, 'National Law: A Small but Neat Utensil in the Toolbox of International Criminal Tribunals' (2010) 10 Int CLR 209

Vanek DC, 'Is International Law Part of the Law of Canada?' (1950) 8 UTLJ 251

Verdier PH & Voeten E, 'Precedent, Compliance, and Change in Customary International Law: An Explanatory Theory' (2014) 108(3) AJIL 389

Verdross A, 'Entstehungsweisen und Geltungsgrund des universellen völkerrechtlichen Gewohnheitsrechts' (1969) 29 Zeitschrift für ausländisches öffentliches Recht und Völkerrecht 635

Verhoeven J, 'Considérations sur ce qui est commun: Cours général de droit international public' (2008) 334 RdC 9

Villalpando S, 'On the International Court of Justice and the Determination of Rules of Law' (2013) 26 LJIL 243

Virally M, 'Panorama du droit international contemporain: cours général de droit international public' (1983) 183 RdC 9

Voyiakis E, 'A Disaggregative View of Customary International Law-Making' (2016) 29 LJIL 365

Waltz KN, 'The Stability of a Bipolar World' (1964) 93(3) Daedalus 881

Walzer M, 'The Moral Standing of States: A Response to Four Critics' (1980) 9(3) Philosophy and Public Affairs 209

Weatherall T, '*Jus Cogens* and Sovereign Immunity: Reconciling Divergence in Contemporary Jurisprudence' (2015) 46 GeorgetJIntLaw 1151

Weil P, 'Vers une normativité relative en droit international?' (1982) 86 RGDIP 5

Weil P, 'Le droit international en quête de son identité' (1992) 237 RdC 9

Weisburd AM, 'Customary International Law: The Problem of Treaties' (1988) 21 VandJTransnat'lL 1

Widdows K, 'On the Form and Distinctive Nature of International Agreements' (1981) 7(1) Australian YBIL 114

Wiener JB, 'Something Borrowed for Something Blue: Legal Transplants and the Evolution of Global Environmental Law' (2001) 27 Ecology LQ 1295

Wight M, 'Why is There no International Theory?' (1960) 2 International Relations 35

Wolfke K, 'Some Persistent Controversies Regarding Customary International Law' (1993) 24 NYIL 1

Wood M, 'The Interpretation of Security Council Resolutions' (1998) 2 UNYB 73

Wood M, 'The Present Position within the ILC on the Topic "Identification of Customary International Law": In Partial Response to Sienho Yee, Report on the ILC Project on "Identification of Customary International Law"' (2016) 15 ChinJIntLaw 3

Wood M, 'The Interpretation of Security Council Resolutions, Revisited' (2017) 20 UNYB 1

Wood M & Sender O, 'Identifying the Rules for Identifying Customary International Law: Response from Michael Wood and Omri Sender' (2014) 108 AJIL Unbound 198

Yasseen MK, 'L'interprétation des traités d'après la convention de Vienne sur le droit des traités' (1976) 151 RdC 1

Ziccardi P, 'La consuetudine internazionale nella teoria delle fonti giuridiche' (1958) Comunicazioni e studi 190

Ziccardi P, 'Consuetudine (diritto internazionale)' (1961) IX *Enciclopedia del diritto* 476

Zürn M, 'Global Governance and Legitimacy Problems' (2004) 39(2) Government and Opposition 260

Unpublished/Online/Working Paper Series

Barkholdt J & Kulaga J, 'Analytical Presentation of the Comments and Observations by States on Draft Article 7, paragraph 1, of the ILC Draft Articles on Immunity of State Officials from Foreign Criminal Jurisdiction, United Nations General Assembly, Sixth Committee, 2017' (April 2018) KFG Working Paper Series No 14 <https://bit.ly/3AxOdhx>

Bellal A & Casey-Maslen S, 'Rules of Engagement, Protecting Civilians through Dialogue with Armed Non-State Actors' (*Geneva Academy of IHL and Human Rights*, 2011) <https://bit.ly/3DAwiZK>

Bellal A, Bongard P & Heffes E, 'Research Brief: From Words to Deeds: A Study of Armed Non-State Actors: Practice and Interpretation of International Humanitarian and Human Rights Norms' (*Geneva Academy of IHL and Human Rights*, December 2019) <https://bit.ly/3lzwCl7>

Cress K, 'Preliminary Observations on the ICC Appeals Chamber's Judgment of 6 May 2019 in the Jordan Referral re Al-Bashir Appeal' (2019) TOAEP's Occasional Paper Series

Kahombo B, 'Africa Within the Justice System of the International Criminal Court: The Need for a Reform' (May 2016) KFG Working Paper Series No 2 <http://dx.doi.org/10.2139/ssrn.3129009>

McMahon E, 'The Universal Periodic Review: A Work in Progress: An Evaluation of the First Cycle of the New UPR Mechanism of the United Nations Human Rights Council' (Friedrich Ebert Stiftung, Dialogue on Globalization, September 2012)

Purcell K, 'Faltering at the Critical Turn to History: "Juridical Thinking" in International Law and Genealogy as History, Critique, and Therapy' (2016) Jean Monnet Working Paper Series, JMWP 02/15

Sadat LN, 'Heads of State and Other Government Officials Before the International Criminal Court: The Uneasy Revolution Continues' (2019) Washington University in St. Louis Legal Studies Research Paper No 19-01-12 <https://papers.ssrn.com/sol3/papers.cfm?abstract_id=3321998>

Sassòli M, 'Transnational Armed Groups and International Humanitarian Law' (2006) Winter 2006(6) HPCR Occasional Paper Series 1 <https://bit.ly/3oW3F4Y>

Skillen JW, 'Development of Calvinistic Political Theory in the Netherlands, With Special Reference to the Thought of Herman Dooyeweerd' (PhD Thesis, Duke University 1973)

Van Woudenberg R, 'Theories of Thing-Structures' in Philosophical Foundations I Reader (International Masters in Christian Studies of Science and Society Program, Vrije Universitet Amsterdam 2006–7)

Websites

Akande D, 'ICC Appeals Chamber Holds that Heads of State Have No Immunity Under Customary International Law Before International Tribunals' (*EJIL: Talk!*, 6 May 2019) <https://bit.ly/3iU7sMz>

Ammann O, 'On the Interpretability of Customary International Law: A Response to Nina Mileva and Marina Fortuna' (*Opinio Juris Blog*, 7 October 2019) <https://bit.ly/3v7sJr2>

Bachand R, 'L'interprétation en droit international: une analyse par les contraintes' (*Société européenne de droit international*, 2007) <https://esil-sedi.eu/wp-content/uploads/2018/04/Bachand.pdf>

Bellal A & Casey-Maslen S, 'Rules of Engagement, Protecting Civilians through Dialogue with Armed Non-State Actors' (*Geneva Academy of IHL and Human Rights*, 2011) <https://bit.ly/3DAwiZK>

Bellal A, Bongard P & Heffes E, 'Research Brief: From Words to Deeds: A Study of Armed Non-State Actors' Practice and Interpretation of International Humanitarian and Human Rights Norms' (*Geneva Academy of IHL and Human Rights*, December 2019) <https://bit.ly/3lzwCl7>

Branca E, '"Yet, it moves . . . ": The Dynamic Evolution of State immunity in the "Comfort Women" case' (*EJILTalk!*, 7 April 2021) <https://bit.ly/3GLpkm7>

Cisney WV, 'Differential Ontology' (*Internet Encyclopedia of Philosophy*, 2021) <www.iep.utm.edu/diff-ont/>

Dickson J, 'Interpretation and Coherence in Legal Reasoning' (*Stanford Encyclopedia of Philosophy*, Winter 2016) <https://plato.stanford.edu/entries/legal-reas-interpret/>

Dupuy PM, 'Intergenerational Reflections on International Law' (*EJIL: Talk!*, January 2020) <https://bit.ly/3sbh9M1>

Fukuyama F, 'The History at the End of History' (*Guardian*, 3 April 2007) <https://bit.ly/2ZEKDpK>

Geneva Call, 'Deed of Commitment under Geneva Call for Adherence to a Total Ban on Anti-Personnel Mines and for Cooperation in Mine Action' (*Geneva Call*, 1 July 2019) <https://bit.ly/3DOwhRC>

Geneva Call, 'What we do' (*Geneva Call*, 2021) <www.genevacall.org/what-we-do/>

Gianelli A, 'Consuetudine (diritto internazionale)' (*Diritto on line*, 2017) <https://bit.ly/3F1QjcG>

Global Initiative to End Corporal Punishment of Children, 'Progress' (*End Corporal Punishment*, 2019) <https://endcorporalpunishment.org/countdown/>

Guillaume G, 'The Proliferation of International Judicial Bodies: The Outlook for the International Legal Order' (*ICJ-CIJ*, 27 October 2000) <www.icj-cij.org/public/files/press-releases/1/3001.pdf>

Hathaway O & Shapiro SJ, 'What Realists Don't Understand About Law' (*Foreign Policy*, 9 October 2017) <https://bit.ly/3kxeVlf>

Human Rights Watch, 'ICC: Jordan Was Required to Arrest Sudan's Bashir' (*Human Rights Watch*, 6 May 2019) <https://bit.ly/300ozFL>

Hyde D & Raffman D, 'Sorites Paradox' (*Stanford Encyclopedia of Philosophy*, 26 March 2018) <https://plato.stanford.edu/entries/sorites-paradox/>

ICRC, 'Increasing Respect for International Humanitarian Law in Non-International Armed Conflicts' (*ICRC*, 2008) <https://bit.ly/3GK1K9y>

ILC, 'Analytical Guide to the Work of the International Law Commission' (*ILC*, 10 December 2019) <http://legal.un.org/ilc/guide/gfra.shtml>

Louth J, 'How Much Public International Law Scholarship Is There?' (*EJILTalk!*, 10 January 2017) <https://bit.ly/3o3pTBq>

Lugo G, 'The Dominican Republic's Epidemic of Domestic Violence' (*Guardian*, 23 November 2012) <https://bit.ly/30z5jzW>

Mack M, 'Increasing Respect for International Humanitarian Law in Non-International Armed Conflicts' (*ICRC*, 2008) <https://bit.ly/3GK1K9y>

Milanovic M, 'ICJ Delivers Chagos Advisory Opinion, UK Loses Badly' (*EJIL: Talk!*, 25 February 2019) <https://bit.ly/3FdrXNq>

Mileva N & Fortuna M, 'Emerging Voices: The Case for CIL Interpretation: An Argument from Theory and an Argument from Practice' (*Opinio Juris*, 23 August 2019) <https://bit.ly/3yGm7BD>

Moloney A, 'Break Silence on "Terrifying" Femicides in Dominican Republic: Minister' (*Reuters*, 16 July 2017) <https://reut.rs/31TmrkD>

Office of the High Commissioner for Human Rights, 'Press Release: Pillay Hails Completion of First-Ever Human Rights Review of All 193 States' (*OHCHR*, 13 October 2011) <https://bit.ly/3HZdLsj>

Peters A, 'Let Not Triepel Triumph: How To Make the Best Out of Sentenza No 238 of the Italian Constitutional Court for a Global Legal Order' (*EJILTalk!*, 22 December 2014) <https://bit.ly/3s9sR9F>

Republic of Korea, 'Comments and Observations on the ILC Topic "Identification of Customary International Law"' (*ILC*, 22 December 2017) <https://bit.ly/3r9bZzp>

Richardson HS, 'Moral Reasoning' (*Stanford Encyclopedia of Philosophy*, Winter 2014) <https://plato.stanford.edu/entries/reasoning-moral/>

Sender O & Wood M, 'The International Court of Justice and Customary International Law: A Reply to Stefan Talmon' (*EJIL: Talk!*, 30 November 2015) <https://bit.ly/3xKvWOd>

Swiss Confederation, 'La pratique suisse relative à la détermination du droit international coutumier' (*ILC*, 2017) <https://bit.ly/3oVWp7G>

Talmon S, 'Determining Customary International Law: The ICJ's Methodology and the Idyllic World of the ILC' (*EJIL: Talk!*, 3 December 2015) <https://bit.ly/3EQMgQ2>

United States Mission to the United Nations, 'Letter to UN Security Council on Article 51' (8 January 2020) <https://bit.ly/3ncI0nu>

UPR Info, 'UPR Info's Database: Action category' (*UPR Info*, October 2014) <www.upr-info.org/database/files/Database_Action_Category.pdf>

US Mission Geneva, 'Statements by the United States at the Meeting of the WTO Dispute Settlement Body Geneva' (*US Mission to International Organizations in Geneva*, 18 December 2018) <https://bit.ly/3zN3oVn>

US Department of Justice, 'Memorandum for Alberto R. Gonzales, Counsel to President 'Re: Standards of Conduct of Interrogation under 18 U.S.C. §§ 2340-2340A' (1 August 2002) <www.justice.gov/olc/file/886061/download>

USTR, Appellee Submission of the United States (30 September 2010) <https://bit.ly/3GEIABH>

INDEX

For EU product safety concerns, contact us at Calle de José Abascal, 56–1°, 28003 Madrid, Spain or eugpsr@cambridge.org.

www.ingramcontent.com/pod-product-compliance
Lightning Source LLC
LaVergne TN
LVHW080529210926
848481LV00020B/1480

* 9 7 8 1 0 0 9 5 0 5 5 0 5 *